LITHUANIAN YESHIVAS OF
THE NINETEENTH CENTURY

T0355663

THE LITTMAN LIBRARY OF JEWISH CIVILIZATION

Dedicated to the memory of
LOUIS THOMAS SIDNEY LITTMAN
*who founded the Littman Library for the love of God
and as an act of charity in memory of his father*
JOSEPH AARON LITTMAN
and to the memory of
ROBERT JOSEPH LITTMAN
who continued what his father Louis had begun
יהא זכרם ברוך

*Get wisdom, get understanding:
Forsake her not and she shall preserve thee*
PROV. 4: 5

*The Littman Library of Jewish Civilization is a registered UK charity
Registered charity no. 1000784*

LITHUANIAN YESHIVAS OF THE NINETEENTH CENTURY

◆

Creating a Tradition of Learning

◆

SHAUL STAMPFER

Translated by
LINDSEY TAYLOR-GUTHARTZ

London
The Littman Library of Jewish Civilization
in association with Liverpool University Press

The Littman Library of Jewish Civilization
Registered office: 4th floor, 7–10 Chandos Street, London WIG 9DQ

in association with Liverpool University Press
4 Cambridge Street, Liverpool L69 7ZU, UK
www.liverpooluniversitypress.co.uk/littman

Managing Editor: Connie Webber

Distributed in North America by
Oxford University Press Inc., 198 Madison Avenue
New York, NY 10016, USA

First published in Hebrew 1995 © The Zalman Shazar Centre for Jewish History
Revised and expanded Hebrew edition 2005 © The Zalman Shazar Centre for Jewish History
English translation first published in hardback 2012
First published in paperback 2014

English translation © The Littman Library of Jewish Civilization 2012

Catalogue records for this book are available from the
British Library and the Library of Congress
ISBN 978-1-906764-60-9

Publishing co-ordinator: Janet Moth
Copy-editing: Tamar Berkowitz, Connie Webber, and Mark Newby
Proof-reading: Philippa Claiden
Index: Christine Headley
Designed by Pete Russell, Faringdon, Oxon.
Typeset by John Saunders Design & Production, Eastbourne

Printed and bound in Great Britain by
CPI Group (UK) Ltd., Croydon, CR0 4YY

This book is dedicated to the memory of

ARYEH TOEG

1938–1973

◆

He was a brilliant biblical scholar, a person whose observance of
ritual was punctilious but who never forgot the search for meaning.
In his life he taught that faith has nothing to fear from truth—
and that without truth there is no faith.
He would have been the teacher of an entire generation,
but he fell on the first day of the Yom Kippur War. Those who lived
lives of hubris remained with us. Those that were pure
were among the first to go.

Acknowledgements

I WISH TO THANK the Zalman Shazar Center for Jewish History and especially Zvi Yekutieli and Yekhezkel Hovav for their support in the preparation of the original Hebrew edition. This book would not have been published without the generous grants given both to the Hebrew edition and this English one by the Bollag Stiftung (Basel). The process of translating this book into English was not at all simple—and I am afraid that my main role was to complicate matters. I am very grateful to Connie Webber, Lindsey Taylor-Guthartz, Tamar Berkowitz, Mark Newby, George Tulloch, Philippa Claiden, and Janet Moth for their immense contribution. Vinyamin Lukin, of the Central Archives of the History of the Jewish People, and Volodya Levine went out of their way to help me with archival materials. My teacher Jacob Katz initially rejected the draft of the first chapter of the thesis on which this book is based. He said that if I have something to say, I don't have to hide behind jargon or big words. I have tried to remain his student in this—and in other—ways.

When I first approached the Littman Library I proposed a translation of my book *Hayeshivah halita'it behithavutah* (The Formation of the Lithuanian Yeshiva), which had appeared in two editions in Israel, in 1995 and in 2005. As the work of translation proceeded I was the beneficiary of queries and comments from exceptional translators and editors. This led me to make innumerable corrections. I also added many sources and tried to sharpen my argument. Thus this is not a simple translation but a revised and expanded edition of the book.

Corrections to the Hardback Edition

Page 150

My discussion of the Purim rabbi in Volozhin omits to mention that Yirmiyahu Flensberg is known to have been honoured with this position in 1859. My thanks to Dan Rabinowitz for pointing this out (http://seforim.blogspot.co.il/2010/01/r-flensberg-donkeys-antelopes-and-frogs.html). R. Flensberg appears, in a different context, on page 156; his name should be spelled thus, and not 'Felsenberg', as it appears there and in the bibliography and index. Yehoshua Mondshine critically reviews some of the sources I employed on the Purim rabbi in his article 'Gilgulo shel sipur: rav shel purim' (http://www.shturem.net/index.php?id=1446&section=artdays).

Page 152

Rabbi Naftali Tsevi Yehudah Berlin's second wife, Batya Miryam, was the daughter of Rabbi Yehiel Michel Halevi Epstein, rabbi of Novogrudok and author of *Arukh hashulḥan*. I am grateful to Rabbi Ben Hecht for suggesting to me that these facts should be mentioned.

Page 163

I mention that Rabbi Naftali Tsevi Yehudah Berlin read newspapers. Eliezer Brodt's article, 'The Netziv, Reading Newspapers on Shabbos, in General & Censorship' (http://seforim.blogspot.co.il/2014/03/the-netziv-reading-newspapers-on.html), offers a careful examination of my comment, with additional sources and some important clarifications.

Page 379

Some of the works attributed in the bibliography to Hayim Berlin should in fact be credited as follows:

Ha'amek davar [Biblical commentary] (Vilna, 1879); *Meshiv davar* [Responsa], 2 vols. (Warsaw, 1904; Jerusalem, 1993) are by Rabbi Naftali Tsevi Yehudah Berlin.

'To Those Who Research the Past' (Heb.), *Hapeles*, 2/15 (1902), 140–3 is by Rabbi Hayim of Volozhin.

Ḥut hameshulash [The Threefold Cord] (Vilna, 1882) was edited by Rabbi Hayim Fried.

Page 380

The description of David Bunimovitsh's *Mikhtav me'eliyahu* (Vilna, 1901) as related to the writings of Rabbi Eliyahu Dessler is incorrect.

Yisra'el Hayim Deiches: the surname should be Daiches.

My thanks to Graham Morris for pointing out these errors.

Contents

Tables

Note on Transliteration and Conventions Used in the Text

THE transliteration of Hebrew in this book reflects consideration of the type of book it is, in terms of its content, purpose, and readership. The system adopted therefore reflects a broad approach to transcription, rather than the narrower approaches found in the *Encyclopaedia Judaica* or other systems developed for text-based or linguistic studies. The aim has been to reflect the pronunciation prescribed for modern Hebrew, rather than the spelling or Hebrew word struc-ture, and to do so using conventions that are generally familiar to the English-speaking reader.

In accordance with this approach, no attempt is made to indicate the distinctions between *alef* and *ayin*, *tet* and *taf*, *kaf* and *kuf*, *sin* and *samekh*, since these are not relevant to pronunciation; likewise, the *dagesh* is not indicated except where it affects pronunciation. Following the principle of using conventions familiar to the majority of readers, however, transcriptions that are well established have been retained even when they are not fully consistent with the transliteration system adopted. On similar grounds, the *tsadi* is rendered by 'tz' in such Anglicized words as barmitzvah. Likewise, the distinction between *ḥet* and *khaf* has been retained, using *ḥ* for the former and *kh* for the latter; the associated forms are generally familiar to readers, even if the distinction is not actually borne out in pronunciation, and for the same reason the final *heh* is indicated too. As in Hebrew, no capital letters are used, except that an initial capital has been retained in transliterating titles of published works (for example, *Shulḥan arukh*).

Since no distinction is made between *alef* and *ayin*, they are indicated by an apostrophe only in intervocalic positions where a failure to do so could lead an English-speaking reader to pronounce the vowel-cluster as a diphthong—as, for example, in *ha'ir*—or otherwise mispronounce the word.

The *sheva na* is indicated by an *e*—*perikat ol*, *reshut*—except, again, when established convention dictates otherwise.

The *yod* is represented by *i* when it occurs as a vowel (*bereshit*), by *y* when it occurs as a consonant (*yesodot*), and by *yi* when it occurs as both (*yisra'el*).

Names have generally been left in their familiar forms, even when this is inconsistent with the overall system.

Introduction

THE YESHIVAS that developed in nineteenth-century Lithuania offered a completely new structure for the study of Talmud—that is, for studying the texts that lie at the core of traditional Jewish elite literary culture. Their development reflected two major characteristics of Jewish society at that time: a conservative reaction to the modernizing trends that were confronting the traditional Jewish world of eastern Europe, and faith in the importance of educational institutions. These characteristics were in themselves a reflection of more general historical phenomena, which is what makes them so significant.

Although the yeshivas of nineteenth-century Lithuania represented a major attempt on the part of traditional Jewry to cope with the challenges of modernity, there has been no comprehensive study of the subject. Much of the existing literature was written by former students by way of tribute: accordingly, such sources present the yeshivas as worthy models, perhaps discuss specific aspects of their history, and provide snippets of information on the famous rabbis associated with them, but that is all. This study, in contrast, is a first attempt at a comprehensive history. It considers the role and functioning of the yeshivas; presents various aspects of their organization and administration, including their funding and the personalities at their helm; and discusses different perspectives of the students' experience, while at all times paying close and critical attention to documentation and sources.[1]

When Jews speak of 'the Lithuanian yeshivas', the borders of the Lithuania they have in mind are not the same as those of the independent state of Lithuania of the interwar period, nor those of modern Lithuania. Jewish geography is a historical geography, so the term is generally used to refer to

---

[1] For a general history of the yeshiva, see J. Katz, 'Jewish Civilization as Reflected in the Yeshivot', and Breuer, *Tents of Torah: The Structure and History of the Yeshiva*. The most important study of yeshivas in medieval Ashkenaz is Breuer, 'The Ashkenazi Yeshiva in the Late Middle Ages' (Heb.). At present, there is no comprehensive study of the history of Jewish education in the modern era. In the meantime, see A. Asaf, *Sources for the History of Jewish Education* (Heb.). There is a wealth of material on education in eastern Europe and on yeshiva education in the fourth volume (*History of Education*) of the *Encyclopaedia of Education* (Heb.), ed. Buber and Ormian. See also Scharfstein, *The History of Jewish Education in Modern Times* (Heb.) Additional bibliographical material on the institutions discussed in this volume appears in the notes below.

the region that constituted the duchy of Lithuania when the Polish–Lithuanian Commonwealth was established in 1569. This region included areas that later became part of the neighbouring Baltic states, Belarus, and Poland.[2]

The Jews of nineteenth-century Lithuania thus defined had several distinguishing characteristics. In religious terms, most were traditional, in the sense that they had withstood the innovations of hasidism; in fact, the strength of the opposition to that movement in Lithuania was such that they came collectively to be known as mitnagedim ('opponents')—that is, opponents of hasidism. Economically, they were mostly poorer than Jews in other major areas of Jewish settlement, such as Poland or Bukovina, and lived in more crowded conditions. Until 1764 they benefited from self-government under the Va'ad Medinat Lita (Council of the Land of Lithuania). By the beginning of the eighteenth century this body had ceased to function, but the distinction between the Jews of Lithuania and those of the neighbouring regions continued to exist—not least because the Lithuanian Jews spoke a distinctive dialect of Yiddish. These and other factors ensured that they continued to maintain a separate identity among the Jews of eastern Europe until the First World War.

This volume traces the history of the Lithuanian yeshivas from 1803, when the first 'modern' yeshiva was founded in Volozhin, until the outbreak of the First World War in 1914. After that conditions changed greatly—thanks also to the Bolshevik revolution in Russia and the independence of Poland and the Baltic states—with the consequence that the subsequent period was so different as to lie beyond the scope of this book.[3]

Because the Lithuanian yeshivas offered a new model of Torah study, they cannot be regarded as a continuation or development of the Polish yeshivas of the Middle Ages and the early modern era. The famous yeshivas of Poland had disappeared in the wake of the Chmielnicki massacres of 1648–9; the precise reasons for their decline have not yet been investigated, but it is clear that they were replaced by small yeshivas, *batei midrash*, and *kloyzim*.[4] The

[2] The Jews of Lithuania have been studied in detail, but no comprehensive work has yet been written on this subject. In the meantime, see Goren et al. (eds.), *Lithuanian Jewry* (Heb.), vol. i; Hasman et al. (eds.), *Lithuanian Jewry* (Heb.), vols. ii, iii; Sudarsky et al. (eds.), *Lithuania* (Yid.). Community memorial books serve as valuable sources, but it is impossible to list them all here. Special mention should be made of Mordechai Nadav's very important work, *The Jews of Pinsk, 1506 to 1880*.

[3] A recent Ph.D. thesis by Ben-Tsiyon Klibansky, 'The Lithuanian Yeshivas in Eastern Europe' (Heb.), gives a very detailed and precise picture of Lithuanian yeshivas between the two world wars, though S. Mirsky (ed.), *The Rise and Destruction of the Torah Institutions of Europe* (Heb.), remains of value.

[4] On the Polish yeshivas before 1648, see Schulwass, 'The Torah and its Study' (Heb.); Breuer, 'The Ashkenazi Yeshiva in the Late Middle Ages' (Heb.); J. Katz, 'Jewish Civilization as Reflected in the Yeshivot'; Reiner, 'Transformations in the Polish and Ashkenazi Yeshivas'

founders of the new Lithuanian yeshivas thus had no contemporary models on which to draw, but their intimate acquaintance with rabbinic literature, in which yeshivas are frequently mentioned, may nevertheless have provided a useful literary model.[5] All the yeshivas discussed here were for advanced students, meaning those who were capable of studying the Talmud and its commentaries on their own. They all attracted students from a wide area, and as such were quite different from the smaller and more local yeshivas attended by younger pupils.

In certain respects the Lithuanian yeshivas were like their medieval Polish predecessors, but in one striking respect they were very different: their complete organizational and sometimes even physical isolation from the local Jewish community. In the past, yeshivas had been communal institutions, but the new type of Lithuanian yeshiva was independent of the community.[6] It was not housed in a community-owned building, nor was it supported financially by the local community, but collected funds by means of itinerant emissaries. Also, while all the great yeshivas of the past had been located in large cities, some of the most important of the Lithuanian yeshivas were to be found in small towns. Since the *rosh yeshivah*—the head of the institution—was not employed by the community, he could run his yeshiva with complete autonomy; and since the students were not supported financially by the community, the local inhabitants had no control over what they did. As we shall see, this isolation from the community and the lack of outside involvement in its administration also had its disadvantages, such as when there was disagreement over the appointment of a new *rosh yeshivah* or on other matters of policy. On such occasions the lack of an external body with the authority to settle disputes was keenly felt.

A rather different consequence of the isolation from the local community was that it encouraged strong student organization. Thus, student organizations

(Heb.). The *kloyz* did not serve as an organizational model for the yeshiva since it was intended as a place for adults to study rather than for young people to be taught. On the *kloyz*, see Reiner, 'Capital, Social Status, and Torah Study' (Heb.).

[5] Copious material on the Lithuanian yeshivas may be found in Dubnow (ed.), *Lithuanian Recordbook* (Heb.). Particularly important for this study is the regulation of 1661, issued by the Council of the Land of Lithuania: 'Forasmuch as our eyes have witnessed the lack of Torah, because of our many sins, in these times, several congregations and towns, even though they have both rabbis and the means of action, do not maintain yeshivas; and young men and youths turn their hearts towards idleness, and this idleness causes, God forbid, obstruction and misfortune. Therefore we have taken counsel to remove this hindrance, and to make this just decree, and to set our approval upon it: every congregation and town that has an *av beit din* is obliged to maintain a yeshiva [for] young men and youths, and to give them sabbaths and a reasonable holiday' (p. 126). However, it is clear from a regulation of 1676 (ibid. 174) that the earlier decree was not carried out, and there is no mention of it in subsequent regulations.

[6] See, however, Reiner, 'Capital, Social Status, and Torah Study' (Heb.), on the ownership of yeshivas.

often provided for medical care and mutual financial aid, organized activities relating to the Jewish holidays and celebrations of different sorts, and so on.[7] While these student bodies were clearly heirs of the Jewish mutual aid societies that were traditional in all Jewish communities, the fact that within the yeshiva the students created a community in miniature was definitely an innovation. Isolation from the wider community made the students more reliant on each other and strengthened their dependence on the yeshiva, especially as it was the source of any financial support they might receive. This endowed the yeshiva, and particularly the *rosh yeshivah*, with great authority, to an extent previously unknown.

In many societies, institutions of higher education serve as gateways to social mobility. In theory this was also true of the Lithuanian yeshivas, but in reality only a very limited degree of mobility was possible because young men from distinguished or wealthy families had a definite advantage in becoming students.[8] This was true from a very early age, since even elementary education of a high standard was expensive. Boys were educated either in a community-funded *talmud torah*, where the level was generally low, or in a private *ḥeder* whose teachers were paid directly by their parents. Naturally, poorer boys studied at less expensive *ḥeder*s staffed by less able teachers, and as a result they generally did not reach a standard that would allow them to study independently as was the practice in the yeshivas. Social divisions were thus perpetuated from one generation to the next. Even if a poor student managed to reach an advanced level, it would still be difficult for him to continue in Torah study because of the need to help support the family. There is absolutely no evidence of a class-based ideology fostered by rabbis or *rashei yeshivah* that deliberately limited poor students in their quest to become scholars, but that was how the system operated in practice.

Prior to the rise of the Lithuanian yeshiva, the community *beit midrash* was the most important, if not the only, institution for advanced Torah study, and in consequence it had a great influence on the character of the yeshivas that developed subsequently.[9] Most of the people who studied in the *batei midrash* were *balebatim*—ordinary members of the community. They studied primarily

---

[7] See below, especially the chapters on Volozhin (Chs. 1–8) and the Telz yeshiva (Ch. 10). It should be noted that students were not organized to the same degree in every yeshiva. The highest degree of organization seems to have been in Telz, with Volozhin not far behind. However, in Slobodka student organizations did not occupy an important part of student life nor did they have significant roles or power.

[8] On the link between Jewish education and social mobility, see Stampfer, 'Heder Study, Knowledge of Torah, and the Maintenance of Social Stratification'.

[9] On the *kloyz*, see Reiner, 'Capital, Social Status, and Torah Study' (Heb.). On the *beit midrash*, see a short discussion in Stampfer, 'Heder Study, Knowledge of Torah, and the Maintenance of Social Stratification'. For a good description of study in a *beit midrash*, see Y. Stern, *Ḥeder and Beit Midrash* (Yid.).

on their own, mostly before or after work, though most seem also to have attended occasional *shiurim* (lectures), whether given by the rabbi or in the framework of various groups organized to promote the study of religious texts. A smaller number of men studied for most of the day—mainly young men who had not yet started working, but also elderly men who no longer worked or worked only for part of the day. A few of the younger men were married and lived with their parents-in-law, but most were single men who came from other towns. The latter studied and slept at the *beit midrash* and relied for their food on invitations they received for meals.

The *beit midrash* had no formal curriculum, no entrance tests, and no examinations. People would study what and how they pleased. Sometimes the town rabbi would give a *shiur*, but this was not a central feature of the educational experience, and attendance was not compulsory. When a student had difficulties with a passage of the Talmud, he would discuss the problem with a fellow student. Such discussion not only provided the necessary clarification but also established the relative standard of both students without any formal system of examination. Supervision of the younger or less advanced students was thus informal but effective. Moreover, students' behaviour was always open to scrutiny by watchful local citizens. A student considered lazy would not be invited to meals with local families: such invitations were issued in order to support and encourage Torah study. A reputation as a *lamdan*—that is, a serious scholar—and, even more, as an *ilui*—a prodigy—would bring a young man invitations for meals, and in the long run ensured him a good marriage with a wealthy man's daughter. This was sufficient inducement to ensure that students concentrated on their studies.

Those studying in the *beit midrash* were not aiming to earn a rabbinical qualification. Their goals were not vocational, but their achievements in study were no secret. Merit was obvious to all, whether in the ability to quote many sources in discussion, to be innovative in textual interpretation, to ask challenging questions, or to demonstrate mental agility by rapid analysis of complex issues. It was these skills that brought a man honour, and in this way the *batei midrash* succeeded in stimulating perpetual study and achievement. This was because Torah study was regarded as the supreme value in Jewish society, and there was a consensus that excellence should be rewarded.[10]

As long as this consensus held, the *batei midrash* flourished; but as new values began to take hold in Jewish society in the second half of the nineteenth

[10] The collapse of traditional social patterns in eastern Europe in the second half of the 19th cent. is generally accepted as a historical fact, but there has been no methodical research into its chronology, extent, and location. However, it seems that the custom of independent study by young men in *batei midrash* had almost completely disappeared in the non-hasidic parts of eastern Europe by the end of the century. Analysis of rabbis' biographies could throw more light on where and when this happened.

century, the link between Torah study and social rank began to crumble. Traditional study began to lose its status among important sectors of the Jewish public, especially the wealthy. This change led to a deepening crisis, both in scholarly circles and among the wider traditional public. The change in values followed in the wake of economic, social, and cultural developments that formed part of a wider process, but their effect on the *batei midrash* was particularly rapid. If wealthy men preferred to marry their daughters to university students rather than traditional scholars, or if a promising student decided to study at a public gymnasium, this was quite enough to damage other young men's belief in the value of Torah study. In this way a gradual process of defection began, which sometimes even led to the closure of *batei midrash*.[11]

Significantly, it was during the period that the *batei midrash* were disintegrating that yeshivas began to proliferate: in the second half of the nineteenth century, yeshivas were founded in Radun, Telz, Slobodka, Novogrudok, Slutsk, Ponevezh, Lida, Malech and elsewhere. This rapid growth seems to have been directly linked to the collapse of the *beit midrash* system in the face of modernity. As we shall see, the various yeshivas differed in their responses to this challenge. The origins of the Volozhin yeshiva, with which this book begins, pre-dated this entire process, but it too was forced to grapple with the challenges of the modern era.

In addition to being independent of the local community, the yeshiva differed from the *beit midrash* in several other ways. Firstly, almost every yeshiva employed one or more rabbis as teachers to give regular *shiurim*. In the Lithuanian yeshivas, these teachers were known as *rashei yeshivah*; sometimes there were several teachers in a single yeshiva, in which case one of them was acknowledged as the head of the institution, with the others subject to his authority. Secondly, whereas those who studied in *batei midrash* were mostly married, the yeshivas were almost exclusively for teenage boys who were not married. Thirdly, yeshivas were usually housed in a separate building dedicated to their exclusive use rather than in a building also used by the community for other purposes. Educationally, the yeshivas had obvious advantages: there was more supervision, more encouragement, and closer personal ties could develop both between teachers and students and among students. However, this advantage was offset by the greater time and effort required in administration and in raising funds.

In spite of these differences, the Lithuanian yeshiva was more similar to a *beit midrash* than to a modern school or college. The main difference was that most study was independent; every yeshiva scheduled a regular lecture by the *rosh yeshivah* but it rarely had any bearing on the subjects or particular tractates studied independently by the students, and attendance was in any case

[11] For an example of the collapse of a *beit midrash*, see Yampolski, 'Memories of My Youth' (Heb.).

not compulsory. As in the *beit midrash*, acquiring rabbinical ordination was not a priority for most students. There was no official date either for the start of the academic year or for its end; students came and went as they wished (except at Telz). The *beit midrash*-like character of the Lithuanian yeshiva, even at the beginning of the twentieth century, is clearly demonstrated by a turn of events in Malech when the *rosh yeshivah* left the town after a dispute with the students but the students carried on studying together for about a year, completely undeterred by his absence.[12] Eventually the local community appointed a new rabbi who agreed to double as *rosh yeshivah*; this was in effect an unintentional movement from the yeshiva model back to a *beit midrash* model. A similar transformation took place at Telz, as discussed in Chapter 10. As in the *batei midrash*, there were generally no regular examinations (although in this regard, too, Telz and, for a short time, Volozhin, were exceptions). In spite of the central importance of the *rosh yeshivah*, the students' discussions with each other were more important than their relationship with the teachers in shaping their character and determining the content of study. This system also made it possible for hundreds of students to study in a yeshiva under the supervision of only a few teachers and perhaps a small number of *mashgiḥim* (literally, 'supervisors') concerned with their spiritual development.

These changes need to be viewed in context. Jewish society changed out of all recognition in the course of the nineteenth century.[13] The question of how traditional Jewish society reacted to modernity is complex and lies beyond the scope of this volume, but considerable research is being devoted to the subject.[14] At the time, however, modernity was a pressing and very real question. Some Jews saw it as beneficial and hoped that progress and Enlightenment would prevail over the old ways; because of their support for the Enlightenment—known by Jews as the Haskalah—they were called 'maskilim'. The attitude of the traditionalists was much more complex, since they felt compelled to resist the changes that came in its wake. For traditionalists, successful confrontation with modernity required the change to be presented in a way that suggested it came from within the traditional system, since in a society based on respecting the wisdom of one's elders, a more radical

---

[12] On Malech, see Ovsay, 'The Yeshivas during the Revival Period' (Heb.).

[13] For a good review of part of this change, see Y. Slutsky, *Russian Jewish Journalism in the Nineteenth Century* (Heb.), ch. 1. This is a major theme in most studies of the Jews of eastern Europe in this period. Another valuable study is M. Levin, *Social and Economic Values in the Ideology of the Haskalah* (Heb.).

[14] It is obvious that economic and social factors played an important role in these changes, along with the policies of the tsarist government and efforts by the maskilim and other social reformers to influence Jewish society. For a bibliography of this complex subject, see Hundert and Bacon, *The Jews in Russia and Poland*, pt. 2; Kahan, *Essays in Jewish Social and Economic History*.

explanation might lead to doubts about the authority of tradition.[15] This problem was not specific to the Jews: every society (but especially traditional societies, which permit no rebellion) experiences difficulty in accounting for mass deviation from accepted norms. For this reason, we cannot expect traditional Jewish literature of the nineteenth century to include open discussion of the success of those who opposed tradition. Moreover, the few discussions of this issue that were published may not reflect genuine contemporary attitudes. Detailed investigation of changes in the traditional attitude to modernity, especially in the field of education, would probably reveal that many people held views of which they themselves were unaware, making this a crucial area for research.

Within traditional Jewish society there were different explanations of the roots of the crisis, and accordingly different solutions for solving the problem. The four main strategies were as follows.

1. Reform in study methods. The first approach attributed the problems to the method of Torah study: this approach was characteristic of Volozhin, especially in its later years, and was later introduced in Telz and elsewhere. Its advocates attributed the abandonment of Torah study and the traditional Jewish way of life to faults in the educational system and felt that an entirely new approach was needed. This view implied partial agreement with the criticism levelled by the maskilim in their opposition to traditional culture, but whereas the maskilim rejected Talmud study per se,[16] the proponents of this approach merely opposed the way in which traditional religious values were transmitted. And whereas the maskilim advocated change in order to conform to contemporary requirements, the advocates of this approach took the opposite view: they regarded their reforms as a return to earlier, correct methods, rather than as the introduction of something new. At the same time, there was a realization that by adopting correct study methods it would be possible to disarm the critics, counter the attractions of the Haskalah, and restore order to Jewish society.

2. Reform in social values. The second approach blamed the collapse of traditional Jewish society on its own shortcomings. In this view, Jewish society no longer reflected Jewish values, and Torah scholars no longer offered positive role models because they were considered hypocritical and haughty—among other failings. Showing some understanding of why young people were abandoning tradition, the advocates of this approach blamed the leaders of the Jewish community for failing to educate young people in Jewish values through the study of *musar* (ethics), a development which they felt would

---

[15] My approach to these questions has been greatly influenced by the works of Peter Berger, especially Berger and Luckmann, *The Social Construction of Reality* (Heb.).

[16] For a concise summary of the Haskalah criticism of traditional study, see Avital, *The Yeshiva and Traditional Education* (Heb.).

achieve the necessary reform of traditional society and stem the abandonment of tradition. Such radical criticism of the traditional leadership naturally caused controversy within the Jewish community but the members of the *musar* movement, as it came to be known, felt that the innovation they were advocating was fully justified. Their programme for action and absolute confidence in their mission was what characterized the yeshiva in Slobodka.

3. Reform in the organization of education. Advocates of this third approach sought to distinguish between outcomes and methods. In their view, the speed with which modernity spread was due less to the superiority of the new values or the shortcomings of traditional society than to the means by which it was disseminated. The traditional public could benefit from these new methods no less than the maskilim did: there was nothing wrong, from a Torah perspective, in journalism, political organization, youth movements, and so on. Similarly in the educational field: there was nothing wrong in adopting modern methods, such as dividing students into classes, or instituting examinations, formal procedures for accepting students, and similar practices. This approach, which placed less emphasis on change in study methods and more on the whole approach to education in Jewish society, underlay many of the innovations of R. Eliezer Gordon at Telz.

4. Reform in the curriculum. The fourth approach claimed that a radical change had taken place in Jewish life and that a certain level of secular knowledge was now essential even for traditional scholars. The problems facing traditional society, in this view, stemmed from the impotence of rabbinic leadership without a secular education. The 'official' rabbis appointed by the government were mostly maskilim, but they had no standing among the traditionally Orthodox Jews; the rabbis who enjoyed the public's trust as spiritual leaders were unable to take up government appointments because of their lack of secular knowledge, which also limited their authority in the eyes of young maskilim. The solution was to integrate secular studies with Torah study in the yeshiva curriculum; this would accord with the government's demands that young people be given a basic secular education, and would have the further advantage of producing yeshiva graduates with a combined traditional and secular education who could take up official rabbinical appointments. Rabbinical leadership that offered traditional Judaism combined with modern knowledge could help halt the process of social disintegration. This approach, advocated by R. Yitshak Ya'akov Reines (1839–1915) and others, was introduced in the Lida yeshiva.[17]

The choice of the yeshivas of Volozhin, Telz, and Slobodka as the focus of this book was therefore no coincidence. Volozhin was the first and archetypical

---

[17] See Salmon, 'The Yeshiva of Lida'.

modern Lithuanian yeshiva and the birthplace of many of its characteristic features. Primarily because of its structural innovations, it was considered *em hayeshivot*, 'mother of the yeshivas', and in many respects it served as a model for all the later yeshivas. Slobodka pioneered the introduction of *musar* study into the yeshiva—the second approach described above—and served as a model for other *musar* yeshivas. Telz exemplified the third approach and put the emphasis on innovation in organizational reforms that were also later adopted elsewhere. The fourth approach, integrating secular studies into the yeshiva curriculum as implemented by R. Reines at his yeshiva in Lida, had limited contemporary influence as the yeshiva only operated for a short time because of the First World War, but it was an important precedent. Extensive research on the Lida yeshiva has elucidated its principal features,[18] and there is little more historical detail that I can add. However, its importance should not be overlooked; indeed, were it not for the Holocaust, the Lida model might have become the most influential.

The choice of these institutions to serve as the focus of this book does not imply that they were the only important yeshivas in Lithuania. The Mir yeshiva, for example, was an outstanding institution, but is not discussed here because in organizational terms it did not differ greatly from Volozhin and Telz. The yeshivas of the *musar* movement, such as Novogrudok and Slutsk, were innovative in their study methods and dissemination of *musar* concepts, but resembled Slobodka in organization and values. Detailed discussion of the histories of other yeshivas would add little to our understanding of the main points. Limitations of space have prevented investigation of the history of the Hungarian yeshivas, which were founded at the same time as those of Lithuania, and likewise of the history of hasidic yeshivas, which were founded later. The Lithuanian yeshivas were not influenced by the Hungarian yeshivas, and any attempt to compare the two would only detract from the main subject matter.

In concentrating on the organization and functioning of the yeshivas, I have not discussed the problems of the study techniques that developed for the analysis of the Talmud nor of the approaches to moral improvement characteristic of the *musar* movement, even though these are important issues and deserve thorough investigation.[19] Nor have I made any attempt to assess the importance and influence of the yeshivas, either in Jewish society in general or

[18] See Salmon, 'The Yeshiva of Lida'

[19] Comparative research on the study techniques used in the Lithuanian yeshivas would clarify the distinctive character of each method and its place in the history of Talmud study. None of the efforts to carry out a study of this nature has yet been very productive. In the meantime, see Zevin, *Personalities and Methods* (Heb.); Z. Kaplan, *From the World of Torah* (Heb.). On the possibility of quantitative investigation in this field, see Solomon, *The Analytic Movement*; see also Wachtfogel, *The Brisker Derech*.

in traditional society in particular. These subjects require separate studies, though I have occasionally touched on issues that have some relevance to the main discussion.

The sources I have used in writing this book—contemporary documents, contemporary newspapers, and memoirs—are worthy of note. The last category is the most important, and like every other source it has both advantages and disadvantages. Memoirs sometimes provide a more detailed picture than official documents, but most were written many years after the events described and are more than likely in consequence to suffer from only partial recall; they also reflect their authors' attitudes at the time of writing rather than at the time of the events they describe. In most cases I have assumed that, although what was written may only be part of the truth, the authors would not deliberately have lied. Moreover, almost all my conclusions are based on several sources, so that if one source proves unreliable it does not usually affect my general conclusions. In order to allow readers to judge the sources for themselves, a large number of quotations are included in the text.

The majority of the book is devoted to the Volozhin yeshiva, while the other institutions have one chapter apiece. There are several reasons for this. First, Volozhin existed for about ninety years, until its closure in 1892, while Slobodka and Telz both existed for only about thirty years, before the First World War. Secondly, since Volozhin was the first modern yeshiva and most of the features adopted by later yeshivas developed there, it warrants more detailed analysis. Thirdly, graduates of Volozhin wrote a great deal about their yeshiva, whereas graduates of Telz wrote much less, and students from Slobodka least of all. I leave it to others to explain this phenomenon. The relative wealth of information on Volozhin obviously encouraged me to focus more on that institution, especially since I have a particular fondness for it; however, I have done my best to neutralize my partiality as far as possible and to use the sources available to reveal the truth.

The reader must be aware that the past is quite different from the present, and familiarity with modern yeshivas can distort our understanding of their nineteenth-century predecessors. If we are to discover the reality of that past, we must take advantage of all the sources available and not seek to avoid contentious issues. Many great figures discussed in this book made remarkable achievements, but this does not mean that facts about them that at first sight seem less than flattering must be expunged.[20] The true stature of such individuals is revealed by showing what they were able to achieve despite their human weaknesses; certainly they would have been the last to call for their faults to be airbrushed out. Those who censor such shortcomings do so from fear; those

---

[20] For an example of this, see Schacter, 'Haskalah, Secular Studies and the Close of the Yeshiva in Volozhin'. Those who impose censorship presumably assume that they are wiser than the author whose text they wish to suppress.

who have true respect for such men know that the shortcomings serve only to highlight the magnitude of what they were able to achieve.

It would have been impossible to write this book without building on the achievements of researchers and writers who came before me such as R. D. Katz, R. S. Mirsky, R. M. Z. Neriyah, M. Tzinovitz, Y. Rifkind, and many others. I discovered most of the sources used here from references they cited. I have checked each source myself, unless noted otherwise, and have therefore generally omitted the original reference, referring the reader directly to the source itself instead. The scope and method of this study differ from those of its predecessors, and it is not designed to replace them; I would thus recommend that the interested reader consult other studies too.

I have generally seen no point in recording errors that I have come across in the work of others, since this type of comment can easily slip into pedantry and adds nothing to our understanding of the phenomena discussed. Moreover, many of these works were written for educational or ideological purposes. In contrast, this book, which aims to describe social processes, people, and institutions in an objective academic manner, attempts to confirm every detail; the reader must be the judge of my efforts. I would therefore be most grateful to readers who can correct details that I have recorded wrongly or who can direct me to sources that I have overlooked.

PART I

THE VOLOZHIN
YESHIVA

ONE

Origins and Early Years of the Volozhin Yeshiva

T HE SMALL TOWN OF VOLOZHIN is not very different from many other Belarusian towns. It has played a very minor role in the history of the region and does not even appear in every atlas. To the casual visitor today it is unimpressive; indeed, it never attracted very many travellers. It is not on a major thoroughfare and not easy to get to. However, for much of the nineteenth century it was one of the focal points of the Lithuanian Jewish world (most of Belarus was regarded by Jews as part of Lithuania), because of the yeshiva that was established there. Even today, in Jewish historical consciousness Volozhin remains a major metropolis—one of the capitals in the Jewish memory map of Europe. This is because the yeshiva of Volozhin represented a novel type of relationship between the Jewish community and Jewish learning: for most of the nineteenth century the Volozhin yeshiva was the most important institution of Jewish learning in all of eastern Europe, and ultimately it served as a model for the rest of European Jewry. The heads of the yeshiva were regarded as leaders of the Jewish community in the Russian empire and beyond; thousands of young men studied there, many of whom went on to have a significant impact on the Jewish world. Patterns that were set in Volozhin are essentially maintained in yeshivas around the world till today—though at the same time much has changed, even if yeshiva students and their social circles are unaware of these changes. There are many curious myths about Volozhin, but the reality was even more interesting. A careful look at the history of the yeshiva can teach us not only about the yeshiva itself but how a society can change in ways that few could have predicted.

1. R. Hayim of Volozhin

The structure and development of the Volozhin yeshiva were directly linked to the life and career of its founder, R. Hayim ben Yitshak of Volozhin. He was born in Volozhin in 1749.[1] His father came from a prominent family and

---

[1] The most important works on R. Hayim and on the Volozhin yeshiva are Etkes, 'R. Hayim

was himself a communal leader. His mother was also of distinguished ances-try.[2] His younger brother, Shelomoh Zalman (1756–88), was an accomplished Talmud scholar who had studied with the great R. Eliyahu ben Shelomoh Zalman, the Vilna Gaon (1720–97).[3] Little is known about his other siblings.

In his youth, R. Hayim studied with two exceptional scholars. First, around the age of 13, he studied in Minsk with R. Raphael Kohen Hamburger (1722–1803), the author of *Torat yekutiel*. R. Hamburger served in later years as the rabbi of Hamburg and was known as a sharp critic of the Enlightenment leader Moses Mendelssohn. After R. Hayim returned home, he studied with R. Aryeh Leib Gunzberg (1695–1785), the author of *Sha'agat aryeh*, who served at the time as the rabbi of Volozhin and later as the rabbi of Metz in France.[4] However, it was the Vilna Gaon who influenced him most. R. Hayim's association with him began in 1768 and lasted until the Gaon's death.[5] During that time he maintained a close relationship with the Gaon, visiting him regularly and consulting him on questions that arose in the course of his study. R. Hayim adopted many of the features of the Gaon's method of

of Volozhin's Method' (Heb.); Gross, 'On the Weltanschauung of R. Hayim' (Heb.); Lamm, *Torah lishmah*; Leone (ed.), *Volozhin* (Heb.); S. Mirsky, 'The Volozhin Yeshiva' (Heb.); Neriyah, *Volozhin Studies* (Heb.); Shmukler [Shapira], *Rabbi Hayim of Volozhin* (Heb.); Tzinovitz, *Tree of Life* (Heb.). For a recent comprehensive study of R. Hayim, see D. Eliach, *Father of the Yeshivas* (Heb.); as the reader familiar with the literature on R. Hayim will sense, Eliach has obviously consulted an even wider range of sources than that suggested by his bibliographical references. He has also published an anthology of R. Hayim's writings, *Kol hakatuv lehayim*.

[2] On R. Hayim's father's family, see the letter from Yehudah Epstein, published in Hebrew under the title 'Mikhtav yakar' ('Precious Letter') as an appendix to Avraham ben Hagra (son of the Vilna Gaon), *Sa'arat eliyahu*, 38. R. Hayim described his father thus: 'My honoured father, of blessed memory . . . was the *parnas* of the town, and the people listened to him, and he carried out his duties with honour' (ibid.). For information on his mother's family, see Shmukler [Shapira], *Rabbi Hayim of Volozhin*, ch. 1; Avraham Simhah of Amtchislav, *Binyan shel simhah*, intro.

[3] For details of his life, see Feivel b. Zeev Wolf, *Toledot adam*. Wolf was the *moreh tsedek* of the Holy Congregation of Vilna. The introduction to R. Hayim's *Nefesh hahayim*, which was written by his son, R. Yitshak, notes that the eldest brother was R. Simhah, and that R. Shelomoh Zalman was younger than R. Hayim. I am grateful to Rabbi Boruch Oberlander of Budapest and Shai Gerson of Yeshivat Har Etsiyon for clarifying this.

[4] See the letter from Eliezer Lipman Rabinowitz appended to Avraham ben Hagra, *Sa'arat eliyahu*, 41. The biography of R. Raphael Hamburger records that, during his period of study with R. Raphael, R. Hayim travelled around as a preacher 'in order to instruct the people and to reprove them with moralistic teachings and the fear of God' (Eliezer Katzenellenbogen, *Zekher tsadik*, 50, col. 1), and that R. Hayim was already studying with the Vilna Gaon. This last detail is chronologically impossible, and it is also doubtful that the first assertion is correct since it would imply that the 12-year-old R. Hayim was living the life of a wandering preacher—which might be possible but seems unlikely.

[5] See Kahana, *Tosafot ma'aseh rav, She'iltot*, 56, and, for a parallel description, Ezekiel Katzenellenbogen, *Tsava'at keneset yehezkel*.

study and always regarded him as his principal teacher.[6] Throughout his life he spoke of the Gaon with absolute reverence. R. Hayim's son wrote of his father that, 'when he taught his children and his students and told them about the time [when he had studied] with the Vilna Gaon, his reverence for his master was apparent as a great awe, as if he stood before him in Heaven'.[7]

R. Hayim's first rabbinical appointment was as the rabbi of Volozhin.[8] This was probably around 1776 and not later than 1779.[9] 'He had already earned a reputation as an outstanding pupil of the Gaon and had rapidly achieved a position of honour among the rabbis of Lithuania. This is clear from the fact that in 1784 he was invited to write an approbation, alongside important and veteran Vilna rabbis, for a commentary on the Torah by R. Shelomoh Dubno (1738–1813), even though Volozhin was just a small town and he was only 35 years old.[10]

[6] The methods of R. Hayim and of the Vilna Gaon were by no means identical. One striking difference was the Vilna Gaon's willingness to resolve textual difficulties by suggesting textual emendations (see Landau, *The Pious Gaon of Vilna* (Heb.), 108–23), an approach that R. Hayim did not adopt. No methodical comparison has yet been made between the two men's methods, though the surviving writings of R. Hayim would permit this. R. Betsalel Dablitski has pointed out to me that the Vilna Gaon would suggest a textual emendation not only when he encountered a particular difficulty on account of the phraseology but also when he noticed an error or corruption, even when this made little or no difference to the practical implications. On R. Hayim's attitude to textual problems in the Talmud, see Spiegel, *Studies in the History of the Hebrew Book* (Heb.), 480–1. From the quotation there it seems that R. Hayim was aware of textual variants. Spiegel states that R. Hayim was not a pupil of the Vilna Gaon in the usual sense (p. 387). See also ibid. 241 for R. Hayim's attitude to poorly edited books.

[7] Hayim of Volozhin, *Nefesh haḥayim*, intro. by his son, R. Isaac.

[8] According to Shmukler [Shapira], he was about 25 when he was appointed rabbi of the town, which would yield a date of 1774 (*Rabbi Hayim of Volozhin* (Heb.), 23). Shmukler apparently relied on the letter by Yehudah Epstein, 'Mikhtav yakar' (see n. 2 above). Here Epstein linked R. Hayim's appointment as rabbi to R. Raphael Hamburger's journey to the west in 1773. However, as R. Eliezer Lipman Rabinowitz explained in the letter appended to Avraham ben Hagra, *Sa'arat eliyahu*, 40, this story seems unlikely and should not be cited as evidence of the date. Mikhal Rabinowitz published a document recording the renewal of R. Hayim's appointment as rabbi of Volozhin in 1782 (see M. Rabinowitz, 'Documents Relating to the History of the Volozhin Yeshiva' (Heb.)). Since this document deals with the renewal of an appointment, the original appointment must have been before then, though the date cannot be determined with any accuracy.

[9] D. Eliach, *Father of the Yeshivas* (Heb.), i. 282, 285 n. 5. Mikhal Rabinowitz, printed a three-year extension of his appointment as rabbi dated to 1782 ('Documents Relating to the History of the Volozhin Yeshiva' (Heb.), 221). If this was the first extension, the original appointment would probably have been in 1779. However this may have been a second or even later extension as Eliach reasonably suggests.

[10] Fuenn, *Safah lane'emanim*, 135–7. On R. Hayim's approbation for R. Dubno's book, see also Mondschein, 'Suppressed Approbations from Volozhin and Vilna' (Heb.), which describes attempts to cover up the matter (in his words: 'another example of a generation that judges its judges', p. 154). Mondschein appends the text of R. Hayim's approbation and that of his brother R. Shelomoh Zalman, and includes a photograph of the originals.

In 1790 R. Hayim was appointed rabbi of Vilkomir.[11] This was a real promotion: Vilkomir had an important Jewish community, more than twice the size of that of Volozhin,[12] and his appointment there could have led to subsequent positions with even more important communities. However, for reasons that are not entirely clear, he stayed in Vilkomir for only one year before returning to Volozhin. Much later it was said that he had asked for a monopoly on the sale of certain goods so that he would not be dependent on the community for his income, a demand that aroused opposition in the community and eventually led him to resign. One can question the veracity of this story, but there is no doubt that he left Vilkomir after one year and returned to his previous post in Volozhin. Never again did he leave his home town to serve in another community.[13] Given his fame, he could undoubtedly have been appointed as rabbi of a prominent community if he had wanted, but apparently he preferred to remain in Volozhin. This was perhaps a result of his experiences in Vilkomir; whatever the reason, his decision to stay had far-reaching consequences.[14]

The death of the Vilna Gaon in 1797 left a vacuum in the rabbinic leadership of Lithuania. Because the authority of the Gaon had been a product of his personal charisma rather than an official position, the void left by his death could not simply be resolved by appointing a replacement. The Va'ad Medinat Lita, which for many years had been the co-ordinating council of the Jewish communities of Lithuania, had been dispersed in 1764 and thus could not provide a framework for communal leadership. The Vilna rabbinate also could not serve as a power base for an authoritative rabbi because the Vilna community had abolished the position of communal rabbi even in the Gaon's lifetime.[15] There were many rabbis in Vilna, but no one had the title of the rabbi of Vilna.

By this time R. Hayim was generally regarded as the leading disciple of the Vilna Gaon, the 'first' among his students, as the Gaon's sons put it.[16] They

[11] See the letter from Hillel Noah Steinschneider appended to Avraham ben Hagra, *Sa'arat eliyahu*, 42.

[12] According to the 1766 census of the Jews of Lithuania, there were 383 Jews in Volozhin and 716 in Vilkomir. The census was not properly published, but the data appear in the *Evreiskaya entsiklopediya*, v. 571, 727. The number of Jewish inhabitants was probably higher by the early 19th cent., but the data do at least suggest the relative sizes of the two communities.

[13] As recorded by Steinschneider in the letter mentioned above (n. 11). However, Eliezer Lipman Rabinowitz, who was also an expert on rabbinical history, was not familiar with this story (see his letter appended to Avraham ben Hagra, *Sa'arat eliyahu*, 41), although he admitted that he trusted Steinschneider's account.

[14] According to D. Eliach, R. Hayim rejected an offer of the position of rabbi of Vilna (*Father of the Yeshivas* (Heb.), i. 116–17). However, the sources for this are late, and contemporary accounts do not mention this story, according to which R. Hayim claimed that the yeshiva could not be moved.

[15] See Yisrael Klausner, *Vilna, the Jerusalem of Lithuania* (Heb.); I. Cohen, *Vilna*.

[16] Introduction by the sons of the Vilna Gaon, *Shulḥan arukh* with commentary by the Vilna Gaon (Shklov, 1803, often reprinted).

described him as 'the holy man, R. Hayim, *av beit din* of the Holy Community of Volozhin . . . a servant of his master, whose reverence and awe of his teacher match his reverence for Heaven'.[17] The first biographer of the Vilna Gaon, R. Yehoshua Heshel Levin (1818–83), who was himself a famous rabbinic scholar, wrote that after the Gaon's death 'his pupils were scattered . . . and they [appointed as their leader] . . . the *gaon*, the light of the exile, the pious and wise man, our teacher, our rabbi, Hayim of Volozhin'.[18] This was not just rhetoric, R. Hayim had won quasi-official recognition as the Gaon's intellectual successor. The introduction to the Gaon's commentary on the book of Jonah, published by his sons in 1800, stated that anyone who wished to publish works by the Gaon should first bring them to be examined by R. Hayim, and described the case of a man in Lithuania who wanted to print the Gaon's commentary on the mishnaic tractate *Tohorot* but was refused: 'The great *beit din* [court] and the head of the court forbade him to print them unless he brought them to . . . the rabbi and *av beit din* of the Holy Community of Volozhin. He handed over the first part, and when the rabbi came with the book to our town he told the great *beit din* that there were many errors in it.'[19]

R. Hayim was also renowned as a prominent *posek*, an authority on the interpretation of halakhah (Jewish law). Only about twenty of his written responsa survived the great fire that devastated Volozhin in 1815, but his stature is still very evident.[20] Six are dated, and three of these were written before 1803. In one of them, written in 1802, R. Hayim writes: 'And thus now, because of our many sins, in our regions this generation is orphaned of wise men, and from all around [people] have placed upon my neck the yoke of instruction, and they do not permit anything at all unless it is with my unworthy agreement.'[21] These are the words of a rabbi who is modest but also aware of his worth and willing to take responsibility for making halakhic decisions. Two years later, he was summoned to act as arbitrator in a complicated case in Minsk between the town rabbi and the community;[22] he also acted in this capacity in a case that involved the rabbis of Mir and Novogrudok.[23] Only leading rabbis were given such responsibility.

R. Hayim was active in organizing support for the followers of the Vilna Gaon who had emigrated from eastern Europe and gone to Palestine following the Gaon's death: when one of these followers, R. Yisra'el of Shklov was sent back to eastern Europe in 1808 to raise funds, one of his first steps was to

[17] Ibid.; see also R. Menahem Mendel of Shklov's edition of the Vilna Gaon's book, *Tsurat ha'arets* (Shklov, 1801).　　　　　　　[18] Y. H. Levin, *Aliyot eliyahu*, 76.

[19] Jonah with the commentary of the Vilna Gaon (Vilna, 1800). The text is on the verso of the title page.

[20] They were printed in H. Berlin (ed.), *Ḥut hameshulash*, responsum 8.　　　　　　　[21] Ibid.

[22] Shabad, *Toledot hayamim*, 17. I have not been able to trace the source for this in the manuscripts of the Minsk community registers, which are now in the National and University Library in Jerusalem.　　　　　　　[23] Bunimovitsh, *Mikhtav me'eliyahu*, 19–20.

turn to R. Hayim for assistance. R. Yisra'el subsequently recorded in the *pinkas* (general register) of Safed that he had merited the 'aid of the *gaon* of Volozhin, in his great wisdom and wonderful righteousness'. His mission succeeded largely thanks to the aid he received from R. Hayim.[24]

R. Hayim did not shirk public responsibility, and emerged as a major leader of Lithuanian Jewry though he had no formal communal position. Indeed, by the nineteenth century, there was no recognized supra-communal structure of Lithuanian Jewry in which he could have played a role. The main meeting point for prominent Lithuanian Jews was the annual Belarusian fair at Zelva, and he went there often.[25] An event that took place near the end of his life reflected his leading role. In 1815 a group of Lithuanian Jewish leaders met in Minsk. Ostensibly, the aim of the meeting was to organize support for Jewish 'colonists' settling as farmers in the Kherson region, and it was indeed decided to offer them aid. However, the hidden agenda was a desire to organize and fund a delegation to St Petersburg to lobby on behalf of the Jews.[26] In effect, the participants were functioning as an ad hoc committee in place of the Va'ad Medinat Lita, which had been disbanded about fifty years earlier. The participants signed the resolutions as members of the council but added at the end of the list, 'his honour, the renowned *gaon* and rabbi, etc., our teacher, R. Hayim, *av beit din* of the Holy Community of Volozhin'. This was clearly done to add weight to their decisions. Three years later when the delegation left for St Petersburg, the participants went by way of Volozhin in order to be able to consult R. Hayim. Some sources claim that R. Hayim himself travelled to St Petersburg, but there is no real evidence of this.[27]

[24] The register has been lost, but part of it, including this quotation, appears in Frumkin, *History of the Scholars of Jerusalem* (Heb.), iii. 139. According to family tradition, one of the emigrants, R. Yitshak of Haslowicz, took the trouble to pass through Volozhin on his way to Palestine. See Hasin, *Divrei yeshayah*, intro. On R. Hayim's role in the emigration of the Vilna Gaon's disciples, see also Morgenstern, 'Two Traditions about the Beginning of the Emigration to Palestine' (Heb.). Morgenstern notes that R. Yisra'el of Shklov emigrated to Palestine in 1810, but was sent back to eastern Europe the same year to organize financial support. For a fine general study of this topic, see Morgenstern, *Hastening Redemption*.

[25] See Bunimovitsh, *Mikhtav me'eliyahu*, 19, in the name of Nahum Kabak and Hillel Fried. In B. Kaplinski (ed.), *Zhetel* (Heb.), 50, it is recorded that R. Hayim ordained Hayim Lipschitz at the Zelva fair, as did R. Shaul Katzenellenbogen of Vilna and R. Abraham Possveller of Vilna.

[26] The resolution regarding the 'colonists' was published in *Hamelits*, 29/251 (17 Nov. 1889). The resolution on the delegation appeared in *Hapeles*, 1/10 (1901), 636–8. On the Minsk conference, see also Lederhendler, *The Road to Modern Jewish Politics*, 54, 68. A copy of the original decision with the signature of R. Hayim appears in Zeira, *Our Sages in the Diaspora* (Heb.), ii. 205.

[27] The visit to Volozhin is recorded in *Hamelits*, 17/6 (22 Feb. 1881), based on the reminiscences of Yitshak Sasson, the secretary of the delegation. Ya'akov Lifschitz claimed, in *Hakerem*, 1 (1888), 180, that R. Hayim himself travelled to St Petersburg, and he was followed in this by Zitron, *Intercessors* (Yid.), 119, and H. Berlin, 'Forgotten Sheaf and Corner of the Field' (Heb.). Sasson, who was a member of the delegation, made no mention of R. Hayim's

In spite of his reputation, R. Hayim wrote few approbations (*haskamot*) to books, and only eleven have survived. It seems likely that many authors requested approbations from him but that he followed the Vilna Gaon's custom of avoiding doing so.[28]

Towards the end of his life R. Hayim suffered partial paralysis. He had to give up teaching, and the administration of the yeshiva was delegated to his son and ultimate successor R. Yitshak (see below).[29] However, judging from the eulogy given by R. David of Novogrudok, he was still closely involved: 'Even in his old age, when he was not strong enough to teach himself, nevertheless he personally supervised the welfare of all the yeshiva students.'[30]

R. Hayim died on 14 June (14 Sivan) 1821. He published no books during his lifetime, but his surviving responsa were published after his death, as was *Sefer nefesh hahayim*, a theological text, and *Ruah hayim*, a commentary on tractate *Pirkei avot* of the Mishnah.

2. R. Hayim's Motives for Founding the Volozhin Yeshiva

The yeshiva in Volozhin, which as we shall see was a major innovation in many respects, was undoubtedly R. Hayim's most important achievement. There has been much discussion about his motives in establishing it. The three principal hypotheses are (a) that he did so on the Vilna Gaon's instructions, (b) that he saw it as an integral part of the struggle against hasidism, and (c) that it was a response to a drastic decline in Talmud study. Each of these explanations is problematic.

Several scholars have rightly dismissed the first hypothesis, since there is no contemporary evidence of any such instruction from the Vilna Gaon: all the sources that mention this theory are late. Similarly, no such directive is mentioned in the promotional literature that R. Hayim distributed on behalf of the yeshiva. If it had been started on the Gaon's orders, he would surely have mentioned that fact.[31]

accompanying them, though he surely would have had this been so. By 1818 R. Hayim was already old and ailing, and it seems doubtful that he would have been able to set out on such a journey. Lifschitz thus seems to have been misinformed.

[28] For a detailed discussion of this, see Stampfer, 'R. Hayim of Volozhin and his Approbations' (Heb.). R. Yitshak, R. Hayim's son, once refused to write an approbation, claiming: 'What shall I do? . . . I cannot break my father's rule.' It would thus seem that his father deliberately wrote few approbations. See also Ze'ev ben Yehezkel Feivel, *Avodah tamah*.

[29] Steinschneider and Zalkin quote a passage written by R. Yitshak at the request of his father found in a manuscript of responsa by R. Abraham Avli: 'I do not say, Accept my opinion, especially now that I am deprived of the use of my hands and feet, may God have mercy, and nothing survives of my body and my mind' (*The City of Vilna* (Heb.), i. 31).

[30] David of Novogrudok, *Galya masekhet*, 66.

[31] For an example of the claim that R. Hayim was obeying instructions from the Vilna Gaon, see Berdyczewski [Bar Bei Rav], 'History of the Ets Hayim Yeshiva' (Heb.), 232. This historical

The theory that R. Hayim saw the yeshiva as part of the struggle against hasidism is more widespread. The anti-hasidic nature of his book *Nefesh haḥayim*[32] would at first seem to support this idea. Additional evidence of his opposition to hasidism may be seen in his strictures against those hasidim who accused the Vilna Gaon of deviating from R. Isaac Luria's kabbalistic teachings:

And as often as I mention the greatness and wonders of the holy Torah of our great rabbi [the Vilna Gaon], may he rest in Eden, I am reminded of something that lights a fire in my heart, for my ear has heard the slander of the many empty-headed fools in far-off regions, who have never seen the light of his holy Torah in their lives, men with no curb on their mouths, whose tongues speak loudly, casting aspersions on the holy ones of Heaven; dead flies, who befoul the holy oil of anointment of our great master, may he rest in Eden, by claiming that he did not think highly, God forbid, of the holy rabbi upon whom the Holy Spirit rested, the Ari [R. Isaac Luria], may his memory be for a blessing. And this and more besides; some of them sink even further into speaking slander, saying also that the Holy Zohar was not pure enough in his eyes, God forbid, for him ever to have studied it—may those lying lips be struck dumb which speak vilely against the righteous man, the foundation of the world; may they be punished, may they be destroyed, may they be silenced, may there be none such in Israel; for their eyes can behold this commentary [on the Zohar], which rests entirely on awesome foundations . . . and the Holy Zohar, and the *Ra'aya meheimna*, and the *Tikunim* [kabbalistic works]. In his works on revealed knowledge [i.e. non-kabbalistic lore] and his commentary on the *Shulḥan arukh* . . . he explained many halakhic rulings on the basis of the Holy Zohar. And even though lies cannot last and their words are void and worthless, nevertheless my heart mourns, and woe to my ears that have heard this, and I feel that I have an obligation to make the truth known.[33]

The problem with this hypothesis is that R. Hayim's opposition to hasidism at the theoretical level was not reflected at the practical or social level. In spite of his close relationship with the Vilna Gaon, who was a great crusader against

error clearly demonstrates the yeshiva's image in the late 19th cent. Criticism of this hypothesis may be found in Etkes, 'R. Hayim of Volozhin's Method' (Heb.), 18–21; Lamm, *Torah lishmah*, 25–6.

[32] On the book's anti-hasidic bias, see Etkes, 'R. Hayim of Volozhin's Method' (Heb.); Lamm, *Torah lishmah*. On R. Hayim's attitude to hasidism in general, see Etkes, 'Review of N. Lamm, *Torah lishmah*' (Heb.); Tishby, 'God, the Torah, and Israel are One' (Heb.), 486–7; id., 'R. Yisra'el of Shklov's Criticism of the Hasidim' (Heb.), 300–3; Hildesheimer, 'R. Hayim of Volozhin's Opinion of Hasidism' (Heb.). Rabbi Boruch Oberlander has pointed out that, despite its anti-hasidic character, *Nefesh haḥayim* reflects the influence of Shneur Zalman of Lyady's *Sefer hatanya* and incorporates some of Shneur Zalman's characteristic idioms without explicitly saying so. See also Greenwald, 'Soul and Hasidic Spirit'; Teitelbaum, *The Rabbi of Lyady and the Habad Party* (Heb.), ii. 90–4. I am not qualified to express an opinion on this claim.

[33] R. Hayim's introduction to *Sifra ditseniuta* with the commentary of the Vilna Gaon (Vilna and Grodno, 1820). On the Vilna Gaon's studies of kabbalah, see Avivi, *The Kabbalah of the Vilna Gaon* (Heb.).

hasidism, his name does not appear on any ban (*ḥerem*) issued against the hasidim.[34] Silence alone does not prove much,[35] but there is also written evidence of his tolerant attitude to hasidism.[36] According to a letter that R. Shneur Zalman of Lyady (1745–1813) sent to the rabbis of Vilna in 1811, R. Hayim permitted ritual slaughter with polished knives according to hasidic custom, a practice to which mitnagedim were generally opposed.[37] There was nothing about the practice that was contrary to halakhah, but given the controversy surrounding it R. Hayim's willingness to approve it publicly was highly significant. He could have repudiated the letter had he so wished, thus weakening R. Shneur Zalman's claim, but there is no evidence that he did so—a fact that argues in favour of the truth of the claim.

Further proof of R. Hayim's tolerant attitude to hasidism is to be seen in reports of his personal contacts with hasidim. For example, one of R. Hayim's

[34] See e.g. Etkes, 'Review of N. Lamm, *Torah lishmah*' (Heb.); Shmukler [Shapira], *Rabbi Hayim of Volozhin* (Heb.), 21–6; Wilensky, *Hasidim and Mitnagedim* (Heb.).

[35] D. Eliach notes that he saw a photograph of a copy of the Vilna Gaon's ban on hasidism in R. Hayim's handwriting (*Father of the Yeshivas* (Heb.), i. 295). The significance of this is not clear. Eliach does not note the source of the photograph; it would have been desirable for the owners of the manuscript to publish it, along with any other sources in their possession.

[36] See the Hebrew edition of Lamm, *Torah lishmah*: 'R. Hayim maintained good, fair, peaceful, and even friendly day-to-day relations with hasidic *tsadikim* and scholars' (p. 24). The parallel passage in the English edition is more restrained. Lamm presents a number of proofs for this statement, and I agree with his conclusion. Nevertheless it should be noted that not all of Lamm's evidence is convincing. A few examples are based on the book *Matsref ha'avodah*, which Lamm admits is a forgery (*Torah lishmah*, 119). Mondschein ('The Book *Matsref ha'avodah* and the Book *Vikuaḥ raba*' (Heb.)) provides detailed evidence of the forgery and shows that the book cannot be used to obtain a picture of R. Hayim's world. Lamm also relies on a story about a meeting with a hasid recorded in Y. Litvin, 'Rabbi Hayim', which appeared with no source cited. The basis of this story seems to be the approbation written by R. Hayim for the edition of the Jerusalem Talmud published in Kopust in 1808, which appeared alongside an approbation from R. Levi Yitshak of Berdichev. However, the storyteller did not notice that each rabbi wrote his approbation in his home town, and that there is no evidence of a meeting between the two figures. The moderation of R. Hayim's language in *Nefesh haḥayim* is also no proof. It might be a product of his personality and style and not a reflection of his attitudes. Similarly, one cannot form conclusions about R. Hayim's opinion from stories about his disciples. However, it might be worth noting that R. Hayim's nephew, R. Avraham Simhah, sent at least one halakhic question to the Habad leader R. Menachem Mendel Schneersohn. See S. D. Levin, 'The Tsemah Tsedek and his Generation' (Heb.), 80; and see also the responsa in M. M. Schneersohn *She'elot uteshuvot al tsemaḥ tsedek*, pt. 2, 114 in the note on responsum 253. Rabbi Boruch Oberlander has pointed out that there is very little discussion in R. Hayim's works of the main thesis of the Vilna Gaon's argument against hasidism, which is the issue of *tsimtsum* (a form of divine self-withdrawal). See also M. M. Schneersohn, *Sacred Letters* (Heb.), i. 19–20, his reply to a letter from R. Eliyahu Dessler. See also Sorski, *Torah and Musar Teachers* (Heb.), iii. 66. I am not qualified to express an opinion on this complex issue.

[37] See Hillman, *Letters of the Master of the Tanya* (Heb.), 205. On the use of polished knives, see Stampfer, 'On the History of the Dispute over Polished Knives' (Heb.).

grandsons became a hasid, but the rabbi did not sever connections with him.[38] When one of his grandsons married the daughter of a hasid, her dowry was deposited with R. Hayim.[39] Another of his grandsons recalled that in his youth, his grandfather had sent him with a message to the hasidic *rebbe* Yisra'el of Ruzhin, requesting him to intercede with the government to prevent Jews being drafted into the military.[40] Another tradition preserved in the family was that R. Hayim visited several hasidim, including a *tsadik* who had a reputation as a great scholar (perhaps R. Shneur Zalman of Lyady);[41] although this is a later tradition, it is difficult to believe that this staunchly mitnagdic family would have made up such a story.

R. Hayim wrote approbations for six books issued by publishers known to have links with hasidim.[42] Had he wanted to demonstrate his distance from hasidism, he could easily have refrained from doing so. One of these publishers, Meir ben Shelomoh, wrote in a preface to the book *Arba me'ot shekel kesef*[43] that he had visited 'my master, my champion, and my instructor, the great *gaon* who is mighty in both the revealed and the hidden lore, our teacher Hayim, may his light shine, head of the yeshiva and *av beit din* of the Holy Congregation of Volozhin' in order to show him the manuscript of a book attributed to R. Hayim Vital. He clearly did not feel uncomfortable with R. Hayim despite his hasidic ties.

The most important evidence regarding R. Hayim's attitude to hasidism is apparent in the circumstances of the publication of his book *Nefesh haḥayim*, in which he discusses hasidic ideas.[44] R. Hayim wrote it in his old age, many

---

[38] This is recorded in R. Hayim's *Teachings and Practices*, based on the Pardo manuscript: 'Our rabbi spoke to one of his family who was inclined towards the hasidim of the time. In any event, be heedful of three things: (1) study the Talmud and its discussions, and let this be your service before the Holy One, Blessed Be He, in your eyes; (2) keep the law of the Talmud; (3) do not speak about our master the Vilna Gaon.' This clearly does not constitute encouragement, but nor is it rejection. See also D. Eliach (ed.), *Kol hakatuv leḥayim*, 147, §4; see ibid. 185 for the story of how R. Hayim prevented a young man from joining the hasidim by means of a miracle. For our purposes, it is important to note that this was not depicted as taking place in the course of an argument, nor was it accompanied by an attack on hasidism. In reality, there was a grandson who was attracted to hasidism; see Katzman, 'The Family of R. Hayim of Volozhin' (Heb.). [39] Alexandrovsky, *Sha'arei yitshak*, 111–12.
[40] According to Lifschitz, *Zikhron ya'akov*, i. 27–8, he related this in the name of R. Yitshak Ze'ev Soloveitchik.
[41] Frumer, 'Memories of R. Zalman Sender' (Yid.). R. Hayim himself noted in *Nefesh haḥayim* (pt. 4, ch. 1) that he had visited a distant region, apparently populated by hasidim. This accords with Zalman Sender—or perhaps it is the source for his tradition.
[42] On R. Hayim's approbations, see Stampfer, 'R. Hayim of Volozhin and his Approbations' (Heb.). [43] Vital, *Arba me'ot shekel kesef*.
[44] On this book, see Etkes, 'R. Hayim of Volozhin's Method' (Heb.); Gross, 'On the Weltanschauung of R. Hayim' (Heb.); Lamm, *Torah lishmah*, ch. 2. On R. Hayim's attitude to hasidic literature as expressed in *Nefesh haḥayim*, see Greenwald, 'Soul and Hasidic Spirit'; Hildesheimer, 'R. Hayim of Volozhin's Opinion of Hasidism' (Heb.); A. M. Katz, 'On the Path

years after he founded the yeshiva,[45] but in accordance with his wishes it was published only after his death. In this book he clearly rejects basic hasidic approaches, and there is no question about the authenticity of these passages.[46] If he had been seriously concerned about hasidism, why would he have postponed its publication? It was not that he contented himself with distributing handwritten copies during his lifetime, since there is no evidence that any of his anti-hasidic pronouncements were circulated in manuscript among his disciples.[47]

We can also learn from an agreement that R. Yisra'el of Shklov signed with hasidic leaders in 1812 dividing up eastern Europe for purposes of collecting funds for hasidic and mitnagdic causes in Palestine.[48] In the light of the close ties between R. Yisra'el and R. Hayim, it seems highly unlikely that R. Yisra'el

Leading Up To Beit El' (Heb.). On *Nefesh haḥayim*, see Magid, 'Deconstruction of the Mystical'; Pachter, 'Between Acosmism and Theism' (Heb.).

[45] See the approbation of R. Avraham Avli at the end of the book.

[46] Not all copies of the first edition contain these sections; see Lamm, *Torah lishmah*, 60. D. Eliach notes that he saw copies of the first edition that included the missing chapters. He raises the possibility that these pages were torn out of the copies hitherto known and that the book was originally published with all the 'missing' material (*Father of the Yeshivas* (Heb.), i. 308). Yeshayahu Vinograd has suggested that it is possible that some copies originally had this passage bound in the book from the start while other copies were bound without it. If this was the case, it would explain two unusual bibliographical characteristics of the book: first, that the pages of each section are numbered as a separate unit and do not run continuously through the book, and second, that the passage containing the anti-hasidic material was not printed as a numbered section (§4), but appears as extra chapters between §3 and §4. These two features would have made it easier to distribute two different versions of the book without making it obvious. However, if this is what actually happened, the question arises as to why. Apparently it is related to the fact that the book was printed in separate fascicles that were only later bound together (see Vinograd, *A Treasury of the Works of the Vilna Gaon* (Heb.), 248). *Likutei hagra* (New York, 1999), ed. Nehemyah Fefer, includes 'Leket nefesh haḥayim' (pp. 261–7) which is presented as portions of *Nefesh haḥayim* that were not printed. The text includes some anti-hasidic statements but it is not clear why it would have been deleted by the editors any more than the anti-hasidic elements that were left in. It is difficult to determine whether the text is authentic or not. I consulted with R. Eliezer Brodt, who is an expert in such topics, and he informed me that there is good reason to assume that the text is authentic.

[47] Eliach notes that he saw a handwritten copy that was slightly different from the printed text (*Father of the Yeshivas* (Heb.), i. 309). However, from what he writes it seems that this was not a copy made by one of his disciples for circulation but a draft version in R. Hayim's hand. The location of this manuscript is unknown to me, and it is regrettable that its owners have not published it or made it available in facsimile. It is possible that it is the manuscript cited in *Likutei hagra*, ed. Fefer.

[48] See Tishby, 'R. Yisra'el of Shklov's Criticism' (Heb.). Dr Aryeh Morgenstern informed me that Tishby told him explicitly that the identification of the author of the manuscript was speculative (personal communication, 8 Nov. 1999). Dr Morgenstern added, 'I know that R. Yisra'el demonstrated a positive attitude to the hasidim in Safed. His second wife was actually from the "sect" of the hasidim, and as a result he was attacked by the *perushim* in Jerusalem.'

would have signed such an agreement without R. Hayim's approval.[49]Again, as Isaiah Tishby has shown, R. Hayim took a strongly anti-hasidic stance ideologically.[50] However, while R. Hayim was opposed to hasidism at the theoretical level, at the practical level he was not interested in fomenting controversy or fighting personal battles.[51]

It is rather improbable that R. Hayim was so concerned about hasidism that he felt compelled to found a yeshiva in order to combat it, but at the same time never found it necessary to take a public stance against either the hasidic movement or individual hasidim. No contemporary sources mention any such opposition, and R. Hayim himself does not refer to it. Thus the attempt to link the founding of the yeshiva to an anti-hasidic campaign seems to be no more than a later interpretation of R. Hayim's actions.[52]

The hypothesis that R. Hayim founded his yeshiva in response to a decline in Torah study assumes that there was indeed such a crisis in Lithuania at the beginning of the nineteenth century.[53] Some would add hasidism into the equation, yielding the theory that the spread of hasidism led to a decline in study, which in turn led R. Hayim to establish the yeshiva. At first glance, there seems to be solid evidence for a decline in Torah study, whatever the cause. Just before the yeshiva opened, R. Hayim himself wrote that 'the Torah

[49] This description accords well with the image of a person who did not want to deal with *balabatim* (the lay membership of the community) nor be dependent on the community. However, see also D. Eliach, *Kol hakatuv leḥayim*, 185, where a passage is cited from a late manuscript by R. Aryeh Levin hinting that study at Volozhin was intended to protect students from hasidism. On R. Hayim's opposition to schism, see the sources listed by Eliach (ibid. 119), concerning R. Hayim's instructions to a student to pray according to the *nusaḥ* (liturgical rite) of the local community.

[50] The compromise of 1812 and another arranged in 1818 are described in the anonymous pamphlet *Record This for a Later Generation* (Heb.), published in Jerusalem in 1845. For additional details, see Frumkin, *History of the Scholars of Jerusalem* (Heb.), iii. 141; S. Halevi, 'R. Yisra'el of Shklov' (Heb.).

[51] As noted above, R. Hayim's nephew, R. Avraham Simhah, sent a halakhic question to the Habad leader known as the Tsemah Tsedek; see S. D. Levin, 'The Tsemah Tsedek and his Generation' (Heb.), 80. See also the responsa of the Tsemah Tsedek, M. M. Schneersohn, *She'elot uteshuvot al tsemaḥ tsedek*, pt. 2, 144, in the notes on responsum 253. Had the approach in Volozhin been to avoid contact with hasidim, it would be difficult to understand how R. Avraham Simhah could have turned to a hasidic rabbi with a question.

[52] On the hasidim in Volozhin, see Mondschein, 'The Pious *Gaon*' (Heb.), 28. R. Yehonatan of Satanov was a hasid who moved to Volozhin after the death of his first wife and was received with great honour by R. Hayim. When he needed advice he used to consult R. Akiva Eger (1761–1837) and not R. Yitshak, but he respected R. Hayim's son. Kinder's *Terrible Stories* (Heb.) mentions R. Hayim as having a positive attitude towards hasidim, but the accuracy of this source is questionable.

[53] Etkes, 'R. Hayim of Volozhin's Method' (Heb.), 16–21. On p. 1, Etkes mentions the crisis evident in the Torah institutions of Lithuania, and on p. 18 he describes the crisis affecting Jewish society in Poland. A similar view is expressed by Shochat in 'Messianic and Mystical Principles' (Heb.).

is being forgotten . . . and is vanishing and disappearing . . . because they have ceased to maintain yeshivas . . . all those who seek God and who seek His Torah . . . have been scattered'.[54] In *Nefesh haḥayim* he wrote: 'The crown of the Torah is abandoned in a dark corner, and with my own eyes I have seen a certain region where this custom has spread to such an extent that in most of their *batei midrash* there is nothing but books of *musar*, and not even a single complete copy of the Talmud.'[55] R. Yosef of Krynki, a disciple of R. Hayim, wrote similarly about the state of Torah study in Lithuania on the eve of the founding of the yeshiva:

> The world was laid waste, in utter chaos, for the very name 'yeshiva' was unknown in the world, let alone the nature of a yeshiva and what is done there. Nor was public Torah study known, for the world was empty of the Torah, and also of holy books. The Talmud could not be found anywhere except in the possession of a chosen few, prominent and wealthy men. Even in *batei midrash* in large towns there was no complete set of the Talmud, for such a thing was not needed, since nobody used it. When our holy master founded the yeshiva, there was a need for many sets of the Talmud. They had to send to large towns and gather Talmuds for the yeshiva students. When the *gaon*, the rabbi of Slavuta, may his rest be in Eden, saw that Talmuds were needed in the world, he printed several hundred sets, both large and small.[56]

R. Yosef's description of the framework for study was accurate. Indeed, at the beginning of the nineteenth century there were no famous yeshivas in the Polish–Lithuanian Commonwealth, and advanced Talmud study was carried out mainly in the informal framework of *batei midrash*. All these sources would seem to demonstrate that there was a crisis in the study of Torah, but complaints of a decline should be treated with caution. Every generation hears that Torah study is not what it was in the past. R. Yosef's words resonate, but as far as they can be checked they seem to be inaccurate. For example, the Slavuta edition of the Talmud was printed in 1801, before the founding of the yeshiva.[57] Nor does the large number of distinguished scholars in R. Hayim's generation and in the generation that followed lend weight to R. Yosef's words. Moreover, much of the 'proof' of a decline in study which R. Hayim mentions refers to the situation in Poland or the hasidic regions of Belarus, and it is misleading to cite evidence from Poland, a region with its own cultural identity, when discussing Lithuania. Even the suggestion that there was a crisis in Torah study in Poland that was linked to the spread of hasidism has not been substantiated. In spite of R. Hayim's complaint about the proliferation of books on *musar*, most of the books printed in the early nineteenth

---

[54] Shmukler [Shapira], *Rabbi Hayim of Volozhin* (Heb.), 53.

[55] Hayim of Volozhin, *Nefesh haḥayim*, pt. 4, ch. 1. See Etkes, 'R. Hayim of Volozhin's Method' (Heb.), 12.   [56] Shmukler [Shapira], *Rabbi Hayim of Volozhin* (Heb.), 46.

[57] Rabbinovicz, *An Account of the Printing of the Talmud* (Heb.), 168.

century in hasidic regions were intended for Talmud scholars and were not about *musar*. Similarly, many classic rabbinic texts were published with appro-bations from hasidic *rebbes*,[58] and hasidic groups that excelled in Torah study, such as Habad or Ger, could not have sprung out of a void. Nor should one ignore the fact that major non-hasidic scholars were active even after R. Hayim's death in the part of Poland under Russian rule ('Congress Poland') and in Galicia. They too could not have arisen in a vacuum.

In reality, it is difficult to establish whether traditional study was even in mild decline in R. Hayim's time and if so where it began, since almost all the surviving sources that deal with the topic are suspect. Certainly there is no hard evidence for the claim, and the large number of gifted rabbis who appeared in the period of 'crisis' suggests, on the contrary, that it was a period when Torah study flourished. The term 'crisis' is surely too strong a term to be used unless there is supporting evidence. At the same time R. Hayim clearly *felt* that Torah study was in decline: it is understandable that having himself studied with the Vilna Gaon, he saw the next generation as infinitely inferior. So while it is difficult to show that the founding of the Volozhin yeshiva was related to a real crisis in Torah study, it may have been the by-product of a subjective sense of crisis. However, there are good grounds for thinking that this too was not the main reason for the founding of the yeshiva.

The most important source of information on R. Hayim's motives in founding the yeshiva is an open letter which he wrote on Sunday 3 October 1802 addressed to 'lovers of the Torah'.[59] R. Hayim began by noting that, although he was unworthy to write the missive, he was acting on behalf of the community. He described the decline he perceived in Torah study, adding that in his opinion it was not caused by contempt for study but rather by lack of opportunity: some wished to study but lacked sufficient means, while others had both the desire and the means but had no rabbi to teach them 'the ways of true logic', because 'yeshivas are no longer maintained in this country'. He continued: 'Those who are great in the fear of God in this region have appealed to me to be among those who awaken others to perform this

[58] The link between Hebrew printing in eastern Europe at the beginning of the 19th cent. and cultural processes has not yet been adequately investigated. On the links between hasidism and printing, see H. Lieberman, 'Legends and Truth about Hasidic Printing Shops' (Yid.). For a preliminary list of Polish presses at this period, see Friedberg, *The Hebrew Press in Poland* (Heb.). See also Vinograd, *A Treasury of the Hebrew Book* (Heb.), vol. ii, and Gries, *Book, Scribe, and Story in Early Hasidism* (Heb.), which open up this area to methodical research.

[59] For an accurate though incomplete version, see Y. Broda, *Beit ya'akov*, 2. The Schwadron Collection in the National and University Library in Jerusalem contains a copy of the letter that bears the incorrect date, Sunday, 7 Tishrei (23 Sept.) 1803. For the complete letter, see the anonymous article 'For Researchers of Antiquity' (Heb.). At a public auction I saw a sheet with the yeshiva's letterhead from the 20th cent. that gave the date the yeshiva was founded as 1807, but this must be an error. On this letter, see Vinograd, *A Treasury of the Works of the Vilna Gaon* (Heb.), 247.

mitzvah.' R. Hayim said that yeshivas were needed in order to safeguard the future of Torah study, and that he had therefore taken upon himself the responsibility of running a yeshiva and was appealing to the public for support. After expanding further on the importance of Torah study, R. Hayim returned to the need to 'repair the breach' in the wall of Torah and called both for more students to dedicate themselves to Torah study and for more individuals to support the institution financially. He observed that the yeshiva in Volozhin already had students, and that 'the taste of the Torah has been instilled in most of them, and they have truly accepted the yoke of the Torah'.

It is worth summarizing the four main points R. Hayim makes in the letter:

1. Many young people wish to study Torah but need support in order to do so.

2. Students need a teacher to lead them in study and set an example through their personal behaviour. This theme recurs throughout R. Hayim's writings, especially in his commentary on *Pirkei avot*. Obviously this idea was not original to R. Hayim, but he was one of the few people of his time to emphasize this point. In his opinion, one of the factors that had led to the sorry state of Torah study that he perceived was that communities had ceased to maintain yeshivas and scholars remained 'enclosed in the four cubits of the Law', rather than teaching others.

3. It is important to adopt the correct way of studying: 'the way of logic in Torah study'. This seems again to reflect the influence of the Vilna Gaon, whose distinctive approach to study—characterized by an emphasis on studying *peshat* (the overt meaning of a text) and on clarifying the halakhah according to the Talmud and only to a lesser degree on the basis of the decisions of later rabbis—left a deep impression on contemporaries. In fact, R. Hayim played an important role in popularizing the Vilna Gaon's method of study. One of his disciples writes: 'The distortion of the [true] study [of Torah] which was customary [before the Gaon] led them to spend their days . . . in twisted casuistry . . . only in Vilna and its environs did they grasp the method of study of our master Eliyahu, the pious *gaon*, of blessed memory, and afterwards our teacher R. Hayim of Volozhin developed and established this study method ... in his yeshiva at Volozhin.'[60]

4. By studying at the yeshiva, the students truly took upon themselves 'full acceptance' of the responsibility of Torah study. The reference to 'full acceptance' hints at R. Hayim's view that the study of Torah is the true service of God. This position was later developed in detail in *Nefesh haḥayim*, but this letter suggests that he had already begun to formulate it before founding the yeshiva.

[60] Z. Epstein, *Minḥat yehudah*, intro.

Thus, R. Hayim's main motive for establishing the yeshiva seems to have been simply a desire to help young men realize the ideal of studying the Torah—not a desire to change Jewish society or to fight against certain trends within it. While hardly a revolutionary idea nor a new one, this certainly fits both with R. Hayim's writings and his deeds. However, this was not the only factor.

3. The Choice of Location

Why was the yeshiva set up in the small town of Volozhin rather than in a big city? At the beginning of the nineteenth century the Haskalah had not yet reached even the largest cities of eastern Europe, so there was no need to seek a location far from the 'harmful' influences of urban life. Indeed, before R. Hayim's time almost all the famous yeshivas had been located in big cities. This was not surprising because yeshivas are expensive to maintain. Large communities could attract great rabbis and often promised not only a salary but also financial support for a certain number of students. Thus a well-known rabbi who aspired to direct a large yeshiva would try to find a post in a big city. Indeed, even later in the nineteenth century, there were important yeshivas in cities such as Kovno and Vilna. R. Hayim could have adopted this strategy. His reputation was great enough to obtain him a rabbinical position in almost any community he wanted, even outside Lithuania.[61] Volozhin, however, was a small town that could not support very many students. It would have been natural for R. Hayim to move to a larger community, yet he did not.

R. Hayim seems to have chosen not to move to a large town for personal reasons. His unpleasant experience in Vilkomir may have deterred him, and the risk of conflicts with community leaders and the many responsibilities that were the lot of a rabbi who served a large community may have discouraged him from moving. Perhaps he was influenced by the Vilna Gaon, who was an outstanding scholar in many fields but never served in a rabbinical position that would have distracted him from his studies. Other suggestions could also be offered.

What is clear is that it was impossible both to stay as a rabbi in Volozhin and still teach all the students he wanted to influence. For some time R. Hayim tried to overcome the limitations of a small community by supporting his students at his own expense, but as the number of students rose it became clear that this was not feasible. He was left with two options: to give up the

---

[61] There was considerable mobility among rabbis in his time. R. Aryeh Leib Gunzberg, one of R. Hayim's teachers, served at one time as rabbi of Volozhin, but towards the end of his life was appointed rabbi of Metz (now in France); R. Hayim's second teacher, R. Raphael Kohen Hamburger, moved from Minsk to the famous Hamburg Jewish community.

idea of teaching a large number of students or to find a way of overcoming the limitations of a small town. The only way to support all the students who wanted to study with him was to raise funds outside the local community. This required an institutional framework that could call on the general Jewish public for support. In other words, it was necessary to establish a yeshiva that was independent of the local community: this alone would make it different from any yeshiva that had ever existed in eastern Europe.[62] However, there is no evidence that R. Hayim founded the yeshiva as part of a conscious attempt to change institutional frameworks or to separate yeshivas from communal structures.[63] He had good enough reasons even without this particular goal. It should be noted that since he had no contemporary model in eastern Europe of a large yeshiva,[64] he was free to invoke the memory of the great central yeshivas, by then known only from books, and adapt it to his own perception of contemporary needs and opportunities.

The exact date on which the yeshiva was founded is not mentioned in the sources and there was probably never a formal transition from a group of students who clustered around R. Hayim to a formal institution that could support a larger number of students. However, judging from the letter mentioned above, the changeover seems to have been completed by late 1802.

4. Funding the Yeshiva: Methods and Consequences

As the number of students in Volozhin rose, R. Hayim wrote to the Jewish communities of eastern Europe to ask for financial support. The response seems to have been positive. Leaders of the Vilna Jewish community made donations, and in 1804, about a year and a half after he sent out his original letter, an open letter was published to encourage others to follow suit.[65] A

[62] See Berdyczewski [Bar Bei Rav], 'History of the Ets Hayim Yeshiva' (Heb.), 232.

[63] Etkes, 'R. Hayim of Volozhin's Method' (Heb.), 19: 'The method that R. Hayim chose in attempting to revive the yeshiva system was appropriate to contemporary circumstances. He probably thought that the earlier system of communities supporting yeshivas could not be successfully reintroduced and therefore preferred to appeal to individual "lovers of Torah", wherever they were to be found.' This is very logical, but I have not found any sources that confirm that this is what R. Hayim had in mind. Communal support for yeshivas in large communities was not at all out of the question; see Zalkin, 'City of Torah' (Heb.).

When observing the behaviour of others it is natural to credit them with deliberate intentions, and to explain their actions in terms of their character even when no such connection exists. On this, see Jones and Nisbett, 'The Actor and the Observer' (I would like to thank my wife for bringing this research to my attention). In R. Hayim's case, too, care must be taken not to attribute intentions to him *ex post facto*.

[64] There were still yeshivas in Germany that served entire regions, as in Fulda, but R. Hayim was not in touch with them, nor is there any indication that he modelled his yeshiva on them.

[65] See *Hapeles*, 2 (1902), 293. The article was published anonymously.

[66] Ibid. On Zeitlin, see Fishman, *Russia's First Modern Jews*, 56–9.

similar letter, probably from the same period, was written by R. Yehudah Zeitlis (Zeitlin) of Shklov,[66] and in 1809 some Vilna notables circulated yet another letter in support of the yeshiva.[67]

There may have been opposition to R. Hayim's initiative, and possibly expressions of jealousy in regard to his plan, at least at the beginning. According to his great-grandson (R. Hayim Berlin, 1832–1912),[68] the *av beit din* of Brisk R. Aryeh Leib Katzenellenbogen wanted to share in the direction of the yeshiva, but R. Hayim would have none of it. R. Ya'akov Barit, a Vilna rabbi, was reported to have said: 'There were many of the holy ones of Israel who were hesitant as to whether this was the way to attract the hearts of the people, and if the *gaon* . . . had not done it himself, permitting himself no slumber nor sleep . . . he would not have achieved his purpose.'[69] No further details were given.[70] In spite of these hints, opposition—if there was any—seems to have been weak. Perhaps surprisingly, R. Hayim also received support from the government: in 1813, at the height of the war between Russia and France, he received a letter promising the protection of the Russian military governor.[71]

In the wake of his successful appeal, R. Hayim organized a structured system for raising funds. It had three stages: first, he made personal appeals to wealthy friends;[72] second, he appointed resident *gaba'im* (financial representatives) in various large cities to collect funds within their communities;[73] and third, in order to reach smaller communities, he began to appoint itinerant

[67] Steinschneider and Zalkin (eds.), *The City of Vilna* (Heb.), i. 21 n.

[68] H. Berlin, 'Forgotten Sheaf and Corner of the Field' (Heb.), 73.

[69] This is according to his son, writing in 1892; see Barit, 'Glory of Israel' (Heb.), 56. The origin of this story is not clear, nor whether it is authentic or was made up at a later date.

[70] There is also a veiled reference to opposition in the Pardo manuscript of R. Hayim's customs. See Hayim of Volozhin, *Teachings and Practices* (Heb.), 25; Lamm, *Torah lishmah*, 26–8.

[71] The letter reads: 'In the name of His Majesty, Commander of the Armies and Troops, to all men of the Great Army in the Field. You are ordered to protect the chief rabbi of Volozhin, R. Hayim Itzkovich, together with his school and its building, from the billetting of soldiers, damage, and levies, and to extend every protection and assistance to the chief rabbi. You are hereby warned that if anyone transgresses this order he will be severely punished, according to military criminal law. As proof that the aforementioned chief rabbi is under the protection of His Majesty, this letter of protection has been written by me and sealed with my seal.' See Gessen, 'The Fate of the Volozhin Yeshiva' (Rus.), 19. Gessen probably found the document in the archives of the Russian Ministry of Education; see Lozinsky and Ginzburg, *Jewish Government Schools* (Rus.), 130. I am most grateful to Shimon Kleiman for his help with translation.

[72] Four of these can be mentioned, though there were probably several more: Ya'akov Ladsiner (see Hirschman, *Beit avot*, 5), Moshe Shemuel Harkavi (see Harkavi, *Generation of the Upright* (Heb.), 80; he is recorded as paying the salaries of 'the rabbis, *rashei yeshivah*, and administrators' in an emergency), Yitshak of Iwaniec (see Hirsch, *Shema ya'akov*, 70), and Lipa of Iwaniec (see Lifschitz, 'A Generation and its Authors' (Heb.), 181, which states that he was 'R. Hayim's foremost supporter when he founded the yeshiva').

[73] See e.g. Lilienthal, 'My Travels in Russia', *American Israelite*, 2/52(33).

emissaries who would go from town to town, in neighbouring and more distant areas, in order to collect funds.[74] Through their fundraising efforts, the *gaba'im* and the emissaries also advertised the yeshiva, thus attracting talented students. R. Hayim probably assigned regions to each emissary, since according to a description written by an emissary in 1838 each one had a particular region allotted him for that year.[75] Although this description reflects the arrangements current after R. Hayim's death, its author was a veteran emissary who had been active during R. Hayim's lifetime. Since he did not describe this division of regions as a recent innovation, it seems likely that it should be attributed to R. Hayim himself.

These methods were unprecedented in the history of east European yeshivas. While, as noted above, at the beginning of the nineteenth century, there were no famous yeshivas in eastern Europe of even regional significance, such yeshivas had existed in Poland and Lithuania before the mid-seventeenth century. However, these yeshivas had been local institutions supported by local communities or a small number of local people. R. Hayim's yeshiva was different because it was not dependent on local support. He may have been unconsciously modelling the support for his yeshiva on a framework with which he was intimately familiar—the system for supporting the followers of the Vilna Gaon, his former teacher, who had gone to live in Palestine. In his time, immigrants from eastern Europe who lived there were supported by a similar and recently established network of *gaba'im* and emissaries who collected money in eastern Europe and regularly transferred the proceeds to Palestine. R. Hayim applied this type of system to fund his yeshiva. In the distant past, fundraising in one town in aid of a yeshiva in another town would have been impossible. There had been a yeshiva in almost every large town, and there was an established halakhic principle that 'the poor of one's own town take precedence'. People who wanted to support advanced Torah study would have made their donations locally. Now, however, when large communal yeshivas did not exist or were not so significant and study took place mainly in *batei midrash*, it was possible to claim that the Volozhin yeshiva was unique, just as the settlement of Palestine was unique. In both cases there were by definition no local equivalents, and in both cases this justified donating money outside the local community. By supporting the yeshiva in Volozhin, donors could feel that they had a part in the uniquely advanced study there, just as they sensed that supporting the residents in Palestine earned them a

---

[74] Moshe Tzinovitz, an expert on the history of the yeshiva, claims that the first two emissaries were R. Yitshak Halevi Horowitz and R. Me'ir Hakohen, and that the former had once been a student of R. Hayim (Tzinovitz, *Tree of Life* (Heb.), 95), but he adduces no evidence. If he is correct, then R. Hayim did not begin using emissaries immediately upon opening the yeshiva but only after some time, which seems quite possible.

[75] Bunimovitsh, *Mikhtav me'eliyahu*, 48.

share in the commandment to live in the Holy Land. There was no reason
for communal leaders to perceive R. Hayim's emissaries as a threat to the
income of similar local institutions, and it was reasonable to regard the yeshiva
that he directed as providing a service which local institutions did not.[76]

The fundraising methods adopted by the Volozhin yeshiva completely
changed the basis of the relationship between the community and the yeshiva
relative to that which had prevailed between the community and the *beit
midrash*. Students in east European *batei midrash* had been dependent on local
hospitality for food, and they customarily slept on the benches of the women's
section of the *beit midrash*. The local rabbi, with whom *beit midrash* students
could have consulted, was employed by the community and therefore dependent on the goodwill of communal leaders. Now, at Volozhin, funds came from
all over Lithuania and beyond, and they were transmitted directly to the *rosh
yeshivah*. Neither the students nor the yeshiva was dependent on the community—quite the reverse: at Volozhin, every needy student received a weekly
stipend from the yeshiva so he could pay for board and lodging with local families (rather than rely on their hospitality),[77] and staff were also paid salaries by

---

[76] Some communities apparently aspired to match or surpass the achievements of Volozhin
and other yeshivas. On such initiatives to support Torah study in larger cities, see Zalkin, 'City
of Torah' (Heb.). This was a very important phenomenon, though these yeshivas did not acquire
the fame or prestige achieved by others.

On the matter of fundraising, Dr Aryeh Morgenstern has told me that, at some early stage, the
emissaries of the Volozhin yeshiva and those of the Jews of Palestine were probably one and the
same (personal communication, 8 Nov. 1999). According to Z. H. Lehren, money was taken
from the funds collected for the poor Jews of Palestine and sent to the Volozhin yeshiva: this was
the reason for the feud between R. Mordekhai Minsker and R. Yisra'el of Shklov. Lehren wrote
to R. Moshe Sofer in Pressburg on 18 June 1839 that the followers of the Vilna Gaon who
settled in Palestine 'permitted this matter, from that which was collected by the permanent emissaries in the country of Lithuania, who receive pay and travel from city to city to collect alms for
the Land of Israel, that they might take part of it to aid the yeshiva'; see Lehren, *Igerot pakuam*
(MS), viii. 160. R. Yisra'el of Shklov opposed this practice, claiming that 'the mitnagedim give
alms for Palestine and not to the yeshiva of Volozhin' (ibid.). Lehren added: 'and this decree
still stands, and because of R. Avraham Fassweiler and the head of the yeshiva [R. Yitshak] it
must be publicly forbidden' (ibid.). This description accords well with the evidence for the
decline in the yeshiva's authority under R. Yitshak (see below). It is doubtful whether anyone
would have dared to criticize R. Hayim in this manner. R. Tanhum Frank cites a report in
Hakarmel, 1/16 (26 Oct. 1860), 1, which supports the claim for a link between fundraising for the
Volozhin yeshiva and for the Jews who had settled in Palestine; see Frank, *The History of God's
House in Volozhin* (Heb.), 31. An obituary for R. Meir Jacobstadter states that he was a trustee of
the fund for the poor Jews of Palestine and also a trustee of the Volozhin yeshiva (ibid.).

[77] Berdyczewski describes a transitional stage in providing for students' needs: 'From the
yeshiva's funds he hired a woman who cooked food and drink in a great pot for all the yeshiva
boys, and at night they slept on the benches of the yeshiva' ('History of the Ets Hayim Yeshiva'
(Heb.), 233). If this is accurate, the solution does not seem to have lasted for long, perhaps
because of the increasing numbers of students. There is no other evidence of such an
arrangement at Volozhin, and all the other descriptions refer to rented rooms and meals supplied

the yeshiva rather than the community. In other words, local Jews depended on income from the yeshiva rather than the other way round. This increased the status of the yeshiva and its students with the local community, while also increasing students' dependence on the *rosh yeshivah*.

The Volozhin yeshiva soon occupied a building of its own, which also influenced the character of the institution. At first the students had studied in the local *beit midrash*, but because this had been built to meet the needs of a small town and could not accommodate dozens of full-time students it soon became too crowded. The local community did not seem to have either the money or the desire to enlarge it. R. Hayim's solution was to use funds raised for the yeshiva to construct a purpose-built study hall. It is not clear exactly when this actually took place but it must have been during the early years of the yeshiva—according to one source, when the number of students rose to over a hundred.[78] The yeshiva building was not located near the *beit midrash* but in a separate compound. There is no evidence that this was intended to isolate the yeshiva from the local community, though this was the inevitable consequence.

The construction of the yeshiva building had both symbolic and practical consequences. On the symbolic level, it emphasized the institution's independence from the local community. In practical terms, it meant that students no longer had daily contact with either the local youth of the town or its learned elite. The fact that students now paid for meals rather than relying on the generosity of local families further diminished the influence of the latter on the former. In contrast, the importance of social relations between the students (most of whom came from outside Volozhin) increased, and their social life became quite separate from that of the local community. Student celebrations at Purim or Simhat Torah increased the social cohesion of the yeshiva;[79] such separate celebrations were only possible because of the separate building.

Isolation from the local community and financial independence were the main characteristics of the new type of Lithuanian yeshiva. All the major yeshivas founded subsequently followed Volozhin's lead, though during the nineteenth century there were also some community-based yeshivas of

by the landlords. I have found no evidence of hostels or dormitories at any of the Lithuanian yeshivas before the First World War; see Ch. 4 n. 34 below.

[78] Berdyczewski [Bar Bei Rav], 'History of the Ets Hayim Yeshiva' (Heb.), 233.

[79] R. Yosef Zundel of Salant recorded an incident from the early days of the yeshiva. A group of friends got drunk on Simhat Torah and started fighting each other; see Rivlin, *The Tsadik Rabbi Yosef Zundel* (Heb.), 29. R. L. Cohen retold the story, apparently with some inaccuracies, in *Hamodia*, 4/6 (21 Nov. 1913). According to this version, the incident took place at Purim, when R. Zundel was the 'Purim rabbi'. The evidence provided by R. Zundel's letter seems more trustworthy. However, Cohen's version demonstrates that festivities were also held at Purim, since he regarded the occurrence of a drunken incident at Purim as perfectly feasible.

significance.[80] As religious observance declined in the late nineteenth century, the increased isolation of the yeshivas became inevitable. In fact, the yeshivas were able to continue only because of their independence from the local communities. Some people attributed R. Hayim's innovation to his anticipation of this process, even though it began some decades after his death. There is no real evidence that this was the case, and it seems more likely that his remarkable innovations in yeshiva organization were introduced solely as a way of solving immediate practical problems without any awareness of their long-term consequences.

5. The Framework of Study

R. Hayim introduced new elements into the structure of the traditional Ashkenazi yeshiva. These too seem to have sprung from local and contemporary constraints rather than being the result of planning for the long term to solve problems that had not yet arisen.

One of the features that distinguished the Volozhin yeshiva from most of its predecessors was that R. Hayim usually had a deputy who gave *shiurim* too, and there were also several other teachers (*magidei shiur*). Some of these people can be identified. From 1803 to 1810 R. Yehiel Mikhal ben R. Tsevi Hirsh lectured at the yeshiva,[81] and between 1815 and 1818 R. Asher Hakohen Ashkenazi served as R. Hayim's deputy.[82] It is the information available on these two figures that suggests that this was the usual model followed at the yeshiva. In 1821 R. Hayim's son-in-law, R. Hillel, became the deputy head of the yeshiva,[83] and from then onwards the position was held by relatives of R. Hayim. Additionally, from R. Hayim's time onwards, distinguished rabbinical guests would also be invited to address the students, in addition to the regular *shiurim*.[84]

---

[80] Dr Mordechai Zalkin has prepared a systematic study of this topic; see Zalkin, 'City of Torah' (Heb.).

[81] See Yehiel Mikhal ben Tsevi Hirsh, *Lezekher leyisra'el*, intro.; Rivkind, 'An Anonymous *Rosh Yeshivah* at Volozhin' (Heb.). [82] See Ashkenazi, *Birkat rosh*.

[83] See H. Berlin (ed.), *Ḥut hameshulash*, intro. He was not the first of R. Hayim's relatives to serve as his deputy. See Neishtater, *Words of Peace and Truth* (Heb.), 10, which records that R. Moshe Yehoshua Rabinowitz, who was married to the daughter of R. Shelomoh Zalman, R. Hayim's younger brother, 'lectured at Volozhin in the yeshiva there on "Yoreh de'ah" . . . and if he was not otherwise occupied he used to travel to Volozhin to shelter in the shadow of his father-in-law's brother'. R. Moshe Yehoshua's wife was born in 1782 (see Steinschneider and Zalkin (eds.), *The City of Vilna* (Heb.), i. 175), and he was probably older, and if his teaching career preceded his involvement in business, he probably would have been teaching at Volozhin before 1815.

[84] This practice is well documented from later years at Volozhin. See Aryeh Halevi of Volkovysk, *Penei aryeh*, 20. Writing about his teacher R. Ya'akov Meir of Yalovka, he recorded that, when the rabbi visited Volozhin, R. Hayim honoured him by asking him to give several

We have no contemporary evidence as to why R. Hayim appointed a deputy. It is possible that his public activities and frequent travels forced him to do so. In the traditional yeshiva, responsibility for the institution rested with the local community, so there was always a local figure available to look after the yeshiva when the rabbi was away. With the yeshiva isolated from the community, there was no obvious substitute to manage affairs when its director was absent and very possibly this led to the appointment of deputies. Perhaps, too, there were students who found it hard to understand R. Hayim's advanced *shiur*, and needed tuition at an easier level.[85] There is no reason to think that contemporaries saw such an innovation as a radical or even important step. In many *batei midrash* there was a variety of study groups, each with its own teacher. The presence of more than one teacher in the yeshiva may not have been regarded as a significant change, but it had clear benefits for the yeshiva. With a deputy on call, R. Hayim's absences did not interrupt studies, and the students had the advantage of being exposed to a variety of approaches to study as well as having an additional source of guidance and counselling.

The isolation from the local community had additional consequences. New positions were created that were not directly linked to the curriculum and had not existed in the traditional yeshiva: the director (*menahel*) and supervisor (*mashgiaḥ*). These titles appear to have been used interchangeably: a certain R. Eliakum is mentioned in one source as the director and elsewhere as the supervisor.[86] He seems to have been responsible for overseeing the students. In *batei midrash* supervision was informal and no one individual was responsible for it. The need to institutionalize functions and roles was part of the price to be paid for the yeshiva's isolation from the community. Similarly, the need to pay staff required a financial system far more complex than that needed for the traditional yeshiva.

The order of study differed from that of the earlier medieval yeshivas and the yeshivas of early modern Poland, and in practice many of the habits of independent study in Volozhin survived from the *batei midrash*.[87] In the medieval yeshivas there were study terms and 'vacation' breaks, and there

lectures at the yeshiva. Although the date of 1825 given for this incident is about four years after R. Hayim's death, it is noteworthy that the author regarded this as a perfectly plausible occurrence.

[85] For difficulties in understanding R. Hayim's *shiurim*, see the letter by Yehudah Epstein appended to Avraham ben Hagra, *Sa'arat eliyahu*, 38.

[86] A. L. Cohen describes him as the *mashgiaḥ* (*The Life of R. Yisra'el Me'ir Hakohen* (Heb.), 2); he is described as the *menahel* by Hayim Feivelsohn in *Hamodia*, 4/6 (21 Nov. 1913).

[87] Breuer has a different view. In his opinion, R. Hayim intended to establish an educational institution and not simply a place for study (*Tents of Torah* (Heb.), 48 n. 75). However, the lack of any emphasis on teaching in the yeshiva suggests that in R. Hayim's time the yeshiva was more similar to a *beit midrash* than to earlier or later yeshivas.

were special *shiurim* at the beginning and end of the study term. The practice
in both the *batei midrash* and at Volozhin was quite different. There were no
study breaks and no special periods of study. In *batei midrash*, study was daily,
and at Volozhin the daily *shiur* took place all year round, with no special
shiurim to mark seasons. In the traditional yeshivas, a single talmudic tractate
was chosen for study each term, while at Volozhin the *shiurim* generally followed the order of the Talmud: they began with tractate *Berakhot* and ended
with *Nidah*, and so on in an endless round, with no omissions (see Chapter 6
below). This may have been because of the importance R. Hayim attributed
to studying the entire Talmud. The choice of the text to be studied was not a
major issue for students. At Volozhin, as in a traditional *beit midrash*, the
emphasis was on independent study rather than on participation in the daily
shiur, and there was no required curriculum that all the students had to follow.
Students studied whatever part of the Talmud they wanted. Attendance at the
daily *shiur* was not compulsory; some students never came at all. In short, the
Volozhin yeshiva was more a place for individual study than for following
taught courses, even though teaching was accorded a place of honour.[88]

Volozhin differed from most yeshivas before and after it in that students
were encouraged to study at all hours of the day and night. As students who
studied through the night left the study-hall, they would often meet the first
of the early risers arriving.[89] In other words, study never stopped in the study
hall except for prayer. R. Kook wrote that before the introduction of oil lamps,
which burned for a long time, students studying on a Friday night used to
study by heart after the sabbath candles had burned out.[90] This unceasing
study is a remarkable expression and application of R. Hayim's view that the
very existence of the world was dependent on Torah study. This was not
unprecedented in Jewish education, but it was new to Lithuania,[91] and there
is no reason to suppose that R. Hayim was familiar with the custom of continuous study from other institutions.[92]

[88] On the medieval yeshivas, see Breuer, 'The Ashkenazi Yeshiva in the Late Middle Ages'
(Heb.); Reiner, 'Transformations in the Polish and Ashkenazi Yeshivas' (Heb.).

[89] See R. David of Novogrudok's eulogy for R. Hayim, *Galya masekhet*, 66: 'Even on the night
of the sabbath these watches did not cease, and he [R. Hayim] himself used to make an effort to
go in and out on sabbath night from time to time to make his presence felt where the students
were studying, so that they should not stop.' He does not state whether this study was organized
or not.   [90] Neriyah, *Volozhin Studies* (Heb.), 24.

[91] In 1703 in the *beit midrash* of Posen, study continued day and night, and 'while the first
group was sleeping, another group was studying' (Evron, *The Register of the Qualified* (Heb.),
325, para. 1824). The decision dates from the intermediate days (*hol hamo'ed*) of Pesach of 1703.
See also Reiner, 'Capital, Social Status, and Torah Study' (Heb.); Shohet, 'Study Groups in the
Seventeenth and Eighteenth Centuries' (Heb.), esp. 409–10.

[92] Breuer notes that R. Yeruham Leibowitz, the *mashgiah* of the Mir yeshiva, wrote that the
custom of study-watches every night in Volozhin was a tradition from the time of R. Hayim and
was based on the view that, just as the court of a king has guards day and night, so should there

6. The Students

We do not have enough information to precisely characterize the student population at Volozhin during R. Hayim's time. Most seem to have been the sons of merchants or of rabbis and other religious functionaries. There are no records of students from very poor families or those whose fathers were artisans.[93] Children from such families rarely had the opportunity to study with a good *melamed*, so they had very little chance of preparing properly for advanced study of Talmud. However, some contemporaries did apparently regard the yeshiva as an institution intended for the poor. A eulogy on R. Hayim asserted: 'Thus this *tsadik* took steps to maintain yeshivas and to teach Torah to orphans and the children of the poor and to supply all their needs, so that Torah might emanate from them.'[94] The description of Torah scholars as poor is a venerable cliché, but it is doubtful whether it ever really was the situation. Naturally, those trying to drum up support for the yeshiva had good reason to describe it as intended for the poor: donors could then feel that they were fulfilling two religious obligations simultaneously—supporting Torah scholars and helping the needy. Most students were probably not rich, however, and they definitely did not live like rich men during their years of study at the yeshiva. This made it easy to regard them as poorer than they actually were.

Most of the students were unmarried, though some came to the yeshiva after marriage and left their young brides in their parental homes. These were arranged marriages rather than love matches: in such cases, separation did not necessarily cause any great suffering. It might even be advantageous, since it had the effect of delaying the young and still immature bride's first pregnancy. A spell at yeshiva also served as a temporary solution for an unsuccessful match.

The students in R. Hayim's time were generally young, not only by modern standards but also in comparison with yeshiva students at the end of

be in a yeshiva (*Tents of Torah* (Heb.), 278). This implies that in Mir there was no tradition of day and night study. Such a practice would have been difficult to establish in a yeshiva like Mir, where the study schedule during the day was very important. See Leibowitz, *The Torah Viewpoint* (Heb.), 'Bamidbar', 7a.

[93] On the limited mobility in the sphere of education, and especially on the role of the *heder* as a means of preserving social stratification, see Stampfer, 'Heder Study, Knowledge of Torah, and the Maintenance of Social Stratification', in *Families, Rabbis, and Education*, in which is discussed the slender chance of a poor child entering scholarly circles. However, see also D. Eliach (ed.), *Kol hakatuv lehayim*, 152.

[94] David of Novogrudok, *Galya masekhet*, 66. Betsalel Dablitski commented that, since Lithuanian Jewry was poor, R. David Tevele's words can be taken literally. However, poverty is a relative matter, and should be considered in its contemporary context. In R. David's time, Torah scholars did not usually emerge from the lower social strata (nor do they now), as may be seen from a study of the pedigrees included in almost every rabbinical biography. There were of course occasional exceptions, but they were rare.

the nineteenth century. Eliyahu Hayim Meisel came to Volozhin at the age
of 8, Yosef Dov Soloveitchik at 10, Naftali Tsevi Yehudah Berlin at 11, and
many others at 13.[95] Although it is difficult to generalize on the basis of
random evidence, the arrival of such young students does not seem to have
been exceptional in the first half of the nineteenth century. Over the years the
average age rose; by the end of the century, the arrival of Solomon Polachek
at the age of 13 aroused considerable attention.[96] Even the married students
were often young. At the beginning of the century many Jewish parents in the
upper strata of society were accustomed to marry off their sons around the
age of 13.[97] This is not to say that the average age was very low, but that the
age range was wider than it became later. This was probably associated with
changes in the concept of 'maturity' in east European Jewish society, but this
is not the place for a full discussion of the issue.

It was not the institutional innovations that led young men to study at
Volozhin instead of at the local *beit midrash*. According to a letter that R. Yosef
of Krynki, one of R. Hayim's first pupils, wrote in his old age, they came
chiefly because of the uniqueness of the study experience. 'In the first year
after the founding of the house of God at Volozhin, I saw that many merchants went out of their way to visit Volozhin to see the nature of the yeshiva
and what they did there, and when they saw that there were dozens of Torah
scholars sitting and diligently learning all day and all night, they were amazed
and astounded.'[98] This clearly suggests that it was the numbers of the students
and the quality of study (and perhaps the hours of study) that made an impression, rather than how the yeshiva was organized. The yeshiva was large by the
standards of the time: when R. Hayim died, the number of students had risen
significantly.[99] No *beit midrash* could boast such numbers. The presence of so
many young men at a single institution must have created a unique atmosphere, and it is easy to understand the tremendous impression the yeshiva
made on visitors. There was also great educational advantage in the concentration of a large number of talented individuals in a single location, in that it

[95] See Stampfer, 'Three Lithuanian Yeshivas in the Nineteenth Century' (Heb.), 223, and
references there.

[96] M. Y. Goldberg et al. (eds.), *Ideinu*, 8–9. R. Isser Zalman Meltzer also arrived in Volozhin
before he was of barmitzvah age. By then this was seen as a very early age to be on one's own, and
the rabbis did not leave him to fend for himself. His grandson records: 'The youngest students
in Volozhin [in 1883] were usually 16, so it is no wonder that when the 13-year-old Isser Zalman
arrived, Rav Berlin and R. Hayim Soloveitchik expressed their dismay that such a young boy
had been sent to the yeshiva. However, once they had realized his nature and his talents . . . they
welcomed him with special affection . . . they appointed R. Zelig Reuven, who was about six
years older than Isser Zalman, to be his study partner' (Meltzer, *Derekh ets ḥayim*, i. 39).

[97] On this phenomenon, see Stampfer, 'The Social Significance of Very Early Marriage'.

[98] The letter has been published in Shmukler [Shapira], *Rabbi Hayim of Volozhin* (Heb.), 47.

[99] As recorded by R. Hayim's son, in Lilienthal, 'My Travels in Russia', *American Israelite*,
2/52(33).

provided even the most advanced scholars with a real challenge if they wanted to prove themselves to their contemporaries.[100]

The main role of the Volozhin yeshiva, as of later yeshivas, was not to train rabbis or prepare students for rabbinic ordination, but to provide a place for intensive study for its own sake. During the nineteenth century the yeshiva was sometimes presented to non-Jewish bodies and to the more modern maskilic Jews as a rabbinical college, comparable to the seminaries set up by the maskilim themselves. This led to many misunderstandings. In the traditional Jewish world of eastern Europe, rabbis were usually ordained on the basis of an oral examination on the 'Yoreh de'ah' section of the *Shulḥan arukh*. Ordination depended on the demonstration of knowledge rather than on the length of study, and could be conferred by any rabbi, though ordination by a well-known rabbi was preferred: the greater the status of the rabbi who conferred the ordination, the more prestigious the ordination itself. Since ordination was conferred on the basis of knowledge rather than of attendance at an educational institution, there was no need to pursue a special course of study in order to obtain it, nor to study with a particular rabbi in order to be ordained by him.

Some students at Volozhin did make every effort to be ordained by R. Hayim before they left the institution,[101] though it is difficult to be sure whether ordination in these cases was a consequence of the students' decision to leave the yeshiva, or the reverse. Many of the rabbis ordained by R. Hayim had never studied at Volozhin but came only to be examined. There were also students who returned to Volozhin to be ordained some years after ending their studies there. It has been claimed that R. Hayim wanted to establish a centralized framework for ordination in Lithuania, but there is no evidence for this.[102] Only at the beginning of the twentieth century was an attempt made to establish a standard for ordination and to permit only certain rabbis to award it.[103]

The procedure for student admission in R. Hayim's time is unknown; it seems probable that there was no formal process though there must have been some procedure to begin to receive a stipend from the yeshiva. It is known that after R. Hayim's death, candidates were sometimes examined, but there is no evidence as to whether this practice had begun while he was still alive.[104] There were no special admission days, and students could begin and end their studies on any date. Nor do we know how long the average student spent at

[100] After R. Hayim's time, another reason emerged to study at a yeshiva: the protection it afforded from conscription into the Russian army; see Shohet, 'The "Rekrutshchina"' (Heb.).

[101] See David of Minsk, *Beit david*, intro.

[102] See Neriyah, *Volozhin Studies* (Heb.), 16, and the sources cited there. On ordination at Volozhin in later times, see B. H. Epstein, *Mekor barukh*, iii. 1204–8. There is no indication that the situation described by Epstein differed from what was customary in R. Hayim's day.

[103] See the series of anonymous articles entitled 'Major Decrees' (Heb.).

[104] Bunimovitsh, *Mikhtav me'eliyahu*, 21.

Volozhin, though some stayed less than a year and others studied there for over six years.[105] In these respects the yeshiva still resembled the *beit midrash*.

7. The Curriculum

Students at Volozhin in R. Hayim's day studied halakhic codes as well as Talmud. For some time there was a *shiur* in 'Yoreh de'ah', taught by a specialist teacher.[106] One student wrote that he studied 'Talmud and *posekim*', and acquired a fundamental knowledge of halakhah. He added that the purpose of this study was 'to understand and delve deeply into the Talmud and *posekim* and to study texts in light of the halakhah'. Others also emphasized the importance accorded to the study of halakhah at Volozhin.[107] Over time, however, the emphasis on drawing practical conclusions from the Talmud gave way to study only for the sake of knowledge, rather than with a view to practical application in real life.

The study of Bible and kabbalah was also important. R. Hayim himself gave a daily *shiur* on the weekly Torah portion to the townsfolk, which many of the yeshiva students also attended.[108] On the sabbath R. Hayim gave a *shiur* on the mishnaic tractate *Pirkei avot*.[109] There were no public *shiurim* on kabbalah or esoteric teachings; students interested in such matters studied them with R. Hayim privately, as will be discussed below. Like the Vilna Gaon, R. Hayim valued the study of *musar* very highly, especially as expressed in the writings of R. Moshe Hayim Luzzatto (Ramhal, 1707–46).[110] The main emphasis in Volozhin, however, was always on the Talmud.

[105] For example, Yehiel Mikhal stayed more than six years; see Yehiel Mikhal ben Tsevi Hirsh, *Lezekher leyisra'el*, intro.

[106] See Neishtater, *Words of Peace and Truth* (Heb.), 10. It is not clear whether this *shiur* was designed for the study of halakhah for its own sake or in order to prepare students for ordination as rabbis—a purpose that is not supported by any other source. Neishtater was the son-in-law of R. Hayim's brother.

[107] See Hirsch, *Shema ya'akov*, intro.; David of Minsk, *Beit david*, intro. On the study of halakhah, see Neriyah, *Volozhin Studies* (Heb.), 13.

[108] In his introduction to his father's book, *Nefesh hahayim*, R. Yitshak wrote: 'Nor did he neglect to speak on the weekly portion every day to the townsfolk, after morning prayers.' R. David of Minsk refers to the students' attendance at these lectures in his introduction to *Beit david*: 'I learnt the method of exegesis of the words of the sages and the Scriptures from him.' See also Neriyah, *Volozhin Studies* (Heb.), 13.

[109] See Hayim of Volozhin, *Ruah hayim*, his commentary on *Pirkei avot*, title page, and also D. Eliach, *Father of the Yeshivas* (Heb.), i. 219.

[110] On the study of Luzzatto's works and the attitude towards him in the circle of the Vilna Gaon and his disciples, see Tishby, 'The Dissemination of Luzzatto's Kabbalistic Writings' (Heb.), 154. He quotes a letter written by R. Hayim's nephew, R. Avraham Simhah, in which he says that R. Hayim greatly admired Luzzatto. The importance R. Hayim attributed to the study of the ethical works and other writings of Luzzatto is also apparent in a letter written by Naftali Amsterdam (in Salanter, *Or yisra'el*, 124).

The question of secular studies only became an issue towards the end of the nineteenth century. At the beginning of the century, the Haskalah had barely reached eastern Europe, but R. Hayim was nevertheless aware of developments in the west. For example, he had given an approbation to R. Shelomoh Dubno for his commentary on the Torah. The latter had collaborated with Moses Mendelssohn, the great German leader of the Haskalah, in the writing of the *Biur* (the commentary on the Torah published with Mendelssohn's German translation) though by the time R. Hayim was in contact with him, he had distanced himself from Mendelssohn.[111] According to his nephew R. Avraham Simhah of Amtchislav, R. Hayim 'yearned for the translation of secular sciences from other languages into the holy tongue, and for the translation of the works of Josephus, for they would enable us to achieve the goal of [understanding] the intentions of our sages of blessed memory in the Talmud and the Midrash'.[112] In this his attitude was apparently similar to that of the Vilna Gaon, which would not be surprising.

According to a later source, R. Hayim demonstrated his support for reforms in Jewish society in the spirit of the Haskalah by siding with R. Menasheh ben Yosef of Ilya (1767–1831), a well-known Lithuanian rabbi who had called for reforms in a number of areas of Jewish life but also remained in the traditionalist camp. However, he strongly opposed R. Menasheh when the latter suggested explaining a mishnaic passage in a way that contradicted the talmudic explanation.[113] We know that R. Hayim's son, R. Yitshak, was interested in science and medicine and knew several European languages;[114] he may have received encouragement at home to learn these languages, though there is no evidence of this. From these examples it seems that R. Hayim had a marked openness to general studies, although such interest was not yet a matter of real controversy.

8. The Role of the *Rosh Yeshivah*

R. Hayim's relationship to his students was somewhat paternal. According to contemporary descriptions, he not only taught Talmud but also tried to

[111] Fuenn, *Safah lane'emanim*, 137. Dubno later distanced himself from Mendelssohn. On R. Hayim's approbation to R. Dubno's commentary, see Mondschein, 'Suppressed Approbations from Volozhin and Vilna'. See Y. Ben-Sasson, 'The *Musar* Movement and the School of Volozhin' (Heb.).

[112] From R. Avraham Simhah's approbation to Kalman Schulman's translation of Josephus, *The Jewish Wars*.

[113] In R. Yisrael Lipschitz's commentary on the Mishnah, *Tiferet yisra'el*, *Bava metsia*, ch. 1. This is also discussed in B. H. Epstein, *Mekor barukh*, iii. 1332. See Wohlman MS, National and University Library, Jerusalem, pp. 18–19. This is a comment by R. Menasheh of Ilya on a passage of the Tosafot—a much less serious matter. I am grateful to A. Morgenstern for bringing this important source to my notice. On this manuscript, see Morgenstern, 'The 1840 Controversy in the Minsk Community' (Heb.); B. H. Epstein, *Mekor barukh*, iii. 1332.

[114] For information on R. Yitshak see the next chapter.

develop a close relationship with students and influence their conduct. Promising students ate at his table on sabbaths and festivals; an invitation to eat at his house was considered a great honour.[115] Because of the atmosphere, many people regarded Volozhin as a good place to learn *derekh erets* (proper behaviour) no less than Talmud. At least one young man was sent off to Volozhin because of his bad behaviour; to the joy of his family, after a year and a half at the yeshiva he returned home a reformed character.[116] R. Hayim was so greatly admired that several works were written about him, like the hagiographical literature that developed around the figure of the Vilna Gaon.[117]

Only a small part of the day was devoted to the Talmud *shiur*, since the emphasis was on independent study. However, the importance of R. Hayim's *shiur* should not be underestimated; it was on an advanced level, and some students invested great effort in preparing for it.[118] R. Hayim encouraged questions and devoted considerable time to answering them.[119] He followed the Vilna Gaon in studying halakhic sources according to their *peshat* (literal meaning) rather than by means of *pilpul* (elaborate argumentation),[120] and felt that it was his duty to teach this method to his pupils. R. Hayim was quite aggressive towards students who insisted on pursuing *pilpul*, as R. Yehiel Mikhal records: 'On some occasions my teacher reproached me for the *ḥidushim* [new interpretations of the text] which I made using the customary method . . . and for almost two years my teacher struggled with me until he had established this method [i.e. *peshat*] and its benefit in my heart.'[121] When

---

[115] See Ashkenazi, *Birkat rosh*, biographical introduction by his son David, p. 2: 'Our teacher, R. Hayim, of blessed memory, used to take him to his table on festivals and sabbaths to eat the bread of holiness with him, giving him living waters to drink, and granting him the honey of the teaching of his mouth.' Yitshak Rivkind recorded that students who did not travel home for Pesach used to celebrate the Seder with R. Hayim in his house, though he cites no source for this; see Rivkind, 'From the Volozhin Collections' (Heb.), 366.

[116] Bunimovitsh, *Mikhtav me'eliyahu*, 19.

[117] For a bibliography of works on his conduct, see Stampfer, 'R. Hayim of Volozhin and his Approbations' (Heb.), 169 n. 27. See also the anonymous publication *Book of Instructions and Guidelines of Our Rabbi Hayim of Volozhin*, which is based on the Pardo manuscript and another manuscript owned by R. Aryeh Levin. The most useful compilation on R. Hayim's conduct is D. Eliach (ed.), *Kol hakatuv leḥayim*. See Gries, *The Literature of Correct Conduct* (Heb.).

[118] Avraham ben Hagra, *Sa'arat eliyahu*, 38.

[119] R. Hayim even felt the need to apologize to his veteran students for this; see Yehiel Mikhal ben Tsevi Hirsh, *Lezekher leyisra'el*, intro.

[120] This is not the place for a detailed definition of *pilpul* and *peshat*; it is sufficient to note that in R. Hayim's time there was a sense that there were two approaches to study. R. Hayim was seen as a follower of the approach of the Vilna Gaon, known as *peshat*. See the introduction to Z. Epstein, *Minḥat yehudah*, for a comment by Yehudah Epstein. On R. Hayim's method of study, see Zevin, *Personalities and Methods* (Heb.), 17–20; Z. Kaplan, *From the World of Torah* (Heb.): 'R. Hayim of Volozhin's Approach to Halakhah' (pp. 9–43), 'A Responsum of R. Hayim of Volozhin' (pp. 44–9).   [121] Yehiel Mikhal ben Tsevi Hirsh, *Lezekher leyisra'el*, intro.

students voiced the suspicion that R. Hayim preferred the Vilna Gaon's method of study because he was not expert in elaborate argumentation, he immediately demonstrated his mastery of that method in order to correct their misapprehensions.[122] R. Hayim apparently did not innovate with regard to the accepted pattern of independent study. As previously, most of the young men studied independently, rather than in pairs as is customary today.[123]

Some students who were already expert in Talmud came to Volozhin specifically in order to study kabbalah with R. Hayim. Thus, R. Eliyahu Rogoler was already an accomplished scholar when he 'determined to become proficient in the wisdom of kabbalah, and made his way to Volozhin to learn Torah from the pious *gaon* R. Hayim'.[124] He was not alone. A contemporary wrote: 'Several individuals forced an entry into his private residence in order to gain a private interview with him, in particular asking the rabbi about the nature of man [*torat ha'adam*] and the proper service of God, as is well known.'[125] Some students had private lessons with R. Hayim; R. Eliyahu Rogoler was given a study-room of his own and R. Hayim used to come and talk to him there.[126] The study of kabbalah was completely different from Talmud study and was conducted privately.

9. Volozhin as a Model for Other Yeshivas

R. Hayim apparently supported the founding of other yeshivas, and may even have encouraged several of his students to set up their own but this was not a common phenomenon.[127] It is recorded that he took greater pride in these

---

[122] See Segalovitz, *Mekor ḥayim*, intro. He mentions a student by the name of Rubinevitzer who whispered that 'the *gaon* R. Hayim's powers in *pilpul* are weak'. R. Hayim heard him, taught an amazing passage of *pilpul*, and ended with the words, 'Now, Rubinevitzer, don't say that my powers in *pilpul* are weak.' See also Tzinovitz, *Tree of Life* (Heb.), 143.

[123] In the letter appended to Avraham ben Hagra, *Sa'arat eliyahu*, 38, Yehudah Epstein wrote: 'My teacher, the *gaon* R. David Tevele . . . told me that it was his custom, when he lived in the great house of study at Volozhin, to study with the great *gaon* R. Shimon of Keidan.' It is thus evident that study in pairs did exist at Volozhin. However, it is not mentioned in other sources, even in contexts where it would seem obvious to have mentioned such a practice. Study was probably not carried out in pairs in the *batei midrash*; the usual framework was individual study. It makes sense that the pattern of individual study carried over to Volozhin.

[124] Frumkin, *Toledot eliyahu*, 18.

[125] Hirsch, *Shema ya'akov*, 70. [126] Frumkin, *Toledot eliyahu*, 18–19.

[127] In his eulogy of R. Hayim, R. David of Novogrudok wrote: 'And when his disciples reached the level where they were qualified to determine halakhah, he encouraged those who had studied with him to found yeshivas in several places for orphans and the children of the poor' (*Galya masekhet*, 66). According to Frumkin, R. Hayim sent R. Meir Shalom Hakohen to Vilna to run a yeshiva there, and even stayed in Vilna for several months when the latter encountered difficulties (*History of the Scholars of Jerusalem* (Heb.), iii. 176). He also told the grandfather of Shelomoh Zalman Altschul to establish a large yeshiva at his home in Bobruisk; see S. Asaf, 'A Pedigree' (Heb.), 135. Another student headed a yeshiva in Antokol, a suburb of

yeshivas than in his own, perhaps because he was not responsible for maintaining them.[128] However, these yeshivas differed from his and did not compete with it. The features of the Volozhin yeshiva that impressed contemporaries were its size, the quality of its students and teachers as well as the perpetual studying, but these were hard to reproduce. The employment of teachers to teach advanced students and the clearly defined student body seem to have been the characteristics that justified the use of the term 'yeshiva'. The organizational innovations do not seem to have inspired imitations.

Only two yeshivas headed by R. Hayim's students are known to us in any detail, demonstrating the relative rarity of yeshivas directed by Volozhin graduates. Perhaps there were others that are not known to us but their numbers could not have been great. One of those about which we have information was founded in Minsk by R. Yehiel Mikhal ben Tsevi Hirsh[129] He was one of R. Hayim's first students, and he even taught at Volozhin for a while. In a book published to commemorate the expansion of his yeshiva, he noted that he hoped to appoint a second instructor (*magid shiur*) at the yeshiva, and emphasized the importance of the correct study method—'the way of true study'. Both were features characteristic of Volozhin. He did not mention the use of emissaries, perhaps because he did not think that his institution was famous enough, but tried to amass contributions to invest in property that would yield an annual income. As an encouragement to potential donors, he promised to list their names in his forthcoming book—a practice common among contemporary authors but unknown at Volozhin. He also introduced an innovation of his own: promising donors priority should their offspring seek admission to the yeshiva. It is possible that his desire to acquire a secure financial base in property may have been related to his hope for independence from the local community, but this was not emphasized and does not seem to have found expression elsewhere. The level of his students was lower than at Volozhin; R. Yehiel Mikhal was dealing with 'the student who is not yet ready to study a page of Talmud with the commentaries of Rashi and Tosafot except with someone who is at a higher level'. The institution that he directed was actually a combination of the form of studies of Volozhin—including the study of halakhah and *posekim*[130]—with a framework resembling that of a

Vilna, though no details are known about this institution. On this student, see the comment of R. Yitshak ben Aryeh, in Steinschneider and Zalkin (eds.), *The City of Vilna* (Heb.), i. 53. See also D. Eliach, *Father of the Yeshivas* (Heb.), i. 273–6. A yeshiva was set up in Bobruisk as a result of R. Hayim's appeal; see Nissenbaum, *Pages of My Life* (Heb.), 14.

[128] See the letter written by R. Yosef of Krynki, in Shmukler [Shapira], *Rabbi Hayim of Volozhin* (Heb.), 47.

[129] The only source of information on him is his book, *Lezekher leyisra'el*, which provided the basis for Rivkind's article 'An Anonymous *Rosh Yeshivah* at Volozhin' (Heb.).

[130] He noted that he gave 'a Gemara *shiur* to all the students, on a single tractate, but with the *posekim*, I study all four divisions of the *Shulḥan arukh* with the *aḥaronim* [later halakhic

kloyz, viz. a private *beit midrash* financed by a single donor (rather than by the community).[131]

The other yeshiva, that of R. Ya'akov Meir in Jałówka, is less well known.[132] The daily *shiur*—unusually, on the great halakhic code written by R. Yitshak Alfasi (the Rif, 1013–1103)—was accorded great importance, and lasted 'about five hours, delivered with great ingenuity and expertise'. The founder paid special attention to the education of poor children, hiring a teacher for them and personally examining the more advanced.[133] The fact that he hired a special teacher proves that this was not for rich youths, whose parents chose teachers for them, and the very fact that this was noted shows that it was unusual. No details are known of the financial organization of his yeshiva. It had only one *rosh yeshivah*; since only seven students attended in 1825, there was obviously no need of another teacher.[134]

The most important of the other Lithuanian yeshivas during the lifetime of R. Hayim was that of Mir. However, no significant link between Volozhin and Mir has been demonstrated other than the possibility that the model of Volozhin may have inspired the founders of the yeshiva in Mir.

As we have seen, R. Hayim's yeshiva was extremely innovative. Although it still occupied only a secondary role in the system of Torah study in eastern Europe, alongside the numerous *batei midrash* that were still flourishing and some community yeshivas, it had an enormous impact in the long term primarily due to the esteem in which R. Hayim was held. The decisive stage in its development lay in its transformation from a yeshiva that reflected the personality of its founder to an institution respected in its own right. This took place with the change of leadership after R. Hayim's death.

authorities] in groups, since I do not have enough [copies of the works of the *posekim*] to learn a single work with all the students. And at the moment I do not have sufficient means to employ another teacher to aid me.' About 600 people subscribed to the book in advance of its publication, not only from Minsk but from Vilna, Grodno, and elsewhere. Had R. Yehiel Mikhal wished to imitate the organizational framework of Volozhin, he could have done so; however, since he lived in Minsk, which was a large city, he probably relied principally on local support.

131 Reiner, 'Capital, Social Status, and Torah Study' (Heb.).
132 See Aryeh Halevi of Volkovysk, *Penei aryeh*, 17.
133 Yehudah ben Eliezer, *Kol yehudah*, 56.
134 Aryeh Halevi of Volkovysk, *Penei aryeh*, 17.

TWO

The Volozhin Yeshiva in the
Second Generation

R. HAYIM DIED IN 1821,[1] and his son R. Yitshak succeeded him as *rosh
yeshivah*. It is often difficult to replace the founder of a successful institution.
This is especially the case with charismatic individuals, since their very presence at the helm discourages the emergence of suitable successors. At
Volozhin, R. Hayim had attended to all the affairs of the yeshiva himself, and
until his last years no one else took administrative decisions. The appointment
of a successor could have been problematic. Fortunately, the presence of a
natural heir—R. Yitshak—solved the problem: he was considered the obvious
person to take up his father's responsibilities. In contrast, as we shall see, the
appointment of a *rosh yeshivah* in later generations was often surrounded by
controversy.

1. R. Yitshak as *Rosh Yeshivah*

R. Yitshak had already begun to take on some of the *rosh yeshivah*'s duties in his
father's lifetime but this had been on an ad hoc basis. After R. Hayim's death,
R. Yitshak became both *rosh yeshivah* and the rabbi of Volozhin. The transfer
of authority from father to son set a precedent for the future transfer of
authority in the yeshiva. R. Yitshak was not as distinguished a scholar as his
father, and it seems very doubtful whether he would have been chosen as *rosh
yeshivah* had he not been R. Hayim's son. He was learned, hard-working, and
a natural leader, but not outstanding. The yeshiva's success under his leadership demonstrates that the institution was no longer dependent on the man at
the helm. It continued to function and to attract students by virtue of its reputation and because it responded to the needs of those who wanted to study. It
was the position that endowed its occupant with prestige and importance,
rather than the reverse.

---

[1] According to Berdyczewski, he died on 14 June 1821 ('History of the Ets Hayim Yeshiva'
(Heb.), 239).

R. Yitshak was born in 1780[2] and, as mentioned above, had already begun to play an active role in the yeshiva before his father's death. He had examined prospective students,[3] acted as an administrator,[4] and given the daily *shiur* when his father was ill.[5] R. Yitshak himself recorded that his father had chosen him as his successor and had commanded him 'to strengthen myself with all my power to maintain his house of study so that the Torah should not depart thence, Heaven forbid'.[6]

Several sources hint that although R. Yitshak was learned, he was not one of the outstanding scholars of his generation. He was noted for many qualities, but not for brilliance. According to R. Yitshak Meisel, he had 'exalted qualities and his holy practices, especially his moderation and tremendous patience, and all his deeds were heard and done in a pleasant manner'.[7] Similarly, several of his students praised his *shiurim*, though generally those on the weekly Torah portion rather than on the Talmud, which were considered less taxing.[8] However, judging from a comment by R. Eliyahu Hayim Meisel (1821–1912), it seems that even at R. Yitshak's *shiurim* on the Torah, regular attendance was unusual: 'The *gaon* Eliyahu Hayim often used to say that the reason why he had merited more wisdom and greatness than his fellows was that he had regularly attended the lectures on the Pentateuch given by his teacher.'[9] Apparently his fellow students had not been regular attendees. R. Mordechai Gimpel Jaffe (1820–91) writes: 'He taught the more advanced of his students the way to fear God and walk humbly [with him], and guided them concerning the establishment of an improved rabbinate, that they might become members of it.'[10] There is no mention of Talmud *shiurim* here.

R. Yitshak's grandson, R. Yosef Paimer, notes: 'Nobody really appreciated my grandfather. They thought he was just a regular scholar, but I can bear witness that he was expert in Talmud and Tosafot.'[11] This is a very hedged evaluation, and much can be learnt from what it does *not* say. He did not publish responsa or halakhic works, but only commentaries on parts of the Torah[12] and on the mishnaic tractate *Pirkei avot*.[13] He was not a halakhic

---

[2] He visited the Vilna Gaon, with his father; see Neriyah, *Volozhin Studies* (Heb.), 21.

[3] Bunimovitsh, *Mikhtav me'eliyahu*, 21. There is no evidence that all candidates for admission were examined.   [4] David of Minsk, *Beit david*, sermon 9.   [5] Ibid.

[6] See his introduction to his father's book, *Nefesh hahayim*.

[7] From a letter published in Trivaks, *Nod demaot*, 2.

[8] See Kopernik, 'And the Third Text Will Come and Decide' (Heb.); Kopernik fondly recalled R. Yitshak's classes on the Pentateuch and R. Eliezer Yitshak's lectures on the Talmud; see Edelman, *Hatirosh*, 55.   [9] Shmukler [Shapira], *Rabbi Moshe Shemuel* (Heb.), 41.

[10] Jawitz, *Jewish History* (Heb.), xiv. 11, quoting R. Mordechai Gimpel Jaffe. Of course, it is possible that R. Mordechai Gimpel saw no need to single out R. Yitshak's *shiurim* for special mention.

[11] Recorded in the name of R. Aryeh Levin; see Neriyah, *Volozhin Studies* (Heb.), 31.

[12] Yitshak of Volozhin, *Peh kadosh*.   [13] Yitshak of Volozhin, *Milei de'avot*.

authority. When a complex halakhic problem arose concerning the *kashrut* of an animal with defective lungs, he preferred to consult the rabbis of Vilna rather than to rule on the matter himself—even though he could have relied on an explicit ruling by his late father on this matter had he so desired.[14]

It is instructive that in R. Yitshak's time there seems to have been a group of students who felt the need to consult rabbis outside the yeshiva on halakhic matters. A collection of letters sent to R. Yisra'el Salanter in 1836 by students at Volozhin includes one from R. Shemuel Salant (dated 31 August), which not only contains questions about the laws of constructing a parapet but also includes a request for guidance about dealing with distractions when wearing *tefilin*. R. Shemuel had been closely associated with R. Yisra'el before going to Volozhin so this correspondence was not surprising. The second letter, from Tsevi Hertz Mazokhovitz, relates to the laws of parapets, and the third, from Mordechai Friedburg, also asks about both distractions and parapets. The request for guidance on dealing with distractions is particularly interesting, implying that there was nobody at the yeshiva who could provide advice on this topic.[15]

The inevitable comparison of R. Yitshak with his father tended to diminish his status. Some sources mention opposition to his appointment. R. Moshe Shapira records a tradition that one student objected so strongly to the nomination as to throw a cat on to R. Yitshak's copy of the Talmud in the middle of the *shiur*.[16] Doubt may be cast on the veracity of the story, but R. Moshe certainly considered it possible. At the same time, it is clear that R. Yitshak directed the yeshiva with considerable success until his death.

R. Yitshak continued his father's policies in his management of the yeshiva, though he was open to new ideas and approaches. One of the most important sources of information on his views are the memoirs of Max Lilienthal (1815–82), a German rabbi and maskil who was active in the tsarist empire in the early 1840s. In 1841 he was appointed by the government to prepare a programme to spread enlightenment among the Jews, and was commissioned to work among the Jewish population to encourage support for his activities.[17] In 1842 he met R. Yitshak in Volozhin, and his memoirs describe the meeting in

---

[14] See B. H. Epstein, *Mekor barukh*, iii. 1178–83.

[15] Tikuczynski, *The Teachings of R. Shemuel Salant* (Heb.), iii. 46–54. Another student who left Vilna, where he had been studying with R. Yisra'el, and came to Volozhin, was R. Hillel Salanter Milikovsky. He was given the honour of delivering a lecture at the yeshiva. See Zalmanovich, *Zikhron hilel*, 16–17.

[16] Shmukler [Shapira], *Rabbi Moshe Shemuel* (Heb.), 209. The fact that R. Yosef Zundel of Salant left Volozhin after R. Hayim died and moved to Posen to study with R. Akiva Eger is of no importance in this context, since he was roughly the same age as R. Yitshak and would not have had any reason to study with him. See Rivlin, *The Tsadik Rabbi Yosef Zundel* (Heb.), 4.

[17] See Etkes, 'The "Official Haskalah"' (Heb.); Stanislawski, *Tsar Nicholas I and the Jews*, 69–96.

minute detail. Lilienthal could never be suspected of excessive enthusiasm for traditionalist rabbis, and this lends added credence to his positive evaluation of R. Yitshak:

He spoke perfect German, Russian, and Polish, although he knew little about the literature of these languages. He understood that it was no longer possible to delay reforms in the field of education, and even though he feared for the fate of his yeshiva once these reforms were carried out, he would never refrain from suggesting the reform of educational methods. 'Do not think', said R. Yitshak, '. . . that all Jews trust me. They suspect that I lean towards the reforms, that I am in favour of the government's programmes.'[18]

Of course, R. Yitshak knew exactly what Lilienthal wanted to hear and what he should say to ensure the yeshiva's welfare, so Lilienthal's evidence cannot be used as the only source for the rabbi's opinions. However, his observation that R. Yitshak knew several languages can be relied on because it is confirmed by other sources. A non-Jewish Polish traveller who visited Volozhin noted that R. Yitshak could read Latin and Greek, and spoke fluent Polish.[19] After his death, 'many books of Polish literature' were found in his house.

One tradition claims that R. Yitshak wanted to travel to Germany in his youth but was prevented from doing so by his father.[20] He was always interested in medicine, and even tried his hand at treating medical problems.[21] When his granddaughter's husband, Yehoshua Heshel Levin (1818–83), tried to publish a rabbinic journal—a great novelty at that time—R. Yitshak was one of the first to offer his support.[22] R. Yitshak corresponded with Wolf Tugendhold (1796–1894), a well-known maskil and official censor, calling him 'my learned, perfect, and excellent friend'.[23] As with Lilienthal, this may not have been a genuine friendship but rather the cultivation of an acquaintanceship that might be of benefit to the yeshiva, so the correspondence should not be taken at face value. Even so, it is significant that he wanted to maintain good relations with a man like Tugendhold.

R. Yitshak was by no means a closet maskil, however. His intellectual curiosity may have been broader than his father's, but he was still firmly rooted

[18] Lilienthal, 'My Travels in Russia', *American Israelite*, 2/52(33), 3/1(34).

[19] Chodzko, *Lithuanian Figures* (Pol.), 189. The author wrote 'R. Solomon' for 'R. Yitshak' but it is clear that he was referring to the latter. For his knowledge of Polish, see ibid. 190. On Chodzko, see Shatzky, *Cultural History of the Haskalah in Lithuania* (Yid.), 181–5.

[20] Rivkind, 'From the Volozhin Collections' (Heb.), 379.

[21] See Posner, 'Kalman Schulman' (Heb.), *Hatsefirah*, 26/23: 1, which records an unsuccessful attempt by R. Yitshak to cure Kalman Schulman. On his attempt to treat cholera, which may have been more successful, see §2 below.   [22] See the first issue, Y. Levin, *Peleitat soferim*.

[23] From a letter in the Schwadron Collection, National and University Library, Jerusalem. It was written in response to an appeal by Tugendhold to R. Yitshak in connection with a relative who needed help.

in traditional society and was not torn between the two cultures. Like his father, he followed kabbalistic practices. Thus, he wrote amulets for two yeshiva students who were epileptics. Before doing so he fasted, immersed himself in a ritual bath, visited his father's grave, and immersed himself once again. The text of one such amulet read: 'Yitshak son of Hayim—a suffering soul.'[24] Unlike his father, however, he is not known to have taught kabbalah. There may have been a decline in kabbalah study at the Volozhin yeshiva in his time: a letter he wrote to his nephew, R. Avraham Simhah, after the latter had left Volozhin, encouraged him to study kabbalah.[25] Nevertheless, a decline in kabbalah study at the yeshiva does not necessarily indicate a conscious shift, which would have been a major break with the past. The words of R. Naftali Tsevi Yehudah Berlin (often referred to as 'the Netsiv') in his eulogy for R. Avraham Simhah are significant in this context:

He was one of the last surviving disciples of the *gaon*, the great shepherd, our teacher and master, R. Hayim, of blessed memory, and received the kabbalistic tradition in several matters and secrets from him, and also practical kabbalah, in which he was most proficient . . . it will be long before God raises up another to take his place, for in these generations there is none from whom to learn this, and who will come to engage in this? . . . There is sorrow in Heaven that there is no man left like him who is able to aid those who are broken-hearted.[26]

There is no hint here of rejection of either theoretical or practical kabbalah, but rather emphasis on R. Avraham Simhah's special prowess in these fields— and a suggestion that such knowledge and study were rare in the next generation. The Netsiv expresses no regret at not having studied kabbalah himself and asserts that there is no one from whom to learn in his generation—in other words, that the chain of tradition had been broken. He clearly valued kabbalah, but did not include it in his curriculum.

It is difficult to determine the impact of R. Yitshak's limitations as *rosh yeshivah* on the number of students who chose to study at Volozhin, since there is conflicting evidence on the student population during his time. Micha Yosef Berdyczewski, who was one of the first to attempt to write a history of the yeshiva, in 1888, claimed that at the beginning of his term of office R. Yitshak raised the number of students to 200, though this later declined to about 100,[27] or even fewer according to other sources.[28] Lilienthal, who visited the yeshiva in 1842, seven years before R. Yitshak died, estimated that

[24] See Yudlov, 'The Book of *Helkat re'uven*' (Heb.).

[25] Ibid. 150. The letter was sent in 1823.

[26] N. Berlin, *Sermons of the Netsiv* (Heb.), sermon 18 (pp. 120–1).

[27] Berdyczewski [Bar Bei Rav], 'History of the Ets Hayim Yeshiva' (Heb.), 234. He was aided in his project by the Netsiv, who was head of the yeshiva at the time.

[28] M. M. Horowitz puts the number at 50–60 students (*Derekh ets hayim*, 112). However, he was not an eyewitness and he does not reveal his sources.

between 200 and 300 young men studied at the yeshiva, in contrast to the 300 he thought had studied there in the days of R. Hayim. In other words, there had been some degree of decline, but it was not large. Lilienthal recorded some problems of which R. Yitshak told him, but the recruitment of students was not among them.[29]

2. Change and Continuity in the Yeshiva under R. Yitshak

Since Volozhin's attraction for students lay in its special features and excellent reputation rather than R. Yitshak's own reputation,[30] it is easy to understand why he preserved the patterns that his father had established. Among these was the practice of the *rosh yeshivah* having a deputy: R. Avraham Simhah, R. Yitshak's nephew, served in this capacity until 1827, sharing the teaching and helping R. Yitshak publish his father's book *Nefesh hahayim*.[31]

In a letter written while he was teaching at Volozhin, R. Avraham Simhah praised the students for studying round the clock on weekdays and sabbaths, and reaching an advanced level. He notes that he himself had little time to devote to preparing his *shiurim*, but nevertheless still managed to produce *hidushim*, or new textual interpretations.[32] Another of his letters seems to imply that there was some sort of study term or semester (*zeman*), and if this was so, it was an innovation. However, no further details are known. He apologizes for not sending any of his interpretations, but 'at the beginning of the term, until the holy flock has been gathered in . . . our troubles are mighty and redoubled'.[33]

Following the great fire at Volozhin in 1826, R. Avraham Simhah took up a new post as the rabbi of Rakov. From there he moved to Stary Bykhov, and then to Mstislavl.[34] The available sources offer no explanation for his departure from Volozhin, but it may be supposed that his precarious financial situation was one of the factors. In a letter written while he was still in Volozhin, he notes that he had to give private lessons in order to support his family.[35] R. Hillel ben Simhah, R. Hayim's son-in-law, also seems to have served in some capacity at the yeshiva at this time, perhaps as a supplementary *rosh yeshivah*, though no further details have survived.[36] In 1827 R. Eliezer Yitshak, son of

---

[29] Lilienthal, 'My Travels in Russia', *American Israelite*, 2/52(33), 3/1(34).

[30] Even Chodzko noted that rich Jews were proud to say that their sons studied with the rabbi of Volozhin (Chodzko, *Lithuanian Figures* (Pol.), 188). He emphasized the institutional role of the yeshiva head rather than his personal qualities.

[31] See the introduction to *Nefesh hahayim*.

[32] See Avraham Simhah of Amtchislav and Shalom of Rubezhevichi, 'Correspondence' (Heb.), 145–50.   [33] Ibid. 147.

[34] See the introduction written by Hayim Yosef to his father Avraham Simhah's book *Binyan shel simhah*.   [35] The letter was published in *Tevunah*, 1/12 (Elul 1941), 148.

[36] In the introduction to H. Berlin (ed.), *Hut hameshulash*, his son recalled that R. Hillel 'gave

R. Hillel and grandson of R. Hayim, was appointed as deputy *rosh yeshivah*. He was only 18 and was married to his cousin, R. Yitshak's daughter.[37] He seems to have discharged his duties well, but in 1839 he contracted a serious illness that greatly weakened him; thereafter he could barely teach two *shiurim* a week. R. Yitshak appointed his other son-in-law, R. Naftali Berlin, as an additional deputy *rosh yeshivah*, and this arrangement continued until R. Yitshak's death.

In summary it can be said that during R. Yitshak's term of office, all the teachers were relatives: both of the last two deputy *rashei yeshivah* were his sons-in-law. There were no 'outsiders' on the yeshiva staff, as there had been in R. Hayim's day, but it cannot be asserted that family connections guaranteed an appointment. R. Yitshak had a son who does not seem to have held any post at the yeshiva: suitability for the position was a clear precondition, and R. Yitshak's son does not seem to have fulfilled this criterion (though he later claimed rights to the institution). In a system based on inheritance, sons occasionally proved unsuitable, but it was always possible to choose appropriate sons-in-law. The advantage of appointing a son or son-in-law is that there is never any doubt as to who is the senior figure: during R. Yitshak's time as *rosh yeshivah* there is no evidence of conflict. Only after his death did the issue of seniority become unclear, as will be discussed below.

Like his father, R. Yitshak had close relationships with his students. He cared for their physical well-being and would take walks with them in the afternoons both in order to encourage them to get some fresh air and to forge personal ties.[38] The only marked change from the customs of his father's time was R. Yitshak's opposition to study at all times of the day and the night. He would tell students studying late at night to go to bed so as to protect their health, although the custom of round-the-clock study seems nonetheless to have been maintained.[39] He would sometimes arrange lodgings for his students with his relatives, and organized hospitality with local families for students who did not

a *shiur* in the yeshiva of this holy community for ten years, some of the time in the lifetime of his father-in-law, the *gaon* . . . our teacher and master, R. Hayim'. For most of the time he would have been teaching during R. Yitshak's term of office. However, Friedenstein recorded that R. Hillel succeeded his father as *moreh tsedek* (teacher) in Grodno (*City of Heroes* (Heb.) 177). His father died in 1813 (ibid. 68), so it seems that he did not replace his father immediately.

[37] For the inscription on his tombstone, see Berdyczewski [Bar Bei Rav], 'History of the Ets Hayim Yeshiva' (Heb.), 'Appendices', p. 241. According to this, he died in 1853 at the age of 44; if this is correct, he must have been born in 1809. The certificate of ordination that he received from his father in 1828 mentions the son's novel Torah insights and notes that he regularly gave the daily *shiur* (M. Rabinowitz, 'Documents Relating to the History of the Volozhin Yeshiva' (Heb.), 222). This implies that he had already begun teaching at the yeshiva by 1827. [38] Eliasberg, *The Golden Path* (Heb.), 8.

[39] See Shmukler [Shapira], *Rabbi Moshe Shemuel* (Heb.), 42–3, 209; Avraham Simhah of Amtchislav and Shalom of Rubezhevichi, 'Correspondence' (Heb.), 145–50.

travel home for festivals.[40] Like his father he gave a Torah *shiur*, and he maintained the *shiur* on *posekim*.[41] Admissions were not his responsibility: it seems that this remained the province of the deputy *rosh yeshivah*.[42]

R. Yitshak maintained the funding system set up by his father, and even expanded it. In several towns there were *gaba'im* who collected donations for the yeshiva throughout the year, recording the funds they received in a register. The donations amassed by the local *gaba'im* were collected by emissaries (*shadarim*), each of whom had his own designated area that he visited regularly. The emissaries brought the funds to the yeshiva, after deducting a certain amount as their fee. R. Yitshak would send the *gaba'im* receipts and letters of encouragement, thus spurring them on to collect larger amounts.[43] The emissaries also persuaded wealthier individuals to make direct donations. Little is known of the backgrounds of such emissaries, but as representatives of the yeshiva they must have had to possess a certain level of Torah learning; it is known of one that he had studied at Volozhin, and this may have been true of others as well.[44]

One important innovation made in R. Yitshak's time was the use of *pushkes* (household collection boxes), the practice used to collect money to support the Jewish community in Palestine, to amass funds for the yeshiva. In 1838 an official agreement was reached on how to divide the money collected in these *pushkes* between the two causes.[45] The use of *pushkes* had far-reaching consequences because it made it possible to collect money efficiently even from poor people who could only afford very modest donations. It was not practical for a local *gabai* to visit people of this sort weekly, but the coins dropped into the boxes slowly accumulated into sums that justified an occa-

<hr>

[40] Lilienthal, 'My Travels in Russia', *American Israelite*, 3/1(34); Dolitski, *A Model for the Masses* (Heb.), 8.

[41] This is R. Yitshak's description of the yeshiva day, as recorded by Lilienthal ('My Travels in Russia', *American Israelite*, 3/1(34)): 'We pray as early as possible in the morning, and all the students of the yeshiva are obliged to be present. After the prayers I deliver a *shiur* on the weekly Torah portion . . . and then the students prepare for the *shiur* . . . which is given by R. Leibele [= R. Naftali Tsevi Yehudah Berlin] from ten until twelve o'clock. In the afternoon they study on their own until the afternoon prayer, and then there is a *shiur* on *posekim* . . . after the evening meal they continue to study by themselves until after midnight.'

[42] Miller, *Toledot menahem*, 41–2. Some of the material in this book seems to be apocryphal.

[43] Two letters of this sort written by R. Yitshak have been published in Malakhi, 'A Letter from Rabbi Yitshak of Volozhin' (Heb.). See also passages from another letter in Neriyah, *Volozhin Studies* (Heb.), 30–1 n. 11*a*. On the appointment of R. Yitshak Eliezer as the person responsible for collecting funds, see *Kerem shelomoh*, 8/8(78) (1985), 57.

[44] See the letter of recommendation written by the *av beit din* of Warsaw for R. Yitshak Eliezer in 1836, which was addressed to 'the generous of Israel' (*Kerem shelomoh*, 8/8(78) (1985), 57).

[45] This was embodied in a halakhic ruling given in Vilna in 1838. The document is being prepared for publication by Dr Aryeh Morgenstern, and I am most grateful to him for showing it to me before publication.

sional visit. Broadening the basis of support in this way had important implications, since the poorer people tended to be more conservative whereas the
wealthier were attracted to frameworks that furthered modernization. It also
strengthened the link between the yeshiva and the Jewish public: even small
donors felt some connection to the institution, and the yeshiva's fame spread
as a result. Perhaps most significantly, the *pushke* system enabled women to
support the yeshiva: a large proportion of the money collected seems to have
come from women who dropped a coin or two into the *pushke* before lighting
the sabbath candles.[46]

The publication of *Nefesh hahayim* in 1824 was also related to R. Yitshak's
fundraising efforts. He appended a letter addressed to those 'who are filled
with love and wish to gladden the soul of my master and father, of blessed
memory' and asked them 'to give charity to his house of study for the purpose
of the remembrance of his soul'. Money was needed that year for more than
the usual expenses: in the same year the book was published, the government
ordered the yeshiva's immediate closure, but the order seems to have been
rescinded by means of a bribe.[47]

R. Yitshak tried actively to uphold the interests of the yeshiva, though he
was not always successful. In 1823 the yeshiva claimed that, with the exception
of raising funds for the Jews living in Palestine, Volozhin had the exclusive
right to raise funds by means of emissaries. The Mir yeshiva, which had been
founded in 1815, contested the claim. The matter was brought before R.
Avraham Abeles Posweler, the *av beit din* of Vilna, who ruled that every yeshiva
had the right to employ emissaries.[48]

It seems that Volozhin often had financial difficulties in R. Yitshak's time
though such problems are endemic to educational institutions (and indeed
other institutions). Although students continued to receive financial support
from the institution, they received no more than 35 copecks a week—a small
sum even by the standards of the time.[49] R. Avraham Simhah's need to give
private lessons to supplement his salary has already been mentioned. R.
Yitshak complained to Lilienthal that 'the donations are not arriving as they
used to—all my strength is needed to maintain the institution, savings must
be made everywhere, and sometimes I do not know how to carry on'.
Nevertheless it is significant that during this period, R. Yitshak managed to
put up a new building of masonry construction to replace the original wooden
structure.[50]

[46] For more details, see Stampfer, 'The *Pushke* and its Development'.
[47] See Gessen, 'The Fate of the Volozhin Yeshiva' (Rus.), 19.
[48] M. Y. Goldberg, *Rabbi Hayim Yehudah* (Heb.), 8.
[49] Berdyczewski [Bar Bei Rav], 'History of the Ets Hayim Yeshiva' (Heb.), 234.
[50] Lilienthal, 'My Travels in Russia', *American Israelite*, 2/52(33). On the new building, see
Berdyczewski [Bar Bei Rav], 'History of the Ets Hayim Yeshiva' (Heb.), 233. I have not been
able to establish its exact date of construction.

A letter written by R. Yitshak in 1849 provides some information on the financial state of the yeshiva at the time:

And also in these last three years, which have been as years of drought to us, I have had to take thought on my own as to how to find the resources to obtain food to feed the students, may they live . . . and now . . . when no place is free of the cholera, God have mercy on us, I also have the responsibility of the students who are living at the yeshiva, and the cholera has begun to spread and make inroads; may God help me, that they may all be saved alive as on this day, by the medicines that I have prepared with the help of God, may He be blessed, and nobody is missing from our study hall.

In the main part of the letter, he thanks the donors and notes that 'everything delivered since last year by the bearer of this letter has arrived safely, as is noted in the registers kept by the bearer of this letter, and will be mentioned for a memorial in the book, as befits those who fear the Lord'. In closing, R. Yitshak again bemoans the yeshiva's financial situation, adding: 'I am alone and poor, and my soul has been weighed down under the yoke of foreign [non-Jewish] creditors from the very first years, and by the extra sum from last year.'[51] It is not known who these creditors were.

Despite R. Yitshak's interest in languages and science, the yeshiva's curriculum did not change under his leadership: in that sense, the institution did not reflect the personality of its *rosh yeshivah*. We have no evidence of whether students studied secular subjects in secret at this time, nor of any demands from the Jewish community for changes in the yeshiva's study programme. R. Yitshak was slow to alter his father's arrangements and was conscious that change might arouse opposition. Moreover, despite his openness to new ideas it is doubtful whether he saw any need for major changes.[52]

3. The Role of the Volozhin Yeshiva in Lithuanian Jewish Society

In the vacuum created by the dissolution of regional Jewish councils (*va'adei aratsot*) in 1764, the *rashei yeshivah* of Volozhin often served as *de facto* regional leaders, as did the rabbis of the larger cities. In his day, R. Hayim had been regarded as a leading authority in the region, and R. Yitshak inherited this role along with the position of *rosh yeshivah*. He similarly retained his father's role as an important figure in the affairs of the Jewish community in Palestine. When the committee of Vilna notables (*rozenei vilna*) that organized support for Jews in Palestine announced the appointment of R. Moshe ben Hillel Rivlin as communal preacher of Jerusalem, it was R. Yitshak's name that

[51] Published in Yitshak of Volozhin, *Peh kadosh* (ed. Shapira), 290–2.

[52] According to Lilienthal, he realized that reforms in education were inevitable, but feared them ('My Travels in Russia', *American Israelite*, 2/52(33)).

appeared at the head of the list of signatories.[53] However, his most prominent
public role was his participation in the government-sponsored conference on
Jewish education held in 1843 in St Petersburg. The participants were invited
personally by the Ministry of Education: the Jewish communities neither
chose them nor elected them. However, the ministry was interested in the
participation of leaders whom it felt could sway Jewish public opinion, so invitations were an indirect but relatively accurate reflection of communal status.
R. Yitshak represented the mitnagedim, while R. Menachem Mendel
Schneersohn of Lubavitch represented the hasidim; additional participants
included the German maskil Max Lilienthal, the Russian minister Sergey
Uvarov, and others.[54] At the conference, participants were pressed into agreeing to the establishment of a network of schools that would provide Jewish
children with a 'modern' education, including the study of languages and
secular subjects, as well as two rabbinical seminaries.

R. Yitshak's opinions on the question of the reform of Jewish education
in the tsarist empire are unclear. Some held that he opposed the very con-
vening of the conference, suspecting the motives of those who had initiated
it and doubtful of its possible results.[55] Lilienthal saw him as supporting the
government's aims, if not very enthusiastically.[56] R. Yitshak definitely tried
to please Lilienthal, but this may merely have been a tactic. Before the conference he sent his student R. Hillel Salanter to Lubavitch, to consult about
the meeting, and probably to co-ordinate positions. Lubavitch sources
emphasize R. Schneersohn's opposition to government interference in
Jewish education, but his name definitely appears on the list of those who
agreed to the government initiative. Of course, there was little alternative,
and undoubtedly all those participants who adhered to a traditional Jewish
way of life felt that they had done their best to minimize the impact of the
changes. Archival material published after the Russian Revolution reinforces

---

[53] Brinker, *The Shemuel [Salant] Charitable Foundation* (Heb.), 8. I would like to thank Dr
Aryeh Morgenstern for explaining the role of *rozenei vilna* and clarifying the identity of the
person appointed as preacher of Jerusalem.

[54] On this conference, see Stanislawski, *Tsar Nicholas I and the Jews*, 78–82. On R. Yitshak's
contacts with Uvarov, see also Lederhendler, *The Road to Modern Jewish Politics*, 71–3.

[55] See the sources referred to in Neriyah, *Volozhin Studies* (Heb.), 28–30. Neriyah cites sources
that mention a sermon given by R. Yitshak on Yom Kippur, in which he attacked Lilienthal.
Lilienthal himself described the sermon (see the next note) but did not mention any attack on
himself, and, according to his account, it seems to have been on an entirely different subject.
He had no reason to distort R. Yitshak's words, and if he described the latter as one of his
supporters it seems probable that this was true, and that at least some of the descriptions of R.
Yitshak's opposition to Lilienthal are inaccurate.

[56] Lilienthal, 'My Travels in Russia', *American Israelite*, 2/52(33). In a letter written about a
fortnight after his meeting with R. Yitshak (18 July 1856), Lilienthal describes the rabbi as
agreeing with his plans, and there is no mention of any hostile sermon; see Zederbaum, *Collected
Articles* (Heb.), 88.

Lilienthal's statements that R. Yitshak was co-operative, at least ostensibly.[57] His participation may have contributed to the renewal at that time of the licence to operate the yeshiva that his father had originally been granted in 1813.[58]

R. Yitshak's communal role illustrates the unusual position of the Volozhin yeshiva in Jewish society in Lithuania. In a society that tended to regard 'greatness in Torah' or serving in an important community as the main prerequisites for rabbinic leadership, R. Yitshak was neither a great halakhic authority nor an outstanding Talmud scholar: his status was purely a product of his position. As *rosh yeshivah* he was referred to as 'rabbi', or 'rabbi and master', of Volozhin, and it was this that gave him his authority, even more than being the son of R. Hayim.

Being *rosh yeshivah* was a convenient base on which to build a personal reputation. A *rosh yeshivah* did not have to contend with the feuds and conflicts of a community, was aided by emissaries, and could count on the support of former students who had enjoyed their time at yeshiva and remembered the assistance they had received, however meagre it had been. In fact, much the same process took place among the mitnagedim as had already happened among the hasidim: leadership generally passed from the rabbis of the large communities to the more independent leaders of institutions as will be illustrated by the discussion of R. Eliezer Gordon below.

4. R. Yitshak's Successor: R. Eliezer Yitshak Fried

R. Yitshak died on 18 May 1849.[59] Once again the yeshiva faced the question of succession, but this time the problem was more complex. R. Yitshak's son does not seem to have been a suitable candidate and may not have wanted to assume the position of *rosh yeshivah*. One of his daughters was married to R. Shemuel Landa, who was also not a candidate, but their daughter had married her cousin, Hayim Hillel ben Eliezer Yitshak Fried,[60] who became a candidate later on. Meanwhile it was R. Yitshak's two sons-in-law, R. Eliezer Yitshak and R. Naftali Berlin, who inherited the mantle of leadership. They had

[57] Lozinsky and Ginzburg, *Jewish Government Schools* (Rus.), 70, 129. In this book R. Yitshak is described from the Russian point of view as a man with good intentions who understands the need for changes. Here too it is impossible to know whether R. Yitshak actually meant this or whether he thought quite differently. However, his very willingness to attend the conference is significant. On his messenger, see Zalmanovich, *Zikhron hilel*, 36–7. As part of a follow up to Lilienthal's project, Benjamin Mandelshtam undertook to deal with the publication of new textbooks. R. Schneersohn was very much opposed, but Mandelshtam reported that R. Yitshak was rather supportive. See Lurie, *A Community and the State* (Heb.), 73 n. 39.

[58] Publisher's intro. to Landa, *Ḥayei ya'akov*.

[59] For his epitaph, see Kamenetsky, *The Making of a Godol*, i. 234–5.

[60] Publisher's intro. to Landa, *Ḥayei ya'akov*.

effectively been running the yeshiva during R. Yitshak's final years in any case. R. Eliezer Yitshak was already described as the acting *rosh yeshivah* in a report to the government in 1847.[61]

R. Eliezer Yitshak was born in 1809;[62] his father, R. Hillel Fried, was from Grodno, and his mother, Esther, was R. Hayim's daughter. In 1827 he married his cousin Rivkah, the daughter of R. Yitshak, and began to give *shiurim* at the yeshiva.[63] Although he was not a well man, two days after the death of his father-in-law he received a letter from the Volozhin community appointing him as rabbi and *av beit din* of Volozhin: 'It is right and fitting for us to appoint in his stead one of his descendants or close relatives, and we have diligently inquired and found that his son-in-law . . . with the help of God, Blessed Be He, will take the place of his late father-in-law.'[64]

Two days later, the yeshiva's *gaba'im* in Ivenets asked him to accept the position of *rosh yeshivah*.[65] The exact nature of the authority possessed by the yeshiva's *gaba'im* in Ivenets is not known; nor is it clear whether they sent the offer on their own authority or after consulting other active supporters of the yeshiva elsewhere who formed part of a larger organization. What is clear is that these separate invitations reflect a strong and institutionalized sense of separation between the community and the yeshiva.

One of R. Eliezer Yitshak's first acts as *rosh yeshivah* reinforced the separation between the yeshiva and the community. He asked R. Shimshon, a former *dayan* (rabbinical judge) in Volozhin, to return to the town to serve as *av beit din* and to take care of the everyday halakhic queries of the townspeople. He probably did this because of his illness and his wish to devote all his remaining energy to the yeshiva. Whatever the reason, the result was that the gulf between the community and the yeshiva widened still further, though it should be emphasized that it did not amount to estrangement. R. Shimshon gave a *shiur* in halakhah at the yeshiva, but it is not clear whether this was for a small group or for the general student body.[66] This tendency for allegiance to be given to the yeshiva or the community but not both was not exclusive to Volozhin; it was also true in Mir. I have not come across any sources which indicate that the pattern of events at Volozhin was imitated at Mir; they seem to have been parallel processes, resulting from the fact that administering a

[61] D. Eliach, *Father of the Yeshivas* (Heb.), ii. 594.

[62] According to his tombstone (Berdyczewski [Bar Bei Rav], 'History of the Ets Hayim Yeshiva' (Heb.), 240–1). His father is mentioned in the previous chapter as a *magid shiur* at Volozhin.

[63] See the poem written by his relative, Adam Hakohen [Abraham Dov Lebensohn], in honour of his wedding, and also M. Rabinowitz, 'Documents Relating to the History of the Volozhin Yeshiva' (Heb.), 222.   [64] M. Rabinowitz, 'Documents' (Heb.), 223.

[65] Ibid. Katzman rightly notes that there was something strange about R. Eliezer Yitshak's appointment, 'which was carried through in great haste, within the week of mourning' ('The Wonder of His Generation' (Heb.), 663).   [66] Shimshon of Volozhin, *Memoirs* (Heb.).

yeshiva was not compatible with attending to the daily needs of a Jewish community.[67]

The transition was not a simple one, as we learn from a letter of condolence written by R. Yitshak Ze'ev Soloveitchik, the father of R. Yosef Dov Soloveitchik, on the eve of Shavuot in 1849, to R. Eliezer Yitshak, who was his cousin by marriage. After expressing his shock at hearing of R. Yitshak's death, he adds:

Now, beloved of God, be strong to maintain and raise the honoured reputation of our lord and master, the rabbi your father-in-law, of blessed memory . . . to raise high the fame of the Torah in your exalted yeshiva . . . and may [God] grant that your hand may not cease in that work which our lord and master, your glorious father-in-law, supported . . . during his life . . . and may the merit of the holy ancestors benefit you, to prosper your way, which is the way of God, and may He grant you mercy before our merciful brethren . . . to maintain the house of God . . . and if it is insufficient to come before you with these words of support, yet, my friend, forgive my words, which are spoken from the very heart, for is this not a matter which needs support?[68]

From this we can glean some idea both of the challenges facing R. Eliezer Yitshak and also of the concern that the change in the yeshiva's leadership might adversely affect its finances. In the light of what is known about the yeshiva's financial situation, R. Eliezer Yitshak's concerns are understandable. In addition to the ongoing expenses, the yeshiva building needed basic repairs and books had to be replaced.[69]

Little is known about R. Eliezer Yitshak as a person. He is rarely mentioned in contemporary sources, which may indicate that he was not considered a *gadol hador* ('giant of the generation') in Torah scholarship. Nevertheless, there is no doubt that he had a reputation as a scholar, and some responsa that he wrote have survived.[70] A letter written by R. Yehiel Heller and other leading figures from Volkovysk who worked to raise support for the

[67] On the Mir yeshiva see Tzinovitz, *The History of the Mir Yeshiva* (Heb.); see also Kinstlicher, 'A Chapter in the History of the Mir Yeshiva' (Heb.); id., 'Letters Concerning the Mir Yeshiva' (Heb.); M. Y. Goldberg, *Rabbi Hayim Yehudah* (Heb.), 34, and the sources quoted there; Y. Eliach, *There Once Was a World*, 181–2.

[68] Yitshak of Volozhin, *Peh kadosh*, intro.

[69] See R. Yitshak Ze'ev Soloveitchik's letter in Yitshak of Volozhin, *Peh kadosh* (ed. Shapira), 294. Beneath his signature R. Yitshak Ze'ev added another line: 'I send affectionate regards to my friend, the God-fearing and renowned rabbi . . . R. Hirsh Leib [i.e. R. Naftali Tsevi Yehudah Berlin], long life to him . . . and may God be with him, that he may keep his sacred watch, to aid his honoured brother-in-law, the great rabbi, long life to him, as to his soul and the soul of his friend in this matter.' This could well be a purely formal and polite gesture, of no particular importance, but it might equally be an appeal to R. Berlin to help R. Eliezer Yitshak.

[70] See R. Hayim Hillel Fried's introduction to his father's book H. Berlin (ed.), *Ḥut hameshulash*, and the responsa published there.

yeshiva expressed joy at R. Eliezer Yitshak's acceptance of the position of *rosh yeshivah*.[71] A more significant letter was sent by the leading halakhic authority, R. Yitshak Elhanan Spektor (1817–98), who was rabbi of Nesvizh at the time.[72] R. Spektor wished R. Eliezer Yitshak success in his new position, and reported that 'the *geonim* [great Torah scholars] of the generation have already been strengthened by you'. It may be that R. Eliezer Yitshak's illness prevented him from making the most of his talents; a student expressed his admiration thus: 'we studied before him in fear and trembling, and regarded his utterances as myrrh'.[73] His scholarship notwithstanding, he was not a major halakhic authority: when he consulted R. David of Minsk on a complex halakhic question about an *agunah* (a 'chained woman' who cannot obtain a divorce),[74] he did not even suggest a possible solution, but asked R. David to find a way of granting permission for the remarriage. Among the responsa of R. Yosef Paimer of Slutsk are two in answer to queries from R. Eliezer Yitshak.[75] Again, both suggest that although he was a Torah scholar, he did not exercise halakhic authority. Nevertheless, from a Russian report on the yeshiva dated 1879 we learn that R. Eliezer Yitshak was greatly respected by all the Jews and was considered a holy man.[76]

We also do not have much information about the yeshiva in R. Eliezer Yitshak's time. In one place Berdyczewski writes that the number of students remained steady throughout his term of office, while elsewhere he claims that they rose.[77] He also states that the yeshiva's annual income was about 4,000 roubles, which was sufficient to support about a hundred students—which would suggest that the number of students had declined.[78] Much funding seems to have come from the Jews of Vilna,[79] and the *gaba'im* in Ivenets continued to work for the yeshiva. In 1851 two young men who wanted to study

---

[71] The original letter is in the Rabinowitz Collection, in the National and University Library, Jerusalem. See also Katzman, 'The Wonder of his Generation' (Heb.), where the entire letter is published (pp. 663–5).

[72] The letter is dated 1850. The original letter is in the Rabinowitz Collection.

[73] Halperin, *Mosedei yeshayah*, intro.

[74] See the book of responsa *Beit david*. I am most grateful to Professor Chimen Abramsky for directing me to this source.

[75] Paimer, *Responsa of Our Master Rabbi Yosef of Slutsk* (Heb.), §16 (p. 83), §50 (p. 168).

[76] Gessen, 'The Fate of the Volozhin Yeshiva' (Rus.), 22. The original report was found in the historical archive in Vilna, now the Lithuanian State Historical Archive, under the heading *fond* 419, *opis'* 2, *delo* 660a, *listy* 14–22; see Agranovsky, 'Naftali Berlin and the Volozhin Yeshiva' (Rus.), 131.

[77] Berdyczewski [Bar Bei Rav], 'History of the Ets Hayim Yeshiva' (Heb.), 234–5. An official document of 1847 records that R. Fried claimed that thirty pupils studied at the yeshiva (D. Eliach, *Father of the Yeshivas* (Heb.), ii. 594), but he seems to have wanted to conceal the true number. Eliach includes a photograph of the document but does not record its source.

[78] Berdyczewski [Bar Bei Rav], 'History of the Ets Hayim Yeshiva' (Heb.), 235.

[79] Yashar, *The Hafets Hayim* (Heb.), i. 65.

at Volozhin turned to their uncle, Shemuel Eliasberg, a prominent figure in Ivenets, for assistance. He gave them 'a letter of request addressed to the exalted *geonim* of the great house of study, asking that the young men related to his great family should be received with the respect they deserved. Throughout their time at Volozhin, the young men were treated with great consideration by the head of the yeshiva, who drew them close with his righteous right hand.'[80] It is evident that the link with Ivenets continued, and that the *gaba'im* there could exert some influence on the yeshiva.

The only surviving primary source about the yeshiva's financial affairs in this period is a list of donors in Warsaw, compiled in 1851. The contributions listed amount to about 750 roubles, sufficient to pay all the salaries of the yeshiva staff for about six months (at the level operative three years later).[81] This was a very large sum and it is not clear if support at this level was sent from Warsaw every year. While the list appears genuine, there is no other evidence of such large contributions from Warsaw, even at the end of the nineteenth century. If there had once been support from Warsaw and it declined, the reason for the decline is unknown.

Review of the donors' names reveals a preponderance of Lithuanians who had moved to Warsaw, and of more modern Jews. The largest contribution, 100 roubles, was made by Zalman Epstein, who had moved from Lithuania to Warsaw only in 1833 and was also noted for his sympathy for the Haskalah.[82] The sons of Yisakhar Baer Vilner, who were apparently of Lithuanian origin, contributed 50 roubles, and another 20 came from Hayim Janas, who seems to have been an inspector and a supporter of educational reforms.[83] A similar sum was given by Yisra'el Gesundheit, a native of Warsaw who came from a mitnagdic family.[84] The document dates from shortly after R. Eliezer Yitshak's appointment, and the size of the donations suggests that the general Jewish public supported his appointment. The large number of donors (almost 120) is to some extent a demonstration of the yeshiva's success in attracting support even from outside Lithuania, although in fact most were either of Lithuanian origin or are known to be mitnagedim.

In this period, attempts were also made to gain supporters in western Europe. Eliyahu Tsevi Halevi Soloveitchik, who travelled to Berlin in 1853, agreed to R. Eliezer Yitshak's request to find someone there who would be willing to collect donations for the yeshiva.[85] It is not clear whether this was

[80] Zalmanovich, *Maḥazeh avraham*, 8. On the Eliasberg family, see Z. Rabinowitz, 'Six Generations of the Great Persons of Pinsk and Karlin' (Heb.).

[81] The original is in the Rabinowitz Collection in the National and University Library, Jerusalem. On salaries in 1854, see M. Rabinowitz, 'Documents Relating to the History of the Volozhin Yeshiva' (Heb.), 229. These salaries were probably somewhat higher than those of earlier years.   [82] See Shatzky, *History of the Jews of Warsaw* (Yid.), ii. 86–7.

[83] Ibid. 98, 283.   [84] Ibid. 87.

[85] See his letter in the Rabinowitz Collection in the National and University Library,

to be a paid or a voluntary post. R. Soloveitchik later wrote that he had found a man by the name of Efrayim Hertz, a native of Germany, who had expressed willingness to collect money for the yeshiva during his travels in France, Holland, and England. It is not known whether anything came of this, but the effort invested in expanding the basis of support is worthy of note.

The first evidence of an interest in the Haskalah or general studies among the students of the yeshiva comes from this period. Avraham Eliyahu (Albert) Harkavy (b. 1835), later an orientalist of note, was one of the first to go on from yeshiva studies in Volozhin to academic general studies. He was first exposed to Haskalah literature at Volozhin, and as a result continued his education at the rabbinical seminary in Vilna set up by the Russian government and designed to provide students with the elements of a secondary general education. Harkavy went on to study at the University of St Petersburg and then in Berlin and Paris.[86] Although he left the world of Torah scholarship he remained supportive of the yeshiva and was close to R. Naftali Berlin. Eliyahu Neuwidel was also first attracted to the Haskalah during his time at the yeshiva; he left Volozhin for Raseiniai in order to get a secular education and then moved to Warsaw where he contributed to a Hebrew grammar written in German and was employed as a private teacher.[87] The case of R. Yitshak Ya'akov Reines (1839–1915) is instructive as regards unexpected ways in which the Haskalah penetrated the yeshiva:[88] he was sent there to distance him from a maskil who was teaching him foreign languages, mathematics, and other subjects, so in fact he brought to the yeshiva a considerable amount of general knowledge that he could pass on to his fellow students. Young men attracted to the literature of the Haskalah found in the yeshiva ample opportunities to explore it, far away from their disapproving fathers. A similar story is recorded by R. Aharon Eliezer Efron of Vilna, who studied at Volozhin shortly after the time of R. Eliezer Yitshak.[89] His description is fascinating not only as an illustration of the ways in which new ideas could reach Volozhin but because it discusses changes in education from the point of view of contemporaries rather than in retrospect:

Jerusalem. R. Yehoshua Mondschein pointed out to me that the signature is that of Eliyahu Tsevi Halevi Soloveitchik, the grandson of R. Hayim of Volozhin and the uncle of R. Yosef Dov Soloveitchik; on whom, see Karlinski, *Founder of the Brisk Dynasty* (Heb.), 42.

[86] Marek, *Great Men of Our Time* (Yid.), 302.

[87] See Leone, 'History of the Volozhin [Jewish] Community' (Heb.), 53.

[88] M. Cohen, 'R. Yitshak Ya'akov Reines' (Heb.), 84. On R. Reines' road to secular studies, see Bat-Yehudah, *Man of Light*, 5–9.

[89] The story appears in the introduction to Efron, *Ḥamishah alafin*, 3–5. See Katzman, 'On the *Gaon* R. Yehoshua Heshel Levin' (Heb.), pt. 2, 704–6. He was the son of a wealthy citizen of Vilna, 'who was very close to all the leading Torah scholars, especially to the *gaon*, R. [Moshe Yehoshua] Yehudah Leib Diskin, of blessed memory, the *av beit din* of Brisk, who even stayed for a fortnight in his house in Frankfurt'.

I studied in one of the yeshivas of the town [Vilna], until, relying on the advice of several of his friends and acquaintances, my father determined to teach me Torah and Haskalah together at the rabbinical seminary, which many citizens of Vilna then considered the desired goal and a powerful combination, a sanctuary of Torah, practical wisdom, and reverence. They did not know that several of the Jewish teachers there had set themselves the goal of misleading the young flowers of Israel from the ways of life to the ways of death, and that every syllable that proceeded from the mouths of these teachers was a cup of poison to our sacred faith. My father, of blessed memory, who was innocent in all his ways and knew nothing of evil, could only see the honourable name 'rabbinical seminary' given to the institution, and he was deceived by this noble name . . . and he always repeated the same cry: 'How could it be, that from this rabbinical seminary, whose students should utter Torah and knowledge and serve as the eyes of the community, venomous serpents should issue forth, or that it should bear fruit that would be a death-dealing drug to our faith? This is nothing more than malicious slander and envy!' . . . But during all the time that I studied at the rabbinical seminary I did not depart from the Torah of the living God, and I studied with the best teachers in the city . . . I was like the dove in the days of Noah, and I found no rest for my soul in this seminary. And when I was a student in the fifth class, a spirit of purity woke me, like a man who awakes from sleep, moving me to travel to the great yeshiva of the town of Volozhin, in order to hear teaching and doctrine from the great teachers there, the famous and renowned *geonim*, our teacher R. Naftali Tsevi Yehudah, known as the Netsiv, and our teacher R. Yosef Dov Ber Halevi, the author of *Beit halevi*, of blessed memory; and also the great master R. Shabetai Rashkes of Shnipishak . . . who had been my teacher and master for several years, strictly ordered me to go to Volozhin, and there I studied diligently for two and a half years. My relations sent me plenty of money from Vilna, so that I was able to support a rabbi or a few poor students, for my father was successful in all he did, and was considered one of the richest men in Vilna.

Someone like this, who had attended the rabbinical seminary, could easily have transmitted knowledge about the Haskalah, even if he himself was opposed to it.

The extent of interest in the Haskalah at the yeshiva during this period is unknown, but it was probably not significant. If R. Reines' father sent him there to get him away from maskilic influences, the yeshiva could not yet have acquired a reputation as a hotbed of the Haskalah. Talmud remained the main subject of study: R. Eliezer Yitshak gave a Talmud *shiur* twice a week, and R. Berlin taught on the other days.[90] Despite the first stirrings of the Haskalah, the traditional patterns still held sway in Volozhin.

At the end of his life, R. Eliezer Yitshak became embroiled in a battle over the leadership of the yeshiva. The rival claimant was R. Yehoshua Heshel Levin, who as we have seen was married to a granddaughter of the late

---

[90] See the introduction by R. Hayim Hillel Fried to H. Berlin (ed.), *Ḥut hameshulash*; and Ch. 3, §2, below.

R. Yitshak,[91] and the battle spilled over into the public arena. A letter to R. Eliezer Yitshak,[92] written on 21 June 1852, suggested that two arbitrators— R. David Tevele of Minsk and R. Yosef Paimer of Slutsk[93] —should come to Volozhin to deal with the dispute, but it is not known whether they did so. Berdyczewski briefly alludes to the episode: 'when God gave rest to the rabbi, our teacher Eliezer Yitshak, a wind passed over the waves of the quarrels and they subsided, then he was summoned to the yeshiva on high'.[94] R. Eliezer Yitshak died on 22 September 1853,[95] but the dispute continued after his death.

5. R. Naftali Berlin and the Question of Leadership

The Volozhin yeshiva occupied a unique place among the educational institutions of eastern Europe: it was dependent neither on the local community nor on a single philanthropist. It was not even clear exactly who owned it. The yeshiva building had been constructed with money donated by Jews from many different towns, and thus could not be regarded simply as belonging to the *rosh yeshivah* or his family. It was obvious that the *rosh yeshivah*, rather than the local community, had the authority to make decisions concerning the yeshiva. However, who possessed authority when the *rosh yeshivah* was absent or when his authority was called into question? Up until the mid-nineteenth century, no special problems had ever arisen. The authority of its leaders was unquestioned, and it had always been relatively obvious who was going to inherit the position of *rosh yeshivah*. The institution was staffed by relatives of the founder, and the status of each member of the family was clear. Problems of authority first arose in the mid-nineteenth century. They proved particularly awkward to resolve, both because of the lack of any mechanism for taking decisions (except for the *rosh yeshivah* himself) and because of the complex relationships between the individuals involved.

The central figure in all the controversies that raged after the death of R. Eliezer Yitshak was R. Naftali Berlin, the second son-in-law of R. Yitshak. He began teaching at the yeshiva during R. Yitshak's lifetime, and later served as

[91] For further details about him and his bitter dispute with R. Naftali Berlin, see the next chapter.

[92] The original is in the Rabinowitz Collection in the National and University Library, Jerusalem. It was written by R. Shaul Hayim Horowitz, the son-in-law of R. David Tevele. Katzman published extracts from R. Horowitz's letter in his article, 'On the *Gaon* R. Yehoshua Heshel Levin' (Heb.), pt. 1, 781–2.

[93] These two rabbis were summoned to Volozhin in 1858, together with R. Ze'ev Wolf ben Feivel of Vilna and R. Yitshak Elhanan Spektor of Novogrudok, to arbitrate in a similar dispute between R. Naftali Berlin and R. Yosef Dov Soloveitchik.

[94] Berdyczewski [Bar Bei Rav], 'History of the Ets Hayim Yeshiva' (Heb.), 234.

[95] Ibid. 241.

R. Eliezer Yitshak's deputy. After the latter's death, R. Berlin was in many ways the obvious candidate to succeed him, but in fact there were several rivals for the position. These struggles were significant in themselves, and also reveal the structural weakness of the yeshiva, which were a consequence of the lack of an authoritative supervisory body.

R. Naftali Berlin was born in Mir in 1817.[96] His father was R. Ya'akov Berlin, a distinguished scholar from a distinguished family, who moved to Palestine in his old age and died in Jerusalem. R. Naftali Berlin arrived in Volozhin at the age of 11, and two years later was married to R. Yitshak's second daughter, Rayna Batya,[97] in a marriage arranged by their parents. R. Yitshak presumably wanted to marry his daughter to a boy who would become an exceptional scholar, since by the time of the marriage it was probably obvious that his own sons were not destined to be great Torah scholars. However, it is very difficult to predict whether a 12-year-old boy is going to become an important scholar, and since early marriage was the social norm the decision had to be made before the prospective groom had reached intellectual (or physical) maturity.[98]

The early years of R. Berlin's marriage were not easy. He did not fit into the family well, and was regarded as an outsider. Worse still, he did not achieve sufficient distinction in his studies. According to his nephew, he was despised in the yeshiva, his wife was ashamed of him, and his father-in-law made no attempt to make him welcome.[99] In light of the descriptions of these years, it is hard to understand why R. Yitshak chose him as his son-in-law. Perhaps the young Berlin was very impressive as a 12-year-old but did not maintain his reputation as time went on, or perhaps his distinguished ancestry played a major role. It is also possible that the accounts of his early hardships were exaggerated, in order to throw the happier times of later years into sharper relief.

Be that as it may, the early years of his married life are described as years of high expectations and low achievement. The boy was under tremendous pressure. He reacted by withdrawing and applying himself to his studies,

[96] See the bibliographical references appended by Tsevi Kaplan to the entries he wrote on R. Berlin in *Encyclopaedia Hebraica*, ix, cols. 782–4, and *Encyclopaedia Judaica*, iv, cols. 660–2. See also H. Kets [Kehat], *The Doctrine of Rabbi Naftali Berlin* (Heb.), which includes a methodical analysis of his thought. For a very perceptive and important intellectual biography of R. Berlin, see Gil Perl's Harvard Ph.D. thesis, 'Emek ha-Neziv'.

[97] Neriyah, *Rabbi Naftali Tsevi Yehudah Berlin* (Heb.), 365.

[98] See Stampfer, 'The Social Significance of Very Early Marriage'.

[99] B. H. Epstein, *Mekor barukh*, iii. 1679–80. He does not explain the reasons behind the match between R. Berlin and R. Yitshak's daughter. On Rayna Batya, see Seeman, 'The Silence of Rayna Batya'. This very original article illustrates the potential benefit of applying anthropological methods to the study of Jewish history. However, there is good reason to doubt the accuracy of Epstein's descriptions; see D. Rabinowitz's excellent article 'Rayna Batya', 55–69.

shunning the company of other students and refraining from revealing his growing knowledge. He eventually became an outstanding scholar, even by the standards of his generation, which was rich in talmudic scholars. Again according to his nephew, 'my uncle's natural talents were average and in no way unusual, but by dint of hard work . . . he reached the very highest level of all.'[100] A family tradition recorded that his brilliance was only revealed when his father-in-law found some correspondence between him and R. David Luria of Bychow (1798–1855), one of the greatest rabbis of the generation.[101] R. Berlin later described R. Luria as his saviour, since he gave the young boy encouragement at a time when he was considering abandoning Torah study for the world of commerce.[102]

6. The Dispute between R. Naftali Berlin and R. Yehoshua Heshel Levin over the Leadership of the Yeshiva

R. Berlin's first rival for the post of *rosh yeshivah* was R. Yehoshua Heshel Levin, who was born in Vilna in about 1814 and was thus slightly older.[103] His father was a distinguished scholar, and his principal teacher was the rabbi of Kalisz, R. Eliyahu Rogoler (1794–1850), who had been born in Žemaičių Naumiestis and was a great scholar and a renowned kabbalist. R. Rogoler apparently knew some Latin and German and is known to have admired the book *Talmud leshon ivri*, the Hebrew grammar published in 1796 by Judah Leib Ben Ze'ev.[104] According to Shmuel Zitron—not always a reliable source—R. Levin was influenced by the atmosphere in Vilna and by the 'moderate Haskalah' though he did not fall neatly into established categories.[105] Zitron claims that R. Levin was well versed in the world of literature and was friendly with prominent maskilim such as Mordekhai Aharon Guenzburg (1795–1846) and Shemuel Yosef Fuenn (1818–90). At the same time, in the

[100] B. H. Epstein, *Mekor barukh*, iii. 1678.

[101] As related by R. Berlin's son, R. Meir Bar-Ilan. See M. Berlin [Bar-Ilan], *Rabbi of Israel* (Heb.), 24–5. B. H. Epstein does not mention the discovery of the correspondence with R. David Luria, though he probably would have known of this incident (*Mekor barukh*, iii. 1678). R. Luria seems to have been related to R. Berlin; in a letter he sent to R. Berlin, he referred to him as 'my relative' (Steinschneider and Zalkin (eds.), *The City of Vilna* (Heb.), i. 158).

[102] B. H. Epstein, *Mekor barukh*, iii. 1681–4.

[103] According to Steinschneider and Zalkin, who are usually accurate about such details (*The City of Vilna* (Heb.), i. 162–3). According to Berdyczewski, R. Levin was born in 1818 ('History of the Ets Hayim Yeshiva' (Heb.), 234). The difference is hardly significant. See also Lunski, 'The Rabbi's House' (Yid.), 2. On R. Levin, see Katzman, 'On the *Gaon* R. Yehoshua Heshel Levin' (Heb.).

[104] For R. Eliyahu Ragoler's biography, see Frumkin, *Toledot eliyahu*, 16. On the ritual recitation of texts related to sacrifices, see Ze'ev ben Yehezkel Feivel, *Avodah tamah*; Morgenstern, *Natural Redemption* (Heb.), 200–22.

[105] See Zitron, 'Dynastic Wars in the Volozhin Yeshiva' (Heb.).

1830s R. Levin supported an organization devoted to the monthly public recitation of texts about the ancient sacrifices (*ma'amadot*). In his opinion, 'the recitation of sacrifices in public by groups protects and atones just as did the real sacrifices'. This was a remarkable liturgical innovation, perhaps linked to messianic tensions, but in a definitely anti-reformist direction. He was a controversial figure, but even his enemies seem to have acknowledged that he was lively and had a quick intellect.[106] He even published a letter containing a philological study of the meaning of the name 'Todros', citing non-Jewish sources, in 1845 in the journal *Zion*, which was founded by the historian Marcus Jost.[107] This was rather exceptional for a traditional rabbi in mid-nineteenth-century Vilna. His manners were polished in the Western mode and, according to Zitron, he wore modern dress, though this cannot be established with certainty.[108]

In 1847 Levin tried to publish a rabbinical journal called *Peleitat soferim* (Remnant of Scribes)—the first attempt of its kind in eastern Europe. Particularly noteworthy is his intention of using the modern media of his day for the purpose of shoring up traditional society. The journal was modelled on the Orthodox journalism that had begun to appear in western Europe and the maskilic journalism of eastern Europe. The project received support from leading rabbis, including R. Yitshak of Volozhin and R. Eliezer Yitshak, but was never implemented. The material assembled for it remained in Levin's hands, and some was published when he finally managed to release a single issue of the journal in 1863.[109]

R. Levin's first wife, the daughter of a prominent figure from Kalvarija, died young. Shortly before 1851[110] he married the daughter of R. Eliyahu Zalman, the son of R. Yitshak, and settled in Volozhin. R. Eliyahu Zalman was not a distinguished Torah scholar but a successful businessman. He may have chosen this nearly 40-year-old son-in-law as a way of realizing the right

---

[106] 'In what did his real strength lie? Only in searching through and interpreting alien books and in his rapid memory and comprehension. But I call heaven and earth to witness that he never sat still anywhere for more than a day, he just travelled over seas and rivers and through cities and villages, and when did he study?' (Kovner, *Sefer hamatsref*, 139 n. 18).

[107] *Zion*, 1 (1845), 16. The editor quoted part of the letter, adding that he had omitted 'derogatory remarks on famous German scholars'. Even then Levin combined an interest in the new with an aggressively conservative attitude. *Zion* was edited by Y. Goldenthal and published in Leipzig. This was the only issue.

[108] Kovner wrote of him: 'He was a real dandy as he walked through the streets wherever he went, a hundred times a day, in summer wearing a black silk coat cut in the old style, and in winter, in a fur cloak with tails hanging down all around it, and with *tefilin* on his head and his arm' (*Sefer hamatsref*, 146).

[109] On this pioneering attempt in the field of Jewish journalism, see Rafael, '*Peleitat soferim* and *Safah lane'emanim*' (Heb.), especially the letter by M. S. Aharonzohn, p. 391.

[110] The date is derived from a letter by R. Yitshak Elhanan Spektor, entitled 'Safah lane'emanim', which was published in an appendix to Y. H. Levin, *Peleitat soferim*.

of his branch of the family to head the yeshiva. Since it was not clear to whom the yeshiva belonged, any member of the family could regard himself as the rightful heir and entertain the idea that he had the right to decide who should be its *rosh yeshivah*. At some point R. Yehoshua Heshel Levin began to give *shiurim* in his home: they became very popular with the students of the yeshiva, and the yeshiva administration apparently responded by prohibiting students from visiting private homes in Volozhin—including his. R. Levin was of course not invited to give a *shiur* in the yeshiva building. At the end of 1853, when it became clear that R. Eliezer Yitshak did not have long to live, R. Levin undertook the publication of R. Hayim's commentary on *Pirkei avot*.[111] He was given the manuscript by his father-in-law, who also helped him obtain approbations for the book. Like R. Berlin, R. Levin was not a direct descendant of R. Hayim, the founder of the yeshiva. It is very possible that his father-in-law encouraged him to edit the book for publication in order to strengthen the public perception of the link between him and R. Hayim's dynasty.

Shortly afterwards R. Eliezer Yitshak died.[112] R. Eliyahu Zalman was in Kovno on business; before he could return to Volozhin and press his claim, R. Berlin had taken over the management of affairs at the yeshiva. He did not do so without some soul-searching. In his eulogy for R. Ya'akov Me'ir Padua, the rabbi of Brisk, R. Berlin noted that R. Ya'akov Me'ir 'strengthened and encouraged me not to cease teaching after the death of my brother-in-law . . . and it is well known how hard he laboured for the welfare of the yeshiva'.[113] This strongly suggests that R. Berlin hesitated but was urged to continue 'for the good of the yeshiva'. Despite the support R. Berlin enjoyed, when R. Eliyahu Zalman returned a fierce and protracted dispute ensued that was resolved only after the intervention of several prominent Lithuanian rabbis some months later.[114]

[111] See the introduction by R. Eliyahu Shelomoh Zalman, son of R. Yitshak, to R. Hayim of Volozhin's commentary, *Ruah hayim*.

[112] The dates are recorded in the approbations to the commentary on *Pirkei avot*.

[113] N. Berlin, *Sermons of the Netsiv* (Heb.), sermon 20 (p. 124).

[114] The main sources recording the struggle for the leadership of the yeshiva are Berdyczewski [Bar Bei Rav], 'History of the Ets Hayim Yeshiva' (Heb.); Levin-Epstein, *Memoirs* (Heb.), 28–32, 343–7; Steinschneider and Zalkin (eds.), *The City of Vilna* (Heb.), i. 90, 277–8; Zitron, 'Dynastic Wars in the Volozhin Yeshiva' (Heb.); and a halakhic ruling on the leadership of the yeshiva, published in M. Rabinowitz, 'Documents Relating to the History of the Volozhin Yeshiva' (Heb.), 226–9. Berdyczewski obtained most of his information from R. Berlin; according to his account, the main controversy was between R. Levin and R. Eliezer Yitshak, while R. Berlin only played a peripheral part in the dispute. This account is not consistent with either the content or the date of the ruling. Zitron's version seems to be based on rumours and second-hand information. He did not know of the existence of the halakhic ruling, and his sources do not seem to have been particularly accurate. Levin-Epstein probably knew Zitron's article (see Levin-Epstein, *Memoirs* (Heb.), 342), but he also used family traditions and material written by his uncle—R. Levin. There is thus no single source that describes all aspects of the affair, so we have to reconstruct the course of events.

The feud was not only between two branches of the family who claimed rights to the yeshiva. There were also important ideological differences between the two rivals, as R. Levin's nephew records:

Among the books and papers that my uncle left when he died, I found a manifesto, written on parchment, which 'spread throughout all the dispersions of the Exile'. In it he expressed his opinion that the Volozhin yeshiva should be organized to produce rabbis for the Jewish communities of Greater Russia, but the yeshiva was [currently] being managed in a different fashion . . . and my uncle wanted order to be established in the studies pursued at the Volozhin yeshiva. He demanded that the students be divided into classes and that prominent rabbis should come each year to hold examinations for the students and to determine their strength in Torah. The more advanced would be transferred to a higher class, and the most outstanding would receive *semikhah* [ordination]. And another matter: since as rabbis they would have to mediate between the Jews and the government, they would have to learn the Russian language, history, geography, and arithmetic.[115]

This raised a very sensitive matter. A few years earlier, in 1847, government rabbinical seminaries had been founded in Zhitomir and Vilna, and an attempt had been made there to combine rabbinical training with a general education.[116] This had aroused fierce opposition in traditional circles—and now here was R. Levin proposing to turn the Volozhin yeshiva into a sort of seminary for traditional rabbis. He saw this as an essential tactic in the campaign against the 'reformers', and wanted to use this model from the West in order to strengthen tradition. There is some similarity here to his attempt to found a rabbinical journal, which was another example of the use of a modern tool in order to combat what he saw as negative aspects of modernity. He was highly suspect in the eyes of the conservatives in traditional Jewish society, but it was clear to contemporary maskilim that he was not one of their own:

All the geniuses and the great ones and the maskilim and the wealthy and the members of the new generation and so on will write of him that he is a genius; but as for us, since we saw him and spoke with him face to face, we have never seen any wonders or genius in him. Only flights of words and quick thought, as in every imaginative man, mixed with a little madness.[117]

R. Levin knew perfectly well what a rabbinical seminary was like. He had been friendly with both R. Ya'akov Barit (1797–1883), who had taught at the rabbinical seminary in Vilna, and with R. Yisra'el Salanter, who was also familiar with the institution.[118] Contrary to R. Levin's opinion that new challenges

---

[115] Levin-Epstein, *Memoirs* (Heb.), 342. I searched for this pamphlet among Levin's literary bequest but could not find it.

[116] On this, see Stanislawski, *Tsar Nicholas I and the Jews*, chs. 3, 4.

[117] Kovner, *Sefer hamatsref*, 136 n. 14.

[118] R. Ya'akov Barit wrote him a letter in 1862 (see 'Safah lane'emanim', in Y. H. Levin,

should be met with new tools, R. Berlin would not agree to any change in existing practices and opposed all institutional innovations,[119] whether in the content and organization of studies or in their goal.

When R. Berlin took over the leadership of the yeshiva after the death of R. Eliezer Yitshak, R. Levin was already a familiar and respected presence in Volozhin—and on very poor terms with R. Berlin. The latter knew that he did not want R. Levin as his deputy but he had no other obvious candidates.[120] This complicated his position, since traditionally there had been two *rashei yeshivah* at Volozhin. The students split into two camps over this, and there are reports of representatives of the two sides coming to blows. The rivals appealed to prominent rabbis to intervene,[121] but the letters sent by the rabbis proved ineffective. Tensions at the yeshiva remained high. More active intervention from outside was needed, and after some time R. Zalman Ze'ev, the *magid meisharim* (preacher) of the Vilna community,[122] and R. David Tevele, the rabbi of Minsk,[123] arrived in Volozhin. Nothing is known of why they were chosen for this mission. According to Steinschneider, who published their decision, the 'heads of the Volozhin yeshiva', an otherwise unknown body and perhaps an ad hoc group, chose them, and they functioned as arbitrators rather than as an official *beit din*. A delegation of three or five rabbis would have constituted a *beit din*, which would have made the difficult situation even worse.[124]

Peleitat soferim), and in 1868 he wrote an approbation for Levin's book *Tsiyun yehoshua*, published in Y. H. Levin, *Moda'ah mevaseret tsiyon*, 9, addressed to his 'friend'. There is no proof that they had been friends earlier than this, but both were from Vilna and it seems likely that this was not a new friendship. On the link with R. Yisra'el Salanter, see below. The most recent and in many ways, the most interesting study about R. Yisrael's links to the rabbinical seminary is Lvov, 'Rabbi Isroel Salanter'.

[119] See the description of the dispute and the positions of the different sides, below.

[120] All the sources agree on this point.

[121] It is difficult to see who supported whom. According to Zitron, R. Levin appealed to two of the yeshiva's *gaba'im*—R. Zissel Rapaport of Minsk and R. Ya'akov Barit of Vilna ('Dynastic Wars in the Volozhin Yeshiva' (Heb.), 132). There is no other record that they held this position at the yeshiva. Zitron also claims that R. Berlin appealed to R. Betsalel of Vilna and R. Gershon Tanhum of Minsk, who were also *gaba'im* of the yeshiva, according to him. According to Levin-Epstein, R. Berlin sought the assistance of R. Ya'akov Me'ir Padua (the rabbi of Brisk); after hesitating, R. Padua wrote a letter supporting R. Berlin, thus persuading R. Levin to end the conflict (Levin-Epstein, *Memoirs* (Heb.), 342). It is more likely that it was the arbitrators' decision that ended it. The picture that emerges from the eulogy that R. Berlin gave at R. Ya'akov Me'ir's funeral is slightly different (N. Berlin, *Sermons of the Netsiv* (Heb.), sermon 20 (p. 124)).

[122] See Steinschneider and Zalkin (eds.), *The City of Vilna* (Heb.), i. 88–91. Vilna tradition has it that he was not only an excellent preacher but also a great Torah scholar.

[123] See B. Z. Eisenstadt, *Rabbis and Scholars of Minsk* (Heb.) 31–2. He had studied with R. Hayim of Volozhin, and was 'very wise in the ways of the world'.

[124] See Steinschneider and Zalkin (eds.), *The City of Vilna* (Heb.), i. 88–91.

On 24 November 1853, about two months after R. Eliezer Yitshak's death, the two rabbis publicized their decision, which was ratified in due course by other leading rabbis: R. Berlin would remain as *rosh yeshivah*, while R. Yosef Dov Soloveitchik, a great-grandson of R. Hayim, was appointed as deputy *rosh yeshivah*, his 'assistant and helper'. The decision was clear-cut.[125] R. Levin was not appointed to any post. Eliyahu Zalman was ordered to hand over the yeshiva buildings and library to the new administration in return for a payment of 700 roubles: evidently this constituted a renunciation of his 'rights'. A monthly allocation to 'the rabbi's house'—that is, the descendants of R. Hayim—was to be made from yeshiva funds. R. Levin, who had been at the centre of the feud, was only mentioned twice: he was allocated 4 roubles a month, half the sum awarded to his father-in-law, but only 1 rouble less than the amount given to R. Yosef Dov Soloveitchik.[126] The decision established that family members had rights to the 'income' of the yeshiva, but did not own it. It should also be noted that the arbitrators actually decided who would be R. Berlin's deputy. It was clear to everyone that there had to be a deputy *rosh yeshivah*, and the presence of two teachers of Talmud (*magidei shiur*) was seen as an integral element of the yeshiva structure. Thus, probably in contrast to the situation in the past, the senior *rosh yeshivah*, in this case R. Berlin, did not choose his deputy, who was selected by an external body.

The decision was sent to various rabbis and was approved in writing by R. David Luria of Bychow, R. Shelomoh Zalman Rivlin of Shklov, R. Yosef ben Me'ir of Slutsk, R. Ya'akov Me'ir Padua of Brisk, and R. Mordekhai of Raseiniai.[127] The practice of obtaining approbations from leading rabbis for decisions in very complex cases was very common, but in this case there seems to have been another reason for doing so, in that the authority of the arbitrators was not at all clear. They were not local rabbis, and had no standing in Volozhin; their authority came from their public status. This was why it was important to append the opinions of other leading rabbis, in order to reinforce the decision and ward off opposition, especially regarding the sensitive question of the ownership of the yeshiva.

The dispute over the leadership came temporarily to an end. R. Levin left Volozhin and returned to Vilna. From there he went elsewhere, though he occasionally visited Volozhin. He was one of the first supporters of the artist Mordecai Mane,[128] was among the first to propose the creation of a national

---

[125] M. Rabinowitz, 'Documents Relating to the History of the Volozhin Yeshiva' (Heb.), 226–9. The date of the decision indicates that the struggle for the leadership took place immediately after R. Eliezer Yitshak's death.

[126] Katzman, 'On the *Gaon* R. Yehoshua Heshel Levin' (Heb.), pt. 1, p. 764, observes that the decision deprived him of any role in the administration of the yeshiva, and limited his allocation to three years.

[127] Steinschneider and Zalkin (eds.), *The City of Vilna* (Heb.), i. 88–91.

[128] See Mane, *Collected Writings* (Heb.), 145, 162.

library in Jerusalem,[129] published polemical works against the Haskalah,[130] and ended his days as the rabbi of the east European Jews of Paris.

It seems very possible that one of the people behind R. Levin's attempt to take over the yeshiva and change its character was none other than R. Yisra'el Salanter, who was close to R. Levin at this time. In 1851 R. Salanter wrote him a letter supporting his attempts to publish the journal *Peleitat soferim*.[131] About a year later, when it was already obvious to the rabbis of the region that a struggle for the leadership of the Volozhin yeshiva was imminent, R. Salanter was among those who wrote approbations for his edition of R. Hayim's commentary on *Pirkei avot*. This was the period in which R. Salanter was trying to set up a new institution for training rabbis in Kovno,[132] and like R. Levin, he was searching for new tools to meet the challenge of the Haskalah. He often tried to work through intermediaries rather than openly,[133] and it is perfectly possible that he and R. Levin were co-operating. They maintained their close ties after 1853, and in 1863 R. Salanter sent a friendly letter to R. Levin, supporting his second attempt to publish *Peleitat soferim*.[134] As rabbi of the east European Jews of Paris, R. Levin benefited from R. Salanter's support,[135] and the relationship between them endured for many years.

If my suggestion about R. Salanter's role in the dispute is correct, this would constitute the first attempt by an outsider to change the yeshiva in order to pursue goals that were foreign to its founders—interestingly, an internal Jewish attempt, and largely prompted by the yeshiva's success. Volozhin's increasing importance in the Jewish world meant that anyone who wanted to influence the training of the future rabbinic leadership immediately focused their efforts there. For the same reason, famous rabbis were prepared to intervene in order to settle the dispute. Nevertheless, the controversy was resolved on the personal level, by a decision as to who should be appointed rather than by instituting fundamental organizational change that would prevent the occurrence of similar problems in the future. Since R. Soloveitchik's appointment was largely the result of family and institutional politics, it could have been anticipated that the same difficulties would re-emerge.

[129] See *Haḥavatselet*, 2/16 (26 Jan. 1872), 125.

[130] Lifschitz identifies R. Levin as the author of the anonymous pamphlet *Milḥamah beshalom* ('War on Peace'; Vilna, 1870), written by the Hevrat Matsdikei Harabim (Society of Justifiers of the Many) (Lifschitz, *Zikhron ya'akov*, ii. 104–5).

[131] See Rafael, '*Peleitat soferim* and *Safah lane'emanim*' (Heb.), 358.

[132] Rosenfeld, *Rabbi Yisra'el Salanter* (Heb.), 22–3.

[133] See below, Chs. 9 and 10, on Slobodka and Telz.

[134] As recorded on the cover of Levin, *Peleitat soferim*. On a parallel project of R. Salanter's, see Etkes, *Rabbi Yisra'el Salanter* (Heb.), 267–84.

[135] Tzinovitz, *Tree of Life* (Heb.), 289.

7. The Dispute between R. Naftali Berlin and R. Yosef Dov Soloveitchik over the Leadership of the Yeshiva

The decision reached by the rabbis solved the immediate problem but paved the way to another dispute. R. Yosef Dov Soloveitchik was a great-grandson of R. Hayim of Volozhin: his grandmother, Relke, was R. Hayim's daughter. His father, R. Yitshak Soloveitchik, had been a student of R. Yitshak of Volozhin, besides filling some secondary positions at the yeshiva, and had later become the crown rabbi of Kovno.[136] To be appointed 'crown rabbi' usually required some knowledge of Russian and identification with government policies; where R. Yitshak Soloveitchik learned Russian, if he indeed did so, is not known. His acceptance of such a position does not seem to have disturbed his relatives. R. Yosef Dov was born in 1820 and had displayed outstanding talent for talmudic studies from an early age; he was sent to study at Volozhin before reaching the age of barmitzvah. After he had spent several years there, he took a position as a Talmud teacher at Blumke's *kloyz* in Minsk. Nothing is known of his links with Volozhin from this point until his appointment as deputy to R. Berlin in 1853.

R. Yosef Dov's position in the yeshiva hierarchy—a direct descendant of R. Hayim serving as deputy to an 'outsider'—was hardly conducive to harmony. R. Berlin, who was only related to R. Hayim by marriage, had apparently not won the support of the students in his struggle with R. Levin because had he done so he would hardly have needed to secure the intervention of rabbis from outside. The appointment of a 'family' deputy seems to have been imposed upon him, and it must have been difficult for him to ensure that his own authority took precedence over that of R. Yosef Dov, whose lineage was more distinguished than his own. The new deputy *rosh yeshivah* did not owe R. Berlin any gratitude for his appointment, and was used to working independently. Moreover, since they were close in age, R. Berlin could not rely on seniority to increase his authority.

Most significantly, the two men had very different personalities. This was obvious to everyone, and eventually contributed to the conflict. In the 'compromise' of 1853, R. Berlin was described as 'working and labouring in the Torah of God with wonderful diligence, until he has become an expert in the entire Talmud, and teaches halakhah . . . God-fearing since his youth.'[137] R. Yosef Dov is termed 'excellent and effective in instilling students with his *pilpul*'. Within a short while, the students split into those who supported R. Yosef Dov's *pilpul* method and those who preferred R. Berlin's wider

---

[136] On R. Soloveitchik, see Karlinski, *The Founder of the Brisk Dynasty* (Heb.). On his father, see ibid. 44–70.

[137] M. Rabinowitz, 'Documents Relating to the History of the Volozhin Yeshiva' (Heb.), 226–9.

expertise. Each group venerated its own leader and despised that of the other camp—just as had happened during the feud with R. Levin.[138] Once again conflict arose over the question of authority at the yeshiva, and once again rabbis from outside the institution were called in to arbitrate.

No details of this conflict are known. No memoirs from this period have survived, and people who mention the incident play down its importance, whether in order to avoid being seen to take sides or to minimize the damage to the yeshiva's image. All that is known is that in 1856 four distinguished rabbis came to settle the dispute, which in itself serves as an indication of the level of tension at the yeshiva. All the evidence indicates that many of the students supported R. Yosef Dov, since otherwise the dispute would not have gone as far as it did. It seems reasonable to suppose that his method of study, which was more stimulating than the plain *peshat* method favoured by R. Berlin, was one of the factors that attracted students to his camp, as was the case even after the dispute.[139] On this occasion too, there was an even number of arbitrators, emphasizing that this was not a court but an arbitrative body. The group was composed of the two rabbis who had intervened in the previous dispute, together with R. Yosef of Slutsk and R. Yitshak Elhanan Spektor, who was rabbi of Novogrudok at the time.[140] In this case too, it is not clear how or by whom the arbitrators were chosen.

Something of the nature of the dispute can be learned from the text of their ruling. The first paragraph laid down that the yeshiva students were forbidden to 'impugn the honour' of either rabbi; one can assume that there must have been good reason for this prohibition. The second paragraph dealt with regulations for the admission of students. R. Berlin was authorized to decide if a student was accepted or not, unless the candidate arrived with a letter of recommendation addressed to R. Yosef Dov. However, both rabbis had the right to discipline students. According to a later source, the dispute began with an argument between the two rabbis over the rejection of a prospective student who had been recommended by R. Eliyahu Hayim Meisel (a famous rabbi of Łódź), simultaneously with the acceptance of another student who

[138] According to Berdyczewski, immature students were responsible for stirring up the conflict, thus necessitating external arbitrators ('History of the Ets Hayim Yeshiva' (Heb.), 235). However, his information probably came from R. Berlin, who had good reason to avoid negative comment on the Soloveitchik family. Lifschitz expressed the same opinion, probably for the same reasons (*Toledot yitsḥak*, 58). B. H. Epstein follows them, but admits that 'there was a breach that broke out as the result of the influences from the different strengths of the two luminaries', obviously referring to the dispute (*Mekor barukh*, iii. 1696). It is hard to believe that the two rabbis could not have restrained their students had they wanted to do so.

[139] See Kets [Kehat], *The Doctrine of Rabbi Naftali Berlin* (Heb.), 65–74, which presents an analysis of R. Berlin's attitude towards *pilpul*.

[140] For the text of the rabbis' decision, see Lifschitz, *Toledot yitsḥak*, 62–3, and, with a few variations, B. H. Epstein, *Mekor barukh*, iii. 1692–3. Lifschitz's version seems closer to the original.

had been recommended by the *gaba'im* of Minsk—important donors to the yeshiva, but not scholars of the standing of R. Meisel.[141] This may have been the background to the arbitrators' ruling on admissions. The third paragraph stated that *shiurim* were to be given only in the yeshiva building, and not in the rabbis' houses. This was probably intended to prevent rabbis from holding private *shiurim* at home for their supporters. There was nothing novel about this system of private *shiurim*; as mentioned above, it was one of the means R. Levin had adopted to gain support. For a student to be invited to his rabbi's house had tremendous symbolic significance, sometimes marking the student's near-adoption as part of the rabbi's family and strengthening the links between the two. However, acceptance of such an invitation placed the student under an obligation and could provoke jealousy among those who had not been invited. It is obvious, therefore, why the arbitrators opposed this custom—and if such *shiurim* were prohibited, they must have been taking place. The other paragraphs of the decision dealt with the yeshiva's finances. This was to remain in the hands of R. Berlin, but R. Yosef Dov was given the right to veto expenditures.[142] In other words, the arbitrators made no distinction between the teaching and administrative roles of the two men.

R. Yosef Dov benefited most from the new ruling. According to the decision made in 1853, R. Berlin had only to show R. Yosef Dov the yeshiva's accounts: now he could not spend money without the latter's approval. Originally admissions were decided solely by R. Berlin, whereas now R. Yosef Dov could admit students who arrived with a recommendation addressed to him. In addition, from now on the approval of both men had to be obtained before an emissary could be dismissed, and emissaries could not honour one rabbi more than the other. This suggests that the emissaries had also been involved in the dispute. The arbitrators also changed the rabbis' relative financial status: according to the 1853 decision, R. Berlin was paid 10 roubles a week, while R. Soloveitchik received 5, but from 1856 on, R. Berlin received

---

[141] Karlinski, *The Founder of the Brisk Dynasty* (Heb.), 111–14, with no reference to any source.

[142] The only significant difference in the versions of Lifschitz and Epstein is in this section. According to Lifschitz, 'All the yeshiva's cash shall be closed up in a box and remain in the house of the rabbi, our teacher and master, the aforementioned R. Tsevi Hirsh Yehudah Leib *under two locks, and one key will be held by the rabbi, our teacher and master, the aforementioned R. Tsevi Hirsh Yehudah Leib, and the second key will be held by the rabbi, our teacher and master, the aforementioned R. Yosef Dov Soloveitchik, and when it is necessary to obtain money for the expenses of the yeshiva, the rabbi, our teacher and master, the aforementioned R. Yosef Dov Soloveitchik will come to open the aforementioned box* and it will be recorded in the yeshiva register.' In Epstein's version, the passage in italics is replaced by the words 'and the removal of money from the box will be done by both of them'; see Lifschitz, *Toledot yitshak*, 62–3. The specification of two locks indicates mutual suspicion and lack of trust. Lifschitz was R. Yitshak Elhanan Spektor's secretary and probably obtained the text of the decision from him. Epstein was R. Berlin's nephew and probably obtained his version from R. Berlin himself or from those close to him, with a few alterations in order to conceal the tension between the two camps.

13 roubles a week and R. Soloveitchik was paid 8. The 5-rouble difference remained, but the rise in R. Soloveitchik's salary was higher in relative terms.

This intervention was no more successful than the first in bringing peace to the yeshiva. In 1864 R. Soloveitchik left Volozhin and was appointed rabbi of Slutsk. Nothing is known of his reasons for leaving, though it seems doubtful that he would have done so had he been fully satisfied with his position at Volozhin and the state of the yeshiva.[143] He was succeeded by a series of deputy *rashei yeshivah*.

Other than the problem of staffing, the state of the yeshiva was apparently good. In 1865 the building burnt down, but the necessary funds for rebuilding were quickly found. Both R. Berlin and R. Levin played prominent roles at the ground-breaking ceremony which suggests that R. Levin had made peace with his situation. In a letter written in 1868, R. Yisra'el Salanter thanked R. Berlin for sending him a copy of his edition of the *She'iltot*, a gaonic work. This also suggests an improvement of relations with circles that had been close to R. Levin.[144]

8. The Restoration of Tranquillity

R. Berlin's next deputy was a younger man—R. Hayim Hillel Fried.[145] He was the son of R. Eliezer Yitshak, the late head of the yeshiva. His wife was a granddaughter of R. Yitshak, the second head of the yeshiva,[146] and hence like

---

[143] Ya'akov Marek writes that when 'R. Yosef Baer [Dov] [Soloveitchik] left Volozhin and became rabbi of Slutsk, R. Berlin asked him to leave the young Hayim [his son] in Volozhin because he thought he would make a suitable husband for his granddaughter . . . but R. Yosef Baer did not agree to this . . . but after great effort [R. Berlin] prevailed upon R. Yosef Baer to agree to the match on condition that R. Hayim should stay and study at Slutsk. R. Hayim stayed in Slutsk until his marriage [in 1873]' (*In the Company of the Great Men of the Generation* (Heb.), 49–50).

[144] I have no explanation for their presence at the ground-breaking. See the report in *Hakarmel*, 6/6 (31 May 1866), 43. The letter of R. Salanter was published in the anonymously edited *Avraham Dov Vaisfish Memorial Volume* (Heb.), in the section entitled 'Eshed hanekhalim' (p. 130). The location of the original manuscript is not noted there but the handwritten letter is reproduced on p. 131. It is very short (just a few sentences), but it is difficult to understand: 'The valued gift of your honour, the Gaon, part three of your book on the *She'iltot*, has arrived. May the blessed Lord increase your strength in order to spread the Torah. What can I say now during the terrible famine which leads each man to have his hands on his loins (Jer. 30: 6), and the poor call out for bread and there is almost no one to help them?' It is not clear if this is a muted rebuke to the publisher of a book during a famine year or an explanation of why the letter is not longer or more expansive.

[145] Lunski, 'The *Gaon* Rabbi Hayim Hillel Fried' (Yid.), 2. A Hebrew translation appears in Leone (ed.), *Volozhin* (Heb.), 221–3. See also his son's account, in H. Berlin (ed.), *Ḥut hameshulash*, intro.

[146] See publisher's introduction to Landa, *Ḥayei ya'akov*. R. Ya'akov Landa was the son of R. Shemuel Landa, the son-in-law of R. Yitshak; R. Shemuel's sister was married to R. Hayim Hillel Fried.

R. Soloveitchik—and unlike R. Berlin—he too was a descendant of R. Hayim. He taught at the yeshiva for only a few years before he became ill and was forced to abandon teaching. During his time as *rosh yeshivah* he experienced financial difficulties, finding it impossible to live on his meagre salary. In response, the *gaba'im* of the yeshiva raised his salary to 12 roubles a month, while raising that of R. Berlin to 18.[147]

R. Fried's relationship with R. Berlin seems to have been no better than that of R. Soloveitchik. A letter written by R. Eliyahu Hayim Meisel of Łódź in 1870 complains:

Throughout his [R. Fried's] illness he found that there was an adversary who would oppress his pure soul . . . and though everyone should have encouraged him and strengthened him in his illness so that he might recover . . . they increased his depression, which made his illness worse. He is the only son of our master Eliezer Yitshak, of blessed memory, and even so they tried to persecute and drive him away, Heaven forbid.[148]

R. Meisel seems to have felt that R. Berlin used R. Fried's illness as a pretext for dismissing him.[149] R. Yitshak Elhanan Spektor of Kovno also criticized R. Berlin's attitude to R. Fried, but seemingly to no effect.[150]

Ironically, it was precisely at this point, after R. Berlin had emerged victorious from the disputes with R. Levin and R. Soloveitchik, that his position as *rosh yeshivah* became particularly difficult. His wife Rayna Batya, R. Yitshak's daughter,[151] died, severing his personal connection with the dynasty of R. Hayim, or *beit harav* ('the house of the rabbi'), as it was known in Volozhin. With her death, R. Berlin could have lost the dynastic right to direct the yeshiva, opening the way for other family members to claim that one of their number should serve at least as deputy *rosh yeshivah*. However, in the light of

[147] The source is in the Rabinowitz Collection in the National and University Library, Jerusalem. The supplement was naturally more significant for R. Fried.

[148] M. Rabinowitz, 'Documents Relating to the History of the Volozhin Yeshiva' (Heb.), 229. In rabbinic Hebrew, the plural form is often used in reference to honoured individuals. Hence, the use of 'they' appears to refer to R. Berlin, or perhaps to him and those close to him.

[149] His words cannot be interpreted as referring to someone else, since nobody at Volozhin except R. Berlin had the authority to dismiss R. Fried. R. Meisel seems to have been very close to R. Eliezer Yitshak. The brief biography of him records that 'in 1840 the *gaon* R. Eliezer Yitshak sent him to Gorodok to take up a position as rabbi, and the *gaon* R. Eliyahu Hayim Meisel obeyed' (B. Z. Eisenstadt, *The Generation of Our Rabbi and its Scholars* (Heb.), ii. 29). R. Meisel seems to have repaid him with devoted loyalty.

[150] In a letter written by R. Spektor, dated 9 Tevet (13 Dec.) 1869, he mentions that R. Berlin has complained 'about what I wrote . . . concerning my dear friend, the great rabbi . . . Hayim Hillel [Fried]'. The letter is in the Rabinowitz Collection in the National and University Library, Jerusalem.

[151] According to M. Berlin, she was about 55, so she must have died in or around 1871 (*Rabbi of Israel* (Heb.), 126).

what had happened in the past, it was obvious that an administrative team of this type would only lead to more in-fighting and to a renewed battle over the leadership.

Against this background, a new dispute developed over the appointment of R. Avraham Dov of Ihumen, the brother-in-law of R. Fried and son-in-law of R. Eliezer Yitshak, as deputy *rosh yeshivah*. Many supporters were recruited for his cause, and the surviving evidence clearly reflects only part of the picture. As early as the winter of 1870, R. Spektor wrote to R. Berlin, suggesting that R. Avraham Dov should be appointed temporarily, until his brother-in-law, R. Fried, recovered.[152] (R. Spektor had been one of the arbitrators who confirmed R. Berlin's position as head of the yeshiva.)

In the same week, a group of rabbis from Warsaw appealed to R. Yosef Eliyahu Eliasberg and R. Avraham Parnas,[153] in their roles as *gaba'im* of the yeshiva, to support R. Avraham Dov's appointment as deputy to R. Berlin on the grounds of his family connections. In a letter dated 5 Elul (1 Sept.) 1870, addressed to the 'officers' (*amarkalim*) of the Volozhin yeshiva, R. Meisel wrote that R. Avraham Dov should be invited to Volozhin to give *shiurim*.[154] A letter sent by R. Eliezer Simhah Rabinowitz, who was rabbi of Suvalk, makes the same point, so it would seem that R. Meisel and R. Spektor seem to have let their positions be known in order to influence public opinion and exert more pressure.[155] Another letter, sent from Grodno, tells the same story.[156] The letters emphasized that not only did R. Avraham Dov deserve to be appointed to the post but that such a step was necessary in order to avoid depriving R. Eliezer Yitshak's descendants of an income. Their closely similar style and content bear witness to a well-organized campaign—perhaps run by

---

[152] Document in the Rabinowitz Collection in the National and University Library, Jerusalem.

[153] On R. Eliasberg, see Steinschneider and Zalkin (eds.), *The City of Vilna* (Heb.), i. 268–9. He is mentioned in the section on 1854 as the book-keeper of the Holy Congregation of Vilna, together with R. Avraham Parnas. See M. Rabinowitz, 'Documents Relating to the History of the Volozhin Yeshiva' (Heb.), 228. On R. Parnas, see Steinschneider and Zalkin (eds.), *The City of Vilna* (Heb.), i. 273–4. He was linked by marriage to the Eliasberg family.

[154] The letter has been published in M. Rabinowitz, 'Documents Relating to the History of the Volozhin Yeshiva' (Heb.), 230.

[155] The original is in the Rabinowitz Collection at the Jewish National and University Library, Jerusalem. On this rabbi, see the *Evreiskaya entsiklopediya*, xvi. 230. He does not seem to have studied at Volozhin, but was connected to R. Hayim's dynasty. There may have been an unsuccessful attempt in this period to appoint him as the deputy *rosh yeshivah*. See Levinski, 'A Home of the Torah' (Heb.), 109. According to Lipman, he was 'the son-in-law of the *gaon*, our teacher R. Leib Ragover, who was related by marriage to R. Itsele Volozhiner [R. Yitshak of Volozhin]', and thus had some family link to the Volozhin dynasty (*On the History of the Jews of Kovno and Slobodka* (Heb.), 221).

[156] The original is in the Rabinowitz Collection in the National and University Library, Jerusalem.

R. Fried himself—to put pressure on R. Berlin.[157] The latter opposed the appointment none the less, as R. Meisel recorded:

Only the *gaon*, R. Naftali Tsevi, has refused to agree, as though he were the sole founder of this holy yeshiva and the whole world did his bidding, and as though he regarded all the sages of Israel and the great ones of the people and their leaders as of no more account than garlic skin; and it is fitting that he should be shown that this is not so, and that the honourable leaders of Minsk, may God protect and preserve them, should write directly to the *gaon* and rabbi of the congregation of Ihumen that he should come, and that he should give the *shiurim*; and who will defy this? Since most of the *geonim* of the land have agreed to this, who shall stop this? And then the *gaon*, R. Naftali Tsevi, may God protect and preserve him, will know that he is not the only *rosh yeshivah* who is capable of giving *shiurim* regularly, and that he should not oppress pure and innocent souls, may God atone for him.[158]

It was obvious to R. Berlin that the appointment of R. Avraham Dov would lead to further disputes, and this was most probably why he opposed it. Ultimately, he managed to have his son-in-law, R. Rafa'el Shapira, appointed to the post.

Peace returned to the yeshiva by the end of 1870, with the appointment of R. Shapira as the deputy *rosh yeshivah*. He was a distinguished scholar, but he was not a descendant of R. Hayim; it is true to say that he received the position only because R. Berlin was his father-in-law. With R. Shapira's appointment there were therefore no further conflicts of authority. He was succeeded in 1881 by his own son-in-law, R. Hayim Soloveitchik, the son of R. Yosef Dov Soloveitchik. These appointments and R. Berlin's attempts to pass on the leadership of the yeshiva to his son in 1892, during his lifetime, will be discussed in Chapter 8.

The battles over who controlled the yeshiva were largely because of how the institution was organized, and especially because of the lack of a clear line of authority. Another contributory factor was the absence of a body authorized to take decisions regarding the administration. Whereas there were towns, including Volozhin itself, where two men shared authority—a rabbi and an *av beit din*—their roles were separate and clearly defined and their titles

---

[157] The letter was sent from Warsaw, dated 'Monday of the week of the Torah portion "Nitsavim"' (approximately September). I have not been able to decipher the year, but, judging from the contents, it is probably about 1870. It reads: 'At the moment, because of his physical frailty and lack of strength . . . he cannot fulfil his sacred duty of teaching, since he has been warned by the doctors, so he has agreed to our request that he accept his brother-in-law, the great R. Avraham Dov, to stand in for him . . . [therefore we appeal to] the *gaba'im* of the yeshiva in the Holy Congregations of Vilna and Minsk . . . that they should stand at the right hand of our master, the *gaon* and rabbi, our teacher, the *gaon* and rabbi Hayim Hillel, may his light shine, that his request may be fulfilled and his brother-in-law may take his place in peace.' I should like to thank Rabbi Boruch Oberlander for assisting me with this text.

[158] M. Rabinowitz, 'Documents Relating to the History of the Volozhin Yeshiva' (Heb.), 230.

were different. At the yeshiva, both the men in a position of authority had the same title: *rosh yeshivah*. Even though one was officially the other's deputy, this was never given expression in the most public sphere, that of teaching. Both taught the same students, with no division into higher- and lower-level classes. This lack of differentiation in the formal sphere heightened the importance of the informal sphere—such as the links created by family and marriage ties— in shaping the relationship between the two men.

The lack of clarity regarding the legal status and ownership of the yeshiva also caused problems. The need to summon rabbis from outside the yeshiva to adjudicate disputes would never have arisen in a traditional Ashkenazi yeshiva, where the local community leaders made all the decisions. To complicate matters further, the founder's descendants regarded the yeshiva as their family property—a position that was acknowledged in the monthly payments made to them solely in recognition of their descent from R. Hayim.[159] Although the payments stopped the members of the dynasty complaining and also made them dependent on the yeshiva, the custom preserved the belief that the yeshiva belonged to the family rather than to the wider community. The family itself had no mechanism for choosing an heir or an authorized candidate to act as *rosh yeshivah*. Ultimately, they had to accept every compromise, since they needed the yeshiva's support and had little alternative. At the time, nobody saw any contradiction between raising money for the yeshiva and allocating money for R. Hayim's descendants, even though some members of the family, such as R. Eliyahu Zalman, the son of R. Yitshak, were wealthy and did not need financial support.

The yeshiva was really an autonomous public institution, a 'non-profit organization' or 'legal person' in modern parlance. But there was no possibility of registering it as a legal organization according to civil law because of the complications of the Russian legal system; nor was there any suitable model in the Jewish legal tradition. It resembled a corporation from the legal point of view, but was much more complex. The Jewish public regarded the yeshiva as an important institution, as is evident from the enormous prestige of the rabbis who took the trouble to travel to Volozhin in order to resolve the conflicts there. The rabbis of Lithuania wanted the yeshiva to carry on, even though in theory they could have managed without it and made do with the study opportunities offered by the *batei midrash*. Another group interested in the continued existence of the yeshiva were the emissaries, who could have exerted considerable influence over the yeshiva in their role as fundraisers; however, they preferred peace and quiet at the institution, since it provided their livelihood. Public quarrels led to a decline in contributions to the

---

[159] See the letter written by the arbitrators in 1854, in M. Rabinowitz, 'Documents Relating to the History of the Volozhin Yeshiva' (Heb.), 229. The rabbinic dynasty had economic interests in the yeshiva.

yeshiva, which in turn reduced their own income.[160] In the light of all the above, it is clear that there would always be someone who would work for a compromise at the yeshiva, even if the solution found was unconventional.

No long-term solution was forthcoming, and it is not even clear whether such a solution would have been possible as there were no public bodies or institutions that could provide suitable precedents. Tranquillity was thus only maintained when the deputy *rosh yeshivah* was completely subordinate to the *rosh yeshivah* on a personal level.

In concluding the discussion of the internal conflicts at the yeshiva, it is important to emphasize that both sides maintained decent and even good relations on a personal level after the resolution of the disputes. R. Levin's nephew studied at Volozhin after his uncle's feud with R. Berlin, and was very close both to his aunt (R. Levin's wife) and to R. Berlin.[161] Similarly, R. Yosef Dov Soloveitchik's son married R. Berlin's granddaughter. This does not mean that there was no tension between the former opponents: it was their ability to rise above it that was particularly notable and worthy of respect. Those who would wish to ignore the tension also cannot appreciate the achievement of rising above tension.

[160] Levin-Epstein, *Memoirs* (Heb.), 28.   [161] Ibid.

THREE

Study at Volozhin in the Time of
R. Naftali Berlin

Most of the information available on how the Volozhin yeshiva functioned and the atmosphere there comes from the period after the leadership struggles of the 1860s. It was a period of relative tranquillity (so there was no need for outside intervention to resolve disputes) and there were no changes in the mode of study or other procedures. As we shall see, the relative abundance of sources from these later years allows more precise description of phenomena that are only hinted at in the sources that have survived from the earlier years, and since we know that there was little change in most areas, it is possible to describe the different aspects of yeshiva life during this period quite well on the basis of available sources.

While there do seem to have been shifts in Volozhin's reputation during this time, in general it retained its pre-eminent status. After the building burnt down in 1865 and R. Yosef Dov Soloveitchik left, R. Yosef of Krynki wrote: 'And now its glory has been brought low and humiliated, for I have heard slander spoken by many, this one asking, "Why is it so important? There are many yeshivas in the world", and that one saying that the yeshivas of other communities are better in their works and in other matters, and all think that the yeshivas in the large cities are the best.' It is difficult to know which yeshivas R. Yosef had in mind—the nearby Mir yeshiva, urban yeshivas in Lithuania, or yeshivas outside Lithuania.[1] Mir was not particularly well known in this period, and there is no evidence of a stream of students leaving Lithuania for Pressburg (Bratislava) or other yeshivas abroad. Perhaps R. Yosef was writing in response to some isolated event, or in order to galvanize support for Volozhin, though there is a distinct sense of decline in his words. Whatever the circumstances, the fact that R. Berlin managed to raise enough funds for a stone-built building suggests that there were a fair number of donors who had confidence in the yeshiva, for donors do not usually rush to support institutions on the decline.

---

[1] Shmukler [Shapira], *Rabbi Hayim of Volozhin* (Heb.), 46. On urban yeshivas, see Zalkin, 'City of Torah' (Heb.).

In later years too, on occasion there were some who sensed decline. In 1880, probably after the opening of the *kolel* in Kovno (see Chapter 11 below) and before R. Hayim Soloveitchik joined the yeshiva, a student wrote: 'In Volozhin they knew that in Kovno . . . they did not speak of Volozhin with the proper respect, saying that the yeshiva had already declined from its great-ness and was not as important as it had been in former days.'[2] However, the editor of *Hamelits*, wrote in the same year that Volozhin was 'a distinguished yeshiva . . . whose fame has spread throughout the Jewish people';[3] he described it as one of the most important Jewish institutions in Russia. If more proof is necessary, it can be noted that the very fact that there were still public controversies about the yeshiva in the second half of the nineteenth century proves its continued importance.

After the 1860s, although the methods of teaching and study remained unchanged there were important developments in the curriculum, though they attracted little attention at the time. Talmud had always been at the centre of the curriculum but now it became the sole text studied (with the exception of the weekly Torah portion): the *shiurim* on halakhah disappeared, the study of halakhic codes declined drastically, the practical halakhic impli-cations of Talmud study were de-emphasized, and the study of kabbalah ceased. These changes are discussed in more detail below.

1. The Yeshiva as a Place of Study

As in earlier years independent Talmud study was the central activity in Volozhin, with *shiurim* taking a second place. The fact that the core function of the yeshiva was to provide a framework for study found expression in every aspect of its functioning: in its architecture, in the role of the *shiur* in the cur-riculum, in the composition of the staff, in the distaste for display, in the daily routine, and in the admissions procedure. In this respect the yeshiva resem-bled the traditional *batei midrash* rather than a modern educational institution. People unfamiliar with a yeshiva had difficulty in understanding that it was essentially a place for study rather than a framework for teaching. It certainly was not an institution for training rabbis, though many students went on to become rabbis. Regarding the yeshiva as a school often led to misunderstand-ings about the nature of the yeshiva and its function in Jewish society. However, this only became an issue late in the nineteenth century.

The Volozhin yeshiva stood on a rocky hill. The lower floor was essentially a cellar and the upper floor an attic. Because the role of the building was to accommodate individual study in the traditional manner rather than class-room teaching, the main floor was essentially a large study hall—a *beit*

---

[2] Z. Epstein, 'A Forgotten Jubilee' (Heb.), 4.
[3] Zederbaum, 'The Heavenly Yeshiva' (Heb.), 746.

midrash. Students did not study on their own in their rooms or in a quiet library, but all at the same time, in the same place, and out loud—even though they were studying different texts. It was in this central hall that the *rashei yeshivah* delivered their *shiurim*—not the best environment either for follow-ing a lecture or for the ensuing discussion. The absence of classrooms is clear from a description published in *He'asif* in 1885; it adds detail to, but essentially does not contradict, an account from forty years earlier that described the yeshiva as 'a spacious building containing a number of large halls . . . the fur-nishings were very simple: long tables, surrounded by benches, a few long shelves, bearing a great library, a Torah Ark with several Torah scrolls, and a *bimah* for the prayer leader—this was all the furniture within these walls'.[4] No major changes appear to have taken place in the physical character of the yeshiva by the time the *He'asif* article was published:

The yeshiva is located in a wonderful palace, built in three storeys. It has a spacious hall, supported by four great columns, with walls as white as snow or pure wool, and a clean, pure floor; this is the study hall. There is also a large lobby where the students read on sunny days, and a beautiful room in which is the great *gemaḥ* [free loan fund] from which every student may borrow if there is need . . . there is a tidy room in which the *menahel* [director], R. Lipmann, distributes the tractates needed for study, and a smoking room (for it is forbidden to smoke tobacco in the yeshiva). On the lower floor are the *mashgiaḥ* and the *menahel*, and on the upper floor is the yeshiva's great library.[5]

Since the building was purpose-built it could have been designed differently, for example with classrooms, either originally or when it was rebuilt in 1865, had the need for this been felt. Apparently it was not; no sources mention *shiurim* being given in special classrooms.

2. Lessons and the Framework of Studies

The yeshiva day was entirely devoted to study. Here is a description of the daily routine from the yeshiva's final years:

From nine o'clock in the morning to nine o'clock at night all the students studied together [in the yeshiva]. And from nine o'clock in the evening until nine o'clock in the morning there were changing shifts and changing watches. The first three hours constituted the first watch; the second three hours were the second watch; and so on, with one watch relieving another. These watches were compulsory: so many benches [of students] today, and so many benches tomorrow. And anyone who knew that he could not carry out his obligation on the night on which he had to keep watch would change to another watch.[6]

---

[4] Lilienthal, 'My Travels in Russia', *American Israelite*, 3/2(35) (18 July 1856).
[5] Berdyczewski [Bar Bei Rav], 'History of the Ets Hayim Yeshiva' (Heb.), 236.
[6] Ibid.

On Friday nights, half the students would eat their evening meal at midnight, when the two watches changed over.[7] This type of atmosphere encouraged *matmidim*—perpetual students who studied for eighteen or more hours every day.[8]

The attitude to giving *shiurim* was complex. On the one hand, the *rashei yeshivah* saw it as a great responsibility—the highlight of their work in the yeshiva—and took pains to prepare their material. Teaching itself was considered to be a sacred activity, almost a ritual obligation:

> At Volozhin, the *shiur* was a sort of 'daily sacrifice [as in the Temple]' . . . every day . . . on the stroke of half past twelve the *shiur* would be delivered . . . the *shiur* was never cancelled. There were cases when someone was dangerously ill in the house of the rabbi and teacher, and the doctors who were to pronounce on the course of the illness were sitting there at the time of the *shiur*, and everyone was upset, but the moment the time for the *shiur* arrived, the rabbi and teacher would enter the yeshiva, deliver the *shiur*—naturally without any *ḥidushim* [meaning, without raising issues that would drag out the shiur]—and review the entire page [of Talmud], before rushing off to hear the doctors' verdict. The *shiur* was never cancelled.[9]

However, nobody checked whether the students understood the material that had been studied. This was because the *rashei yeshivah* saw independent study as the students' main obligation. They were thus very strict about constant attendance in the study hall, but less concerned about quantifying achievement, measuring the acquisition of knowledge, or providing *shiurim* that met students' needs. The practice of holding a single *shiur* at an advanced level for all the students assumed that even if a student initially found it difficult to follow, with the passage of time he would gradually comprehend more; eventually he would understand everything and would be able to take part in the discussions that accompanied the *shiur*. While somewhat strange to modern ears, this description would have a familiar ring for students at medieval universities. The rabbi giving the *shiur* did not have to try to make it comprehensible to the students, since everyone assumed that yeshiva students were self-sufficient and did not need the help of a teacher. The *shiur* was a particularly good framework for outstanding students: participation in the *shiur* with other advanced students presented them with a challenge. Indeed, this model would seem like paradise for gifted schoolchildren today, who have to sit for years in classes aimed at the average student. For the less gifted it was far from paradise: since the teachers made no effort to ensure that the *shiur* was accessible, the less able students developed a sense of inferiority that made it even harder for them to grapple with the material. The

[7] B. H. Epstein, *Mekor barukh*, iii. 1787.

[8] M. A. Eisenstadt, 'The Volozhin Yeshiva' (Heb.), 163. The sources do not explain when those who stayed awake half the night or more found the time to pray.

[9] M. Berlin [Bar-Ilan], *From Volozhin to Jerusalem* (Heb.), i. 90.

heavy social and educational price this exacted from the more mediocre students is described by R. Barukh Epstein, the nephew of R. Berlin, himself a student at Volozhin:

The fellow students [of a particularly weak student] at the yeshiva, whose regular seats in the yeshiva were near his, would avoid him, and would not include him in Torah discussions or in friendly conversation; there would hardly be any ties or closeness between them, and they would not pay attention to him. The reason for this was that they valued themselves far more highly than him in the level of their Torah study, sharpness, knowledge, expertise, taste, reasoning, and logic, as well as in their method of learning and their worldly knowledge.[10]

Students were expected to study as much as possible and the tradition of uninterrupted study day and night was maintained,[11] but attending *shiurim* was optional. They had almost total freedom in the organization of their time as long as they used it productively. Students were disciplined for not coming to *shiurim* only if they were not using their time productively; if they were studying on their own during *shiur* time, they were not penalized.[12] One student claimed that 'only those who received the weekly stipend' attended *shiurim*,[13] but this was probably an exaggeration since another recalled, probably equally inaccurately, that in his time only a few dozen students used to attend.[14] Both claims were undoubtedly overstated, but they reflect the reality of obligatory study and optional classes. The fact that classes were optional reflected the tradition of independent study in the *beit midrash*.[15]

During R. Berlin's time as *rosh yeshivah*, he delivered the *shiur* on the first three days of the week, with his deputy replacing him on the other weekdays; each started his *shiur* at the page of the Talmud where his predecessor had left off.[16] In this way each student had the opportunity to hear both *rashei yeshivah* if he wished. One of the factors affecting attendance at *shiurim* was thus the *rosh yeshivah*'s personality, but the subject of study was also important: 'When [R. Hayim Soloveitchik] taught about matters of *taharah* [ritual purity], few students attended, because of the esoteric nature of the subject matter; but when he gave *shiurim* on damages and the laws relating to women, hundreds

[10] B. H. Epstein, *Mekor barukh*, iii. 1682.

[11] Berdyczewski [Bar Bei Rav], 'A Bundle of Letters' (Heb.), *Hamelits* 28/56. Zlatkin wrote of the good students at the yeshiva: 'There were no demands from the *mashgiah*: they did not examine them, they did not check whether they attended the yeshiva at the proper hours or not. They were even allowed to study wherever they wanted' ('The Volozhin Yeshiva in Bialik's Time' (Heb.), 59).   [12] M. A. Eisenstadt, 'The Volozhin Yeshiva' (Heb.), 162.

[13] Z. Epstein, *Writings* (Heb.), 122.

[14] On lack of attendance at *shiurim*, see Kamenetsky, *The Making of a Godol*, i. 714–17.

[15] Balosher, 'Bialik at Volozhin' (Heb.), 28.

[16] Berdyczewski [Bar Bei Rav], 'History of the Ets Hayim Yeshiva' (Heb.), 237; M. Berlin [Bar-Ilan], *From Volozhin to Jerusalem* (Heb.), i. 88.

of students flocked to hear him.'[17] Another description gives additional details:

Some students only attended the *shiurim* given by one of the *rashei yeshivah*,[18] while others only attended when talmudic passages in which they had some interest were being discussed. At one time, when the order of *Nezikin* had been completed and they were just about to start the order of *Kodashim* in the *shiur*, some of the students expressed their opinion that most of the students were not knowledgeable about the subject matter of *Kodashim* and that it would be difficult for them to understand the *shiurim*. The *rashei yeshivah* decided to accede to their request, though not to interrupt the usual order of study, and they instituted two *shiurim* each day. At the usual time for the *shiur* they began again with tractate *Berakhot* [the first tractate in the Talmud, i.e. they skipped the difficult orders of *Kodashim* and *Tohorot* entirely], and in the early evening they gave another *shiur*, carrying on with *Kodashim*.[19]

The material a student chose to study was influenced by the absence of an academic calendar, the goal of study, and the perception that the yeshiva was basically a place for individual study—not for taught classes. Right up to the yeshiva's final days in the last decade of the nineteenth century, students could arrive to start their studies on any day of the year and continue to study independently, round the clock and all year round. As mentioned above, there were no vacations, except for the Jewish religious festivals when no *shiurim* took place. R. Berlin would no doubt have been somewhat surprised by the recognized vacation periods of contemporary yeshivas. If yeshiva study had been cumulative and sequential, the lack of defined periods of study would have made things very difficult; but since the main emphasis was on independent study, there was no logic in limiting the admission of new students to particular times during the year.

3. The Staff of the Yeshiva and their Functions

The staffing of the yeshiva reflected its nature as an institution that emphasized study rather than teaching. Because it was assumed that all students would know how to study on their own and could use their time profitably even if they had difficulties in understanding the *shiur*, there were only two teachers: the two *rashei yeshivah*. The rest of the staff were responsible for the daily functioning of the yeshiva and for making sure that the students did not waste their time in idle pursuits. Several people were engaged in this in the 1860s: there was a *menahel*, described as 'head of the *mashgihim*' (supervisors),

[17] Don-Yihia, 'Memoirs' (Heb.), *Netivah*, 11/29.

[18] It was said of Bialik that 'like all those from Vilna, he preferred *breadth* to *depth*. He never used to attend the *shiurim* of R. Hayim [Soloveitchik]' (see Don-Yihia, 'Memoirs' (Heb.), *Netivah*, 11/34). On lack of attendance at R. Berlin's *shiurim*, see below.

[19] M. Berlin [Bar-Ilan], *From Volozhin to Jerusalem* (Heb.), i. 61.

implying that there were several *mashgiḥim* under his authority. Their job was to confirm that the students were actually in the study hall and studying: easy in theory, but according to one student more difficult in practice:

The *rashei yeshivah* and the *mashgiḥim* were struck with blindness, so that in those moments when R. Hirsh Leib or one of the *mashgiḥim* entered the building, all the students made a great noise and pretended that they were studying with great enthusiasm; but the moment they left the yeshiva most of the students stopped studying and began to whisper together about other matters.[20]

Supervision extended outside the yeshiva too:

A man by the name of R. Shelomoh, the *menahel*, played the part of a spy in this yeshiva. He used to steal out every night and sneak by the windows of the students' residences or into their rooms, to see how they were spending their time there, and if he found anything reprehensible about one of them, he brought his slander to R. Hirsh Leib so that [the student] might be punished.[21]

Most memoirs give little attention to the *mashgiḥim*, which says something about the lack of importance that students at the yeshiva attributed to the position. In consequence the names of *mashgiḥim* have generally not been preserved, though we know of a certain Hirshel Shaike who fulfilled this function in the 1880s.[22]

Later descriptions yield evidence of changes in the number of *mashgiḥim* and of variations in the yeshiva's policy. The goals and requirements seem to have remained the same, but the means to attain them changed in accordance with contemporary circumstances. The reliance on supervision seems to have declined in some periods, and its reimposition was then regarded as an innovation. The sense that the appointment of a *mashgiaḥ* was something new emerges from a description of 1874: 'In this year a *mashgiaḥ* came to the yeshiva, R. Shimon Novogrodski of Vilna. He was about 60 years old, a great *talmid ḥakham*, and he used to sit in the yeshiva all day in front of an open Gemara. Most of the students were not pleased about his arrival. They regarded it as humiliating that a *mashgiaḥ* should be appointed to supervise them.'[23] Obviously this was not actually an innovation, but collective memory can be very short in an educational institution with a rapid turnover of students from year to year. Evidence of changes in the organization of supervision comes from the memoirs of another student from roughly the same period. He does not mention a *mashgiaḥ*, but describes a *shamash* (beadle), 'who used to pass by the students' residences and investigate . . . whether any of them were reading heretical literature'.[24] The calibre of the *mashgiḥim* varied.

[20] Shomer, *Poems and Memoirs* (Heb.), 61. [21] Ibid. 60.
[22] Mashvitski, 'In the Dwelling-Places of Torah' (Heb.), *Baderekh*, 3/38(105).
[23] A. Z. Horowitz, *Memoirs of Two Generations* (Yid.), 227.
[24] Levin-Epstein, *Memoirs* (Heb.), 31.

N. M. Shaikevitch (Shomer) recorded that the head *mashgiaḥ* in his time, Yitshak Eliezer of Nesvizh, used to give the *shiur* when one of the *rashei yeshivah* was absent.[25] However, most were neither great scholars nor very efficient in their supervision of the students, as the following story demonstrates:

> The rabbi and the *mashgiaḥ* decided that owning modern books came under the prohibition of possessing forbidden objects and anyone who read them was to be considered as though he were reading heretical books. But they did not search thoroughly, and only by chance would the *menahalim* [this was the term for those who lit the lamps, distributed the books, and drew the water at the yeshiva] find anything. The *mashgiaḥ* would give them details of signs by which they might recognize the new books. They could be distinguished by the use of dashes, question marks, and exclamation marks, and sometimes they would give them lists of titles, such as: *Ahavat tsiyon*, *Ashmat shomron*, *Ayit tsavua* [novels by Avraham Mapu], *Ha'avot vehabanim* [a novel by Sholem Yankev Abramovitsh (generally known as Mendele Moykher Seforim)], etc. Once the *menahalim* found a book called *Ahavat tsiyon*, by the *gaon* [R. Eleazar] Fleckeles, and with great rejoicing they carried it off to the *mashgiaḥ*, who turned their joy into grief and sorrow [when they realized that it was not the book by Mapu] . . . This [supervision] had always been the practice but recently they have renewed it with ever greater severity. They have ordered the *menahalim* to go through the students' lodgings and to search in every nook and cranny, like bloodhounds, after forbidden books.[26]

Some students considered supervision a custom alien to Volozhin, and attributed it to the influence of the *musar* movement founded by R. Yisra'el Salanter.[27] However, it is clear from the sources that supervision was practised at Volozhin long before the birth of this movement.[28] Indeed, there is no

[25] Shomer, *Poems and Memoirs* (Heb.), 60. This was probably R. Yitshak Eliezer Rabinowitz, who died in 1874. See the article in *Halevanon* (Heb.), 11/18 (16 Dec. 1874), 5, where he is described in somewhat different terms from those used by Shomer: 'The beloved deceased from his youth onwards served as a rabbi in one of the communities of Lithuania. For about fifteen years the *gaba'im* [wardens] of the yeshiva recognized his worth and placed him in charge of the yeshiva's funds, and he served faithfully to the end of his life.' He seems to have been appointed to this post in the wake of the conflict between R. Berlin and R. Yosef Dov Soloveitchik.

[26] Shirotkin, 'The Dew to which All Turn' (Heb.), *Hashaḥar*, 8/3: 115. I am not convinced that the story is true, but it seems to reflect the image of the *mashgiaḥ* and the attitude towards him. It should be noted that it was not R. Eleazar Fleckeles (1754–1826) who wrote the book *Ahavat tsiyon* but his teacher, R. Yehezkel Landau (1713–93).

[27] Mashvitski, 'In the Dwelling-Places of Torah' (Heb.), *Baderekh*, 3/38 (105): 4: 'The great rivalry [between the *musar* yeshivas of Slobodka and the Kovno *kolel*] brought confusion to the leaders of the Volozhin yeshiva and our complete freedom [there] was gradually suppressed. In conformity with the demand of the *musar* leaders, a special *menahel* was appointed then [1885] to make sure that the students came every day to the yeshiva to pray together. A painstaking watch and thorough supervision has been maintained ever since then over everything done by the students, even in their residences.'

[28] Shmuel Zitron studied there in 1876, and wrote about this period: 'Strict discipline was always observed in the famous yeshiva of Volozhin. For example, the tiniest suspected infraction,

evidence of widespread interest in *musar*, though at least some students were familiar with it. For example, Jacob Joseph, a future chief rabbi of New York who studied in Volozhin, later went to Kovno in order to study *musar* with R. Salanter.[29]

Staff members performed a number of different duties and functions, and it may be supposed that their responsibilities changed from time to time. At one stage the *menahalim* were responsible for distributing books and lamps to the students.[30] In the 1880s there was a *menahel* by the name of R. Lipman, one of whose duties was to stop students talking during prayers.[31] In 1886 yet another, Avramele, 'was charged with waking the students and urging them to hasten to the [prayer] service'. He took his job very seriously, carrying out the instructions of the *rosh yeshivah* or the head *mashgiaḥ* with the utmost gravity.[32]

The changes in the allocation of administrative duties suggest a conscious attempt to make things run more smoothly, and in particular to make supervision more effective and to increase the time the students spent in study. It contrasts strongly with the lack of change in the study framework and the absence of any attempt to make teaching more effective, for example through additional *shiurim* or *shiurim* at different levels. However, it was precisely because of the somewhat casual attitude to *shiurim* that students had complete freedom in their studies. Additional *shiurim* and closer supervision of the method and material of study would have reduced and eventually destroyed this freedom.

4. The Perceived Functions of the Yeshiva and their Consequences

The yeshiva was not seen as a place for religious or spiritual growth nor as a framework offering preparation for a rabbinical career. It was simply a place for study.

Both staff and students at Volozhin disapproved of excessively pious behaviour and demonstrative and emotional prayer.[33] According to R. Barukh Epstein, the nephew of R. Berlin:

such as arriving late for prayers, was sufficient for the *mashgiaḥ* to punish a student' (Zitron, *Three Literary Generations* (Yid.), 160).

[29] See K. Kaplan, 'Rabbi Jacob Joseph' (Heb.), 5.

[30] Berdyczewski [Bar Bei Rav], 'History of the Ets Hayim Yeshiva' (Heb.), 236: 'the *menahel* R. Lipman will distribute the necessary tractates for study'; Shomer, *Poems and Memoirs* (Heb.), 61: 'each had a lamp by whose light he would study at night'.

[31] Mashvitski, 'In the Dwelling-Places of Torah' (Heb.), *Baderekh*, 3/38(105).

[32] M. A. Eisenstadt, 'The Volozhin Yeshiva' (Heb.), 64.

[33] On R. Berlin's attitude to *musar* and the 'fear of Heaven', see H. Kets [Kehat], *The Doctrine of Rabbi Naftali Berlin* (Heb.), 134–40.

My uncle could not bear it if one of the students at the yeshiva cut short his study time in order to pray more than the regular prayers, and he used to say that the time of life when a man devoted all his time and all his being to the goal of acquiring the blessing of Torah [knowledge], like those yeshiva students who came and studied enthusiastically at the yeshiva for several years—all that time his Torah study was necessary, essential, and equal [in importance] to every other commandment, and that each hour [of study] was far more valuable than gold and silver—and than extra prayers.[34]

The students felt the same: 'If one of the students occasionally behaved in a pietistic manner and spent a long time praying, he became one of the weakest students and an object of mockery.'[35] It was in fact customary to study during the prayer services:[36] 'We used to talk among ourselves during prayers, even when the *rosh yeshivah* or the chief *mashgiaḥ* was present. During the reading of the Torah most of us were immersed in our Gemaras.'[37] It can be assumed that the conversations during prayer services were thus not idle talk but rather discussion of the material studied.

One student described the negative attitude in Volozhin towards excessive piety as follows:

Once one of the students was caught up by enthusiasm for *musar*; he began to neglect his Talmud study and to delve into *musar* and kabbalistic books, and fasted and practised self-mortification. The rabbi summoned him and warned him that Volozhin was a place purely for Torah and that there were no duties there but Talmud study, which is the basis of [true] *musar*; fasting on the days appointed for fasts; and eating properly on the days on which eating is permitted according to the law. When this student ignored three warnings and did not learn his lesson, they put him on a cart and sent him to the nearest railway station. Eventually we heard that he had reached Kovno . . . where he devoted himself to the *musar* ideal . . . [among the disciples of R. Yisra'el Salanter] until he went completely mad.[38]

This description clarifies R. Kook's comment that yeshiva students 'could never quite accept me, since from their point of view I used to behave with excessive piety and devotion'.[39]

Just as studying at the yeshiva was not intended to deepen students' spirituality, in Volozhin as elsewhere it was also not intended to provide practical training in rabbinics. Over the years, students obviously acquired tools that

---

[34] B. H. Epstein, *Mekor barukh*, iii. 1786.   [35] Z. Epstein, *Writings* (Heb.), 123.
[36] Balosher, 'Bialik at Volozhin' (Heb.), 130.
[37] M. A. Eisenstadt, 'The Volozhin Yeshiva' (Heb.), 163.
[38] Balosher, 'Bialik at Volozhin' (Heb.), 25–6.
[39] Tsoref, *Life of Rabbi Kook* (Heb.), 30–1. R. Kook's room-mate from his time in Volozhin recalled that he would light sabbath candles in his room. His fellow students saw this as exaggerated piety, to the extent that once one of them even extinguished the candles (see Neriyah, *On Rav Kook* (Heb.), 64). For a more recent and very valuable study of Kook's early years, see Y. Mirsky 'Intellectual and Spiritual Biography'.

enabled them to study halakhah and prepare themselves for rabbinical ordination, and also acquired a scholarly style, but there was no requirement to study at a yeshiva in order to be ordained as a rabbi. As in the past, any man could go to a rabbi with established credentials and ask to be examined, and if successful he would receive his document of ordination.

Outsiders tended to misunderstand the role of the yeshiva and the nature of the yeshiva way of life, as mentioned above. The Russian authorities, for example, saw the yeshiva as an institution for training rabbis. This is evident from the Russian law on Jewish education published on 13 November 1844. It describes yeshivas as 'large educational institutions for young men who have studied in a *talmud torah*, a secondary *ḥeder*, or with private teachers, who wish to study talmudic science and the sources of the laws and faith in a thorough-going manner, or who wish to prepare to become rabbis',[40] and makes no mention of Talmud study for its own sake. Many Jews similarly regarded yeshivas in general (and Volozhin in particular) as institutions for training rabbis. Precisely because of their belief in the importance of the institution as a training-ground for rabbis, they felt it necessary to intervene in its internal affairs. Among the maskilim of the end of the nineteenth century, 'the desire to reform the yeshiva and transform it into a seminary' was widespread.[41] Alexander Zederbaum, the editor of the maskilic journal *Hamelits*, could thus write:

So let us aid those who are trying to obtain the government's agreement concerning the Volozhin yeshiva, for it will aid us to replace the crown of the rabbinate to its former glory . . . the rabbis must be trained to act in accordance with the spirit of the children of the new generation . . . and thus it is the duty of those who lead the yeshiva to make every effort to train such rabbis.[42]

This attitude reflected a complete misunderstanding of the goal of the yeshiva as understood by its leaders and students. The idea that Torah study had no integral worth and was only valuable if it led to some definable achievement spread among the wider public, and not only among maskilim, exposing the yeshiva to pressures from several different directions. When the young Me'ir Pisiuk expressed his desire to study at Volozhin,[43] his employer asked him, 'Why would you want to join those idlers at Volozhin?' Such a question reflected a belief that professional advancement was of greater value than study for its own sake. The yeshivas could not ignore such attitudes because they relied on the financial support of the general public; in the long term, the training of rabbis thus became one of the cornerstones on which the

---

[40] The law was published in Russian and Yiddish under the name 'Temporary Regulation' (Vilna, 1844).   [41] Berdyczewski [Bar Bei Rav], 'The World of Emanation' (Heb.), 65.

[42] Zederbaum, 'The Heavenly Yeshiva' (Heb.), 746.

[43] Pisiuk, *Pages of Memories* (Yid.), 99–101.

yeshivas based their appeal for funds. This can be seen in the discussion of the foundation of the Kovno *kolel* (Chapter 11).

Many yeshiva graduates *were* rabbis. This lent support to the belief that the yeshiva's function was to train rabbis, as did the fact that the *rosh yeshivah* himself ordained rabbis. The more famous the rabbi who granted ordination, the more valuable the ordination certificate; it was only natural that ordination by the *rosh yeshivah* would be particularly prestigious. Moreover, R. Berlin was known to be very careful about granting ordination; this made his ordination even more valuable, and also enhanced the importance of Volozhin as an institution in which to receive ordination. The following passage, written by a student at Volozhin in the 1880s, reflects this well:

There were some young married yeshiva students who rushed off to R. Naftali Tsevi [Berlin] from other places or yeshivas in order to be ordained by him—and this gave them the title of 'religious rabbi' [in contrast to 'government rabbi']. In truth, every rabbi is authorized to ordain others. But each of them wanted his ordination certificate to bear the signature of a famous authority. The best candidates [for ordination] were prepared to be examined by a more scrupulous examiner. Those who were interested knew in advance that R. Yitshak Elhanan [Spektor] of Kovno was more lenient in his examinations . . . an ordination endorsed by the name of R. Naftali Tsevi was quite different. The candidates stayed in Volozhin for week after week just in order to get a letter of ordination that he had signed. R. Naftali Tsevi used to test the candidates again and again on their knowledge in all branches of talmudic literature, and the ordinations he issued under his signature were very highly respected by Jewish communities.[44]

The general feeling in Volozhin was that unmarried students should be studying for the sake of study itself and not for purposes of ordination; those with a more pragmatic goal in mind usually kept quiet about it. For married students it was different: since they had to worry about making a living, studying for the purpose of ordination was seen as a legitimate objective.[45]

R. Berlin's attitude to training for the rabbinate was somewhat ambiguous. On one hand, he regarded preparation for the rabbinate as something that interfered with studying Torah for its own sake: 'Once R. Moshe [Lindinski] asked R. Berlin, his teacher, to ordain him so he could serve as a rabbi and he answered him: "You do not need it as these [other students] do." He simply did not want R. Moshe to serve as a rabbi, since this would distract him from his unusually long hours of study. He wanted R. Moshe to be *rosh yeshivah*,

[44] M. A. Eisenstadt, 'The Volozhin Yeshiva' (Heb.), 170.

[45] Eisenstadt notes that in 1886 'there were several dozen married *perushim* who came here in order to complete their knowledge and receive ordination from the *rosh yeshivah* . . . the *perushim* used to devote their time and attention primarily to the *posekim* [i.e. halakhic literature] and used to look forward eagerly to their future careers. Several of them already had a rabbinic post awaiting them, either by inheritance or tradition [i.e. thanks to family links]' (ibid. 164).

and his wish was fulfilled.'[46] On the other hand, according to a description by R. Berlin's son from the final years of the Volozhin yeshiva, 'it was common practice for every student, before he left Volozhin, to go to my father of blessed memory to receive ordination'.[47] R. Berlin was thus not opposed to granting ordination, and even encouraged married students to come to the yeshiva for the sole purpose of being ordained; but the yeshiva itself did not train rabbis.[48]

The method of study at Volozhin did not change over the years: what was done at the yeshiva in R. Berlin's time did not differ from what had been customary in the time of his predecessors. The yeshiva remained what it always had been, a place of study. What changed was people's expectations of a yeshiva education, both among the general public and among the yeshiva students themselves. In the latter years many students were ordained as rabbis at the end of their studies, following a thorough oral examination by R. Berlin. That was something quite new. Even if R. Meir Berlin's statement that 'it was common practice' is something of an exaggeration, it is clear that students' expectations had changed. Whereas in the early years yeshiva graduates had expected to marry girls from rich families and either go into the family business or start up on their own with the help of a generous dowry, by the 1870s the economic future was becoming less secure and a rabbinical position became one of the few remaining options.[49] Because young men had to worry more about their future, they were more concerned to equip themselves with a certificate of rabbinical ordination as formal confirmation of their knowledge. This necessarily changed the prevailing atmosphere of the yeshiva.

[46] Yashar, *The Hafets Hayim* (Heb.), ii. 664–6. It should be noted that the split between the community rabbinate and the *rashei yeshivah* is portrayed as obvious and even desirable.

[47] M. Berlin [Bar-Ilan], *From Volozhin to Jerusalem* (Heb.), i. 154.

[48] Zederbaum, 'The Heavenly Yeshiva' (Heb.), 746.

[49] Stampfer, 'The Social Significance of Very Early Marriage'; and see Ch. 11, §2, below, on changes in the status of Torah students, especially the discussion of the Brodsky and Kovno *kolelim*.

FOUR

The Organization and Operation of the Yeshiva

THE WAY IN WHICH the yeshiva was administered largely reflected the personality and values of its leaders. There was no supervisory body, and the staff had wide leeway in determining goals and procedure, though there were often practical limitations on what could be done. In fact, it was the gap between reality and aspiration that determined much of what went on in the yeshiva.

1. Supervision and the Assessment of Progress

Supervision and the assessment of progress are common elements of educational programmes. In most Western educational institutions the teacher is also the assessor. There are formal ways of evaluating achievement such as tests or papers, and these are often the cause of tension between students and teachers. The yeshiva framework was very different: the *rashei yeshivah*'s principal activity was giving *shiurim*, not assessing achievement. Examinations occupied a very peripheral place in yeshiva life, and there were long periods when there was no formal testing at all. Tests were certainly not a central factor in establishing the relationship between students and teachers, and in fact the absence of formal grading was conducive to strengthening ties between them because it eliminated an obvious source of tension.

There were good reasons for the lack of emphasis on testing. Where teaching is based on lectures and when it is assumed that the function of teaching is to transmit knowledge or skills, examinations are necessary. Students in such conditions are basically passive participants in the educational process and teachers find it difficult to assess comprehension or success. The teacher knows best what was taught and therefore the teacher is the best person to test the students. If a student demonstrates knowledge or ability, the educational process is assumed to have succeeded—irrespective of whether the student invested any major effort to achieve this level. The system in Volozhin was quite different: the *shiur* was not a forum for transmitting information, like a university lecture, but rather a framework for discussion. Students were active participants, and this gave ample opportunity for the demonstration of ability and knowledge without the need for examination. This public participation created a general consensus as to who was more knowledgeable or perceptive and who was less so. Indeed, examinations would have been contrary to the outlook that prevailed at Volozhin, where the emphasis was on the act of studying rather than on achievements alone. Even participation in a *shiur* was not deemed necessary for advancement: at best it was a useful supplement to independent study and thought. Tests are intended to spur students on, to justify the granting of a certificate, or to confirm the attainment of knowledge—none of which was necessary at Volozhin. A grade that is achieved by cheating is no less useful than a grade acquired honestly once grades replace informal examination as the mode of assessment. Moreover, a student who did well in examinations without having spent much time studying would effectively have discouraged diligence among others. This would have been problematic because what concerned the yeshiva was assiduousness in study, which is why there were strict rules of attendance in the study hall. Significantly, in the *beit midrash* model on which R. Hayim had based the yeshiva, students had not been examined.[1] Without any pedagogic need or external pressure to institute examinations and with no obvious precedent, there was little reason to introduce examinations as a basic element of the educational programme.

Nevertheless, examinations are occasionally mentioned in memoirs. Thus, in an attempt to present the yeshiva to a critical maskilic audience in 1886, Berdyczewski wrote: 'Twice a year the rabbi and *gaon*, R. Hayim, and the rabbi and *mashgiaḥ* hold an inquiry in a special room, and they examine the students to see whether they are expert in what they have learned, and they assign grades which are known to all who pass beneath the rod of this inquiry.'[2] This description suggests that all students were regularly examined and graded. If this was standard practice, the topic should have come up often in memoirs but it does not. There are no dramatic descriptions of anxiety over examinations or excitement about the results. This suggests that examinations were only held for a short period, that they did not concern all the students, or that Berdyczewski's account was not totally accurate.[3]

Sometimes a student would be examined because of special circumstances, such as when a question arose about his knowledge and progress. The student would be asked to prepare a passage of Talmud and then discuss it.[4] This

---

[1] For a different view, see Breuer, *Tents of Torah* (Heb.), 251.

[2] Berdyczewski [Bar Bei Rav], 'History of the Ets Hayim Yeshiva' (Heb.), 237.

[3] 'But the best students . . . were not examined' (Zlatkin, 'The Volozhin Yeshiva in Bialik's Time' (Heb.), 58). Naturally, many memoirs were written by those who had demonstrated talent from a young age.

[4] 'The rabbi placed [a book] in front of him . . . showed him a *sugiyah* [talmudic passage] which

assessed his ability to study on his own rather than his competence in repeating what he had heard in a lecture.[5] Examinations of this sort were held not to threaten students with failure, but to encourage them.[6] Thus, Solomon Polachek of Maitchet, considered a child prodigy, was examined weekly.[7] In his case, regular examinations were part of the special care accorded to the young boy. They were mentioned in his biography because he knew they were exceptional. Had all students been examined in this way, it would not have been worth noting. One also finds descriptions of examinations that were intended to educate rather than to assess. For example, R. Berlin once asked a student who had a taste for *pilpul* to present an argument found in a particular book. Soon after he began, R. Berlin interrupted him to demonstrate that the author had in fact made an error and had added the word 'not' to the text of the Talmud—and this very negation had been the basis of the *pilpul*. In this case the lesson was perfectly obvious.[8] Thus in so far as examinations were held in Volozhin, they generally differed both in nature and scope from the tests we are familiar with in contemporary education.

Some memoirs mention the lack of regular and organized examinations as a negative point, though it is not clear whether they thought this at the time or only later, after they had become familiar with other educational institutions. One student from the 1860s wrote of the *rashei yeshivah*: 'None of them paid any attention to finding out whether his words had penetrated their students' ears, as at the yeshiva of Mir, and they did not examine the students. Each student studied what he wanted to.'[9] The author did not claim that the level of studies was low or that students wasted time, but he was critical of the fact that students were free to choose their own subjects of study because he felt that learning to accept discipline was important, but this idea was foreign to the ethos at Volozhin—at least in so far as the choice of study material was concerned.

he had to study for an hour or two, and then required him to summarize it . . . as was customary in these examinations' (Druyanow, *Selected Writings* (Heb.), i. 170–1).

   [5] Don-Yihia has described the way in which R. Hayim Soloveitchik used to examine students: 'He used to raise a query or a law and ask for its basis in the Gemara, and when one of the students would demonstrate his strength in reasoning, he used to say to him, "Know, my friend, that I too am no lightweight in reasoning; please produce an explicit proof from the Gemara"' (Don-Yihia, 'Memoirs' (Heb.), *Netivah*, 11/29).

   [6] As in the case of Bialik: 'The *rosh yeshivah* [R. Hayim Soloveitchik] who examined him found that he was doing well in his studies, and congratulated him' (Zlatkin, 'The Volozhin Yeshiva in Bialik's Time' (Heb.), 59).

   [7] M. Y. Goldberg et al. (eds.), *Ideinu*, 27.

   [8] A. Litai, biography of Druyanow, in Druyanow, *Selected Writings* (Heb.), i. 170–1.

   [9] Shomer, *Poems and Memoirs* (Heb.), 60. His comment is not completely accurate. The Mir yeshiva was not famous for holding examinations.

2. The *Shiur*

The tradition in Volozhin had been that the Talmud was taught page by page, from the beginning to the end. When it was completed—a process that took seven years—a new cycle began. In 1875, something new occurred. R. Isser Zalman Meltzer records that when the complex order of *Kodashim*, which deals with sacrifices, was reached, it was decided that it would be too difficult for most of the students, and another order was taught instead.[10] However, so as not to abandon tradition, 'in the afternoon, a *shiur* on *Kodashim* was held for a few elite students. R. Hayim [Soloveitchik] himself personally decided which students would attend.' The young Isser Zalman was invited, but declined. Later one of his best students 'expressed the opinion . . . that the main reason . . . was that he probably feared that his participation in this special *shiur* would arouse jealousy among his friends . . . and by going to this *shiur* he would give the impression that he was puffing himself up above them'.

Holding a *shiur* in which participation was by invitation only was one way of establishing relative status and of rewarding outstanding students. Such a practice would have been impossible in the days of R. Hayim. The rule then was that all *shiurim* were open to everyone, both those who understood and those who did not. Only in the esoteric field of kabbalah studies was it usual to limit participation to those deemed 'suitable'. The young Isser Zalman's concerns about participation in the special *shiur* are perfectly understandable. This arrangement was never repeated: when the study of *Kodashim* was completed, the yeshiva went back to the tradition of holding a single *shiur*, open to all the students. Nevertheless, the incident raised the possibility of change.

The *shiur* had indirect effects of which some students were unaware. Two will be described here: first, the way in which the *shiur* served as a way of ranking the students and second, its function as a forum for the release of tension.

As we have seen, students at Volozhin were ranked not on the basis of examinations but in informal ways. Studiousness was apparent to all, since all students studied in the same hall. Those who devoted themselves constantly to study may have felt alienated from their less studious peers, but their diligence was visible, noted, and respected. The extent of their comprehension, of course, was not so immediately apparent.

Students attending *shiurim* were encouraged to challenge the *rosh yeshivah* by asking questions. Each teacher had his own style both as regards encouraging questions and answering them, which influenced students' evaluations both of the *shiur* and of the teacher who delivered it.

The posing of questions was an integral element in the ways intellectual ability was tested. Questions could be raised in the conversations between

[10] Meltzer, *Derekh ets ḥayim*, 44.

students during study, and, above all, in the course of the *shiur*: 'The *rashei yeshivah* used to deliver their *shiurim* from twelve o'clock to two o'clock in the afternoon. They would sit at the head of a very long table, with almost all the students sitting and standing around them. The students often used to take part in their teachers' discussions of problems and *pilpulim*, in order to prove their ability.'[11] The harder it was for a teacher to answer the question, the greater the prestige of the student who posed it. The quality of the questions, the nature of the reaction (dismissal or consideration), and the answer itself enabled all those present—both teachers and students—to draw conclusions about the ability of the individuals concerned. The respect accorded active participants encouraged students to develop their critical abilities, the speed of their reaction, and their powers of expression. Students who were willing to engage in public discussion obviously had an advantage over shy students. There were other ways, though, to gain prestige. Some students visited the *rosh yeshivah* privately to pose questions. Others presented their ideas to small groups of their peers.[12] A good example is provided by a story about R. Barukh Ber Liebowitz:

When R. Barukh Dov thought up a new Torah question he longed to publicize his *ḥidushim* [new ideas]. However, in the Volozhin yeshiva it was impossible [because of the emphasis on humility] to speak of innovations in public. R. Barukh Dov thought of a plan, and invited some of the yeshiva students for *se'udah shelishit* [the 'third meal', eaten on sabbath afternoon] on the sabbath; he placed beer on the table, and at the same time he revealed his *ḥidushim* to them.[13]

Apparently Yitshak Eizik Halevi used a similar method to publicize a *pilpul* 'which amazed his friends' just before he left the yeshiva.[14] Participation through questioning was characteristic of study in Lithuanian yeshivas generally, and not just in Volozhin.[15]

Adolescent boys often want role models while simultaneously feeling the need to prove their own ability. Open debate with a *rosh yeshivah* offered a convenient framework for both.[16] Displays of aggression towards the authority figure tested a student's ability, and the *rashei yeshivah* encouraged this behaviour. At the same time, the *rashei yeshivah* almost always came up with

[11] Levin-Epstein, *Memoirs* (Heb.), 29.
[12] 'I studied constantly. R. Berlin was pleased with me and so was the *mashgiaḥ*. I often went to R. Berlin's room, and to R. Hayim's, to ask a question. I was considered one of the best students at the yeshiva' (A. Z. Horowitz, *Memoirs of Two Generations* (Yid.), 232).
[13] Edelstein, *Rabbi Barukh Dov Liebowitz* (Heb.), 20.
[14] *Der Israelit*, 23 May 1929.   [15] See the discussion of Telz, Ch. 10, §4, below.
[16] A distinction must be drawn between cause and effect. The patterns of behaviour in the *shiur* were not determined on the basis of some psychological theory, but the unintentional advantage of the *shiur* framework as it developed in Lithuanian yeshivas in general and at Volozhin in particular should not be ignored.

answers, proving their authority time and again. The *shiur* thus assumed an almost ritual character. The *rosh yeshivah* taught, the students attacked with questions, and the teacher ultimately won. Having demonstrated his ability in the *shiur*, the student had shown his independence and could still treat the same teacher with admiring respect.

Sometimes the students' adolescent emotions were displayed more crudely. Zalman Epstein, who studied at Volozhin in 1880, told the following story:

R. Alexander Lapidot, the rabbi of Raseiniai, once came to Volozhin as a guest of the *rosh yeshivah* . . . he was known to be experienced in the ways of the world, besides being a great Torah scholar, and had written articles for *Halevanon* [an Orthodox newspaper] . . . an achievement which was then very rare among great rabbis, who usually devoted all their time to Torah study. The yeshiva students were particularly eager to gain the approval of such a distinguished rabbi, and to show him the best of the Volozhin yeshiva and its students. As was customary, the *rosh yeshivah* honoured the visitor by asking him to deliver the *shiur*. They were then studying tractate *Shabat*, at the beginning of the chapter 'Bameh madlikin'. The students had known about this several days earlier, before the time came for the *shiur*, and the whole yeshiva decided to 'prepare' . . . usually, the daily *shiur* attracted only a few dozen[!] students, since according to the system of study at the yeshiva attendance was not considered compulsory. Now, however, all the students assembled—more than two hundred young men—to attend the *shiur* given by the visiting rabbi. The great study hall of the yeshiva was packed. All the students stood up in their places when the rabbi of Raseiniai appeared, an elderly and dignified figure, accompanied by the *rosh yeshivah*. The guest sat down in the *rosh yeshivah*'s place . . . and the *shiur* began: 'What may one use to light [the sabbath lights] and what may one not use . . .'—but before the rabbi had had time to complete a few lines, a student at the end of the table stood up . . . 'Rabbi, I have a question!' The rabbi stopped, listened to the question, thought for a few moments, and answered it. The answer was accepted. The rabbi went back to the text. Once again, he had to stop! At the other end of the table another student had risen to pose a question. By the time the rabbi had dealt with him, there were new questions from all directions . . . the poor rabbi had no respite for the rest of the *shiur*, which went on for more than two solid hours, and was inundated by a hail of questions and complicated problems marshalled from every possible *sugiyah* [talmudic unit] and method, from the Talmud and the halakhic literature, the earlier and later halakhic authorities, each more complicated than the previous one . . . one of the youngest students, regarded as a prodigy at the yeshiva, distinguished himself by asking a particularly difficult and intractable question. The rabbi became confused. After thinking for some time, he answered—but his answer was inadequate, and it was only out of respect that the questioner did not point out that such an answer was not worthy of the name . . . everyone was satisfied with the results of the *shiur*: 'The rabbi of Raseiniai has found out what it means to give a *shiur* at Volozhin, and he'll remember it for a long time!', the young men shouted and exulted . . . the students who had posed the most outstanding questions were surrounded on all sides, while their fellows shook their hands and cheered them for maintaining the honour of the yeshiva.[17]

The use of questions as weapons and the representation of the *shiur* as a battlefield is clear from the story. The students made sure that they taught their guest a lesson about Volozhin and its standards. The rabbi for his part saw the delivery of a *shiur* as a mark of honour, which indeed it was. The fact that people wanted to come and listen to him was sufficient to confer honour—but he had to earn that honour. Quick answers would have earned the students' admiration, but the rabbi was unable to cope with the sort of onslaught he faced. The *rosh yeshivah*, who was present, did not interfere. To do so would have caused his guest greater damage, since it would have emphasized his weakness. As it was, the students were able to express their loyalty to their institution without any open display of personal hostility to the visiting rabbi.

The story also suggests that there was an additional function to this event. Although there is no hard evidence about the facts, it does indicate how the students regarded the situation. Zalman Epstein has this to say about the background to the 'attack' on R. Alexander Lapidot:

A rumour was circulating among the various groups of students that the 'top brass'—the *rosh yeshivah* and those close to him—had hinted to the best students, obviously unofficially, that it would be good to 'build a rampart and siege-wall' around the *shiur* given by the rabbi of Raseiniai. They said that it was a special political strategy for scoring one over Kovno. At Volozhin they knew that in Kovno (which was also considered to be a major Torah centre, distinguished by the presence of the *gaon* of the generation, R. Yitshak Elhanan [Spektor]) they regarded Volozhin with a lack of proper respect, claiming that the yeshiva had already declined from its former greatness and was not as distinguished as it once had been; and since the rabbi of Raseiniai was close to R. Yitshak Elhanan and was respected in Kovno, this was a golden opportunity for the Volozhin yeshiva to show 'them' that it was still as flourishing and strong as before.[18]

There are relatively few sources that illustrate the teaching methods of R. Yosef Dov Soloveitchik or of R. Rafa'el Shapira, but there is abundant evidence for those of R. Berlin and R. Hayim Soloveitchik. R. Berlin excelled in many areas. He was famed for his halakhic rulings and as a commentator on the Bible who searched for the *peshat* (the simple meaning of the text) and displayed enormous erudition. He composed commentaries on the Torah, on tannaitic literature, and on gaonic works, and wrote many responsa, earning himself recognition throughout the Jewish world. His *shiurim* were characterized by the same erudition. According to Y. L. Radus, one of his students, 'When he gave a *shiur*, he would penetrate deep into the heart of the law, into

---

[17] Z. Epstein, *Writings* (Heb.), 121–2.   [18] Ibid. 121.

the depth of the halakhah, a master of clarity who explained and interpreted each issue according to his method, in a wonderful explanation, until there remained no room for any objects or for problems or excuses.'[19] However, while all his students apparently recognized his erudition, there was less agreement about the appeal of his teaching.

R. Hayim Soloveitchik's strengths, on the other hand, lay less in his talents as a halakhic authority or his textual commentaries but rather in his method of analysis and his teaching. As Radus recalls: 'He jumped from place to place and raced through the page of Talmud at great speed, like someone reciting Ashrei [Psalm 145, recited three times in the daily prayers and therefore usually very quickly]. He demonstrated his strength and greatness in his *pilpul*, which he would deliver at every *shiur*. The yeshiva students saw his sharp-wittedness and genius in his *pilpul*, which astonished those who heard it.'[20]

The different approaches elicited varying responses from the students. A vivid expression of these differences comes from a student who attended the yeshiva in its final years:

Those who attended the *shiurim* of [R. Berlin] included both *perushim* [married students whose future careers were often dependent on recommendations from R. Berlin] and [unmarried] students. There were often more *perushim* than unmarried students. When [the rabbi] appeared at the yeshiva to give the *shiur*, nobody moved from their place until he had rapped on the table as a sign that it was time for the *shiur*; but when [R. Hayim Soloveitchik] had barely reached the door of the yeshiva, all the students rapped on the tables together as a sign that R. Hayimke had arrived, to demonstrate the love they felt for him.[21]

The greater display of enthusiasm for one *rosh yeshivah* than for another obviously did not contribute to the maintenance of cordial relations between the two *rashei yeshivah*.

There is no doubt that R. Hayim Soloveitchik's *shiurim* were fascinating. His way of posing problems—exposing contradictions and then resolving them—added excitement and vivid interest to his *shiurim*. One student recalls that he 'explains, resolves, and fights with all his mighty intellect against the opponents of Maimonides; he used to emerge from his *shiurim* like a victorious hero returning from the field of battle, full of happiness and joy from his

[19] Radus, *Memoirs* (Heb.), 65. A less flattering description is given in Z. Epstein, *Writings* (Heb.), 121: 'The late R. Naftali Tsevi Yehudah was not noted for his mental agility and sharp wits. The students knew this and the more conceited of them, in the brazenness of youth, loved to take advantage of this and would sometimes lead the rabbi into open confusion, suddenly springing some intractable and complex problem on him, which he would not be able to answer immediately. But on the other hand he had tremendous expertise in all the fields of Torah knowledge, and a sound and honest intelligence.' See also the important Ph.D. thesis of Gil Perl, 'Emek ha-Neziv'.

[20] Radus, *Memoirs* (Heb.), 65. On R. Hayim's method of study, see below.   [21] Ibid. 66.

victory over Maimonides' opponents'.[22] The metaphors of battle and of struggle used in this very typical description are worthy of note. The students served as an audience, rooted to their seats, as well as participants in the 'war' in their role as questioners and listeners.

3. The Importance of the New Study Method

The importance of R. Hayim Soloveitchik's *shiurim* lay not only in the enthusiasm for study that they engendered, or in the students' increased understanding of the Talmud and its commentaries in consequence. Rather, students seem to have felt that his *shiurim* opened a wholly new path to understanding the Talmud, and even to understanding larger existential questions.[23] One student describes the feeling thus:

> He used to approach every talmudic matter like a surgeon, meticulously checking the logical elements of the *sugiyah*, revealing different aspects; and on the basis of this logical analysis he used to explain and comment in front of his audience. Then he would mention a disagreement in the Gemara or between Maimonides and R. Avraham ben David of Posquières and resolve it according to both logical sides . . . I loved his *shiurim*, which were free of any taint of twisted casuistry and showmanship but full of deep insights . . . a special effort was necessary to understand the precise nature of his reasoning, but he who could comprehend it 'rejoiced over it as one who has found great spoil [Ps 119: 162]'.[24]

The word 'logic' constantly recurs in descriptions of R. Hayim Soloveitchik's *shiurim*, and this is not by chance. R. Hayim Soloveitchik did not function in a vacuum. In the last third of the nineteenth century Torah scholars accorded great importance to 'logic', at a time when there was mounting criticism of traditional society in general and of its methods of

---

[22] Don-Yihia, 'Memoirs' (Heb.), *Netivah*, 11/34.

[23] The subject of R. Hayim's method of study ('the Brisker method' as it was known, after the town where R. Hayim served as rabbi after the Volozhin yeshiva closed in 1892) is extremely complex and requires research of a completely different type from that underlying this book. I will limit myself to a description of his method as it was generally understood and will not address the problems of the definition of the method and its originality. One of the problems in discussing this subject is the fact that we cannot be sure that the written word adequately reflects the living reality of his teaching method. On this issue, see the chapters on R. Berlin and R. Hayim Soloveitchik in Zevin, *Personalities and Methods* (Heb.), 85–9. See also Solomon, *The Analytic Movement*, and *Supplement to the Book of Shiurim* (Heb.). A short but excellent introduction to R. Hayim Soloveitchik's method of study is Wachtfogel, *The Brisker Derech*. See also the stimulating and perceptive articles by Krumbein, 'From R. Hayim of Brisk . . .' (Heb.); M. Lichtenstein, 'What Hath Brisk Wrought'; and Shapiro, 'The Brisker Method Reconsidered'. A more recent and very good discussion of Soloveitchik's innovations in talmudic methodology is Saiman's 'Legal Theology'. Soloveitchik's method and that of the Netsiv are contrasted in detail in Tikochinski, 'Methods of Learning' (Heb.). See also Yosef Blau (ed.), *Lomdus*.

[24] Don-Yihia, 'Memoirs' (Heb.), *Netivah*, 11/29.

Torah study in particular.[25] For the first time since the Rabbanite–Karaite disputes, there was widespread criticism within the Jewish world of Talmud study. The critics were maskilim—men who were themselves well versed in the rabbinic texts but who thought that both the exigencies of the period and intellectual honesty required Jews to engage in an alternative form of intellectual activity—and that such a shift would lead to material success.[26] The challenge was hard to ignore. Part of the maskilic criticism was levelled against *pilpul*, which they considered artificial, divorced from reality, and irrelevant. Just as the Karaite challenge had persuaded an earlier generation of rabbis to emphasize biblical associations in their work, rabbinic literature now had to be justified in terms of the 'scientific' and 'logical' norms of 'modern' Western thought.

Pilpul was regarded as the antithesis of modern ways of thinking. The term *pilpul* is very hard to define. It is used in different ways by different people and very often one scholar's *peshat* (simple interpretation) is seen as *pilpul* by others. The concept can be roughly described as an attitude or approach that focuses on forcing texts into agreement (or disagreement) with each other rather than focusing on what was most likely the original intent of the statement though the term is not suited to a formal and explicit definition. It is only a little less difficult to define the unique character of R. Hayim Soloveitchik's method of study, known as the 'Brisker method'.[27] It is sufficient to note that his students saw his method as truly 'logical' in elucidating the plain meaning of the talmudic text, in contrast to the methods of other scholars, which they described as *pilpul*—by their definition, a superficial reading. Even more importantly, those who adopted R. Hayim Soloveitchik's 'logical' method felt that it offered a refutation of the modernist critique, and therefore constituted an important new development. The question of whether it was genuinely new will not be discussed here, but there is no doubt that his students were convinced it was.

R. Hayim Soloveitchik's students felt that they had an answer to the criticism levelled by the maskilim and were able to blame the shortcomings of the older methods for having caused talented and intelligent young men to turn their backs on Talmud study. They were convinced that fewer young men would abandon the study of Talmud and turn to the Haskalah if R. Hayim's

[25] See e.g. Berdyczewski's criticism of Rav Berlin's method of study: 'A study method that was old-fashioned and rusty . . . if in his *shiurim* our master had proposed startling words, founded on pure logic . . . we would have trooped to his *shiurim* . . . but now . . . since our master devoted most of the *shiur* to *pilpul* . . . only a few of us attended' (Berdyczewski [Bar Bei Rav], 'A Bundle of Letters' (Heb.), *Hamelits*, 28/56: 574).

[26] There was no fundamental opposition to Talmud study among the hasidim, so the only precedent was that of the Karaites, though of course their reasons were completely different from those of the maskilim.

[27] See n. 23 above for references to the relevant literature.

method were adopted more widely. They firmly believed that it contributed no less to a person's intellectual development than the study of secular subjects in the Western manner. In this way they felt confident in justifying—to themselves, perhaps, as much as to others—the advantages of studying Talmud in a traditional institution. This can be seen from Don-Yihia's description of Bialik's time at Volozhin:

Once the conversation turned to Jewish *pilpul*, and Bialik turned to mocking the twisted mental exercises [characteristic of *pilpul*]. As he was talking he opened a volume of Talmud and said [parodying *pilpul* style], 'It says on the title page that the book was printed in Zhitomir, but I think it was printed in Vilna, and if not, what does this teach us?' . . . Knowing that Bialik was destined to be a great Jewish writer, I wanted him to gain some idea of lucid talmudic logic. Once we were walking together for a few hours, and I went over one of R. Hayim's excellent *shiurim* with him. In spite of the fact that he did not usually attend . . . R. Hayim's *shiurim* and that, judging from his talents and the way in which he had been educated, he was very distant from this method of study, he enjoyed it immensely when I explained the talmudic logic to him according to R. Hayim's wonderful exposition.[28]

Bialik of course was not convinced, and did not become one of R. Hayim's supporters; he did not even attend his *shiurim* regularly. The person who was convinced by Don-Yihia's arguments was Don-Yihia himself. He was able to convince himself that Bialik's alienation from Talmud was the result of his upbringing and education, and particularly his lack of familiarity with the correct method of study. At the same time, Don-Yihia maintained the traditional view about the inherent value of Talmud study. His expressions of understanding for Bialik's attitude were certainly a rather revolutionary view.[29]

R. Hayim Soloveitchik's innovation cannot be explained as the result of external influences; in fact, there is no evidence that he was influenced by the Haskalah or Western literature. On the contrary: he did not read any foreign languages, was not interested in the new Western literature, and was an opponent of the Haskalah. In his view, his method was based on the traditional method. What is easier to explain is why it aroused such excitement. Approaches that had attracted many students in the past had become less appealing, and his method, which may have been known earlier in an undevel-

---

[28] Don-Yihia, 'Memoirs' (Heb.), *Netivah*, 11/34.

[29] Obviously it would be desirable to quote more sources to demonstrate the role played by the new method of study in coming to terms with new ways of thinking, but I have not found any. However, even this evidence lends support to the assumption that an unconscious sense of competition with 'modern, Western' approaches underlay the excitement about the 'Brisker' method. This does not detract from R. Hayim's interpretations or their importance in the development of study methods. The existence of an external stimulus diminishes neither the originality of a response nor its value for later generations, which can continue to be significant even after the stimulus has disappeared.

oped and less publicized form, now became far more attractive because it was seen as meeting the challenges of contemporary life. However, it is clear that this was not the only reason for the enthusiasm displayed for R. Hayim Soloveitchik and his method. He had great personal charm, formulated his thoughts clearly, and his *shiurim* provided tremendous intellectual pleasure.

A link between R. Hayim's *shiurim* and the response to the Haskalah is suggested by one of his opponents, R. Ya'akov David ben Ze'ev Willowski (Ridbaz, 1845–1913). In the introduction to his volume of responsa, *Beit ridbaz*, R. Willowski expressed his desire 'to tell the generations what happened in my lifetime down to today in the history of the Jewish people, in spirituality and Torah study and the crown of the rabbinate and material matters'.[30] In this context he seems to have discussed R. Hayim's method of study:

At that time[31] the study of the Torah changed completely . . . a certain rabbi invented the study of 'chemistry' . . . and many call it logic, and this has been very harmful for us, for it is a foreign spirit from outside which they have brought in to the study of the Oral Law, which is the Torah handed down to us from Moses, the mouthpiece of God, and this study method has spread among yeshiva students who barely have any grasp of the Gemara.[32]

R. Willowski was careful not to mention any names, but it would be hard to think of any study method that had spread more widely than R. Hayim Soloveitchik's. And if he was thinking of another study method, it is hard to explain why he ignored that of R. Hayim. R. Willowski's terminology is not accidental. He mentioned the term 'logic', as did Don-Yihia though he added

---

[30] Willowski, *Beit ridbaz*, 1. I would like to thank Dr Benjamin Brown for correcting this reference. He supports (*The Hazon Ish* (Heb.), 321) the identification of the 'chemist' as R. Reines, following Professor Saul Liebermann's suggestion to me in a conversation. Brown's most convincing claim is that R. Willowski was principally objecting here to the movements that called for modernization; in this context, his words would be more appropriate to R. Reines than to R. Hayim Soloveitchik. However, since many of R. Hayim's students founded yeshivas or taught in them, R. Willowski's words could apply to them too. Reines apparently had few disciples. However, I was more convinced by A. Lichtenstein: 'Those who did not openly oppose [R. Hayim] spoke of him disparagingly. They called him *der kemiker*, "the chemist". Indeed there was something of chemistry in his method: the detailed analysis of the talmudic passage into its components and fundamental principles. Mainly, however, there was attention to the same element that occupies a central place in the world of the science of chemistry: an emphasis on sorting and classification' ('This Was the Rav's Method' (Heb.), 107). Bialik said much the same. Oded Schechter has drawn my attention to a comment by Bialik in *Devarim shebe'al peh*, 233: '[R. Hayim] was, in his own way, the way of *pilpul*, a complete modernist, quite literally. R. Hayim invented the most accurate chains of reason for his students in such a plastic way that they even had an aesthetic value. There was a special beauty in his logic.'

[31] The period under discussion is not clear in the original.

[32] Willowski, *Beit ridbaz*, 4.

the term 'chemistry', obviously used in a derogatory sense. In his opinion, this method of study was foreign to the traditional Jewish approach even if it grew out of internal sources. Nevertheless, anyone unhappy at the mass abandonment of Torah study and the failure of the traditional approach to respond to the new challenges might find R. Hayim's method attractive because it looked logical. Criticism of the type voiced by R. Willowski actually led Don-Yihia to support R. Hayim's new method.

4. Staff–Student Relationships: Financial Support and Discipline

After teaching and study, ensuring students' material welfare and maintaining discipline were the most important tasks of the staff of the yeshiva. In modern educational institutions, discipline is based to a large extent on the institution's ability to award or withhold grades, certificates, or degrees. In religious contexts, discipline is often based on faith, with the individual's access to God controlled by a leader who derives his or her authority from this faith. In Volozhin the authority of the *rashei yeshivah* was grounded in the respect and admiration accorded them. This was reinforced by the economic power at their disposal, since the students were dependent on them for financial support. However, here as in other areas, there were differences between R. Berlin and R. Hayim Soloveitchik. The former, who was of course much older, maintained a degree of distance from his students,[33] while the latter was closer to them.

The surviving sources of evidence about financial support come from the 1870s and 1880s, and there is no way of telling whether there had been any change since the yeshiva's earliest days. There do not seem to have been any remarkable innovations, but there is no proof of this.

The overwhelming majority of students received a weekly allowance from the yeshiva—or more accurately, from the *rosh yeshivah*, as described above.[34]

---

[33] See the letter of R. Berlin to R. M. G. Joffe of Rozhinoy from 1856, published in *Moriyah*, 18/5–6 (Nisan 1992), 56. Jaffe had apparently written to thank R. Berlin for keeping an eye on his son. R. Berlin responded that the boy was studying well because of his own merits and added: 'Closeness in matters that are not related to study hurts the desired goal, and I also restrain myself even from relatives studying in the holy yeshiva except for a few occasions.' He went on to note that each student has to study in their own way.

[34] Ch. 1, §4. On the many consequences of this arrangement, see below. There was no dormitory accommodation at Volozhin. Only after the First World War did yeshivas have dormitories (see Ch. 1 n. 77 above and Stampfer, 'Dormitory and Yeshiva in Eastern Europe'). Maintaining a dormitory involves not only a substantial investment but also a system for cleaning and tidying, and for long-term planning in order to ensure that there are sufficient places. The system of renting rooms worked very well; as long as there was no need to protect students from the influence of the surrounding society there was no need for dormitories.

There was no standard allocation; the *menahel* or the *shamash* reported on the behaviour of every student, and the *rosh yeshivah* allocated money accordingly.[35] In the mid-1870s a rouble per week was considered a large allowance, and some students only received half a rouble.[36] Around 1890 students received between 60 copecks and a rouble and a quarter per week,[37] so there had been little change. They used this money to rent rooms and arrange for meals from the family that rented out the room. The larger the allowance received, the better the room a student could rent and the more (and better) the food that a student could afford. At that time R. Berlin used to go over the list of allocations once a fortnight, on Saturday evening, with the aid of R. Hayim Soloveitchik, the *mashgiah*, the *menahel*, and the *shamash*.[38] According to R. Berlin's son, students were discussed according to the name of their landlord rather than in alphabetical order or the order in which they had arrived at the yeshiva, and the money was given directly to the landlords.[39] The system reduced the need for written records since payments did not have to be made out to each student and eliminated concerns that allocations might not reach the intended destination.

According to Moshe Reines, it was not only the students' devotion to study and behaviour that determined the amount of their allowances but also the student's marital status, his behaviour, and, more unexpectedly, his town of origin:

This was the way in which money was allocated to the students: the students used to receive 2 to 3 roubles per month, and the married students would receive from 4 to 9 roubles, but not all the students were equal, nor was there one standard for them all in this poor allocation, but their origin was what determined it. According to the decree of the *rosh yeshivah*, the best share went to those whose native towns gave most money to the yeshiva, though even these received 75 copecks a week at most from the allowance money that was distributed twice a month. Those who were 'born under an unlucky star' in a small town or in one whose inhabitants closed their hands and hardened their hearts in the matter of charity—these unfortunates received even less. And this was only if there was only one student from that town, but if others arrived, their allowance was reduced to 60 copecks or less![40]

Under this system, a donor to the Volozhin yeshiva was actually giving charity to his fellow townsmen, since students from his town would thereby receive a higher allowance. There are no further details of this practice or its back-

---

35 Berdyczewski [Bar Bei Rav], 'A Bundle of Letters' (Heb.), *Hamelits*, 28/53: 544.
36 A. Z. Horowitz, *Memoirs of Two Generations* (Yid.), 232.
37 M. Berlin [Bar-Ilan], *From Volozhin to Jerusalem* (Heb.), i. 91.
38 Ibid. In the yeshiva's later years R. Berlin's wife played an important part in allocating money, which made her very unpopular among the students; see below.
39 Berdyczewski [Bar Bei Rav], 'A Bundle of Letters' (Heb.), *Hamelits*, 28/53: 544.
40 M. Reines, 'Dwelling-Places of Torah (Heb.)', 15–16.

ground, and it is not mentioned before R. Berlin's time. It is possible that R. Berlin introduced it, not only from a desire to 'reward' generous towns but also on the assumption that this would help the yeshiva's fundraising efforts.[41] In order to be awarded a larger allowance, students from 'poor' towns used to try to obtain a letter of recommendation from the rabbi of a 'generous' town.[42] The system was open to unexpected distortions: 'And there were some who came here for the weekly allowance that was paid here, and not for study.'[43]

There was little need to enforce discipline. Students attended the yeshiva of their own free will, and were free to leave whenever they wished. Study, particularly towards the end of the nineteenth century, did not necessarily lead to economic success, so leaving the yeshiva did not necessarily damage a young man's economic prospects. In order to be accepted into the yeshiva, the candidate had to have reached a fairly advanced level, so that every student there was already experienced in Talmud study; if study did not attract him, he would never have reached the level required for acceptance. Of course, those who studied in yeshivas attracted considerable acclaim, but respect could be obtained in other ways. The overwhelming majority of students had thus come to the yeshiva of their own free will. Factors such as family pressure and social influence also played a part, as did the approval of important rabbis, and all these influences together encouraged young students.

Even so, there were occasional problems with discipline. Students were meant to devote every possible moment to study. As already discussed, there were hardly any students who questioned the importance of study in general, and Talmud study in particular, though there were some who wanted to spend part of their time on other matters. In some of these cases the staff felt they had to intervene and mete out punishment. The different types of punishment at the yeshiva demonstrate both the authority wielded by the staff and the relative gravity with which they viewed the various 'offences' committed.

The lightest punishment was to bar the culprit from receiving the honour of reading from the Torah during services. To deprive a student of this was to humiliate him publicly, although since the number of students who would receive such an honour in any given week was relatively small, people would not necessarily be aware that the punishment had been incurred. If a student was afraid of social sanctions, the threat of such a punishment could be effective; but if he was confident in what he had done and his friends supported him, the punishment lost its force. Berdyczewski records that this punishment was incurred by a certain student who, as a way of insulting R. Berlin (or perhaps his wife), had been dismissive of some new interpretations suggested

---

[41] This system was also practised at the Telz yeshiva; see Ch. 10, §4, below.

[42] M. A. Eisenstadt, 'The Volozhin Yeshiva' (Heb.), 166.

[43] Levin-Epstein, *Memoirs* (Heb.), 342.

by R. Berlin's father-in-law (from his second marriage) while visiting the yeshiva:

This student brought proof of a logical contradiction in every single idea that the visiting rabbi presented, and now this student has not been called up to the Torah for three years . . . and you should know that this matter—banning a student from receiving an *aliyah*—was a regular form of punishment among us, and any student who was lax about attendance at the *shiur* and only came now and then would lose many *aliyot*.[44]

There were more severe punishments for more serious infractions. Reducing a student's allowance hurt his pocket, and led to a decline in the standard of his housing and food. This punishment was meted out to students who 'behaved light-headedly in relation to some custom or mitzvah'.[45] According to Berdyczewski: 'He who misses the time for prayer will lose half his allowance; he who scatters around heretical books will not be paid anything . . . he who does not attend the *shiur* or the lesson on the Pentateuch will receive forty stripes (i.e. 40 copecks will be deducted from his allowance).'[46] Students were fined 15 copecks for coming late to prayers;[47] this was the lowest fine we find mentioned. The effectiveness of this punishment was limited to those students who needed the yeshiva's financial support. There is no mention of fines being demanded of students who did not receive such support, and it seems doubtful whether it would have been possible to do so.

A more severe punishment was a slap from R. Berlin. 'All those who were slapped by the rabbi were awarded the title of *der gepatshter* ['the slapped one'], and this was a kind of badge of shame to him who had earned it, shaming him and sometimes even ruining his prospects of a good marriage.'[48] This seems to have been a rare punishment—'Only very rarely did such a disgraceful thing happen as the rabbi striking a student'[49]—but it did happen a few times in the course of the fifty years discussed here.

Sometimes a student was slapped for cutting off his *pe'ot* (sidelocks). Not every student at the yeshiva had long *pe'ot*, and cutting them to a certain length was not forbidden by halakhah. However, those students who arrived at the yeshiva with *pe'ot* came from families to whom the custom was important, so cutting them off would have brought the yeshiva into disrepute. In 1877 a student who cut off his *pe'ot* received a resounding slap from R. Berlin, who exclaimed, 'People will say that there is no fear of God at Volozhin!'[50] In

---

[44] Berdyczewski [Bar Bei Rav], 'A Bundle of Letters' (Heb.), *Hamelits*, 28/56: 574.

[45] M. A. Eisenstadt, 'Revolution in the Yeshiva' (Heb.).

[46] Berdyczewski [Bar Bei Rav], 'A Bundle of Letters' (Heb.), *Hamelits*, 28/53: 544 (parentheses in the original).

[47] Mashvitski, 'In the Dwelling-Places of Torah' (Heb.), *Baderekh*, 3/13(80), 3/38(105).

[48] M. A. Eisenstadt, 'Revolution in the Yeshiva' (Heb.).   [49] Ibid.

[50] Levin-Epstein, *Memoirs* (Heb.), 59. Wiener, *A Beard Is the Glory of the Face* (Heb.), 398,

a similar incident in 1886 R. Berlin similarly burst out: 'See how much influence the yeshiva of Volozhin has had on you, you've already managed to destroy your *pe'ot!*'[51] Everything that happened in the yeshiva was taken as a sign of the atmosphere there, and it was essential to take swift action against any threat to the yeshiva's image.[52]

One student records that he was afraid of being similarly punished after a donor from his native town stopped contributing to the yeshiva on learning that he used to read a Russian newspaper.[53] He was convinced that if R. Berlin found out, he would be slapped twice and would have his allowance cut. Luckily for him, the emissary who had brought the news went to the *mashgiah* first, who made do with reprimanding him since he knew that he was a good student.[54]

On at least one occasion the slapping of a student who had cut off his *pe'ot* led the other students to a strike in protest.[55] They did not regard the student's action as a serious infringement of halakhah and considered the punishment as an affront to their collective dignity. However, there is no evidence of any such reaction to a punishment when its reason was obvious and it did not seem too severe. Thus, for example, a student was slapped after coming into the yeshiva on Yom Kippur 'with his *pe'ot* neatly combed'—though the halakhic ruling on combing hair on the holy day is problematic.[56] Another received a slap after being caught reading Smolenskin's *Hato'eh bedarkhei hahayim*—a maskilic work—on Yom Kippur.[57] No protest by other students is mentioned in either of these cases.

The most extreme punishment was expulsion. M. Eisenstadt gives a detailed account of an expulsion and the circumstances that led up to it:

Expulsions from the yeshiva were usually carried out in one of three ways: the gentlest was the suggestion, concealed from the public eye, to 'leave' the yeshiva. This treatment was generally reserved for students who wasted their time . . . once they

quotes a letter sent to him by a former student of R. Isser Zalman Meltzer: '[Students] also cut their beards at Volozhin, but there they only trimmed them.' (I found this book from a reference in Y. Meltzer, *Derekh ets hayim.*) R. Wiener also quotes from R. Berlin's commentary *Ha'amek davar* (Lev. 19: 27), where he justifies the prohibition on cutting *pe'ot.*

[51] Levin-Epstein, *Memoirs* (Heb.), 31.

[52] M. A. Eisenstadt, 'Revolution in the Yeshiva' (Heb.). For a similar statement, see Mashvitski, 'In the Dwelling-Places of Torah' (Heb.), *Baderekh*, 3/23(90).

[53] B. Goldberg, *Memories of the Past* (Heb.), 14.

[54] Another student, who became a fierce critic of Volozhin, claimed that R. Berlin hit students who complained that he had misused yeshiva funds (see Shirotkin, 'The Dew to which All Turn' (Heb.), *Hashahar*, 8/4: 164. In this case, yeshiva funds had been used to provide a dowry for one of R. Berlin's relations.

[55] M. A. Eisenstadt, 'Revolution in the Yeshiva' (Heb.), 1–2.

[56] Shmukler [Shapira], *Rabbi Moshe Shemuel* (Heb.), 60.

[57] B. Goldberg, *Memories of the Past* (Heb.), 14.

had reached their homes, the exiles would reveal that they had been thrown out, and would enlarge on the fact that they had not wanted to go . . . how different was the fate of those who had committed some unforgivable sin, such as playing at cards! These unfortunates were publicly expelled. In these cases, letters were sent to their parents or to the local rabbi with explanations of the reasons for this terrible punishment. It was obvious that these pariahs would not be able to hide the truth from local society, and they usually ended up by going into trade, becoming artisans, finding a job, or devoting themselves to secular studies. But if the outcast was slapped as well—and such cases, though rare, did occur from time to time—he left with the mark of Cain upon him for ever. He would escape from Volozhin as though chased by a demon and would not even dare to go back to his parents. The names of these unfortunates were engraved for years in the memories of their fellow-students.[58]

Expulsion was an extreme sanction that was implemented in order to warn others against similar behaviour, despite the possibility that it might cause the individual concerned to abandon the traditional way of life completely because of the public humiliation. Indeed, both the names of those expelled and the nature of their misdemeanours were apparently transmitted from student to student for generations.

The common element of the 'serious crimes' Eisenstadt mentions is the misuse of time. An institution based on achievement would not have taken so much notice of time-wasting, but in one that placed so much emphasis on constant study, wasting time stood in opposition to the fundamental nature of the institution and could lead other students astray. This was why a game of cards was regarded as such a sin: it was a pastime that offered neither meaningful content nor sharpened the intellect, and moreover was addictive.

Obviously there were other misdemeanours, such as courting local girls,[59] but such cases were very rare. The watchful eyes of the other students were no less efficient than those of the *rashei yeshivah*. There was little room at the yeshiva for open revolt against traditional values, since anyone who wanted to rebel could leave the institution. Wasting time was thus the most common misdemeanour.

It was not always easy to expel a student. If a student was willing to take the risk of gaining a bad reputation and was not dependent on the allowance, it was difficult to throw him out. As a last resort, the townsfolk of Volozhin might be called in to help. R. Berlin was one of the largest employers in the town, and could threaten a landlady that she would not be allowed to rent rooms to students in future if she continued to provide housing and food for

[58] M. A. Eisenstadt, 'The Volozhin Yeshiva' (Heb.), 165.

[59] Once the father of a student who was courting a local girl turned up and accused R. Berlin of running an impure institution and being responsible for his son's spiritual deterioration (see Shirotkin, 'The Dew to which All Turn' (Heb.), *Hashahar*, 8/4: 168; although this is a hostile source, it seems more likely that the story was distorted rather than entirely made up).

a student facing expulsion. Sometimes a threat of this sort was enough to force the student to leave the town.[60] In the absence of any means of physical compulsion, expulsion required the support of the general public.

In 1886 a student left the yeshiva in order to join a cantor's choir, and then wanted to return. R. Berlin rejected his request, but several students protested and supported the student from their own pockets. In their view, the yeshiva was meant to be a place of study; if a talented student who had left wished to return, there was no reason not to accept him. There was no ideological opposition to R. Berlin's system of values here but simply disagreement over a particular case, in which the students claimed that they were acting in accordance with R. Berlin's own principles. The students' support for their rejected colleague was clearly and openly damaging to the *rosh yeshivah*'s authority, and he ended the affair by paying the young man off. The latter finally agreed not to return to the yeshiva, 'but he made a condition with him, that he [R. Berlin] would give him money for his travel expenses and also a letter of recommendation, and he [R. Berlin] agreed to this request. The next day, the student went to the office of the *rosh yeshivah* and after some negotiation obtained 25 roubles from him, and the letter, and then left Volozhin.'[61] This was not the only time that the yeshiva paid a student to leave. Another student was expelled for playing cards, 'and he stayed in Volozhin until the *rosh yeshivah* made a compromise with him, giving him a fair sum of money to leave the town, but this was the only incident of its kind and was never repeated'.[62]

The sanctions employed against the students affected their dignity and their pockets. However, there were wealthy and independent students at the yeshiva, as well as the possibility of organizing alternative financial support from that supplied by the *rosh yeshivah*, and these factors limited the effectiveness of the sanctions. The yeshiva administration was thus forced to take account of the attitude of the student body before meting out punishments.

[60] B. Goldberg, *Memories of the Past* (Heb.), 20.
[61] Radus, *Memoirs* (Heb.), 67–9; see Ch. 5, §6, below.
[62] Goldberg was wrong in this claim; see B. Goldberg, *Memories of the Past* (Heb.), 20.

FIVE

The Student Body

1. The Decision to Study at Volozhin

A variety of reasons and considerations led young men to travel to Volozhin to study at the yeshiva. Not all were equally conscious of the factors that had influenced their decision, but even so one may try to classify the reasons cited in memoirs and to identify trends. The most common reason given is simply the desire to study Torah and to make progress as a scholar. This is obvious. The practical advantages of study in Volozhin were rarely mentioned. Although these descriptions were usually written many years after leaving home, it seems that these were accurate descriptions of what they felt at the time they actually made their decisions. In fact, very little was written about the decision to study, since in some circles it was self-evident that, at the appropriate age, a bright young man would leave home to study Torah. However, there were occasionally other reasons. As might be expected, 'among the students were the sons of wealthy men, who only came to Volozhin to acquire a scholarly reputation',[1] while some students came in order to escape from an arranged marriage that had failed.[2] Of course, even the students who came simply out of a desire for quality study were aware that distinction in Torah scholarship opened the way to a good match and brought rewards. A young man who studied at Volozhin in the 1860s gives a very cynical description of this point:

Most of the young men who came to Volozhin to draw up the pure waters from the well of its yeshiva did not study there for the sake of Heaven, but hoped to gain the reputation of being scholars, so that they might find a beautiful wife with a beautiful dowry and beautiful maintenance at a rich father-in-law's table. How true were the words of one of these clowns, who once remarked at a student gathering: 'We, the sons of the Volozhin yeshiva, will be able to take pride in saying that we learn Torah for her own sake, in other words, for the sake of the bride we imagine in our hearts . . . it was also my family's aim, in sending me to the yeshivas of Mir and Volozhin, to acquire "the reputation of a scholarly young man" for me, so that many people would leap [at the chance of having me as a son-in-law]'.[3]

---

[1] Shomer, *Poems and Memoirs* (Heb.), 66.   [2] Ibid. 61.   [3] Ibid. 62.

It has been said of the situation at the end of the nineteenth century that 'the diploma of a Volozhin graduate helped a young man to get on in life, whether in the rabbinate, in marrying, or in being honoured throughout his life'.[4] However, the fact that study in Volozhin had its rewards does not necessarily mean that this was the main incentive for study. Indeed, even when the practical benefits diminished, as the rich Jews of eastern Europe sought to become part of modern society, students continued to flock to Volozhin.

The benefits to be gained from study in Volozhin were certainly sufficient for students to fear expulsion or even lesser punishments that could damage their reputation and their chances of a good match.[5] In fact, good marriages were sometimes arranged within the walls of the yeshiva: wealthy parents of eligible daughters would consult the *rosh yeshivah* about a suitable match. R. Shimon Shkop (1860–1940), who later became *rosh yeshivah* at Telz, was married off in this way: when R. Moshe Mordekhai Idelvitz came to Volozhin and asked R. Berlin to pick out a good young man for his daughter, R. Shimon was recommended, and the marriage was duly arranged.[6]

Some students came to the yeshiva with the aim of becoming rabbis. The *perushim*, the married students who had left their wives in order to come to Volozhin, study, and obtain ordination from R. Berlin, obviously did this to increase their chances of finding a position.[7] Parents could also encourage sons to study in Volozhin for the same reason. Levin-Epstein wrote: 'My father wanted, and perhaps even hoped, that I would be a rabbi.'[8] Some felt that this goal was shared by many students—'every young man who aspired to reach the lofty position of rabbi came to Volozhin'[9]—though few students spoke openly of their hopes of becoming rabbis, as noted above (Chapter 3, §4). It is safe to say that while the decision may not have been motivated by practical concerns, that the benefits of study in Volozhin were generally recognized. Consequently, the decline in the economic prospects for yeshiva graduates at the end of the late nineteenth century should have led students to rethink their objectives and, as we shall see, this apparently was the case.[10]

2. The Admission Procedure

Volozhin never had a totally rigid and formal admission procedure. There was no need to register in advance, and there was no fixed date on which studies

[4] Zaltzman, *From the Past* (Heb.), 111.
[5] M. A. Eisenstadt, 'Revolution in the Yeshiva' (Heb.).
[6] Sorski, *Rabbi Shimon Shkop* (Heb.), 90. The truth of the story is less important than the fact of its existence as a demonstration of student aspirations.
[7] M. A. Eisenstadt, 'The Volozhin Yeshiva' (Heb.), 164.
[8] Levin-Epstein, *Memoirs* (Heb.), 26.
[9] Zlatkin, 'The Netsah Yisra'el Secret Society and H. N. Bialik' (Heb.), 181.
[10] See Part II.

began—because there was never a date when they stopped. In practice, many students arrived immediately after the High Holidays, but this was not a requirement. Prospective students would usually bring a letter of recommendation from a rabbi or prominent figure in their home town. Some former students mention having to demonstrate their ability in Talmud study before being accepted, or before being allocated a particular level of allowance, but not all. The custom may have varied over time, or else was deemed so unimportant that not everyone bothered to mention it. In any event, few sources mention apprehension before an entrance test, and few applicants seem to have been rejected. It seems that examinations were more likely to be employed when a candidate did not have a letter of recommendation. A student of the 1860s wrote: 'From Minsk I travelled to Volozhin, and I handed the letter from the rabbi of Nesvizh to the *rosh yeshivah*, R. Hirsh Leib, and he instantly took me into the yeshiva, and allocated me ten gulden a month from the yeshiva treasury.'[11] There is no mention of a test here, though the letter of recommendation seems to have been important. The allowance seems high, however, and the author may not have recalled this detail accurately. Another example, from the 1880s, records: 'Before I entered the yeshiva there was a superficial examination, as was customary in those days. I came to the *rosh yeshivah* armed with my letter of recommendation. The rabbi's opinion of me seems to have been very positive, since after reading the letter, the *rosh yeshivah* contented himself with asking me a few questions.'[12]

There seem to have been more rejections during the yeshiva's last days, but even then there were ways of getting around the official procedure by taking advantage of the tensions between the *rashei yeshivah*:

When I arrived in Volozhin I visited R. Berlin. He told me that . . . because of the yeshiva's dire financial straits . . . he would have to turn down my request. I was very young. When I heard this answer my heart sank and I prepared to return home . . . some of the yeshiva students approached me and told me, 'Don't worry, go to R. Hayim [Soloveitchik], and if he likes you, you'll be accepted.' And indeed, after I visited R. Hayim and spoke to him of Torah matters, he told me that I could stay at Volozhin.[13]

Sometimes in those cases where candidates were examined, it was the *mashgiah* who did the testing, as in this case from 1886:

I went to see the *rosh yeshivah*, who lived opposite the yeshiva. I went into his office and the secretary took me to the room where he sat and studied. I waited until he

---

[11] Shomer, *Poems and Memoirs* (Heb.), 60.

[12] M. A. Eisenstadt, 'The Volozhin Yeshiva' (Heb.), 162. Rabbi Boruch Oberlander pointed out to me that the warmth of the letter and the character and fame of the rabbi who signed it would have influenced the decision as to whether to examine a student and also the nature of the examination.   [13] Don-Yihia, 'Memoirs' (Heb.), *Netivah*, 11/29.

turned to me, and showed him my papers and the letters from rabbis. He read them quickly and told me that I would see the *mashgiaḥ*. The *mashgiaḥ* tested me and gave me a note for the supervisor of books, so that he would give me a volume of Talmud.[14]

These descriptions suggest that letters of recommendation were generally the most important element in the admission of candidates.

Underlying all of this was a natural process of self-selection that obviated some of the need for a formal admission procedure. A youth who was not sufficiently able would not want to risk the shame of failure, nor indeed the cost of travel to Volozhin. The young men who went there did so with the confidence that they were able to undertake independent study at an advanced level. Self-selection is less effective with regard to behaviour. Therefore, letters of recommendation were particularly useful. Why then the interest in letters of recommendation? The yeshiva was principally a place of independent study, and therefore the students' behaviour, and in particular their assiduousness, was critical. Simply testing knowledge would have implied that knowledge was the key value, rather than the investment of effort in Torah study. Moreover, such an examination would also say little about whether a student was responsible enough to become a yeshiva student. A letter of recommendation was a reliable source of information because it not only came from someone who had knowledge of the student, but because the writer of such a letter would know that if his assessment turned out to be inaccurate it would reflect poorly on him. Moreover, candidates were aware of this and this knowledge encouraged good behaviour.

The system was far from perfect, however. Sometimes, letters of recommendation turned out to be a means of pressuring the *rosh yeshivah* rather than tools for assisting him. R. Berlin's sensitivity on this point stands out in this official announcement from the yeshiva, signed by R. Dynkin, the yeshiva's *mashgiaḥ*, which appeared in the newspaper *Hamelits* on 7 May 1886:

Volozhin, 24 Nisan 5646 [29 April 1886]: At the end of the last year, at the order of the *gaon* and *rosh yeshivah*, we announced in this newspaper, *Hamelits*, and also in *Hatsefirah*, that the yeshiva will not accept young students of the Torah without a travel permit according to the law of the land, nor those who cannot study a page of Talmud with Rashi and Tosafot independently. Many have transgressed this order and been punished by being sent home, and many of them have caused the *gaon* and *rosh yeshivah*, long may he live, agony and mental grief, since it is difficult for him to reject the letters from rabbis or important people pleading on the students' behalf. Therefore we request these rabbis and important people, wherever they dwell, not to rush to give such letters to young people who long to come to the yeshiva here before examining them well, to see whether they can study a page of Talmud with

---

[14] Radus, *Memoirs* (Heb.), 65.

Tosafot without any help, for if they cannot do this they cannot hope to succeed in their endeavours.[15]

R. Berlin's extensive involvement in raising funds for the yeshiva and his ties with big donors exposed him to pressures as regards the admission of students. Were it not for the announcement in *Hamelits* mentioning the abuse of personal ties to gain acceptance to the yeshiva, the following description, apparently by a former student, would seem quite unbelievable:

The rich men who crouch over their moneybags extended their rule over the Volozhin yeshiva and broadcast their opinions far and wide; they gave letters of praise to ignorant young men as stupid as milk, and in spite of his feelings the rabbi was forced to accept them in the yeshiva, disregarding his anger and irritation. For who could offend the rich men without paying for it? When the rabbi saw that more and more students arrived every day, and that the yeshiva had become a refuge for every Tom, Dick, and Harry, and for every young man empty of knowledge and wisdom, and that there was not enough money to furnish all their needs, he stopped giving every student enough to meet his needs, and he only supported some of them, this one with much money and this with a little, and made no distinction between those who understood Torah and those as stupid as milk; and only those who had a letter from an important rich man, even if they did not understand the basic phrase *Mai kamri rabanan* ['What did our teachers say?'], were deemed fit to receive the money; and if someone brought a letter from an unimportant man, even if he was a genius, he would receive less money than an idiot.[16]

Shirotkin's account, though undoubtedly exaggerated, reveals how vulnerable the admission procedure at Volozhin was to pressure and how unsuitable students could be admitted. At the same time, it is important not to exaggerate the importance of connections. One student, who did not see himself as exceptional wrote of his apprehension before his entrance examination. He had arrived at the yeshiva without a letter of recommendation and felt that his acceptance depended entirely on his performance in the examination. Given a page of Talmud at random he looked it over, identified a good problem for discussion, made his case well, and was accepted.[17]

The absence of a formal admission procedure had its own logic and some advantages. Since study was continuous and students were not assigned to classes or grades, there was no particular difficulty in joining in at any time and no reason to artificially delay the beginning of study. The yeshiva did not have to deal with large groups of students turning up at the same time, which

---

[15] *Hamelits*, 26/32 (7 May 1886). It is interesting that this appeal to potential students was published in a Haskalah newspaper.

[16] Shirotkin, 'The Dew to which All Turn' (Heb.), *Hashahar*, 8/3: 114. Had the situation really been this bad, the yeshiva could not have maintained its reputation.

[17] A. Z. Horowitz, *Memoirs of Two Generations* (Yid.), 227–30.

could have put the small staff under enormous pressure. In the long run, students who did not do well in their studies were not given financial support, and eventually left. There was thus a kind of trial period rather than faith that a short examination or a quick conversation could provide an accurate picture of a student's abilities.

A disadvantage of the absence of a fixed date for admission was that it was very difficult to construct a long-term budget, since the precise number of students could never be anticipated. Moreover every time a candidate was examined, the question arose as to whether a more talented student would arrive the next day and perhaps have to be turned away. This situation added yet another unknown that the yeshiva needed to reckon with.

By the end of the nineteenth century many east European Jews were intimately familiar with the very formal and rigid structures of the general educational system and began to see them as a model of how education should be organized. In these circumstances the informality of the admission procedure was damaging the yeshiva's reputation. Many saw it as yet another example of the lack of order that characterized traditional society. Thus, even Moshe Reines, who was a strong supporter of Torah study, was critical of the informal admission system: 'The admission of students to the yeshiva, which is conducted without proper regulations, is painful to behold! The number of students is huge—about four hundred . . . and a great deal of money is needed.'[18] He repeats the charge that the level of the students declined because students were accepted on the basis of the intervention of wealthy supporters rather than their suitability for yeshiva. This issue was not resolved in R. Berlin's lifetime.

3. Adapting to Yeshiva Life

Induction into the yeshiva was not very complicated and was largely informal: the person in charge of the books would give the new student a volume of the Talmud, and that was it.[19] The yeshiva did not arrange food or accommodation for the students. New arrivals had to find a room to rent, but there was always a local householder happy to have the income that a boarder brought. No information has survived from the 1870s and early 1880s that indicates control of rental prices, but students do not seem to have been exploited. Most students paid for their board and lodging out of funds they received from the yeshiva, and prices were kept to reasonable levels for obvious reasons. Volozhin was a small town: if a new student were to have been cheated, word would have soon got round. People who overcharged would soon have found themselves without any lodgers. Students with relatives in Volozhin obviously

---

[18] M. Reines, 'Dwelling-Places of Torah' (Heb.), 18.
[19] Radus, *Memoirs* (Heb.), 65.

benefited from their assistance in finding a room; the majority did not, and had to manage on their own or the help of friends when they arrived:

Once the student arrived at Volozhin, the carter would bring him from the railway station . . . to the inn that served as the only hostelry in the town . . . The student did not spend a long time there but tried to find a place in a regular hostel—in other words, to rent a room together with a friend or two. Sometimes four young men would share a room. Everything depended on his ability to pay. There was also a difference between a 'room' and a 'residence' [*maon*]. A 'room' literally meant a room in the landlord's house, with access via other rooms, with the consequence that domestic affairs sometimes proved to be a disturbance, while a 'residence' was a small separate room at the side of the house where the student lived on his own. The richer students and those who were married lived in the 'residences'.[20]

The carter who transported the student from the railway station could serve as a go-between for negotiations with a landlord. One student records that the carter noticed that he was new, and since he knew that there was a vacant room at the tailor's, he took the student straight there. The tailor explained in great detail the qualities of the room and his wife's cooking, and the student agreed to rent the room.[21] It seems that the local people had just as much need of tenants as the students had of rooms.

The most usual way of finding accommodation, however, seems to have been by consulting veteran students, often from the new arrival's home town. Mutual assistance between students from the same town is mentioned repeatedly in the sources: the geographical link operated as a substitute for family ties. 'A student from my town . . . found me a place to live (a *taḥanah*, in yeshiva slang) in advance, with his landlord', writes one student.[22] Another records: 'At this yeshiva I found three other young men from Nesvizh, and together we rented a "residence" in the house of one of the Volozhin landlords. A young man from Slutsk joined us, and the landlady undertook to prepare meals for us.'[23]

Most of the students were satisfied with the living arrangements in Volozhin, which do not seem to have changed much over time. The following description comes from the 1880s, but is just as true of other periods: 'Our landlady saw to all our needs. She served us our meals, cooking in accordance with her tastes. Once a week we would settle our bills. Sometimes problems would emerge as we were doing this. Sometimes the bill was not correct, but usually the yeshiva students did not make any problems.'[24]

After arranging accommodation, and sometimes even before, the student

[20] M. Berlin [Bar-Ilan], *From Volozhin to Jerusalem* (Heb.), i. 88.

[21] A. Z. Horowitz, *Memoirs of Two Generations* (Yid.), 228.

[22] M. A. Eisenstadt, 'The Volozhin Yeshiva' (Heb.), 161, parentheses in the original.

[23] Shomer, *Poems and Memoirs* (Heb.), 60.

[24] M. A. Eisenstadt, 'The Volozhin Yeshiva' (Heb.), 167.

went to the study hall of the yeshiva and began to study. There was no need to fit the student into a *shiur*, since there was only one *shiur* for all the students. He did not even need to look for a study partner, since most study was carried out individually.[25] As we saw, early in the century visitors could be more impressed by the yeshiva's size than by the novelty of its organization.[26] The late nineteenth-century descriptions of Volozhin reveal that not only had the arrangements for study not changed, but that reactions to them were identical. Yehoshua Radus, who had already studied in a large yeshiva in Slobodka–Kovno, writes: 'When I entered the yeshiva and looked around, I was amazed by the sight; I had never in my life seen a yeshiva that could compare with this for glory and beauty.'[27] Another student reports that he was struck dumb and could not move, paralysed by his excitement.[28] Yet another writes: 'I felt as though I had entered another world, a strange and wonderful world.'[29] These reactions are not at all different from the responses of students shortly after the founding of the yeshiva.

It took time for the first surprise to wear off. A student who came in 1874 described how stunned he was by the numbers of students studying day and night and how learned they appeared. He recalled how when he first came, he felt that he was like a nothing in comparison to them:

I thought that each of them was a great Torah scholar and was no doubt a master of the Babylonian Talmud and the Yerushalmi Talmud and what am I and my knowledge in comparison to them? However, with time I discovered that the reality was not as I had imagined. From all of the lads and young men, only two were truly masters of the Babylonian Talmud and they were R. Shmuel Lando, now a rabbi in Helusk . . . and R. Herzl of Nesvizh who was later a rabbi in Saluk . . . but at the time I didn't know this.[30]

4. Students' Geographical Origins

Little can be said about the geographical background of the students of the Volozhin yeshiva for most of the years it existed. Clearly most of the students it attracted were from the regions of Lithuania and Belarus, the area Jews termed 'Lite'. However, without statistical data, it is impossible to tell which parts of 'Lite' supplied most of the students and whether they came from cities or towns. Certainly, it is impossible to follow changes over time. However, there are two lists of students, from 1879 and 1888, that while far from being

[25] On study partners, see Ch. 6, §2, below.
[26] See Shmukler [Shapira], *Rabbi Hayim of Volozhin* (Heb.), 47.
[27] Radus, *Memoirs* (Heb.), 64.
[28] A. Z. Horowitz, *Memoirs of Two Generations* (Yid.), 229.
[29] Turberg, *Works of Pinhas Turberg* (Heb.), 131; see also M. A. Eisenstadt, 'The Volozhin Yeshiva' (Heb.), 161–2.   [30] Zakheim, *Nitei eitan*, 48.

ideal, shed light on the geographic background of Volozhin students in those years.

In the documents Genrikh Agranovsky discovered in the Vilna archives related to an attempt to close the Volozhin yeshiva in 1879 (discussed in §6 below, and Chapter 8) are two lists of students of the yeshiva that are of particular interest. These lists were published and analysed by Agranovsky and Sid Leiman.[31] The first was prepared in Hebrew by the administration of the yeshiva. It contains the names of sixty students along with their home towns. This was submitted to the government as a list of the students of the yeshiva. At the same time, the government obtained a list of 147 Jews who were present at the time in the town of Volozhin but who were not permanent residents.[32]

In the archives there is also a list of students in the Volozhin yeshiva in 1888 in addition to the list published by Agranovsky and Leiman. Analysing both of the lists makes it possible to consider changes over time even though it is necessary to be cautious about coming to quick conclusions because there is no reason to think that the list is complete.

It is not even clear how many students really were in Volozhin in 1879. It was certainly more than 147 but what we do not know is exactly how many more. While according to some sources, there were hundreds of students in the yeshiva, in a letter R. Berlin wrote in 1875, he stated that the yeshiva was supporting 150 students.[33] In this internal letter, there was no reason for him to cite a lower figure than the reality and if so, then the list of 147 students may not have been so far off. This means that all the lists are very incomplete and we have no way to determine in what way the picture they give is a

[31] Agranovsky and Leiman, 'Three Lists of Students Studying at the Volozhin Yeshiva in 1879'.

[32] As Agranovsky and Leiman correctly observed, there is no doubt that almost everyone in the list of 147 non-residents was a student of the yeshiva. The relationship between the lists is unclear. Ostensibly, the first was prepared and submitted by the yeshiva administration while the second was prepared by a local government official. However, while 18 of the names on the first list appear, scattered in the first 100 names of the second list, almost all of the remainder, 39, are found in the last 42 names of the second list. This is certainly not a case of random distribution, and it seems that there was some co-ordination between the yeshiva administration and the local official. Indeed, it would have been mildly surprising had there been no collusion between a local government official who had years of contact with the yeshiva and the yeshiva leadership. However, while such ties are clear, the mechanism is not. The first list has almost all of the students from the Kovno region who appeared on the third list (16 out of 23) and from the Mogilev regions (8 out of 12) but only a quarter of those from the Grodno and Vilna regions (7 out of 27 and 6 out of 20) and only a third of those from the Minsk region (11 out of 33). Certainly there was a reason, but I do not know what it was. It is not clear why the yeshiva administration submitted such a short list of 60 names and how they intended to reconcile it with the longer list submitted with the local official. It is also not clear why the names of some individuals appear on both lists, others just on the list submitted by the official and an unknown quantity of others, not at all.   [33] N. Berlin, *Letters of the Netsiv* (Heb.), 66.

distorted one. However, the numbers are large enough to warrant some analysis though it would be foolhardy to rely blindly on the results.

These sources shed light on the question of how many students there were in the Volozhin yeshiva at its height. There are many reports of 300 students at that time and some claim that that there were even 400 or more. However, the lists are corroborated by less formal material. In a letter written by a resident of Volozhin in 1890, a teacher of Russian in the yeshiva who knew what was going on, claimed that there were 225 students in the yeshiva.[34] Given the precarious situation of the yeshiva with regard to the authorities, it does not seem likely that the leadership would have countenanced the presence of hundreds—or even tens—of unrecorded students. The risks were too great. It was clear to all that the authorities knew what was going on in the yeshiva. Certainly the Russian teacher would not have missed an opportunity to report on a mass of illegal students had this been the case. However, there is additional evidence for a student population of a bit more than 200 that is not dependent on trust or lack of trust in external sources.

The physical dimensions of the Volozhin yeshiva did not allow for a student body of 300 students or even near that number. Any visitor to Volozhin who sees the yeshiva building is startled by how small it is. The internal dimensions are 71.2 by 42 feet which yields a total of 2,987 square feet.[35] On the main floor of the yeshiva there was the main study hall as well as rooms for the charity fund, the clerk of the yeshiva, and a smoking room.[36] In the study hall there were aisles and a *bimah* for reading the Torah. Even with 225 students, it was no doubt crowded. Significantly more students would have required special arrangements for times such as prayer when all of the students were present—and the sources do not refer to exceptional crowding at these times.[37] There seems to be no simple answer to the question as to how many students there were in Volozhin.

The information recorded on home towns is not always clear. In some cases, it seems that people from small towns reported themselves as having come from the nearest well-known community and this could explain some of the differences between the reported home community on the yeshiva list and the government lists. However, the province of origin is almost always clearly noted. If we consider the students from the four provinces that provided the bulk of the students on the lists (106 out of 147 of the official list), we can

---

[34] Lithuanian State Historical Archive, *fond* 568, *opis'* 1, *delo* 761, *list* 29.

[35] I am grateful to the Center for Jewish Art at the Hebrew University, and particularly to Dr Vladimir Levin, for this information.

[36] See Berdyczewski, 'History of the Ets Hayim Yeshiva' (Heb.), 236.

[37] Lithuanian State Historical Archive, *fond* 568, *opis'* 1, *delo* 806. This material has been microfilmed and a copy is held in the Central Archives for the History of the Jewish People in Jerusalem. I am extremely grateful to Vinyamin Lukin for locating the material, recognizing its importance, microfilming it, and bringing it to my attention.

compare the breakdown of students to the relative weight of the Jewish population of these provinces about twenty years later. Unfortunately, there was no census in 1879 so that the 1897 data we have is the only data we can rely on.

There is a significant difference between the lists from 1879 and 1888. In the first list, there are no students recorded as coming from Poland or Mogilev–Vitebsk. In the second list, 24 out of the 182 yeshiva students listed are recorded as coming from Poland and 16 from the region of Mogilev–Vitebsk. It could be that there was a dramatic jump in yeshiva students from these regions in the nine years between the two lists. It is perhaps even more likely that these regions were excluded in the first list for reasons that were not stated. In order to compare the two lists, the accompanying table was created for the students in the regions covered in both lists. It would appear that there is an over-representation from the Minsk and Kovno provinces, while from the Vilna province, in which Volozhin was located, there was under-representation.

Table 5.1. Volozhin yeshiva students by region, 1879 and 1888

Province	Male Jewish population, 1897		% of students		No. of students	
	No.	% of aggregate	1879	1888	1879	1888
Grodno	135,000	27	26	29	28	41
Kovno	100,000	20	22	27	23	39
Minsk	165,000	33	39	30	41	42
Vilna	100,000	20	13	14	14	20
Total	500,000	100	100	100	106	142

Sources: See text, and Brutskus (ed.), *Statistics of the Jewish Population*, suppl., table 2.

What is more significant is that it appears that there were relatively few students from the big cities of Vilna and Kovno. In 1888, there were no yeshiva students at all recorded as coming from Vilna even though it was a major city. If this was indeed the case, it would fit in well with what we know from other contexts that the youth in urban centres were quicker to adopt new behaviour patterns, in this case, to seek out modern education, while small town youths remained attached to traditional values and educational patterns longer. This would also fit with the over-representation of the Minsk and Kovno provinces and the under-representation of the Vilna province. The Minsk and Kovno regions were relatively stagnant from an economic and cultural point of view during this period and the major industrial and intellectual movements in the late nineteenth century were focused in the Vilna region. The regions that were not developing economically seem to have been relatively traditional while the developing regions seem to have been populated by individuals who were quick to adopt new values. In other words, this data suggests that by 1879 modernization, however one defines the term, was well advanced among elite urban Jewish youth and even more so in 1888. This was also the case in the Slobodka yeshiva a few years later.

5. Finding One's Place at the Yeshiva: Integration and Differentiation

The students at Volozhin were very conscious of themselves as a group, and had a high opinion of their own worth. They felt special, and were proud to be studying at the yeshiva. Their social life and the ties between them were richer and more varied than those that existed among students at *batei midrash*, as a result of the large number of students and the way in which life in the yeshiva was organized. A student at a *beit midrash* had to get to know the local inhabitants—if only in order to find out where he could go each day for his meals—but the yeshiva student had no reason to get involved in town life. The students at Volozhin studied in the yeshiva building and were not supervised by local townsfolk in any way; they thus built an independent social framework, which gave them a sense of importance.[38]

Going away to yeshiva, or to a *beit midrash* for that matter, obviously meant leaving home and being cut off from one's family; it became almost a formal rite of attaining maturity. Visits home were rare, even for festivals. The student body thus became a substitute family, with the *rosh yeshivah* playing the role of father. The importance of the Seder on the first night of Pesach, when many students ate at the *rosh yeshivah*'s table, demonstrates this (see below, Chapter 6, §4). Leaving home at a relatively young age was not in itself a rare occurrence. It was the practice even among the unlearned, with apprentices commonly leaving home to live in the house of their master. Similarly, a high percentage, perhaps most, of the youths who went on to study in *batei midrash* travelled away from their native town in order to do so. Only married students studied at local *batei midrash*, and even they usually lived and studied in their bride's native town so while they were not totally removed from a family framework, they were not in the family home in which they had grown up. Entering a yeshiva to study Torah was an important rite of passage because of this break with home, and accordingly the social framework that the yeshiva offered assumed great importance.

Officially, as we have seen, it was the yeshiva that decided who would be admitted. However, there was a parallel process of acceptance that was no less important from the student's point of view. This was not a formal initiation

---

[38] Their social life was not very organized. Nevertheless there was some organization for the celebration of festivals, and, in the final days of the yeshiva, some activity in connection with the election of a successor to R. Berlin, besides the Zionist organizations; on these, see below.

ceremony but a process of informal induction into yeshiva life. Part of this process was acquiring a new name: 'When we came to Volozhin, we were all deprived of our names and surnames, and each of us was given the name of the town from which he came, or even of the town which had provided his written recommendation . . . nicknames were added to these regular names since there were several students from the same town.'[39] Receiving a new name was just one part of the student's break with home and childhood. Another part was making friends—though this was not always easy. As one student noted:

The conditions there did not make it easy for the yeshiva student to acquire friends and acquaintances. There were no student societies or leagues at the yeshiva . . . in which . . . they could get to know each other and make friends. There was nowhere in the town . . . where they could spend some time in the company of their friends and fellows . . . [the new student] did not know most of the other students, even though he spent most of his time with them in the yeshiva.[40]

However, with time, most students seem to have found a circle of friends. Moreover, as we shall see, at certain times there were indeed student societies in Volozhin.

Marital status was a factor that divided students. As already noted, most students were single; married students came principally to obtain ordination. The fact of marriage was not in itself a reason for single students to be jealous since the married students came alone, but it led to jealousy for other reasons. Married students received larger allowances, as well as more attention from the *rosh yeshivah*.

Another source of differentiation was economic status. The more support a student received from home, the less his dependence on the institution and the less he felt himself subject to yeshiva discipline. Economic status also had implications for daily life: since there was no dormitory or dining hall that could create a common standard for all, wealthy students could live better than those who depended on the yeshiva for their sustenance. As one wealthy student put it:

We, the richer students, lived in better rooms. For instance, I lived in a large room . . . we used to drink sweet tea and buy white *ḥalot* [plaited sabbath loaves], cheese, and butter. For our midday meal we used to eat meat, often even chicken . . . in the other room at the house of R. Lazer, the *menahel*, three students lived together . . . they did not actually starve, but lived in a very modest way.[41]

This description demonstrates that differences in economic status did not lead to completely separate accommodation, since rich and poor students could

[39] M. A. Eisenstadt, 'The Volozhin Yeshiva' (Heb.), 167.
[40] Zlatkin, 'The Volozhin Yeshiva in Bialik's Time' (Heb.), 56–7.
[41] M. A. Eisenstadt, 'The Volozhin Yeshiva' (Heb.), 167.

live together in the same house. However, there were few attempts to down-play differences.

Wealthy young men who came to Volozhin in order to obtain a reputation for scholarship even though they were really not suited to it found themselves subject to criticism that may well have been partly prompted by envy. The economic gap may have led to more obvious social tensions, as emerges from a description of the struggle over the election of a 'Purim rabbi' at Volozhin in the 1870s. There were two candidates, one from Sventsyany and the other from Denenburg. 'There was a long battle between the Sventsyany and the Denenburg factions, and the hatred between these two groups grew daily. The Sventsyany faction called us Denenburgers "the barefoot lot", since most of our members were poor. And we called them "the wicked sons".'[42] There is little additional evidence, however, of social tensions due to economic factors—not because the yeshiva tried to cover up the differences but rather because since students studied all day long there was little opportunity for demonstrating economic or social status.

The period of study at Volozhin, as at every yeshiva, was an important transitional stage in a young man's life. The separation from home, the new name, and the lessened importance of one's economic status (and naturally of family connections, thanks to the change of name) combined to create an experience akin to the puberty rites known from other societies. This type of rite, in which a young man becomes part of a community outside his family, typically includes 'a sense of break with the past (a "marginal environment") together with segregation from the family and from those of the other sex, and chastisement under the direction of elders for didactic purposes'.[43] Going to yeshiva fits this description in many respects, even though the context is completely different. The yeshiva student was separated from his family and the company of women, was subject to the perpetual supervision of the *rashei yeshivah*, and was punished if he did not obey their orders. The *rosh yeshivah* served as a substitute father; it was not by chance that the students were called *benei yeshivah*, 'sons of the yeshiva'. Most of the students had to make do with much less than at home, and had to study for hours with no break. The requirement of constant study under difficult conditions constituted a test of the student's will power, his loyalty to certain social values, and his commit-ment to Torah study. Those who passed the test could be proud of their success for the rest of their lives. Ironically, easier living conditions might have undermined the impact of the yeshiva experience. The pressure to study, the separation, and the loneliness created conditions whereby it was easier for the *rashei yeshivah* to influence the young men and shape their personalities. At Volozhin they did this by setting a personal example of devotion to constant

[42] Shomer, *Poems and Memoirs* (Heb.), 66; see Ch. 6, §4, below.
[43] Ong, 'Latin Language Study as a Renaissance Puberty Rite', 235.

study. At other yeshivas, as we shall see, there were different and more direct attempts to influence the student's character.

Entering the yeshiva was thus a very important stage in the student's life. While he remained solitary in his independent study and isolated from the external world, simply being part of the yeshiva world gave him a sense of belonging and a shared destiny. Once he had settled down into his new status and identity, he would discover that there were several frameworks within the yeshiva that would afford him opportunities for developing new ties and associations. He arrived at the yeshiva as a solitary individual, but left it as one of a fellowship—a status clearly emphasized in the custom whereby yeshiva students would accompany departing students to the railway station.[44]

6. Student Activities, Student Solidarity, and Staff Reactions

Although students devoted most of their time to study, there was one particular extra-curricular interest that brought certain students together outside the study hall: a desire to gain access to the books and journals that were not available in the yeshiva library because they were considered 'Haskalah literature'. Such books were not cheap, and nor were they easy to obtain in a small town like Volozhin. Books of this type that found their way into the yeshiva were therefore eagerly circulated among interested students;[45] at least one maskil is known to have begun his secular education under the influence of books he had borrowed from other students at his yeshiva because he was too poor to buy them for himself.[46]

Groups of students also subscribed jointly to journals, as Binyamin Goldberg describes:

Several students . . . subscribed to a single copy of an issue. I recall there were four subscribers to *Voskhod* [a Jewish newspaper in Russian]: one from Moscow, one from Boisk, one from Derechin . . . and myself. The student who had signed up as the subscriber, and to whom the copy was sent, had to go to the post office himself to get it . . . and each issue, before its subscribers could read it, was bound between two boards, lest it be crumpled from overuse and passing between grubby hands; and eventually, after several days, it would return to the main subscriber, who collected

[44] It is said of Bialik that 'when he left Volozhin and the yeshiva to travel to Odessa, more than a hundred of his friends and acquaintances from the yeshiva accompanied him for a long way, far from the town . . . such a number of people accompanying a yeshiva student . . . was a very rare sight at Volozhin, and only a few lucky students merited this treatment' (Zlatkin, 'The Volozhin Yeshiva in Bialik's Time' (Heb.), 56). About a quarter of the student body accompanied Bialik, which was quite unusual. But even a much less important student such as A. Z. Horowitz remembered that many students accompanied him beyond the town (*Memoirs of Two Generations* (Yid.), 238). [45] Levin-Epstein, *Memoirs* (Heb.), 31.
[46] A. Z. Horowitz, *Memoirs of Two Generations* (Yid.), 235.

all the issues for the year and bound them in a single volume, so that others could also enjoy them later.[47]

This practice was very common, so much so that Goldberg even states, doubtless with some exaggeration, that 'there was no yeshiva student who would not give his last penny to subscribe to some newspaper'.[48]

According to a friend of Bialik's who studied at the yeshiva during its final years, much the same method was employed to obtain books:

[There was a student] from Courland who was outgoing and enterprising, and an entrepreneur of Haskalah for the pleasure of it. He had a remarkable talent for sniffing out heretical opinions from a distance, and for discovering heretical books packed away in boxes. He used to sniff out the 'new faces' who arrived at the yeshiva, probe into their characters, and check their boxes. If he found any Haskalah books there, he would write down their names in a notebook, and by this cursory inspection he would acquire these books, and they passed from their owner's possession into his. He used to dispose of all the Haskalah books that were hidden and concealed by their owners just as though they belonged to him, taking them from one person and giving them to another without their owners knowing anything about it, and taking as much delight in the whole exercise as though he were performing a mitzvah.[49]

This was a remarkable example of private initiative responding to what was clearly a great demand. Although the books were distributed without their owners' permission, permission was apparently granted after the fact since the owners were given other books in exchange—an unofficial library system.

Relationships between students were not always smooth. For instance, although outstanding students who were close to R. Berlin or the other *rosh yeshivah* would generally be highly regarded by their fellow-students, their closeness to the rabbinic authorities could sometimes be a source of friction and even lead to their ostracization. Binyamin Goldberg describes this:

One sabbath I visited a young man from my town, Yisra'el Aharon Kravtschik. He was the son of a poor tailor from Rozin, and at that time was considered the most outstanding student. The *gaon* R. Hayim Soloveitchik would not give his *shiur* to the students before consulting him as to which passage of *pilpul* would be best to present . . . as a result of their inordinate envy, the yeshiva students had nicknamed him 'Baḥ' [abbreviation of *ben ḥayat*, 'tailor's son'], hinting at his father's trade.[50]

Another account records: 'The students looked unfavourably on those of their fellows who excelled in their studies, and they especially disliked me, since I was one of the youngest and smallest of all the students.'[51] In both these cases

[47] B. Goldberg, *Memories of the Past* (Heb.), 5–6.
[48] Ibid. 4.   [49] Baloshcr, 'Bialik at Volozhin' (Heb.), 120.
[50] B. Goldberg, *Memories of the Past* (Heb.), 12–13.
[51] Levin-Epstein, *Memoirs* (Heb.), 30.

success in studies was not the direct cause of envy, but rather the perception that the student was receiving respect of which he was not 'worthy', whether because of his origins or his youthfulness. Nevertheless, brilliant students were generally not pressured into hiding their abilities, and the other students did not harass them except in unusual cases like these.

Students who developed close relations with the teachers out of a desire to curry favour with the authorities came in for worse treatment:

A new student came to Volozhin, the son of a *gabai* [communal leader] and of a good family, and he began to curry favour with the 'court', and often went in there for no good reason, and his fellows gave him a warning. Anyone who ignored a first and a second warning was punished: they took him out of the yeshiva and decreed a certain length of time during which he had to stay at home, isolated from everyone else, and was forbidden to enter the yeshiva.[52]

It was difficult for a single student to stand up against the entire student body. The existence of a close relationship between a student and the teaching staff was not a matter for disapproval unless the student used it as a way of arrogating importance to himself. The punishment meted out by the student body for what they considered an infraction of social mores was therefore social rather than physical: a boycott, which must have been a very severe punishment indeed for a student with no other social milieu with which to interact.

The students felt a sense of solidarity in facing their teachers that was sometimes strong enough to overcome what were otherwise major ideological differences between them. This was true of the attitude to the Haskalah and its literature, for instance. The yeshiva staff were unambiguously opposed to any involvement in the Haskalah; they differed only in the punishments they imposed. Their basic view of the Haskalah as a distraction from Torah study, or even as a major source of deviation, never altered—even if they also admitted that it was not a total waste of time. Many students shared this opposition, but if they knew that another student was reading Haskalah literature they would generally not turn him in. Berdyczewski describes it thus: 'The students of Volozhin possess another virtue, in that they do not suffer from the plague of slander [*lashon hara*], as in other yeshivas, and even if a student were to be offered all the wealth of the world he would not slander his fellow.'[53] There is evidence that some cases of informing did occur, though the fact that they were regarded as exceptional indicates that it was not a common practice.[54] Further proof of this attitude comes from the following anecdote:

Because I read [the newspaper] *Ha'ivri*, I was given a thorough dressing-down by the student Mr Klapfisch, the son of the well-known R. Zanvil Klapfisch of blessed

[52] Balosher, *Bialik in Volozhin* (Heb.), 38.
[53] Berdyczewski [Bar Bei Rav], 'A Bundle of Letters' (Heb.), *Hamelits*, 28/53.
[54] See the story recorded by Don-Yihia in 'Memoirs' (Heb.), *Netivah*, 12/5.

memory [a well known rabbi in Warsaw], and this is how it happened; this student lived in the same room as a boy from London whose father used to send him *Ha'ivri* to read, and this boy, who was one of my friends, knowing my love for newspapers, used to give it to me to read. I had skimmed through the works of Mapu and Smolenskin and had been struck by several points, and I did not scruple to go to this friend of mine on the eve of Yom Kippur, after the afternoon prayers, to borrow the newspaper from him, for in this matter I made no distinction between this day and other days. When I came to his room, I found his room-mate there, the student Klapfisch, and when he found out the purpose of my visit, he reproved me to my face for my wicked ways, displaying interest in newspapers on the eve of Yom Kippur. And had it not been for the horror of informing, which was sacred among the students, who knows whether I might not have been handed over by this fanatic to the gallows, in other words, to the judgement of R. Berlin, who would have proceeded with all the severity of the law against the wretched *vakhernikim* [students who received the weekly allowance from the yeshiva].[55]

Student solidarity also had negative consequences. Shomer describes a situation in the 1870s when some students laid claim to several seats in the study hall and took more than their fair share of the candles and afterwards 'sold' the seats and the candles to other students. He adds: 'If one of the students dared to complain to the *mashgiah* or the *rosh yeshivah* about those who used the seats and candles as a means of enriching themselves, many of these wicked ones would rise up against them and would make their lives bitter and beat them cruelly.'[56] He might be suspected of exaggeration, except that another student describes a similar occurrence in the 1880s:

The students never let go of their volumes of Talmud for a moment and would carry them under their arms as they came in or went out, because people used to steal books from each other and were not ashamed if they were caught red-handed. If a student left his place and went out for a few moments he would have to ask the student standing next to him to keep an eye on his volume so that it would not be stolen.[57]

Solidarity in opposition to the teaching staff and internal solidarity were clearly two distinct matters.

Nevertheless, the solidarity that prevented informing on fellow students found even stronger expression where there was cause for dissatisfaction with the teaching staff. Thus, on the eve of Pesach one year the students announced that they refused to attend the Seder at R. Berlin's house because they opposed his wife's involvement in allocating allowances and imposing fines:

---

[55] B. Goldberg, *Memories of the Past* (Heb.), 8.
[56] Shomer, *Poems and Memoirs* (Heb.), 61.   [57] Radus, *Memoirs* (Heb.), 65.

The messengers came to invite us to come for the Seder, but nobody stirred from his place until our rabbi came himself and asked us to enter his house for the Seder. We did not have the strength and audacity to refuse this great sage, and we decided to go to the Seder. Then we found out that one student, who had been so heavily fined that he had not been allocated the usual allowance, did not want to go to the Seder. Our rabbi also found out about this, and sent a special messenger to [the student] to ask him not to disrupt the Seder, and we waited until he arrived. This great act of humility and the love that he showed us, like a merciful father, washed away all our grievances against him, and we went in for the Seder with singing and music . . . but though we had made peace with our rabbi, our anger against his wife had not slackened, and we took revenge on her in all sorts of ways, and did not allow her to rest for a moment. We removed the cups, the forks, and the spoons and threw them under the table so that she would have to go and find replacements.[58]

In a similar case one eve of Shavuot, the students felt that R. Berlin had insulted one of their number and in protest none would give him the customary festival greeting at the end of prayers. R. Berlin capitulated and publicly asked the student's forgiveness.[59]

The students had a special method of demonstrating dissatisfaction very publicly: 'When the *mashgiah* entered or left the yeshiva everyone stopped studying and whispered "Sha–sha–sha", and as he passed through the hall his face was burning.'[60] They resumed their studies immediately he had passed, but they had satisfactorily succeeded in demonstrating their collective dissatisfaction. This method even had a name. It was known as the 'Volozhin Sha'. The power of this custom lay in its being an expression of the sentiments of the student body as a whole. The joint pause in study, even if only for a moment, constituted a violation of the yeshiva's values and symbolized the students' stand that, if the staff did not do what they wanted, they in their turn would not do what the staff wanted.

There were also more emphatic ways of expressing collective opposition than the 'Volozhin Sha'. 'Suddenly the sound of a table top banging was heard, as it was ceaselessly raised and lowered, and this was like a sign for the start of the revolution. All the students were sitting at their places and studying, while raising and lowering the table tops, and their voices mingled with the banging of the tables—and there was pandemonium.'[61] Thus began one of the revolts that characterized the final years of the Volozhin yeshiva.[62] The rioting stu-

---

[58] Mashvitski, 'In the Dwelling-Places of Torah' (Heb.), *Baderekh*, 3/13(80). He recorded a similar event one Purim. R. Berlin refused to call a doctor to a student who was ill, and by way of retribution the students boycotted the rabbi's Purim feast (see ibid. 3/38(105)).

[59] M. A. Eisenstadt, 'Revolution in the Yeshiva' (Heb.).

[60] A. Z. Horowitz, *Memoirs of Two Generations* (Yid.), 237.

[61] M. A. Eisenstadt, 'Revolution in the Yeshiva' (Heb.). On the 'Volozhin Sha', see also Radus, *Memoirs* (Heb.), 68; Mashvitski, 'In the Dwelling-Places of Torah' (Heb.), *Baderekh*, 3/38(105).

[62] See below.

dents broke windows, threatened the *mashgiaḥ*, and called him a 'scoundrel and a spy'. The staff was powerless in the face of such behaviour. 'R. Berlin tried unceasingly to walk around the hall and ask the students to calm down, but to no avail. Angry and full of exasperation, R. Berlin left the yeshiva without giving his *shiur* that day.'[63]

Such disturbances were generally an organized reaction to the insulting of a student. A. Z. Horowitz tells of the collective opposition to the arrival of a new *mashgiaḥ*, on the grounds that 'they regarded the appointment of a *mashgiaḥ* to supervise them as a humiliation'.[64] R. Berlin sometimes received a similar reaction for slapping a student's face. This was particularly humiliating for the student involved and indirectly insulted the other students too. After one incident of this kind the students got together and made a plan: 'When all us students had gathered together in the yeshiva, we decided to stop studying immediately and to take counsel, as to what appeasement we should seek from our rabbi and teacher, R. Berlin, for the insult to all the students of the yeshiva. For this was the sort of action to be expected of a *melamed* in a *ḥeder*, and such things ought not to be done at the Volozhin yeshiva.'[65] This was not an instance of opposition to the *rosh yeshivah*'s authority in principle, but to what the students felt to be misuse of it.

The dispute over the appointment of R. Berlin's son as his successor, which will be discussed below, was also described in terms of a battle over honour: 'The yeshiva students, to whom the honour of the yeshiva was very precious, thought that if an unsuitable *rosh yeshivah* were to be appointed, it would be a great disaster for the yeshiva and [lead to] a terrible decline in its reputation.'[66] It seems that the boycott of the Seder mentioned above was also inspired by the feeling that a woman's interference in yeshiva matters was an affront to the students' dignity: the yeshiva was an exclusively male world.

The students did not take issue with action taken by staff over issues that they recognized as legitimate. Thus, for example, students did not oppose measures taken to prevent a student becoming involved in the Haskalah, even if they were thus involved themselves. It is recorded of a certain *mashgiaḥ* that 'this man knew no mercy, but he could do no evil against a single student, for the fear of the students was constantly upon him, lest they band together against him and turn him out, as they once did'.[67] In spite of this, there are no descriptions of organized opposition to the searches for Haskalah books, even by those who were reading them. The students seem to have accepted that the staff had a right to watch out for this, even if they themselves saw no

[63] M. A. Eisenstadt, 'Revolution in the Yeshiva' (Heb.).
[64] A. Z. Horowitz, *Memoirs of Two Generations* (Yid.), 237.
[65] Mashvitski, 'In the Dwelling-Places of Torah' (Heb.), *Baderekh*, 3/23(90).
[66] Zlatkin, 'The Volozhin Yeshiva in Bialik's Time' (Heb.), 63.
[67] Shirotkin, 'The Dew to which All Turn' (Heb.), *Hashaḥar*, 8/3: 116.

harm in dabbling in Haskalah on the side. The yeshiva's strict rules about this were not regarded as an affront to the students' honour.

7. The Individual Student and the Teaching Staff

Individual students also had ways of expressing opposition to yeshiva policy, although their abilities were more limited. The simplest method was to ask questions designed to embarrass rather than to enlighten. Thus, for example, when R. Berlin prevented a student from taking a walk outside on Shavuot, the student prepared a particularly difficult question and posed it to the rabbi at the *shiur* the next day. He derived great satisfaction from the fact that R. Berlin had to make a great effort and think for ten minutes before coming up with an answer.[68] As already mentioned, one student tried to contradict everything that R. Berlin's father-in-law (by his second marriage) said in a *shiur*, with the express aim of hurting him.[69] Questions were also used as a weapon in the campaign against the appointment of R. Hayim Berlin as *rosh yeshivah*, as described below.

Another method available to the individual was mockery. While the custom of having a 'Purim rabbi' (see Chapter 6), was still practised, it constituted a sanctioned outlet for criticism and satire even if the right to criticize was reserved exclusively for the 'Purim rabbi' alone. However, this was not the only opportunity for mockery. In the final years of the yeshiva there were students who distributed handbills or pamphlets critical of what was happening. The attempted boycott of the Seder in R. Berlin's house that was mentioned earlier began when a student posted an anonymous announcement on the door of the yeshiva. In the case of another student, the 'genius from K—z [Kremenitz?]', who was not allowed to return to the yeshiva after leaving to join a cantor's choir:

His spirit was saddened and his mind grieved, and he was in despair, and hatred for the leaders of the yeshiva, especially the *rosh yeshivah*, burnt like fire with him . . . he thought up a plan and devised a way of taking revenge on his enemies, and thus he often stuck up lampoons on the walls of the yeshiva . . . it was said that once he affixed a lampoon to the *rosh yeshivah*'s door; the staff and also the rabbi's wife read the lampoon and burst out laughing. Shortly thereafter a poster with large letters appeared on the door, and it read as follows: 'Listen, my brothers and fellows! We have seen the dogs laughing, and we thought that Elijah the Prophet must have come to town; but to our sorrow, and in spite of our desire, we saw that a bitch was among them, the great bitch, the daughter of the rabbi'. This hurt the rabbi's wife to the depths of her soul.[70]

[68] A. Z. Horowitz, *Memoirs of Two Generations* (Yid.), 237.
[69] Berdyczewski [Bar Bei Rav], 'A Bundle of Letters' (Heb.), *Hamelits*, 28/56.
[70] Radus, *Memoirs* (Heb.), 67–8. On this student, see above.

A similar incident occurred during the dispute over the appointment of R. Hayim Berlin: 'Every morning, when the students arrived at the yeshiva, they would find the entrance door covered with lampoons about R. Hayim Berlin; most of them were written in the form of parodies of *piyutim* [liturgical poems], *seliḥot* [penitential prayers], *kinot* [lamentations], and so on, and in them he was held up to ridicule, mockery, and insult.'[71]

There were other ways in which students managed to bring their claims against particular staff to the attention of the other students and to outsiders despite the absence of social frameworks or meeting places outside the study hall. Posters were one such method, but much use was made of written material, and particularly in the case of disputes over appointments. Thus, as part of a campaign to dissuade R. Berlin from appointing his son as his successor, students sent him abusive anonymous letters;[72] they also wrote to rabbis and other important figures outside the yeshiva, asking them to intervene in this matter.[73] More violent methods were also employed:

Judgement also struck [the rabbi's wife] one day, when fanatics from the yeshiva acted disgracefully and threw a stone through her window; she became ill from fear and took to her bed, and almost stood at the gates of death. And so greatly had hatred destroyed all proper behaviour, that just when the doctors had despaired of her recovery and there was sorrow and grief throughout the rabbi's household, the rabbi found a piece of paper in his volume of Talmud which bore an inscription to be engraved on her tombstone.[74]

Another strategy, similar in its extreme nature and far-reaching implications, was to appeal to the general public through the Hebrew press, in order

[71] Zlatkin, 'The Volozhin Yeshiva in Bialik's Time' (Heb.), 64.

[72] Ibid. A similar incident seems to have happened at the Mir yeshiva. In 1881 an announcement in *Hamelits* asked readers' help in finding a man who had abandoned his wife in Mir and had left her an *agunah* [unable to remarry according to Jewish law]. The husband's name resembled the name of the *rosh yeshivah*, and shortly thereafter a clarification appeared in the newspaper, explaining that the announcement had been submitted as a hoax designed to embarrass the *rosh yeshivah*. See *Hamelits*, 17/50 (3 Jan. 1882); 18/6 (28 Feb. 1882). Attempts to embarrass the *rosh yeshivah* were obviously not confined to the students at Volozhin.

[73] Zlatkin, 'The Volozhin Yeshiva in Bialik's Time' (Heb.), 64.

[74] Berdyczewski, 'A Bundle of Letters' (Heb.), 28/56: 573. Mashvitski may have referred to this incident (which was completely exceptional) when he wrote: 'And it happened, one Saturday evening, when R. Berlin and his assistants were calculating fines, that a stone was thrown through the window, and those sitting there only escaped by a miracle. Those who knew about the incident claimed that he who threw the stone had not done so out of wickedness of heart and resentment, but that he was one of the most outstanding students in the yeshiva, who sat in R. Berlin's house when they were discussing capital offences, and from over-excitement had left the house and done this deed. And if this account is true, he is one of the outstanding scholars of our generation today'; see Etkes and Tikochinski, *Memoirs of the Lithuanian Yeshivas* (Heb.), 129. The purpose of this passage is clear; violence needed a very strong justification, so the discussions about the allocation of allowances had to be interpreted as study of capital offences.

to encourage external intervention in the yeshiva's affairs. A distinction should be made between articles about the yeshiva written by guests or former students and those submitted by current students in an attempt to influence the course of events. Journalism was a totally new phenomenon in Jewish society in eastern Europe. Articles written in order to disseminate information or to analyse processes in Jewish society did not necessarily influence what happened, and did not pose problems for the yeshiva; there were many articles about the Volozhin yeshiva in the Jewish press.[75] But the publication of reports and articles that were intended to exert influence was a different matter. Students do not seem to have wielded much influence during the disputes of the 1860s and 1870s, partly because they had no way of contacting the important donors and no chance of winning over the rabbis who came to the yeshiva. However, this changed with the rise of the Jewish press: access to newspapers could give them considerable power. Since newspaper editors in the 1880s were often critical of R. Berlin and the rabbinical establishment, students had little difficulty publishing their opinions in the newspapers. Indeed, several articles of this type—urging outside intervention—did appear in the Hebrew press during the 1880s. The first example seems to have appeared in 1879 in *Hashahar*,[76] and similar pieces were published in 1883,[77] 1888,[78] and in other years.[79]

The most extreme act of protest that a student could take was to inform on the yeshiva or its teachers to the tsarist authorities. During R. Berlin's time, the yeshiva's legal status was not entirely above question, in spite of the letters that R. Hayim and R. Yitshak had received (see above, Chapter 1, §4, and Chapter 2, §3); most definitely it did not have permission to operate a countrywide network of financial support. The danger from informers was thus very real, and we know of one case that did indeed cause severe problems.[80]

The case unfolded as follows. In 1879 R. Berlin was accused of involvement in a currency counterfeiting scam. The authorities suspected him of receiving counterfeit coins from England and distributing them throughout Russia. The basis of the accusation was a forged letter, ostensibly sent by R. Berlin to an English rabbi,[81] which contained a receipt and thanks for money sent to him, a claim that he bribed local officials, and a request for a consignment of counterfeit coins. The author made sure that the letter reached the police, with the obvious intention of getting R. Berlin into trouble; and indeed, in the wake of the 'discovery' of the letter, the police confiscated documents

[75] See the list compiled by Leone (ed.), *Volozhin* (Heb.), 173 ff.

[76] Shirotkin, 'The Dew to which All Turn' (Heb.).

[77] 'Shevik' [pseud.], *Hamelits*, 15/61 (8 Aug. 1883); 'Ish Deretschin' [pseud.], *Hamelits*, 15/69 (5 Sept. 1883). [78] Berdyczewski [Bar Bei Rav], 'A Bundle of Letters' (Heb.).

[79] See the discussion below of the students' battles with the staff on the eve of the yeshiva's closure. [80] See Ch. 8 below on these years.

[81] Either R. Ettlinger or Dayan Reinowitz—the reports of the case differ. See next note.

relating to the yeshiva. Yehoshua Steinberg and Yonah Gerstein, two Jews who worked as advisors to the authorities, examined them, and R. Berlin was summoned for interrogation. The forgery was soon detected by comparing the differences between the signature in the letter with R. Berlin's own: the rabbi signed his name with only one letter *yod* in the names Tsevi and Yehudah, while the forger had used two.[82] But the affair did not end there: because the authorities had taken note of the fact that the yeshiva in Volozhin was collecting money throughout Russia without any authorization to do so, the yeshiva could have been closed down. Fortunately, however, Yonah Gerstein had burnt all the documents that mentioned the collection of money—the most sensitive issue—claiming that they were merely family correspondence.[83] A bribe probably solved the other problems, as Binyamin Goldberg recalls:

Every year, in the summer, the district director used to come and visit the yeshiva, and in spite of the unpleasant impression it made on him, he never harmed it. Local experts claimed that the *rebbetzin* won the official over to the yeshiva's side so that he did not invoke the law against it, for after his visit to the yeshiva they used to invite him to dinner at R. Berlin's house, prepared by the *rebbetzin*; but others believed that when the director shook hands with the honoured rabbi as they parted, the rabbi slipped him a little something.[84]

[82] A report on the search, by someone signing himself 'Ish Yemini', was published in *Hamelits*, 9/25 (12 June 1879). In issue 28 (3 July 1879) Zederbaum, the editor, wrote that he had received letters from R. Berlin and others about the incident, and, according to him, the forged letter had been addressed to R. Ettlinger. It recorded that R. Berlin had received 30,000 roubles, of which a third had been distributed to the students, a third had been given to local officials as bribes, and a third was intended for bribing senior ministers. The forger had written to the authorities telling them where to find the forged letter. According to R. Berlin's son, the letter was addressed to Dayan Reinowitz; see M. Berlin [Bar-Ilan], *From Volozhin to Jerusalem* (Heb.), i. 85.

[83] M. Berlin [Bar-Ilan], *From Volozhin to Jerusalem* (Heb.), i. 86–7. Another description of the false denunciation appears in Milikovski-Samsonov, *Ohalei aharon*, 208–18. I thank both Rabbi Betsalel Dablitski and Professor Marc Shapiro for the reference. There are no real differences between his description and Berlin's other than the ending of the affair. While Berlin described Yonah Gerstein as burning the documents, R. Milikovski wrote: 'When he came to the minister of the region, he was pleasantly received; he was given a chair and the results of the inquiry into this matter were announced in this manner. First, it was determined that he did none of the crimes that the forged letter accused him of having committed. As such, all of the writings and notebooks that were taken from him at the time of the search in his house are being returned to him. Secondly, it was announced that since the Interior Minister together with the Minister of Education had found that, for the whole time that the yeshiva in Volozhin had been closed by the government, students continued to flock to the yeshiva to advance in the study of Torah and nothing wrong had been found in them. Therefore the Interior Minister and the Minister of Education recognize the yeshiva in Volozhin from this day on as open under the auspices of the government and the right is given to R. Berlin to continue his teaching as he has done until now' (*Ohalei aharon*, 220). It is doubtful that this is the whole story.

[84] B. Goldberg, *Memories of the Past* (Heb.), 15.

The identity of the forger was never established, though rumour had it that he was a student who had been expelled from the yeshiva.[85] From the very existence of such rumours it is clear that the students regarded informing as a possible way of settling scores with the staff. It was, not necessarily one that should be used: informers aroused enormous antagonism in Jewish society.[86] The failure to reveal the informer's identity—or more accurately, his failure to boast of his deed—suggests that there was widespread disgust at the incident. No other cases of informing are known from 1879 until the final years of the yeshiva.

The existence of events such as have been described here does not mean that the atmosphere at the yeshiva was one of constant tension. The dramatic cases were the exceptions and not the rule. Most students were very happy during their stay in Volozhin, identified with the yeshiva and its teachers, and were concerned for its reputation. We have already seen that if a guest arrived who threatened the yeshiva's honour, the students felt it was their duty to defend it and to teach him a lesson. Another indication of the general level of satisfaction was that students played an active role in recruiting other students for the yeshiva.[87] Bringing in a particularly talented student was regarded as an achievement for both the institution and the person who had recruited him. In addition, when a student succeeded in persuading a young man whom he respected to follow in his footsteps, it strengthened his confidence in his own choice of path. Demoralized students would hardly have encouraged others to come to the yeshiva.

8. The Relationship between the Students and the Local Community

The students at Volozhin had few points of contact with the local community. Even though they lived in rented rooms in local houses, the long study day at the yeshiva limited the possibilities of forming close ties with the local people. In any case, the students were generally contemptuous of them. As one student who arrived in Volozhin around 1890 wrote:

I was accepted to the yeshiva and became one of the students. I was longing to see how the students lived and how they were received in local society, and this amazed

[85] According to Goldberg (*Memories of the Past* (Heb.), 15), it was probably a student whom R. Berlin had slapped. In Zederbaum's words, 'according to one of the letters there were three suspects: one in Volozhin, who hated the honoured rabbi, and two students, one from Minsk and the other from Vilna, whom the rabbi had banned from coming to his *shiur*' (*Hamelits*, 9/28 (3 July 1879)). According to M. Berlin his father did not know who the culprit was, but suspicion fell on a student who had been rebuked on Yom Kippur and had been expelled from the yeshiva (*From Volozhin to Jerusalem* (Heb.), i. 85).

[86] See Zederbaum's account in *Hamelits*, 9/28 (3 July 1879).

[87] See M. Y. Goldberg et al., *Ideinu*, 8.

me greatly. I was used to yeshiva students being submissive to the local inhabitants and accepting their criticisms, for [the latter] supported them and provided their food. Here I saw the exact opposite. The yeshiva students were the ones who arranged all the business of the town, and everything was done according to their orders, for most of the townsfolk were simple people and respected the students. And since the latter did not need the townsfolk's support and were independent, they were the aristocrats of the town, and their opinions on public matters were listened to.[88]

The students unflatteringly called the townsfolk *stopkes* ('corks' or 'bottle stoppers').[89] A yeshiva student was 'urbane, well-mannered, dressed respectably, in contrast to the local Jew, who was a simple man'.[90] There were no cases of riots or violent clashes with the local inhabitants, of the sort associated with the educational establishments of other cultures—there was simply no time available for this type of activity.

Very occasionally the local residents would come to celebrations at the yeshiva. Some came to watch what went on in R. Berlin's house on Pesach Eve, after they had finished celebrating their own Seder at home,[91] or to listen to the *shiur* given by the 'Purim rabbi'.[92] But a certain tension remained: 'A slight insult by a *stopak* to a student's dignity was sufficient to set the whole yeshiva in turmoil and cause an almighty fuss.'[93] These incidents were relatively small, however. A memoir by A. Mashvitski describes the means available to the students in their clashes with local residents and the circumstances that justified such actions as follows. There was an incident in 1885 in which a student died before a doctor could reach the yeshiva. In response, the students decided not only to demand that R. Berlin see that a doctor be employed on a permanent basis in the town, but also to take steps to ensure the local community's support for this essential project:

We solemnly undertook not to buy meat slaughtered by the Volozhin community but to bring in meat from another town near Volozhin. This threat did indeed terrify the Volozhin community [because the communal organization depended on revenues from the kosher meat tax]. At first they promised to give a certain sum towards the cost of underwriting the scheme, but they did not keep this promise. In addition, many of the students could not keep to their plan of refraining from eating meat, and annulled their vows after consulting a rabbi. Then it came to the week before Purim . . . the news came that a student from Krakizov had fallen dangerously ill, and there was no doctor in the town . . . the affair ended when about ten students

---

[88] Turberg, *Works of Pinhas Turberg* (Heb.), 131.

[89] Z. Epstein, *Writings* (Heb.), 118. Evidence of the contempt that yeshiva students displayed towards the townspeople can be seen in B. H. Epstein, *Mekor barukh*, iii. 1816–20, and M. Berlin [Bar-Ilan], *From Volozhin to Jerusalem* (Heb.), i. 108.   [90] Z. Epstein, *Writings* (Heb.), 118.

[91] M. Berlin [Bar-Ilan], *From Volozhin to Jerusalem* (Heb.), i. 168.

[92] Zitron, *Three Literary Generations* (Yid.), 163.   [93] Z. Epstein, *Writings* (Heb.), 119.

took their sabbath clothes to the *gemaḥ* [loan society] and several students pawned their watches, and this provided the sum necessary to send a messenger and pay the doctor [to come from another town].[94]

According to M. Berlin, the boycott extended to yeast sold locally, since this also carried a tax payable to the local community. The students therefore baked matza (which contains no yeast), rather than bread, and imported meat from a nearby town in order to put pressure on the local treasurers to support their Society for Visiting the Sick. His account of the incident has a more dramatic ending:

Once, on a Thursday evening . . . eight butchers burst into the yeshiva, wielding clubs and axes, and set upon the students whom they suspected [of organizing the boycott]. However, the students were strong in more than Torah and fought back. They surrounded the eight butchers and beat them . . . after an hour or so my father, of blessed memory, came out and quietened the crowd, and the butchers, not the students, went home shamefaced and covered with bruises.[95]

There is no other source that can corroborate this dramatic story, and it may be somewhat exaggerated. However, its teller was familiar with the reality in Volozhin and obviously considered the students as a strong group.

The students were indeed powerful when they worked together as a collective. However, their behaviour, their consciousness of their own strength, and the fact that the local inhabitants depended on them economically tended to limit the points of conflict.

    [94] Mashvitski, 'In the Dwelling-Places of Torah' (Heb.), *Baderekh*, 3/38(105).
    [95] M. Berlin [Bar-Ilan], *From Volozhin to Jerusalem* (Heb.), i. 108–11.

SIX

Life at the Volozhin Yeshiva

1. The Daily Routine

The daily routine at Volozhin reflected the values and goals of the *rashei yeshivah*. Though not identical to that of modern yeshivas, it was broadly similar. A description of the daily routine in the 1880s by M. A. Eisenstadt reads as follows:

> I would get up at nine o'clock and hurry off to the yeshiva for morning prayers, which took only fifteen to twenty minutes. From the very first day, I noticed that they did not drag out the prayers unnecessarily . . . Talmud study was the centre of everything. The students saw it as an advantage of our yeshiva over others, where students were forced to spend hours and hours in prayer and in reading books of *musar*. When prayers finished I hurried back to my room for my morning meal, and at ten o'clock I went back to the yeshiva. The *rosh yeshivah*'s *shiur* began at exactly eleven o'clock and continued for over an hour . . . on the days when I did not stay to listen to the *shiur* I went straight back 'home'; otherwise I came home only at two o'clock in the afternoon, and stayed there about an hour for lunch and reading the Bible. At the third hour of the afternoon I returned to the yeshiva—this time until ten o'clock at night. At half past ten I left home and went back to the yeshiva and stayed there until two in the morning. Each night, before going to sleep, I used to go over Weber's general history.[1]

One can raise questions about the details in this description. Nine o'clock in the morning seems a rather late hour for morning prayers, though sunrise in mid-winter in Volozhin can be after nine o'clock. Berdyczewski's description from the same period records that prayers began at eight o'clock.[2] The time taken up by prayers also seems unusually short, but since none of the memoirs mention prayer at Volozhin as being in any way a special activity or emotional experience, Eisenstadt may be correct in saying that little importance was attached to them. Berdyczewski reports that after prayers, the students returned to their rooms for breakfast except that those who wanted to hear R. Berlin's *shiur* on the weekly Torah portion stayed on at the yeshiva. Presumably

---

[1] M. A. Eisenstadt, 'The Volozhin Yeshiva' (Heb.), 162.
[2] Berdyczewski [Bar Bei Rav], 'History of the Ets Hayim Yeshiva' (Heb.), 237.

they had breakfast after the *shiur*. At eleven o'clock all the students had to
return to the study hall, where they studied on their own until it was time for
the daily *shiur*. He adds: 'the learned . . . R. Shelomoh David Dynkin, used to
check the seats, and nobody was missing'.[3] According to Eisenstadt the daily
shiur started at eleven o'clock, but according to Berdyczewski it started at one
o'clock. It is not clear whether the timings changed or whether one or other
of the sources is inaccurate. In Berdyczewski's day, R. Hayim Soloveitchik
taught on Sunday, Monday, and Tuesday, and R. Berlin on Wednesday,
Thursday, and Friday. After lunch, at three or four o'clock, all the students
returned to the study hall, where a roll-call was taken again prior to afternoon
prayers. After that, they studied continuously until ten o'clock at night. When
evening prayers were said is not clear—nor terribly significant. After a late
evening meal, most came back to study until midnight or even later, though
some went to sleep and got up before daybreak in order to begin studying
again. While one can raise questions about some of the details, all the descriptions we have suggest that the study day at the yeshiva was long and demanded
considerable effort and a high degree of concentration.

2. Study Routine

Students at Volozhin generally studied on their own and not in pairs (*havrutot*).
Since in later periods study in pairs was the norm, it is important to examine
the information we have from Volozhin carefully in order to provide a base for
this claim. The descriptions of study in Volozhin usually do not dwell on the
fact that study was not in pairs. It was presumably considered a natural state of
affairs. There was of course interaction between students. Shomer writes:
'Both of us were then studying the tractate *Berakhot*, and he used to bring
everything which he found hard to understand to me, and I used to explain
every obscure point to him very clearly, and for this he respected and loved me
greatly.'[4] However this is a reference to passing conversations, with no mention
of studying together on a regular basis or use of the term *havruta* (study
partner). Another student describes how he fell asleep while trying to study all
through the night between Thursday and Friday, a custom known as *mishmar*;
he does not mention a study partner trying to keep him awake or letting him
doze,[5] so he must have been studying on his own. Descriptions of perpetual
students, such as in Bialik's famous poem *Hamatmid*, also do not mention study
partners but rather focus on the scholarly prowess of the individual.

   The physical arrangement of the study hall, which was dictated to some
extent by the desire to check that the students were present, was not conducive
to study in pairs, as is clear from the following description:

---

³ Berdyczewski [Bar Bei Rav], 'History of the Ets Hayim Yeshiva' (Heb.), 237.
⁴ Shomer, *Poems and Memoirs* (Heb.), 63.   ⁵ Levin-Epstein, *Memoirs* (Heb.), 30–1.

[It was] a great and spacious hall, with tables running across and along it from wall to wall, crammed in next to each other. Only a narrow aisle separated them. The tables sloped downwards on either side, so that one student's volume of Talmud did not touch that of his fellow opposite. Benches stood on either side of the tables. They were marked with numbers, running from 1 to 400. Every student who was accepted was allotted a numbered seat, and it was written down in a ledger, and three times a day the *mashgiah* would check that all the students were present in the yeshiva. The checking was carried out in this way: the *mashgiah* would read the number of each seat from the ledger and the student had to answer, 'Present'.[6]

These conditions made it difficult to study in pairs. For example, because students had fixed places and had to sit in their assigned place during roll calls (as several sources record) it would have been difficult to study with different partners in the different study sessions—morning, afternoon, and night. Indeed, it is common in contemporary yeshivas to place the volumes of the Talmud on a 'stender' or individual book stand, an arrangement conducive to rearrangement and group study. The seating in Volozhin did not make study in pairs impossible, since students could have gone back to their own seats for the roll call—but 200 students changing seats simultaneously would have caused considerable upheaval. The use of tables and benches also presented an obstacle, since the relatively crowded conditions impeded movement around the hall and made prolonged conversation with other students difficult.

If students had studied in pairs, the link with the study partner would have been one of the strongest memories of the yeshiva experience; but in fact such links are never mentioned, even in passages where they would naturally have been recalled, such as the following:

For the new student, meeting and making friends with the other yeshiva students generally started with his neighbours at his lodgings, since every lodging-house had between two and eight students, in accordance with the number of rooms available; another method was for the newcomer to get to know his neighbours at the yeshiva or in the *beit midrash* who studied at the same table; or he might meet those who came to hear the *rosh yeshivah*'s *shiur*—the students who sat next to him and with whom he sometimes discussed matters arising from the *shiur*. If there were other students who came from his home town he would make their acquaintance and seek them out.[7]

It is noteworthy that the detailed list of social settings here makes no mention of study in pairs.

Nevertheless, the practice of study in pairs was not completely unknown at the yeshiva, as the following description by Levin-Epstein suggests:

[6] Radus, *Memoirs* (Heb.), 64.
[7] Zlatkin, 'The Volozhin Yeshiva in Bialik's Time' (Heb.), 56–7.

As was customary at Volozhin, my father arranged for a friend, who was truly my rabbi, to study with me each day the page of Talmud on which the *shiur* was to be given . . . I used to study with my rabbi-friend every day, from nine o'clock until twelve in the morning, and we used to penetrate the very depths of the Talmud page scheduled for the *shiur* that day. From twelve o'clock until two o'clock we listened to the *shiur*. Then we ate lunch. After an hour I sat with another friend, a real friend, and studied another tractate. I studied *Bava kama* with him.[8]

The first 'friend' was basically a tutor. Levin-Epstein was a wealthy student and therefore it is safe to say that hiring a tutor was not typical; when he describes something as 'customary at Volozhin', he could mean that it was customary among students from wealthy families like his own. Weak students from poorer families could not have afforded this luxury (although clever students from poor families were of course only too happy to tutor for payment). The 'real friend' was a study partner in the contemporary sense. It is therefore difficult to establish how frequently study in pairs occurred on the basis of Levin-Epstein's account alone; he was a weak student, and that might have been the reason he sought out a study partner.

R. Berlin himself had studied alone as a young man, and apparently he worked alone in writing his commentaries on rabbinical texts. At the same time, according to the memoirs of his nephew, Barukh Epstein, R. Berlin encouraged study in pairs:

My uncle used to attribute a greater development of intellect and spirit to those students at the yeshiva who used to study in pairs, and [did not think] that he who studied on his own was greater in Torah and better in his studies; and even though he did not insist that the students follow this custom and learn in pairs, nevertheless everyone knew that he regarded this custom with approval and found a special pleasure in such pairs. And whenever he spoke of this matter, he would say that in his opinion, everyone who studied by himself, everyone who interpreted the halakhah by himself, and everyone who wrote books by himself, without the help of friends and pupils, would almost certainly fall into error and make many more mistakes than might be expected . . . since when he made a mistake nobody would alert him to the fact, and thus he would be sunk in error and inaccuracy . . . but this was not the case with the man who studied or interpreted halakhah or wrote books together with friends and pupils. He would come and learn about this, and his words would rise up pure and shining, clear and refined and truthful.[9]

Epstein's account suggests that students were generally not interested in studying in pairs and needed to be encouraged to do so. The lack of a tradition of studying in pairs—and perhaps also a feeling that it was a sign of intellectual weakness—might explain why this practice was not common at Volozhin.

[8] Levin-Epstein, *Memoirs* (Heb.), 30–1.   [9] B. H. Epstein, *Mekor barukh*, iii. 1772.

However, it seems that there were nonetheless students who studied in pairs, purely from an awareness of the mutual benefit this practice offered.[10]

The pattern of independent study at Volozhin should not surprise us. As in the *beit midrash*, the only reason for being there was independent study. The ability to do so was apparent to all, and the insistence on independent study served to exclude those who were not sufficiently able. This changed in later years, when even the advanced students studied in pairs; but conditions in general had changed, and there was more supervision and fewer students seeking admission. R. Hayim Soloveitchik is described as having matched up students for study in pairs. However, these may have been only or mainly exceptional cases, for instance if a student was very young.[11]

3. The Annual Cycle

In the medieval Ashkenazi yeshivas and the early Polish yeshivas, students were present only part of the year. The chronicle *Yeven metsulah* provides a picture of what was customary at Polish yeshivas before the Chmielnicki massacres of 1648–9, from which it emerges that there were two periods of study, summer and winter, each lasting three and a half months.[12] Each period was divided into two, with the first half devoted to Talmud and the second to halakhic writings. When the yeshivas were not in session, the students would study elsewhere. In this respect, the *beit midrash* was a very different place of study. In these local institutions, study was a daily activity with no real breaks.

Volozhin offered a curious combination. There were days that were seen as the beginning of a study period (*zeman*) but no day that was seen as ending a study period. Moreover, studies continued in the same format every day, with very few exceptions. There were no special periods for particular types of study, and certainly no 'vacations'. According to A. Mashvitski: 'The New Moon of Iyar was considered the beginning of *zeman* in the summer, and on this day those students who had travelled to their parents' house for Pesach returned, and those who had returned from the towns where they had celebrated the festival, all gathered [at the yeshiva], as well as the new students, who hastened to the yeshiva in order to be accepted, since there was a very limited number of places.'[13]

[10] R. Kook, who was very close to R. Berlin, studied with a partner in Volozhin. See Neriyah, *On Rav Kook* (Heb.), 70, where the author describes R. Kook's excitement when, later in life, he met a *ḥavruta* partner from his yeshiva days. R. Kook explained his excitement very simply: 'After all, we studied together as a *ḥavruta*.'

[11] See Kamenetsky, *The Making of a Godol*, i. 717, and see his description there on study in pairs in the Slobodka yeshiva. For an opinion that differs from mine, downplaying the role of pair study in Volozhin, see Breuer, *Tents of Torah* (Heb.), 248.

[12] Hannover, *Abyss of Despair*, 110–16; see also Breuer, 'The Ashkenazi Yeshiva in the Late Middle Ages' (Heb.), 56–9.

[13] Mashvitski, 'In the Dwelling-Places of Torah' (Heb.), *Baderekh*, 3/23(90).

The first day of a *zeman* was important for students. Shomer, who studied at Volozhin in the 1870s reported: 'The seats on the benches in the yeshiva were claimed by the students as follows: if a student left an open book on a particular seat at the beginning of the *zeman*, then he became lord of that seat, and no other student, whoever he might be, had the right to sit there.'[14] This was echoed in R. Meir Berlin's memoir of a later period: 'On the first sabbaths after the beginning of the *zeman*, the yeshiva was full of students. That was the time when every student "bought" the right to the seat he had chosen. The seat in which a student sat and studied on the sabbath after the festival stayed in his "possession" throughout the summer or winter.'[15] However, there was no day that was a formal end to a *zeman* and no period in which a break from study was normative. In Mashvitski's words,

In the Volozhin yeshiva there was no beginning or end of the *zeman* in relation to Talmud [study]. Only in those yeshivas where the rabbi's *shiur* was the main event could it be said that there was an end of the *zeman*, in other words that the *shiur* ceased to be given, and afterwards, when the students assembled again, the *shiur* recommenced; but this did not happen at Volozhin. The *shiur* was not the central feature, but the great gathering of students of different types made it into a true haven of the Torah. The end and beginning of the *zeman* could only be sensed in the shrinking and expansion of this gathering. But study at the yeshiva never ceased, except during prayers and on one day each year—Yom Kippur, which was devoted to prayer and supplications.[16]

The *rashei yeshivah* gave their regular *shiurim* every day irrespective of how many students were present and students studied whether or not the *rashei yeshivah* were present. Thus in Volozhin a *zeman* could begin but never end.

4. Sabbaths and Festivals

Sabbaths and festivals were breaks in the daily study routine at the yeshiva. Friday, the eve of the sabbath, was characterized by a slackening of the effort spent in study. This is partly because many students spent the entire night between Thursday and Friday studying, a custom known as *mishmar*, after which they were understandably rather tired. In addition, preparations had to be made for the sabbath. For both these reasons, Friday became a day of relaxation from the tensions of study: 'Most of us used to spend Friday reading newspapers and books, writing letters, going to the bathhouse, visiting friends, and so on. At the beginning of the sabbath, after prayers, we went to

[14] Shomer, *Poems and Memoirs* (Heb.), 61. There is a description from 1874 of a custom that, on the night after Simhat Torah, students would take places that would be their permanent seats in the study hall (see Zakheim, *Nitei eitan*, 50).

[15] M. Berlin [Bar-Ilan], *From Volozhin to Jerusalem* (Heb.), i. 117.

[16] Mashvitski, 'In the Dwelling-Places of Torah' (Heb.), *Baderekh*, 3/23(90).

sleep again, in turns: I would either stay awake until two o'clock in the morning, when one of my friends came to take my place, or we would exchange our times [of study].'[17]

In contrast to Friday, the sabbath did not have an especially important social function. There was no shared activity on the sabbath in which all the students took part, except for the prayers. Since there was no dining hall at the yeshiva, sabbath meals did not occupy an important place in the yeshiva's social life. The *rosh yeshivah* did not give a *shiur*, and nor were there other educational activities or sermons. Thus, the difference between sabbath and weekdays lay in the prayers and in the fact that no *shiur* was given, but the rest of the daily routine hardly differed. Concern over maintaining continuous study on the sabbath related not just to Friday night, as we saw above, but also to during the day. As one student recalled: 'Even on sabbaths and festivals some students would go to eat while others would sit and study until their fellows came to relieve them.'[18]

The High Holidays at the yeshiva do not seem to have made a great impression on the students; they are barely mentioned in the memoirs, and there is not a single nostalgic description of a special atmosphere in the yeshiva during this period. One description records: 'On Yom Kippur, too, which is a day of prayer for all Jewish communities, they would cut down the additional prayers and songs, entirely omitting the liturgical poems, and then they would study together for three hours between the Musaf and Minhah services.'[19]

The students do not seem to have taken any special notice of prayer in the yeshiva during the High Holidays. There was certainly no sense that the 'High Holiday experience' in the yeshiva differed from what students were familiar with in their home communities. The difference between the yeshiva and ordinary life did not lie in the strength of religious experience but in the intensive Torah study; the time spent in praying was cut short in favour of longer hours of study.

Sukkot was different because it was not celebrated in the yeshiva the same way it was celebrated in the home communities. The students celebrated the festival together with the *rosh yeshivah*, singing and dancing together until the small hours.[20] The festivities served as an expression of their relationship with the *rosh yeshivah*, and of their own solidarity. One of the students, recalls the celebrations during the intermediate days of Sukkot as follows:

It was an ancient custom at Volozhin that all the students assembled in the yeshiva on every festival in order to rejoice and celebrate. The rabbi used to sit in his chair

---

[17] M. A. Eisenstadt, 'The Volozhin Yeshiva' (Heb.), 163.
[18] Balosher, 'Bialik at Volozhin' (Heb.), 29.　　[19] Ibid.
[20] Turberg, *Works of Pinhas Turberg* (Heb.), 133–4.

like Solomon in days of old with the staff of the yeshiva around him. The other students stood further off and played instruments and sang songs. After each song a student would go up to the *bimah* and strike the cushion that rested there with his hand and shout, 'Hurrah for His Honour the Rabbi!', and all the others would answer him, 'Hurrah! Hurrah!' The rabbi regarded this custom as sacrosanct. Nothing could compel him to do away with it, and thus would he say: 'It is not for us to uproot the customs of the ancients, for our predecessors were like angels, and as for me, I am dust beneath their feet. Perhaps I am not worthy of all this honour; in any event, Jephthah in his generation was as great as Samuel in his generation, and I am only in Volozhin and the *rosh yeshivah* of the yeshiva of Volozhin!' And the rabbi looked approvingly at the student who called out first and almost kissed him on the lips.[21]

The nature of the celebration gave symbolic expression to the *rosh yeshivah*'s role as head of the yeshiva. Even though it is evident from the description that the writer did not like R. Berlin, he offers an important insight into R. Berlin's perception of his own role.

In the 1860s and 1870s Purim was a major event at Volozhin, and the heart of the Purim celebrations was the election and coronation of a student as the 'Purim rabbi' for the day. This was a common tradition in medieval yeshivas and has many parallels in other cultures.[22] In Volozhin it was understood that R. Hayim, the founder of the yeshiva, had instituted the custom for educational purposes:

He wanted to know of the defects in his management of the yeshiva which he had not discerned and of which no student would dare to tell him, and therefore he singled out one day in the year, the day of Purim, when the sages of old too gave permission to make merry, so that one of the students would be free to do what he liked the whole day and would be in sole charge of the yeshiva and its management, and then all the undesirable deeds of the 'all-year-round rabbi' would come to light, and he would know and understand how to correct what was wrong afterwards, and would not repeat his mistakes thereafter.[23]

There is no other evidence that R. Hayim was looking for feedback and that this was the reason behind the establishment of the custom of having a 'Purim rabbi'. The story certainly does not fit in with what we know of R. Hayim's character. He did not seek criticism in other spheres and could have easily obtained the necessary information by simply talking to the students. Besides, the 'Purim rabbi' voiced his criticism in front of everyone, not only to the *rosh*

[21] Shirotkin, 'The Dew to which All Turn' (Heb.), *Hashahar*, 8/3: 114.

[22] Zilberzweig, *Lexicon of Yiddish Theatre* (Yid.), iii. 1677, s.v. *Purim rov*, and see the bibliography listed there.

[23] M. A. Eisenstadt, 'The Purim Rabbi' (Heb.). A similar explanation appears in the article by Mashvitski: 'In the Dwelling-Places of Torah' (Heb.), *Baderekh*, 3/38(105).

yeshivah. This explanation seems to have been a late invention and says more about the person who invented it than it does about the practice itself. As we shall see, R. Berlin was not an enthusiastic supporter of this custom, though for many years he continued it as part of the pattern he inherited. The attribution of the custom to R. Hayim may have been a ploy adopted by those who wanted to maintain the custom, but ultimately it was indeed abolished.

The students elected the Purim rabbi themselves. They organized the election, the coronation ceremony (which took place in the bathhouse), and the festivities in the yeshiva. The Purim rabbi was always one of the veteran students, chosen not because of his ability as a jester but rather in recognition of his status as a scholar. As mentioned in the previous chapter, Shomer records how the Purim rabbi was elected in the 1860s and the social factors that influenced the election.[24] As he describes it, there were two candidates, one from Denenburg and one from Sventsyany. Preparations for the election began a month before the festival and were very competitive, since the position of Purim rabbi was extremely prestigious. The yeshiva became quite divided over the election, with most of the poorer students supporting the student from Denenburg and the more affluent supporting the one from Sventsyany (see Chapter 5, §5, above). On election day, the two factions arrived at the yeshiva armed with cudgels. One student stood on the *bimah* and asked the assembled crowd who should be elected. Each student shouted out the name of his candidate, and the building shook with the noise. When the uproar threatened to give way to blows, R. Berlin entered the study hall and suggested that one candidate should be the Purim rabbi on Purim itself and the other one on Shushan Purim, the next day. The compromise was accepted and peace returned to the yeshiva.

The election did not always cause so much excitement, and did not always take the same form. In 1876, for example, the students apparently split along geographic lines: 'The day before the Fast of Esther, hundreds of students split up into groups on the basis of their native regions: Poland, Lithuania, Samogitia, Ukraine, Latvia, the Caucasus, and so on. Each group elected its own *gabai* [secretary], and together these *gaba'im* chose the Purim rabbi.'[25] Their choice fell on a certain Barukh Moskver, a veteran student with leanings towards the Haskalah who was consequently embroiled in a feud with the *rosh yeshivah*. He used his Purim speech to lampoon R. Berlin's *shiurim*, delivering a *shiur* that surveyed the entire Talmud but was spiced with jokes about the *rosh yeshivah*, the *mashgiah*, and the rest of the staff. The festivities ended in dancing, in the course of which Barukh Moskver donned R. Berlin's fur-trimmed *shtreimel* and R. Berlin danced with a student's cap on his head.

[24] Shomer, *Poems and Memoirs* (Hcb.), 64–6.
[25] 'The Old Purim Constitution in the Volozhin Yeshiva', in Zitron, *Three Literary Generations* (Yid.), 165.

The custom of choosing a Purim rabbi and the reversal of roles (and clothes) that this involved reflected the tensions between the students and the *rashei yeshivah*, but also bears witness to the respect and admiration with which the latter were regarded. The lampooning of the *rosh yeshivah* merely reflected the tensions that are always present between the individual and those in authority over him: the frustration at such tensions could only be expressed on Purim because it is a day when what is normally forbidden is permitted. Moreover, the role reversal was limited to very specific areas. Firstly, it was forbidden to express contempt for religion or other unacceptable opinions: the reversal of roles was not accompanied by a reversal of values. Secondly, both sides had to acknowledge that the reversal was only temporary: at the end of the day, the Purim rabbi had to return the *rosh yeshivah*'s hat to its owner. It was obvious to all that this was not a real take-over; the power of the criticism expressed was therefore limited, and could not undermine the authority of the staff or the structure of the institution on a long-term basis.

Indeed, the entire Purim rabbi tradition was only possible because of the students' respect for the *rosh yeshivah* and admiration for the yeshiva and its values. When students have no respect for their teachers, such role-reversal is impossible since it may stop being a game. Even though it has no practical implications and the 'impostor' has no access to financial resources, the position could serve as a platform for demagoguery—a risk that the authorities could not take. In conditions of real conflict, an 'impostor' might not always be able to restrain himself from furthering his own goals. Thus, during the years in which a Purim rabbi was elected at Volozhin, it can be assumed that students and staff generally saw eye to eye. When tensions mounted, there was no room for this type of custom.

At the end of the 1870s the custom of choosing a Purim rabbi was abolished, following a period in which the lampooning had become increasingly more personal and more pointed.[26] The decision seems to have been linked to R. Berlin's second marriage, shortly after the death of his first wife, to a beautiful young divorcee. The marriage took place at the beginning of the 1870s; R. Berlin was about sixty by this time, while his new wife was in her twenties. An aggressive woman, she was reputed to have obtained a divorce from her first husband because he was not learned enough for her liking.[27] The match set off a storm among the students, and in consequence the wife was made the subject of much of the lampooning in the Purim festivities in the years that followed. Furious, she commented: 'They begin by dancing with my husband,

[26] M. A. Eisenstadt, 'The Purim Rabbi' (Heb.). Only Zitron describes student organization before Purim as being based on their places of origin. Zakheim, *Nitei eitan*, 50, describes such a framework when students organized before Shemini Atseret in 1874. This was around the time when Shomer was at Volozhin.

[27] According to her son; see M. Berlin [Bar-Ilan], *Rabbi of Israel* (Heb.), ch. 14, 'His Helpmate'.

and then they make fun of me.' She persuaded her husband to abolish the custom, probably in 1879 or shortly thereafter.[28]

But the absence of a Purim rabbi did not stop the joy of Purim at Volozhin. Instead, the role of arranging the festivities passed to the *gaba'im* who were elected to co-ordinate student life: 'and as part of their duties they arranged all the Purim festivities observed there in great joy and mirth, and for the Purim feast we were all invited to the *rosh yeshivah*, and we used to spend the whole night until dawn in songs and dances'.[29]

The joy of the festival survived, but some of its unique quality disappeared. As the above quotation suggests, with the abolition of the Purim rabbi the celebrations were moved from the yeshiva, which was the students' territory, to R. Berlin's house. Here there could be no doubt who was in charge: as head of the house, he was in control. Henceforth the joy of Purim was expressed only in song and dance, and no longer in lampooning and satire.[30]

Pesach was of course also a major event at the yeshiva. Many and probably most students did not travel home for the holiday and more than 150 of them stayed in Volozhin.[31] They received special supplements to their allowances in order to cover the extra expenses associated with the festival but they still had to go somewhere for the Seder. In the early nineteenth century families had formerly competed for the honour of hosting a yeshiva student for the festival, but in R. Berlin's time there were only enough invitations for twenty to thirty students. The solution was the two enormous Seders held each year in R. Berlin's house,[32] events that created a true sense of family.[33] They were the

---

[28] M. A. Eisenstadt, 'The Purim Rabbi' (Heb.); Ben-Ezra, 'Kings of Purim' (Heb.), col. 347. The source of the quotation is Zilberzweig, *Lexicon of Yiddish Theatre* (Yid.), iii. 1677. Zilberzweig quotes sources that deny there ever was a Purim rabbi at Volozhin, but most of the evidence indicates otherwise.

[29] Zilberzweig, *Lexicon of Yiddish Theatre* (Yid.), iii. 1677. He studied at Volozhin in 1880 and was already familiar with the ban on the Purim rabbi.

[30] R. Kook was elected Purim *gabai* while a student at Volozhin. See Z. A. Rabiner, *Or mufla*, 119: 'The fact that R. Kook was elected to serve as Purim *gabai* is evidence of his high status. The role of Purim rabbi was a great honour in the yeshiva and dozens of yeshiva students would go to his residence with torches in their hands in order to bring the "rabbi" to the yeshiva building and to R. Berlin's house with great pomp and circumstance.' It is not clear from Rabiner's description if R. Kook had been both rabbi and *gabai* or had held just one of the positions. It seems likely that he was just a *gabai* and that 'rabbi' was a slip of the pen.

[31] On Pesach in Volozhin, see Mashvitski, 'In the Dwelling-Places of Torah' (Heb.), *Baderekh*, 3/38(105).

[32] Rabiner writes: 'The yeshiva students celebrated the Seder in the house of the rabbi [Berlin]. About a hundred people were at the Seder at his house, twenty-five in the house of R. Hayim [Soloveitchik], and twenty-five in the house of the *mashgiah*. When the Seders were finished at the house of R. Hayim and at the house of the *mashgiah*, all would come to the house of R. Berlin' (*Or mufla*, 180). He does not explain how it was determined who would go where.

[33] As a family-style event, the Seder could also lead to tension: thus the student boycott of the Seder in solidarity with a student whom the rabbi had rebuked, as described above.

solution for most of the students who did not go home.[34] Organizing such
large Seders was complicated but they created a framework that strengthened
and demonstrated group solidarity. Attendance served to reinforce the students' ties with the *rosh yeshivah* because their participation was as children
and his role was that of the father. The students helped out. They used to elect
gaba'im from their ranks, 'from among the outstanding and important students', to act as waiters at the Seder.[35] The family role playing is clearly
reflected in this description of how Pesach was observed in 1885: on the eve
of the festival the students prayed in the yeshiva hall and then sang and
danced, until it was announced that everything was ready at the rabbi's house.
They went off to the house 'singing with great cheer and rejoicing'. R. Berlin
sat at the head of the table, flanked by his two small sons, and the students sat
at the tables that filled the entire room. The *rebbetzin* sat at a small table next
to the door. R. Berlin read the Haggadah and expounded it,[36] and his sons
asked the Four Questions. The students used to sing songs they had composed,[37] spiced with witticisms and talmudic references, and the celebration
continued late into the night. At dawn the students returned to the yeshiva to
pray.

The practice of holding Seders at the rabbi's house with mass participation
of students seems to have developed under R. Berlin. Prior to that time, students had often stayed with families in nearby towns not only for Pesach but
for most of the month of Nisan. The reason for travelling away from the
yeshiva for Pesach is not spelled out in any of the sources I have seen; it was
customary in medieval yeshivas, but that should not necessarily have
influenced patterns of behaviour in the nineteenth century. The reason may
simply have been the lack of a good alternative for students who could not
squeeze into a Seder at one of the rabbis' houses (or who were not invited),
since the option of participating in a Seder where they were rooming was
problematic. They were not invited, but paying, guests, and participation in
the Seder would have been a role shift. More seriously, those who rented out
rooms were generally from the poorer economic strata and their conduct at
table would have been far from that of the yeshiva students. Students who
went to small towns would have been hosted by the more affluent local families and not the abject poor. Hence, from a class point of view, they would

[34] Zakheim, *Nitei eitan*, 49, describes the departure of yeshiva students to *yishuvnikim* (isolated
Jewish families), for Pesach. Interestingly, the students trusted the *kashrut* of these simple Jews
and did not feel the need to require more stringent standards.
[35] M. Berlin [Bar-Ilan], *From Volozhin to Jerusalem* (Heb.), i. 114–17. The description of the
Seder is based on his account and on that of Mashvitski (see previous note).
[36] His explanations at the Seder table formed the basis for his commentary on the Haggadah,
in *Seder hagadah shel pesah ... im perush imrei shefer*.
[37] According to S. A. Rabiner, R. Kook used to participate in these Seders, and composed
poems in very literary Hebrew for the occasion ('At the Dawn of his Days' (Heb.)).

have been more at home with these hosts then with the families that rented them rooms in Volozhin.

R. Abraham Zakheim records that there was an annual ceremony on the *yahrzeit* of R. Hayim: 'On the fourteenth of Sivan, the day R. Hayim died, all the students went to the cemetery to visit his grave. They said the customary prayers as found in the book *Ma'aneh lashon*, and so on. This procession made a great impression and remained as a memory deep in the hearts [of the participants].'[38] I have not found any other descriptions of such a ceremony, so perhaps it was practised for only a short time.

The annual cycle reflected the values of the *rosh yeshivah* and the student body. It also influenced their self-image and sense of social solidarity and institutional cohesiveness. But while students appear to have perceived the cycle as fixed, in reality the turnover among students was such that they were unable to judge the degree of change in the way holidays were marked.

5. Extra-Curricular Activities

Although students invested most of their time and energy in Talmud study, they did have a little free time in the afternoons. It was not time to be wasted. Some students would stay in their rooms until three or four o'clock, and many used the time to read. Some considered this a good time to engage in reading the Bible, which was not something studied formally at the yeshiva at all:

To read in the Holy Scriptures and in the holy tongue, which is considered at most yeshivas as a waste of time . . . and in a few is regarded as the sign of a freethinker, was important and desirable at Volozhin. R. Berlin, who was an expert on Scripture, wrote commentaries, and knew Hebrew (unlike most other *rashei yeshivah*) . . . [and] felt a special affection for those students who studied the Holy Scriptures for an hour a day, and who knew Hebrew well.[39]

The more conservative students might read a book of talmudic *ḥidushim*, responsa, or sermons.[40]

The view of the yeshiva was that time should not be spent frivolously. But with most of the day devoted to study, how could social needs be met without frivolity? Meals were taken at one's lodgings, so one met only fellow lodgers at dinner. The yeshiva disapproved of students' meeting in their rooms in the evenings,[41] and the nearest coffee-house was several hundred kilometres away. For many students, going for a walk was the answer and the practice is

[38] Zakheim, *Nitei eitan*, 50.
[39] Balosher, 'Bialik at Volozhin' (Heb.), 127. M. A. Eisenstadt describes leisure-time reading habits and notes that reading the Bible was considered 'kosher' ('The Volozhin Yeshiva' (Heb.), 261). [40] Zlatkin, 'The Volozhin Yeshiva in Bialik's Time' (Heb.), 60.
[41] Shomer, *Poems and Memoirs* (Heb.), 60.

mentioned in a number of memoirs.[42] While walking one could converse with a friend or discuss a topic with a group of friends. Moreover, walking was not considered frivolous: on the contrary, it was seen as necessary to preserve health and maintain the strength necessary to study Torah. One student records: 'My father brought me to Volozhin. Before he went home he laid out a daily routine for me. He said: First of all—physical health, that I should eat nourishing food, and walk for an hour each day, and so on.'[43] Obviously, the time spent on a walk could be used in different ways. Many students used to 'add to their Torah study time, arguing, posing difficult questions, analysing them, and disputing on halakhic matters'[44]—though of course they could not do so over an open Talmud. In fact it was generally felt that there was no obligation to study during walks, and most students just used the time as an opportunity for physical and mental relaxation. In other words, taking a break from study in order to take a walk was not regarded negatively. One student who was prevented from taking a walk because R. Berlin ordered him back to the study hall felt justified in taking revenge by posing a particularly difficult question during the *shiur*.[45]

6. The Haskalah at the Yeshiva

Reading Haskalah literature was never permitted at Volozhin, but it happened none the less. However, the extent of such activity varied in different periods, as did the attitudes towards it.[46] A student at Volozhin in the 1860s wrote: 'Those things that were considered sins and misdeeds by the *rashei yeshivah* and the *mashgihim* were: (a) if several students gathered together in one room and discussed secular matters, in other words things related to the world of deeds; (b) if a student wrote down words of *pilpul* or of commentary; and (c) if a student read secular books, known as Haskalah books.'[47]

However, not everyone saw a contradiction between Haskalah literature and Torah study. Yirmiyahu Felsenberg, one of the outstanding students at Volozhin in the late 1850s, had received a copy of Mapu's novel *Ahavat tsiyon* from his teacher, before he ever came to the yeshiva, as a prize for demon-

[42] 'They used to take a walk on summer evenings or on sabbaths and festivals after lunch' (ibid.).
[43] Levin-Epstein, *Memoirs* (Heb.), 29. On Rav Berlin's concerns about health, see B. H. Epstein, *Mekor barukh*, iii. 1788–94.
[44] Zlatkin, 'The Volozhin Yeshiva in Bialik's Time' (Heb.), 62.
[45] A. Z. Horowitz, *Memoirs of Two Generations* (Yid.), 237.
[46] An excellent long article on this subject, with copious sources relating to the attitude to secular studies at Volozhin, is Schacter, 'Haskalah, Secular Studies and the Close of the Yeshiva in Volozhin'. The relationship between Torah study and an interest in the Haskalah was quite complex (see T. Cohen, 'The "Maskil" as "Lamdan"').
[47] Shomer, *Poems and Memoirs* (Heb.), 60.

strating his knowledge of 300 pages of Talmud at his barmitzvah celebration. He went on to study at Volozhin but retained his interest in the Bible and in Hebrew literature.[48]

By the 1860s there were several students at Volozhin who were interested in the Haskalah, though little is known about them. Hayim Zhitlowski records that when his father studied at Volozhin in this period he wrote poems in Hebrew—a typical maskilic activity—and he was probably not the only student doing so.[49] There is no mention that he was punished for this. More is known about the 1870s and 1880s, and there is no doubt that many more students were interested in the Haskalah then. Levin-Epstein gives us a glimpse from 1877: 'Yisra'el Goldenblum used to receive maskilic books from Warsaw, and students who wished to taste a little Haskalah used to gather in his room in secret and read whatever was available. Even though my father was a bookseller, I first read Mapu's books *Ahavat tsiyon* and *Ashmat shomron* in Goldenblum's room.'[50] Another student is known to have studied the Bible and read *Ahavat tsiyon*, Hebrew poetry, and other maskilic books.[51] Yet another source recorded that the forbidden books were *Ahavat tsiyon*, *Ashmat shomron*, *Ayit tsavua*, *Avot uvanim*, *Kehal refa'im*, *Galut sefarad*, *Ḥatserot shir*, and the journal *Hamelits*.[52]

However, interest in the Haskalah was generally limited to interest in literature; secular subjects never became serious rivals to Talmud study. Not all maskilic literature was equally attractive to the students, according to Zalman Epstein:

My memory retains the image of several typical Volozhin students of the 1870s. That was the period of the Haskalah of *Hashaḥar*, simultaneously innocent and extreme, voluble and strident, but actually powerless, undefined, and superficial. This type of Haskalah did not penetrate the yeshiva. A few individuals read *Hashaḥar* in deepest secrecy, but the yeshiva continued along its accustomed path and remained outside its sphere of influence. The free criticism of the Talmud and halakhic literature which was then finding a place in Haskalah literature, with the works of [Moses Leib] Lilienblum [1843–1910], [Reuben Asher] Braudes [1851–1902], and their colleagues, did not breach the walls of the Volozhin yeshiva. Most of the students there were not maskilim in the accepted sense of the term. They knew and studied the Holy Scriptures. They also read the books of the early maskilim from Vilna, and tried their hand at composing flowery letters about the purity of Hebrew and occasional verses, but it was just light reading, a

---

[48] See his son's introduction to his book on Exodus, *Divrei yirmiyahu*, p. v. I am grateful to Esther Goldberg for directing me to this publication.

[49] H. Zhitlowski, *Memories of My Life* (Yid.), i. 140. He quotes some of his father's poems.

[50] Levin-Epstein, *Memoirs* (Heb.), 31.

[51] A. Z. Horowitz, *Memoirs of Two Generations* (Yid.), 234–5.

[52] Shirotkin, 'The Dew to which All Turn' (Heb.), *Hashaḥar*, 8/3: 115–17.

toy from the outside world, that never entered the sphere of real life and left no lasting impression.[53]

It is not surprising that yeshiva students were more interested in the literary side of the Haskalah than in its more practical applications. Yeshiva study was not obligatory, and those who studied at yeshiva did so of their own free will.[54] A student who had a negative attitude to Torah study would have had no reason to stay, especially since taking up secular studies could have improved his economic position. Even Shirotkin, who attacked the yeshiva fiercely in the pages of *Hashahar* in 1877,[55] had been a good Talmud student when he studied there in 1874,[56] and seems to have become critical of it only after leaving. Additionally, literature was perceived as a symbol of culture, perhaps because it had no practical application. In that sense it resembled Talmud study, which also lacked practical application but was a characteristic element of culture, making it somewhat easier for the yeshiva student to take an interest in it.

It is difficult to know the extent of maskilic activity, both as regards the number of those who took part and as regards its role in life at the yeshiva. There was of course no formal record of Haskalah enthusiasts, and the available memoirs are not very helpful on this subject. No conclusions can be drawn from an expression such as 'many maskilim'. Nevertheless, it seems that Haskalah activity at Volozhin was always peripheral. According to the description by Epstein quoted above, in 1880 most of the students studied the Bible, wrote flowery prose, and read the books of the early maskilim, but the time devoted to this was all very minor compared to Talmud study. The situation remained the same at the end of the decade:

As for beliefs and opinions, the overwhelming majority of the yeshiva students were devout—observing all the commandments, as befitting Torah scholars. Some were even fanatically pious, distancing themselves from secular studies and all innovations. But there were also a small number of students who did study secular subjects, whose [inhibitions] had already collapsed, and who were freethinkers and transgressed certain commandments of the Torah, though only in secret, of course. Generally it can be said that the yeshiva students who set the tone of the institution and left their mark on it were those who displayed a high level of intelligence and morality, possessed great talents, studied the Torah and kept all its commandments, and were outstanding in their ethical behaviour, as befitting Torah scholars. Only

[53] Z. Epstein, *Writings* (Heb.), 119.

[54] Even though there was no apparent reason for someone not interested in the study of Talmud to come to a yeshiva, one cannot overlook the role of parental pressure. I thank Rabbi Boruch Oberlander for this observation.

[55] Shirotkin, 'The Dew to which All Turn' (Heb.).

[56] A. Z. Horowitz, *Memoirs of Two Generations* (Yid.), 230.

a small and unremarkable minority of students differed from the main body in their opinions and deeds, and they were of little account.[57]

The image of the yeshiva as a centre of Haskalah activity that was current in some circles thus did not match reality, although there are discrepancies between the various sources on this point.

It is instructive in this regard to compare the accounts by Berdyczewski and Hayim Nahman Bialik. Writing in *He'asif* in 1885, Berdyczewski says: 'Many worked diligently within the doors of the Haskalah there, with no interference. This one studied Russian and German, and this our Hebrew language and its grammar; this one read Jewish literature, and this Russian or German literature; this one studied engineering and this, history.'[58] Reading this it is easy to envision Volozhin as a hotbed of modernization. However, Bialik's impression when he arrived in Volozhin in 1890 was very different. As he noted in a personal letter: 'Nothing may be studied here except sacred subjects, and everything that Berdyczewski wrote in *He'asif* . . . is completely untrue. May God grant that I may be diligent in my studies and derive lifelong benefit from them.'[59] Bialik's piety was short lived, however; it seems that after he had been at the yeshiva for longer and had himself joined the circle of Haskalah enthusiasts, he learnt that there was more activity of that type than had met the untutored eye. His letter records only his first impressions, however, and relates only to the extent of open Haskalah activity there. The difficulties inherent in using memoirs for information on this subject are obvious.

The factors that led students to take an interest in the Haskalah are also difficult to determine. As is the case with hasidism, Zionism, and other movements, the means by which the Haskalah spread still await detailed research. In general, however, it seems that students read maskilic literature out of curiosity rather than rebelliousness. They do not seem to have seen any contradiction between this activity and their allegiance to the beliefs and opinions of the world of Torah. We must also remember that traditionally there was a positive attitude towards writing in Hebrew and elegance of style, as well as an appreciation of expertise in all fields of Jewish literature. As we have seen, R. Berlin was famous for his skill in these areas; as well as being a Talmud scholar and halakhic authority, he wrote commentaries on the Pentateuch and on tannaitic texts and on the *She'iltot*, an eighth-century halakhic text. A. Z. Horowitz, who studied at Volozhin in 1874, notes the importance R. Berlin accorded to Hebrew style:

---

[57] Zlatkin, 'The Volozhin Yeshiva in Bialik's Time' (Heb.), 59.
[58] Berdyczewski [Bar Bei Rav], 'History of the Ets Hayim Yeshiva' (Heb.), 237.
[59] Bialik, *The Letters of Hayim Nahman Bialik* (Heb.), 21–2.

When R. Berlin went over my letter, he said to me, 'Bereziner [alluding to Horowitz's home town, Berezen], you will study, with God's help, and if you study, you will learn. But you simply don't know how to write.' His words made a great impression on me, and the very same day I picked up a Bible and began to study it. In the evening I used to read a Haskalah book before going to sleep . . . it was forbidden to read secular books at the yeshiva. I used to say that it was like the Egyptian exile—one had to make bricks but they gave you no straw. It was forbidden to look at a Haskalah book, but you had to know how to write [good Hebrew].[60]

It seems unlikely, though, that most of those who studied Haskalah literature did so at the encouragement of the *rosh yeshivah*, but the anecdote makes clear that the ability to write good Hebrew—often regarded as a preoccupation of the Haskalah—was considered a desirable skill for a Talmud scholar. Many who encountered maskilic literature felt that something was lacking from their training as a scholar and drew similar conclusions to Horowitz.

7. The Yeshiva's Stand on Secular Knowledge

The *rashei yeshivah* opposed the reading of secular literature, though R. Berlin did not issue an outright ban. This might be because he was concerned about opposition from the students or because it would have been interpreted as opposition to government efforts to promote secular studies; but one can assume that had he considered it a serious infraction he would not have kept silent. Moreover, his position was not consistent over time. Horowitz claims that R. Berlin knew that students were reading Hebrew literature and learning modern languages and made no real effort to stop it. It was forbidden, but those who engaged in it were not punished.[61]

In 1883 two items appeared in the Haskalah newspaper *Hamelits* foreshadowing a hardening of attitudes towards Haskalah activity in the yeshiva, and thus implying that the reins had been somewhat slacker the previous year. The first item, which was sent in by a student signing himself 'Shvik', informed readers that R. Berlin had 'strictly forbidden his students to read *Hamelits* and to make matters clear had also ordered them not to set foot in the post office in order to receive letters and journals, so as not to fall prey to temptation'.[62] It further described how R. Berlin had wanted to expel a student who had been caught reading a newspaper, but had contented himself instead with burning all the issues of the newspaper found in the student's possession. According to Shvik, this new campaign was the result of a desire to support a competing Orthodox newspaper (perhaps *Halevanon*) and to take

---

[60] A. Z. Horowitz, *Memoirs of Two Generations* (Yid.), 234.

[61] See Kets [Kehat], *The Doctrine of Rabbi Naftali Berlin* (Heb.), 11–12, and the sources cited on p. 18; A. Z. Horowitz, *Memoirs of Two Generations* (Yid.), 235.

[62] *Hamelits*, 19/60 (20 Aug. 1883).

revenge on *Hamelits* for having published articles of which the *rosh yeshivah* did not approve.

The second article, which appeared in *Hamelits* a month later, was signed by 'A Man of Derechin'.[63] He admitted that a ban had recently been imposed on reading newspapers at the yeshiva, but claimed that Shvik had exaggerated matters: the ban on newspapers was only because 'the reading of journals was a waste of time that could be spent studying Torah', rather than a desire to take revenge on the editors. Which student is correct is immaterial; of far greater significance is the fact that an internal dispute in Volozhin had become public knowledge.

Although reading newspapers was not officially allowed, in the 1880s many students are known to have done so. As we have seen, Goldberg confidently asserted that all the yeshiva students read newspapers despite the lack of permission, and that the ban was generally disregarded.[64] Eventually, the policy itself changed, and by the 1890s students were allowed to read newspapers undisturbed. An item written in defence of the yeshiva's change in policy by a student calling himself 'Aba Arash' makes the following point:

These days are different from those of the past: now nobody stares at a yeshiva student who drops a 'heretical book', and the *mashgiaḥ* does not chase after copies of the *Moreh nevukhim*, the *Kuzari*, or the *Akedah* [*Akedat yitshak*] . . . on the contrary, not only do they not rebuke the one who reads books of *ḥokhmat yisra'el* [Wissenschaft des Judentums], the vernacular is studied there quite openly, as well as all the knowledge which is necessary to mankind.[65]

The description seems accurate, and is consistent with a memoir by a student who was at Volozhin in 1890.[66]

It is not clear exactly when the ban on newspapers was eased but it seems to have been in the late 1880s. In 1885 there was still a *menahel* who went around the students' lodgings at night 'and peeped through chinks so that he might report on them to R. Berlin'; this may have been a result of the influence of the *musar* movement.[67] Berdyczewski notes that in 1888 a *menahel*

---

[63] *Hamelits*, 19/69 (17 Sept. 1883).

[64] B. Goldberg, *Memories of the Past* (Heb.), 4–6.   [65] *Hamelits*, 17/61 (26 Mar. 1891).

[66] Zlatkin records: 'Although the *rosh yeshivah* knew that there were students who were studying secular subjects and reading Haskalah books, he deliberately looked the other way. The period of searches for heretical literature, works by Mapu, Smolenskin, and others, among the belongings of new students because of this, and the persecution of students who took part in the Haskalah, as had happened earlier (according to the books written by those who had studied at the yeshiva in earlier times), had already ended. For the *rosh yeshivah* recognized the spirit of the times by then, and that the publication of such matters in the newspapers would damage the yeshiva. For in any event there was already much criticism of the yeshiva by the maskilim and by the government' ('The Volozhin Yeshiva in Bialik's Time' (Heb.), 61). Balosher mentions that Haskalah literature was read, but does not mention searches or punishments ('Bialik at Volozhin' (Heb.), 126–7).

[67] Mashvitski, 'In the Dwelling-Places of Torah' (Heb.), *Baderekh*, 3/38(105).

found a letter that he had written, but he does not mention systematic searches for books in students' lodgings.[68]

Interest in the Haskalah persisted partly because the yeshiva's ability to control the students was limited.[69] Thus, for example, R. Berlin rebuked a student who was caught with Lilienblum's book, *Kehal refa'im*: 'I shall not continue to give you the allowance that I gave you from the yeshiva's funds, and if you are stiff-necked and, like a deaf viper, close your ears against listening to my orders, as God lives, you shall no more pass the threshold of the yeshiva.'[70] The main tool at his disposal was the monetary allowance, but financial penalties only affected those who were dependent on the yeshiva for an allowance, and expulsion was not so easy to enforce.[71] Since the yeshiva did not award grades or diplomas, it could not threaten to withhold a graduation certificate. Moreover, the more financially independent a student, the less his dependence on the *rosh yeshivah*—and especially if the yeshiva was beholden to his family for donations. In addition, the *rosh yeshivah*'s moral and emotional power was effective as long as the student agreed in principle with the basic premisses underlying this power. The moment a student thought that the *rosh yeshivah* was wrong, or did not have the right to use force against him, the *rosh yeshivah* lost control.

Even the financial dependence of students from poor families did not always help the situation as the unequal weighting of the support system exposed the *rosh yeshivah* to claims that he was acting unjustly. Second, the students were not equally dependent, so financial pressure could not be exerted equally. Thus, when R. Berlin wanted to expel Barukh Moskver (the student elected as Purim rabbi despite his maskilic tendencies),[72] he could not do so as he was related to one of the yeshiva's most important supporters, the philanthropist Shmuel Zuckerman. It was inherently difficult to take action against wealthy students, but the precedent made it difficult to punish poor students too.

A further problem for the yeshiva administration was that parents sometimes encouraged their sons take an interest in Haskalah literature. This made it difficult for the yeshiva to act against it, as the following description highlights:

A thorough search was carried out at the lodging of the student from Mstislavl, and there they found plenty of booty. The *menahalim* carried off nine books to the rabbi's house, but they were bitterly disappointed; nothing evil might be done to this student, and he emerged from his trial an innocent man. Five of the books were

---

[68] Berdyczewski [Bar Bei Rav], 'A Bundle of Letters' (Heb.), *Hamelits*, 28/53.

[69] On student involvement with the Haskalah and the yeshiva's response in its final year, see Ch. 8 below.   [70] Shirotkin, 'The Dew to which All Turn' (Heb.), *Hashahar*, 8/3: 117.

[71] See Ch. 4 n. 59 above.

[72] On Moskver, see Zitron, *Three Literary Generations* (Yid.), 162–3.

in Russian, and this was why the rabbi had to relent and hold his peace, since he had come across a letter from the student's father in which he ordered his son to study Russian.[73]

If the yeshiva had taken a clear stand against the Haskalah, this type of problem would never have arisen. It would have been clear to all that being a student at Volozhin and engagement in the Haskalah were diametrically opposed. The father would not have sent his son to Volozhin at all, or if he had done so, he would not have encouraged his son to violate the policy. In any case, the yeshiva would not have gone along with the father's request. But at Volozhin, unlike other yeshivas, especially those of the *musar* movement, opposition to the Haskalah was not self-evident, and there was no clear dividing line between the permitted and the forbidden; this was why it was not obvious to students that Talmud study was totally incompatible with other studies. The simplest solution would have been to tell this student that learning modern languages was forbidden at the yeshiva and his father had been wrong to tell him to do so, but R. Berlin did not do this. Paternal authority was very important in traditional Jewish society and he was not prepared to undermine it.

The main reason that the yeshiva did not employ its full powers against the Haskalah was R. Berlin's own attitude, as noted above. He did not see it as inherently evil, but merely a waste of time. He was himself familiar with many fields of Jewish literature, and ensured that his son Me'ir learned Russian.[74] Both R. Berlin and R. Hayim Soloveitchik read newspapers. R. Berlin felt that a good knowledge of the Hebrew language was important and had even published well-written newspaper articles in Hebrew.[75] He also permitted the reading of newspapers on the sabbath, so it is clear that he did not think this activity objectionable in and of itself.[76] He was not opposed to the Haskalah per se but to *bitul torah*, the waste of time that could be used for Torah study

[73] Shirotkin, 'The Dew to which All Turn' (Heb.), *Hashahar*, 8/3: 117.

[74] M. Berlin [Bar-Ilan], *From Volozhin to Jerusalem* (Heb.), i. 131.

[75] B. H. Epstein, *Mekor barukh*, iii. 1795. On R. Hayim Soloveitchik reading newspapers, see B. Goldberg, *Memories of the Past* (Heb.), 6: 'And the deputy to the *rosh yeshivah*, the *gaon* R. Hayim himself reads *Hamelits* in secret.' Rabbi Boruch Oberlander pointed out that, in the latest edition of R. Berlin's responsa, *Meshiv davar*, there is a curious omission. The original reads 'as published in *Hamelits*, 137 in 5687', but the new edition reads simply 'as published in 5687' (H. Berlin, *Meshiv davar*, ii. 71 (responsum 8)). Despite the omission in the current edition, it is clear that R. Berlin read newspapers.

[76] A responsum of R. Berlin was published in Kook, *Itur soferim*, 22–3: 'In the *Shulḥan arukh*, "Oraḥ ḥayim", 307: 3, it is ruled that it is forbidden even to leaf through non-urgent letters without reading them, but one may leaf through non-urgent letters when one does not know what is in them, for other reasons. According to this view, it is forbidden to skim through journals except for those in the holy tongue, and even this permission is not at all obvious, as is seen in the writings of the later sages of blessed memory. It seems to me that it is certainly permitted simply to glance through them.'

or to certain extreme trends in the Haskalah movement. However, it seems doubtful whether these distinctions were understood at the time, and some students definitely interpreted his tolerance as a sign of weakness.

R. Berlin's attitude complicated matters in the campaign against Haskalah activity among the students. However, there were reasons for his tolerant attitude:

R. Berlin saw the decline of this generation, and realized that if he were too strict about the students' dress and haircuts they would dwindle in numbers year by year, and in the future the Torah would be forgotten in Israel, God forbid. So he began to be slightly more lenient in these matters, and students without *pe'ot* began to appear at Volozhin, together with semi-maskilim, and the old type of student almost disappeared. Every young man who studied at Volozhin, with a few exceptions, had a fair amount of worldly experience, especially in politics and every current political question.[77]

Thus a modern appearance and familiarity in those fields labelled as 'Haskalah' became more common—if still marginal—among students at Volozhin yeshiva in its last years.

It is important to distinguish between Haskalah in the sense of scientific or practical knowledge and Haskalah as a term referring to a movement that demanded changes in Jewish society. With regard to knowledge, R. Berlin's attitude was generally pragmatic, but he was totally opposed to most of the demands of the Haskalah movement for far-reaching changes in the Jewish community. His positive attitude to this type of knowledge certainly does not mean he thought it necessary to teach it in the yeshiva.

R. Berlin wrote on the question of how to respond to the challenges of his time: 'We have to strengthen ourselves for the study of Torah. The rabbis and the heads of the communities must involve themselves in this issue so that the teachers will be Torah scholars. Even if the government should demand that secular studies be taught, this too has to be done under the supervision of the rabbis and community leaders, who should ensure that the teachers be pious.'[78] He went on to add that since it was impossible to find private teachers with knowledge of general studies who were also pious, it was necessary to establish the appropriate frameworks. In his view it was impossible to prohibit the study of secular topics, and that the attempt to do so only drove the young generation further away from tradition. As he put it, 'this too is a responsibility on the community and the community leaders, not to prohibit secular studies entirely, but [to ensure that] the chosen teachers should be supervised so that they will not stray from the path of Torah, and so that they will devote

---

[77] B. Goldberg, *Memories of the Past* (Heb.), 4. On R. Berlin's tolerant attitude to hasidism, see *Meshiv davar*, ii. 10–11 (responsum 10).

[78] H. Berlin, *Meshiv davar*, i. 51–5 (responsum 44).

substantial time to the study of Torah, with the ultimate result that both goals will be achieved.'[79] In other words, R. Berlin supported the integration of general studies, presumably at the elementary school level, with the study of Torah. At the same time, he did not see general studies as an end in themselves and claimed that it was impossible 'to be a great Torah scholar if one is also dealing with other topics'. This was the root of his opposition to involvement in secular studies at the yeshiva. In his opinion, 'all the great Torah scholars who are also wise in secular matters received their secular education either before they devoted themselves entirely to the study of Torah or acquired their knowledge after becoming Torah scholars. However, to do this simultaneously precludes reaching the desired goal of study.'[80] This implies that it is possible to study secular studies in elementary school and nonetheless to become a great Torah scholar later in life. This approach to Haskalah and general studies was the norm and far from exceptional in Lithuanian rabbinical circles in his time.

8. Prohibited Leisure Pursuits

The leisure pursuits that were tolerated at Volozhin were those which combined enjoyment with benefits to health or intellectual development. Leisure activities that were purely recreational contradicted the fundamental values of the yeshiva. Thus, playing cards was cause for immediate and severe punishment—though according to Binyamin Goldberg, 'there was never any lack of card games at Volozhin in the winter'.[81] The players had to hide from the *shamash*, and if they were caught, had to bribe him not to report them. They did not consider themselves to be rebelling against the yeshiva's ethos, but only having a bit of fun. They knew they were wrong and did not claim that punishment was unjustified, but nevertheless wanted to avoid it.

An uncommon leisure pursuit indulged in by students was the development of relationships with local girls. Very few cases are recorded, though there may have been more than we know of. R. Berlin tried to prevent students living in houses where there was a risk of romantic entanglement,[82] but it was difficult for him to foresee all possible risks or changes in family situations. In one case, a student did not come to morning prayers because he preferred to have a chat with his landlady, whose husband was in America at the time.[83] Another

---

[79] It appears that R. Yisra'el Salanter shared this view. See D. Katz, *The Musar Movement* (Heb.), ii., chs. 17 and 18, on his position on the *talmud torah* in Kelme and Grobin. See also Beer-Marx, 'Confrontation of the Rabbis who Wrote in *Halevanon*' (Heb.), ch. 3, and Ch. 8 below. [80] H. Berlin, *Meshiv davar*, i. 51–5 (responsum 44).

[81] B. Goldberg, *Memories of the Past* (Heb.), 19–22. On card games, see M. A. Eisenstadt, 'The Volozhin Yeshiva' (Heb.), 165.

[82] Shirotkin, 'The Dew to which All Turn' (Heb.), *Hashahar*, 8/4: 165.

[83] M. A. Eisenstadt, 'The Volozhin Yeshiva' (Heb.), 164.

student sent love letters to his landlord's daughter while he was at home on holiday; when this was brought to the attention of R. Berlin he immediately expelled the young man, even though he was an outstanding student.[84]

An interesting example of a relationship between a yeshiva student and a local girl occurred in 1890. The student fell in love with the girl, and R. Berlin agreed that they could marry. Surprisingly, the other students opposed this, seeing the incident as an affront to the honour of the yeshiva—though perhaps the students' concern for the yeshiva's honour was accompanied by a tinge of jealousy.[85] Hundreds of young men studied at the yeshiva during their adolescent years, and each must have had some level of sexual drive. If they had lived a generation earlier, most of them would have been married already. The postponement of marriage among the scholarly elite created new tensions. The years of study at the yeshiva demanded self-restraint and patience, and it helped if all the other students at the yeshiva were in the same situation. Any deviation, however small, could awaken doubts about their chosen path and attract considerable jealousy. The safest method of coping with a phenomenon of this sort was fierce criticism of deviation, together with encouraging the conviction that restraint and postponement was truly the best and the most correct path to take. It was easier for R. Berlin to take a tolerant stand than it was for the students.

The students at Volozhin held a variety of opinions on matters of ideology and did not all share the same values. One way to measure the breadth of opinions and their personal values is to consider their leisure pursuits. Analysis of 'unusual' behaviour shows that there was a high level of agreement between the staff and the students on fundamental questions. The few examples of deviant behaviour underscore the general aspiration to devote all one's strength and energy to the study of Torah.

[84] Shirotkin, 'The Dew to which All Turn' (Heb.), *Hashaḥar*, 8/4: 165–8.
[85] Balosher, 'Bialik at Volozhin' (Heb.), 125–6.

The Last Years of the Volozhin Yeshiva

IN THE 1880s and 1890s the Volozhin yeshiva found itself in difficult circumstances. Its finances were catastrophic, its relations with the Jewish
community at large were deteriorating, and it faced many calls for far-
reaching structural changes in the institution. There was also an internal split
over the question of R. Berlin's successor, as will be described in the next
chapter. These challenges did not significantly change the atmosphere of the
yeshiva, though the increasing importance of student societies was a noteworthy development. By surveying these organizations and other aspects of
student life in the last years of the Volozhin yeshiva and giving a careful look
at the finances of the yeshiva it is possible to come to some important insights
into the changing realities of yeshiva life during these critical years.

1. Welfare and Aid Societies

During the latter years of the nineteenth century, the attitudes, interests, patterns of behaviour, and plans for the future of the students at Volozhin
changed significantly. The reasons for this are not entirely clear, but one of the
consequences was the strengthening of student societies.

When new types of organizations appear, they are often a response to new
circumstances. In Volozhin the main factor in the sudden appearance of an
entire range of organizations seems to have been the sense that an organized
body could solve problems better than individual initiatives or ad hoc groups.
However, there were additional consequences to this development. Student
societies reinforced the students' collective identity, reduced their dependence
on the yeshiva, and made it easier for them to present their demands. The
phenomenon seems to have been influenced by the contemporary practice in
the wider society of establishing organizations to achieve political, social, and
economic change. The student societies in Volozhin, however, aimed less at
political change than at dealing with students' daily needs, welfare, and providing charitable assistance.

A charitable society seems to have come into existence in the early 1880s; a source from 1886 records that there was a 'room for the *gemaḥ* [an association that loaned money to students against a pledge] founded by the students about four years ago (the local inhabitants take no part in this charitable work) to provide money for students in need'.[1] The same source discusses the students' financial problems and how they were resolved:

We have founded a society of 'Supporters of the Torah' here [in Volozhin], with donations from each student according to the generosity of his heart, week by week, to support students who fall into difficulties, but the society cannot pay those who are owed huge sums of interest from their fellows, such as 50 roubles. Moreover, the loan society, which we have founded, only makes loans to students against a pledge, with no differentiation made in their hour of need.[2]

A description of the items destroyed in the fire of 1886 suggests that the society was both active and well endowed:

Two *batei midrash* were burnt down, together with the holy yeshiva, the *gemaḥ* room with the pledges it contained, to the value of 2,000 roubles; and almost all the items belonged to poor students, their best household vessels and their sabbath and festival clothes, and valuable pieces of jewellery that the poor had borrowed from the rich to serve as pledges . . . according to the regulations of the *gemaḥ* that the pledge should be worth three times the amount of the loan.[3]

A simple calculation reveals that the loan fund must have had over 700 roubles at its disposal, a sum that seems quite impressive for an institution of this sort.

As noted above, the charity was supported by contributions from the wealthier students. One such student wrote: 'I used to receive 12 roubles a month from home. This sum was sufficient for me to purchase everything I needed and also to donate 1 rouble a month to the mutual support fund of the yeshiva.'[4] The fund did not usually cover all the expenses of a needy student. They had first to try to obtain assistance from home and from the yeshiva itself. However, the very existence of the fund did help the students and could give them a considerable degree of independence. One may recall Y. L. Radus's account, quoted above, of how a student whom R. Berlin wanted to expel in the mid-1880s was supported by the students' charity fund. Indeed, 'in spite of what the *rosh yeshivah* wanted, he remained at the yeshiva and the "Supporters of the Torah" society gave him money for food'.[5]

As we have seen, such power as the *rosh yeshivah* had was linked to his control of the yeshiva's finances. The students responsible for the *gemaḥ*, as an independent source of funds, thus had power that in some areas resembled that of R. Berlin himself, though to a more limited degree. They could not

[1] Bunimovitsh, 'The Burden of Volozhin' (Heb.), 1098.   [2] Ibid.
[3] 'Letter from the Notables of Volozhin' (Heb.), *Hamelits* (25 Aug. 1886), 1180–1.
[4] M. A. Eisenstadt, 'The Volozhin Yeshiva' (Heb.), 166.   [5] Radus, *Memoirs* (Heb.), 67.

teach or confer rabbinical ordination, but they could determine whether a certain student would study at the yeshiva, so in that sense they could overrule R. Berlin—and there was virtually nothing he could do to prevent it.

Over the years, other social welfare societies were founded by the students for the benefit of the student body.[6] They provided for needs that were sometimes seen as the responsibility of the yeshiva but which the students felt were not being met.[7] The existence of these associations thus freed the yeshiva from having to deal with the various emergencies that students were confronted with, but at the price of a certain decline in authority because the self-help organizations increased the students' sense of self-reliance.[8]

2. Zionist Societies

Only a minority of students ever belonged to Zionist societies, but even so their impact in the yeshiva was significant. In the early 1880s several attempts were made to found a branch of Hovevei Tsiyon (Lovers of Zion) at Volozhin. The first attempts were unsuccessful, though it is not clear whether this was because of personal issues or because the yeshiva intervened.[9] The impetus for setting up Zionist societies was completely different from that for setting up charitable societies. The latter were a response to urgent, local problems; there was no political agenda that could rile the yeshiva or the government. The students could therefore easily agree who would discharge the various functions involved and determine policy, and the yeshiva had no difficulty allowing them to operate openly. The situation with Zionist societies was quite different, particularly because they could arouse the ire of the government. The yeshiva therefore also opposed them. Any Zionist activity had to be clandestine and concealed not only from the authorities but also from the *rosh*

---

[6] A. Litvin mentions the Supporters of the Torah *gemaḥ*, 'Oneg Shabat', and the lodgings committee (*Jewish Souls* (Yid.), 6).

[7] See Ch. 5, §8, above, on a dispute between the students and the *rosh yeshivah* over the provision of appropriate medical care for a student. An organization devoted to providing medical care is described in Binyamini, *Yesteryear* (Heb.), 7–8. Binyamini was born in 1875. After he had been exposed to Haskalah literature at a small yeshiva in Ruzhany, his father sent him to Volozhin. In his memoirs he wrote that the son of the rabbi of Jašiūnai organized the Tomkhei Torah society, as well as a hospital for yeshiva students. A Minsk doctor who had once studied in Volozhin would come to treat students in emergencies.

[8] See Breuer, *Tents of the Torah* (Heb.), 421.

[9] It was recorded that 'one association that was founded among the students for this purpose [i.e. settlement in Palestine], whose members were numerous although heterogeneous in character, disbanded after its existence became known to the supervisors, and nothing came of the members' labour' (Friedland [Had ben Hevraya], 'Hibat Zion at Volozhin' (Heb.), 11). Yosef Rotstein recorded in his memoirs that 'we met several times to found an association of "Lovers of Zion" among the students, but each time we failed, and for various reasons related to questions of imagined honour the associations we founded were destroyed' (see Yisrael Klausner, *History of the Nes Ziona Association in Volozhin* (Heb.), 118).

yeshivah. Of course, any attempt by yeshiva students to do things that they did not want the *rosh yeshivah* to know was necessarily problematic.

The first Zionist society to be successfully established at Volozhin was Nes Ziona (Banner to Zion), which was founded in 1885 at the initiative of Yosef Rotstein, a keen Zionist who had chosen to study at Volozhin less from a desire to immerse himself in Torah study than from an ambition 'to spread [his] opinions throughout the entire people by means of this famous yeshiva'.[10] The intention was 'to found a secret society with no limitations of time or place, which would be joined only by chosen individuals, the best and most outstanding faithful Jews, and its members would swear a solemn oath to be faithful to their covenant and to preserve its secrecy'.[11] In other words, they wanted to create an elite group to influence future leaders—rather like Benei Moshe (Sons of Moses), the secret league that had been founded by Ahad Ha'am with the intention of spreading Zionist ideas. The yeshiva was intended to serve as the centre for the society's operations.

A large part of the society's success, in contrast to the failure of earlier groups, was due to the decision to institute a membership oath. The idea of a secret society having an oath was not a novel idea in general but it was an innovation for yeshiva students. It was of great importance in the yeshiva world since Jewish law regards an oath as a very serious undertaking and of a more binding nature than a simple word of honour. Halakhah strongly discourages the taking of oaths, and Torah scholars generally refrain not only from taking oaths but also from using expressions that resemble oaths. Thus the use of an explicit oath as a condition of membership emphasized the commitment that membership implied. The idea came from Eliyahu Rosenkrantz, a wealthy Torah scholar of repute who was also attracted to the Haskalah.[12] Some people opposed the use of an oath on religious grounds, as we shall see, but their opinion was overruled by the founders because of the seriousness it conferred on membership. Obviously, once members had sworn faith to the society they were determined that it should succeed—though it seems likely that it would have flourished even without this measure.

The society started off slowly, but then expanded: 'At first its activity was limited to accepting new members, but when its numbers grew, and especially after Yehudah Leib Berger of Minsk joined, we began to organize ourselves and make plans.'[13] In its first phase, it seems to have had about fifty members.[14] Berger did not restrict himself to yeshiva students but enlisted secondary

---

[10] Rotstein, 'Memoirs' (Heb.), 117.

[11] Friedland [Had ben Hevraya], 'Hibat Zion at Volozhin' (Heb.), 11.

[12] On the foundation of the society, see Rotstein, 'Memoirs' (Heb.); Friedland [Had ben Hevraya], 'Hibat Zion at Volozhin' (Heb.). Friedland described Rosenkrantz and identified him as the figure described in Berdyczewski [Bar Bei Rav], 'The World of Emanation' (Heb.), 75–6.

[13] Rotstein, 'Memoirs' (Heb.), 118.

[14] Friedland [Had ben Hevraya], 'Hibat Zion at Volozhin' (Heb.), 12.

school students as members too. But the society's centre was still the yeshiva, and most of its members were students there.[15] Members who lived in other towns were kept in touch by letter.

Members engaged in a number of activities to further the Zionist cause, but because of the clandestine nature of the society's operations the public perceived them as be spontaneous actions carried out by individuals.[16] The nature of the activities to be undertaken and the resources to be allocated to them were specified in the society's constitution: 'three-quarters of [its income] should be allocated to the distribution among our people of books, pamphlets, and journals which support the settlement of Palestine'.[17] Members did indeed distribute this literature. They also collected letters of support from leading rabbis, hoping to publish them as a book.[18] However, they never got as far as practical action on behalf of the settlement of Palestine. There was a suggestion that some members be sent to Constantinople to study, but nothing came of this.[19]

There were constant arguments, not only about modes of action but also about organizational matters. The question of the oath as a condition of membership, with its associated halakhic problems, aroused much passion. For a short period these arguments almost brought activity to a halt, but after some organizational changes—the most important being the election of representatives from the local committees—activity resumed.[20]

In the winter of 1889, however, Nes Ziona came to the attention of the tsarist police. They knew about its main activists but thought that the centre of the movement was in Minsk, and that the group in Volozhin was only a branch. According to a Vilna police report, the Jews of Volozhin co-operated with the police from fear that the yeshiva could be endangered by the 'revolutionary activity' among its students. Yosef Rotstein was arrested and the society's archives were confiscated. Rotstein was soon released, and thanks to 'negotiations' the confiscated archive 'disappeared',[21] but the society never recovered.

---

[15] Rotstein, 'Memoirs' (Heb.), 118.

[16] Friedland [Had ben Hevraya], 'Hibat Zion at Volozhin' (Heb.), 8.

[17] §1, para. 5; see Yisrael Klausner, *History of the Nes Ziona Association in Volozhin* (Heb.), 29.

[18] The material was not published at the time, but most of it appeared later in A. Y. Slutsky (ed.), *Return to Zion*. See Yisrael Klausner, *History of the Nes Ziona Association in Volozhin* (Heb.), 16.

[19] It is not clear what they were going to study there—perhaps law. See Rotstein, 'Memoirs' (Heb.), 120.

[20] Yisrael Klausner, *History of the Nes Ziona Association in Volozhin* (Heb.), 14–15.

[21] Rotstein, 'Memoirs' (Heb.), 122; see also Broides, *Zionist Vilna and its Activists* (Heb.), 40; Druyanow, *Writings on the History of Hibat Zion* (Heb.), i. 48–9. On the Vilna police report, see MS GAOR (Central State Archive of the October Revolution, Moscow), *fond* 102, *delo* 460. I am most grateful to Binyamin Natan, who informed me of the existence of this material and its contents.

Nes Ziona's rapid decline was due not only to fear of the police but also to opposition from R. Berlin. He considered a secret society within the yeshiva a threat to its functioning and while he was a supporter of settlement in Palestine, he thought that its members were wasting time that could be better spent on Torah study. R. Berlin took the unusual step of nullifying the oath that the members had taken. Once the requirements of secrecy and loyalty had been lifted it was easier to discover who the members were and to persuade them to leave the society. R. Berlin probably did not object to the society's activities per se, judging from his restrained reaction when he learnt of its existence: 'When the *rosh yeshivah* released them from their vow, the existence of the society was revealed, along with details of its members and activities. The *rosh yeshivah* did not expel the society's members from the yeshiva and did not punish them, though they had to cease their activities and the society was disbanded.'[22] However, other sources indicate that the members did not in fact get off scot free: 'After the affair, about 20 copecks were docked from the weekly allowance they each received . . . and during those days they told us on several occasions that we had no hope of staying here in the summer . . . they had already begun to carry out [these threats], by removing financial support from several students. However they also told us that they would treat us strictly according to the rules and would not expel us now in a shameful manner. Accordingly we all prepared to leave.'[23]

The negative publicity that the society received once its existence was discovered discouraged any attempt to re-establish it: 'After all this it was obvious that our activity would not fare well, and apart from this, all our affairs were known and revealed to all, and gathering new members and spreading our ideas would not be easy here.' Rotstein mentions another reason for the suppression of the society in his memoirs: renewed controversy over the use of an oath.[24]

These reasons seem insufficient to account for the disbanding of the society, however. If its members had so wished, they probably could have reorganized in secret. The main factor was probably that no one came forward to devote time and energy to the difficult task of rebuilding it after Rotstein's arrest. Managing an extensive network of correspondence with members in distant towns and running activities was all undertaken at considerable risk and with no social or financial compensation. Setting up an organization requires a person with commitment and strong ideological convictions. Rotstein could not carry on after his arrest, and no successor emerged. Several students displayed interest in the society's goals, but were not prepared to sacrifice their time and energy for them.

[22] Zlatkin, 'The Netsah Yisra'el Secret Society' (Heb.), 181.

[23] Yisrael Klausner, *History of the Nes Ziona Association in Volozhin* (Heb.), 95.

[24] Rotstein, 'Memoirs' (Heb.), 123–4.

The Nes Ziona episode shows that the yeshiva students were interested in the nascent Zionist movement and were familiar with contemporary methods of organization and action. Many students were prepared to join the society, even though—and perhaps precisely because—admission involved taking an oath. They were also ready to contribute some of their scanty funds to the society. However, the fact that after Rotstein was arrested no one came forward to replace him suggests that the students' desire for involvement in Hibat Zion, or indeed in political movements in general, was not as strong as their commitment to Torah study. Membership of the society reflected a certain openness to the new ideas then current in the Jewish world, but not a complete change in values.

One could perhaps attribute the whole affair to Rotstein's charisma, but the subsequent establishment of another Zionist organization some time later shows that students were seriously attracted to Zionism or proto-Zionism, even if was not a top priority for them. In the summer of 1890 a new secret society, Netsah Yisra'el, was founded at Volozhin. At the initiative of three former members of Nes Ziona, eight young students were persuaded to set up a secret association and run it on the much the same lines as Nes Ziona,[25] including using an oath as a means of preserving secrecy. The three initiators undertook to help the society but did not join it themselves so that it would not be considered as a continuation of Nes Ziona,[26] which had been ordered to disband. The platform of the new association was published in *Hamelits* on 9 April 1891, in an article entitled 'The Idea of Settlement' written by one of its members, Hayim Nahman Bialik. The society attracted members from among the best students of the yeshiva,[27] and was active without being discovered until the yeshiva shut its doors in 1892. It is not clear how many members it had at its height. Like Nes Ziona, it aspired to attract only the elite students, and only a minority of the students seem to have been members.[28] After the closure of

[25] This description is based on the account given by Zlatkin, 'The Netsah Yisra'el Secret Society' (Heb.), 181. Yisrael Klausner quotes a letter from Rafael Sasanhohn that gives a slightly different explanation: 'A few weeks ago there was a preacher here from Saragan whose pleasant speech and words attracted the hearts of the young yeshiva students . . . this caused them to set up an association with the aim of spreading the idea of settlement [of Palestine], and whose members will support speakers on this topic. On the eve of the holy sabbath of the Torah portion "Pinhas", the association was founded, taking on the obligation to be faithful to the idea of settlement and not to reveal the secret of the association. There were ten founding members . . . the management of the society is currently in our hands, and they will listen to everyhing we command them' (*History of the Nes Ziona Association in Volozhin* (Heb.), 103). On Netsah Yisra'el, see also Balosher, 'Bialik at Volozhin' (Heb.); Don-Yihia, 'Memoirs' (Heb.); Friedland [Had ben Hevraya], 'Hibat Zion at Volozhin' (Heb.); Goldstein, 'Bialik's Beginnings' (Heb.); Nissenbaum, *Pages of My Life* (Heb.), 105–96; and Y. Katz, 'The "Ahuzot" Campaign in Palestine' (Heb.), esp. 119–22, 144.

[26] Zlatkin, 'The Netsah Yisra'el Secret Society' (Heb.), 181. [27] Ibid. 182.

[28] Yisrael Klausner, *History of the Nes Ziona Association in Volozhin* (Heb.), 108–9, on the society's regulations and on the admission of new members.

the yeshiva the society continued to operate for a while, but maintaining contact by post proved unworkable and activity soon foundered.[29]

Netsah Yisra'el's goals included not only the development of Jewish settlement in Palestine but also 'the awakening of love for our religion and people among our brethren living here'.[30] In other words, a secondary aim was to strengthen religious fervour among the Jews of eastern Europe by means of new methods. This clause in the society's regulations was added as a result of pressure from two members—Zalman Yaffe and Yehudah Don-Yihia.[31] The desire to strengthen religion went back to the days of Nes Ziona, but Rotstein, who was a passionate nationalist ideologue, had rejected the suggestion of combining the two goals: 'When the number of members increased and included many pious individuals, they did not emphasize unity and they did not want to be together with those who are estranged from religion. Nevertheless, the breach was not so very wide, since the more pious were afraid of their great responsibility and agreed to compromises.'[32] In other words, Rotstein did not want questions of religion to influence his organization and its membership. Thus, whereas the first Zionist society in Volozhin was concerned only with the goal of Jewish settlement in Palestine, the second was a more religious movement that was also clearly conscious of developments in the surrounding society and responded to them. In Netsah Yisra'el the majority opinion generally prevailed, while the leadership seems to have had a more prominent role in its predecessor. Not surprisingly, Netsah Yisra'el was less passionate about settlement in Palestine, and in this regard was more conservative than its predecessor. It also managed to attract many members, whether because students were thirsty for organized extra-curricular activity or because they wanted greater involvement in contemporary events in Jewish society.

In 1889 another society was founded with the aim of setting up 'a colony in our holy land, so that there may be vine growers and farmers on the mountains of Israel'.[33] According to its founders, many students were interested in this new development: 'About a hundred of us joined.' It is difficult to be sure of the exact number, though, and this figure seems to have been an exaggeration intended to impress the recipient of the letter. The society reflected a trend that was becoming familiar in the wider Jewish society to set up popular organizations—such as the Agudot Ha'elef (Societies of the Thousands)—in order to purchase land in Palestine and encourage settlement there.[34] The

---

[29] Yisrael Klausner, *History of the Nes Ziona Association in Volozhin* (Heb.), 24.

[30] Regulations of the Society; see Yisrael Klausner, *History of the Nes Ziona Association in Volozhin* (Heb.), 105.   [31] Zlatkin, 'The Netsah Yisra'el Secret Society' (Heb.), 182–3.

[32] Rotstein, 'Memoirs' (Heb.), 119.

[33] Druyanow, *Writings on the History of Hibat Zion* (Heb.), ii. 797–800; see also the introduction in Yisrael Klausner, *History of the Nes Ziona Association in Volozhin* (Heb.), 24–5.

[34] On the *agudot ha'elef*, see Yisrael Klausner, *From Katowice to Basle* (Heb.), i. 16–17.

idea of the students establishing a settlement in Palestine was never implemented, of course, but the fact that such an organization was established reveals that there was interest in the yeshiva in such an idea and enthusiasm for settlement as an organized group. In this period the yeshiva seems to have been not only a place of Torah study, but also a focus of social and political activity, like other contemporary educational institutions in Russia.

None of these societies achieved any tangible results, though one of the more active members of Hibat Zion called them 'exciting and delirious'.[35] The idea of the return to Zion penetrated the yeshiva in other and perhaps more important ways, however. R. Berlin himself belonged to Hovevei Tsiyon well before the founding of Nes Ziona, and the discovery of its activity in the yeshiva did not prevent him from publicly supporting the Zionist idea. In 1890, around Shavuot, he gave a lecture on the subject:

After the morning prayers, he spoke to his students and instructed them, as is his custom every year, and with words that kindle flames of fire he planted in their hearts the love of Torah, and this time he also touched on the idea of settling the Land of Israel, and aroused the hearts of his audience to support those who till the holy soil; and because of his tremendous enthusiasm for this matter, his eyes were constantly filled with tears. His words made a great impression on the students' hearts, and many of them who had hitherto hesitated between the two alternatives and had not known whether the idea of settling the Land of Israel was acceptable or not, now became enthusiastic supporters of the idea.[36]

R. Berlin's attitude reflects the traditional feeling for Palestine as a holy place; he had worked on behalf of the Jewish community there even before this date, continuing in this regard the work of R. Hayim and R. Yitshak of Volozhin. The enthusiasm of his students for the Zionist idea was a reflection of this traditional attitude but the new organizations reflected new methods—the clandestine nature of the activity stands out most prominently—and new attitudes, such as the acceptance of some aspects of the Haskalah at a time when many religious traditionalists were actively campaigning against such ideas. Although the Haskalah was not specifically mentioned in Nes Ziona's articles of association, Rotstein records in his memoirs that:

[Y. L. Berger] introduced friends of his who were gymnasium and university students to the society. At first everyone rejoiced and welcomed them, since they all knew that it would be impossible to build up the land without [secular] knowledge and the advantage of training in worldly experiences, and it was absolutely necessary to co-opt these individuals who were prepared for the future, to serve as experts in all spheres of knowledge and wisdom.[37]

---

[35] Judah Leib Appel, in Druyanow, *Writings on the History of Hibat Zion* (Heb.), iii. 60.

[36] Berdyczewski [Bar Bei Rav], in *Hamelits*, 30/120 (13 June 1890), 4.

[37] Rotstein, 'Memoirs' (Heb.), 119; a clear sense of inferiority is apparent in this passage.

Netsah Yisra'el's articles of association state, in contrast:

No one shall be admitted as a member to our society unless he knows Torah and behaves accordingly like all Israel and is of good character, and does not despise the Haskalah, and besides all these characteristics, he must excel in one of the three following spheres: Torah or Haskalah or wealth, or else he must be moderately learned in Torah and Haskalah.

Candidates for membership in Netsah Yisra'el also had to demonstrate 'love of our religion'.[38]

It is difficult to evaluate how such societies influenced students' experience of the yeshiva: because they were secret organizations most students were not aware of their existence and were blissfully ignorant that they had not been judged worthy of membership. Joining such a society was thus not a way of demonstrating one's social standing, but merely conferred a personal sense of self-worth. The societies certainly did not lead to rifts between students or conflict with the yeshiva authorities.

Indirectly, however, the societies do seem to have influenced the atmosphere at the yeshiva. Members of Netsah Yisra'el distanced themselves from the conflicts over the appointment of R. Hayim Berlin and later of R. Hayim Soloveitchik that will be described in detail below.[39] Perhaps this was because of R. Soloveitchik's opposition to Hibat Zion,[40] but for the most part the involvement in Zionist activities in addition to the ongoing Talmud study did not leave time for involvement in what would have been regarded as minor issues of succession.

Membership of a society provided a framework for action, a much-valued outlet for bookish students. The yeshiva was in some disarray at this time, as we shall see, so membership of a society actually had a moderating effect on volatile young students. As Yosef Rotstein notes, the foundation of Nes Ziona was accompanied by a decline 'in the spirit of rebellion and mockery that had characterized the yeshiva'.[41] The young men behind the initiative, including Rotstein, made great efforts to persuade 'many of the students to devote the best of their talents . . . to the welfare of our people'. A similar situation developed in 1892 in connection with the appointment of a new *rosh yeshivah*. N. Zlatkin writes of Bialik: 'Zionism did not possess his whole being like most of the members of the society, who pondered on it all day long and hardly took any notice of what was happening at the yeshiva at the time . . . most of

---

[38] Yisrael Klausner, *History of the Nes Ziona Association in Volozhin* (Heb.), 108.

[39] See Ch. 8 below.

[40] For this letter of Benei Zion care of Zaks, see Druyanow, *Writings on the History of Hibat Zion* (Heb.), iii. 140–1. It was said of R. Hayim Soloveitchik that 'even though it was clear to us that he prided himself on his hatred for the settlement movement, and also made a great effort to persecute us', the members of Nes Ziona 'had a deep respect for R. Hayim Soloveitchik' (ibid.).   [41] Yisrael Klausner, *History of the Nes Ziona Association in Volozhin* (Heb.), 117.

the students took part in this movement of rebellion, but none of the members of Netsah Yisra'el did, except for Bialik.'[42] Taking into account the characters and talents of the Netsah Yisra'el activists, it is obvious that their Zionist activities contributed to the stability of the yeshiva, if only indirectly.

3. Other Societies

In 1887 an attempt was made to found an association of maskilim at Volozhin. The following article appeared on the 'Jewish news' page of *Hatsefirah*:

> We have been informed from Volozhin that one of the yeshiva students, both a Talmud scholar and a maskil, is founding a society of select young men who gather on winter evenings in his residence to hear a discourse on Jewish studies and history, with exposition and investigation. This is a very good and honourable innovation, but the members of the aforementioned society do not possess the necessary books of wisdom, and they therefore request scholars and authors to assist them by donating books at no cost.[43]

The article is unsigned and gives no address and it is not clear where the 'scholars' and 'authors' were meant to send their books, all of which raises questions about the veracity of the report. The publication of the announcement brought a swift reaction, however. The edition of *Hatsefirah* that appeared two weeks later contained the following letter:

> I read in *Hatsefirah* . . . about the announcement from Volozhin . . . and I have written, not only to deny these things—for what has been announced are deeds that should not be done, because the winter evenings in Volozhin were created only for study. I have also come to request of the editor of this newspaper not to accept anything else from Volozhin that has not been confirmed and approved by the *gaon*, our master and teacher, the *rosh yeshivah*, may he merit a long and prosperous life. Written on behalf of the *gaon*, our master and teacher, may he merit a long and prosperous life, by Moshe Friedlander, secretary of the holy yeshiva of Volozhin.[44]

Things were thus not as simple as would appear from the letter written by the secretary (a post known only from the signature on letters to newspapers). Shortly afterwards, Micha Yosef Berdyczewski wrote:

> We did in truth found a small society to investigate our people's history and literature, although most of the yeshiva students truly have no contact or dealings with academic Jewish studies and no knowledge of Jewish history or the development of its literature. And when the secretary wrote his letter our society had in fact already been dissolved at the order of our rabbi and teacher, R. Berlin, may he merit a long and prosperous life, and many of those who were involved have already been

---

[42] Zlatkin, 'The Netsah Yisra'el Secret Society' (Heb.), 184. He may have exaggerated somewhat, but the phenomenon is important in this context.

[43] *Hatsefirah*, 14/250 (25 Nov. 1887), 2.   [44] *Hatsefirah*, 14/261 (8 Dec. 1887).

punished . . . Haskalah is permitted at Volozhin and the *rosh yeshivah* does not protest against it, but he does not think it appropriate to set up an association for this purpose.[45]

There was no need to organize a society in order to engage in the Haskalah, apart from the faint hope of receiving free books. Moreover, the members of this association might have guessed that R. Berlin would not react positively to the announcement in the newspaper, but they sent it in anyway. The motivation for founding the society seems to have been not material gain but reinforcement of the founders' self-image. The publication in *Hamelits* won them recognition as maskilim and represented the yeshiva as a place of maskilic studies. Considerations of this sort—the search for recognition and the sense of working within an official framework—probably outweighed concern of the *rosh yeshivah*'s disapproval. The moment the *rosh yeshivah* condemned their actions in public, however, they had no basis on which to justify opposition. In spite of the large numbers of students interested in the Haskalah, we know of no other attempt at organizing maskilic studies in this way. The dissolution of the society did not lessen interest in the Haskalah at Volozhin, and such study could be pursued independently. The attempt to found a society would seem to demonstrate the students' desire for social engagement no less than their interest in the Haskalah.

4. Student Newspapers

During the yeshiva's last years the students began to publish newspapers. The members of Nes Ziona published a newspaper or, more accurately, a 'circular', run off on a hectograph.[46] There was a strict ban in tsarist Russia on the use of these devices without a licence. When the society was uncovered, the authorities found and confiscated the hectograph, which was one of the reasons why its members feared for Rotstein's fate. There were also other attempts to publish newspapers that were not related to formal organizations, as Pinhas Turberg notes:

The yeshiva students often used to publish newspapers devoted to their affairs. It was not printed but was simply written by hand, in several copies. The editors and assistants were students and used to carry out their 'literary' work at night in their lodgings, and even then they used to hide away to avoid the searching eye of the *shamash*, who used to go round the windows at night and peep in through cracks in the shutters to see what each student was doing. Shemuel Hayim Goralski, who later became a well-known merchant in Łódź, published a newspaper of this sort,

---

[45] *Hamelits*, 28/30 (17 Feb. 1888).

[46] See Pesah Friedlander's letter to Druyanow, in Druyanow, *Writings on the History of Hibat Zion* (Heb.), iii. 48–9, 997 n. 4.

called *Haboker* [The Morning],[47] at the yeshiva, and a few months before the yeshiva closed down I published a newspaper called *Haḥayim* [Life] . . . At the top of the newspaper appeared the words '*Haḥayim*, a weekly scientific and literary newspaper for all Jewish affairs in general and for the Ets Hayim yeshiva [i.e. Volozhin] in particular. Edited by Bar Bei Rav.' Its motto was 'Its ways are ways of pleasantness, and all its paths are peace' [Prov. 3: 17]. Eight issues of *Haḥayim* appeared, most of which were devoted to the controversy surrounding the appointment of a successor to R. Berlin.[48]

The Rivkind Collection of the National and University Library in Jerusalem has copies of the eight issues of *Haḥayim*, and a quick glance shows that Turberg's description is accurate. The issues were hand-written, copying the format of *Hamelits* down to its questions-and-answers page. The first issue appeared on 4 December 1891; the other issues are not dated. The articles discussed the settlement of Palestine and literary matters, but were mostly concerned with the affairs of the yeshiva—for instance, the campaign against the appointment of R. Hayim Berlin as *rosh yeshivah*. This poem, published in the second issue, is typical of the newspaper and reflects its style:

> I will not be amazed, my rabbi [R. Hayim Berlin], I will not be surprised.
> Why do you have a paper in front of you during the *shiur*?
> For I know indeed that you have no memory,
> and how [else] would you remember what you have seen in your books?
> Nor will I ask where your memory is
> for it is the Bible and not I who alludes to you;
> you have taken on the post of rabbi and teacher
> and your heart is lofty and forgetful [see Deut. 8: 14]. [signed] Favis"t Minen[49]

Why did the students publish a newspaper? It does not seem that their motive was to disseminate news, since distribution was limited to the yeshiva. Nor did it serve as a platform for the dissemination of ideas: even within the yeshiva, circulation was restricted to small groups of people who could be relied on not to betray its existence to the *rosh yeshiva*. For these small groups, verbal communication would have been much more effective than investing hours in writing out a newspaper by hand and copying it in secret. A manifesto would have also achieved the same goal with far less effort. Accordingly, it seems that the main reason for publishing a newspaper was the satisfaction it gave to those who produced it: they could feel that they were following in the footsteps of those maskilim who published proper Hebrew newspapers. It was a mode of self-expression rather than a means of communication. Literary

[47] On *Haboker*, see the memoirs of Don-Yihia as cited in Etkes and Tikochinski, *Memoirs of the Lithuanian Yeshivas* (Heb.), 161.   [48] Turberg, *Works of Pinhas Turberg* (Heb.), 134.

[49] The 'Favis"t Minen' with which the letter ends is apparently an acronymic allusion to the author's name, but I have not been able to identify who it might be.

expression was something quite new in the yeshiva, reflecting the influence of the Haskalah in values as well as in style. Another noteworthy point is that the work required to produce these newspapers was such that no student could have accomplished it alone; in other words, the existence of a newspaper is evidence of change in the values of many students rather than of a few specific individuals.

5. Involvement in Political Issues

The information available on the students' interest in political events in Russia and their involvement in Russian revolutionary activity is very scanty. The only evidence of student interest in Russian politics comes from a comment on the events of 1881 by Binyamin Goldberg in which he relates how he met a friend from Sadov the day after the coronation of Tsar Alexander III:

On the following sabbath the Sadover suggested a little walk outside the town to me and to several of our friends, and we agreed. There our ears heard what our ancestors' ears had not heard on Mount Sinai. The young man, who had entered the 'orchard' [that is, the world of secret knowledge] and peeped and been some- what affected [a reference to the talmudic account of the four sages who entered 'the orchard', three of whom suffered varying degrees of injury; BT *Ḥag.* 14*b*], began to explain to us the theory of constitutionalism, and opened our eyes to see how much foolishness, hypocrisy, and humbug there was in the ceremonies we had witnessed that week. In our eyes everything [that he said] seemed as though it had been written in those books the readers of which were now being exiled to the swamps of Siberia and to the banks of the Lena as punishment for having read them. We stood in amazement and listened to his words in fear and trembling . . . we feared that the birds in the sky might betray us.[50]

They listened, but went no further. This account suggests mere interest rather than any attempt to act in this sphere. Goldberg also claimed that the stu- dents, 'led by the *gaon*, R. Hayim Soloveitchik', supported Osman Pasha during the Russo-Turkish War.[51] He does not record R. Berlin's attitude.

6. The Financial Situation of the Yeshiva

The financial situation of the yeshiva in its final years was particularly bad. Even in better times it had been short of funds, both because the tendency was to expand the student body to the very limit of the available resources and because the organizational structure made financial planning almost impos- sible. But in the final years, the financial difficulties were so bad as to cause unrest among the students and adversely affect R. Berlin's ability to manage the yeshiva, as he himself recorded in a private letter written during this period:

[50] B. Goldberg, *Memories of the Past* (Heb.), 12.   [51] Ibid. 4–5.

I do not know any longer how to answer clearly, since the ways of the holy house of study have changed as a result of many obstacles. For the past year the students' allowances have not been paid, and debts to landlords alone amount to 2,000 roubles. And whoever has not already taken in a student in this fashion does not wish to take in any [new students] now. In general, what should I say to my dear and honoured friend? My heart breaks when I mention the practical difficulties in sustaining the holy yeshiva . . . I myself do not know how to do what is right and honest. And there is no one to help me, and being by myself, what can I do? Only God can give strength to one as powerless as I am. I trust in Him, and He will help me, and uplift me.[52]

Exaggeration is to be expected in a letter intended to elicit a donation, but nevertheless it seems that there had been a real change in the situation. A year's delay in paying the students' allowances had never been mentioned in the past, and it is unlikely that R. Berlin would have invented this. Even the landlords' reluctance to take in new students seems to be a new phenomenon.

No details are available on the yeshiva's finances for most years, but between 1883 and 1885 details of its income and expenditure were published in *Hamelits*.[53] In 1883, its income was 16,675 roubles.[54] The following year, it was probably 15,000 roubles, and the year after that about 17,800 roubles. It is difficult to be any more accurate because there are inconsistencies between the sums given for individual items as compared with the totals reported. Even so, the accounts reward careful scrutiny—for example, because the geographical distribution of the donors is listed. The significance of this breakdown is made clear in Table 7.1.

That an enormous effort was expended in raising funds for the yeshiva is immediately obvious. Methods varied from place to place and from year to year. The notes accompanying the budget for 1883 state that most of the money raised in the United States was collected by *gaba'im*, whereas in the previous two years it had been collected by emissaries. It seems that *gaba'im* were local residents who represented the yeshiva, while emissaries were travelling representatives. Their number and identity is unknown. In England the money was similarly collected by *gaba'im*, while in Germany it was rabbis who

[52] See A. Y. Katz, *Personalities and Deeds in the Mirror of the Past* (Heb.), 326–61, and the letter on p. 346. Katz did not record the date of the letter, and my efforts to locate the original have been unsuccessful. Katz says the letter was addressed to a man who died in 1885, so it must have been sent before this date. There is no information from other sources on the cessation of support before 1885, and the mood of the letter points to the end of the 1880s. Later in the same letter R. Berlin expressed his sorrow at the state of the Jewish world. The date of the letter needs to be clarified.

[53] For details from Iyar 1883 to Nisan 1884, see *Hamelits*, 25/9 (13 Feb. 1885), 137–40. For summer 1884 to winter 1885, see *Hamelits*, 25/34 (18 May 1885), 556. For summer 1885 to winter 1886, see *Hamelits*, 26/40 (4 June 1886), 623–5.

[54] As mentioned above, the detailed list has omissions.

Table 7.1. Income of the Volozhin yeshiva by source, 1883–1885[a]

Source	1883	1884	1885
England	568	407	538
Germany	200	343	534
Russia (collected by emissaries)	7,006	10,308	10,960
(collected by local *gaba'im*)	n.a.	190	370
(sent by individuals)	n.a.	634	580
(sent by rabbis)	116	176	785
Siberia[b]	858	1,274	1,359
United States	1,786	1,453	1,671

[a] The currency is apparently roubles, but the source does not state this explicitly.
[b] Siberia is listed separately from Russia in the sources because it was outside the Pale of Settlement.

Sources: 1883: *Hamelits*, 25/9 (13 Feb. 1885); 1884: *Hamelits*, 25/34 (18 May 1885); 1885: *Hamelits*, 26/40 (4 June 1886).

were credited with collecting funds. The management of this fundraising framework must have been enormously complex; it could not be relied on to function on its own.

The small amount received from individual wealthy donors is of great interest. The proportion of the budget donated in these three years by wealthy Russian Jews remained stable, at about 5 per cent of all the contributions from Russia. Another important fact is that about 90 per cent of donations were collected by representatives of the yeshiva—in other words, in small donations from the general public. The total number of donors is unknown. There were great differences in the amounts donated by individuals; for instance, there was one individual in Kovno who gave a single massive contribution of 900 roubles. Unfortunately, there are no details on his identity or the circumstances of the donation. One also sees that in 1885 large sums were donated to the yeshiva's *keren kayemet* (endowment fund); there is no mention of this fund elsewhere, and it is not known how it operated.

R. Berlin tried to expand the financial base of the yeshiva, and to make contact with additional communities that might support the yeshiva. In 1886 he made major efforts to send a fundraiser to the Caucasus: this was the father of R. Kook.[55] He also tried persistently to enlist the support of wealthy assimilated Jews. He corresponded with Dr Abraham Harkavy, one of the central figures in the Jewish community of St Petersburg in his time who knew many such individuals, but to no avail.[56]

Some of the most famous of the wealthy Jews in the Russian empire

[55] Neriyah, *On Rav Kook* (Heb.), 146–7.
[56] N. Berlin, *Letters of the Netsiv* (Heb.), letters 49 and 50.

donated relatively small sums to the yeshiva. Baron Guenzburg made a yearly donation of 100 roubles and the Polyakov family donated 140 roubles annually. This was not because they were by their nature ungenerous, but because they preferred other organizations. Contemporary reports of the Society for the Promotion of Culture among Jews, an organization that supported the spread of secular studies among Jews by allocating grants, show that it had 23,406 roubles at its disposal at the beginning of 1885. More than 22,000 roubles were collected that year, against expenditure of about 23,000 roubles. In the same year Baron Guenzburg donated 1,000 roubles to the society, while the Polyakov family gave 190 roubles. These were regular contributions, which were augmented by 'special' donations: in 1885 Guenzburg gave no less than 6,900 roubles as a special donation, and Polyakov 200 roubles, while L. M. Rosenthal (whose name does not appear at all in the list of donors to the yeshiva) donated 4,700 roubles. Others gave donations of several hundred roubles.[57]

Comparison of the donations that these wealthy individuals made to the yeshiva with those they made to the Society for the Promotion of Culture among Jews illustrates their alienation from the yeshiva world. Financial support for the yeshiva came almost exclusively from individuals who were suspicious of modernity; only a small portion came from those who supported change. Those wealthy men who were hoping for and investing in major change in Jewish society could easily have solved the yeshiva's financial problems, and in doing so bought themselves the possibility of exerting considerable influence there; but because they did not see the yeshiva as a means of achieving their goals they contented themselves with making merely symbolic donations. It was a vicious circle: since the yeshiva was not beholden to them they had little influence over what happened there, and in consequence it served as a focus for activity that was not always to their taste. Among those who supported the yeshiva, its image as an institution that maintained traditional practices and was resistant to change could actually encourage donations, while the same image deterred potential supporters from more modern circles. In fact, the more conservative donors pressured the yeshiva to resist change. R. Yitshak Elhanan Spektor of Kovno put it this way: 'Since [the yeshiva] receives only limited support from generous individuals [i.e. the famous and affluent] of our nation, it must also act according to the will of the people [i.e. the masses].'[58]

This same point was made by Moshe Reines:

In my opinion, the *rosh yeshivah* was right in preventing this favourite practice of the maskilim [i.e. introducing secular studies into the yeshiva's curriculum] . . . the

[57] See Society for the Promotion of Culture among Jews, *Report for 1885* (Rus.), 22–33, esp. 29–31.　　[58] Lifschitz, *Zikhron ya'akov*, iii. 144.

Volozhin yeshiva subsists entirely on the contributions of donors, and most of these donors, who are poor, downtrodden, and simple people, give their money purely in order to fulfil a mitzvah ... and now, if R. Berlin decides to change the nature of the yeshiva, and institute compulsory secular studies for even a single hour, or even a single minute each day, he will instantly ruin the yeshiva ... what will the donors say when they hear this news? ... for the donors are neither maskilim nor authors ... but the simple masses ... then they will stop giving money to [the yeshiva] ... and the yeshiva, that holy and exalted building, will collapse![59]

Contributions from outside Russia also seem to have come from people who were persuaded that the yeshiva represented the embodiment of traditional society and a way of life that they wanted to support. Mostly these would have been relatively recent emigrants from eastern Europe who looked back sentimentally on the yeshiva world and wanted to support it even if they were themselves still rather poor. In general, in the late nineteenth century only a small proportion of donations came from outside Russia—less than 15 per cent—and the proportion coming from the United States was particularly small: in 1884 and 1885, the donations from America were only a little larger than those from Siberia.[60] R. Berlin did all he could to encourage donations from the United States,[61] and even appealed to American Jews via the pages of *Hamelits*,[62] but to little effect. The Jews of the United States began to play an important role in funding yeshivas in Europe only after the First World War.

At the beginning of 1885, as noted above, emissaries operating in the Russian empire brought in most of the yeshiva's income. Organizing their work was not easy, and there were often problems. One was that the emissaries kept back part of the money they collected as payment for their services. Many felt that the share they were taking was too large though no one claimed that the emissaries were rich. Zederbaum, writing in *Hamelits*, reported that 'at least half the income they collect is wasted on travel expenses and food, even if these are limited';[63] and it seems possible that in fact the proportion retained might have been even higher.[64] R. Berlin could not easily change the arrangement, however, since it was an arrangement of long standing, and it would

[59] M. Reines, 'Dwelling-Places of Torah' (Heb.), 12. Similar comments were made by 'Erez' (Zederbaum), in *Hamelits*, 32/47 (8 Mar. 1892).

[60] All these calculations assume that all income was disclosed; if some sources were not revealed, the picture would be different. The figures seem likely, however, even in the light of external factors.

[61] On these efforts, see Rivkind, 'History of the Volozhin Emissaries in the United States' (Heb.).

[62] *Hamelits*, 25/10 (31 Jan. 1881). It is not known whether he thought that many Jews in the United States would read this newspaper.   [63] *Hamelits*, 32/50 (11 Mar. 1892).

[64] There were complaints that only a third of the money collected reached its destination. See the comments of Yitshak Rivkash, in *Hamelits*, 31/112 (2 June 1891): 'They complain ... that 70 per cent of the donations went on their expenses.'

Table 7. 2. Expenditure by the Volozhin yeshiva by category, 1883–1885

Type of expenditure[a]	1883	1884	1885
Students' allowances	5,939	7,754	10,769
Students' travel expenses	1,501	1,788	1,612
Salaries	3,618	3,758	3,914
Emissaries' travel expenses	573	281	373
Care of the sick	n.a.	256	283
Books	464	406	458
Candles	348	365	465
Clothing	161	117	109
Building repairs	324	396	210
Holidays and Purim	387	408	386
Mail	85	107	148
Insurance	36	75	35
Miscellaneous	n.a.	11	136
Excess of expenditure over income[b]	299	1,584	2,545[c]

[a]   The currency is apparently roubles, but the source does not state this explicitly.

[b]   The data in this table are given according to the original. According to my calculations, using the totals reported and cited in the text of the original (and not the sum of the categories, which is less), in 1883 the budgetary deficit came to 3,239 roubles; in 1884 to 807 roubles; and in 1885 to 1,946 roubles.

[c]   According to the report, this sum includes the deficit brought forward from the previous year.

Sources: 1883: *Hamelits*, 25/9 (13 Feb. 1885); 1884: *Hamelits*, 25/34 (18 May 1885); 1885: *Hamelits*, 26/40 (4 June 1886).

not have been easy for the yeshiva to bring in new emissaries. Another problem was competition from other institutions, of which there was no shortage[65] and the growing impoverishment of Jews in the tsarist empire. Because of all this, the yeshiva had little chance of increasing its income in the late nineteenth century.

Analysis of the yeshiva's expenditure (see Table 7.2) reveals its internal problems and budgetary constraints. The stability of the expenditure on staff is striking, in contrast to the major instability in the amounts spent on student allowances. The amount allocated for salaries each month—for R. Berlin, R. Hayim Soloveitchik, the *mashgiaḥ*, the *shamash*, and others—was about 320 roubles. However, the total sum of the salaries paid to all these individuals was far below 320 roubles per month. The discrepancy may be explained by provision in an agreement between R. Berlin and R. Yosef Soloveitchik that

---

[65]   For a description of rivalry on this with the yeshiva in Slobokda, see D. Katz, *The Musar Movement*, ii. 306; Kamenetsky, *The Making of a Godol*, ii. 1204–6. See also Rakov (ed.), *Sefer vayal ya'akov*, 221–40, for a description of tensions between the Jewish community in Palestine and the *kolel* in Kovno over the use of collection boxes. The Volozhin yeshiva was not involved.

members of R. Hayim of Volozhin's family would receive allowances from the yeshiva (see Chapter 2, §7, above). This probably explains the discrepancy between the amount paid to the yeshiva staff and the item of expenditure labelled 'salaries'.

According to the yeshiva's published budgets, in 1885 it was supporting about 260 students.[66] This is consistent with other available evidence. Each student appears to have received an average of 31 roubles per annum, which is consistent with statements made in personal memoirs. Thus, Berdyczewski states that students received 2 to 3 roubles a month or 24 to 36 roubles per annum.[67] Another source states that in the 1880s a month's food cost about 8 roubles,[68] which makes it clear that students could not subsist on the yeshiva's allowance alone in this period. The data also shows that the level of the allowances varied over time. In 1883 students received about 23 roubles a year, while in 1885 this rose to 41 roubles. When the yeshiva's income rose, so did the allowances; the converse was also true.

This financial insecurity had a detrimental effect on the atmosphere in the yeshiva. As we saw in Chapter 4, R. Berlin and other members of staff fixed the level of the allowance for each student on a personal basis. They did not use objective standards, or criteria that were clear and acceptable to the students, but relied on their assessments of the student's personal attributes and family connections. Students who received less considered this unfair, but because the finances were controlled by R. Berlin, criticism of financial practices involved criticism of one's teacher, which made the situation very difficult. The existence of a *gemaḥ* to provide financial assistance to students also suggests dissatisfaction with the allocation of financial support.

A striking expression of tension and conflict over financial matters is seen in an article by 'He Who Sees But Is Not Seen', published in the *Yidishe folksblat* in 1884, which reported that after R. Berlin had turned away a student who had requested urgent financial assistance, the student picked up a knife and tried to kill himself. [69] R. Berlin published a response in *Hamelits*,[70] in which he explained that the background to the incident had been the financial failure of the student's father. However, he did not justify his behaviour, and said 'I cannot escape recrimination in this affair, for am I not a mere mortal?' He also noted that he had sent the student home with someone who would keep an eye on him.

[66] See R. Berlin's comments in *Hamelits*, 25/9 (11 Feb. 1885), 137–40.

[67] Berdyczewski [Bar Bei Rav], 'History of the Ets Hayim Yeshiva' (Heb.), 237; following him, M. Reines, 'Dwelling-Places of Torah' (Heb.), 15.

[68] M. A. Eisenstadt, 'The Volozhin Yeshiva' (Heb.), 166.

[69] 'He Who Sees But Is Not Seen' (Yid.). It should be noted that the editor of the newspaper inserted a comment stating that he found the report hard to believe.

[70] *Hamelits*, 25/9 (13 Feb. 1885), 137–40. This description reveals R. Berlin's great integrity and humility far more than censored biographies do.

The relationship between the students and R. Berlin was very complex. They were attracted by his personality, his behaviour, his fame, his status, and his vast knowledge of the Torah, but because he was responsible for the yeshiva's finances their economic welfare was entirely under his control. It seems reasonable to suppose that the students did not fully realize the yeshiva's difficult financial situation. It is even possible that there was a link between the tension arising from R. Berlin's ambiguous position and the outbursts against his wife described above: her involvement in allocating financial support was common knowledge. For many students, the fact that a woman held such authority may in any case have been a novelty that was not necessarily welcome. At the same time, her involvement was helpful to R. Berlin, both in practical terms and from the point of view of his public image. Even though he was officially responsible for the level of the aid granted, her involvement meant that he could retain his positive image as the much-loved head of the yeshiva since his wife could be blamed for all the problems.

Evidence of the financial crises of the yeshiva is to be found in letters from the rabbi of Kalvarija. After visiting Volozhin he noted, 'I never saw such an exalted yeshiva and it is the pillar of Torah in our generation . . . it is the Temple in the diaspora', but he was so appalled by its finances that he tried to raise money for it by writing to Ovadiah Lachman, a well-known philanthropist in Berlin who played a major role in financing the *musar* yeshivas, as we shall see below, and to the Rothschilds in Frankfurt. He also asked his friend, R. Eliyahu David Rabinowitz-Theomim (known as 'the Aderet') to write to them too and encourage them, ideally, to set up an endowment fund for the yeshiva.[71]

In the late 1880s there was a whole new series of financial problems. The worst was the fire in the winter of 1886 that destroyed the yeshiva as well as much of the town.[72] Fires were common in Lithuanian towns: most houses were built of wood and fire-fighting was inefficient. Neighbouring communities responded by sending carts loaded with food and other necessities, but their aid was insufficient. The Volozhin community therefore appealed to the wider Jewish public through the Hebrew press, asking for support for both themselves and the yeshiva. Three types of contributions were received: for the yeshiva alone, for the townspeople alone, and for both together. By the end of the summer of 1886, about 2,000 roubles had been donated to the yeshiva, about 250 roubles had been collected for the exclusive use of the Volozhin community, and about 680 roubles had been sent to the townspeople and the yeshiva together.[73] Rebuilding the yeshiva started immediately after the fire and was finished by the beginning of the following winter.[74] Most of the students seem to have left town while the building was in

[71] See Kook, *Letters* (Heb.), 532–3.
[72] See the letter from the leaders of the Volozhin commuity in *Hamelits*, 26/88 (1 Mar. 1886).
[73] *Hamelits*, 26/105 (14 Sept. 1886).   [74] *Hamelits*, 26/151 (21 Nov. 1886).

progress,[75] returning after the High Holidays. The building itself cost about 10,000 roubles, and R. Berlin organized a campaign to raise the money. He published two reports. The first, in September 1886, listed all the donations to the town, as cited above. About two months later he announced that the yeshiva had received another 1,200 roubles and 25 marks, while the sum of 1,350 roubles had been raised for the yeshiva and town together.[76] The yeshiva thus received less than 5,000 roubles, not even half of what it needed to cover the cost of rebuilding.

R. Berlin may have exaggerated the cost of rebuilding the yeshiva, but there was unquestionably a wide gap between income and expenditure. In June 1887 a letter appeared in *Hamelits* from Moshe Friedlander, the secretary of the yeshiva, addressed to R. Yehoshua Zeitlin of Dresden, thanking him for his donation of 150 roubles—a third for the students, a third for distribution among ten scholars on the anniversary of the death of the donor's wife, and a third 'to lighten the burden of debt that saddles the neck of the *gaon*, may he merit a long and prosperous life, as a result of the rebuilding of the yeshiva last year'.[77] In other words, apart from the annual deficit resulting from usual expenses, there was still a heavy burden of debt left over from the rebuilding. Only a few of the famous rich Jews in Russia appear in the two lists of donors, and it is clear that not all of them made a contribution in proportion to their wealth.

The year 1891 seems to have been particularly difficult for the yeshiva. Because it was a leap year according to the Jewish calendar and therefore had a thirteenth month, an extra monthly allowance was needed with no parallel increase in the yeshiva's annual income. A poem by Bialik, who was then a student at the yeshiva, mentions that it was decided to cancel the monthly allowance for the extra month that year,[78] though this is not mentioned elsewhere. A slight reduction of the monthly allowance throughout the entire year would have enabled the yeshiva to pay the allowance for the extra month, but, if Bialik's statement is true, perhaps the yeshiva miscalculated the anticipated level of donations over the year. Alternatively, perhaps the decision was never implemented, or had in any case been only a rumour.

R. Berlin was forced to publish an announcement in the newspaper to the effect that the yeshiva could not support any new students:

Since many *haverim* ['friends'—the meaning of the term is unclear] and students remain at the holy yeshiva during the summer, I have found it necessary to announce that no *haver* or student should come next summer, for we are unable to accept

---

[75] *Hayom*, 1/160 (30 Aug. 1886).

[76] *Hamelits*, 26/151 (14 Sept. 1886).   [77] *Hamelits*, 27/122 (15 June 1887).

[78] 'Beleil hara'ash', a fragment from *Hamatmid*, published in *Keneset*, 1 (1936), 4–7. According to Lachover, Rivkin mentions this decision, and he relies on this source (see Lachover, *Bialik* (Heb.), i. 93). However, Rivkin did not study at Volozhin himself, and it is difficult to know his sources and their reliability.

more, both because of the laws of the government, may its majesty be exalted, and because of the burden of debts, which have proliferated, to the point where I am concerned that the holy yeshiva should not collapse, Heaven forbid, under the weight of the burden of debt and under the weight of its expenses, which far outstrip its income.

And the rabbis and the *geonim*, may they merit long and prosperous lives, are asked not to urge us to accept the candidates they recommend, for [if they do so], they are showing no concern for the existence of the holy yeshiva, whether from their lack of faith in us or from their lack of concern for our difficulties, and may God make atonement for them.

Even those who come at their own expense are too numerous for us to accept in accordance with the laws of the government, may its majesty be exalted, and therefore they study in the *beit midrash* or elsewhere, and their parents should know that we cannot supervise them and are not responsible for them; and may God have mercy on us and make us worthy to increase Torah.

Naftali Tsevi Yehudah Berlin[79]

In 1892, the year the yeshiva closed, the situation was dire. R. Hayim Berlin wrote in *Hamelits* a description of the economic situation of the yeshiva upon its closure:

On the occasion of the closure of the yeshiva by order of the ministers of the government, may its majesty be exalted, my honoured father, the *gaon* and righteous man, may he merit a long and prosperous life, is in a terrible plight, with the foreclosing of huge debts with which he is saddled, to the sum of over 10,000 roubles, which he owes to others,[80] and which he borrowed from them for the expenses of running the yeshiva during the years he headed the yeshiva until this day, for about forty years.[81]

Perhaps the debts were not quite so enormous, but there is no doubt that they were large. R. Hayim Berlin even travelled to Amsterdam in the hope of raising money there,[82] and R. Naftali Berlin spent his last year running fundraising campaigns.[83] In these circumstances it was difficult for him to continue teaching and to maintain his contact with the students in the yeshiva's last years. These financial difficulties also made it harder to find the funds to bribe government officials—a strategy that might have saved the yeshiva. Perhaps the only positive development during this difficult period was the receipt of a large donation for the establishment of a *kolel*, a new type of institution in eastern Europe, within the framework of the yeshiva. This will be discussed in Chapter 11.

[79] *Hatsefirah*, 18/52 (13 Mar. 1891).

[80] This provides additional evidence that the yeshiva was not a legal entity but a sort of business venture belonging to the *rosh yeshivah*, who was personally responsible for its debts.

[81] *Hamelits*, 32/151 (19 July 1892).   [82] See his letter in *Hamelits*, 32/151 (19 July 1892).

[83] See B. H. Epstein, *Mekor barukh*, iii. 2030.

EIGHT

The Closure of the
Volozhin Yeshiva

O N 2 FEBRUARY 1892 the authorities ordered the closure of the Volozhin yeshiva. The hundreds of students were dispersed and an institution that had represented a pinnacle of Talmud study for generations ceased to exist except as a memory. Although it reopened a few years later, it never regained its former status, either in importance to the Jewish community or, apparently, in its level of scholarship. Analysis of the developments that brought about its closure leads to surprising conclusions that illuminate both the yeshiva's internal politics in the late nineteenth century and its precarious status.[1]

The ostensible reason for the closure of the yeshiva was its refusal to accept the government demand for far-reaching changes in the curriculum so as to incorporate secular studies and to devote a significant number of hours to these studies. However, it is highly probable that this was not the real reason.

If the concern for general studies was so important to the government, it is difficult, if not impossible, to explain why it was only the Volozhin yeshiva that was required at this time to include such an extensive programme of secular studies and why it was only the Volozhin yeshiva that was closed down. Other yeshivas were active in eastern Europe at this period, but only one, the Ramailes yeshiva in Vilna, was also required to introduce secular studies, though to a lesser extent than Volozhin: it was 'forced to introduce the study of the official language and of arithmetic'.[2] If the government really wanted to change the nature of the yeshivas of the Russian empire, why did it not present similar demands to all of them? The theory that it made an example of Volozhin in order to show other institutions the fate that awaited them is untenable, because after the closure of Volozhin there was no attempt to change the curriculum elsewhere. Nor was the closure of Volozhin used as a threat to those who did not accede to its demands. If Volozhin was intended to be an example, this was certainly a rather odd policy. What is more, it reopened after a relatively short time and without a programme of secular studies.

---

[1] For a penetrating and interesting analysis quite different from my own, see Kamenetsky, *The Making of a Godol*, i. 442–55.   [2] Kaplan, 'Rabbi Jacob Joseph' (Heb.), 7.

It might be possible to claim that the authorities did not take action against the other yeshivas because they were concerned about international public opinion. This is also hard to understand. First, the Volozhin yeshiva was the best-known yeshiva in its time and if the closing of any yeshiva would have aroused world opinion, it would have been Volozhin. Secondly, after the closing of the Volozhin yeshiva, the government should have concluded that there was nothing to be concerned about. While the closure of Volozhin attracted attention among the Jews in the Russian empire, it did not cause significant protest in the rest of the Jewish world, nor did it spur the wealthier and more influential Jews of Russia to lobby the authorities. There is thus no doubt that the authorities could have taken action against the other yeshivas with no fear of repercussions. Since this did not happen, it seems that another factor lay behind the authorities' demand for radical change in the curriculum of the Volozhin yeshiva.

The opening of the archives of the former Soviet Union allows the examination of internal government documents from the tsarist period, and enables us to learn from them more about what really motivated the authorities in various episodes affecting the Jewish community. The wealth of detail they contain shows that the authorities knew a great deal about the internal affairs of the yeshiva, and certainly far more than most Jews ever imagined.

1. The Yeshiva and the Authorities

In the late nineteenth century, tsarist policy was to encourage the modernization of the Jewish community. However, views on how to achieve this varied periodically, and the government had difficulty in defining its goals. In addition, even when a particular policy was adopted, it was by no means certain that it would be implemented properly because of inefficiency and widespread corruption.[3] It is against this background that we must try to trace the development of the relationship between the yeshiva and the government.

The first contacts between the government and the yeshiva date back to the time of R. Hayim, when the yeshiva received a document granting it official recognition, as discussed in Chapter 1. At that time official 'recognition' was not particularly important, since the government did not interfere very much in the internal affairs of the Jewish community. However, it apparently was regarded as desirable enough to justify efforts to gain such recognition.

In 1824 the authorities ordered the closure of the yeshiva, for reasons that are unclear. We know this from a government clerk who wrote about the incident more than fifty years later, noting that there was such an order but that

---

[3] I thank Professor Michael Stanislawski and Professor Israel Bartal for clarifying aspects of these matters. Vladimir Levin's 'Jewish Politics in the Russian Empire' (Heb.) is instructive on this topic.

it was never carried out.[4] In fact, the yeshiva continued to function as before. It should be remembered that Volozhin was a small town, far from the centre of government. Few government officials lived there, and it was easy to 'persuade' them to ignore the yeshiva's existence if necessary.[5] When R. Yitshak, the son of R. Hayim, travelled to St Petersburg in 1843 to take part in a conference of rabbis with Max Lilienthal, the German Jewish educator who advised the government on Jewish education, and with Sergey Uvarov, the Minister of Education (on which meeting see Chapter 2), he took the opportunity to request recognition for the yeshiva, and his request was accepted—despite the closure order of 1824, which was still valid and, technically, had never been rescinded.[6]

In the 1840s the tsarist government carried out a number of initiatives related to the education of Jews,[7] and among them was the establishment of rabbinical seminaries under government auspices. These were intended to prepare a new cadre of rabbis who could lead the Jewish communities to enlightenment and modernization.[8] Naturally, many of the maskilim greeted this innovation enthusiastically, but conservative circles opposed it. In the late 1850s there was a fierce dispute in Vilna between supporters of the rabbinical seminary and traditionalists. On several occasions the traditionalists tried to change the nature of the institution, if not to close it down completely,[9] but failed. The question of the future of the seminary graduates became increasingly important. They were ostensibly trained to serve as community rabbis, but the communities did not want them. A compromise was eventually worked out: many communities had two rabbis: a government or crown rabbi with a certain level of secular education and a 'spiritual' rabbi with halakhic authority.[10]

There were also less well known education initiatives in the 1840s, among them a requirement that every *rosh yeshivah* submit an annual report on his curriculum—this even though the government did not insist on the teaching of secular studies in the yeshivas. A report of this type from the Volozhin yeshiva in 1847 has survived. It states that thirty students studied at the yeshiva, though there were clearly more. There is no mention of the curriculum and there is no hint that the yeshiva had altered it in any way.[11]

---

[4] See Gessen, 'The Fate of the Volozhin Yeshiva' (Rus.), 19–22. This is the best article on the legal status of the yeshiva and forms the basis of the discussion here.

[5] A later example appears in M. A. Eisenstadt, 'The Volozhin Yeshiva' (Heb.), 156: 'The police commander or the superintendent of the local police would also treat a yeshiva student with respect. In return for this, they used to receive handsome tips on their festivals.'

[6] Gessen, 'The Fate of the Volozhin Yeshiva' (Rus.), 19; see also above, Ch. 2, §2.

[7] On this period, see Stanislawski, *Tsar Nicholas I and the Jews*.

[8] On the rabbinical seminaries, see ibid., esp. ch. 4; Zalkin, *At Dawn* (Heb.).

[9] Y. Slutsky, 'The Rabbinical Seminary of Vilna' (Heb.), 35.

[10] Shohet, *The Official Rabbinate in Russia* (Heb.).

[11] See *Takanot sha'ah* issued in Vilna in 1844, esp. §§28–36 (pp. 8–10). A. Tscherikower

In 1856 the Russian Ministry of Education decided to close the yeshiva.[12] It is not clear what exactly was the background to this decision, though it may have been linked to the desire to support general studies. The governor of the Vilna district asked the authorities to rescind the decision, since he saw no advantage in closing it—particularly because the yeshiva students who would leave in the wake of a closure would not transfer to government schools—and thought it would merely antagonize the Jews. He suggested instead applying pressure on the yeshiva to force it to adopt a curriculum similar to that of the government schools. It is not clear what made him take this 'enlightened' stand; it may be that he had received a bribe, but there is no evidence for this. There were some tolerant officials, and not every liberal or charitable act was the result of a material inducement—but some were.[13] In the end, nothing was done to the yeshiva.

The status of the Volozhin yeshiva may have been related to developments in Vilna. On 22 December 1855 the crown rabbi of Vilna, R. Yisra'el Gordon, died. He had been active in campaigns against the rabbinical seminary in the city, and both sides felt it was extremely important that his successor should be from their camp. The interest in this position may have been heightened by the fact that, since the days of the Vilna Gaon, the Jewish community of Vilna had not appointed a traditional rabbi to the lead the entire community. The dispute was fierce, involving appeals to the authorities and to public opinion. The police intervened actively to ensure the election of a rabbi with a secular education. Several people were reported to have fainted in the tumult, and one was killed. Eventually the traditionalist candidate, R. Gershon Amsterdam, was elected, though only for three years.[14] The outcome put students of the rabbinical seminary on notice that they might have difficulty in securing rabbinical posts if they had to compete with candidates with a traditional education. This may have been what lay behind an anonymous proposal of 1857 sent to the government committee on Jewish affairs by a Jew who wanted to accelerate change, suggesting that all the yeshivas be closed because they were training fanatical rabbis.[15] The proposal was rejected on the grounds that according to a law enacted in 1855 rabbis would in any event have to possess a general education from 1875 onwards. Indeed, R. Amsterdam was succeeded by

published an introduction to the partial translation into Yiddish of the document in 'The Archives of Simon Dubnow'. According to a personal communication from Professor Stanislawki, this is an accurate translation of the regulations in the publications of the Russian Ministry of Education. For the surviving report, see D. Eliach, *Father of the Yeshivas* (Heb.), ii. 594.

[12] Gessen, 'The Fate of the Volozhin Yeshiva' (Rus.), 19.

[13] On the phenomenon of bribery and corruption in the Russian empire, see the fascinating and sophisticated study by Chwalba, *Empire of Corruption* (Pol.).

[14] On Vilna at this period, see Yisrael Klausner, *Vilna, the Jerusalem of Lithuania* (Heb.), 330–47.   [15] Gessen, 'The Fate of the Volozhin Yeshiva' (Rus.), 19.

R. Ephraim Cohen, who was a graduate of the rabbinical seminary and a teacher there.[16]

On 6 April 1858 the superintendent of education in the Vilna district once again ordered the closure of the Volozhin yeshiva. The official justification was the yeshiva's failure to comply with section 33 of the temporary laws of 1845, which stipulated that yeshivas must operate under the supervision of the superintendent of education. According to a letter from a clerk of the Ministry of Education dated 12 January 1859, the yeshiva was closed on 16 August 1858.[17] However, there is no mention of any closure in the Jewish sources, and judging from the complaints by the Ministry of Education about R. Naftali Berlin's continued activity, it is clear that the yeshiva was not closed. There is also no contemporary evidence of any change in the yeshiva's routine or of increased supervision by the superintendent.

The closure order of 6 April 1858 was very possibly linked to circles associated with the rabbinical seminary. There is no evidence of a basic change in the government's policy on yeshivas; for many years yeshivas had functioned without problems, and there are no indications of great concern about them at this time among government officials. Those officials who supported the closure displayed familiarity with the need to guarantee positions for rabbinical school graduates, but they do not seem to have known a great deal about the yeshiva itself. This suggests that officials who were prepared to help those who supported the Haskalah were being fed tendentious information on the Volozhin yeshiva by interested parties. In light of the tactics adopted in the Vilna rabbinical dispute, the willingness of some Vilna Jews to inform on the yeshiva does not seem exceptional. Indeed, this would not have been the first time.[18]

In fact, there was no serious attempt to carry out the closure. This also suggests that the order was the result of external attempts to influence the Ministry of Education rather than an internal policy decision. Had it been an initiative of the ministry, it is difficult to understand why greater efforts were not made to ensure its implementation. It thus seems that the order was given at the request of other parties.

The closure order prompted an immediate Jewish response. On 22 April 1858 R. Gershon Amsterdam, the newly elected crown rabbi of Vilna, and a group of prominent citizens presented a request to the superintendent of

[16] See Steinschneider and Zalkin (eds.), *The City of Vilna* (Heb.), ii. 79.

[17] This discussion derives from a group of sources in the government archive in Vilna that formed the basis of Gessen's detailed article, 'The Fate of the Volozhin Yeshiva' (Rus.). I am most grateful to Genrikh Agranovsky for giving me photocopies of the sources, which I have used to complete and correct Gessen's data. The material is in the Lithuanian State Historical Archive, *fond* 567, *opis'* 6, *delo* 598, of which pp. 3–5 were available to me. See also Agranovsky, 'Materials on the History of the Volozhin Yeshiva' (Rus.).

[18] Gessen, 'The Fate of the Volozhin Yeshiva' (Rus.).

education to rescind the order.[19] The signatories described themselves as 'the elders [*starshiny*] of the yeshiva' and claimed that several other elders from other cities and the heads of the yeshiva had given their approval to the letter. They requested formal recognition of R. Naftali Berlin as the *rosh yeshivah* and emphasized the institution's importance to the Jewish community. They claimed that the younger students were being taught secular subjects, and even supplied details of the curriculum and the names of the teachers. The two-year curriculum they described was as follows:

Year 1

Bible: Pentateuch and early prophets, with Rashi's commentary and the *Biur*[20]
Mishnah: orders *Zera'im*, *Mo'ed*, and *Nashim*
Talmud: tractates *Berakhot*, *Shabat*, *Pesaḥim*, and *Eruvin*, with the commentary of the Rosh[21]
Jewish law: *Shulḥan arukh*, 'Oraḥ ḥayim'
Hebrew grammar: the first two parts of Ben-Ze'ev's *Talmud leshon ever*
Languages: Russian and German, reading and preliminary grammar
Arithmetic: the four principal operations

Year 2

Bible: later prophets and writings, with Rashi's commentary and the *Biur*
Mishnah: orders *Nezikin* and *Kodashim*, with explanation
Talmud: tractates *Ḥulin*, *Nidah*, *Yevamot*, *Ketuvot*, *Gitin*, *Kidushin*, with the commentary of the Rosh
Jewish law: *Shulḥan arukh*, 'Yoreh de'ah' and 'Even ha'ezer'
Hebrew grammar: completion of Ben-Ze'ev's *Talmud leshon ever*
Languages: continuation of Russian and German, grammar and writing
Arithmetic: fractions and decimal fractions

The teacher's name is recorded as Mafeus Levitis.[22]

Only some of the material on the closure order has survived. However, a letter from the district authorities to the district office of the Ministry of Education from April 1858 records that in September of the preceding year the district office of the Ministry of the Interior had reported to the district office of the Ministry of Education that the district court at Oshmyany had testified that the yeshiva had been closed, and that R. Naftali Berlin had signed a statement to that effect. It had not been closed of course, and nothing is known of any document with the signature of R. Berlin. This misleading

---

[19] Ibid. For some reason Gessen states that the letter dates from November, but the original clearly shows that it was sent in April.
[20] This must refer to Mendelssohn's *Biur*; I am grateful to Rabbi Boruch Oberlander for his assistance on this.
[21] It is not clear if the reference was to Rashi or to the halakhic summary of R. Asher b. Yehiel.
[22] I have not been able to locate any information on him.

report obviously served the interests of the yeshiva, and one can only speculate about the motives for it.

There was no immediate response to the appeal of the Vilna Jews. After several months, in December 1858, some Jews from Minsk similarly appealed to the Ministry of Education on behalf of the yeshiva. At the same time, the Jews of Vilna wrote directly to the Ministry of Education and asked for a reply to their appeal. This emerges from a letter from the Ministry of Education to the district superintendent of education, in late December 1859, asking him to report on the reaction of the superintendent in Vilna to the order. The Vilna superintendent of education could not ignore the letter from the Ministry of Education, and sent an answer three weeks later. His letter noted that the yeshiva did not serve the purposes of the government, that it was breaking the Jewish Education Law of 1835, and that its graduates were competing with graduates of the rabbinical seminaries.

The authorities realized that the demand to produce a curriculum was insufficient, and on 4 May 1859 a law was enacted requiring the teaching of secular subjects in yeshivas.[23] However, this law, like the closure order, was never enforced and did not change anything at the yeshiva.

In October 1862 the superintendent of education sent another complaint to the district authorities regarding the yeshiva's continued operation in spite of the closure order. The district authorities ordered the Oshmyany court, which as we have seen apparently co-operated with the yeshiva, to close the yeshiva immediately and to take action against those guilty of ignoring the order. A few months later, in March 1863, the Oshmyany court filed a report that the yeshiva was no longer operating, and that R. Berlin was only giving private lessons in Hebrew reading to a few young members of his family in his house. The district authorities seem to have been satisfied with this transparent untruth and reported it to the superintendent of education.[24]

However, that was not the end of the story. In September 1863 a teacher from the elementary school in Volozhin wrote to the superintendent of education, informing him that the yeshiva was still operating, and that a new stone building was being constructed for it. He also said that the rabbis were unwilling to comply with the authorities' instructions for the teaching of Russian. This information naturally led the superintendent of education to complain to the district authorities. They merely responded that the Oshmyany court had again been instructed to close the yeshiva: a month later, they reported that

---

[23] See Y. Katznelson, 'Why Was the Volozhin Yeshiva Closed Down?' (Rus.), 3.

[24] The material that Genrikh Agranovsky found in the archives (see n. 17 above) included a draft version of a letter ordering the closure of the yeshiva, but not the final version. However, the archive does contain a response, dated 6 Oct. 1862, to the letter that was sent, so the final letter must have been sent by that date. Neither the Volozhin yeshiva nor the Tomkhei Temimim yeshiva in Lubavitch was legally licensed (see S. D. B. Schneersohn, *Sacred Letters* (Heb.), 26–7).

the Oshmyany court said that the yeshiva was not functioning but that there
was a synagogue named after R. Hayim of Volozhin in the town, where local
Jews gathered to read psalms and sacred books. One can imagine the anger
of the education officials upon receiving these excuses. It seems that in early
January 1864 there was yet another complaint about the yeshiva, since there
are some declarations from later in the month, signed by the Volozhin community leaders and by R. Berlin, stating that the signatories were aware of the
ban on the yeshiva and that it was not operating.[25]

Nothing is known of further developments, and for the next fifteen years
the yeshiva seems to have operated without interference. Since there are no
relevant sources that explain this silence, one can only offer informed specu-
lations; perhaps after the Polish rebellion of 1863 the authorities decided that
there was nothing to be gained by antagonizing the Jews, or perhaps the
graduates of the rabbinical seminary were more successful in finding jobs.

In 1879 there was another attempt to close the yeshiva, as mentioned in
Chapter 5. This was in the wake of an informer's presentation of a letter that
purported to describe R. Naftali Berlin's involvement in smuggling and with
a secret society, along with a report that the yeshiva was describing itself as a
school or a house of prayer in order to avoid the legal requirements imposed
on yeshivas.[26] An investigator was sent to Volozhin to collect information on
the yeshiva. In the wake of this investigation, R. Naftali Berlin was summoned
to an interrogation. Ultimately the investigation determined that the letter
was forged and that he was innocent of any involvement in criminal activities,
but the fact that the yeshiva had been operating illegally since 1824
remained.[27] R. Berlin's defence was simple. He claimed that since it was traditional for every town to support a yeshiva, he did not realize that he needed
special permission—and he claimed that there were only sixty students in his
yeshiva.[28] In fact there were certainly far more, and this was no secret. The
government investigator was given a list by a local official of 147 non-residents who were living in Volozhin, almost all of whom were students at the
yeshiva; he was also informed by a local Jew that there were 400 students in
the yeshiva. However, R. Berlin explicitly denied these reports.[29] A local Jew
may have informed the investigator that there were hundreds of students in
the yeshiva, but he was not willing to put this in writing.[30] The superintendent

[25] This is clear from the archive material mentioned in the previous note. See also Agranovsky,
'Naftali Berlin and the Volozhin Yeshiva' (Rus.), 131 and see the postscript to this chapter (p.233).
[26] Lithuanian State Historical Archive, *fond* 419, *opis'* 2, *delo* 660a, *listy* 14–22. This source is
quoted in Agranovsky, 'Naftali Berlin and the Volozhin Yeshiva' (Rus.).
[27] Gessen, 'The Fate of the Volozhin Yeshiva' (Rus.), 19.
[28] Agranovsky and Leiman, 'Three Lists of Students Studying at the Volozhin Yeshiva in
1879', 7.   [29] Agranovsky, 'Materials on the History of the Volozhin Yeshiva' (Rus.), 332.
[30] Agranovsky and Leiman, 'Three Lists of Students Studying at the Volozhin Yeshiva in
1879', 10.

of education prepared a closure order and actually dispatched it, but the investigation was not followed up. The Minister of Interior opposed the measure, claiming that the yeshiva was very important in the Jewish world, even outside Russia, and that closing it would create difficulties for the government. He further noted that it had existed for many years, and that if it had been a threat in any way it would already have attracted the attention of the authorities. He proposed that it simply be ordered to comply with the law, including the requirement of teaching secular subjects, and that it should only be closed if it failed to meet these demands. The Ministry of Education agreed and the order was cancelled. Ultimately the yeshiva seems to have been given a licence to continue even though the curriculum had not been changed.[31]

The cancellation of the order was not a simple matter, as Binyamin Goldberg explains:

The order to close it was issued with no investigation or prior demand. Then R. Berlin remembered his student Harkavy [Albert Harkavy, librarian at the Imperial Library and a renowned scholar] and travelled to Petersburg to see him, and [Harkavy] displayed great interest in him and introduced him to important people, like Polyakov and Guenzburg, and they interceded for him with the famous liberal Count Pahlen, who was privy to the secret affairs of the ministries, to obtain a license to open a yeshiva that would only teach religious subjects without having to teach national languages, and the license was granted.[32]

R. Berlin was thus able to rely on the help of Harkavy, a former student, in order to exert influence on the right people. Yitshak Eizik Halevi also seems to have been involved though the details are not clear.[33]

---

[31] Gessen, 'The Fate of the Volozhin Yeshiva' (Rus.), 19. In 1879 there was not only an attempt to forge R. Berlin's signature, but also an accusation of a different type. A letter dated 7 Sept. 1879 sent from the Third Department (i.e. the secret police) to St Petersburg claimed that there were 250 disloyal Jews in the town of Volozhin, but in the absence of any supporting evidence government secretary Nabokov closed the inquiry. It is not clear if the minister of the interior who did not press charges was Makov (as Gessen says), or Loris Melikov (as Agranovsky says). See Gessen, 'The Fate of the Volozhin Yeshiva' (Rus.); Agranovsky, 'Materials on the History of the Volozhin Yeshiva' (Rus.), 334.

[32] B. Goldberg, *Memories of the Past* (Heb.), 15. Berdyczewski also claimed that the yeshiva received a licence to operate, and from then on was subject to inspection by the superintendent of education in the Vilna district ('History of the Ets Hayim Yeshiva' (Heb.), 236). Yitshak Dov Markon discussed the appeal to Polyakov. He wrote that 'at the end of the 1870s a meeting was held in the house of Samuel Polyakov', at which there was discussion of 'the government's decision that several hours a day be devoted to Russian and secular studies at the Volozhin yeshiva'; he records R. Yosef Dov Soloveitchik's sharp rejoinder to Polyakov (Markon, 'From Generation to Generation' (Heb.), 342). It is not clear whether R. Yosef Dov had also travelled to the meeting or whether there is an error in one of the descriptions.

[33] His biography (*Der Israelit* (23 May 1929), 1–3) states that he arranged the licence with Smirnov, the regional superintendent of education in Vilna. It is not clear how the licence was obtained, but it must have been a complex and possibly expensive process.

2. Secular Studies at the Yeshiva

The threats to close the yeshiva from the mid-nineteenth century on were linked to the authorities' desire to bring about change in Jewish society. The teaching of secular subjects at the yeshiva, and especially the teaching of Russian, was seen as an important step in this direction. This became a focus of tension between the authorities and the yeshiva administration, as we have seen.

By the end of the nineteenth century it was clear to all, including the most traditional Jewish circles, that the ability to speak, read, and write Russian was essential for a variety of functions and professions. This realization was not a break with the past. For generations, ordinary people, and especially members of the elite in Jewish society, had been sending their children not only to the *melamed* at the *ḥeder*, but also to the *shreiber*, who taught arithmetic and writing, since anyone engaged in commerce needed these skills. Mastery of a foreign language was also considered useful. However, these practical subjects were not studied in the *ḥeder*, but with a different teacher and in a different place. This emphasized the difference between religious study and study that prepared one for worldly activity.

R. Berlin's attitude to secular studies was quite traditional. Precisely for this reason he did not rule out secular knowledge nor think it unnecessary—quite the reverse. Like many other scholars before and after him, he thought that secular knowledge was of benefit in Torah study and important for earning a living. However, he did not feel that secular study should be integrated with Torah study and certainly not confused with it. It was those who were influenced by modernization who were categorically opposed to such studies.

R. Berlin even mentioned the benefit of secular knowledge in his commentary on the Torah: 'There are seven external forms of wisdom that are supplementary to the Torah, and which the Torah needs in order to be interpreted in full detail.'[34] Similarly, he wrote in a letter:

I do not deny in the slightest the importance of teaching secular subjects at the yeshiva, especially the Russian language, and I think that it is my duty, as far as I am able and it is possible, to further the development of this cause at the yeshiva. However, I also bear another responsibility: to strengthen the yeshiva's reputation as an institution in which young men study religious subjects thoroughly and in detail. The donors to the yeshiva and all religious Jews have charged me with this responsibility.[35]

---

[34] *Ha'amek davar* (Exod. 37: 19). I thank Professor Gershon Bacon for this reference.
[35] Appendix: Document D.

He went on to observe, however, that in practice it is impossible to combine the two spheres of study.[36] In other words, secular studies were desirable, but not within the framework of yeshiva studies. Such opinions were widespread at that time among Jewish scholars in Lithuania. The editor of R. David Friedman's book *Emek haberakhah* (apparently R. Michel Pines) wrote: 'Study of languages has never been forbidden to individuals studying by themselves at home.'[37] R. Friedman, who served as rabbi of Karlin and was a leading rabbinic authority in his time, himself wrote approvingly: 'when outside the Land of Israel . . . they [the Jews] hand over their children to the *talmud torah* and to the elementary yeshivas, so that . . . they may devote a few hours each day to teaching them reading, writing, the local language, and the arithmetic that merchants need'.[38]

R. Berlin practised what he preached and hired a private teacher to teach Russian to Ya'akov and Me'ir,[39] his children by his second wife, though he does not seem to have provided this sort of education for Hayim, the son of his first wife. It seems likely that this change in the education he gave his children bears witness to a shift in his views. The memoirs of Ya'akov Lifschitz, the secretary of R. Yitshak Elhanan Spektor, provide evidence that the study of Russian was tolerated at Volozhin. 'The yeshiva administration did not protest at all against the actual study of Russian, since they already recognized the necessity of knowing the state language.'[40] Lifschitz was not himself a maskil, but he knew people who were.

R. Berlin's opinions were not unique at Volozhin. It is known that when R. Shelomoh Dynkin, who served as *mashgiah* during the yeshiva's last years, was in Warsaw for a consultation with doctors, he took the opportunity to visit the editorial offices of *Hatsefirah* and to meet its famous editor, Hayim Slonimsky, 'whose articles made a great impression on readers at that time'.[41] In other words, R. Dynkin read newspapers and valued what was written in them, though his attitude to secular studies at the yeshiva is not known.

The fact that the *rosh yeshivah* of Volozhin recognized the importance of secular studies does not imply that he wanted to introduce them into the curriculum: on the contrary, he and the other teachers at the yeshiva were

[36] Notwithstanding all his reservations about introducing general studies into the yeshiva, R. Berlin ended his letter by asking to receive 'practical instructions as to how to implement the above demand without harming the yeshiva's primary and particular purpose'. This is a good example of the yeshiva's delaying tactics.

[37] David Friedman, *Emek haberakhah*, 12*a*.   [38] Ibid. 12*b*.

[39] The information about R. Ya'akov comes from a conversation with his daughter, Bertha Papish. On Me'ir Berlin [Bar-Ilan], see his book *From Volozhin to Jerusalem* (Heb.), i. 131.

[40] Lifschitz, *Zikhron ya'akov*, iii. 144. According to Tzinovitz (*Tree of Life* (Heb.), 322), similar opinions are recorded in Ben-Tovim, 'In the Volozhin Yeshiva before its Closure' (Heb.). However, this late article cannot replace contemporary evidence.

[41] Shmukler [Shapira], *Rabbi Moshe Shemuel* (Heb.), 73.

completely opposed to such a move, from a conviction that students should devote all their time to Torah study during their yeshiva years. General knowledge should be acquired before or afterwards. Engagement in secular studies was thus regarded as a distraction from Talmud study, but it was not considered heretical; punishment for such studies (in so far as it was possible at all) was generally light.

Thus, while the Ministry of Education and other bodies made regular demands that secular studies be incorporated in the yeshiva curriculum, the *rosh yeshivah* consistently objected. Since the yeshiva did not receive government funding or support of any kind, there was nothing the authorities could do to promote their position, short of closing the yeshiva. Such a decision was in fact taken in 1880, as emerges from an internal report written about a decade later by the Ministry of the Interior in Vilna:

Later, in 1880, even though the Ministry of the Interior and the Ministry of Public Education did indeed recognize the need to close the Volozhin yeshiva, nevertheless, in view of the fact that it had gained great significance, not only among the Jews of Russia but also abroad, and that its immediate closure might well make an extremely unfavourable impression not only among our Jewish population but also abroad, and would give rise to accusations that under contemporary circumstances would have been not at all desirable, it was required of the administrators of the Volozhin yeshiva only that they comply with the general regulations, though the order was given to resort to the closure of the aforementioned yeshiva in the event of their refusing or being evasive.[42]

However, the decision was not carried out immediately. On 4 September 1880 the superintendent of education of the Vilna district suggested to the supervisor of primary schools in Vilna that the yeshiva be permitted to function, on condition that it comply with the regulations established for Jewish educational institutions on 13 November 1844. These regulations included the requirement that general studies be introduced into every yeshiva.[43] R. Berlin apparently signed an undertaking to comply with the order, but (as might have been expected), he never did so. As the above-mentioned government report notes:

even though steps were taken at that time to bring this institution to order on precisely the basis of the law and the regulation of 13 November 1844, with the procurement of an official undertaking by the yeshiva administration acknowledging its agreement to comply with this law in every particular, in spite of this, however, the Volozhin yeshiva showed no serious proof of any inclination to obey the demands made of it by the government.[44]

[42] The report is dated 10 Apr. 1890; see Appendix: Document B.
[43] See also Appendix: Document E.
[44] Appendix: Document B.

R. Berlin employed delaying tactics by dragging out the correspondence on the topic, correctly assuming that the authorities were in no hurry to take action. In this way the affair went on for a long time.[45]

At the same time, R. Berlin made a great effort to maintain a good relationship with the government and with representatives of the government.[46] One of the ways in which he did so was by marking the Russian holidays connected with the imperial family with great pomp and ceremony. Speeches were read out in the study hall and special prayers were recited, and the *rosh yeshivah* drank a toast to the tsar and his family. In 1883 the local commander (*pristav*) was replaced on the very day of Alexander III's coronation, and the entire yeshiva, staff and students alike, had to repeat the ceremony twice—once in the morning, in the presence of the outgoing commander, and again in the afternoon, in the presence of the new commander.[47]

In fact, the authorities permitted the yeshiva to continue. Thus, for instance, on 24 June 1885 R. Berlin was given an official document recognizing his right to run the yeshiva. A similar document was given to R. Hayim Soloveitchik, recognizing his position as deputy head of the yeshiva.[48] This seems to have been done because the yeshiva was a recognized institution; according to bureaucratic logic, the staff of recognized institutions also had to be recognized. However, recognition had a price: if staff members were recognized, changes in personnel had to be reported and approval requested for new appointments. As will be seen below, this had complex ramifications.

We learn from a report written by a student that appeared in *Hamelits* in 1885 that in the early 1880s approval was tacitly granted for the private study of secular subjects at Volozhin: 'Nor do they [the *rashei yeshivah*] prevent them from devoting time to the education necessary to mental and physical success, as may be seen by the fact that every year a Russian inspector comes to examine the yeshiva students in secular subjects, as required in this sort of school, authorized and established by the government, and he is always pleased with their knowledge and talents.'[49] This comment is not about the organized teaching of secular subjects under the yeshiva's auspices, but rather about private study. The reason for the increased tolerance towards secular

[45] Appendix: Document D: 'the yeshiva administration prefers to gain time by engaging in fruitless correspondence.'

[46] These efforts were not in vain. Thus, for instance, Ivan Fedorovich Starovich, son of the superintendent of schools for the Vilna district (which included Volozhin), apparently wanted to write about the significance of the yeshiva as a place in which study was pursued ceaselessly as a form of spirituality. It seems likely that he got this positive attitude from his father. See Kogan, *In the Storm of History* (Yid.).

[47] B. Goldberg, *Memories of the Past* (Heb.), 9–11. Other descriptions of ceremonies of this sort appear in the reports of Yosef Ben-Tsiyon Demant in *Hamelits*, 28/113 (7 June 1888); 28/281 (3 Jan. 1889). [48] Appendix: Document E.

[49] *Hamelits*, 25/68 (21 Sept. 1885), signed by 'Menahem Mendel Bunimovitsh'.

study is not known, but it seems likely that the interest in these subjects was so great that the yeshiva had little alternative but to acquiesce.

The question of secular studies came up again in 1887, when Shemuel Polyakov, who was one of the richest Jews in Russia, convened a conference of rabbis in St Petersburg to discuss the issue.[50] Polyakov was a determined man with excellent contacts with the authorities. He was interested in promoting the study of secular subjects by Jewish youth and wanted the conference to agree to an entire series of educational reforms. In fact most of his demands were rejected but some of the rabbis, including R. Berlin, were reluctant to antagonize the wealthy philanthropist and therefore accepted some of the measures he proposed:[51]

On the matter on which we were consulted, as to whether the state of the yeshivas in our land could be improved if Russian language and script were taught there . . . we respond:

1. The study of Russian language and script in yeshivas: even though most of those who come to study at the yeshivas already know the Russian language and script, as they have learnt it before they come to the yeshivas, nevertheless the *rosh yeshivah* must employ a teacher of the language and script of our country, Russia, and there must be a house near the yeshiva with space and equipment for these studies, and the yeshiva students who have to learn the Russian language and script will go there to learn from the teacher, who will teach them at a regular time.

2. The aforementioned teacher will teach them nothing but Russian language and script . . . this teacher will not be permitted to keep freethinkers' books there . . . and it is also forbidden for the teacher in his conversations with the students to speak of subjects that arouse freethinking opinions . . .

3. So that we may be assured that what was stated in point 2 is fulfilled, the teacher will be appointed only by the *rosh yeshivah* . . . and nothing will be placed in this house . . . except those books on which the *rosh yeshivah* has written that they may be brought into this house.

4. However, as for the study of knowledge and sciences, and also the study of language and writing . . . not only will they not improve the state of the yeshiva, but they will make it worse, for those philanthropic men who maintain and support them with their money . . . will withhold their donations . . . and worse than this, in a short time the yeshiva will lose its form . . . and the end of the yeshiva, God forbid, will be like the end of the rabbinical school.[52]

---

[50] A. Katz, 'The Background to the Rabbis' Conference in Petersburg' (Heb.). Lifschitz, *Zikhron ya'akov*, iii. 153–7, states that the conference took place in 1885, but the other details match. It is unlikely that there were two conferences on the same subject only two years apart, so the date seems to be wrong.

[51] See 'The Opinion of the Rabbis Led by R. Yitshak Elhanan Concerning Yeshivas' (Heb.), 1 Mar. 1887. A photographic reproduction appears in *Evreiskaya entsiklopediya*, v. 725–6; for a transcription, see Shimoff, *Rabbi Isaac Elchanan Spektor*, 28–30.

[52] N. Berlin, *Letters of the Netsiv* (Heb.), 70–1. R. Berlin was the first signatory. Among the others were R. Yitshak Elhanan Spektor, R. Yosef Dov Soloveitchik, and R. Yitshak Ya'akov Reines.

There were probably other conditions. *Hamelits* reported that the rabbis had decreed that 'as regards the yeshivas . . . only in a special room in a corner of the building may they teach the required subjects to students in the first division, and then only at a time which is neither day nor night'.[53] The rabbis thus agreed that there would be a framework for Russian studies at the yeshivas, though they took pains to ensure that it would not change the atmosphere. Agreement was one thing, but implementation was quite another; as before, R. Berlin was in no hurry to implement the decision.[54]

While R. Berlin was in St Petersburg for the rabbinical conference, the superintendent of education in the Vilna district sent the district supervisor of elementary schools to Volozhin at the head of a deputation to check whether the yeshiva was carrying out its duty to teach Russian according to the 1844 law concerning Jewish education.[55] It is not known if the timing of this inspection was intended for a period when R. Berlin was away or if it was coincidental. Among the members of the delegation was Yehoshua Steinberg, a teacher at the Jewish teachers' college in Vilna.[56] His name crops up repeatedly in the description of the closing of the yeshiva in 1892, several years later, and some accused him of being responsible for it.[57] R. Berlin attributed the closure to 'traitors and plots', without naming anyone or making specific accusations. However, his son, R. Me'ir Berlin, attributed some of the responsibility to Steinberg.[58] Indeed, Steinberg was not reputed to be a great fan of the yeshiva.[59] He was known to be devoted to the Hebrew language and biblical studies but opposed to Talmud study,[60] though he was rather lax in doing anything about it. According to one of his pupils, he displayed no initiative at the teachers' college; he did not fight to introduce Hebrew studies and in general was not particularly active.[61] He published some works but was not known for his honesty.[62] Thus, it might have been anticipated that he would have an

---

[53] *Hamelits*, 27/88 (3 May 1887), according to Tzinovitz, *Tree of Life* (Heb.), 323.

[54] Schacter, 'Haskalah, Secular Studies and the Close of the Yeshiva in Volozhin', 107.

[55] Appendix: Document B.   [56] See J. Gottlieb, 'Joshua Steinberg'.

[57] See the report by Perets Shalom Sach in *Hatsefirah*, 14/35 (16 Mar. 1887), and also *Hamelits*, 37/40 (28 Feb. 1887).

[58] M. Berlin [Bar-Ilan], *Rabbi of Israel* (Heb.), 141. However, J. Gottlieb states that the yeshiva was closed despite Steinberg's objections, though no evidence is given ('Joshua Steinberg').

[59] D. Eliach, *Father of the Yeshivas* (Heb.), 603.

[60] 'Hamashkif' [Joseph Klausner], '"Steinberg, Yehoshua"' (Heb.). The identification of Klausner is based on Attia, *The Hebrew Periodical Ha-Shiloah (1896–1919)*.

[61] H. Y. Katznelson, 'Yehoshua Steinberg' (Heb.).

[62] In a critical book review in *Knizhki Voskhoda* (Dec. 1902), 165–9, his former pupil Y. Katznelson proved that Steinberg's commentary on the book of Joshua (Vilna, 1902) was actually a translation of a German commentary by Herxheimer (see the entry on him (attributed to the editors) in *Encyclopaedia Judaica*, viii, col. 401). A similar claim of plagiarism was made by Goldblum about Steinberg's book *Ma'arekhei leshon ever* (Goldblum, *Book Reviews* (Heb.)). See also the pseudonymous account (by Yasbab Hasofer) in *Hamelits*, 26/30 (30 Apr. 1886), in the

inimical attitude to the yeshiva but, at the same time, it would not have been entirely surprising if in spite of his declarations of loyalty to the tsar he would have been prepared to accept a bribe to present a positive report.[63]

The deputation stayed in Volozhin for a week. They checked the students' documents, and living conditions, and also examined their knowledge of Russian. It seems likely that the timing of the visit—during R. Berlin's absence—was not accidental; certainly it did not work to the yeshiva's advantage.[64] It is not clear exactly what the deputation found. However on his return R. Berlin demanded the students' documents and certificates of exemption from military service, so that there would not be any problems during future visits.[65]

It is possible that some of the students themselves tried to engineer government involvement in the question of general studies. In a letter written by R. Yitshak Elhanan Spektor on 30 January 1890 to 'one of the wealthy philanthropists' of St Petersburg he claimed that there were young people who were spreading false information about the yeshiva in an attempt to get the government to intervene in this regard. He therefore asked his correspondent to lobby on behalf of the yeshiva in government circles and explain what it was trying to achieve.[66]

Such student denunciations may have been a factor in the decision of the governor of the Vilna district on 21 December 1889 to close the yeshiva on the grounds that the commitment to add secular studies to the curriculum had not been fulfilled.[67] There were also those in government circles who claimed that the prolonged tolerance shown to the yeshiva was publicly regarded as a sign of weakness, and that the affair was damaging both to the implementation of educational policy and government dignity. He estimated that between 400 and 450 young men studied at the yeshiva, and its annual budget was about 14,000 roubles. He also claimed that the yeshiva served as a refuge for undesirables, draft-dodgers, and others disloyal to the government.[68] In his opinion, the Zionist activity at the yeshiva, in the form of the secret organization led by Rotstein,[69] proved the danger in the yeshiva's continued operation; it was a branch of the 'Secret Jewish Kahal'.[70] The use of this term reflects the widespread belief in contemporary Russia that a secret Jewish organization (the 'Kahal') was trying to gain control of Russia (or of the

section *Dikdukei soferim*, 470–1. On the way in which Steinberg used his position as censor to persecute literary enemies, see Yosef G. Klausner, *History of Modern Hebrew Literature* (Heb.), iv. 184–6.

[63] Abramowicz, *Disappeared Images* (Yid.), 200–1. [64] *Hatsefirah*, 14/53 (16 Mar. 1887).
[65] *Hatsefirah*, 14/68 (3 Apr. 1887). [66] Lifschitz, *Zikhron ya'akov*, iii. 143–4.
[67] The data come from Appendix: Document B. [68] See ibid.
[69] On Rotstein and the Nes Ziona organization, see Ch. 7 above.

[70] The term 'Secret Kahal' was common among Russian antisemites, and was based on the publications of Ya'akov Brafman; on whom see Klier, *Imperial Russia's Jewish Question*.

world), a belief that increased fears about secret Jewish activity. But again the closure order was not carried out, possibly as the result of rabbinic intervention with the authorities.[71]

The pressure exerted on the yeshiva to introduce secular studies eventually bore fruit. In 1890, apparently fearing that the authorities would in fact close down the yeshiva, R. Berlin decided to set up a framework for secular studies under the yeshiva's aegis, and began to take steps to carry out his decision.[72] This was a great innovation, of course, even though such study was not compulsory, did not take up much time, and did not take place in the yeshiva itself—though where exactly these studies took place is not clear. However, for the first time secular studies were given an official place in the study programme at the yeshiva. At first there were twenty-five participants and the number rose to fifty—which was about 20 per cent of the student body.[73] Ultimately, fifty students were registered for the lessons, thirty-five in the beginners' class and fifteen in the advanced class.[74] According to the evidence of the son of one of these students, students 'whose piety was more outstanding than their learning' were chosen; they were regarded as 'volunteers' who would save the yeshiva by their participation.[75] Even so, it seems likely that at least a few of the participants actually wanted to learn Russian, even if they did not admit it. R. Berlin made sure that the teacher was not Jewish, probably fearing that a Jewish teacher who supported the Haskalah might have a bad influence on the students, while a non-Jewish teacher would content himself with teaching Russian. This angered the local maskilim, of course. Secular studies were held initially once a week, in the evening, and lasted for about

[71] Lifschitz, *Zikhron ya'akov*, iii. 143–4.

[72] See the report from 7 Jan. 1892 in Appendix: Document D; see also M. Berlin [Bar-Ilan], *Rabbi of Israel* (Heb.), 136; id., *From Volozhin to Jerusalem* (Heb.), i. 164; Don-Yihia, 'Memoirs' (Heb.), *Netivah*, 12/11; H. L. Gordon, 'The Son Will Honour the Father' (Heb.); Ben-Tovim, 'In the Volozhin Yeshiva before its Closure' (Heb.); Schacter, 'Haskalah, Secular Studies and the Close of the Yeshiva in Volozhin', 107–9. According to Kamenetsky, this attitude was supported by R. Mordechai Solomonov, one of the most important *gaba'im* of the yeshiva (*The Making of a Godol*, i. 447). R. Tanhum Frank published a partial quotation from a letter by R. Berlin on this step, but did not note the source; see Frank, *The History of God's House in Volozhin* (Heb.), 130. R. Berlin wrote: 'This term we were studying the tractate *Eruvin*. The reforms . . . were according to the wishes of the director of authorized schools, and we were compelled to fulfil his desires to impose the Russian language on the students who were leaving, from a non-Jewish teacher for an hour and a half, so that they might derive benefit from this . . . for the public when they would merit a rabbinic appointment, but indeed even though there are students, thank God, from every place, this lesson was only made compulsory for twenty of them, and nothing harmed the students.'

[73] Lithuanian State Historical Archive, *fond* 568, *opis'* 1, *delo* 761, esp. *listy* 29–30.

[74] As recorded in Appendix: Document D. This does not match the number given by R. Berlin.

[75] H. L. Gordon, 'The Son Will Honour the Father' (Heb.); see also Binyamini, *Yesteryear* (Heb.), 8.

two hours.[76] They were not intensive and the students did not always take them very seriously; attendance was irregular. It seems that, over time, the number of students attending rose.[77] Their progress was not very impressive, as the authorities noticed, but it was progress.[78] A demand was made that the number of students learning Russian should be raised to a hundred,[79] but it was not implemented.

R. Naftali Berlin did not want the yeshiva students to study secular subjects as part of their studies at the yeshiva, but was prepared to submit to the demand that a few dozen students should engage in such studies once a week, for an hour and a half, in order to prevent the yeshiva being closed. According to a report in the London *Jewish Chronicle* on 1 September 1893, R. Naftali Berlin made efforts to reopen the yeshiva with a limited amount of general studies as part of the programme:

> The Jews in Russia have lost a distinguished Hebrew scholar and one of their foremost rabbinical authorities by the death of Rabbi Naphtali Zevi Berlin, Principal of the great Yeshiba at Wolozin, which was closed by order of the Government about two years ago. Subsequently to this occurrence Rabbi Berlin travelled through Western Europe, with the object of obtaining funds for the extension of the Yeshiba as a secular as well as a theological college, but the Government has not sanctioned the alteration. The closing of the College considerably affected the health of Rabbi Berlin, who settled in Warsaw, where he died.[80]

The well-documented evidence for R. Berlin's recognition of the importance of secular studies and his grudging willingness to introduce a small amount of such studies into the curriculum contradict the well-known version of events written by his son R. Hayim Berlin in his will:

> The *gaon* my father commanded me . . . before his death, concerning how he had sacrificed himself in the matter of the Volozhin yeshiva, not to introduce any secular study there, and for this reason they closed down the yeshiva and this is why he became ill with a mortal illness, and he commanded me with a warning never to agree to this matter in any way . . . and said that this was alluded to in the Torah which requires to us to distinguish between the holy and the profane, that is that when the profane mixes in with the holy without distinction, not only do secular studies not become sanctified, but sacred studies are spoiled by them.[81]

---

[76] Don-Yihia, 'Memoirs' (Heb.), *Netivah*, 12/11; Lifschitz, *Zikhron ya'akov*, iii. 144–5.

[77] Lithuanian State Historical Archive, *fond* 568, *opis'* 1, *delo* 761, esp. *list* 69.

[78] Appendix: Document D.

[79] See the letter from the superintendent of education, Appendix: Document D: 'the director of elementary schools in the Vilna district issued a demand that the number of those learning general studies should be raised to at least one hundred.'

[80] I was led to this source by <http://onthemainline.blogspot.com/2009/06/what-happened-to-volozhiner-roshei.html>.

[81] Schacter, 'Haskalah, Secular Studies and the Close of the Yeshiva in Volozhin', 78; see also H. Berlin, *Nishmat ḥayim*, 121.

It is impossible to check the original quotation today since R. Hayim Berlin's handwritten will has 'disappeared', though contemporaries attested that this was indeed in his handwriting. However, even if we suppose that this is an accurate quotation, it raises several problems.

There is no doubt that classes in Russian and mathematics were given to some of the students within the framework of the yeshiva. In the Lithuanian State Historical Archive there are detailed reports of these studies by the teachers.[82] In one of these letters Yunovich, a Jewish teacher who graduated from the government Jewish Teachers' Institute, wrote that fifty students attended but that these were religious fanatics who did not really want to study secular topics. He reported that a yeshiva student who expressed a desire to participate in the programme of secular studies was specifically excluded because the heads of the yeshiva did not want students to be distracted from the study of Talmud. Yunovich went on to claim that advanced yeshiva students recognized that a solid knowledge of Russian was essential for a rabbinical career but that they were afraid to ask R. Naftali Berlin to expand the programme for them—so they took private tutors and studied Russian late at night and in secret.[83]

R. Hayim Berlin was in Volozhin when the yeshiva was closed, and had no need of his father's dying words to know what led to its closure. It is not likely that R. Naftali Berlin felt on his deathbed that he had to tell his son about what they no doubt had discussed many times and to which the son had been an eyewitness. The continuation of the will is also problematic. R. Hayim Berlin relates of his father that 'this is why he became ill with a mortal illness'. It is well known that he fell ill before the yeshiva's closure, since this is why he wanted to hand over the running of the yeshiva to his son. Even more perplexing is the passage where R. Hayim Berlin quotes his father as saying: 'not only do secular studies not become sanctified, but sacred studies are spoiled by them'. This contradicts R. Berlin's own words in his commentary *Ha'amek davar*, as noted above. It is difficult to explain these contradictions. In general, it is difficult to accept the words of a dying man, even when reported by a scholar as great as R. Hayim Berlin, as accurate historical evidence. When he was in the presence of his ailing father he must have been upset, and this would doubtless have influenced his memory of the occasion. In addition, R. Hayim's will was written in Jerusalem, where he might have been influenced by the widespread opposition in certain circles to secular studies. Whatever the case, it is difficult to accept this single late piece of evidence as representing the entire truth and to entirely reject all the evidence presented above that R. Berlin regarded certain secular studies as acceptable.

Elsewhere secular studies were incorporated into curricula on the government's orders. The Agudat Yisra'el movement in Poland between the world

[82] Lithuanian State Historical Archive, *fond* 568, *opis'* 1, *delo* 806.   [83] Ibid., *listy* 32–3.

wars was led by R. Yisra'el Me'ir Hakohen (the Hafets Hayim, 1838–1933), who was well known for his opposition to any change in traditional education. Nonetheless, when the Polish government demanded the inclusion of secular studies in the yeshiva curriculum, Agudat Yisra'el complied fully. R. Yisra'el Me'ir Hakohen did not fully or explicitly support this but tacitly accepted the situation.[84] R. Yosef Leib Bloch of Telz took a similar stance,[85] as did other leading rabbis, such as R. David Friedman of Pinsk who was cited above.[86] Even central figures in the *musar* movement followed suit, such as R. Simhah Zissel of Kelme (a follower of R. Yisra'el Salanter) and R. Yeruham Leibowitz, and very possibly R. Yisra'el Salanter himself,[87] as will be discussed in the following chapters. It thus seems that among Lithuanian rabbis, categorical opposition to secular studies was the exception; most rabbis were prepared to compromise.

3. The Choice of R. Berlin's Successor

In the yeshiva's last years, besides the mounting pressure from the authorities to introduce secular studies there was also a bitter internal struggle going on. R. Berlin was old and ailing and wanted to retire and spend his last years in Jerusalem, and there was the question of who should succeed him.

During this period, the yeshiva did not function as well as previously. The Russian Ministry of Education in the Vilna region saw the situation at the yeshiva in these terms:

Until recently the yeshiva administration fulfilled its duty to present lists of the students to the educational authorities, according to the regulations of 13 November 1844, in a more or less satisfactory manner. Now the yeshiva is no longer carrying out even this duty: in spite of repeated reminders from the director, lists of students at the yeshiva have not been presented to the school administration. As a result, the administration cannot check the true number of yeshiva students, and cannot verify whether all the yeshiva students have presented their passports as required, nor whether there are any among the students who have no passport or who are evading military service.[88]

This state of affairs does not seem to reflect a shift in policy but simply a failure in administration. For decades, all the responsibilities of managing the yeshiva

[84] See London, 'The Hafets Hayim and the Struggle over the Form of Jewish Education'. On changes in the interwar period, see Bacon, *The Politics of Tradition*, ch. 7, 'The Quiet Revolution'. On the Satmar hasidim's agreement to include secular studies in elementary schools in the United States, see the entertaining description by a non-Jewish teacher, Albarelli, *Teacha!* Obviously there is a difference between elementary and advanced studies, but the principle is the same. On readiness to compromise in eastern Europe, see Kamenetsky, *The Making of a Godol*, i. 534. [85] See the sources in Altman, '"And his head reached heaven"' (Heb.), 7.
[86] See n. 38 above, and see Kamenetsky, *The Making of a Godol*, ii. 1031.
[87] On R. Simhah Zissel Ziv, see Ch. 10 below; on R. Yeruham, see Kamenetsky, *The Making of a Godol*, i. 511. [88] Appendix: Document D.

had fallen on R. Naftali Berlin; his frailty now had serious consequences, making it imperative to appoint a successor as swiftly as possible. It is important to remember that the *rosh yeshivah* was responsible for many other tasks in addition to teaching. This is made very clear from an interesting correspondence between R. Eliyahu David Rabinowitz-Theomim and the Mir yeshiva in 1899. R. Rabinowitz-Theomim was invited to become *rosh yeshivah* in Mir, but he declined on the grounds that it would be difficult for him to teach every day. His correspondents replied: 'The main thing is not the teaching . . . [but] running the yeshiva, its financial affairs, [supervising] the collectors of donations and the students . . . and writing letters.'[89] A *rosh yeshivah* thus had to be a good administrator as well as a good teacher. It was not easy to find such a man.

During this period an attempt seems to have been made to bring in R. Eliezer Simhah Rabinowitz as *rosh yeshivah*. He had many qualifications for the job: he was a scholar of some repute who had married into the family of R. Yitshak of Volozhin, and he also spoke Russian and was familiar with government procedures. However, the negotiations with him, which lasted about two years, got nowhere. It was then that R. Berlin seems to have decided to appoint his son R. Hayim Berlin to the post.[90]

Family ties had always played a role in the appointment of a *rosh yeshivah*. After the death of the founder R. Hayim, his son R. Yitshak had taken his place. His sons-in-law, R. Eliezer Yitshak and R. Naftali Berlin, succeeded him. Thus, when R. Naftali Berlin felt that his time was over, it was natural for him to seek a successor from his family. However, there were only three possible candidates. R. Hayim Berlin, his son by his first wife, was an outstanding scholar and was eventually chosen. His sons by his second wife, Ya'akov and Me'ir, were still too young.[91] R. Naftali also had two daughters, Sarah and Dreizl, by his first wife. Sarah had married R. Rafa'el Shapira, and after she died at a young age he married her sister Dreizl. R. Shapira served as R. Naftali Berlin's deputy for over a decade. In 1881 he took up the post of rabbi of Novoaleksandrovsk, giving up the position of deputy *rosh yeshivah* in favour of his son-in-law, R. Hayim Soloveitchik. R. Shapira could theoretically have returned to Volozhin, though we do not know whether this idea was ever suggested. He might not have wanted to harm the prospects of the third candidate—his son-in-law R. Hayim Soloveitchik. This would have been in keeping with his personality. R. Shapira was known for his humility; he once

---

[89] See R. Rabinowitz-Theomim's autobiography, *Seder eliyahu*, 103. On the incident, see Kinstlicher, 'A Chapter in the History of the Mir Yeshiva' (Heb.).

[90] Lifschitz, *Zikhron ya'akov*, iii. 145; Zeira, *Our Sages in the Diaspora* (Heb.), i. 148–50; A. Y. Katz, 'The Great Yeshivas of Volozhin and Mir' (Heb.), 107 n. 9. R. Naftali Berlin may not have taken the decision on his own to choose R. Hayim Berlin as his successor, but the sources do not reveal evidence of consultation on the matter.

[91] On R. Ya'akov, see his daughter's autobiography: Papish-Berlin, *Unforgettable Sounds* (Heb.), ch. 3.

remarked to R. Naftali Berlin, 'My son-in-law is more talented than your son-in-law [i.e. himself].'[92] It is also possible that he felt responsible for his community and did not want to leave it.

R. Hayim Berlin, born in 1832, was the son of R. Naftali Tsevi Berlin and played a major role in the history of the yeshiva.[93] As a young man he had married the daughter of a wealthy resident of Shklov, and his father-in-law had supported him. In 1865 the father-in-law became bankrupt and the son-in-law was forced to take a post as rabbi in Moscow. He had a reputation as a talented preacher and a great Talmud scholar, though he never attained the level of his father or of R. Hayim Soloveitchik. He remained in Moscow until his wife died in 1883. Not long after her death, and to the surprise of many, he became engaged. R. Hayim Berlin's fiancée, Tila, was the daughter of a prominent hasid and businessman, R. Isaac Shachor, in Biała, but when R. Hayim married her she was already a personality in her own right. She was not willing to move to Moscow and take on the role of 'the rabbi's wife', and it seems that one of the conditions of the marriage was that the couple live in Biała. At the time this caused a sensation because R. Hayim was known as the rabbi of the non-hasidic Jews in Moscow and now he was moving to a town that was mainly hasidic.[94] Tila was born around 1842, and in her first marriage she had been the wife of a well-to-do timber dealer. However, a freak accident led to the sinking of a large raft of logs that he had sent to Danzig with huge financial loss. The catastrophe broke his heart; he died shortly afterwards, and she was left on her own. The couple had been childless and the widow took over the business full-time with the intention of paying off the accumulated debts. However, she did not stop when they were paid off, and she turned into one of the major timber dealers in the region—which was a high-risk and high-profit field. It was at this point that she married R. Hayim Berlin in 1884. He settled in Biała in her luxurious dwelling and spent his days studying Torah while she continued in business. He showed no interest in teaching or in getting involved in yeshiva matters. However, on a sabbath afternoon walk in 1891 with two nieces, Tila complained that she felt weak, collapsed, and died of a heart attack. She was only 50 years old. After the mourning period, the family opened up her iron safe and found in it 560,000 roubles as well as many promissory notes and other valuables. She also owned a number of buildings. This would have been enough to cover the debt of the Volozhin yeshiva many times over, but nothing is known of support from Tila for the yeshiva. It is not known how much R. Hayim Berlin inherited, but it is known that each of her siblings received 60,000 roubles. Shortly after getting his share, he left Biała for Volozhin.[95]

[92] Rivkind, 'Rabbi Rafa'el Shapira' (Heb.), 228.
[93] Eliezer Leone wrote his biography; see Leone (ed.), *Volozhin* (Heb.), 215–20, and the bibliography there.
[94] See Zederbaum, in *Hamelits*, 20 (24 Oct. 1884), 80.   [95] Shain, 'Tila Berlin'.

R. Hayim's arrival in Volozhin coincided with the departure of his son-in-law, Ephraim Samunov, who had played an important role in the yeshiva. In the light of R. Hayim's vocal opposition to secular study in his later years, it is worth noting that Ephraim Samunov was far from coming from a radically anti-modernist family. His grandfather served as rabbi in Mitau in Courland. There, as is many other places, the elite sent their children to study in gymnasiums (high schools) even though these schools had classes on the sabbath. He did not launch a campaign to try to convince parents not to send their children to such schools. Instead, he embarked on a successful effort to arrange for Jewish gymnasium students to be freed from the requirement to attend classes on the sabbath—and implicitly accepting the reality of secular study.[96]

At the age of 15, Ephraim was sent to study in Volozhin. He studied very well there, and quickly acquired a reputation for being a talented talmudist. While he was in the yeshiva he was very close to R. Hayim Soloveitchik. After three years of study, he returned to Mitau and continued studying Talmud and Jewish law in his father's house. This he could have done in Volozhin, but he also studied other subjects that he could not have studied there—secular studies and languages. At the age of 20 he was offered an exceptional match—the granddaughter of R. Naftali Tsevi Yehudah Berlin. Her father was R. Hayim Berlin who was then serving as a rabbi in Moscow. According to his uncle, the match was vetted by the family in Volozhin and approved. Clearly, they were aware of his secular studies and this apparently did not lead to any complications. It may even have been a positive factor in the eyes of R. Hayim Berlin. As was customary, the groom moved into his father-in-law's household in Moscow. It would have been rather difficult for him to function in that city without a good knowledge of Russian.[97]

While in Moscow, R. Ephraim Samunov went into business, using his dowry as capital. However, he lost his money and returned to Volozhin in 1887 with the goal of studying until he could find a rabbinic position. His arrival coincided with increasing government supervision of the yeshiva. One of the government demands was that the yeshiva should employ a teacher for every fifty students. Yeshiva study was based on independent study, but the government policy made the reasonable assumption that a yeshiva was like a school and that therefore a minimal ratio of teachers to students was necessary. The yeshiva got round this by reporting on its books that R. Dynkin, the *mashgiah* of the yeshiva, was a secondary teacher in addition to R. Berlin and R. Soloveitchik. However, this was not enough because there were more than 200 students. Therefore, R. Samunov was reported as a second secondary teacher—though there is no evidence that he ever taught Talmud in the yeshiva.[98] However, he was intelligent

[96] Milikovski-Samsonov, *Ohalei aharon*, 168.   [97] Ibid. 202.

[98] Lithuanian State Historical Archive, *fond 568, opis' 1, delo 982.* See especially *listy 5–8.* In this document, R. Hayim Hillel Fried is recorded as a fifth teacher.

and he did play an important role in the yeshiva because he handled much of the institution's Russian-language correspondence.

In 1890 R. Samunov was offered the position of rabbi in Jacobstadt, in what today is Latvia, and he accepted the invitation. In the same year, his father-in-law, R. Hayim Berlin returned to Volozhin. It is not clear if the two events were linked and if the son-in-law found it prudent to relocate. In any case, his absence did not help the yeshiva in its dealings with the government.

R. Hayim Berlin was seen as a capable administrator who could successfully deal with all the tasks necessary to run the yeshiva. A hint that this is what influenced R. Naftali Berlin in appointing him may be seen in the wording of the announcement published in *Hamelits* on his appointment. His role was described as being 'to collect . . . to maintain . . . to fill the empty coffers'.[99] Even after the closure of the yeshiva, R. Hayim Berlin threw himself into raising money to pay off the yeshiva's debts.[100] While he was clearly a serious scholar, he had not built up a reputation over the years as a teacher or interpreter of the Talmud. It might have been possible to split the teaching and administrative roles, but no suggestion of doing this was ever made, as far as we know.

There were those who accused R. Naftali Berlin of nepotism in appointing his son as head of the yeshiva because R. Hayim Soloveitchik was a greater scholar. Binyamin Goldberg, who was a student at the yeshiva during these years, records:

He decided to crown his son, R. Hayim Berlin, as his successor. This rabbi, with all respect, displayed several negative traits . . . he deceived his father, R. Berlin, with talmudic plagiarisms, for he had a very rich library of all the fields of Hebrew and rabbinic literature. From these infinite and mighty depths he used to draw up pearls of wisdom and present them to his father as though they were his own ideas, and his father thought that he must be a true genius, worthy to succeed him. But when he began to give *shiurim* before the outstanding students . . . they plied him with questions as complicated as the matter of Akhnai's oven [a famous talmudic debate], and they forced him to the wall. His father was astounded and dumbstruck, and asked him hoarsely, 'Hayim, why do you not demolish this refutation with the famous Tosafot from tractate *Zevaḥim*, page such-and-such . . . and this refutation with the answer given in *Sha'agat aryeh*?', and so on. In spite of this, his son did not decline the position, and his father did not change his mind, and [his son] stood at his right hand, for love overrides discipline.[101]

In spite of his love for his son, R. Naftali Berlin was well aware of how important it was that a scholar of acknowledged authority be appointed *rosh yeshivah*.

---

[99] *Hamelits*, 31/45 (6 Mar. 1891).

[100] It should not be concluded from this that R. Soloveitchik made no effort at all in the financial sphere. See Kamenetsky, *The Making of a Godol*, ii. 1070–1, on the raising of a very large donation for the Volozhin yeshiva from Barukh Zeldovitz of Minsk. The year in which this happened is not recorded.   [101] B. Goldberg, *Memories of the Past* (Heb.), 16–17.

It is thus difficult to accept Goldberg's claim that it was no more than paternal affection that determined the appointment, or even that this was the main factor behind it. In order to understand R. Berlin's motivations, R. Hayim Soloveitchik's attributes must also be taken into account.

Many people thought that R. Soloveitchik was the most suitable candidate for the post. He was a superb scholar and his innovative ways of thinking have influenced generations of Talmud scholars. It is difficult to describe the deep impression that he made on young scholars of his time. His grandson, R. Yosef Dov Soloveitchik, said of his grandfather that in his understanding (but apparently, not in his mastery of sources) he surpassed even the Vilna Gaon.[102] He also developed a close relationship with his students, who loved and admired him. However, his abilities as an administrator and disciplinarian do not seem to have matched his intellectual gifts. From Binyamin Goldberg's memoirs we learn things about R. Soloveitchik that may shed light on R. Naftali Berlin's preference for his son:

When R. Berlin was old he saw that his strength was failing, and that he could not continue to go out and in and manage the administrative affairs of the yeshiva, especially the financial side, and he saw that he could not possibly hand over the reins to his deputy, the *gaon* R. Hayim Soloveitchik, of blessed memory; for because of his intensity and sensitive nature, he would never be able to deliver the slaps that R. Berlin, of blessed memory, used to give the students when he was angry at them for some sin they had committed during prayers, or in cutting their *pe'ot*, or reading secular books, but because of [R. Soloveitchik's] love for all mankind he would have given away all he owned to the first person who asked for it, and if he received a donation for the yeshiva, he would have immediately given it to some poor and unhappy individual, to furnish his bride with a dowry or buy him a horse or repair his house.[103]

It thus seems that R. Naftali chose his son to succeed him partly because he thought that R. Hayim Soloveitchik was less capable as an administrator.[104] R. Naftali had experienced the difficulties of managing the yeshiva's complex financial system and knew the importance of sound administration. A *rosh yeshivah* had to pay careful attention to financial matters, since the yeshiva could not otherwise fund all those who wanted to study there. In previous chapters we saw cases of students who were rejected on financial grounds but who then appealed to R. Soloveitchik, who accepted them with no regard for the practical economic consequences. While this is a clear sign of his compassion, it also demonstrates his lack of concern or awareness of the financial realities of the yeshiva.

---

[102] Kamenetsky, *The Making of a Godol*, i. 432.

[103] B. Goldberg, *Memories of the Past* (Heb.), 16.

[104] Kamenetsky, *The Making of a Godol*, ii. 988. On R. Soloveitchik as a teacher (not a lecturer), see p. 926.

After the closure of the yeshiva, R. Soloveitchik became rabbi of Brisk. Many students came to him there, but he did not set up his own yeshiva. He seems to have lacked the enterprise to run a yeshiva, and may have feared that running an institution would have interfered with his studying.[105] R. Naftali Berlin thus had good reason to think that R. Soloveitchik was not suited to dealing with the disciplinary issues, institutional affairs, and fundraising for a large yeshiva like Volozhin.

R. Soloveitchik's own attitude to the struggle over the succession is still not totally clear. It is not known whether he really wanted to be *rosh yeshivah*. He never expressed a view on the matter in public though some idea of his opinions can be gleaned from the memoirs of the son of R. Yitshak Eizik Halevi Rabinowitz, who was a *gabai* of the yeshiva:

My father and mentor of blessed memory and R. Hayim of Brisk [i.e. Soloveitchik] had nothing against the personality of R. Hayim Berlin, but they did not approve of his appointment, though they hesitated to distress R. Berlin, of blessed memory, or to affront R. Hayim's honour; so they waited for an appropriate time when matters would become clearer and they could both argue that [the appointment] would be a mistake.[106]

In Volozhin, it was generally believed that R. Soloveitchik wanted to be *rosh yeshivah*, and even the Russian authorities felt this to be the case;[107] in this view, his silence about the matter did not mean that his opinions were unknown. True, he did not publicly seek to succeed R. Naftali Berlin; but despite his desire not to distress the latter and despite his concern for the honour of R. Hayim Berlin, he did not appeal to his students to support R. Hayim Berlin and nor did he himself express public support for R. Hayim Berlin's appointment.[108] It seems reasonable to assume that his students, who knew him well, reflected his feelings in their behaviour.

[105] However, it seems likely that R. Naftali Berlin feared at one point that R. Soloveitchik would open a yeshiva of his own that would compete with Volozhin, though he never did so (ibid. 911–13).   [106] Auerbach (ed.), *Yitshak Eizik Halevi Memorial Volume* (Heb.), 27.

[107] See Appendix: Document D.

[108] After the closure of the Volozhin yeshiva, R. Hayim Berlin tried to obtain the post of rabbi of Międzyrzec Podlaski. The previous town rabbi, R. Israel Isser Shapira, had died in 1894 and the position was in theory available. However, his son, R. Dov Nahman Shapira, presented himself as a candidate for the position and apparently claimed he had an inherited right to the position. R. Soloveitchik made a visit to Międzyrzec Podlaski for the express purpose of supporting the heir. It could be claimed that this was a settling of accounts. However, it seems reasonable to suppose that he was motivated in this by a desire to do justice. R. Soloveitchik indeed claimed that, in Jewish law, R. Hayim Berlin's rival had a right to the position. However, it is not known whether R. Soloveitchik ever intervened in any other question of inherited rabbinical posts in Lithuania, and it certainly was most unusual for a nephew to take sides against his uncle, especially since the two rabbis were not on friendly terms. In any event, R. Hayim Berlin was not appointed to the position. See Kamenetsky, *The Making of a Godol*, i. 451–3, ii. 1286–8, and Edelbaum, 'Rabbi Dov Nahman Shapira' (Heb.), 264.

4. The Dispute Over the Succession

The precise timing of the appointment of R. Hayim Berlin as head of the yeshiva is not clear. The succession was mentioned in a letter he wrote in the summer of 1889 as something to prepare for:

My honoured father, the *gaon* and righteous man, may he merit a long and prosperous life, has strictly charged me to dwell in Volozhin and to immerse myself in the management of the holy yeshiva, the eternal ideal of our ancestors. And its management and maintenance has for some time been too much for him, now that he is advanced in years, and I must prepare myself to take his place, may God lengthen his days and his years.[109]

At this stage, R. Hayim Berlin was assisting his father but did not yet have an official position; this came only in the spring of 1891 or perhaps a little earlier. When the appointment was made, it immediately split the yeshiva. Most of the students had wanted R. Soloveitchik to be the next *rosh yeshivah*, on the grounds that R. Hayim Berlin was not sufficiently distinguished as a scholar; some went so far as to regard his appointment as an insult.[110] Clearly, their years of familiarity with R. Soloveitchik worked against R. Hayim Berlin, who had had no links with the students. After his appointment, however, he did try to establish greater contact with them by lending them books from his extensive private library,[111] but to no avail. The students remained far closer to R. Soloveitchik, as will be seen below.

According to R. Hayim Berlin's half-brother, R. Me'ir Berlin, there were other reasons that the students did not want R. Hayim Berlin:

Even though my brother was no less distinguished in Torah, righteousness, and good qualities than most of the great scholars of his time, as *rosh yeshivah* he did not continue the tradition of the *rashei yeshivah* of Volozhin. There was in particular a striking opposition between his views and those of my father, of blessed memory, concerning the management of the yeshiva. The decades my brother had spent as a rabbi in Moscow, and the period afterwards when he lived as a wealthy private citizen, had influenced him in directions that were not customary at the yeshiva. He set regular hours for meeting the students and discussing Torah matters with them. This was an innovation at the yeshiva. They had been used to the idea that any time was suitable for a discussion of Torah matters or for going to see the rabbi, whether day or night.[112]

[109] The letter is in the Yerushalimski Collection in the Schocken Library and is dated Sivan (June) 1889.

[110] See the detailed descriptions in Zlatkin, 'The Volozhin Yeshiva in Bialik's Time' (Heb.), 64; B. Goldberg, *Memories of the Past* (Heb.), 16. Zlatkin wrote: 'He had no right to this, except his ancestral merit and the merit of his father, R. Berlin. And at the same time the man who deserved the post of rector, R. Hayim Soloveitchik, was already there in the yeshiva.'

[111] Zlatkin, 'The Volozhin Yeshiva in Bialik's Time' (Heb.), 63.

[112] M. Berlin [Bar-Ilan], *From Volozhin to Jerusalem* (Heb.), i. 162. In the continuation of this passage, he emphasizes R. Hayim Berlin's responsibility for financial matters.

Many of those who campaigned against R. Hayim Berlin's appointment justified themselves by saying that his appointment would be an insult to R. Soloveitchik, as will be discussed below. But it seems that behind this concern for R. Soloveitchik's honour lay another factor: the fear that if R. Hayim Berlin were chosen, R. Soloveitchik would leave Volozhin.[113] This was a serious possibility. R. Soloveitchik was married to R. Naftali Berlin's grand-daughter and thus had to defer to him, but he had no direct familial ties with R. Hayim Berlin, and it was very doubtful whether he would agree to work under him. There seem to have been rumours that R. Naftali Berlin tried to find R. Soloveitchik a rabbinical post outside Volozhin. Had R. Soloveitchik accepted a proposal of this sort, the situation would definitely have been much simpler.[114] However, he did not. The atmosphere in the yeshiva resembled that which had prevailed during the conflict between R. Yosef Dov Soloveitchik and R. Naftali Berlin—and R. Hayim Soloveitchik would surely not have forgotten the outcome of that dispute.

The rift over the unpopular appointment soon became public knowledge and both R. Naftali Berlin and the yeshiva students appealed to external bodies for support. The students wrote letters to rabbis and public figures,[115] and addressed the wider public by means of the newspapers. In a report from Minsk published in *Hamelits*, a certain Eliezer Bran described a large meeting held there at which R. Hayim Berlin had been chosen, though he did not supply any further details.[116] In the issue of *Hamelits* that appeared less than a fortnight after the meeting, there was fierce criticism.[117] A writer using the pen name Mordecai Gamzu criticized the choice of R. Hayim Berlin without any preliminary announcement to the general public, and stated that *ḥokhmat yisra'el*—which may be roughly translated as 'modern Jewish studies'—should be included in the yeshiva curriculum. It should be noted that this criticism apparently did not actually come from yeshiva circles. A response appeared about a week later, signed by 'Aba Arash'. It claimed that both Jewish and secular studies were being taught at the yeshiva, and added that R. Hayim

[113] Don-Yihia, 'Memoirs' (Heb.), *Netivah*, 12/11.

[114] Kamenetsky, *The Making of a Godol*, i. 191–2, 449.

[115] Zlatkin, 'The Volozhin Yeshiva in Bialik's Time' (Heb.), 64.

[116] *Hamelits*, 31/45 (6 Mar. 1891), 5, signed by Eliezer Bran. The report stated that the meeting had been convened in Minsk 'to take advice on the improvement of the material and ethical status of the Volozhin yeshiva . . . and to appoint a *rosh yeshivah* . . . and documents and letters were sent to the rabbis of the region, asking them to come to our city to take counsel with our teacher, the *gaon*, the town rabbi; and thus the meeting took place, and after long discussions the *gaon*'s son, R. Hayim, may he merit a long and prosperous life, who had been the preacher and *moreh tsedek* in the capital Moscow, was chosen unanimously by all those gathered there as the *rosh yeshivah* of Volozhin, to collect money from the generous among our people to maintain the yeshiva, so that Torah and light might proceed from it, [and] to fill its empty coffers and to pay its outstanding debts.' [117] *Hamelits*, 31/54 (17 Mar. 1891).

Berlin would not wish to take up the post since he was a wealthy man and would not wish to take upon himself the burden of administering the yeshiva, and when he had visited the author's town not long before he had told several well-known people that Eliezer Bran was not telling the truth as regards the yeshiva.[118] The writer did not specify the points on which Bran was inaccurate. In another reaction published three days later, Shmuel David Zaks of Shkod disagreed with Gamzu, and wrote that important people had been present at the meeting, and that R. Hayim Berlin deserved to be appointed.[119] About a month later, Yitshak Rivkash announced in a report from Vilna that R. Naftali Berlin had appointed his son as his successor, a piece of information that could hardly be regarded as news at this point.[120] According to Rivkash, R. Naftali Berlin had emphasized the yeshiva's pressing debts, and thus 'his son would be the best and right [person] . . . and he would manage this matter with good sense and wisdom and justice and honesty'.

After these reports, Elazar Shulman, signing himself 'the *menahel* of the yeshiva', announced in *Hamelits*:

I hereby announce that all which has been said by the letter-writers, claiming that our master, teacher, and rabbi, may he merit a long and prosperous life, has resigned his post and ceased to give *shiurim*, and that he has been replaced by his son, R. Hayim Berlin, is absolutely false, since upon the advice of the yeshiva's *gaba'im* and the rabbi and preacher of Vilna,[121] who were here for a meeting last week, it has been decided that our master, teacher, and rabbi will remain at his post and will remain rector and will give his *shiur* as before, and the *gaon* R. Hayim Soloveitchik will be his deputy, and all will carry on as before, and from now onwards let all these writers cease arguing with each other, and if anyone wishes to communicate something to our rabbi and teacher, let him send a letter to the usual address.[122]

It is difficult to take this announcement at face value, but it was effective in halting the public discussion of the situation in Volozhin in the newspapers. On 16 December 1891, an 'open letter' from the editor to a would-be author who was identified only by his initials Sh. AL. of B"k [perhaps Shmuel Aleksandrov, who was living in Bobruisk] was published in *Hamelits*: 'This *bat kol* [divine voice] issues forth from Mount Horeb to destroy the world of the famous yeshiva, and such a voice should not be heard upon the mountains of Israel.' In other words, the editor had refused to publish an article supporting the students. It is almost certain that he had done this not from lack of interest

---

[118] *Hamelits*, 31/61 (27 Mar. 1891).

[119] *Hamelits*, 31/63 (29 Mar. 1891).   [120] *Hamelits*, 31/112 (2 June 1891).

[121] It is not clear to whom the reference is. It may have been R. Tsevi Hirsh Rabinowitz, son of R. Yitshak Elhanan Spektor, who had succeeded R. Jacob Joseph as rabbi preacher of Vilna in 1889; see Steinschneider and Zalkin (eds.), *The City of Vilna* (Heb.), i. 101.

[122] *Hamelits*, 31/122 (16 June 1891). The announcement is dated 5 June, so it must have been published almost immediately upon its arrival.

in the affair, but in response to an appeal from R. Naftali Berlin to stop the publication of comments about the dispute at the yeshiva.[123]

The *menahel*'s announcement in the newspaper, on the instructions of R. Naftali Berlin, was clearly an attempt to create the impression that nothing had happened, and demonstrates that the publicity on the subject was deemed damaging to the yeshiva—and certainly as regards the ability to raise funds. In fact, Shulman's announcement conceals more than it reveals, as evident from a fuller description of events:

> In order to calm the mood, the three main *gaba'im* came to Volozhin: R. Mordekhai Solomonov of Minsk, R. Eizik Rabinowitz of Vilna,[124] and the famous philanthropist R. Barukh Zeldowitz.[125] The students elected a deputation of ten of their number, who were charged with presenting the claims of those who opposed [R. Hayim Berlin] to the delegation [of *gaba'im*]. They spoke of the two types of *shiurim*: the deep and wonderful *shiur* given by R. Hayim Soloveitchik, and the *shiur* overflowing with wide-ranging talmudic knowledge [*bekiut*] given by R. Hayim Berlin, proving that it would be a terrible loss to the yeshiva if the brilliant *shiurim* of R. Hayim Soloveitchik were to cease.[126] R. Mordekhai Solomonov answered, 'Do you expect all the *geonim* to penetrate to the depths like R. Hayim Soloveitchik, who would be capable of giving a *shiur* to R. Akiva Eiger himself!'[127] And the second member of the delegation, R. Barukh Zeldowitz, defended R. Hayim Berlin . . . saying, 'To him you may apply the verse, "There is a righteous man that perishes in his righteousness [Eccles. 7: 15]", for he was zealous for his father's honour.' Ultimately everyone stood by their opinions and no compromise was reached.[128]

The students are presented here as an organized body, whose representatives had the right to take part in the process of making appointments at the yeshiva. They elected a representative deputation and their opinion was listened to, although their claims were not accepted. According to this report, it was clear to all that R. Soloveitchik was a greater Torah scholar than R. Hayim

[123] *Hamelits*, 31/270 (16 Dec. 1891), 7.

[124] This was R. Yitshak Eizik Halevi Rabinowitz.

[125] On Zeldowitz, see Kamenetsky, *The Making of a Godol*.

[126] He knew—or assumed—that if R. Hayim Berlin were to be chosen, R. Soloveitchik would leave the yeshiva.

[127] 1761–1837; a renowned talmudist and rabbi in Posen.

[128] Don-Yihia, 'Memoirs' (Heb.), *Netivah*, 12/11. It is not certain that the director and Don-Yihia are describing the same event, but both descriptions mention the rabbi of Vilna and the *gaba'im*. However, according to the director, it was agreed that no change should be made at the yeshiva, while in Don-Yihia's description it is noted that 'no compromise was reached'—in other words, that the *gaba'im* did not succeed in persuading the students to accept R. Hayim Berlin as *rosh yeshivah*, although it is not necessarily clear that they decided not to appoint him. In the light of all these elements, if there were two meetings, it must be assumed that Don-Yihia would have mentioned them. It would thus seem that these are simply two interpretations of a single event. On the affair of the 'troublesome student', see n. 132 below.

Berlin. Indeed, if the main consideration in choosing a *rosh yeshivah* had been his teaching skills, the *gaba'im* would doubtless have chosen R. Soloveitchik. However, R. Solomonov's attitude reflected the traditional stance that the main purpose of attending a yeshiva was to engage in independent study rather than to listen to *shiurim*. Given this, it is clear that for him, administrative rather than educational considerations were dominant in the choice of a *rosh yeshivah*. For the students, however, the most important factors seem to have been the quality of the *shiur*, the relationship with the teacher, and the sense that they were studying at an elite institution. Perhaps in previous times the students had regarded the yeshiva as a place for independent study, but by the end of the nineteenth century it is clear that they saw it as a place where they would be taught.

Both Shulman and Don-Yihia mention the *gaba'im* of the yeshiva. There is very little information on the identity and functions of the *gaba'im* during this period, as also in earlier periods. Aba Balosher claims that in his time, in most yeshivas the *rashei yeshivah* were all-powerful, both in relation to the students and the money donated to the yeshiva, but that the situation was different at Volozhin:

Even though the *rashei yeshivah* were two of the best scholars of the generation, who were absolutely and unhesitatingly trusted in everything, they could not act entirely according to their will there, but had to consult with a board of scholars and sages, who were not rabbis but merchants and businessmen. The members of this board, who lived in different towns, were occasionally invited to the yeshiva and would visit it, and they used to check the account books and allocate such and such a sum to the *rashei yeshivah* and their assistants, and such and such a sum to each class of students. The students used to go and talk with them on Torah matters and secular affairs; and the students would bring all their claims and complaints against their rabbis to them, and they would decide each matter with no favouritism.[129]

This is the only source that mentions the intervention of the *gaba'im* in the everyday affairs of the yeshiva, such as the distribution of the weekly allowances. If this was an established custom, it would surely have been mentioned by other former students. Since I have not found it mentioned elsewhere, I am forced to conclude that the description is inaccurate and that either the involvement of the *gaba'im* was more restricted, or that it was true but only for a short period. R. Me'ir Berlin wrote that the main role of the *gaba'im* was the collection of funds, and this seems more credible.[130] According to this view, they functioned like ordinary charity *gaba'im*: they would have had some influence over what happened in the yeshiva, but would

[129] Balosher, 'Bialik at Volozhin' (Heb.), 129. This description accords well with R. Meir Berlin's description of the *gaba'im*; see M. Berlin [Bar-Ilan], *From Volozhin to Jerusalem* (Heb.), i. 153.   [130] M. Berlin [Bar-Ilan], *From Volozhin to Jerusalem* (Heb.), i. 153.

not usually have taken the initiative in the management of the yeshiva, and nobody expected them to do so. The students were thus probably correct in crediting R. Naftali Berlin with the appointment of R. Hayim Berlin as *rosh yeshivah*.

5. Student Involvement in the Dispute

The dispute over the appointment of R. Naftali Berlin's successor kindled tempers within the yeshiva, and in this atmosphere, every confrontation, however small, served to fan the fire of conflict:

One incident acted like oil poured on a fire . . . it inflamed the spirits of the 'lower ranks' of the yeshiva. A certain troublesome and stubborn student came to R. [Naftali] Berlin and asked for a large sum of money to pay his travel expenses home. R. Berlin offered him a smaller sum, and when the student held his ground and argued with the aged *gaon*, R. Hayim Berlin, who was present, rebuked the student and actually drove him out of the house. This incident left a bad impression on the students, since they were used to R. Soloveitchik's fatherly attitude to each student. Opposition to R. Hayim Berlin's appointment continued to increase.[131]

The students were quick to take the lead in this:

The best students and married students opposed this appointment and tried to cancel it by all available means. First of all, whenever R. Hayim Berlin began to deliver his *shiur*, the most sharp-witted students would surround him and pose difficult questions that he was unable to answer, and they used to embarrass him in this way. And they harassed him in other ways. They would write to his father, R. Berlin, expressing their opposition to the appointment. And they also wrote to famous rabbis and great scholars, asking them to intervene in the matter and to prevent the yeshiva from falling into the hands of someone who did not deserve to be its *rosh yeshivah*. They did not content themselves with this. Every morning, when the students arrived at the yeshiva, they would find the main door covered with posters about R. Hayim Berlin, most of them composed as parodies of liturgical poems, supplications, dirges, and so on, in which he was ridiculed and mocked.[132]

---

[131] Don-Yihia, 'Memoirs' (Heb.), *Netivah*, 12/11. R. Yehezkel Rozovski pointed out to me that a few years later, when R. Hayim Berlin was living in Jerusalem, he was regarded as one of the foremost rabbis of the city of scholars and therefore the contemptuous attitude expressed towards him by many yeshiva students should be regarded with caution.

[132] Zlatkin, 'The Volozhin Yeshiva in Bialik's Time' (Heb.), 64. For similar descriptions, see B. Goldberg, *Memories of the Past* (Heb.), 16–17; M. Berlin [Bar-Ilan], *From Volozhin to Jerusalem* (Heb.), i. 159–62. Y. Meltzer, *Derekh ets ḥayim*, i. 51, published a letter from 1908, sent to R. Hayim Berlin by one of the students who had opposed him, asking for his forgiveness. In his reply, R. Hayim Berlin wrote: 'already in those days when they were troubling me, I used to say every night . . . "Forgive him for everything that he has troubled me with", and you should feel no necessity to ask me for forgiveness, since for my part I have already forgiven.' This is evidence of R. Hayim Berlin's moral stature. However, R. Hayim added that he could not forgive the

The dispute intensified. On at least three occasions R. Hayim Berlin tried to give a *shiur* and students disrupted it.[133] Once he was physically prevented from ascending the rostrum.[134] There were posters attacking him, and there were also violent incidents in which yeshiva property was destroyed. We know this from the first draft of Hayim Nahman Bialik's poem *Hamatmid*:

Then a myriad of hands loosened their bonds and restrained angers were released
and windows were smashed and candles extinguished
benches, tables were overturned
and the *mashgiah* was terrified and fled
the *shamash* hid, the *menahalim* ran off
for they saw the terrible uproar,
for when the day of reckoning came they would not be held innocent;
and like lifeless corpses, the tables and benches
lay abandoned in darkness on the floor of the hall
the thresholds trembled, the walls shook,
the young men caught and young scholars smitten
But one candle survived in a corner;
the whirlwind of destruction did not dare to extinguish it.
There a space of two cubits served as the fortress of the Shekhinah
and for the choicest of her sons—may God guard him.
There was the place of the young man we are describing.[135]

Many students devoted most of their time to the dispute. Those diligent students who wanted to continue studying were forced to abandon the stormy study hall and take refuge in study halls in the town:

In this emergency the character of the yeshiva was spoiled: the routine was disrupted and supervision was relaxed. The *matmidim* uprooted themselves from the yeshiva and fled to small *batei midrash* in the town or gathered together in their rooms with their volumes of Talmud. The campaigners milled around in the streets and markets, going from house to house and engaging in politics. Those in the middle, who stood between these two extremes, sat on their benches in the yeshiva and rocked above their books, but their hearts were elsewhere. Their eyes were fixed

student for the desecration of God's name (*ḥilul hashem*) that he had caused and for the pain his letters had given R. Berlin, which might have brought on the illness from which he died. I thank R. Shaul Bar-Ilan for this reference.

[133] See Appendix: Document D.

[134] Shmukler [Shapira], *Rabbi Moshe Shemuel* (Heb.), 75–6. He did not witness the incident himself, but was told about it.

[135] *Keneset*, 1 (1936), 6. See also Lachover, *Bialik* (Heb.), i. 92–5. A discussion of this passage appears in the critical edition of *Hamatmid*, ed. Dan Miron, 21–7 (the text is on p. 88) as well as an explanation of why it was left out of the printed version. Bialik described the disturbances as a reaction to cuts in financial support. According to Bar-Ilan and Lachover, the incident was linked to the dispute over the succession. See Lachover, *Bialik* (Heb.), i. 92–5; M. Berlin [Bar-Ilan], *From Volozhin to Jerusalem* (Heb.), i. 128–9.

on the open volumes of Talmud in front of them, but their ears were straining outwards, to catch the rumours from the battlefield.[136]

Some students broke into R. Hayim Berlin's house and stole his *lulav* and *etrog* during Sukkot of 1891. R. Naftali Berlin and R. Soloveitchik threatened that if they were not returned immediately, the entire student body would be required to undergo a rigorous examination in Talmud and that anyone who failed would have to leave the yeshiva. The threat worked and they were returned, but none the less, after the festival R. Hayim Berlin decided to cut the allowances of those who had been involved in the disturbances. This merely provoked fresh outbursts. When R. Naftali Berlin and R. Soloveitchik renewed the threat of an examination, some of the students broke into R. Soloveitchik's house, apparently feeling that he had publicly betrayed them by agreeing to such examinations:

Then the students caused unpleasantness for Soloveitchik too, even though he had enjoyed the greatest respect and esteem of his students until recently. The glass in the windows of his apartment was broken; and once, in the yeshiva, coming to himself after one of his moments of absent-minded inattention, he found a piece of paper in his hand bearing a verse from Genesis: 'and the serpent was more wily than all the beasts of the field.'[137]

Shortly after Sukkot tempers flared again, as a report to the government authorities made clear: R. Hayim Berlin apparently intended to ban the troublemakers from the yeshiva and to stop their allowances. When the students found out, they reacted by disrupting studies, breaking lamps, and so on. They even threw stones through the yeshiva windows and posted notices critical of the yeshiva's leadership. In an effort to halt the disturbances, it was decided that R. Soloveitchik should examine the students in the talmudic tractates that they had been studying independently, and the people of the town were forbidden to house the ringleaders. The latter, so it is claimed, having nowhere to sleep, went to R. Hayim Berlin's home to find shelter and food. The next day, they begged for mercy, swearing henceforth to correct their ways and to be diligent students. The only troublemaker who actually left Volozhin was Yossel Mordukh ben Leib Glasstein, who died in late October, after he had been expelled, as reported by Captain Dubelt.[138]

The students who had been expelled wrote to Yehoshua Steinberg and Feivel Getz, apparently after Glasstein's death, asking them to intervene. In a letter written in Hebrew they described the background to their expulsion as follows:

And behold, now, when he wanted to prove to the donors [to the yeshiva] that he hates the maskilim very fiercely—and in any event he knows the Torah . . . and he

[136] Balosher, 'Bialik at Volozhin' (Heb.), 124.   [137] Appendix: Document D.   [138] Ibid.

is the colleague of the *gaon* R. Hayim Soloveitchik, his deputy, who is also known as the head of those who rebel against the light [a leading opponent of the maskilim], he gave an order to the landlords about nineteen individuals who were held to be maskilim, in other words those who know a little both in the sacred tongue and in other languages, that they should drive them out of their lodgings and should not give them lodging for a single night. And not a single meal. And behold, now, alas! We have been flung out at the head of every street, at such a time, the time of snow and rain falling from heaven and cold and snow.[139]

The letter is signed 'The Students of the Yeshiva', followed by twenty-one signatures. It was translated into Russian and handed to the authorities, but apparently to no avail. It seems that R. Naftali Berlin supported his son's strategy:

It is known in Volozhin that, after the death of Glasstein, who had been expelled from the yeshiva by Hayim Berlin, Hirsch [Tsevi] Berlin gave an address concerning this, in which he referred to the divine punishment meted out to the sons of Aaron for not showing full obedience to higher authority, and linked this to the deceased. This address made a very painful and unpleasant impression on all the yeshiva students, since they had all loved and respected the deceased.[140]

6. The Authorities' Reaction to R. Hayim Berlin's Appointment

The Russian authorities did not approve of the transfer of authority to R. Hayim Berlin. This was partly because they were not officially informed of the change, despite the law requiring every recognized institution to report on staff changes. They found out about it in any case, so the attempt to conceal it had only damaged the yeshiva:

When he took on the administration of the yeshiva without permission, Hayim Berlin also decided, likewise without permission, to take the teaching duties upon himself . . .

At present, substantive changes are taking place in the composition of the teaching staff and administrators of the yeshiva, but it is not from the yeshiva administration that the educational authorities have learned of this. The most important change is the replacement of Naftali Hirsch Berlin by his son, Hayim Berlin. This major change is an undoubted fact, yet the proprietor of the yeshiva, Naftali Hirsch Berlin, has taken pains to conceal this fact from the authorities and continues to style himself as 'rector of the Volozhin yeshiva' in his dealings with them. This

---

[139] Ellipsis in the original. The authorities checked the names of the signatories and realized they were all false.

[140] Appendix: Document D. It also states that R. Berlin did not regret the decision to expel the students.

deliberate concealment from the educational authorities of an event that undoubtedly took place and is well known in Volozhin demonstrates how little trust may be placed in the yeshiva administration.[141]

R. Naftali Berlin probably knew that it was not worth seeking approval for the appointment. R. Hayim Berlin had no secular education, and since the authorities were increasingly demanding that students study Russian, it is reasonable to suppose that they made similar demands of the teachers too. It is also possible that R. Naftali Berlin might simply have forgotten to apply for approval, or might not have understood that this was compulsory, but the authorities interpreted his action as deliberate.

At the end of December it became clear to the authorities that the management of the yeshiva was deteriorating. An official report records:

At present, the members of the yeshiva administration are almost all scattered elsewhere. The self-styled rector, Hayim Berlin, went off to Vilna at the beginning of December, for personal reasons; Hayim Soloveitchik went away about a month ago, according to some people to Warsaw, to recover his health, and according to others, to a variety of places in order to collect donations for the yeshiva; Samunov left Volozhin altogether at the beginning of the term and moved to Jacobstadt, where he took up the post of spiritual rabbi;[142] because of his age and frail health, Fried takes no part in teaching; Hirsch Berlin himself rarely visits the yeshiva and has given up teaching altogether. In this way the entire management of the yeshiva is left in the hands of the Jew Dynkin, who is not even a teacher but performs the functions of a supervisor and tutor.[143]

In this atmosphere of growing disorder and despair, a letter was sent to the superintendent of schools in the Vilna district, complaining of the failure to teach secular studies at the yeshiva:[144]

Your Excellency! Do not reproach us for daring to importune Your Excellency now with a letter so full of a great quantity of mistakes. Believe us that we too want very much to be enlightened men, useful to the motherland, but the fault is not ours— it is the head of the yeshiva, H[ayim] Berlin, who should be blamed . . . even someone who educates himself at home can come off very badly, because Rabbi H[ayim] Berlin is a very nasty and terrible enemy of enlightenment. Nobody who studies enlightened subjects, and in general the Russian language, escapes unharmed from his hands.

The letter was written in poor Russian and signed 'The Voice of the Entire Yeshiva'.[145]

[141] Appendix: Document D.
[142] See D. Levin (ed.), *Encyclopaedia of Jewish Communities* (Heb.), s.v. Jēkabpils/Jacobstadt, p. 146.   [143] See the letter of the superintendent of education, Appendix: Document D.
[144] B. Goldberg, *Memories of the Past* (Heb.), 17. On the government's demands, see below.
[145] Appendix: Document C.

Informing against the yeshiva was an extreme step because it could lead to its closure or the arrest of its leadership. The informers apologized for their poor Russian and stressed that they wanted to know the language better, but that this was currently impossible at the yeshiva. They claimed that R. Hayim Berlin punished students who wanted to learn Russian and feared that they would share the fate of nineteen students who had been expelled from the yeshiva in the middle of the winter.[146] They claimed that R. Hayim Berlin censored the outgoing mail and that they had therefore had difficulty in contacting the superintendent and were appealing to him now to protect them. They concluded their letter 'Save us, save us!' It is not hard to imagine the impression such a letter must have made.

In fact it is not absolutely certain that it was yeshiva students who sent this letter. R. Reuven Pyatigorsky, who examined the language of the letter very carefully, came to the conclusion that the author knew literary Russian well and that the mistakes were deliberate. In his opinion the letter was a forgery and not the work of a yeshiva student at all.[147] Whatever the truth of the matter, the letter spurred another visit to Volozhin by government officials:

In view of the importance of the information received, the acting inspector of elementary schools, Ilin, in whose sphere of responsibility Volozhin lies, was instructed to inspect the yeshiva. After discharging this duty, Ilin presented a report to the superintendent of elementary schools on 29 December, in which he depicted the present state of the yeshiva as very poor indeed.[148]

While in Volozhin, he was apparently given a letter identical or very similar to the letter sent to the superintendent of schools in the Vilna district. In the letter Hayim Berlin is described as 'an opponent of enlightenment and a poor talmudist', and it includes a request not to permit his appointment as head of the yeshiva. The conclusion reached by the officials who visited the yeshiva was unambiguous:

In the light of all this, and in accordance with Your Excellency's proposal . . . I have the honour most respectfully to request instructions from Your Excellency regarding the closure of the Volozhin yeshiva. In addition, in order to avoid possible inconveniences consequent on the presence in Volozhin of the Berlins and of Soloveitchik after the closure of the yeshiva, it would be timely to carry out the banishment of Berlin and Soloveitchik from Volozhin, as proposed by the governor-general of Vilna, Kovno, and Grodno, at the time of closure.

The governor-general, whom I have informed of these measures, has expressed full agreement with them.[149]

---

[146] See p. 224 above.

[147] Pyatigorsky, 'The Point of a *Yod*' (Rus.). I thank Mrs Miriam Kaidanov for drawing my attention to this important article.   [148] See Appendix: Document D.

[149] See the letter of the superintendent of education, Appendix: Document D.

Yehoshua Steinberg also personally checked the claims made in the letter. On 7 January 1892 he reported to his superiors in the Ministry of Education that he had received the letter signed by the students and noted their claim that they risked death from cold and hunger. Steinberg probably did not want to ignore the letter and may have been frightened to do so. However, he reported to the authorities that some details in it were untrustworthy.[150] Indeed, as we shall see, it was not this letter that sealed the fate of the yeshiva.

7. The Decision to Close the Yeshiva

On 22 December 1891, well before Yehoshua Steinberg officially presented his report, new regulations were published concerning the yeshiva,[151] requiring among other things that its 'leaders' should prove that 'they had completed studies at no lower a level than those of a district school',[152] and the authorities began to take steps to enforce this.[153] These regulations thus effectively prevented both R. Hayim Berlin and R. Soloveitchik from serving as *rosh yeshivah* since neither of them could prove completion of such studies. Additional requirements were also imposed on the yeshiva:

The content, order, and arrangement of the Hebrew studies and number of hours allocated to such studies shall be decided by the owner of the yeshiva with the limitations specified below:

1. The hours between 9 and 3 shall be allocated to general studies.
2. The total number of hours of study time shall not exceed ten hours.
3. Nocturnal study will not be permitted at the yeshiva under any circumstances.[154]

Thus, according to the new regulations, no more than four hours could be spent in Talmud study each day. By demanding that six hours of secular studies be taught daily, the authorities went far beyond the basic legal requirements. Both sides understood that the demands were excessive and completely unrealistic. Indeed, the *rashei yeshivah* could not have accepted such guidelines,

---

[150] Ibid.

[151] For a Hebrew translation of the Russian original, see 'Concerning the Volozhin Yeshiva' (Heb.).

[152] According to 'Concerning the Volozhin Yeshiva' (Heb.), *Hamelits*, 32/46.

[153] In a letter of reply sent in 1892 to R. Moshe Nahum Yerushalimski, who had been enquiring about a position, he was informed that 'the school officials in the Vilna district, on whom the appointment of the rabbi and the *rosh yeshivah* depends, will all say that they will not judge simply from seeing a certificate [since it was possible to obtain a certificate fraudulently] . . . [but they will check themselves] whether he can speak the national language fluently and knows what is necessary for a district school. Therefore all those who have tried to obtain this post have been rejected.' The letter is in the Yerushalimski Collection in the Schocken Library.

[154] *Hamelits*, 32/46 (24 Feb. 1892).

which were in opposition to their values and to those of the people who supported the yeshiva. Anyone who had the slightest familiarity with the yeshiva knew that R. Naftali Berlin would never consider reducing study hours so drastically. Those who framed the new regulations must have known this, so it is clear that their aim was to bring about the yeshiva's closure—as indeed happened. However, these regulations created the impression that the yeshiva was not being closed due to the direct instructions of the authorities but due to its failure to comply with the laws concerning secular studies.

What led the authorities to draft the regulations that led to the yeshiva's closure? There is no trace in the official documents of a desire to take concerted action against the Jews or Judaism, nor is there any hint of satisfaction at the damage done to Jews in general or to Torah study in particular by the yeshiva's closure. It is also difficult to make the simple assertion that the authorities' goal of introducing secular studies led to the new regulations and their consequences. As noted above, we do not know of demands that secular studies be included in the curriculum at other yeshivas during these years, nor is there any mention in contemporary sources of an intensive policy of popularizing secular studies among the Jews.

What the surviving documents do reveal is the authorities' great interest in every expression of unrest and their fear of any deviation from the law. The regime, which by this period was already facing the threat of revolutionary movements, was afraid of the potential danger that might emerge from large groups of unsupervised youths. R. Hayim Berlin's inability to impose his authority on the yeshiva students would have been a source of anxiety to the authorities. The students who appealed to Steinberg undoubtedly thought that they would find a receptive audience. However, these sources suggest that this was not so. The authorities did indeed support secular education, but they did not approve of the students' appealing against their superiors. For the authorities, active support of the Haskalah or of R. Hayim Soloveitchik were both evidence of a lack of discipline in the yeshiva. Underground political activity, such as the clandestine Zionist societies, only strengthened this fear.

Indeed, any outside observer of the events at Volozhin in 1891 would immediately have taken particular notice of the disturbances and lack of order at the yeshiva, and of the dispute over the succession. From the authorities' point of view, a person who opposed the *rosh yeshivah* and would resort to violence in pursuit of his goal might also raise his hand against the tsar. A state of disorder at an educational institution looked dangerous to the authorities, and if the yeshiva staff could not impose order, the authorities would have to do so.

The key to understanding the thought processes of the Russian officials seems to lie in the last paragraphs of the document dated 7 January 1892:

From the facts noted above the conclusion emerges that the Volozhin yeshiva is currently disintegrating, and there is no reason to hope that the present yeshiva administration, if it exists at all, is capable of restoring a proper way [the original has the mistake 'meaning'] of life to this institution . . . Soloveitchik, who until recently was the mainstay of the yeshiva, has stirred up the students against him by his intrigues, and has turned from a guardian of law and order into a propagandist of the most vile sort . . . there seems to be no administration at all now at the yeshiva, since its principal members have dispersed to various places . . .

Let the Jews of the North-West Region see from these regulations what demands the authorities have made of the yeshiva. And if there are among them individuals who would like to take upon themselves the duties of proprietor of the yeshiva, a role that men like Berlin and Soloveitchik are completely incapable of performing, the educational authorities will not prevent the reopening of the Volozhin yeshiva on new foundations.[155]

The authorities were interested in the students' education, but were immeasurably more concerned with order. They kept their word: after several years the yeshiva reopened, with no secular studies, but with a *rosh yeshivah* who maintained order and discipline, R. Rafa'el Shapira.

Many factors led to the situation that brought about the closure of the yeshiva. Secular studies was one of them, but since R. Naftali Berlin had agreed to introduce a minimum of secular studies into the curriculum it is clear that this obstacle could have been overcome. Student support for the Haskalah was still very limited, in any case. A more significant problem was the lack of order in the yeshiva. In other words, it was not external factors that led to the closure as much as the behaviour of the yeshiva students themselves. Their campaign to support R. Hayim Soloveitchik and depose R. Hayim Berlin had results that they could never have anticipated.

Even after the decision to close the institution had been taken, the Russian bureaucracy still had to come up with formal grounds. Their fears concerning illegal activity were not something they wanted to publicize. There is no record of discussions of this matter, perhaps because it is not the type of consideration that would ever be recorded. However, it seems that the exaggerated demands made by the authorities over secular studies—which were completely unparalleled elsewhere and went far beyond the actual requirements of the law—demonstrate their intentions. It was much more convenient to present an impossible demand, which would look perfectly reasonable to the St Petersburg bureaucracy and accorded with several laws promulgated in the past, than to publicly admit to concerns about disorder in the yeshiva. Anyone who knew the yeshiva would know that R. Naftali Berlin would not be able to agree to devote so much of the day to the study of secular subjects.

[155] Appendix: Document D; see also Document F, on the disorder at the yeshiva as a factor in its closure.

By demanding something that could not possibly be accepted, the authorities created the grounds for closing the yeshiva. And indeed it is when R. Berlin rejected this demand that the authorities announced its closure.

This interpretation is supported from what might be seen as an unanticipated source. The London *Jewish Chronicle* had the following piece of news in the issue of 22 April 1892, under the heading 'Expulsion of Rabbis':

Further information has reached us, under date of March 2nd, respecting the closure of the Talmud School in Woloshin (Wilna Government). By order of Kochanov, Governor-General of Wilna, the head-masters—Rabbi Hirsch Leb Berlin, Rabbi Chaim Berlin, his son, and Rabbi Chaim Solowejzig (the celebrated son of the Rabbi of Brest)—have been forbidden to reside in any part of the Government of Wilna for the term of three years, the police thinking that only when the three principal teachers were removed from their sphere of action, would there be security that the college would not be re-opened secretly. It is reported that the school was closed on the strength of a denunciation by the police and Ispravniks, who represented the school as a 'nest for Nihilists'.[156]

8. The Closure of the Yeshiva

On 22 January 1892 the Volozhin yeshiva was closed by order of the government. Five days later, a report from a student appeared in *Hamelits*:

Slonim, 27 January—The yeshiva of Volozhin was officially closed last Wednesday, 22 January, and the students were sent back to their native towns. On the morning of 22 January, the governor of Oshmyany [the district town] and the deputy prosecutor of that town came to the yeshiva, and many policemen and peasants from the villages were summoned by the district governor. The Volozhin area officer demanded that the rabbi, the *gaon*, our teacher and master, R. Naftali Tsevi Yehudah Berlin prepare all the documents of the students present that day which had been deposited with him. Then he asked our rabbi and teacher whether all the students were then present together at the yeshiva, and when our rabbi and teacher answered that none were absent, he gave the order that nobody was to leave until he had finished his speech, and the district governor read the government's order concerning the yeshiva and its students out of a book, saying thus: 'From today and henceforth the yeshiva is closed according to the laws of the state, since they have not observed the school regulations; the students must leave the town within three days. Students' documents as well as travel letters and certificates of completion of army duties will not be given to them but will be sent to the police stations in their places of residence, where they will be returned to them. They will receive travel permits for their journey home from the clerks' bureau of the Volozhin area officer.' When he finished reading from the book, he ordered the students to leave the building immediately, and they were able to receive their travel documents and leave

---

[156] I was led to this source by <http://onthemainline.blogspot.com/2009/06/what-happened-to-volozhiner-roshei.html>.

Volozhin the same day. When the students had left the yeshiva, they placed the tsar's seal on the building, and the students went to the Volozhin area officer to receive their travel permits. As stated, the yeshiva was closed because it did not adhere to the school regulations, and thus a charge has been laid on the *geonim* of our generation and on the wise men of our times to publish their suggestions as to how we may re-establish the Volozhin yeshiva in a proper fashion, with governmental permission.

A former student of the yeshiva, Moshe Hayim Graiver[157]

There seems to have been another order, which Graiver does not mention and perhaps did not know about. This order forbade R. Naftali Berlin, his son R. Hayim Berlin, and R. Soloveitchik to be in the Vilna district (to which Volozhin belonged) for the next three years.[158] R. Soloveitchik travelled to his father in Brisk, and R. Naftali Berlin went to Warsaw. He and his son immediately set about collecting money to pay off the yeshiva's remaining debts, which amounted to about 10,000 roubles.[159] R. Hayim Berlin travelled to western Europe,[160] while his father made the rounds of the cities of eastern Europe.[161]

The closure of the yeshiva sent shock waves through the Jewish public, but did not spark off a storm.[162] Both *Hamelits* and *Hatsefirah* printed the full version of the regulation on the basis of which the yeshiva had been closed,[163] and A. Zederbaum, the editor of *Hamelits*, wrote a series of articles explaining his interpretation of the reasons behind the yeshiva's closure and the process

---

[157] *Hamelits*, 32/28 (15 Feb. 1892).

[158] Don-Yihia, 'Memoirs' (Heb.), *Netivah*, 12/11. Don-Yihia wrote his account from memory. He records that the officials who came to close the yeshiva excused their actions by claiming that R. Berlin had resigned, but it seems very doubtful that they would have used such an excuse. On the order of expulsion, see also M. Berlin [Bar-Ilan], *From Volozhin to Jerusalem* (Heb.), i. 181.

[159] See the discussion of the yeshiva's finances above.

[160] The stops on his itinerary included Paris (see *Hamelits*, 32/139 (5 July 1892)) and Amsterdam (see *Hamelits*, 32/151 (19 July 1892)).

[161] M. Berlin [Bar-Ilan], *From Volozhin to Jerusalem* (Heb.), i. 182–6.

[162] R. Eliyahu Aharon Milikovski-Samsonov described the closing of the yeshiva in his book *Ohalei aharon*, 213–14 (my thanks to Rabbi Betsalel Dablitski for this reference). His eyewitness account tells how the closure order was given on a Wednesday; on the following Sunday a meeting took place in Vilna with the participation of R. Berlin, R. Yosef Dov Soloveitchik, R. Mordekhai Solomonov of Minsk, R. Yitshak Eizik Rabinowitz (the author of *Dorot rishonim*), and others. The meeting had no real results. R. Hayim Karlinski describes a very similar meeting, based on the account of a relative, R. Naftali Tsevi Yehudah Rif, who had heard about it from his grandfather, R. Rafa'el Shapira; see Karlinski, *The Founder of the Brisk Dynasty* (Heb.), 416. However, according to R. Karlinski, the meeting took place before the closure of the yeshiva. This is consistent with the account by M. M. Yashar, based on the account given him by R. Tsevi Levinson (Yashar, *The Hafets Hayim* (Heb.), i. 223–4). I prefer R. Milikovski-Samsonov's eyewitness version to second-hand accounts. However, it is possible, though not very probable, that there were two meetings. I would like to thank Yosi Sofer for drawing my attention to these sources.

[163] *Hamelits*, 32/46 (24 Feb. 1892); *Hatsefirah*, 19/56 (18 Mar. 1892); 19/57 (20 Mar. 1892).

it involved.[164] The Russian Jewish press also commented on the affair.[165] The most unusual reaction came from the students of the Telz yeshiva, who wrote and staged a play about the closure of Volozhin. It was staged at other yeshivas in Lithuania, and handwritten copies of the script were distributed to students.[166] However, as mentioned, the reaction of the Jews of the Russian empire to the yeshiva's closure was muted. No serious attempts were made by wealthy Jews of St Petersburg and Moscow or even within the Pale of Settlement to appeal against the closure, and the affair did not occupy a prominent place in the Russian-language newspapers. Nor did rabbis and leaders outside Russia intervene to help.

The closure also shocked those who were close to the yeshiva, who tried to account for what they had witnessed. It is not hard to understand why there were some who saw the closing of the yeshiva as a deliberate attack on Torah study. By the mid-nineteenth century, and even earlier, conservative circles tended to attribute enormous power to the maskilim, beyond anything they actually possessed. In addition, although Jews were aware of the activity of the Russian police, they were not generally able to gauge the extent of their surveillance of the yeshiva and their understanding of what went on there. Moreover, it was hard for the Jewish public to imagine that disturbances at the yeshiva and the dispute over the succession could inspire concern among government officials.

The general belief among those close to the yeshiva was thus that the authorities and the maskilim had plotted together to oppose Torah study, a view supported by the fact that the official excuse for the closure was the lack of secular studies. The thought that unruly yeshiva students were a potential danger to the mighty tsarist empire and that this could determine the attitude to the yeshiva would have seemed ridiculous to Jews who were familiar with the common run of yeshiva students. Lacking accurate information, a conspiracy between the maskilim and the authorities was the most logical explanation they could come up with.

The mistaken attribution of the closure to a plot of this sort is not the only case of this type in the history of the Jews of the tsarist empire. A similar phenomenon occurred in connection with the anti-Jewish pogroms in southern Russia in 1881, known in Hebrew as *sufot hanegev* ('the storms of the south'). Many Jews saw these pogroms as linked to a government-engineered plot;

---

[164] *Hamelits*, 32/47 (8 Mar. 1892); 32/50 (11 Mar. 1892); 32/55 (18 Mar. 1892).

[165] Y. Katznelson, 'Why Was the Volozhin Yeshiva Closed Down?' (Rus.); Rivkin, 'The Last Years of the Volozhin Yeshiva' (Rus.).

[166] Rivkind, 'From the Volozhin Collections' (Heb.), 365–75, where the full text appears. The play impressed those who saw it, and R. Eliezer Gordon of Telz ordered it to be staged at the yeshiva. It was performed on the eve of Shemini Atseret, and the rabbi himself helped to set up the stage.

like others in Russia they saw the state as all-powerful, and could not imagine that so many pogroms could be the simply the result of spontaneous local riots that the Russian police were unable to control. Only when the archives were opened and the affair was investigated in depth did the truth emerge.[167]

Attempts to reopen the Volozhin yeshiva began immediately after its closure, but they did not succeed until three years later. It never regained its former glory, however, and always operated under the shadow of its distinguished past. Meanwhile, other yeshivas continued what Volozhin had started and attained similarly distinguished reputations in the Jewish world.

∗

In the final stages before printing, the following information came to my attention:

In 1865 the yeshiva narrowly escaped major difficulties that could have led to its closure. In that year Petr A. Bessonov became head of the Vilna Rabbinical Seminary. He was very energetic and committed to transforming (and russifying) the Jews. In the words of Mikhail Dolbilov, the young maskilic teachers of the seminary 'enthusiastically planned an attack, under Bessonov's protection, on such centers of traditional Jewish learning as for example the famous yeshiva in Volozhin'.[168] Bessonov set himself a goal to weaken the authority of yeshivas such as Volozhin. Thus, after the fire there in 1865, he tried to pressure Potapov, the governor-general of the region, to forbid fundraising for a new building. Luckily for the yeshiva, he was unsuccessful in his lobbying.[169] Bessonov resigned his position in 1866, and no successor had the same intense ties with the Jewish teachers as he did. In 1869 a number of maskilic educational projects were discussed. There had been a change of personnel among the government authorities, and this time 'the officials were particularly irritated by the point about the attack on the yeshivas and heders, which threatened to draw the authorities into a conflict with the traditionalist Jews'.[170]

[167] On this fascinating episode, see Aronson, *Troubled Waters*.
[168] See Dolbilov, 'Russifying Bureaucracy', 127. Dolbilov cites as his source OPI GIM (Manuscript Division of the Russian State Historical Museum in Moscow), *fond* 56, *delo* 335, *listy* 129–30, 137–8 (ibid. 127 n. 48).
[169] See Dolbilov, 'The "Cleansing" of Judaism': the statement about Bessonov's aversion to yeshivas is on p. 193. In the same article (p. 203 n. 94), Dolbilov refers to a denunciation of the yeshiva by maskilim found in Bessonov's archive (OPI GIM, *fond* 56, *delo* 335, *listy* 129–30, 137–8).
[170] Dolbilov, 'Russifying Bureaucracy', 139, citing RO RNB (Manuscript Division of the Russian National Library in St Petersburg), *fond* 523, *delo* 114, *listy* 12–20 (a memorandum by the inspector of the Vilna Educational District, N. Novikov).

Documents from the Tsarist Archives about the Volozhin Yeshiva

DOCUMENT A

The Third Department of His Majesty's Private Chancellery
Department 3
7 September 1879,
no. 5685

To the Acting Minister of the Interior[1]

The Minister of Justice has passed on for my consideration the results of the inquiry into the rabbi of the town Volozhin, Oshmyany district, Vilna province, Naftali Hirsch [Tsevi] Yehudah Berlin. An accusation was made against him that up to 250 Jews of undesirable character are living in the above-mentioned town under his protection, forming a separate society, denigrating the authorities and harbouring various criminal plans. This accusation was found to have no basis, and in accordance with the opinion of State Secretary Nabokov [the Minister of Justice], I think that the investigation into Berlin's file should be halted.

However, when I looked through this file, I could not help but notice that an institution for training learned rabbis (a yeshiva) is operating in Volozhin; it was founded about a century ago. In 1824 it was officially closed, but in fact it is still functioning and enjoys great fame; there are about 200 to 250 students there, from various places in Russia and even from abroad.

If the authorities' order to close the Volozhin yeshiva was based on [the yeshiva's] harmful nature, then it should not be permitted to exist in an unofficial manner. [Therefore] it seems to me that it is my duty to point this out for Your Excellency's consideration, and I hereby request that you inform me as to the outcome.

Adjutant General Drenteln

---

[1] The letter is superscribed: 'Received 8 September 1879. Confidential'. A note written after the date reads: 'Report to the Minister'.

DOCUMENT B

Ministry of the Interior
Governor General of Vilna, Kovno, and Grodno
10 April 1890
no. 431
Vilna

To the Minister of the Interior[2]

At the end of last year the General Administration for Press Affairs forwarded to the inspector of printing houses and the book trade in Vilna an appeal, in the Jewish language, allegedly printed in one of the printing shops of Vilna and signed by several spiritual rabbis living in the Vilna province, in which Jews were invited to contribute to the Jewish colonies in Palestine.

During the investigation that was undertaken on my orders, it was discovered that the appeal had been printed at an unknown location; that the main figure active in its distribution in the North-Western Region was the rector of the Volozhin yeshiva, R. Berlin; and [that] the collector of the contributions was the learned Jew at the directorate of the Vilna educational district, Fin. In addition, the investigation revealed that there is a circle of Jewish activists in the town of Volozhin, known as 'Neyts', which distributes leaflets and makes appeals for donations among the Jewish population. One of the leaders of this circle was a *meshchanin* of Vitebsk province, Yossel [Yosef] Rotstein, who had become a student at the Volozhin yeshiva, as he himself declared, in order to participate in this circle. Rotstein wrote appeals, sent them to various places in the empire, conducted all the correspondence, and took receipt of the donations. In addition to Rotstein, many other students of the Volozhin yeshiva were members of the circle, as well as a student at the University of Dorpat, Pressman, and a student at the University of St Petersburg, Ginzburg. The latter two edited the appeals that Rotstein sent them, and for that reason maintained a regular correspondence with him and with other students of the Volozhin yeshiva.

Even though no aims of a political nature were discovered in the Volozhin circle's activities, nevertheless the very existence of a group of this kind among the students of the Volozhin yeshiva, without the knowledge or permission of the authorities, confirms the validity of the question that has already been raised repeatedly concerning the anomalous status of the Volozhin yeshiva.

The Volozhin yeshiva has existed since 1805, but in 1824, when the rapid increase in the number of its students became apparent, it was closed by order

[2] The letter is superscribed: 'Received: Department of Religious Affairs of Foreign Religions, 15 April 1890.

of the authorities as an unauthorized institution. In spite of this it continued to function without authority for many years, with the enthusiastic support of individuals and entire Jewish communities, in Russia and abroad. Later, in 1880, even though the Ministry of the Interior and the Ministry of Public Education did indeed recognize the need to close the Volozhin yeshiva, nevertheless, in view of the fact that it had gained great significance, not only among the Jews of Russia but also abroad, and that its immediate closure might well make an extremely unfavourable impression not only among our Jewish population but also abroad, and would give rise to accusations that under contemporary circumstances would have been not at all desirable, it was required of the administrators of the Volozhin yeshiva only that they comply with the general regulations, though the order was given to resort to the closure of the aforementioned yeshiva in the event of their refusing or being evasive (response of the Ministry [of the Interior], through the Department of Religious Affairs of Foreign Religions, 28 March 1880, no. 231).

Ten years have passed since then, but even though steps were taken at that time to bring this institution to order on precisely the basis of the law and the regulation of 13 November 1844, with the procurement of an official undertaking by the yeshiva administration acknowledging its agreement to comply with this law in every particular, in spite of this, however, the Volozhin yeshiva showed no serious proof of any inclination to obey the demands made of it by the government. Things continued in this way until 1887, when the superintendent of the Vilna educational district sent the supervisor of elementary schools of the Vilna province to Volozhin, who insisted on the introduction into the curriculum of the teaching of the Russian language. But two years have now passed since the supervisor of elementary schools travelled to Volozhin, and the rector of the institution, Rabbi Berlin, who does not know Russian at all, like the rest of the yeshiva staff members, categorically refuses to introduce the state language into the list of subjects taught at the yeshiva, since he thinks that the teaching of Russian is incompatible with the study of the Talmud. As a consequence of this, and in view of such a manifest and stubborn transgression by the Volozhin yeshiva of the laws and regulations incumbent upon such institutions, the council attached to the office of the superintendent of the Vilna educational district, at its meeting of 21 December 1889, acknowledged the necessity of closing this yeshiva, since continued leniency towards this institution would be a mere indulgence harmful to educational affairs and not in accord with the dignity of legal authority. At the same time, the council declared that it had nothing against the existence of a yeshiva for the study of the laws of Judaism, and, if necessary, this could be permitted even in the town of Volozhin.

In informing Your Excellency of all this, and taking into consideration that: the Volozhin yeshiva is a hotbed of Jewish fanaticism and a refuge for Jews whose loyalty is doubtful and who, when they are admitted to the yeshiva, escape close supervision by the police and can easily evade their military duties and legal prosecution; that this yeshiva, as I noted above, is administered by individuals who not only do not understand a word of Russian, but also regard the study of Russian and other secular subjects with hostility; that Jews of various ages and varying family status are admitted to the yeshiva: 17-year-old youths along with 40-year-old men who have wives and children—and the number of such students at this yeshiva is 400 to 450; that the donations for the upkeep of the institution amount to 14,000 [roubles] per annum, and that all these funds pass into the unsupervised control of Rabbi Berlin, who also issues the students with certificates for various Jewish religious degrees; that the testimony of the yeshiva student Rotstein that he entered this institution with the aim of participating in a circle proves that the Volozhin yeshiva does not justify its designation; that this institution demonstrates the might of the Kahal, which rules the Jews of the North-Western Region despotically and exerts a strong anti-government influence over the Jewish masses—[in the light of all this] I deem that the continued existence of the Volozhin yeshiva is positively harmful, and therefore would consider it absolutely essential, if the decision were taken to close down the Volozhin yeshiva completely, that the most energetic steps should be taken at the same time against the individuals who now direct this institution, [such as] their banishment to different places, in order to put an end, once and for all, to the existence of this anti-government institution. If this is not done, the aim will not be achieved and the yeshiva will continue to function as it has done up to now, only secretly and not openly.

I consider it my duty to add that the opinion of the council attached to the office of the superintendent—that the educational authorities have no [objection] if the existence is permitted in Volozhin of a yeshiva, as an institution specially established for the study of the laws of Judaism—must in no circumstances be given effect, in view of the fact that government supervision of the training of Jewish spiritual rabbis and attempts to subordinate the teaching of Jewish dogma to the general educational order have proved unsuccessful and have not achieved their aim. In consequence of this the government, through the reorganization of the rabbinical seminaries in 1873, removed from itself the responsibility for special religious Jewish higher education.

I respectfully request Your Excellency to honour me with notification of the outcome.

Lieutenant-General Kokhanov

DOCUMENT C

Volozhin, 20 December 1891

To the greatly esteemed Superintendent of Schools in the Vilna Province

Your Excellency!

Do not reproach us for daring to importune Your Excellency now with a letter so full of a great quantity of mistakes. Believe us that we too want very much to be enlightened men, useful to the motherland, but the fault is not ours—it is the head of the yeshiva, H[ayim] Berlin, who should be blamed. It's not just that, like his father, he hasn't turned the yeshiva into a sort of seminary; even someone who educates himself at home can come off very badly, because Rabbi H[ayim] Berlin is a very nasty and terrible enemy of enlightenment. Nobody who studies enlightened subjects, and in general the Russian language, escapes unharmed from his hands.

Until such time as Your Excellency had been here, we could not have the honour of writing to you about everything that is happening at the yeshiva, because the new head of the yeshiva, Hayim Berlin, removes from the post all the letters that we send and checks them to see whether anything has been written about him. However, since Your Excellency has now assured us that you will accept our requests, we have made bold to have the honour to write this petition to you. We write truly to you about everything that is done and heard at the yeshiva. For Rabbi H[irsch] L[eib] Berlin, who has up to now been the head of the yeshiva, has given up because of his advanced age and has handed his post over to his son Hayim Berlin. But he is a big oaf, and when he is teaching at the yeshiva, if he is asked questions he never knows what to answer, which is very shameful. Therefore he really wants to get back at us, which God forbid. And so we beg you to take pity on us, and be so good as not to allow him to be the head of the yeshiva, or else woe to us, for he will no doubt place a *ḥerem* [ban] on us, as he has already done this month to nineteen individuals, and many of them were forced to leave Volozhin and go away, and some are in great poverty. Save us, save us!

The Voice of the Entire Yeshiva

DOCUMENT D

Ministry of Public Education
Superintendent of the Vilna Educational District
Bureau, Desk 3
7 January 1892
no. 49
Vilna

To the Minister of Public Education[3]

At the end of November last year the inspector of the Jewish Teachers'
Institute in Vilna, Steinberg, gave me a letter that he had received from
Volozhin with the signatures of eighteen students of the yeshiva there. The
original letter and a translation are appended hereto. The signatories say that
the rector of the yeshiva has renounced his post and handed it over to his son,
Hayim Berlin, and that the new rector of the yeshiva ordered the landlords
to throw them out of their lodgings and not to give them food or shelter, since
he regarded them as enlightened men, as they knew Hebrew and something
of other languages. And so it is that we, say the signatories, are cast out into
the streets at such a time as this, soaked through from rain and snow and
frozen with cold. We are tormented by hunger, and if other students had not
invited us in by turns to eat something once a day, we would have died from
hunger, with no mercy.

After I had become aware of the contents of this letter, I charged the
inspector of elementary schools in the Vilna province to collect precise information on this subject. The inspector has now presented this information,
received from the deputy commander of the Vilna province gendarmerie, *rot-
mistr* [= Captain] Dubelt, and from the senior teacher of the Volozhin elementary school, Yunovich. The information presented revealed that:

1. The rector of the yeshiva, Naftali Hirsch Berlin, is indeed no longer the
    director of the yeshiva in the full sense of the word. He continues to
    influence the yeshiva and controls its resources, but in all other respects
    he has handed over control to his son, Hayim Berlin.

2. When he took on the administration of the yeshiva without permission,
    Hayim Berlin also decided, likewise without permission, to take the teach-
    ing duties upon himself. However, his lectures do not please the students.
    According to the information supplied by the deputy commander of the
    Vilna province gendarmerie, Captain Dubelt, Hayim Berlin attempted to
    begin his lectures three times, but without success: the students shouted,

[3] The letter is superscribed: 'Received 13 January 1892. Confidential'.

whistled, and walked out of the yeshiva. Berlin senior himself tried to talk over the students, and ordered them, under threat of punishment, to obey his son Hayim, but Naftali Hirsch Berlin's exhortations only influenced the students temporarily. At the time of the Sukkot festival the disturbances were renewed with increased force. Motivated by their unwillingness to submit to Hayim Berlin, a crowd of students went to his house and stole the *etrog* and *lulav* that had been prepared for the festival. Berlin senior and the teacher Hayim Soloveitchik then announced to the students that if the *etrog* and *lulav* were not returned to Hayim Berlin, they would be given a difficult examination after the festival, and anyone who failed would be excluded from the yeshiva. As as result of this threat the students returned the stolen *etrog* and *lulav*. A teacher at the Volozhin elementary school, Mr Yunovich, reports for his part that there were again disturbances after the Sukkot festival. According to him, Hayim Berlin, not finding the yeshiva students to be in sympathy with him, had taken it into his head to rid the yeshiva of the stubborn ones and to stop their allowances. When this became known to the students, they reacted to Berlin's intentions with disturbances during studies, breaking lamps and so forth; on one occasion stones were thrown from the yard at the yeshiva windows; within the walls of the institution anonymous letters began to appear, in which the heads of the yeshiva were unceremoniously criticized. In order to put an end to these disturbances, it was decided to examine all the students in the parts of the Talmud that they had studied independently. Soloveitchik was to hold the examination. Then the students caused unpleasantness for Soloveitchik too, even though he had enjoyed the greatest respect and esteem of his students until recently. The glass in the windows of his apartment was broken; and once, in the yeshiva, coming to himself after one of his moments of absent-minded inattention, he found a piece of paper in his hand bearing a verse from Genesis: 'and the serpent was more wily than all the beasts of the field'. Such grossly improper acts by the students eventually moved the administration of the yeshiva to take decisive steps against the instigators of the disturbances: landlords were forbidden to house the guilty students in their lodgings. The latter, deprived of any shelter, could find no other refuge than at Hayim Berlin's house; they went there to sleep and also requested food. The next day, realizing that their situation was hopeless, the youths began to beg for mercy; they swore that they would renounce the error of their ways and be exemplary and diligent students in future. Only one of those who had been ostracized left Volozhin; this student, Yossel Mordukh, son of Leib Glasstein, died at the end of October, after he had been placed under a ban, according to Captain Dubelt.

3. There is reason to believe that all these disturbances are linked to the unfulfilled dream of Soloveitchik, the elder Berlin's former deputy, who wanted to become the yeshiva's rector after Naftali Hirsch Berlin left. Soloveitchik did not want to come out openly against the Berlins, both father and son, but neither did he want Hayim Berlin to become rector of the yeshiva. In order to attain his goal he chose to incite the students against his competitor. The students, however, were evidently quick to understand Soloveitchik's part in the game. The note reading 'and the serpent was more wily than all the beasts of the field', which was placed in his hand, strongly hints at this. And of course Soloveitchik's hypocrisy was bound to inspire in the students a feeling of disgust with the man whom they had so recently admired. This emotion was expressed in the breaking of Soloveitchik's windows and other attacks on him.

4. In reference to the question whether it was indeed yeshiva students who wrote the letter to Mr Steinberg, this has not yet been entirely clarified. All that is known is that, of those yeshiva students whose passports had been presented to the local Volozhin police, none was among the signatories of the letter. It must therefore be concluded either that the signatories did not dare to use their real first names and surnames, or else that these Jews had been studying there illegally and were not registered anywhere.

In view of the importance of the information received, the acting inspector of elementary schools, Ilin, in whose sphere of responsibility Volozhin lies, was instructed to inspect the yeshiva. After discharging this duty, Ilin presented a report to the superintendent of elementary schools on 29 December, in which he depicted the present state of the yeshiva as very poor indeed. His report showed that:

1. At present, the members of the yeshiva administration are almost all scattered elsewhere. The self-styled rector, Hayim Berlin, went off to Vilna at the beginning of December, for personal reasons; Hayim Soloveitchik went away about a month ago, according to some people to Warsaw, to recover his health, and according to others, to a variety of places in order to collect donations for the yeshiva; Samunov left Volozhin altogether at the beginning of the term and moved to Jacobstadt, where he took up the post of spiritual rabbi; because of his age and frail health, Fried takes no part in teaching; Hirsch Berlin himself rarely visits the yeshiva and has given up teaching altogether. In this way the entire management of the yeshiva is left in the hands of the Jew Dynkin, who is not even a teacher but performs the functions of a supervisor and tutor.

2. It is known in Volozhin that, after the death of Glasstein, who had been expelled from the yeshiva by Hayim Berlin, Hirsch Berlin gave an address

concerning this, in which he referred to the divine punishment meted out to the sons of Aaron for not showing full obedience to higher authority, and linked this to the deceased. This address made a very painful and unpleasant impression on all the yeshiva students, since they had all loved and respected the deceased.

3. As the local non-commissioned officer of gendarmes reported to Mr Ilin, there is a custom in the yeshiva of addressing the students only by their first names and their place of origin (for example Yankel of Minsk), rather than by their real surnames. This can make it extremely difficult for the local police to identify the individuals named on the yeshiva's register by one surname and in police registers by another.

4. The district head of police attested to Mr Ilin that the yeshiva students are quite capable of expressing their protests by violent means, and proved his point by citing recent violent acts directed against the butchers in order to fix the price of meat.

5. A visit to the Russian class and inspection of the student attendance registers for the classes convinced Mr Ilin that attendance at Russian lessons is not at all regular: 35 students were listed in the register for Class A and 15 for Class B, but in reality, according to the teacher, no more than 15 or 20 students attend the lessons. From 1 November to 18 December only 33 study days took place. The students' progress turned out to be very poor: many of them were unable to write their civil status, name, and surname correctly. According to Mr Ilin, the yeshiva students' irregular attendance at Russian lessons and their dislike for secular studies can be explained by that fanatical mood which always has been and still is prevalent at the Volozhin yeshiva, fully supported by those in charge of it.

During the inspection of the yeshiva, a private messenger brought Mr Ilin a letter signed 'The Voice of the Entire Yeshiva'. The letter, appended hereto, describes Hayim Berlin as an opponent of enlightenment and a poor talmudist, and includes a petition not to entrust the administration of the yeshiva to him.

In bringing all this information to the attention of Your Excellency, I think it necessary to add that recently the yeshiva administration has absolutely ceased to carry out the demands of the educational authorities and has almost completely broken off communication with the elementary schools administration.

According to the law of 1859, the yeshiva is obliged to include instruction in certain secular subjects in its curriculum. As in the past, the yeshiva administration continues to pay little attention to this law. The educational authorities have insistently indicated to the administration of the yeshiva many times the need to teach secular subjects to all students, but these efforts have only resulted in the administration permitting some fifty individuals, i.e. about a sixth of the students, to study secular subjects. As to how much attention is paid to the serious conduct of these lessons—this has been spoken of above. Recently the director of elementary schools in the Vilna district issued a demand that the number of those learning general studies should be raised to at least one hundred, but even this modest requirement has not been fulfilled, and the yeshiva administration prefers to gain time by engaging in fruitless correspondence. Naftali Hirsch Berlin's answer to this demand was: 'I do not deny in the slightest the importance of teaching secular subjects at the yeshiva, especially the Russian language, and I think that it is my duty, as far as I am able and it is possible, to further the development of this cause at the yeshiva. However, I also bear another responsibility: to strengthen the yeshiva's reputation as an institution in which young men study religious subjects thoroughly and in detail. The donors to the yeshiva and all religious Jews have charged me with this responsibility.' Thus, to the duty to carry out the law of the state Berlin opposes the duty laid upon him by donors to the yeshiva. And since it is impossible, according to Berlin, 'to combine both duties in equal measure', he has left the director's demand unfulfilled. However, Berlin evidently does not want to halt the correspondence by an unambiguous refusal, so he appeals to the director with a request to give him 'practical instructions as to how to implement the above demand without harming the yeshiva's primary and particular purpose'.

Until recently the yeshiva administration fulfilled its duty to present lists of the students to the educational authorities, according to the regulations of 13 November 1844, in a more or less satisfactory manner. Now the yeshiva is no longer carrying out even this duty: in spite of repeated reminders from the director, lists of students at the yeshiva have not been presented to the school administration. As a result, the administration cannot check the true number of yeshiva students, and cannot verify whether all the yeshiva students have presented their passports as required, nor whether there are any among the students who have no passport or who are evading military service.

At present, substantive changes are taking place in the composition of the teaching staff and administrators of the yeshiva, but it is not from the yeshiva administration that the educational authorities have learned of this. The most important change is the replacement of Naftali Hirsch Berlin by his son, Hayim Berlin. This major change is an undoubted fact, yet the proprietor of the yeshiva, Naftali Hirsch Berlin, has taken pains to conceal this fact from the authorities and continues to style himself as 'rector of the Volozhin yeshiva' in his dealings with them. This deliberate concealment from the educational authorities of an event that undoubtedly took place and is well known in Volozhin demonstrates how little trust may be placed in the yeshiva administration. Not a word about the disturbances at the yeshiva was reported to the school administration.

From the facts noted above the conclusion emerges that the Volozhin yeshiva is currently disintegrating, and there is no reason to hope that the present yeshiva administration, if it exists at all, is capable of restoring a proper way [the original has the mistake 'meaning'] of life to this institution. The former rector, Naftali Hirsch Berlin, who so many times made promises and gave signed undertakings to submit to the demands of the educational authorities, ceased towards the end of his activity to observe even those regulations which he had previously acknowledged as binding on him. Soloveitchik, who until recently was the mainstay of the yeshiva, has stirred up the students against him by his intrigues, and has turned from a guardian of law and order into a propagandist of the most vile sort. Finally, as shown by the report of acting inspector Ilin, there seems to be no administration at all now at the yeshiva, since its principal members have dispersed to various places.

In the light of all this, and in accordance with Your Excellency's proposal of 1 March 1888, no. 3430, I have the honour most respectfully to request instructions from Your Excellency regarding the closure of the Volozhin yeshiva. In addition, in order to avoid possible inconveniences consequent on the presence in Volozhin of the Berlins and of Soloveitchik after the closure of the yeshiva, it would be timely to carry out the banishment of Berlin and Soloveitchik from Volozhin, as proposed by the governor-general of Vilna, Kovno, and Grodno, at the time of closure.

The governor-general, whom I have informed of these measures, has expressed full agreement with them.

I have the honour to add to what has been set out above that, on my instruction, new regulations concerning the Volozhin yeshiva, authorized by Your Excellency, have been published in *Vilenskii vestnik*. Let the Jews of the North-West Region see from these regulations what demands the authorities have made of the yeshiva. And if there are among them individuals who would like to take upon themselves the duties of proprietor of the yeshiva, a role that men like Berlin and Soloveitchik are completely incapable of performing, the educational authorities will not prevent the reopening of the Volozhin yeshiva on new foundations.

Superintendent A. [illegible]
Director of the Bureau [illegible]

DOCUMENT E

Copy

Statement.

22 January 1892. Pursuant to the proposal of the director of elementary schools in the Vilna province of 20 January, no. 402, based on the order of His Excellency the acting superintendent of the Vilna educational district of 20 January, no. 369, the inspector at the Vilna administration of elementary schools, *kollezhskii sovetnik* Ogievich, having arrived at the building of the Jewish yeshiva in the town of Volozhin, along with the head of police of the Oshmyany district, *nadvornyi sovetnik* Solntsev, the deputy commander of gendarmerie of the Vilna province for the Oshmyany district Captain Dubelt, and the police officer of Area 1 of the Oshmyany district, *kollezhskii asessor* Voitkevich, in the presence of witnesses—the elder of the peasants of the Volozhin area, the peasant Vashkevich, and the elder of the townspeople of Volozhin, townsman Persky—Ogievich announced to the rector of the yeshiva, Rabbi Naftali Hirsch Berlin, to the yeshiva teachers who were present, Shelomoh Dynkin and Hayim Fried, and to the 219 students who were present, the order of His Excellency the Minister of Public Education, expounded in his proposal of 14 January, no. 888, issued to the acting superintendent of the Vilna educational district, for the immediate closure of the above-mentioned yeshiva. [Ogievich] required them to discontinue all studies in the yeshiva immediately, and removed from the yeshiva's rector, Berlin, the certificate that had been issued to him by the Vilna elementary schools administration on 24 June 1885, no. 2855, confirming his right to direct the yeshiva; the certificate issued by the same administration on 24 June 1885, no. 2856, to the townsman Hayim Soloveitchik, confirming him as deputy rector of the above-mentioned yeshiva; and the copy of the letter of the superintendent of the Vilna educational district of 4 September 1880, no. 6388, to the director of elementary schools in Vilna, concerning the authorization of the yeshiva's existence in the town of Volozhin on condition that its proprietors comply with the regulations for such institutions of 13 November 1843 [i.e. 1844]; and the register and documents of the yeshiva students. The register and the students' documents were handed over directly to the head of the Oshmyany district police.

Thereafter, for the fulfilment of the above-mentioned order of the Minister of Public Education on the closure of the yeshiva in the town of Volozhin, the head of the Oshmyany district police for his part deemed it necessary to take the following steps: (1) To lock up the yeshiva building with its contents, pending a decision by the appropriate authorities regarding the ownership of the above-mentioned building and its contents by an individual or an association, and to seal the doors with the seal of the officer of police of Area 4 of the Oshmyany district, entrusting the keys to the building and the maintenance of its security to the elder of the townspeople of Volozhin Persky, the yeshiva's rector Berlin, and the former teachers Dynkin and Fried; (2) In order to forestall attempts to resume studies, to procure from the rabbis Naftali Hirsch Berlin, Shelomoh Dynkin, and Hayim Fried a signed confirmation that the order of the Minister of Public Education regarding the closure of the yeshiva in the town of Volozhin had been declared to them, and that they undertook not to resume lessons in any circumstances, either in the former yeshiva building or in private houses; (3) After examining the documents of all the former students of the yeshiva, to prepare and issue to them travel passes for them to proceed immediately to the places of residence where they are registered; the original documents are to be sent to the appropriate police administrations to be returned to the above-mentioned individuals when they arrive at their permanent places of residence; the register of yeshiva students is to be kept in the office files of the officer of police of Area 4 of the Oshmyany district.

It has been resolved: to prepare a statement concerning everything recorded above, with the requisite signatures, and to present it to the educational authorities via the inspector at the Vilna administration of elementary schools, Ogievich, together with the certificates taken from Rabbi Berlin, nos. 2855 and 2856, and the copy of the letter of the superintendent of the Vilna educational district, no. 6388, and the statement of the rabbis Berlin, Dynkin, and Fried.

The original document was signed by: the inspector at the Vilna administration of elementary schools, *kollezhskii sovetnik* Ogievich, the head of police of the Oshmyany district, *nadvornyi sovetnik* Solntsev, Captain Dubelt, the police officer of Area 1 of the Oshmyany district Voitkevich; witnesses: the acting elder of the peasants of the Volozhin area M. Vashkevich, and the elder of the townspeople of Volozhin I. Persky.

Identical to the original: *Director of the Bureau* [as on the previous document]

Copy

Confirmation

22 January1892. We the undersigned confirm to the inspector at the Vilna administration of elementary schools, *kollezhskii sovetnik* Ogievich, and to the head of police of the Oshmyany district, *nadvornyi sovetnik* Solntsev, that the order of His Excellency the Minister of Public Education, in his letter of 14 January, no. 888, to the acting superintendent of the Vilna educational district,

for the immediate closure of the yeshiva in the town of Volozhin, has been declared to us, and we undertake not to resume lessons in any circumstances, either in the yeshiva building that has now been closed or in private houses.

The original document was signed by: Hirsch Leib Berlin (in Hebrew), the third teacher of the yeshiva, Shelomoh David Dynkin, and the fourth teacher, H. G. Fried.

Identical to the original: *Director of the Bureau* [as on the previous document]

DOCUMENT F

On the yeshiva at Volozhin, Vilna province[4]

Yeshivas are educational institutions for young Jews who wish to acquire knowledge of the Talmud and historical Jewish religious laws after completing their studies at special Jewish schools [*ḥeders*]. According to the information gathered by the former Supreme Commission for the Review of Laws Relating to Jews in the Empire, these educational institutions, being fully organized centres of Talmud study, exert enormous influence over the Jewish masses, and facilitate the strengthening of Jewish fanaticism by training spiritual rabbis, which is not allowed by law.

Yeshivas, which on the basis of existing laws (of 13 November 1844 and 4 May 1859) fall within the jurisdiction of the Ministry of Public Education, in common with other Jewish educational institutions, are directly administered by a learned rabbi, called *rosh yeshivah* (head of the institution). It is his duty to see to it that there are suitable premises for his institution; to have at least one appropriately educated (no lower than at district-school level) teacher for every fifty students; to fulfil all the requirements of the educational authorities; and to report to them twice a year on the internal arrangements of the institution. Independently of this, the above-mentioned rabbi must report the curriculum and the number of teachers and their titles to the Ministry of Public Education, through the superintendent of the educational district, before the beginning of each academic year.

The most important yeshivas are located in Volozhin (Oshmyany district of Vilna province), Mir (Minsk province), Eishyshok (Vilna province), and the city of Vilna.

The Volozhin yeshiva, which had been operating in secret since 1805, became better known only in September 1879, in connection with a case pursued by government institutions regarding an accusation against the yeshiva's rector, Rabbi Naftali Hirsch Berlin, to the effect that up to 250 Jews of undesirable character were living in Volozhin under his protection, forming

---

[4] Neither date nor author is noted on this document.

a separate, anti-government society that was harbouring various criminal plans. This accusation was not proved and the further pursuit of the case was halted.

In his report on this to the Ministry of the Interior, the former head of the gendarmerie, Adjutant General Drenteln, noted, among other things, that the above-mentioned Jewish school, which existed without the authorities' permission, had been officially closed as long ago as 1824. He also expressed the opinion that, if the closure order at that date had been made in response to the yeshiva's harmful influence on the local population, then its secret existence [now] should not be tolerated either.

For his part, the former governor-general of Vilna, Adjutant General Albedinsky, also deemed the continued existence of the Volozhin yeshiva impossible without a legal licence. He proposed that it be closed immediately and that those in charge of the institution be allowed to request permission, according to established procedure, to reopen the yeshiva in accordance with existing regulations.

The former Minister of Public Education, Count Tolstoy, also agreed with this opinion, considering that a complete cessation of the Volozhin yeshiva's activity would not achieve the desired aim, since those in charge would not part with the institution that they had founded, and that any negotiations with them before the closure of the yeshiva, about its submission to the existing regulations, would not be compatible with the dignity of government authority.

In 1880 the former Minister of the Interior, State Secretary Makov, deemed the proposed closure of the Volozhin yeshiva to be impossible, since this step would create an extremely negative impression, not only among Russian Jews, but also abroad, and would serve as a pretext for censure of a kind that, in the circumstances then obtaining, would have been not at all desirable.

Further, State Secretary Makov did not regard the culpability of the proprietors of the said yeshiva to be such that it should be subjected to a severe penalty merely for failing to observe the rules prescribed by law; it had not caused harm hitherto, and had only attracted attention by chance. State Secretary Makov deemed that it would be more appropriate to do what had often been done already with various harmless groups that had arisen: to require that the Volozhin yeshiva's proprietors should comply with the general regulations, and to resort to closing the yeshiva only if they refused or prevaricated.

In March 1880 this decision, with the agreement of the Minister of Public Education, was communicated to the governor-general of Vilna, in order that it should be announced to the rector of the yeshiva, Rabbi Berlin, and to the members of the spiritual administration; and that they should sign an undertaking that they were bound to comply fully with the existing regulations concerning yeshivas.

The proprietors of the Volozhin yeshiva under Rabbi Berlin's leadership, despite the official undertaking that they gave in 1880, did not however comply with the demands made of them by the government; indeed, by the very setting up of the yeshiva in a house of prayer they patently contravened the existing law (*Sbornik zakonov*, vol. ix, pt. 1, art. 1064), which strictly forbids any assembly of Jews in synagogues and prayer houses for any purpose other than prayer and the performance of religious ceremonies.

From the records of the council of the superintendent of Vilna [educational district] of 23 October 1889 it is clear that attached to the Volozhin yeshiva lived many young Jews seeking concealment, either to evade military service or for other reasons, including criminal and political offences; for there, under the cover of studying the Talmud, they were afforded broad scope to hide from the supervision of the authorities and to develop social-revolutionary ideas. Since it is located in one of the most out-of-the-way parts of Vilna province, the Volozhin yeshiva has successfully evaded close supervision by the local police. When the need arose, the students would run away from the yeshiva, and the police perforce adopted a lax attitude even to the registration of passports.

In 1890 the governor-general of Vilna raised the question of the need to close the Volozhin yeshiva, by virtue of its being a hotbed of Jewish fanaticism and serving as a refuge for Jews of doubtful loyalty and an anti-government institution, demonstrating the might of the Kahal, which rules the Jews of the North-Western Region despotically. The Ministry of the Interior passed the governor-general's proposal to the Minister of Public Education, who for his part responded that it would be possible not to close this institution, but with the condition that the regulations prepared for this institution by the superintendent of the Vilna educational district would be applied to it, with a view to regulating the yeshiva's activities by submitting it to the control of the authorities.

The Minister of the Interior accounted the projected regulations to be in general expedient, but on the advice of Artillery General Kokhanov he deemed it useful to introduce certain amendments, for the purpose of defining more exactly the conditions of admission to the educational establishment, the rights of candidates applying for teaching posts, etc.

The regulations for the Volozhin yeshiva formulated jointly in this way by the two ministries were transmitted in December 1891 to the superintendent of the Vilna educational district for implementation through instructions to be given from his side. They were accompanied by a warning that any deviation by the proprietors of the yeshiva from full compliance with the demands set out in the regulations would result in the immediate closure of this educational institution.

However, the steps taken by the educational authorities to bring the

Volozhin yeshiva to order did not bring about the desired outcome. As early as January of the following year, 1892, the Ministry of Public Education informed the Ministry of the Interior that, in the light of disturbances that had arisen at the yeshiva, which began as a result of the transfer of the rectorship of the yeshiva from the elder Berlin to his son Hayim and the expulsion of several students from the yeshiva by the latter, the Ministry had found it necessary to order the closure of the Volozhin yeshiva. At the same time, State Secretary Count Delyanov [the Minister of Public Education], in accordance with the petition of the superintendent of the Vilna educational district, asked for the assistance of the Ministry of the Interior in expelling the yeshiva directors, Naftali Hirsch and Hayim Berlin and also Hayim Soloveitchik, from the above-mentioned town, since they were guilty of the above-mentioned disturbances.

As a result, the Ministry of the Interior forbade these individuals to reside in Vilna province for three years. This was communicated to the governor-general of Vilna in January 1892, who was granted the right to allow Naftali Hirsch Berlin to stay temporarily in Volozhin for the final arrangement of affairs regarding his property.

PART II

SLOBODKA, TELZ
AND KOVNO

NINE

The Slobodka Yeshiva

THE SLOBODKA YESHIVA, founded around 1881, was a completely new type of yeshiva, and it became one of the most influential of its time. It was unique in combining intensive Talmud study with a passionate commitment to developing its students' moral character and instilling in them an awareness that a concern with *musar* (ethics) was an essential attribute of a Torah scholar. These innovations were not accepted unquestioningly. This chapter examines the reasons and background for this, as well as the opposition that the founders had to face and the difficulties that eventually split the institution.

The Slobodka yeshiva was founded in very different circumstances from those of Volozhin. Volozhin developed its unique form because the demand for Talmud study of the sort that it offered required greater financial support than the local population could offer. In the absence of an appropriate institutional model that R. Hayim could follow he had to come up with his own solution for the problem; the founders of Slobodka, in contrast, could base themselves on Volozhin, and in fact did so. Like Volozhin, Slobodka had two *rashei yeshivah*, operated a continuous study year, gave allowances to students, and abandoned the traditional pattern of students eating meals with the local inhabitants. Like Volozhin, too, Slobodka used emissaries to raise funds; the difference was that because devotion to Torah study and maintaining Jewish traditions more generally was seen as outmoded by key sectors of Jewish society at the end of the nineteenth century, fundraising was much more difficult and depended less on support from communal elites than on help from individuals with an ideological commitment to the yeshiva's approach.[1]

In the late nineteenth century young men could choose from a number of tempting alternatives to Torah study as a means of advancement and fulfilment: integration into the surrounding society, political activity and membership in the revolutionary movement, secular studies, Zionism, and other spheres. The response of the founder of the Slobodka yeshiva, R. Natan Tsevi Finkel (1849–1927), was to change the curriculum and, in particular, to introduce the

---

[1] On the changes in Orthodoxy in eastern Europe, see e.g. Luz, *Parallels Meet*; Silber, 'The Emergence of Ultra-Orthodoxy'.

systematic study of ethics, or *musar*. In his view, the yeshiva could no longer be exclusively devoted to Talmud study, as at Volozhin: it had to shape students' characters. This necessitated new patterns of organization, as part of which a new type of *mashgiaḥ*, or ethics tutor in modern parlance, became a central member of the yeshiva staff. These changes had many consequences. I shall attempt to explain both the way in which this innovation was implemented and its consequences.[2]

There was a third significant difference between Volozhin and Slobodka. Throughout its existence, Volozhin had always enjoyed the full support of the rabbinical establishment and was widely regarded as a distinguished institution. Slobodka never attained this status because its association with the *musar* movement, which was supported by only a small minority in the traditional camp, placed it towards the periphery of the traditional world. The students who came to Slobodka were not necessarily familiar with the *musar* movement and had no commitment to the study of ethics; they had to be introduced to the topic and persuaded of its importance. Students who came to Volozhin, in contrast, saw it as the embodiment and realization of the values they had learnt at home.

Much has been written about R. Yisra'el Salanter as the founder of the *musar* movement,[3] much less about R. Finkel. Almost no scholarly studies have been written about the Slobodka yeshiva, the dynamics of the *musar* yeshivas, or the influence of social changes on these educational institutions. The *musar* movement in general has been meticulously documented by R. Dov Katz, whose works are a very important source of information on the history of the Slobodka yeshiva. As a member of the *musar* movement, R. Katz made no secret of his admiration for its leaders and their ideals, but he also presented the opinions of those outside the movement, and annotated his sources meticulously.[4] He was apparently secure enough in his beliefs not to feel a need to impose censorship. Some of his successors were less secure. This chapter builds on his work to analyse the Slobodka phenomenon and to try to explain the factors behind its development.

1. The *Musar* Movement

The 1860s and 1870s were a time of change in the circumstances of the Jews in the Russian empire. They began to enter new economic spheres, such as

---

[2] For a comparison between the Volozhin yeshiva and the *musar* movement, see Y. Ben-Sasson, 'The *Musar* Movement and the School of Volozhin' (Heb.), 251–77.

[3] For references to the literature on him, see n. 18 below.

[4] See D. Katz, *The Musar Movement* (Heb.). R. Katz's honesty and fairness in his writing is a practical lesson in *musar* and worthy of imitation. The articles by Yisra'el Dvorets (also known as Yisra'el Paltin) are also very valuable sources. (He published under both names: *dvorets* means 'palace' in Russian, as does *paltin* in Hebrew.)

banking, industry, and the liberal professions, and a new elite was formed, differing from its predecessors not only in its occupations but also in its values.[5] These changes involved more intensive contact with the non-Jewish population and formal training in secular studies, and were not restricted to one sector of the Jewish public. The first signs of a Jewish proletariat began to emerge in the 1870s, and became more obvious as time went on.[6] The lives of both poor and rich Jews were affected by the process of urbanization, as was the speed of social change.[7] The transition from village to town weakened the power of traditional authority, affecting patterns of belief, behaviour, and education.

In particular, there was a notable rise in the numbers of Jewish students attending Russian educational institutions. Whereas in 1863 there were 574 Jewish pupils in secondary schools, in 1880 there were 7,999. Whereas in 1864 there were 129 Jewish students at universities, by 1880 there were 566, and by 1886 there were 1,858.[8] Obviously, these students constituted no more than a fraction of the entire Jewish population of Russia and most came from the elite, but it should be remembered that yeshiva students too had never come from all social strata but had generally come from the upper classes.

This new situation posed a threat and a challenge to the traditional system of education. Hitherto there had always been a close link between the Jewish economic leadership and the world of talmudic scholarship. Supporting Talmud scholars had been a prestigious thing for a wealthy man to do. The link between the philanthropist and the scholar also often had a personal dimension: wealthy Jews often had a talmudic education themselves and were genuinely interested in engaging with scholarship, to the extent that they also chose scholars of distinction as their sons-in-law. Excellence in Talmud study often led to marriage into a wealthy family, or at least to a respected rabbinical position. In other words, study at a yeshiva could be an important route to economic success.

As the status of the old elite declined, however, the importance of this route of entry to its ranks similarly declined. As people increasingly saw secular education as the entrance to a world of new possibilities, the wealthy no longer sought to marry off their daughters to Talmud scholars. A further factor here was a law of 1874 that granted graduates of secondary schools significant reductions in military service.[9] A campaign for a secular education was also of course waged by the maskilim, from a conviction that secular knowledge was essential to every Jew in his search for truth. By 1886 the

---

[5] Slutsky, *Russian Jewish Journalism in the Nineteenth Century* (Heb.), ch. 1, esp. p. 27, which contains an excellent analysis of the phenomenon. See also the superb study by Benjamin Nathans, *Beyond the Pale.* [6] Mendelsohn, *Class Struggle in the Pale.*

[7] On urbanization, see Leshchinski, *The Jewish Diaspora* (Heb.), 88–147, esp. 117–18; see also Kahan, *Essays in Jewish Social and Economic History,* 27–31.

[8] Slutsky, *Russian Jewish Journalism in the Nineteenth Century* (Heb.), ch. 1. [9] Ibid. 25.

number of Jewish students at universities surpassed that of students at the main yeshivas of eastern Europe.[10] The rise in the number of university students probably came at the expense of those dedicating themselves to Talmud study, especially in the *batei midrash*. An anonymous 'Faithful One', writing in *Halevanon* in 1879, described the crisis thus:

Fathers and sons will take heed for the future, since His Imperial Majesty has decreed that anyone graduating from the state schools with a diploma of the second rank will not have to do extended military service but only three years instead of the six years decreed for all. Therefore fathers will take heed for their sons so that their time of service will be reduced to three years, and their sons will make every effort to obey them, so that immediately upon leaving school they may find a position in a shop or in a trading house. Even those boys who would be most talented in Talmud study do not look back . . . all their attention is devoted to learning the language of the state . . . and the writing and language of the state and its ignoramuses seem better to them than learning 500 pages of Talmud by heart, for they profit by it immediately, and they prefer one bird in the cage to ten on the roof; therefore all leaders and upholders of religion should take counsel as to what to do in order to implant love of the study of Talmud, Rashi, and Tosafot in the hearts of our youth, after they leave the state schools, and that *tov torah im derekh erets* [Torah study combined with worldliness is good].[11]

The increasing interest in secular education contributed to the decline in the numbers of Talmud students in the *batei midrash* while the impact on yeshivas was different. As already mentioned, *batei midrash* could collapse very quickly. As soon as the best student in the *beit midrash* decided that he had had enough of Talmud study and wanted to devote himself to secular studies, others followed him. The absence of discipline and teachers in the *beit midrash* meant that students were particularly susceptible to the influence of their peers. For instance, a report of 1879 states that prior to that time, 'up to 150 men, including distinguished pilpulists and masters of halakhah' had studied in the Nevaizer *kloyz* of Kovno, 'but now there are only seven left'—and this was not the only institution that was collapsing.[12]

---

[10] Slutsky, *Russian Jewish Journalism in the Nineteenth Century* (Heb.), 27. In 1886 there were 1,858 Jewish university students. Although there are no accurate data on the number of those studying at yeshivas, a rough estimate can be made as follows: there were about 400 students at Volozhin, fewer than 300 at Mir, about the same number at Telz, and slightly fewer at Slobodka—altogether fewer than 1,858. It should be remembered that the university students came from all over the tsarist empire, not just from Lithuania, and that the total number of yeshiva students does not include the many Talmud students in *batei midrash* or in less famous yeshivas. In hasidic areas there were still many youths who studied in *batei midrash*. Nonetheless, the data do reflect the situation in mitnagdic regions. I thank Rabbi Boruch Oberlander for this observation.

[11] *Halevanon*, 15/30 (28 Feb. 1879), 238–9. The article was sent from Dundee, in Scotland. I have not succeeded in identifying the 'Faithful One'.

[12] N. Amsterdam, in *Halevanon*, 15/37 (25 Apr. 1879), supplement. A description of the same

The traditional public found it difficult to cope with the extent to which young people were abandoning the accepted path, especially as those leaving the fold came from the social and scholarly elite. In the past, isolated cases of deviation could be attributed to weak character, the desire for material gain, the lust for fame and power, or illogical behaviour bordering on insanity. However, the rising numbers of these cases, the social success of those who left tradition behind, and their readiness to devote their lives to different ideals—revolutionary, intellectual, national, or other—demanded new and better explanations if the claim that the new was superior was to be successfully challenged.[13] There was also a growing need to provide material support for the few who continued to study Torah, and to encourage others to join them. This problem was especially acute in the case of older students, either married or on the verge of marriage.

Many members of the traditional camp despaired of stemming the tide of desertion. R. Eliezer Gordon, *rosh yeshivah* in Telz, wrote:

Because of our manifold sins, it is impossible to gauge the extent of the heresy that has broken out among all the 'enlightened' in our country, both girls and boys. Every day we see girls and boys who only yesterday feared God and His Torah but have now thrown off all restraint, Heaven protect us. While my sons and daughters, thank God, follow the way of Torah and the fear of God, who can say how things will be with them, Heaven forbid, in a few years' time?[14]

The supporters of the *musar* movement claimed that the decline was caused by unethical behaviour, especially on the part of scholars, and that if people studied *musar* properly, the decline of traditional society would end. They therefore proposed a clear plan of action, focusing on the transformation of social values through the education system. Many of the central figures of the *musar* movement had been attracted to the Haskalah in their youth, and had clearly struggled with the question of the right path to take.[15] Their interest in *musar* seems to reflect the internal conflict that they had themselves experienced.[16] The movement did not espouse intervention in contemporary social

phenomenon, but from the opposite point of view, appears in Yampolski, 'Memories of My Youth' (Heb.), 859–61. See also his comments as recorded in Slutsky, *Russian Jewish Journalism in the Nineteenth Century* (Heb.), 321 n. 83, and the other evidence collected there.

[13] This argument is influenced by Berger and Luckmann, *The Social Construction of Reality*.

[14] Ostrovsky (ed.), *Man of Jerusalem* (Heb.), 63.

[15] On R. Simhah Zissel Ziv, see A. A. Friedman, *Memoirs* (Heb.), 18; on R. Yosef of Novogrudok, see D. Katz, *The Musar Movement* (Heb.), iv. 179–94; on Maltzan, see ibid. ii. 683; on R. Natan Tsevi Finkel, see above. One must be wary of authors who describe their heroes not only as righteous but also as reformed sinners, but even so the 'modern' features of the *musar* movement—such as its innovative organization, its focus on philosophy rather than kabbalah, its emphasis on man's ability to reform himself, and so on—tend to support their credibility, in my opinion.

[16] On a similar phenomenon of 'reformed sinners' preaching the gospel, see Festinger et al.

questions but nor did it advocate isolation. It aspired to a society in which everyone would engage in *musar*, and in which there would thus be no social injustice. Whereas traditional scholarly society measured status by the time one spent studying and by one's analytical ability and expertise, in the *musar* movement status was related to one's behaviour and ability to influence others.

Involvement in the *musar* movement thus required activity. In addition to the confidence that came with social activism and shared ideology and customs, members also enjoyed the social benefits of belonging to a closed group (sectarianism in the eyes of their critics) as well as from practical assistance from other members. In founding his yeshiva, a leader like R. Finkel could rely on help from fellow members without even knowing them personally. His prestige lent authority to his requests, and saved him having to run around persuading people to support him. Many individuals helped with raising funds, giving *shiurim*, responding to criticism from other yeshivas, advertising the institution, and so on. Since the bond between the leader and the members of the movement was not based solely on friendship or personal charisma but also on a common ideology, the leader could expect personal sacrifices on his behalf, just as were expected of him in his role as leader.

The Slobodka yeshiva, which followed the principles of the *musar* movement in many ways, was a response to the weakening of traditional society. It combined traditional Torah study and observance of Jewish law with a seemingly modern critique of traditional society, and strove for the perfection of society through the ethical reform of the individual. The *musar* movement attributed the crisis in traditional society to religious leaders' indifference to ethics, and considered it only natural that the best of its young people, who had drifted away from tradition, should try to change that situation. Often totally ignorant of a Jewish approach to ethics, these alienated youngsters sought non-Jewish substitutes: their approach was critical of the leaders of traditional Jewish society, considering them, at the very least, outmoded. The *musar* movement offered an alternative that aspired to combine the perfection of the individual with loyalty to Jewish tradition; basing itself on these principles, the Slobodka yeshiva attempted to integrate Talmud study with the study of *musar*. While this framework was not intended for the young Jews of eastern Europe who were set on acculturating, it did provide answers for traditionalists who were sensitive to the critiques of their peers. The remainder

(eds.), *When Prophecy Fails*. It has been noted that the *musar* movement tried to explain the failure of tradition in its encounter with the new society and offered ways in which to deal with this new situation. The need to cope with the failure of a traditional society was not unique to this group; both the situation and the coping strategies are very similar to those described by Festinger. He gave the name 'cognitive dissonance' to the contradiction between belief and a reality that is seen as contradicting that belief. A characteristic reaction to this is the hope of recruiting new believers (ibid. 3–7).

of this chapter will consider how this was achieved, though we shall turn first to some background on the founder of the *musar* movement, R. Yisra'el Salanter, before examining how the methods of the movement were implanted in a yeshiva framework.

2. R. Yisra'el Salanter

R. Salanter was born in 1810 in Žagarė in northern Lithuania, near the present-day border with Latvia, and from a very early age displayed unusual talent. He studied at the *beit midrash* in Salant (hence how he came to be known) and with R. Yosef Zundel (1786–1866), whose charismatic personality made a deep impression on him, as did his insistence that moral rectitude was as important as Torah study. He married the daughter of a prominent figure in the Salant community and in 1840 moved to Vilna, where he became *rosh yeshivah* of the Ramailes yeshiva and worked hard to encourage the study of *musar*. There is good reason to think that he seriously considered accepting a position in the new rabbinical seminary established by the government in Vilna in 1848, but moved to Kovno after he did not receive a senior position there.[17] Clearly the move to Kovno was not undertaken in order to avoid government pressure: Kovno was no less a part of the tsarist empire than Vilna. In 1857 he moved to Germany and in fact he lived most of the rest of his life outside Lithuania.[18] In all these places he tried to disseminate his interest in *musar*, although not always with much success.

Since R. Salanter believed that developing an ethical approach to life should be a central concern for every Jew, he believed that education had to emphasize moral development alongside the study of rabbinic texts. His students developed various approaches to how moral reform was to be achieved,

[17] See Lvov, 'Rabbi Isroel Salanter', esp. p. 123.

[18] There is an extensive literature on R. Salanter and the *musar* movement. This chapter is not intended to provide a full review of his life and the history of the movement, but rather to provide some background. On R. Salanter, see Etkes, *Rabbi Yisra'el Salanter* (Heb.); H. Goldberg, *Israel Salanter*. On the *musar* movement, see D. Katz, *The Musar Movement* (Heb.); id., *The Musar Controversy* (Heb.), and the bibliographies there. Another important article is H. H. Ben-Sasson, 'The *Musar* Movement in Lithuania' (Heb.); also excellent is Ross, 'Conceptual Thought in the Writings of the Successors of R. Yisra'el Salanter' (Heb.), which systematically examines the concepts of the *musar* movement and draws some fascinating conclusions: it is a pity that this has not been published. Much of the copious documentation relating to the *musar* yeshivas is polemical. I have not accepted testimonies that seem unreliable, usually in relation to the nature of the *musar* movement and of the controversy surrounding it. A few of the sources I have used could probably be rejected, and more far-reaching conclusions could be made by using doubtful material. I have tried to base every statement on a range of sources from different factions, in order to avoid relying on a single source. I could not discuss every piece of evidence and justify my acceptance or rejection of it, since this would have made the chapter much too long and would have detracted from its subject.

based on different conceptions of the nature of man and of the divine demands on him, but the basic assumption remained that one should always work actively and consciously on moral self-improvement.[19]

In the 1840s and 1850s R. Salanter's efforts did not make a great impression, at least in terms of the number of people who adopted his approach.[20] His ideas had a strong basis in traditional literature, and while they were widely perceived as novel, were not revolutionary. He based himself to a great extent on such luminaries as Moshe Hayim Luzzatto (Ramhal, 1707–46) and the Vilna Gaon.[21] His originality lay principally in the emphasis he placed on ethics and the means he suggested for implementing his ideas. R. Salanter was acutely aware of the crisis facing traditional society, but not all shared his sense of threat. In the mid-nineteenth century there was no broad consensus among the traditional Jews of eastern Europe that new approaches were necessary. However, as the sense of crisis grew, the traditionalist public became more open to new approaches and R. Salanter was a key figure in this transition. In emphasizing the need to change priorities in education, even in the traditional world, and stressing universal moral values, R. Salanter was an unusual figure among the rabbis of his generation. His ideas even met with approval in circles that were not usually positively disposed towards tradition. For instance, though Peretz Smolenskin was a radical modernist, on the occasion of R. Salanter's move to Paris in 1880 he made the following comment in the journal he edited, *Hashaḥar*:

We regard R. Yisra'el Salanter as a legendary hero in the spirit of the people, whose direct manner of speaking has won him the hearts of all those who know him, and whenever people wish to praise a pleasant idea or an honest act they invoke the name of R. Yisra'el . . . [R. Yisra'el] is now to leave his native land and his people . . . and will travel to a foreign country . . . we, the Jews of Russia, have the first claim on the goodness of R. Yisra'el.[22]

In 1845 R. Salanter undertook to republish Mendel Lefin's book on ethics,

---

[19] Ross, 'Conceptual Thought in the Writings of the Successors of R. Yisra'el Salanter' (Heb.).

[20] Two of the most talented young men then studying in Kovno became friendly with him but did not adopt his *musar* system; they were Eliezer Gordon (1840–1910), who later became *rosh yeshivah* in Telz (see Ch. 10 below) and Yeruham Perlman (1835–96), who later became famous as 'Hagadol Miminsk' (the Great Sage of Minsk; see Heilpern, *The Great Sage of Minsk* (Heb.), 29–33). They were more impressed by his talmudic knowledge. The halakhic writings of R. Salanter have not yet been studied systematically; see Etkes, *Rabbi Yisra'el Salanter* (Heb.), 191–214.

[21] On his links with the Vilna Gaon and R. Hayim of Volozhin, see Etkes, *Rabbi Yisra'el Salanter* (Heb.), ch. 1. For information on Luzzatto, see Tishby, 'The Dissemination of Luzzatto's Kabbalistic Writings' (Heb.); Ross, 'Conceptual Thought in the Writings of the Successors of R. Yisra'el Salanter' (Heb.).   [22] Bernstein, 'Hastening Redemption' (Heb.).

Ḥeshbon nefesh, a text that was very close to the spirit of the Haskalah,[23] and he maintained this interest. Indeed, in a letter written in 1876 he noted that he was interested in books on logic, not necessarily by Jews, but that his know-ledge of German was inadequate for this.[24] It would thus seem that one of the reasons for the considerable success of his system in the late nineteenth century in the traditional camp, especially among young people, was the fusion of an approach that met the standards of contemporary thought with one that preserved traditional patterns of behaviour. When he started his work, however, very few people were aware of his basic premiss—that Jewish society in eastern Europe was facing a crisis. Twenty years later everyone rec-ognized the truth of the situation.

From 1857 onwards R. Salanter was based in Germany, visiting Russia only occasionally. Little is known of his activity in Germany in the 1860s and 1870s except that he kept in close contact with a handful of loyal disciples in Russia and continued to guide and influence them until his death in 1883. They admired him deeply, and their activities reflected to some extent the approach that he promoted. He was active in working against the promulga-tion of new laws affecting Jewish education, and against the establishment of rabbinical seminaries in Russia. He also tried to fight the maskilim with their own weapons, writing for an anti-Haskalah journal.[25] However, most of his efforts went into disseminating his method in the educational sphere. Early on, while still in Kovno, he tried to open an institution called a *beit musar*

---

[23] Lefin's book was based on the writings of Benjamin Franklin, a fact of which R. Salanter was probably unaware; see Etkes, *Rabbi Yisra'el Salanter* (Heb.), 95–6.

[24] Lutske, *History in their Hands*, 56.

[25] This episode has not been described before, but since it is important in the description of the way in which R. Salanter and his disciples fought the Haskalah, I will give a brief outline here. In 1870 the Hevrat Matsdikei Harabim (Society of Justifiers of the Many) in Vilna published a pamphlet entitled *Milḥamah beshalom* (War on Peace), which contained vituperative attacks on the Haskalah. According to Lifschitz, R. Dov Ber Zeitlin and R. Yehoshua Heshel Levin were behind this society (Lifschitz, *Zikhron ya'akov*, ii. 104). On R. Levin's links with R. Salanter, see Ch. 2, §6, above. The pamphlets did not continue to appear for very long. In 1871 a similar publication appeared, called *Hayare'aḥ* (The Moon). Most of its articles were unsigned, but the same group seems to have been behind it. The publisher was the Hevrat Matsdikei Harabim, and R. Dov Zeitlin edited issue 4 in the spring of 1871. An article by R. Salanter entitled 'Imrei binah' (Words of Wisdom) appeared in this issue (p. 91). It had been published ten years earlier, in the first issue of *Tevunah*, a publication edited by R. Salanter himself. R. Salanter is described on the second title page as 'our master and teacher, the rabbi' and the publisher notes: 'I was commanded thus by our master and teacher, not to give him many titles.' R. Salanter must thus have been connected with the Hevrat Matsdikei Harabim. The same journal contained articles by R. Alexander Moshe Lapidot, who was a follower of R. Salanter (on the relationship between them, see D. Katz, *The Musar Movement* (Heb.), i. 141, 186, 195–7). It is difficult to establish how closely R. Salanter identified with the activities of his disciples and admirers, since there is insufficient material available on this (see Etkes, *Rabbi Yisra'el Salanter* (Heb.)). The late and much-missed Rabbi Betsalel Landau gave me the reference to *Hayare'aḥ*.

(house of *musar*)—a sort of *beit midrash* where the ordinary men of the community could study *musar*—but the experiment failed. His disciples' efforts in the field of education were more successful.

The establishment of a *musar* yeshiva, with a view to encouraging students in Talmud study while also shaping their characters, was one of the most important innovations of the *musar* movement. In addition to the regular teaching staff there was a *mashgiah* responsible for the students' moral development; his status within the institution was at least equal to that of the *rosh yeshivah*. The change in values that underlay this took time to be absorbed, but the *musar* movement's apparent ability to offer a remedy for the crisis affecting traditional society in the late nineteenth century and its proven ability to maintain its appeal to students led to the rapid growth of *musar* yeshivas. Slobodka was the first, and the most outstanding example.

3. The Founding and Character of the Slobodka Yeshiva

Slobodka was a suburb of Kovno, but the atmosphere there was rather different from elsewhere in Kovno. As A. A. Friedman put it, 'Kovno is built to the east of the confluence of the Viliya and the Neman. Across the Viliya river lies Lithuanian Slobodka, drenched in the darkness and poverty of Lithuania. It is a stronghold of extreme religiosity, bordering on fanaticism. Across the Neman river is Aleksat . . . where a European atmosphere prevails.'[26] It was there that the Slobodka *musar* yeshiva was founded in about 1880.

The *musar* yeshiva was not the first Torah institution in Slobodka. In 1835 there had been a yeshiva there, with both married and unmarried students.[27] Another yeshiva operated in the 1850s, though apparently not of a very high standard. The *rosh yeshivah* was young and was still studying for the rabbinate.[28] One student records that there was a close and positive relationship between the yeshiva and the local residents,[29] though another from the same period notes that R. Eliezer Gordon, then a young scholar living in Slobodka, once had to climb into the yeshiva through a window, since the door was locked 'because of the street urchins, who used to disturb the students with

---

[26] A. A. Friedman, *Memoirs* (Heb.), 132.   [27] Frumkin, *Toledot eliyahu*, 25.

[28] Marmer, 'Ya'akov Tsevi Sobel' (Yid.). Another yeshiva that operated at the same time was described in Deiches, *Sermons of Rabbi Yisra'el Hayim Deiches* (Heb.). Deiches, who was born in 1852, wrote in the introduction that 'when I was three years old, my father was appointed as *dayan* in Kovno. He was head of the *metivta* [yeshiva] that is in the great *beit midrash* for seven years.' The son himself studied in a yeshiva that operated in Slobodka under the leadership of an otherwise unidentified R. Yosef. It appears that the students were advanced, since he mentions a friend who 'supported me against the protests of the older students who were opposed to the presence of a young child and thus I was accepted into the yeshiva'.

[29] Barnet, *Memoirs* (Heb.), 1.

their childish pranks'.[30] This was clearly a community with a history of talmudic study.

The central figure in the history of the *musar* yeshiva in Slobodka, as already mentioned, was R. Natan Tsevi Finkel. He was born in Raseiniai in 1849 but grew up in Vilna,[31] moving to Kelme after his marriage to the grand-daughter of R. Eliezer Gutman, the rabbi of Kelme. A local resident recalls that R. Finkel showed interest in the Haskalah but R. Simhah Zissel Ziv, a disciple of R. Yisra'el Salanter who lived in Kelme, 'brought him back to the right path'.[32] This story may have a factual basis, but the attribution of a maskilic past to R. Finkel could also be because of his behaviour and style of dress, which were quite usual in Vilna but might have been seen in Kelme as a sign of leaning towards the Haskalah. R. Finkel became R. Simhah Zissel Ziv's most notable disciple and assisted him in his activities in Kelme. However, they did not always agree, and in 1877 R. Finkel left Kelme and settled in Slobodka.

There were at least two yeshivas for young boys in the Slobodka area at this time: Mahazikei Ets Hahayim (Upholders of the Tree of Life), founded in Kovno itself in 1876 and headed by R. Yosef Rabinovitz,[33] and R. Tsevi

[30] Sorotskin, 'From the Paths of the *Tsadik*' (Heb.), 58, citing R. Shmuel Pundiler. See also H. L. Gordon, 'On the Banks of the Viliya and Neman' (Heb.), 57: 'Most of the town's inhabitants were strange creatures, there were very few Christians, and not a single church could be found in Slobodka. The local Jewish population included a stratum of coarse and boorish people and hoodlums. In my time there, only one yeshiva student, called Reuven of Slobodka, actually came from the town. When we went out of the yeshiva, the urchins used to ambush us, attack us (for we were very young), and beat us up. Because of this we always used to walk through the streets in a group, though it did not help much.'

[31] D. Katz, *The Musar Movement* (Heb.), ii, s.v. Finkel, and the sources cited there. For a useful compendium of sources on his life and teachings, see Weinberger (ed.), *The Grandfather of Slobodka* (Heb.).

[32] 'A group of R. Simhah Zissel Ziv's more enthusiastic disciples approached him and welcomed him into their midst . . . a young man, a maskil who knew Hebrew and its grammar and was fluent in German—a true maskil—who was an opponent of R. Simhah, suddenly came over to his side; he got up one morning and burnt all his Haskalah books and joined R. Simhah with all his heart and soul. This young man was R. Natan Tsevi, who with his strong will and powers of speech has ever since been one of the inner pillars supporting the *musarniks* and has had enormous influence on his students' (see A. A. Friedman, 'On the History of the *Musarniks*' (Heb.), 9; Kamenetsky, *The Making of a Godol*, i. 147–8, 343). On R. Simhah Zissel Ziv, see D. Katz, *The Musar Movement* (Heb.), ii. 219–26. The third most important leader of the *musar* movement (after R. Simhah Zissel Ziv and R. Finkel) and the founder of the Novogrudok yeshiva was R. Yosef Yosel Horowitz (1848–1920); he had abandonned the Torah world but returned to it under the influence of R. Salanter (see D. Katz, *The Musar Movement* (Heb.), vol. iv, ch. 10). There seems to have been a link between hesitation over choosing a path in life and the tendency to engage in self-improvement.

[33] On this institution, see Braverman, 'The Jewish Community in Kovno' (Heb.). This yeshiva made use of emissaries; on their activities see 'Yeshivat mahazikei ets hayim bekovno', by a pseudonymous author, 'Sheravya Halevi Ish Elisheva': *Hamelits*, 29/194 (12 Sept. 1889), 1–2, and 'Letters from Kovno' (Heb.), *Hamelits*, 31/61 (26 Mar. 1891), 1–3, signed by another pseudonymous author, 'Hayehudi'.

Hirshel's yeshiva in Slobodka. The two institutions competed for pupils.[34] R. Finkel took a position at R. Tsevi Hirshel's yeshiva, where he had ample opportunity to use his abundant energy. One of his students described the yeshiva as follows:

This yeshiva was very shabby, because of the tremendous poverty of its students. The righteous *gaon*, R. Tsevi, of blessed memory, was a righteous and upright man, and subsisted on the fees paid by the students, and since he was dependent on them his influence was limited. Nor was it possible for the righteous *gaon*, R. Tsevi, of blessed memory, to be too particular in choosing students of high calibre. There was no order in the classes of students, since he was the only teacher there. In addition to all this, he was very poor, and was not clear-minded enough to devote himself properly to the yeshiva. And therefore the first thing done by our master and teacher, the righteous *gaon* and rabbi, the *gaon* R. Natan Tsevi, of blessed and holy memory, was to set a salary for the righteous *gaon*, R. Tsevi Hirshel, of blessed memory, so that he would not be dependent on the students any longer, and he would then only choose those students who were the most talented and were suitable for being trained in the Torah. Besides this, he brought in more teachers to the yeshiva, great Torah scholars who later became famous for their learning.[35]

However, R. Finkel did not stay long at R. Tsevi Hirshel's yeshiva. While teaching there, R. Finkel played a major role in founding a *kolel*—a special institution for young married Talmud students (see Chapter 11)—in Kovno, which also attracted unmarried students of a high standard. The latter were not eligible for admission to the *kolel*, but came in order to study at the *batei midrash* of the city where the students of the *kolel* studied, as reported in 1879 by Naftali Amsterdam in *Halevanon*:

Kovno—come and see . . . the joyous voices of . . . these students, their concentration and the exalted diligence of their study! And how envy has increased wisdom among the younger students who have set their hearts on the day of battle to join themselves to these students of Torah and to hear teaching from their mouths.[36]

Every year the yeshivas of Kovno and Slobodka for young boys—the Ets Hahayim yeshiva and R. Tsevi Hirshel's yeshiva—also produced graduates who wanted to study at the *kolel* but were not allowed to do so because they were not yet married. R. Finkel realized that there was a need for an advanced yeshiva for these unmarried young men, and he founded one. It did not formally open on a particular day; rather, it seems that in the early 1880s some advanced students who had completed their studies at the junior yeshivas simply began to organize as a group. Evidence from 1883 reveals the existence of a more formal framework:

---

[34] Radus, *Memoirs* (Heb.), 40.
[35] Dvorets [Paltin], *The Biography of Our Master and Teacher* (Heb.), 2.
[36] *Halevanon*, 15/37 (25 Apr. 1879), supplement.

And here was a letter from R. Natan Tsevi Finkel, who suggested that I come to Slobodka. So thus I went there in the winter of 1883, and I found that there was already an important place of Torah study there, with about ten advanced students, including some famous Torah scholars, studying there (apart from the students in Kovno, whose numbers I do not know), and some small yeshivas. And there was also a group [*kibuts*] of important young men with no particular *rosh yeshivah*, but our teacher, the *gaon* R. Yitshak Blaser, his memory for a blessing, occasionally gave them a *shiur*, and in the summer, when our teacher, the *gaon* R. Eliezer Gordon, his memory for a blessing, was accepted as the rabbi of Slobodka, he gave two *shiurim*, and once my honoured brother, R. Shmuel Avigdor, may he be spared for a long life, gave a *shiur*.[37]

The institution described here is somewhere between a yeshiva and a *beit midrash*; there was a well-defined group of students who attended *shiurim*, but the latter were not given regularly since there was no permanent teacher.[38] This type of study framework was often described as a *kibuts* ('group'). After 1886 there were regular teachers besides R. Finkel, and the *kibuts* developed into a proper yeshiva. The students sat and studied day and night, as in other yeshivas—though, unlike other yeshivas, there were *shiurim* both in Talmud and in *musar*.

There was a large Jewish population in Kovno–Slobodka, with many active institutions, so the yeshiva had no difficulty in finding a suitable operational base. Studies initially took place in the old *beit midrash* of Slobodka and later moved to other *batei midrash*. Only in 1901 did the yeshiva get a building of its own. The move is barely mentioned in accounts of the yeshiva, and it seems to have been taken for granted.[39]

Musar study was a distinguishing feature of the yeshiva from its earliest days. It was considered its central activity in terms of importance, though not in terms of the amount of time devoted to it. The students used to go over the lectures on *musar* given by the *mashgiaḥ* in exactly the same way that students at other yeshivas used to go over the *rosh yeshivah*'s Talmud *shiurim*.[40] The importance of *musar* study in the yeshiva's early days found formal expression in the fact that only two Talmud *shiurim* were held each week[41]— fewer than was usual at other yeshivas.

The *musar* curriculum included lectures on ethical issues and analytical study of *musar* texts. In an effort to drive home the moral teaching, students used to repeat choice maxims over and over in the *beit midrash*, sometimes

---

[37] Feivelson, 'Memories from the Beginning of the Foundation of Torah Institutions' (Heb.). I have no information on what happened to the yeshiva in later years.

[38] On the teachers in this period, see Kamenetsky, *The Making of a Godol*, i. 398–404.

[39] D. Katz, *The Musar Movement* (Heb.), iii. 49–51.

[40] Ibid. 214. Shmuel Rosenfeld has claimed that there were public confessions of sins (*Rabbi Yisra'el Salanter* (Heb.), 57).

[41] *Hamelits*, 36/266 (14 Dec. 1896), letter from the yeshiva's *shamash*.

shouting them out and weeping as they did so. Not all students approved of such behaviour.[42]

Musar study was intended to train students in self-discipline and the perfect service of God. The focus was the individual: the movement did not demand any change in the structure of society and did not address questions of social organization, poverty, or social wrongs. It therefore never developed any links with the socialist movement, even though both movements aspired to social reform and justice. *Musar* study aroused opposition from several rabbis, who disapproved of the extreme forms of behaviour that sometimes accompanied it, the preference for *musar* study over that of the Talmud—which was interpreted as contempt for the Torah and those who studied it—and the sectarian character of the movement. Maskilim also opposed the movement because of its declared opposition to innovation.[43]

While R. Finkel was the central figure in creating the yeshiva, a German Jew from Berlin, Ovadiah (Emil) Lachman, played the central role in funding it. Until 1896 Lachman covered almost all the yeshiva's expenses himself, though Baron Rothschild and Shmuel Strauss also contributed.[44] In other words, the main donors lived in a different country, and in practice gave the yeshiva a free hand in running its affairs. They supported it even though they themselves identified with German Orthodoxy because they were anxious to prevent the crumbling of traditional society in eastern Europe and felt that the *musar* movement could help achieve this. They were also critical of the Haskalah.[45] The administrative burden on the yeshiva was thus lightened tremendously, since there were no financial worries and no need to devote time and energy to raising funds. Thanks to Lachman's donations, the Slobodka yeshiva was more independent and less influenced by public opinion than Volozhin had been. Although the use of emissaries at Volozhin had limited local pressures on the yeshiva, it was still dependent on public support and therefore susceptible to public opinion in areas where the emissaries were active.

In a letter discussing his arrival as a student in 1901, R. Weinberg, later a key figure in modern Orthodoxy, notes: 'The treasury of the yeshiva was very poor and the Saba [lit.: 'grandfather', i.e. R. Finkel] lacked the financial means to grant the talented students and the studious ones generous support as he

---

[42] For a hostile description of *musar* study at the yeshiva, see D. Katz, *The Musar Controversy* (Heb.), 108, from a rabbinic pronouncement against the *musar* movement of 1897 published as a broadsheet with the title 'Lema'an da'at' ('In the Interests of Knowledge'), The leaders of the *musar* movement did not disagree with the facts in this description but rather interpreted them differently.   [43] D. Katz, *The Musar Controversy* (Heb.).

[44] See R. Yehiel Weinberg's words in Dvorets [Paltin], *Assembly of Israel* (Heb.), 3, 10.

[45] R. Salanter's role in forging this link between the Orthodox in Germany and the *musar* movement requires further study. I searched for information on Lachman, who had such a great influence on the history of the yeshivas, but found very little; the details I gleaned will be discussed below.

did in later years when he gave geniuses and industrious students financial gifts with a free hand.'[46] However, everything is relative and the ability to give support in 1901, even if limited, was unquestioned.

R. Finkel did not hesitate to use the funds at his disposal to influence teachers and students alike. We know that he offered R. Yitshak Ya'akov Rabinowitz, who was a teacher of Talmud in the yeshiva, an additional 20 roubles per week (a considerable sum at the time) if he would agree to teach a *shiur* in *musar* as well as his Talmud *shiur*. R. Rabinowitz was known to harbour reservations about the *musar* movement, so his agreement would have been interpreted by the students as indicating a change in his position; but in fact he turned down the offer and left the yeshiva.[47] R. Finkel was also prepared to give increased support and better conditions to attract talented young men to his yeshiva.[48] This was doubly beneficial: gifted students brought prestige to the yeshiva in which they studied, and their time at the yeshiva might influence them to join the *musar* movement. For this reason R. Finkel used a number of tactics to attract students from other yeshivas.[49] In general, support for students at his yeshiva were better than those elsewhere in Kovno,[50] which made it perfectly reasonable for a poor young man to choose it in preference to others.[51] During a student revolt in the yeshiva which is discussed below, R. Weinberg wrote that the students suspected him of informing on them 'and they almost excommunicated me, and they didn't let any student take me as a tutor, and thus cut down my income, because it

[46] See Weinberg, *Insights into the Talmud* (Heb.), 1–2. On Weinberg, see Marc Shapiro's perceptive and profound study *Between the Yeshiva World and Modern Orthodoxy*.

[47] Z. A. Rabiner, 'Rabbi Itzeleh Ponevezher' (Heb.), *Bamishor*, 3/110: 6.

[48] D. Katz, *The Musar Movement* (Heb.), iii. 258, iv. 20. On R. Finkel's attempt to lure R. Solomon Polachek to his yeshiva, see M. Y. Goldberg, 'The Life of the Gaon of Maitchet' (Heb.), 123.

[49] Radus wrote about what happened to him as a young boy on the way to study in the other yeshiva in Kovno: '[Upon arriving in Kovno,] I was surprised and happy to see two lads from my city standing in front of me. I extended my hand to them; I greeted them and embraced them. I asked them when they had come and where they were living. Had they seen anyone of my family before they left my town? To satisfy my questions they told me that they had left our town a day after I left and that they saw my father before they left and that he told them to tell me in his name that it was his desire and wish that I study in the yeshiva in Slobodka which is near Kovno, and God forbid that I should reside in Kovno because a God-fearing person will not dwell there near headstrong and empty youths . . . in the course of time, by corresponding with my father, I found out that the words that were attributed to him were made up and that my father had not seen my acquaintances, and they did not hear anything from him about me. I found out from a reliable source who had connections with the *mashgiah* from Slobodka that he was involved in this. My friends denigrated the yeshiva in Kovno while praising the Slobodka yeshiva to the skies' (*Memoirs* (Heb.), 40–1).

[50] The Keneset Beit Yitshak yeshiva; for a discussion of this institution, see below.

[51] According to the testimony of S. Lown, who studied at Keneset Beit Yitshak in 1905. His brother chose the *musar* yeshiva for precisely this reason.

was the custom then that the main source of income of the advanced students was from tutoring the younger ones. However, the Saba gave me generous support.'[52] From this we learn something about the composition of the student body: there were students who taught for payment; there were students whose abilities were limited to the extent that they needed tutors; and there were students who came from families wealthy enough to enable them to pay for such tuition. Generally these students were not totally dependent on the yeshiva for support, but it was there if needed.

4. The Students

For many of the students, especially those who had not met R. Finkel previously, their period at the Slobodka yeshiva was their first encounter with *musar* ideology. Despite all the changes that were taking place, they seem to have come to the yeshiva for the traditional reasons—to progress in the study of Talmud, to improve their social standing, and to find a group of companions with shared aims. They could assume that, if they were successful in their studies, their social status would increase, and they hoped, despite all the changes in society, that they would therefore merit a bride from a wealthy family.

Most of these students came from small towns, and this was their first taste of city life.[53] Relatively few of them came from large cities, since by the late nineteenth century, talented young men from the affluent families in larger urban centres were usually more attracted to the local secular secondary schools than to a distant yeshiva. When the young men arrived at Slobodka they were told that the yeshiva aimed not only to advance their studies but principally to assist in their moral development. Few had heard of this necessity before, and not all of them felt that it applied to them. Some accepted the new approach, while others still focused exclusively on traditional study.

Many students, and not necessarily the least gifted, were interested in the Haskalah and in acquiring secular knowledge. For a young city-dweller, going to yeshiva meant a conscious rejection of the Haskalah or secular studies; those who came from small towns came for lack of any alternative, and for them the Haskalah offered fascinating new horizons. Thus there were talented and serious students at the yeshiva who were also interested in the literature of the Haskalah.[54] The attitude to the study of such literature at

[52] Weinberg, *Insights into the Talmud* (Heb.), 5.

[53] H. L. Gordon noted that there was only one student from Kovno at the yeshiva during his time there ('On the Banks of the Viliya and Neman' (Heb.), 57). See also the list of students arranged by home town in Dvorets [Paltin], *Assembly of Israel* (Heb.), 16–17. This list reflects the situation in 1912, and reveals the small number of students from large cities: there were only ten students from Kovno and eleven from Slobodka, even though these were large urban centres.   [54] Mathisson, 'The Tragedy of a Great Man' (Heb.), 284.

Slobodka was complex. The more mature students who were on the verge of marriage were allowed to read secular books, younger students were not. Even so, by the early twentieth century students were using the Jewish library in Kovno that had been set up by supporters of the Haskalah.[55] The following description gives some idea of the clandestine atmosphere associated with an interest in the Haskalah at the yeshiva:

And sometimes you would be slipping through the dark lanes, and a figure would glimmer in front of your eyes and your heart would suddenly miss a beat: surely it must be one of the *mashgiaḥ*'s sleuths, sent to follow you, and you wouldn't know what to do with yourself . . . and then a clear laugh would ring out and a voice would call from the darkness, 'Natan!' And I answer him: 'Moshe Eliyahu!' Two secret readers of David Haselbitzer's library have run into each other . . . so we walk on together . . . and continue to the same small, clean room, where a little bookcase stands in a corner, with beautiful volumes peeping out from it . . . David Haselbitzer welcomes us . . . and engages us in light conversation about Zion that heals all our wounds, and, overcome with awe, his lips murmur the names 'Herzl' and 'Ahad Ha'am', and he licks his lips as though sipping heady wine.[56]

An interest in *musar* and an interest in the Haskalah were not necessarily incompatible. Aharon Bakst, who later became the rabbi of Šiauliai, was said to be 'well versed in sciences, Jewish and world history, knowledge of nature, philosophical method, etc.' Whether or not all of this was accurate is irrelevant. What is important is that it could be said, and it was not seen as improbable. It is important to distinguish between the ideological Haskalah, from which R. Bakst was indeed remote, and the acquisition of knowledge in various fields, which he and others regarded as legitimate.[57] A young man could continue along both paths, although eventually he would feel the tension between them. Students new to both yeshiva life and city life saw both *musar* and secular studies as 'modern' topics that stimulated interest and curiosity:

To slip away from the yeshiva during the *musar* lectures and to hesitate in the dark lanes which led to the 'Potters' Street', the home of the secret Hebrew library owned and run by David Haselbitzer, was neither comfortable nor easy. At first I used to imagine that spying glances were fastening on me, piercing into the inner mysteries of my soul; and in any case, I loved those hours of *musar*, full of suffering and gloom. The struggles with the satanic forces lying in wait stimulated my young imagination and bewitched me with the mysterious enchantment of exalted sanctity. The hundreds of ecstatic young men pouring out their souls in the whispered words of the *Mesilat yesharim* ['Path of the Upright'] . . . in these hours the heart's yearning

[55] A. Litvin, *Jewish Souls* (Yid.), ch. 7.
[56] Grinblat, 'In the Secret Library' (Heb.). Natan Grinblat was a native of Vidaz, a small town.
[57] D. Katz, *The Musar Movement* (Heb.), vol. v, ch. 7 (p. 125).

worked wonders, and it was so good to be drawn to all those young men with their excited faces and their burning souls—and then, suddenly, you would rise and leave that feverish spot and plunge into the darkness outside the town, stepping between gardens . . . and make your way among fences twisted by the darkness into crooked teeth—how your heart thrills then! But the desire grows for those tiny books, saturated with heady and stimulating juices, and twining around the soul like serpents . . . and that desire shakes and entices and impels you, and you hesitate for a moment, with your ears cocked—perhaps they are following you?—and you note every rustle, every echo, as if you were off to commit burglary.[58]

Here we see the strong allure of the Haskalah, standing in opposition to the emotional power of *musar* study in the yeshiva.

The attempt at character-building aroused opposition among many students, as already mentioned. This was not necessarily on ideological grounds: the students were adolescents who had only recently left home, and rebellion against authority was quite natural under the circumstances. Many probably longed for independence and were frustrated to find that the *rosh yeshivah* saw himself in a paternal role—much more so than in Volozhin. M. M. Shuk writes:

Never did the Saba order or command or scold his students. He behaved just like a father to the yeshiva students . . . and he practised what he preached. He was concerned not only with the spirituality of his students but also with their physical needs, and with their future. The old man played a part in his students' lives even after they had left the yeshiva. His students consulted him about everything and eagerly awaited his advice and his decision, which was always worthwhile. The yeshiva students were also educated to behave like brothers to each other. There was no jealousy about honour among the students of Slobodka.[59]

Students from small towns who encountered the opportunities of a modern city for the first time were often plunged into crisis. In the city they learnt of new roads to success that could not be reached by studying Talmud in a yeshiva. The *musar* movement's response to this was to offer different measures of success and to claim that the very way of life in a yeshiva was of enormous value, though in ways that the new students had never imagined. The focus of education in a *musar* yeshiva was not the next world—unlike the teachings of the itinerant preachers, which focused in vivid detail on the pleasures awaiting the righteous and the torments destined for the wicked—but rather on developing a moral attitude to this world.[60] The emphasis was on man, rather than on

[58] Grinblat, 'In the Secret Library' (Heb.).

[59] Shuk, 'The Grandfather of Slobodka' (Heb.), 311.

[60] The issue is presented in a very general way here. In practice, there were considerable differences between different thinkers in the *musar* movement. For a more detailed discussion, see D. Katz, *The Musar Movement* (Heb.); Etkes, *Rabbi Yisra'el Salanter* (Heb.); and, especially, Ross, 'Conceptual Thought in the Writings of the Successors of R. Yisra'el Salanter' (Heb.).

God—just as in the approach of the Haskalah the goal of full realization of ethical potential was seen as the pinnacle of achievement. However, in contrast to the Haskalah, the ultimate goal of *musar* remained the service of God.

The *musar* leaders used language appropriate to the secular challenge they were facing. They used vocabulary borrowed from philosophy and psychology, giving an impression of making logical and intellectual claims even though it was emotion that played a central role in strengthening the moral character. Similarly, R. Finkel required his students to dress properly, so that they would not feel inferior to the gymnasium students. This was no small matter: the latter wore impressive uniforms in keeping with their social status. On the same grounds, R. Finkel stopped the custom whereby students relied like beggars on the hospitality of others.[61] Volozhin had abolished this practice in the early nineteenth century, but it was common elsewhere up to the end of the century.

Those students who attached themselves to the *musar* movement saw themselves as superior to others. According to Saul Lieberman, who studied at Slobodka, the yeshiva's goal was to prove to the students that the external world was inferior and worthless.[62] The idea that they were superior to others logically also applied to great Talmud scholars who had not studied *musar*. A critic of the movement wrote in 1907: 'They teach each other the belief and the idea that those great scholars of the Torah who lack *musar* according to their version are scarcely any better than clever craftsmen, while the least of the *musar* experts is as important and weighty as an old scholar who sits in a yeshiva releasing *agunot* by the true Torah which is in his mouth.'[63] The criticism did not bother the enthusiastic adherents. The students who adopted the way of *musar* were very loyal to the movement's leaders and eager to spread its doctrines.[64]

It seems that most of the students who came to Slobodka in the late nineteenth century did not attach themselves to the *musar* movement,[65] and many

[61] D. Katz, *The Musar Movement* (Heb.), iii. 288–9. The abolition of the custom of eating with local householders—which had actually been abolished much earlier at Volozhin (for practical rather than ideological reasons)—also reflected the sources of funding at the disposal of the yeshiva, and considerable sensitivity to the public perception of yeshiva students. In a generation that revered Torah study, such sensitivity would have been unnecessary. On R. Finkel's limited success, see H. L. Gordon, 'On the Banks of the Viliya and Neman' (Heb.), 42.

[62] Based on a personal interview with Saul Lieberman.

[63] 'Lema'an da'at', *Hatsefirah*, 24/175 (15 Aug. 1897), 870–1. See also Israel Eliashiv's description of his feelings in 'Grabin' (Heb.).

[64] The relationship between leaders of the *musar* movement and their students was very similar to that between hasidic *rebbe*s and their hasidim. The memorial booklet for R. Finkel regularly refers to him as *admor*, a term used for hasidic *rebbe*s (and an acronym of the Hebrew for 'our lord, our teacher, and our rabbi'); see Dvorets [Paltin], *The Biography of Our Master and Teacher* (Heb.), and also below.

[65] My assertion that the majority of students opposed *musar* is based on the fact that, in the split of 1897 (see below), most of the students remained in the Halvayat Hamet *beit midrash*, which later became the Keneset Beit Yitshak yeshiva; only about 20 per cent followed R. Finkel.

actually opposed it.[66] They came in order to study, confident that Talmud study for its own sake was all that was necessary in life. Those who came to a yeshiva considered themselves gifted students, and it was not easy for them to accept the idea that an education in *musar* made one a better person than an education in Talmud. It was usually the best students who rejected *musar* since it threatened their status.[67] Some decided to take up secular studies or abandon Talmud study, but many students stayed in the yeshiva because they enjoyed the Talmud study there, and not necessarily because they considered *musar* important. Thus the number of students in a *musar* yeshiva did not necessarily reflect the number of students committed to the movement's ideals.

Another reason why students were opposed to *musar* was the yeshiva's policy of spying on them.[68] At Volozhin students were expected to devote most of their time to Talmud study, and beyond that there was little supervision of their opinions or leisure-time activities. They could usually engage in secular studies and literature if they did so discreetly. However, since at Slobodka the focus was not on study but on character, the yeshiva felt compelled to keep an eye on all aspects of the student's life.[69] This caused major tensions in the yeshiva and led many students to rebel. Before discussing these developments, however, we shall briefly consider the attitudes of the rabbis who taught Talmud at the yeshiva as well as of the general public, since they too played a part in the conflicts.

5. Talmud Study in the *Musar* Yeshiva

The status of the Talmud teachers, known in many yeshivas as *ramim* (an abbreviation of the phrase *rashei metivta*, 'heads of the college'), was very

[66] See below for descriptions of the struggles over *musar* at Slobodka and cf. Ch. 10, below, on Telz.

[67] On R. Yosef Kahaneman's time as a student at Telz, see Kul, *Alone in his Generation* (Heb.), 33–77.

[68] In Slobodka there was no dormitory; the students lived, as in Volozhin, in rented rooms. Such a room was called a *stantsiya*; on student accommodation, see Kamenetsky, *Rebi Ya'akov* (Heb.), 53. Dormitories developed mainly after the First World War. Although they facilitated supervision, it had not been practical to build them earlier. Stampfer, 'Dormitory and Yeshiva in Eastern Europe', discusses this in detail.

[69] See e.g. Mathisson, 'The Tragedy of a Great Man' (Heb.), 284, on R. Finkel's treatment of R. Yehiel Weinberg: '[He] was one of the most brilliant students at the Keneset Yisra'el yeshiva, and was a favourite of the *mashgiah*, R. Neta Hirsh Finkel. It seems that he was suspected of reading secular books, and they tried to lodge another student in his room as a sort of spy, to watch over his behaviour. But Yehiel managed to avoid this and claimed that he had promised my parents to keep an eye on me, so that he had to live with me . . . in the meantime it seemed that R. Neta Hirsh felt that Yehiel, who came from Ciechanowiec, had reached a parting of the ways. This was when he arranged the match with the daughter of the late rabbi of Pilvishki, and Yehiel was appointed as rabbi of the town by way of dowry. This step was the great tragedy of his life. His heart was not in the match.'

complex. During the early years of the yeshiva, there were no teachers who were hired specifically to teach Talmud. Most of the students came from Slobodka itself, though some did come from further afield because they were attracted to the ideology of *musar*.[70] However, after well-known Talmud teachers were brought in, it became considerably more attractive as a place to study.

The yeshiva developed under the leadership and guidance of R. Finkel; even if people were not always aware of it, he saw himself primarily as a *mashgiah*.[71] The first regular *rosh yeshivah* to be appointed, in 1886, was R. Hayim Rabinowitz; shortly afterwards, R. Avraham Aharon Burstein was appointed as his deputy. Both left the yeshiva in 1890; they were replaced by R. Yitshak Ya'akov Rabinowitz, who left in his turn in 1894.[72] It is known that both R. Yitshak Ya'akov Rabinowitz and R. Burstein left because of their opposition to the emphasis on *musar* study.[73] They had not come from the ranks of the *musar* movement and could not come to terms with the elevation of *musar* study to the same level of importance as Talmud study.

R. Finkel retained control of the yeshiva, in spite of the appointment of *rashei yeshivah*. He controlled its budget and made appointments. At Volozhin, the *rosh yeshivah* had controlled the funds, and any disagreements that had arisen had been between the *rashei yeshivah*. The *mashgiah* there, when there was one, was employed by the *rosh yeshivah*. The situation was reversed at Slobodka, where the *mashgiah* controlled the funds and the entire yeshiva. A *rosh yeshivah* might have been used to having to defer to wealthy donors on account of their wealth, but taking orders from a *mashgiah* was another matter. Not only did he control the institution's funds, but he could also treat the rabbi as an equal. If the *mashgiah* was older, the *rosh yeshivah* could accept this

---

[70] Such as Feivelson; see 'Memories from the Beginning of the Foundation of Torah Institutions' (Heb.).

[71] On the yeshiva in general, see D. Katz, *The Musar Movement* (Heb.), iii. 31–86, and also below.

[72] For details of his departure, see Kamenetsky, *The Making of a Godol*, i. 423–4.

[73] For R. Yitshak Ya'akov Rabinowitz, see S. Bialoblocki, 'Rabbi Itzeleh of Ponevezh' (Heb.), 395. R. Burstein signed the anti-*musar* diatribe 'Lema'an da'at' (see n. 63 above), which would explain his departure from the yeshiva. See also his impassioned article, 'A Secret Society in Israel' (Heb.). R. Hayim Rabinowitz was the first Talmud teacher at the Keneset Beit Yitshak yeshiva, which was founded in opposition to the *musar* movement. It would thus seem that he too opposed the movement, and this may have been the reason for his departure (see H. L. Gordon, 'On the Banks of the Viliya and Neman' (Heb.), 109). An interesting story that throws light on the personalities of R. Yitshak Ya'akov Rabinowitz and R. Finkel is recorded by Z. A. Rabiner in 'Rabbi Itzeleh Ponevezher' (Heb.): the leaders of the *musar* movement appealed to R. Yitshak Ya'akov's wife 'to use her influence with him to persuade him to teach the yeshiva students *musar* once a week, and they would then add 20 roubles a month to his salary. But the attempt did not succeed. R. Itzel [Yitshak Ya'akov] did not follow his wife's advice, and would not change his opinions for the sake of financial profit.'

state of affairs, but if he was a contemporary, or even younger, the situation was much more difficult. This contributed to the instability of Slobodka in its early years.

After R. Yitshak Ya'akov Rabinowitz left in 1894, younger teachers were appointed to replace him—the brothers-in-law R. Moshe Mordekhai Epstein (1866–1934) and R. Isser Zalman Meltzer (1870–1954). Three years later R. Meltzer left in order to found a branch of the Slobodka yeshiva in Slutsk at R. Finkel's request. In contrast to their predecessors, R. Epstein and R. Meltzer had identified with the movement even before coming to the yeshiva. This was a great help to R. Finkel, who no longer had to combine the running of the yeshiva with battling against opponents who were also greatly admired by the students. The yeshiva was now headed by great Torah scholars who supported R. Finkel's methods. The appointment of two young and unknown rabbis initially aroused opposition among the students, although this eventually died away.[74]

R. Finkel delegated a great deal of authority to R. Moshe Mordekhai Epstein as the new *rosh yeshivah*, giving him a central role:

We have recorded his wonderful relationship with our master and teacher, the *gaon* R. Moshe Mordekhai, of blessed and holy memory, and the wide-ranging authority which [R. Finkel] entrusted to him, by appointing him as the official representative of the yeshiva to the outside world, and by arranging that all the money and letters received at the yeshiva were addressed to him, at his private address, and that all the letters and circulars that were sent out from the yeshiva were sent in his name, as though he were the sole *rosh yeshivah* of the yeshiva, without any colleagues.[75]

However, as this description demonstrates, ultimate authority remained with R. Finkel.

As noted earlier, members of the *musar* movement had a complex attitude to Talmud study, especially within the yeshiva. On the one hand, the Talmud was of enormous religious significance as the source of halakhah. On the other hand, they felt that *musar* study also needed time and effort. Thanks to his balanced personality and outlook, R. Epstein offered a practical solution to this problem. In spite of his abundant skill as a Talmud scholar, he managed to fit into a framework in which Talmud was considered less important than *musar* study—even though more time was devoted to the study of Talmud. It was not easy to find someone of this nature in a generation that had grown up regarding Talmud study as the supreme value. However, even finding the right man did not preclude the possibility of further problems developing as a result of the need to determine the place of Talmud study in a *musar* yeshiva.

[74] Dvorets [Paltin], *The Gaon Rabbi Moshe Mordekhai Epstein* (Heb.), 9.
[75] Ibid. 18–19. In this, R. Finkel was following his teacher, R. Simhah Zissel Ziv; see D. Katz, *The Musar Movement* (Heb.), ii. 65.

This was also expressed in study methods. New types of study that emphasized logic, known as *sevara* or *higayon*, were spreading to many yeshivas at this time, and the masters of these new methods—R. Hayim Soloveitchik, R. Shimon Shkop, and R. Barukh Ber Leibowitz—attracted many students. One of the attractions of these methods was the belief that they held the key to coping with modernity. At Slobodka, in contrast, R. Epstein taught using the traditional method of *pilpul*. R. Yisra'el Salanter himself had supported *pilpul*, as a method that sharpened the intellect,[76] and it was accepted at Slobodka, though not without opposition. R. Paltin, a member of the *musar* movement, wrote of R. Epstein:

The other Talmud teachers . . . taught using the new *havanah* [understanding] or *higayon* [logic] methods in Torah study, without giving much consideration to study for the sake of *bekiut* [breadth of knowledge]. The method of our lord, teacher, and rabbi, the *gaon* R. Moshe Mordekhai was built on strong foundations of tremendous breadth, and was entirely practical and good. Many yeshiva students, particularly the youngest, who are the leaven in the 'dough' of the yeshiva, were strongly attracted to the 'sweet and good' *shiurim* [of the non-*musar* teachers]. These lectures became 'fashionable', and the opponents of *musar* used them to fill the vacuum created by the lack of *musar* in the yeshivas under their control. Obviously, the shiurim given at the Keneset Beit Yitshak yeshiva, which was founded solely because of opposition to *musar* study in yeshiva, were necessarily of this second sort.[77]

The attraction of novel methods of Talmud study aroused concern in the *musar* yeshiva. In 1904 R. Barukh Ber Liebowitz was appointed head of the Keneset Beit Yitshak yeshiva—the rival yeshiva in Kovno. He was a famous teacher and the most outstanding pupil of R. Hayim Soloveitchik, and the heads of the *musar* yeshiva of Slobodka, or Keneset Yisra'el as it was then called, were worried that he might lure away some of their students and damage their yeshiva's reputation. Some students from Keneset Yisra'el did go and listen to R. Liebowitz's *shiurim*, but to general relief this had little effect on the yeshiva's functioning in the long run.[78] R. Finkel's charisma and the financial support he provided guaranteed the yeshiva's continued popularity.

In the yeshivas that did not belong to the *musar* movement, the new study methods were the main attraction. At Slobodka, there was no need for these methods since *musar* study—and reliable finances—were what held the students. Study using the older *pilpul* method was less alluring, posing less of a threat to the supremacy of *musar* study at the yeshiva.

[76] See the sources and analysis in D. Katz, *The Musar Movement* (Heb.), vol. i, ch. 19. Study was regarded as a means rather than an end.
[77] Paltin [Dvorets], 'On the History of the Keneset Yisra'el Yeshiva' (Heb.), *Tevunah*, 13/125: 9. R. Paltin also published under the name Dvorets: see n. 4 above.
[78] Edelstein, *Rabbi Barukh Dov Liebowitz* (Heb.), 30.

6. Institutional Growth

The drive to disseminate *musar* led to the setting up of a network of branches. Whereas some Volozhin graduates had founded yeshivas, these were not 'branches' of Volozhin, and were not subject to its authority. There were no financial links between the yeshivas founded by Volozhin graduates and Volozhin itself, nor was there any mutual financial aid or exchange of students. Outstanding students may have moved from the less important yeshivas to Volozhin, but there was no compensatory movement the other way to strengthen the smaller yeshivas. There was no sense of unity among the daughter yeshivas, nor did they form a cohesive social unit.[79] In contrast, R. Finkel set up branches of his yeshiva, helped finance them, and ensured that students moved from the branches to the central yeshiva and back again— both according to their preference and to instructions from the leaders of the movement. A student at a traditional yeshiva like Volozhin came to study for his own intellectual benefit, but those who accepted the authority of the *musar* movement had to sacrifice themselves for the sake of the movement.

Even by 1881, before the Slobodka yeshiva was founded, a yeshiva had been set up at Telz (see Chapter 10) as a result of R. Finkel's efforts. This institution was also funded by Lachman, who placed the money at R. Finkel's disposal and also influenced some of the first students to study at Telz.[80] Despite R. Finkel's initial involvement, however, the Telz yeshiva operated independently, with no link to Slobodka. The first real branch of the Slobodka yeshiva was founded in 1897 in Slutsk, at the invitation of R. Ya'akov David Willowski (the Ridbaz, 1845–1913). At this time, R. Willowski was competing with R. Meir Paimer for the position of town rabbi, and he thought that having a local yeshiva to support him would increase his prestige and help him obtain the position. R. Finkel took up the invitation and sent a group of teachers and students to Slutsk, led by R. Meltzer. Other branch yeshivas of Slobodka were founded in Shklov, Szczuczyn, and elsewhere.[81] These were genuine branches: R. Finkel appointed the principal staff, set up their mode of operation, and also provided financial assistance. However, R. Finkel did not concentrate all authority in his own hands: the *rashei yeshivah* decided on student admittances and appointed local staff. R. Finkel also sent them outstanding students from existing yeshivas in order to influence the atmosphere there.[82] In the case of the Mir yeshiva he took a more extreme step: in order to bring the yeshiva under his influence, he married his son, R. Eliezer Yehudah Finkel

[79] See Tzinovitz, *Tree of Life* (Heb.), 432–54.   [80] See Ch. 10, §1, below.

[81] This emerges from the description in T. Y. Meltzer's 'Ets Hayim Yeshiva' (Heb.); see also D. Katz, *The Musar Movement* (Heb.), vol. iii, ch. 4, 'Its Network of Yeshivas and Activities'.

[82] D. Katz, *The Musar Movement* (Heb.), vol. iii, ch. 4. On the Minsk branch, see Rosenstein, *Writings* (Heb.), 98.

(1879–1965), who was an outstanding scholar, to the daughter of the *rosh yeshivah* at Mir, R. Eliyahu Barukh Kamai, thus gaining a foothold for *musar* study in Mir.[83] His ability to dispatch students and provide funds gave him enormous influence in the world of the Lithuanian yeshivas, which he used not for self-aggrandizement but in order to spread *musar* study more widely.

7. Disputes and Conflicts

The *musar* movement met with opposition from broad segments of Jewish society, both traditionalists and maskilim, for a variety of reasons.[84] Some people were insulted by the implication that their behaviour was not sufficiently ethical, some considered the movement hypocritical, some considered the whole idea unnecessary—and there were additional reasons as well. The supporters of *musar* made little attempt to answer their critics. Rather, they abandoned R. Yisra'el Salanter's initial aim of spreading their ideas widely and concentrated instead on a small circle of students whom they felt were receptive to their message.

Simultaneously with his success in expanding the network of *musar* yeshivas, R. Finkel was forced to deal with opposition from within the yeshiva itself.[85] The first major dispute erupted in 1897. According to R. Finkel's supporters, the challenge to his leadership sprang from 'the jealousy that some of the students who had remained at the Slobodka yeshiva felt towards their colleagues who had gone to Slutsk. Spurred by their jealousy, they began to search for defects in the running of the yeshiva and in the *musar* method'.[86]

However, several additional factors played a role. There had been a history of tension between Kovno rabbis and *musar* leaders with regard to the Kovno *kolel* (see Chapter 11), but R. Yitshak Elhanan Spektor, the chief rabbi of Kovno, had kept this in check. In spring 1896 R. Spektor died. At his funeral, R. Yitshak Blaser (1837–1907), one of the local *musar* leaders, eulogized him, alongside R. Spektor's son, R. Tsevi Hirsh Rabinowitz (1848–1910), but later the same year a rift arose between the *musar* movement and the rabbinical establishment and articles hostile to the yeshiva appeared in the Hebrew-language press. In an effort to calm things down *Hamelits* published a response by Ya'akov Me'ir Shamash accompanied by a letter of approbation from the rabbi of Slobodka, R. Moshe Danishevski, but the apparent peace did not last long, and it seems doubtful whether the two sides had really come to an

---

[83]   D. Katz, *The Musar Movement* (Heb.), iii. 64, and see pp. 66–8 on R. Finkel's influence on other yeshivas.   [84]   See the material collected in D. Katz, *The Musar Controversy* (Heb.).

[85]   The main difference between the conflicts within the yeshiva and those in the Kovno *kolel* (for which, see Ch. 11 below) was that, in the case of the *kolel*, most of the critics came from outside, while in the yeshiva the opposition was mainly internal.

[86]   Dvorets [Paltin], *The Gaon Rabbi Moshe Mordekhai Epstein* (Heb.), 11.

agreement.[87] On 10 May 1897 R. Rabinowitz wrote a scathing attack on the movement and its leaders which was published in the Hebrew press on 9 July 1897. The author was a long-time opponent of the *musar* movement who had meanwhile succeeded his father as rabbi of Kovno.[88]

In Slobodka itself there were students who opposed *musar* study. Some were angered by the financial and other privileges given to those students who specialized in *musar*,[89] some were unhappy with the lack of rabbis of calibre to teach Talmud.[90] There were thus both ideological and economic factors behind the opposition to R. Finkel.[91] The students knew that if they spoke out against *musar* study, and especially against R. Finkel's management, they would find a ready ear among local rabbis. In this respect their situation was very different from that of the students at Volozhin, where the authorities always had the wholehearted support of contemporary rabbis.

Under these circumstances, it is not hard to understand how in 1897 some of the students organized an anti-*musar* campaign. They removed *musar* books from the study hall and deliberately disrupted R. Finkel's lectures by loudly studying Talmud as he was trying to speak, moves that they claimed led their opponents to bring in thugs to beat them up. The two sides eventually presented their claims to the rabbi of Kovno.[92] A letter sent to *Hamelits* at this time by about 150 students claimed that of all the funds that had been donated to the yeshiva, 'except for forty or fifty of the top *musar* students, who have received financial support every month, only about eight or ten of the others—of about two hundred and fifty of them in all—received any support, and the rest have been fed on mouldy bread and the empty words of the *rosh yeshivah*'.[93] If that indeed was the case, is curious that only 150 students signed out of the 200 who did not receive support. There may be some exaggeration here. However, the complaints were taken seriously.

In response to all this, the rabbis of Kovno held a meeting. Various proposals

---

[87] See *Hatsefirah*, 15/53 (24 Mar. 1898); *Hamelits*, 37/266 (7 Dec. 1896).

[88] *Hamelits*, 37/143 (9 July 1897); see also Shmukler [Shapira], 'Rabbi Tsevi Hirsh Rabinowitz' (Heb.).

[89] See the declaration entitled 'Lema'an da'at' ('In the Interests of Knowledge'), published above a list of signatures in *Hamelits*, 37/143 (9 July 1897), 3: 'they have drawn nigh with both hands and have given much support to those young men whose hearts are empty of Torah, and devoid of talent, and open to their false *musar*. The talented and blessed young men, whose souls desire to engage in Torah day and night, these have the *rashei yeshivah* pushed away with both hands and deprived them of all good . . . and every *musar* student who comes up with a new *musar* idea from some superficial article . . . brings his newly thought-up idea to their leaders . . . and if they approve and adopt the *musar* concept presented to them, they honour the inventor and innovator above all his brethren'. See also Y. Lieberman, 'Musarniks in Lithuania' (Yid.).

[90] See Dvorets [Paltin], *The Gaon Rabbi Moshe Mordekhai Epstein* (Heb.), 9.

[91] See the short report by Rosenfeld in *Hamelits*, 37/36 (24 Feb. 1897), 2–3.

[92] See the declaration entitled 'Lema'an da'at' (n. 89 above). Nothing is known about the results of this meeting.   [93] Rosenfeld, 'Letters from Provincial Towns' (Heb.).

were put forward, for instance that R. Finkel should be dismissed, that a deputy should be appointed, or that a committee of six should be appointed to supervise the distribution of financial support. At least some of these committee members were to be opponents of *musar* study, and the committee as a whole would be responsible for ensuring that every student received some money, even if he did not study *musar*.[94] The *musar* movement was represented at the meeting by R. Finkel and R. Blaser. According to one report R. Finkel reacted sharply to the accusations, but R. Blaser merely wished those present 'Good night', rose, and left the meeting.[95]

In practical terms, however, R. Finkel's reaction was much the same as R. Blaser's: he did not argue with the hostile faction but rather transferred those students who supported him to another *beit midrash*. Between forty and seventy students out of the student body of about 250 went with him, forming the core of a new yeshiva, a *musar* yeshiva, which was soon named Keneset Yisra'el after R. Yisra'el Salanter.[96] The students who remained at the large *beit midrash* formed the foundation of the Keneset Beit Yitshak yeshiva, named after R. Yitshak Elhanan Spektor. R. Rabinowitz and R. Danishevski took over the running of this yeshiva.[97] It is said that R. Finkel received a donation of

[94] *Hamelits*, 37/54 (16 Mar. 1897); Rosenfeld, 'Letters from Provincial Towns' (Heb.).

[95] See D. Katz, *The Musar Movement* (Heb.), ii. 251; id., *The Musar Controversy* (Heb.), 99, and the sources he cites.

[96] Rosenfeld puts the number at forty ('Letters from Provincial Towns' (Heb.)); H. L. Gordon gives an estimate of fifty ('On the Banks of the Viliya and Neman' (Heb.), 109); Dvorets suggests seventy (*The Gaon Rabbi Moshe Mordekhai Epstein* (Heb.), 23).

[97] See the announcement of the foundation of the yeshiva named after R. Yitshak Elhanan and the principles on which it was founded (*Hamelits*, 37/76 (13 Apr. 1897), 7). There is no mention of the circumstances surrounding its foundation, apparently to avoid mention of the controversy: 'Slobodka . . . at the end of Adar I last year . . . when the holy *gaon* of Israel was taken from us . . . R. Yitshak Elhanan . . . has been given an eternal memorial . . . that will be called after him "Keneset Beit Yitshak", a place of study for young men who sit immersed in the four cubits of the halakhah and the fear of God in the old *beit midrash* in Slobodka, as a memorial in the temple of the Lord . . . and the two renowned *geonim*, the rabbis of the two towns of Kovno and Slobodka, have begun to protect . . . these young men who sit in Keneset Beit Yitshak . . . and suitable men have been appointed at the gathering of many honoured and pious individuals . . . as supervisors, to aid and help these rabbis and *geonim* with guidance and individual supervision . . . therefore, behold, we believe we are obliged, for the welfare of the public, to announce openly and publicly, that: (1) It has been decided and agreed to emphasize the duty of study of Gemara, Rashi, and Tosafot in Keneset Beit Yitshak, together with the early and later commentators, as well as the study of the books of the earlier and later *posekim* . . . (2) Only those young men will be accepted there who have already reached an advanced level in Gemara, Rashi, and Tosafot . . . and who pass an examination . . . in addition, they must possess certificates attesting their good character, fear of God, and correct behaviour according to both divine and earthly standards. (3) There are no vacancies left for the summer term . . . only, as an exception, we will try to find a place for a very few candidates who are found to be especially distinguished and brilliant after being examined. (4) Anyone who arrives without a letter from a scholar addressed to the *gaon*, the rabbi of Slobodka, has no chance . . . written and signed by one of the supervisors, Shelomoh Zalman Landa.'

300 roubles at this time from R. Yisra'el Me'ir Hakohen (the Hafets Hayim), in order to fund his new yeshiva.[98] He also continued to receive financial support from Lachman in Berlin and was able to construct a new building for the yeshiva though it was necessary to employ *shadarim* or emissaries to raise additional funds in eastern Europe.[99] Thus, two large yeshivas developed in Slobodka—Keneset Beit Yitshak and Keneset Yisra'el. At times the relationship between them was tense,[100] but it did not usually reach the point of open conflict; students from one yeshiva even used to visit the other institution to listen to the *shiurim* there.

The split into two yeshivas, one in favour of *musar* study and one against, did not mark the end of the controversy over the study of *musar* among R. Finkel's students. In 1902 new disturbances broke out in the Keneset Yisra'el yeshiva. R. Paltin, who was at the yeshiva at the time, describes them as follows:

Those who complained pretended that all they wanted was to elevate the role of Torah, and that this was why they opposed the study and supporters of *musar*, who, they claimed, were causing a decline in Torah study . . . and in order to demonstrate their devotion to Torah study, they enticed into their net several of the best yeshiva students, who came up with creative ideas every day in the presence of the most talented students, so that they might develop and advance in Torah study . . . they tried to influence them against the *musar* studies at the yeshiva.

By means of these stratagems they succeeded in luring the greater part of the students into their net . . . and there was a still deeper plan in this stratagem . . . they hoped that they would succeed in influencing our lord, teacher, and rabbi, the *gaon* R. Moshe Mordekhai [Epstein], may his holy and righteous memory be for a blessing . . . so that he would not oppose them in this. And then it would be an easy matter for them to banish our lord, teacher, and rabbi, the *gaon* R. Natan Tsevi Finkel, from the yeshiva, who had withdrawn himself and almost completely given up all official functions at the yeshiva, and his victory for *musar* would be nullified.[101]

According to R. Paltin, this dispute was more dangerous to the yeshiva than the one of 1897. Back then, Lachman had still been supporting the yeshiva, but in the meantime he had lost his fortune, and the yeshiva was now dependent on the general public for support. In addition, he claimed that some of the students who ostensibly opposed *musar* did so in order to conceal their Haskalah leanings.

[98] Yashar, *The Hafets Hayim* (Heb.), i. 329; D. Katz, *The Musar Movement* (Heb.), iv. 30.

[99] Rosenfeld, 'Letters from Provincial Towns' (Heb.); Dvorets [Paltin], *Assembly of Israel* (Heb.), 10. On supplementary fundraising, see the letter from R. Yitshak Blaser of 10 Jan. 1901 to R. Eliyahu Klatskin, reproduced and transcribed in *Avraham Dov Vaisfish Memorial Volume* (Heb.), 140–1, which mentions the construction of a new building for the yeshiva.

[100] See Paltin [Dvorets], 'On the History of the Keneset Yisra'el Yeshiva' (Heb.), *Tevunah*, 12/123: 10.   [101] Ibid.

The controversy dragged on for a long time. To the surprise of his friends, R. Finkel did not become aggressive to his opponents, though his students took a more aggressive stance on their own initiative:

At this time, those students who were loyal to the yeshiva became very interested in how it was run, and they took their own steps against those who had provoked the controversy. One of these measures was this: since the yeshiva was then divided into two camps, those who had provoked the controversy sat on the southern side of the study hall . . . while those who supported *musar* sat on the other side . . . which emphasized the strength of those who stirred up controversy. Therefore several of the most prominent *musar* supporters decided to change their seats in the yeshiva and to mingle with their opponents, so as to cancel out their predominance and reduce their influence.[102]

The crux of the dispute came with the dumping of *musar* books 'in the town's enormous public lavatory . . . all of Slobodka was in a turmoil'.[103] Hirsch Leib Gordon describes how the books were fished out and taken for burial in a *genizah* (a depository for sacred books that have become unusable), and records the eulogies delivered at the event. However, even then R. Finkel did not attack his opponents or drive them out of the yeshiva.[104]

His next step was even more surprising, given the yeshiva's difficult situation: he answered a request from R. Eliezer Gordon, head of the Telz yeshiva, 'and agreed to send him twenty-five of the best students from Slobodka who were loyal to *musar* . . . these students included almost all the veteran students of the Slobodka yeshiva, and when they left to go to Telz, all those who supported the Slobodka yeshiva felt that it had been left like a pool with no fish'.[105] Nevertheless, R. Finkel had tremendous authority, and even this step did not lead to confrontation with his opponents. R. Epstein helped to ensure this: he had not 'intervened in the yeshiva's internal spiritual matters, whatever had happened'. R. Finkel's approach worked. Opposition died down, eventually the opponents of *musar* seem to have left, and peace returned to the yeshiva.

This was the last rebellion in Slobodka and the most severe. No further reports of major public controversies over the management and direction of the yeshiva are to be found in memoirs or in the contemporary press. Nevertheless, the tension between *musar* study and traditional Talmud study still existed, potentially if not openly. Both the conflict and the calm need to be understood.

It is important to remember that Slobodka was not the only yeshiva to experience rebellion.[106] The first years of the twentieth century were years of political ferment in the Russian empire, especially among young people, and its most striking expression was the rebellion of 1905. Ultimately, the unrest

---

[102] Ibid., *Tevunah*, 12/124.
[103] H. L. Gordon, 'On the Banks of the Viliya and Neman' (Heb.), 58.
[104] Paltin [Dvorets], 'On the History of the Keneset Yisra'el Yeshiva' (Heb.), *Tevunah*, 12/124: 5.　　　　　[105] Ibid.　　　　　[106] Ibid., *Tevunah*, 12/123: 7.

of that year changed little in the empire; but at the time there was a sense that everything was about to change. R. Paltin records in his memoirs that some yeshiva students were swept up into the revolutionary movement and left the yeshiva, while others apparently absorbed the atmosphere but did not leave.[107] There were disturbances in many yeshivas during these years. Within the Russian empire, people—and especially young people—turned to extreme methods to solve their problems, and this atmosphere must have contributed to the controversy at the Slobodka yeshiva.[108]

Some students were influenced by the new attitudes but chose less violent ways in which to express their discontent with yeshiva life. Thus, for example, a group of students from Slobodka sent a declaration to the conference of Russian Zionists at Minsk in 1902, with a demand that they deal with the conditions—both physical and spiritual—of yeshiva students. The students criticized the *rashei yeshivah*:

Nobody pays any attention to the development of the young and their demands. Nobody listens to the appeals of the students . . . at the very same hour in which the yeshiva students are bursting to get out and throw off the 'chains of the spirit' and are shouting for air and light, the *rashei yeshivah* are trying to mummify the souls of their pupils and to kill off every live emotion, every spark of life in them . . . to blunt their aspirations and to implant servile feelings in their hearts, to turn them into hypocrites and lickspittles.[109]

[107] Paltin [Dvorets], 'On the History of the Keneset Yisra'el Yeshiva' (Heb.), 7: 'In those days came the war between Russia and Japan and then the days of the revolution, the giving of the constitution in Russia, and then the bloody pogroms against the Jews. The many revolutionary parties that swept across the Jewish quarter attracted almost all the younger generation, including some yeshiva students. Throughout these years there was unrest and changes in leadership in almost all the yeshivas of Lithuania. There was an uprising at the Telz yeshiva, and matters reached such a pass that the *gaon* R. Yosef Leib Bloch (of blessed memory), who was then acting *rosh yeshivah*, left the yeshiva and became the rabbi of Varna. The *gaon* R. Shimon Shkop (of blessed memory) also left his position as *rosh yeshivah* there and became rabbi of Bransk. These *geonim* would never have taken such steps were it not for the controversy raging in the yeshiva. In the Keneset Beit Yitshak yeshiva, too, in the old *beit midrash* in Slobodka, there was fierce dispute, taking the form of brawls between pro- and anti-Zionist students, and the *rosh yeshivah*, the *gaon* R. Hayim Rabinowitz (of blessed memory) left the yeshiva and later went to Telz. The Maltsh yeshiva, which was founded by the *gaon* R. Zalman Sender Kahana Shapira (of blessed memory), the *gaon* and *av beit din* of Maltsh, closed down, and the *gaon* became rabbi of Krynki. Even in the Radun yeshiva of the Hafets Hayim (of blessed memory), which was still run according to the older pattern, new attitudes broke out and quarrels started up, until the Hafets Hayim realized the danger it posed to the yeshiva. The Mir yeshiva declined too, and almost had to close. And in all the other yeshivas there were many unpleasant incidents and constant spiritual danger. The heads of the yeshivas all took great pains to set up their own arrangements for their yeshivas, according to their methods and understanding.'

[108] D. Katz, *The Musar Movement* (Heb.), iii. 52.

[109] Printed with many omissions in *He'avar*, 9 (Elul 1962), 106, under the title 'The Declaration of the Yeshiva Students'.

It is not clear exactly whom this declaration was intended to represent. R. Paltin's memoirs mention conflict between Zionist and anti-Zionist students at the Keneset Beit Yitshak yeshiva, but the position of Zionism at Keneset Yisra'el is not clear. In addition, no details of any Zionist organization at the yeshiva are known, and only a small minority seem to have been interested in the movement.

After 1905 the political upheavals died down, which must have contributed to the return of tranquillity to the yeshivas. Conflict rarely lasted long in a yeshiva: the extremists tended to leave for more congenial institutions while the more moderate went back to their studies. With each year, R. Epstein achieved greater power. The authorities had the advantage of controlling funds, and this may well explain the rapid return of calm to the yeshiva after the earlier disputes.

This description of the Slobodka yeshiva has focused on the link between the changes that were taking place in nineteenth-century Jewish society and the *musar* movement of which the Slobodka yeshiva was a part. This link comes to the fore in two main spheres: in the structure of the yeshiva (the position of the *mashgiaḥ* alongside the Talmud teacher, or even above him) and in events in yeshiva life. The establishment of the yeshiva was linked to the new reality created in the wake of changes in traditional society. The *musar* movement and the yeshiva tried to provide a response to the situation by means of an ideology and a programme for action. This path was too conservative for the maskilim and aroused their opposition. However, it was too innovative for many in traditional Jewish society.

It is difficult to estimate the extent to which Slobodka succeeded in shaping the personalities of its students. Many dropped out, many abandoned the path of *musar*, and some abandoned traditional religious life altogether. However, this was to be expected, given contemporary conditions. A large group continued at the yeshiva and remained committed to Torah study and the religious way of life. From the point of view of the yeshiva, this was judged a success.[110]

---

[110] After the First World War enthusiasm for *musar* study declined, as did the importance of the spiritual *mashgiaḥ* in the *musar* yeshiva. Study focused on the Talmud once again, and many students came to think of the daily half-hour of *musar* study as merely symbolic. This seems to have been linked to a new balance in the yeshiva world. Dropout rates were low, and there was no secret reading of secular works and little ideological competition, with the result that few yeshiva students had doubts about their path. The explanation of how this balance was created lies outside the bounds of this study. For a fine study of the later history of the yeshiva in the Land of Israel, see Shlomo Tikochinski's as yet unpublished Ph.D. thesis, 'The *Musar* Yeshivas from Lithuania to Israel' (Heb.). Ben-Tsiyon Klibansky wrote a fascinating study of the yeshivas in the interwar period in eastern Europe (see his 'The Lithuanian Yeshivas in Eastern Europe' (Heb.)).

TEN

The Telz Yeshiva

TELZ OFFERED a third type of yeshiva. It was not based on a new method of study as Volozhin was, and it set itself no new goals as Slobodka did. It was a reaction to the perceived disintegration of traditional society and the decline in Torah study, but with no new values: its founders wanted to produce Talmud scholars capable of making profound halakhic decisions. Its importance in the history of Lithuanian yeshivas lies in its new organizational patterns: whereas Volozhin and Slobodka modelled themselves on the *beit midrash*, Telz was more like a modern educational institution. Other yeshivas eventually followed suit to varying degrees, so in that sense Telz marked a final stage in the development of the Lithuanian system. Later changes were very minor.

The Telz yeshiva did not associate itself with the *musar* movement, but in spite of this there was an attempt to include the study of *musar* as part of the regular curriculum. The attempt failed, but investigation of this episode and the reasons for its failure can elucidate attitudes to the *musar* movement as well, as the constraints facing a *rosh yeshivah* who wanted to innovate.

Many memoirs have been written about the Telz yeshiva, and many articles on its history have been published. However, there has been little analytical research into its characteristic features and processes.[1] My focus here will therefore be on its history and organization.

1. The Establishment of the Telz Yeshiva

The Telz yeshiva is closely linked to the figure of R. Eliezer Gordon, who was the *rosh yeshivah* for many years, even though its establishment pre-dates his arrival.

---

[1] The first article to summarize the yeshiva's history was by R. Mordekhai Gifter, the *rosh yeshivah* (Gifter, 'The Telz Yeshiva' (Heb.)). Another important article is Shoshanah, 'Chapters on History and Evaluation' (Heb.). The yeshiva is mentioned frequently throughout D. Katz, *The Musar Movement* (Heb.). On R. Eliezer Gordon, the yeshiva's founder and first leader, see Z. A. Rabiner, *The Gaon Rabbi Eliezer Gordon* (Heb.). Most of the rich memoir material about Telz was written much later and from a different perspective, and must therefore be used with care. It is often hard to distinguish between major and minor matters and between imagination and fact. A particularly prominent example of this is A. A. Friedman, *Memoirs* (Heb.), which has been used with great caution.

The town of Telz (Telšiai) lies in north-western Lithuania, about 75 km east-north-east of Memel (Klaipėda). Yehudah Leib Gordon, the well-known maskil, lived there from 1865 to 1872 and was the principal of a government school for boys and girls. A letter he wrote shortly after his arrival describes the town as an old-fashioned and conservative place which the Haskalah had not yet reached.[2] From the traditionalists' point of view, Telz looked quite different: in their eyes great changes had taken place, and not always for the better (the very presence of Y. L. Gordon in the town attested to this), and it was these changes that were probably among the factors that led to the foundation of the yeshiva. This is how David Druck, who heard about Telz from Levi (Louis) Ginsberg, one of the R. Eliezer Gordon's first students at the yeshiva and later a renowned professor of Talmud, described it:

Like all Jewish towns at that time, Telz was a city of Torah and the fear of Heaven . . . but during the short period that the poet Yehudah Leib Gordon lived there the town began to change. It was 'annexed', to use the contemporary phrase, by the tempest of new spirits that had begun to blow in the world. Gordon had an enormous influence on the young people of the generation . . . he introduced something of the spirit of the Haskalah into the town . . . the traditional Jews . . . used to regard with fear and loathing the doings of Yehudah Leib Gordon and his circle and the entire Enlightenment that they advocated, but they comforted themselves with the thought that this strange movement would not last long and would soon disappear as quickly as it had appeared. However, this hope proved ill-founded . . . at that time there were two notable and respected men living in Telz . . . they found that the only cure for the malady of the generation was Torah study, following the maxim 'If this scoundrel [the evil inclination] assails you, drag him to the *beit hamidrash*' [BT *Suk.* 52*b*]. By founding a yeshiva and teaching Torah to many it would be possible to regain former glories, not only in Telz but in other places where the Haskalah had begun to spread. These two men were the principal agents behind the foundation of the great yeshiva of Telz, whose fame spread throughout Jewish towns and which produced many students, noted scholars and famous rabbis.[3]

[2] Letter from Y. L. Gordon to Moshe Hakohen Prager, 10 Iyar (25 Apr.) 1866, in Y. L. Gordon, *Letters* (Heb.), 102. On Gordon's time in Telz, see Stanislawski, *For Whom Do I Toil?*, 105–68. Much material appears in Alperowitz (ed.), *Telz* (Heb.). Some of this is original and some reprinted.

[3] Druck, *Rabbi Levi Ginsberg* (Heb.), 72–82. The biography of Louis (Levi) Ginsberg, written by his son Eli Ginsberg, records that Druck heard many details from Ginsberg himself, who had studied at Telz during its early years; see the introduction to Ginsberg, *Keeper of the Law*. However, there are inaccuracies in what Druck says (for example, he does not mention R. Oppenheim, and it is not clear whether Ginsberg studied there during Oppenheim's time or whether he had forgotten this—perhaps this did not interest Druck). R. Gordon's account was similar to that of Druck, even though he was not among the founders of the yeshiva and only arrived there some years later. R. Gordon stressed that the yeshiva was founded because of the decline in Torah study. This, at any rate, is what R. Yeruham Wahrhaftig reported (see Wahrhaftig, *Offerings of Yeruham* (Heb.), 3). Obviously, in sources of this sort there is always a risk of projecting intentions that only developed later, but the claim is reasonable and there is no evidence to the contrary.

According to Druck it was two local scholars—R. Tsevi Ya'akov Oppenheim and R. Me'ir Atlas—and later a third, R. Zalman Abell, who concluded that the *beit midrash* could not survive in the modern world and that if nothing was done, young men would abandon traditional study. Therefore, in the late 1870s, they decided to open a yeshiva with a permanent teacher and regular lectures.

This description matches what we know from other places. However, there seems to have been more than a purely local impulse behind the yeshiva's foundation. On one hand, R. Natan Finkel of Slobodka used his connections to promote the Telz yeshiva and to encourage students to go there. On the other hand, Ovadiah Lachman of Berlin, the philanthropist who funded the Slobodka yeshiva, also supported the yeshiva in Telz. This is an impressive response to a home-grown initiative. Barukh Feivelson writes:

For behold . . . [in the summer of 1881] a letter [came from] the honoured R. Natan Tsevi Finkel . . . which suggested that my brother . . . and I should travel thither . . . but indeed, who founded the yeshiva? This one too [was founded] by Berlin! The above-mentioned anonymous philanthropist [Ovadiah Lachman] established [a fund to pay for the] salary of our teacher, the *gaon* R. Tsevi Ya'akov [Oppenheim] to be the *rosh yeshivah*.[4]

He added that the yeshiva served as a place of higher Torah education both for his native city and the entire district. It thus seems that the yeshiva was established thanks to a combination of local enterprise and external aid; it is not clear which came first.

Not much is known about the three founders of the yeshiva. Druck gave this description of R. Atlas:

R. Me'ir Atlas was the son-in-law of a wealthy Jew of Telz, Shabetai Zagirer, who owned a large wholesale haberdashery business. Like all proper learned sons-in-law in those good days, he too was dependent upon his father-in-law. Even when his children were grown and had become young men of nineteen and twenty, he was still dependent for his income on his father-in-law. He lived in the upper storey of Shabetai's house and his wife helped her father in the shop.[5]

Eventually he became rabbi of Šiauliai and later served in other important communities.

---

[4] Feivelson, 'Memories from the Beginning of the Foundation of Torah Institutions' (Heb.), 5 and *passim*. Feivelson wrote that R. Oppenheim returned to Telz after working in Kelme and Grobin with R. Simhah Zissel Ziv; R. Natan Tsevi Finkel appealed to his relative, Ya'akov Habas, who in turn enlisted his brother, Yosef Hayim, who lived in Berlin. Yosef Hayim approached Ovadiah Lachman, who had founded the *kolel* in Kovno, to donate money for the foundation of a yeshiva in Telz, and he agreed. Kul wrote that it was Habas who persuaded Lachman to donate 600 roubles 'to enable the opening of the Telz yeshiva' (Kul, *Alone in his Generation* (Heb.), 90).

[5] Druck, *Rabbi Levi Ginsberg* (Heb.), 28.

Likewise, little is known about the yeshiva during R. Atlas's time. A student at R. Atlas's yeshiva in 1871 wrote:

I was the youngest student [he was 15] at the yeshiva of R. Me'ir Atlas, of blessed memory: I studied *Ḥovot halevavot* ['Duties of the Heart', by Bahya ibn Pakuda, eleventh century] there and read *Hashaḥar*. I used to go in and out of the house of the great and devout R. Yehoshua Heller, and also the house of the poet Yitshak Rabinovitz, who came from Kovno and was known as 'the heretic' [*apikoros*] since he had seduced me and my friends into reading Haskalah books . . . I began to practise writing in Hebrew in Telz . . . my first literary work was the publication of a weekly magazine called *Hakokhav* ['The Star'].[6]

This description suggests that already in 1871 there was a yeshiva in Telz.

A little more is known about R. Tsevi Ya'akov Oppenheim. He was born in 1855 and was about 25 years old when the Telz yeshiva was founded. Before going to Telz he had already taught at the *musar* yeshivas of R. Simhah Zissel Ziv in Kelme and Grobin; it is not known why he left Grobin.[7]

R. Zalman Abell had a good knowledge of secular subjects and spoke Russian and German, but devoted most of his energy to sacred studies: 'R. Zalman himself was an enlightened man, and knew Russian, Hebrew, and German well. However, he did not approve of those "little books" [Haskalah books].'[8] He married R. Eliezer Gordon's niece but died at a young age. R. Abell was apparently a man of more than local importance; an obituary was published in *He'asif*, a moderate Haskalah publication,[9] and his book *Beit shelomoh* (House of Solomon) was published posthumously.[10]

The founders were young, and it seems that when the yeshiva was founded they did not hold official positions in the local community.[11] They were aware, however, of the changes taking place in Jewish society. This fact, together with the way in which the Haskalah was spreading in Telz and R. Finkel's involvement, reinforces the claim that the Telz yeshiva was founded in order explicitly to combat the new trends. It was thus the first yeshiva founded for this purpose.

The yeshiva prospered but could not support its young leaders since its income was very small. In 1882 R. Oppenheim left Telz, and the lack of a *rosh*

---

[6] Marek, *In the Company of the Great Men of the Generation* (Heb.), 28.

[7] It seems probable that the idea of dividing the students into graded classes, as in a modern school, came from Grobin. For a discussion of R. Oppenheim, his great-grandson Professor Ya'akov Blidstein referred me to D. Katz, *The Musar Controversy* (Heb.), 211; see also p. 140. R. Oppenheim signed the declaration condemning the *musar* movement in 1897, though he later regretted its publication (ibid. 120). He died in 1926.

[8] Druck, *Rabbi Levi Ginsberg* (Heb.), 34. He does not mention R. Oppenheim; see n. 3 above.

[9] A. A. Abel, 'Rabbi Shlomo Zalman Halevi Abell' (Heb.).   [10] S. Abel, *Beit shelomoh*.

[11] Someone else also seems to have been involved in the foundation. In the introduction to his book, *Tsevi veḥamid*, R. Tsevi Rozansky writes that he taught at the yeshiva.

yeshivah who could attract students and donations was sorely felt. In 1883 R. Eliezer Gordon was invited to serve as rabbi of Telz and to run the yeshiva, even though it does not seem to have had any official status as a community institution.[12]

2. R. Eliezer Gordon

R. Eliezer Gordon was born in 1841 in a small village near Svir.[13] He studied in Svir and Smorgon, and later, probably in the mid-1850s, at the Zaritsa yeshiva in Vilna. R. Yisra'el Salanter had been *rosh yeshivah* there some years previously but had moved to Kovno by this time. R. Gordon also moved to Kovno and married the daughter of the *dayan* Avraham Yitshak Nevisky, the brother of the philanthropist Tsevi Hirsch Nevaizer, who had founded the *kloyz* where R. Salanter taught. R. Gordon was a brilliant student and caught R. Salanter's attention. R. Gordon writes:

I remember that, when I was living with my father-in-law . . . that the pious *gaon* R. Yisra'el Salanter . . . urged me to begin teaching younger students, thinking that my *pilpul* came close to the true meaning of the text and that my efforts to understand everything with straightforward and deep logic and with clear thought, and the accurate comments with which God has graced me would have a great influence on the young students reviewing material and would strengthen their devotion to Torah study, with God's help, and he urged me so strongly that once he said to me that because of his great desire I should teach the best young students that he undertook to teach the students twice a week in the first six months, and that I should [also] teach them; however, later he travelled abroad, but when he returned to Kovno for a short time, he kept his promise and delivered one lecture to the students that I had taught in Kovno.[14]

The extent of the links between R. Gordon and R. Salanter is not clear. R. Gordon's move from the Zaritsa yeshiva to Kovno might have been influenced by R. Salanter's disciples who were still at the yeshiva. Almost nothing is known of what was going on at this yeshiva during these years, so this cannot be verified. R. Salanter may also have been involved in R. Gordon's marriage

---

[12] Druck describes the background to the yeshiva's foundation, though with many inaccuracies (*Rabbi Levi Ginsberg* (Heb.), 93). He probably did not know, for instance, that it existed before R. Gordon's time. However, he may be correct in claiming that the founders wanted R. Gordon, since there were no signs that they opposed his appointment.

[13] Z. A. Rabiner, *The Gaon Rabbi Eliezer Gordon* (Heb.), 31. This is an important source on Gordon's life.

[14] Ostrovsky (ed.), *Man of Jerusalem* (Heb.), 68. R. Salanter seems to have made his appeal to R. Gordon in 1856, since he left Kovno in 1857. If so, R. Gordon would have been 15. Professor Chimen Abramsky observed that it seems unlikely that R. Gordon would have been asked to teach at a yeshiva at the age of 15, and has suggested that there may be some error in the dates. On the *kloyz*, see Etkes, *Rabbi Yisra'el Salanter* (Heb.), 226–9.

to the daughter of his friend's brother, but, again, there is no proof of this. In any event, R. Gordon's words reveal his admiration of R. Salanter, though not the relationship of a teacher and his disciple.

R. Hayim Daiches was also in contact with R. Salanter in his youth, although he never joined the *musar* movement:

When I was 14 [in 1866] my father, of blessed memory, brought me to . . . [the esteemed] R. Yisra'el Salanter . . . who was then living in Kovno, and I presented a talmudic *ḥidush* [novel insight] I had composed before him . . . and he asked me which books of the *aharonim*[15] I had studied, and when I told him that I was studying the *Or ḥadash*[16] on tractates *Pesaḥim* and *Kidushin*, and other works, he said to me, 'My son, listen to my advice. Study "Ḥoshen mishpat"[17] with [the commentaries] *Ketsot haḥoshen* and *Maḥaneh efrayim*,[18] and let most of your study be of the *rishonim* such as Nahmanides, R. Shelomoh ben Adret, Rabenu Nisim,[19] and so on.'[20]

He noted that R. Salanter 'was very fond of him', and that he even came to the synagogue where R. Daiches was ceremonially called up to the Torah on the sabbath before his wedding, but he never mentions *musar*. More than a decade later, in 1879, R. Daiches sent R. Salanter a collection of his new Torah insights and received a reply from him.[21]

R. Shmuel Luvtser was also very close to R. Salanter during his time in Vilna, but the latter's influence on him was confined to Torah study and did not extend to *musar*.[22]

During his time as *rosh yeshivah* at Telz, R. Gordon did not place great emphasis on *musar*. This can be seen from the following text in which a member of the *musar* movement tries to explain how it was that someone who came within R. Salanter's sphere of influence did not identify with the *musar* movement:

This wonderful genius, who had been lucky enough in his youth to learn Torah in the *beit midrash* of our master, the holy *gaon* Yisra'el Salanter, while he was in Kovno, even though he did not merit being counted among his most outstanding disciples

---

[15] Halakhic authorities from the middle of the 16th cent. onwards.

[16] *Or ḥadash* is a commentary by R. Elazar Kalir (1728–1801), rabbi of Kolin and other communities. His commentaries on the talmudic tractates of *Pesaḥim* and *Kidushin* were often reprinted.

[17] A section of the *Shulḥan arukh*, the halakhic code by R. Yosef Karo (1488–1575).

[18] *Ketsot haḥoshen*, commentary on *Shulḥan arukh*, 'Ḥoshen mishpat' and 'Even ha'ezer' by R. Aryeh Leib Heller (1745–1813); *Maḥaneh efrayim*, halakhic work by Efrayim ben Aharon Navon (1677–1735).

[19] The *rishonim* are the halakhic authorities from before the middle of the 16th cent., who include the three prominent figures mentioned by name here.

[20] Deiches, *Sermons of Rabbi Yisra'el Hayim Deiches* (Heb.), p. vi.

[21] Ibid.   [22] R. Hanokh Aiges, intro. to Luvtser, *Olat shemuel*.

in *musar*, nevertheless harboured a great inclination towards *musar* in his soul and always longed to introduce the spirit of *musar* to the Telz yeshiva, but for various reasons he did not succeed in this.[23]

R. Gordon identified more strongly with Ya'akov Lifschitz's circle in Kovno, an informal group known by the maskilim and Zionists as the 'Black Bureau'. He had strong ties with it and was considered one of its main figures.[24] Ya'akov Lifschitz himself was on good terms with R. Salanter, though he too was far from being associated with the *musar* movement.

R. Avraham Yitshak Nevisky, the *dayan* of Kovno, died in 1874, and R. Gordon, his son-in-law, was offered the post. Ya'akov Lifschitz has left us a detailed description of the controversy over the appointment, a controversy between the 'traditionalists', who supported R. Gordon, and the 'intellectuals', who opposed him. R. Gordon was eventually appointed as *dayan*, but three months later he was offered the post of rabbi of Kelme and accepted it.[25] R. Gordon arrived in Kelme in the wake of a fierce and protracted conflict in the community between the majority, who wanted to appoint the previous rabbi's son-in-law, and the elite who supported his own appointment. Eventually a compromise was reached: R. Gordon would be the rabbi, and the son-in-law would be the *dayan*. According to a late source, R. Salanter was responsible for paving the way for R. Gordon's arrival in Kelme.[26]

R. Gordon immediately opened a yeshiva for advanced students. It was innovative in that the students were publicly examined once a month on twenty-five to thirty pages of Talmud; only those who passed the test could continue their studies. There is conflicting evidence on the relationship between R. Gordon and R. Simhah Zissel Ziv, who ran a *talmud torah* in the town and was one of the leaders of the *musar* movement. Friedman, who apparently studied there at the time, claims that it was in fact the students who called for the public examinations, in order to prevent R. Simhah Zissel Ziv's *musar*-oriented *talmud torah* students from joining the yeshiva, but that R. Gordon also had reservations about them.[27] However, Friedman was opposed to the *musar* movement and his statements must be treated with caution. Other sources record warm and friendly relations between R. Gordon and R. Simhah Zissel Ziv.[28] A letter from the latter to R. Gordon suggests that the

[23] Dvorets [Paltin], *The Gaon Rabbi Moshe Mordekhai Epstein* (Heb.), 51.

[24] Lifschitz, *Zikhron ya'akov*, ii. 125.

[25] Ibid. 173.　　　　　　　　　　　　[26] Karlinski, 'The Shtetl Kelme' (Yid.), 1446.

[27] A. A. Friedman, *Memoirs* (Heb.), 100–3. Friedman claims that the examinations were his idea, as was the idea of founding a yeshiva in Kelme. It is impossible to establish whether this is true. If it is, it seems likely his interest in founding a yeshiva came from his studies in a yeshiva for young boys in Veliuona run by R. Jacob Joseph, one of R. Salanter's disciples, and later the chief rabbi of New York (see ibid. 87–90).

[28] For example, see Z. A. Rabiner, *The Gaon Rabbi Eliezer Gordon* (Heb.), 37–8; D. Katz, *The Musar Movement* (Heb.), iii. 32–3 (probably the source of Rabiner's account).

truth lay between these two extremes:[29] they were on good terms but differed in their approaches. R. Simhah Zissel Ziv's letter tried to persuade R. Gordon of the benefit of *musar* study, following the latter's refusal to introduce *musar* into the yeshiva's curriculum.

In 1883 R. Gordon left Kelme for Slobodka, for reasons that are uncertain, but stayed for only a few months; he was chosen as rabbi of Telz the same year. According to Dov Katz, 'some say that R. Natan Tsevi [Finkel] had a hand in this too'.[30] In the same year, R. Oppenheim was chosen to replace R. Gordon as rabbi of Kelme. This may have been a package deal, arranged through R. Finkel.[31] Upon his arrival in Telz R. Gordon took over the management of the yeshiva and ran it until his death in 1910.

R. Gordon's arrival did not lead to changes at the yeshiva or among its staff. Druck describes the curriculum and R. Gordon's impact:

This yeshiva was divided into three classes. In the first, highest, class, R. Lezer [Yiddish form of 'Eliezer'] Gordon and R. Me'ir Atlas taught the *shiur*; in the second class R. Me'ir Atlas and R. Zalman Abell taught; and the third class [was taught by] R. Zalman Abell and R. Yosef Bloch. The reputation of R. Lezer Gordon and the other *rashei yeshivah* was so great in the Jewish world that students and young men immediately began to stream to Telz from every corner of Russia. Five hundred students filled the yeshiva in Telz shortly after it opened, and it immediately began to grow, increasing in power and influence, until its fame extended throughout the world, thanks to its great *rashei yeshivah* and excellent students.[32]

The number of students seems exaggerated, but the evidence of a division into three classes at such an early stage of the yeshiva's development seems reliable.

Within a few years all the teaching staff had changed. Shortly after his arrival in Telz, R. Gordon seems to have arranged a match between his sister's daughter and R. Abell, thus creating a family tie with him.[33] This type of link between the most important figures at a yeshiva is known from other places such as Volozhin as well. In 1884, a year after his arrival, R. Gordon appointed

---

[29] D. Katz, *The Musar Movement* (Heb.), iii. 78–81.

[30] Ibid. 29. See also Sorotskin, 'These Are the Generations' (Heb.), 115. R. Finkel was living in Slobodka at this time, which lends some support to this claim. Sorotskin writes: 'His wife the *rebbetzin*, peace be upon her, died in Kelme; she was the daughter of the *gaon* R. Avraham Yitshak Nevisky. As his second wife he took the daughter of his brother-in-law, the righteous and prominent R. Barukh Broide of Kovno, may his righteous memory be a blessing' (ibid. 113). Katz describes R. Broide as one of 'the veteran *musar* adherents in Kovno' (*The Musar Movement* (Heb.), i. 197). At this period he was one of the treasurers of the Kovno *kolel*. This detail suggests that R. Salanter might have been involved in this match.

[31] Karlinski, 'The Shtetl Kelme' (Yid.), 1447. R. Gordon was not elected unanimously to the post in Telz. See Shisha, 'A Person's Feet . . .' (Heb.).

[32] Druck, *Rabbi Levi Ginsberg* (Heb.), 30.

[33] See R. Gordon's approbation to S. Abel, *Beit shelomoh*.

his son-in-law, R. Yosef Yehudah Leib Bloch, as a teacher in the yeshiva, and also successfully invited R. Shimon Shkop, who was married to his sister's daughter, to serve as a teacher.[34]

In 1885 R. Atlas left to serve as rabbi of the Lithuanian Jews in Libau.[35] There is no information on the relationship between him and R. Gordon, and thus no way of knowing what he thought of the changes at the yeshiva; however, his departure may give some indication of his feelings. R. Abell died about two years later. Both R. Bloch and R. Shkop stayed at the yeshiva for many years, and their respective departures will be discussed below. It is important to note that, within a few years of his arrival, R. Gordon was the head of a group of teachers that he had chosen himself, and could thus direct the yeshiva with little concern for internal opposition. Under his leadership the yeshiva expanded and increased in importance. Its unusual features included its organization, the formation and organization of the student body, and the frequent and bitter conflicts between staff and students.[36] The background to these phenomena will be explored below.

In contrast to Volozhin, Telz did not receive official recognition from the authorities. This had certain advantages, in that it was not subject to bureaucratic pressure like Volozhin; however, as an unlicensed institution, it was in constant danger of being closed down. Ya'akov Marek writes: 'In Telz people used to talk about his clever and subtle ruses and about how he knew how to gain the trust of the local officials—even if they were bigoted antisemites—so that they would not harm the yeshiva, for the yeshiva was illegal and they were capable of closing it down at any time.' The principal means used seems to have been bribery: 'the local police were bribed and pretended not to notice anything'.[37]

3. The Aims of the Yeshiva

Our most important source on the aims of the yeshiva is a pamphlet, *Kol kore* (A Voice Calls), published over R. Gordon's signature in 1894. It is an appeal addressed to rabbis and philanthropists that was entrusted to a *shaliaḥ* (emissary) who toured the country to raise funds for the yeshiva. In order to introduce the yeshiva, R. Gordon listed its aims and current state in eleven paragraphs and attached letters of approbation.

[34] On R. Bloch, see e.g. Bloch, 'The Telz Yeshiva' (Yid.), esp. p. 624; on R. Shkop, see Gindes et al. (eds.), *Festschrift for Rabbi Shimon Yehudah Shkop* (Heb.), 9; Rosenthal, *They Shall Seek Torah* (Heb.); on his philosophy, see Sagi, *Judaism: Between Religion and Ethics* (Heb.), 97–102, 335–49; on his legal thinking, see the perceptive Ph.D. thesis by Shai Wozner, 'Legal Thinking in the Lithuanian Yeshivas' (Heb.).

[35] See the entry on him in Hasman et al. (eds.), *Lithuanian Jewry* (Heb.), iii. 52.

[36] There were conflicts at almost every yeshiva, but they were particularly intense at Telz.

[37] Marek, *In the Company of the Great Men of the Generation* (Heb.), 25.

This was an official publication of the yeshiva, in which R. Gordon referred to himself in the first person, and there is no doubt that it was either written by him or composed under his inspiration.[38] It is dated 7 November 1894, while the approbations were written somewhat earlier (1889 and 1890) but were included in order to demonstrate the support that the yeshiva enjoyed. R. Yeruham Perlman's approbation, dated 1889, mentions a *Kol kore*, but it is not clear whether this refers to the pamphlet in which it was to be published or whether another *Kol kore* had appeared earlier promoting the yeshiva.

The pamphlet we are discussing was published about a decade after R. Gordon came to the yeshiva. It thus throws no light on the yeshiva's beginnings but rather on its development after some years had gone by. It clarifies R. Gordon's goals and his approach in running the yeshiva, both in the spiritual sphere and the material one. Since it is so important, the entire document will be presented here:

To the honoured rabbis and *geonim*, *gabai'im*, and philanthropists who fear and tremble [before God], who are wise and educated in the true Word, each according to his dignity, may the Almighty command his blessing upon them.

Behold, it is known in the gates that here in Telz a great yeshiva was founded some years ago, [organized] along the best lines, that is:

1. Two hundred and fifty outstanding young men study at the yeshiva. They possess excellent abilities, and almost all of them will become good rabbis, if they continue in their studies, and many of them whose talents are particularly great, if the Almighty enables them to engage in God's Torah, will become, if God wills it, great Torah scholars.

2. No young man is accepted at the yeshiva until he has been examined to ensure that he is talented and will rise in the levels of Torah in the best way, and there is a special committee for this purpose, to examine every young man before they accept him.

3. And they are divided into four levels, each higher than the next, and their teachers and guides are Torah scholars of the highest level, distinguished in halakhah and expert in the ways of the Talmud, capable of delving into the depths of halakhah and of inspiring by their example, and of the most excellent character, and I myself teach the highest level.

4. And our entire aim is to teach the students the correct way of studying the Talmud, that is, to understand every matter by means of reasoning acceptable to the honest and healthy intellect, and to teach them to understand one thing from another and to relate issues that share common ground and to distinguish matters that superficially seem similar but that analysis shows are unrelated, and to show them that if they learn perceptively, they will see that in most cases one must bring proof for a new decision or a new line of reasoning developed by the *aḥaronim* [latter-day rabbinic authorities].

[38] For photographs of this document, see Dessler, *Generations Gone By* (Heb.), i. 235–7.

5. And for all the students of each level we have set the number of [Talmud] pages which they must master each month, and at the end of every month the students are tested [to ascertain] whether they have mastered the Talmud pages that they have studied, according to the fixed number that we have set them.

6. And at the 'test' they are asked questions about cases, for which they must bring proof from the Talmud that they have learned in order to decide in each case, so that they become accustomed in this way, so that when they are older and have to judge and teach, they may bring proof from the Talmud in order to make a halakhic decision or decide on questions they may be asked regarding what is permitted and what is forbidden, so that they should not make decisions based upon the books of the *aharonim* without a correct knowledge of the reason and justification for their views, but should only look at the source of the decision in the Talmud and in early legal works, and should give correct instruction with the help of God.

7. An excellent *mashgiah* will watch over all the yeshiva students. He watches and observes every student with attention; he is distinguished for his fear [of Heaven] and his spiritual nobility, is wise, and has the other qualities needed by one entrusted with inspiring the students to Torah study and fear [of Heaven] and good behaviour and good manners, so that they may find favour among God and men.

8. We will sum up: the students at the yeshiva are educated in an excellent way, both in Torah study and in behaviour, and we can justly say of the students of this institution that they combine Torah and fear [of Heaven] and good behaviour and all the qualities required of a man who intends to be a rabbi and teacher in Israel, and they will be men who are of benefit to human society, and will bring great profit to the vineyard of the House of Israel.

9. It is obvious that the provisioning of such a yeshiva, with two hundred and fifty souls, most of whom are from poor families, so that Torah may emanate from them, requires great expense, for we have to give them support and to pay the salaries of the *rashei yeshivah* and the *mashgiah*, and the rest of the necessary expenditures, which amount to a great sum every year, and we cannot diminish these expenditures, for young men come to join the yeshiva at a greater rate than we can take them in, and although we warn the extra students that they will suffer from hunger, and many of them return to their homes, nevertheless many of them persist and enter the yeshiva.

10. And thus we must announce that if we should have enough money to defray the necessary expenditure for this high and lofty purpose, then we will add such good and useful things as are required for the benefit of such excellent students, and we hope that, just as the Almighty has given us the merit of bringing the yeshiva to its present exalted state, He may enable us to bring it to full perfection.

The last paragraph appeals to the public to give their donations to a certain emissary, Barukh Nahum Schonsohn, who is described as travelling to collect funds for the yeshiva. It thus seems that several copies of the pamphlet were made and given to the yeshiva's emissaries to help them collect donations. The document is signed 'Eliezer Gordon, resident here in the Holy Congregation of Telz'.

The first paragraph notes that there were 250 students at the yeshiva and adds that they 'will become good rabbis if they continue in their studies'. There is no trace here of the ideal of Torah study *lishmah*, that is, study for its own sake; rather, study is seen as preparation for the future and a career. This aim is also reflected in the subsequent paragraphs, especially paragraph 8. However, it seems likely that the pamphlet was written to appeal to a wide public for fundraising purposes. This public may not have been familiar with the idea of 'learning for its own sake' or might have known about it but did not identify with it. The yeshiva's actual goal may have been different. Whatever the case, the readiness to present study at the yeshiva as a form of vocational training reflects the change that had taken place in the attitude to yeshiva study: in the past, outstanding students looked forward to a good match and a handsome dowry, and did not ostensibly train to be rabbis. The pamphlet thus demonstrates accommodation to a new set of values that saw educational institutions as a framework for vocational training. R. Gordon's appeal to donors was intended to prove to them that a contribution to the yeshiva was a contribution to the community's future. This is a practical claim, quite different from the traditional position that saw Torah study as a value in itself.

Concern for order is apparent in paragraph 2; a student who wants to be accepted at the yeshiva must be examined 'to ensure that he is talented'. Entrance examinations, so characteristic of Western education, had not featured at earlier yeshivas. The introduction of an obligatory entrance examination reflects that improvements in transportation and communication had made such an innovation possible, but more particularly a desire for order in the yeshiva's affairs.

This is also clear from paragraph 3, which describes the division of the students into 'four levels' according to their expertise. Division into classes promotes efficient study, since the level of the class can be adapted to the students. However, this was not a usual practice at yeshivas, which had hitherto only provided one *shiur*. The traditional assumption was that even if a student did not understand the *shiur* initially, he would gradually understand more and more. This method, characteristic of medieval education, favours the more able student. The division into classes may not have been R. Gordon's innovation,[39] but it is clear that he identified with this practice and wanted to emphasize it.

The rabbis who taught at the yeshiva are described as 'distinguished in halakhah and expert in the ways of the Talmud, capable of delving into the depths of halakhah'. The emphasis on halakhah is worthy of comment: in contrast, the curriculum stressed Talmud study rather than the deduction of practical halakhic conclusions; there is no mention of students learning halakhah in an organized fashion. So why was the teachers' halakhic ability singled out

---

[39] There is no hint there, however, that R. Gordon instituted an organizational revolution, so probably this was a development of an existing feature.

for mention? The question might just as well be posed about the link between the declared goal of training rabbis and the lack of any suitable framework for such training in the curriculum. This nature of the description suggests that it was probably aimed at the general public—potential donors—who wanted to see the yeshiva as an institution for training rabbis, even though this did not always find practical expression.

The method of study is described in detail in paragraph 4. It begins by stating that the aim of instruction is to teach the students 'the correct way of studying the Talmud, that is, to understand every matter by means of reasoning acceptable to the honest and healthy intellect, and to teach them to understand one thing from another'. The use of 'honest intellect' as the yardstick for measuring the correctness of an interpretation does not contradict traditional study, nor is it an innovation. However, it is the emphasis on this point, which accords well with the yardsticks of Western education—and even perhaps of the Haskalah, that is significant.

The next two paragraphs deal with an innovative theme: examinations. The students were obliged to learn a set number of Talmud pages each month and were examined on this material. This is the first we learn of the monthly examination of students at an advanced yeshiva. Until this time, the Lithuanian yeshivas had carried on the study traditions of the *beit midrash*, where each individual learned at his own pace and according to his own ability. There is some evidence that at Volozhin a page of Talmud was studied each day in the *shiur*, but progress in independent study, which was the main goal of the yeshiva, was not measured in terms of the number of pages covered. The Telz system—determination of quantitative goals in advance—was clearly an innovation based on patterns accepted in secular education.

As paragraph 6 notes, the examination was also intended to improve the ability to draw halakhic conclusions on the basis of the material studied. However, since teaching aimed at developing skills in 'understanding one thing from another', or deduction, rather than in drawing halakhic conclusions, students were actually tested on skills that they had not acquired in lessons. It is possible that R. Gordon thought that 'understanding one thing from another' was the same as drawing halakhic conclusions, but few students considered themselves able to serve as *posekim*. Moreover, the descriptions of study written by former students make no mention of an emphasis on halakhic decision-making in their studies. This section may have been written purely to encourage donations, since the public regarded yeshivas as advanced training institutions. But perhaps a real change is reflected here: while previously the training of rabbis in eastern Europe had always been by means of independent study or studying under a respected rabbi, in Telz this process had been turned into an organized sphere of study—once again, a process of institutionalization. R. Gordon also emphasized the need to make decisions based on the Talmud and the *rishonim*. This trend, which resembles classicism, expresses alienation from the tradition of relying on precedent; it was characteristic of the mood of the period and was not confined to R. Gordon.

The role of the permanent *mashgiah* in supervising students was so important to R. Gordon that he devoted a whole paragraph to it (paragraph 7). This was not a *mashgiah* of the type familiar at the *musar* yeshivas. The Telz *mashgiah* did not give *shiurim* or assist with administration, and nor was his role limited to taking the register and similar activities as at Volozhin. He had to be a man of elevated spirituality who could inspire the students to Torah and the fear of Heaven. The introduction of such a position underscores the desire to strengthen the students' devotion to study and to faith, and the fear that without proper guidance they might fail. This shows a very realistic approach to the problem, though here too there is a marked deviation from the customary patterns of the past. In earlier generations there had been no fear that *beit midrash* students might abandon Torah study, and therefore no need for such supervision.

In paragraph 8, R. Gordon describes the aims of a Telz education: to produce students who not only excel in their studies but are also well behaved and well mannered. Emphasis was to be placed not only on transmitting knowledge or study skills but also on shaping personalities. In this respect Telz resembled the *musar* yeshivas. R. Gordon expresses the attributes he wishes to encourage in the following words: 'we can justly say of the students of this institution that they combine Torah and fear [of Heaven] and good behaviour and all the qualities required of a man who intends to be a rabbi and teacher in Israel, and they will be men who are of benefit to human society, and will bring great profit to the vineyard of the House of Israel'. Some very innovative attitudes are reflected here, though it is difficult to know whether these words are R. Gordon's genuine views or whether he was merely trying to please the public to whom the publication was addressed. The mention of decent behaviour (*derekh erets*) echoes the slogan coined by R. Samson Raphael Hirsch (1808–88), the leader of Frankfurt Orthodoxy. Moreover, students were supposed to emerge not only as rabbis but also 'men of human society'; in other words, decent human beings—an objective well beyond the usual objectives of east European *rashei yeshivah*. Even if such expressions were also used by his predecessors, they were very loaded expressions in this period; and if they echoed current trends, the fact that R. Gordon used them shows how deeply contemporary values had penetrated his educational philosophy.

Paragraphs 9 and 10 call for support for the yeshiva. As noted above, the eleventh paragraph records the name of the emissary responsible for disseminating the publication, R. Barukh Nahum Schonsohn, and R. Gordon appealed to his readers 'to help him to gather donations for the Telz yeshiva and to hold an appropriately dignified meeting in their city'. He signed the pamphlet on 7 November 1894.

The publication aimed at emphasizing the innovative aspects of Telz, both in its goals and in the means chosen to achieve them. There is no mention of a crisis in Jewish society or a decline of Torah study, even though both of these were very real problems.

Six letters of support and recommendation were reproduced in the pamphlet. These are instructive principally because they show how the yeshiva was perceived by important rabbis of the time. Memoirs can be coloured by the benefits of hindsight and experiences garnered in later life. These letters, in contrast, provide genuine contemporary evidence, even given the fact that letters of recommendation will obviously only contain positive assessments. However, since only one of the letter-writers had actually visited Telz, while the others followed his lead or relied on hearsay, some degree of caution should be adopted in drawing conclusions.

The order in which the letters are presented is not the same as the order in which they were written, nor is it alphabetical, as can be seen from Table 10.1.[40] R. Spektor's letter was placed first, presumably because he was considered the senior rabbi among the letter-writers and his status among the rabbis of Lithuania was well known to all. R. Soloveitchik, the author of the next letter, was famed for his originality and method of study, though he was less distinguished in the field of public activity. This may be why his letter was given second place. R. Soloveitchik was the only rabbi in the list who achieved the title of 'exalted *gaon*', and was thus greatly respected by R. Gordon. It is more difficult to explain the order of the other letters. They follow the order in which they were written, except for that of R. Eli'ezer Moshe Halevi. The order may reflect the importance of their authors in R. Gordon's eyes, though this is not clear.

Table 10.1. Order of the letters of approbation in *Kol kore*, 1894

Order of composition	Order of presentation
R. Yeruham Perlman of Minsk	R. Yitshak Elhanan Spektor
The rabbis of Vilna	R. Yosef Dov Soloveitchik
R. Yosef Dov Soloveitchik	R. Yeruham Perlman of Minsk
R. Eli'ezer Moshe Halevi Horowitz, *av beit din* of Pinsk	The rabbis of Vilna
R. Yitshak Elhanan Spektor	R. Eliyahu Hayim Meisel
R. Eliyahu Hayim Meisel	R. Eli'ezer Moshe Halevi Horowitz, *av beit din* of Pinsk

[40] I would like to thank Dr Ehud (Udi) Wolf for drawing this to my attention.

R. Spektor's letter is brief but informative. He describes R. Gordon as 'my soulmate' (*yedid nafshi*). In saying at the outset that he was 'very pleased with the good tidings that were made known to me from the ranks of the yeshiva', he emphasizes that his comments are not based on direct knowledge of the yeshiva. He notes in general terms that 'it is desirable to strengthen them as is proper in order to exalt the horn of Torah', but like R. Perlman he adds that everything must be done 'in accordance with the permission of the exalted government and according to the laws of our master, His Majesty the Tsar, and then the horn of Torah will be raised on high'. It is impossible to know whether this is meant as advice or as a demand, or was added simply out of caution.

The first letter to have been written was that of R. Perlman, which is from 15 January 1889. The author explains that he had come to Telz for his son's wedding. It is not clear whether R. Gordon would have approached him if he had not come to Telz. He seems to have come for the wedding of his son R. Eliyahu, later rabbi of Gorodeya who married Hasyah, the daughter of R. Dov Broide of Telz.[41] The bridegroom himself did not study in Telz, but at Volozhin.[42] R. Perlman noted that he found 'a great company of young men outstanding in their continual study and very correct regulations [*sedarim*], and the order [*seder*] of study is also excellent'. The word *seder*, 'order', which was a key concept in R. Gordon's educational philosophy, appears twice in this sentence, suggesting that others also recognized the importance of this concept to Telz's unique nature.

R. Perlman appealed for donations to the yeshiva, but took care to add that this would only happen if 'they would take out a licence for this from the exalted government according to the law'. It is not entirely clear what he was hinting at here. We have no information about official status being granted to the yeshiva, nor of the yeshiva attempting to achieve recognition, nor of problems with the authorities for operating without a licence. R. Perlman did not explain whether this was just offered as advice or expressed the fear that supporting an unrecognized institution might cause difficulties with the authorities. R. Spektor, as noted above, makes the same point, though I have not found anything similar in letters of support written for the Kovno *kolel* or for other yeshivas.

R. Gordon forwarded R. Perlman's letter to the rabbis of Vilna and to R. Horowitz to help enlist their support for the yeshiva, as they testify in their own letters. This suggests that at this stage, R. Gordon did not feel that a direct appeal from him alone would be enough. The letters of the three Vilna rabbis appear under a common heading: 'A Letter [*sic*] from the *Geonim* of Vilna'. The first was written by R. Me'ir Mikhel Shatner.[43] He studied in

---

[41] See Heilpern, *The Great Sage of Minsk* (Heb.), 206–7.

[42] S. N. Gottlieb, *Ohel no'aḥ*, 32.

[43] On R. Shatner, see Zeira, *Our Sages in the Diaspora* (Heb.), i. 110–12.

Kovno at the Nevaizer *kloyz*, where R. Gordon had once studied, but seems to have been there earlier than R. Gordon, being about twelve or thirteen years older. He was styled 'head of the rabbinical judges' in Vilna,[44] and was also the head of the famous Ramailes yeshiva. His letter praised R. Gordon and expressed his hopes for the new yeshiva: 'for I know the rabbi and *gaon*, the former *av beit din*, may he live, and I know how great is his strength in the Torah and his inspirational qualities in discussions of Torah in the way of truth, and surely he will inspire with his own spirit the many students who come to him, to pour water on his hands, and they will mount up on high in the study of the Torah of God'. He does not note any new arrangements or special organization at the yeshiva, though he seems to have attributed special importance to the *rosh yeshivah*'s ability in Torah study and to the number of students.

R. Shatner's letter is followed by a joint letter from two other Vilna rabbis, R. Shmuel Luvtser and R. Shelomoh Hakohen.[45] R. Shmuel, who was about twenty years older than R. Gordon, had been a student of R. Salanter in Vilna, and it seems likely that R. Gordon knew him from there. R. Shmuel was a senior rabbi in Vilna. He kept the seal of the *beit din*, an indication of his high status.[46] The two rabbis wrote that they were appealing to the public to support the yeshiva on the basis of R. Perlman's letter. They do not seem to have visited Telz, but relied on R. Perlman's testimony. In other words, R. Gordon did not meet them by chance but deliberately appealed to them for help, since he respected them and their authority. They knew nothing of the specifics of the curriculum and organization of the yeshiva, which suggests that the yeshiva was not well known at that stage, and most of their comments relate to the importance of supporting those who study Torah.

The letter from R. Soloveitchik is the shortest, and it is somewhat ambiguous. His opening phrase—'After I saw that many great scholars, may they live, were praising the deeds of my friend'—emphasizes that he knew nothing about the yeshiva apart from the fact that other scholars supported it. He commends 'the deeds of my friend, the rabbi and *gaon* of Telz in his strengthening of the study of the holy Torah', and adds, 'I have also contributed to the yeshiva'. He does not mention any of the yeshiva's unique features, nor even state explicitly that R. Gordon was its head. After mentioning his personal donation, he adds 'It is definitely desirable to join those who are performing this mitzvah'; that is the end of his appeal for support. In spite of its brevity, the letter was placed second among the approbations. R. Soloveitchik was linked to the Volozhin yeshiva, and his son was teaching there at the time the letter was written. It may be that he thought that a letter supporting the Telz

---

[44] Zeira, *Our Sages in the Diaspora* (Heb.), i. 111.

[45] On the former see ibid. 103–4, and on the latter see Y. M. Stern, *The Great Ones of the Generations* (Heb.), 888–9.   [46] Zeira, *Our Sages in the Diaspora* (Heb.), i. 104.

yeshiva might be misinterpreted under the circumstances; this may explain the brief and rather tepid letter. Certainly, the nature of his friendship with R. Gordon is not clear.

R. Meisel of Łódź was well known in the rabbinical world of eastern Europe. He lived in Poland, but was closely connected to the yeshiva world in general and to Volozhin in particular. His letter starts by referring to the claim that there were enough yeshivas and therefore no need for another one in Telz. There was no mention of this in any of the other letters, but there is no doubt that R. Meisel was echoing a widely held opinion. R. Meisel rejected the claim of an over-abundance of yeshivas and praised the rabbis who founded yeshivas, 'including the rabbi and *gaon*, famous for his Torah and fear [of Heaven], the glory of the Torah reputation of our teacher and master, R. Eliezer Gordon'. Deep admiration of R. Gordon is evident here, but at the same time the mention of other yeshivas suggests that R. Meisel has no special preference for Telz. He too records that he has heard much about the yeshiva—an indication that he had not actually visited it. He attributes the foundation of the yeshiva to R. Gordon, even though this was not historically true, and this was not corrected by the editor of the publication.

R. Horowitz, the author of the next letter, was *av beit din* of Pinsk.[47] His name is followed by the phrase *zekher tsadik liverakhah* (may the memory of the righteous be a blessing), since he had died in the summer of 1890, about a year after the letter was written. Nothing is known of his links to R. Gordon. His letter relied on that of R. Perlman and on 'a trustworthy source [who reports] that they stream to the paths of the yeshiva for there is much to say in its praise'. It is possible that this 'trustworthy' source was the person who persuaded R. Horowitz to write in support of the yeshiva. He adds that in his time 'lovers of the Torah have become few', and goes on to report that it was a pleasant surprise to hear about the yeshiva, and he wound up by appealing for support for the yeshiva. He expresses his astonishment at the huge numbers of students—about 180—and at their accomplishments, but does not mention any of the innovations that characterized the yeshiva.

Close analysis of the letters reveals that only R. Perlman, the rabbi who knew the yeshiva from a personal visit, mentions the importance of the institutional innovations at Telz. The others merely seem to have been impressed by R. Gordon's reputation and the large numbers of students.

4. Study Arrangements

As at other contemporary yeshivas, most of the day was devoted to the independent study of Talmud in the study hall of the yeshiva building. (The yeshiva had its own building, though it is not known when it was built.) There

---

[47] On R. Horowitz, see Nadav, *The Jews of Pinsk, 1506–1880*, 471–7.

was no dormitory or dining room, and the students rented rooms in the town and ate at their landlords' tables. In these respects, Telz was similar to other yeshivas.

Where Telz was very different from other yeshivas was in the division into classes on the basis of ability, which was a striking innovation. First spelled out in paragraph 5 of the yeshiva's manifesto, it gradually became the norm in all yeshivas. Simhah Asaf, who studied at Telz from 1905 to 1908, describes the system as follows:

There was a special system at the Telz yeshiva, which was unparalleled at other yeshivas in that time. There were five classes there, as in a grade school, that were known at the yeshiva as the *shiurim*, and each new student entered one of these *shiurim* in accordance with his rank. The usual time spent in each *shiur* was three *zemanim* [terms], in other words a year and a half. Outstandingly talented individuals would rise from one *shiur* to the next after only two *zemanim*. However, there were those who stayed in the same *shiur* for four or five *zemanim*. If a young man was not accepted to the first *shiur*, he had to pay one of the older students to teach him for an hour or two each day and groom him for entrance to the first *shiur*. This was a source of income for the older students who studied in the fourth or fifth *shiur*. The youngsters who were not accepted into the first *shiur* were known as the *ḥutsniks*, in other words 'those who study outside', a sort of *rabanan tarbitsei* [external scholars] as in the Babylonian yeshivas, though these students also studied within the yeshiva's walls together with all the other students. The first four *shiurim* were given by the *rashei yeshivah*, who were famous Torah scholars, such as R. Shimon Shkop and R. Yosef Leib Bloch, and later, R. Hayim Rabinowitz, may all their memories be a blessing. The fifth *shiur* was given by R. Eliezer Gordon, who was also the rabbi of Telz, and this *shiur* was therefore known as 'the rabbi's *shiur*' . . . the *shiurim* given to the students in the first two levels did not resemble those given to students in levels 3 and 4 . . . ultimately the main thing was independent study of the Talmud. The *shiur* only served to direct the path of study and to encourage the students to delve deeper and deeper in their study.

The number of students was smaller in each ascending *shiur*, for only the most outstanding merited admission to the rabbi's *shiur*. Usually only about twelve to fifteen students attended. The largest *shiur* was the second, which accepted not only those who had risen from the first *shiur* but also a considerable number of new students. The most lively, spirited, and alert students were concentrated in this *shiur*; most of them had already become accustomed to the yeshiva after studying for a year or two, and this was the 'leavening agent' in almost all the disputes and rebellions that broke out from time to time at the yeshiva.[48]

Asaf adds a description of the yeshiva day:

The order of the day at the yeshiva was fixed. All the students had to arrive at eight o'clock for the Shaharit [morning] prayers. After prayers they went back to their

[48] S. Asaf, 'My Study Years at the Telz Yeshiva' (Heb.), 35–6.

lodgings to eat breakfast. At ten o'clock study began, continuing without a break until half past two. At half past two they said the Minhah [afternoon] prayers and went to eat lunch. At half past four all the students had to return to the yeshiva and study for five consecutive hours until half past nine. After that they studied books on *musar* for half an hour, each by himself—works such as *Ḥovot halevavot*, R. Yonah of Gerona's *Sha'arei teshuvah*, *Orḥot tsadikim*, and R. Moshe Hayim Luzzatto's *Mesilat yesharim*,[49] each student choosing whichever book he wished. The most diligent, the *matmidim* [perpetual students], would extend their Talmud study and shorten their *musar* study. At ten o'clock they prayed the Arvit [evening] prayers and went home. The *matmidim* used to return to the yeshiva and study until one or two o'clock in the morning. This was the daily order during the winter; in summer the prayers and the beginning of study were earlier.

Discipline was strict in the yeshiva and the *mashgiḥim* were very particular that the students should arrive on time. One *mashgiaḥ* used to walk between the benches during the repetition of the Amidah prayer to see which students had not come to prayers, and he would inscribe a small circle next to the absentee's name in the student register, in which they were listed according to their seats, for each student had his own seat. He would do this during the study periods too. A check was carried out ten minutes after the beginning of study. However, the older and more learned students would allow themselves to be late and would even fail to turn up, and R. Eliezer reproved them for this in one of his sermons.

These arrangements were not fixed, as we shall see from the dispute over *musar* study discussed below. Asaf gives further details of the *shiurim*:

The *shiurim* were given . . . on the second floor. The benches of the students in *shiurim* 1 and 2 were arranged on sides, one above the next, so that all could see the *rosh yeshivah*. A small platform stood in the middle of the eastern side, on which the teacher stood. (For the students of *shiurim* 3 and 4, who were less numerous, there was another hall, where they sat around tables covered with green cloth.) Usually each *shiur* lasted for an hour and a half. The *rosh yeshivah* [i.e. the teacher—not necessarily R. Gordon] would present his *ḥidushim*, the students would ask questions and come up with difficulties, trying to refute his ideas, and the *rosh yeshivah* would answer them and parry their objections. However, when R. Hirshowitz was teaching, the students spent so much time in halakhic discussion that he could not finish the *shiur* in less than three or four hours, and he would end up covered in sweat, utterly worn out and exhausted. They did not keep silent [during his *shiurim*], nor did they accord him the proper respect. The students of the fourth *shiur* did not come to the *shiurim* at all and continued their study in the yeshiva hall. If R. Eliezer [Gordon] entered the yeshiva hall during the *shiur* time, some of the students would go upstairs to the *shiur*, but most of them would slink off home.[50]

[49] *Ḥovot halevavot* (Duties of the Heart) by Bahya Ibn Pakuda (11th cent.); *Sha'arei hateshuvah* (Gates of Repentance) by Yonah of Gerona (*c.*1200–1263); the anonymous *Orḥot tsadikim* (Ways of the Righteous; 15th cent.); and *Mesilat yesharim* (Path of the Upright) by Moshe Hayim Luzzatto (1707–46) are classical works dealing with perfection of the personality and behaviour.

[50] S. Asaf, 'My Study Years at the Telz Yeshiva' (Heb.), 39.

The accepted system in other Lithuanian yeshivas up to this time had been that all the students attended the same *shiur*, with no regard for the level of the individual student. The Telz system of dividing students up into classes according to ability reflected the adoption of methods customary in secular schools of the time.

The system was practised at Telz even before R. Gordon's arrival, but he accepted the idea and developed it further. Asaf records the existence of five *shiurim*, but R. Gordon claimed in his manifesto: 'they are divided into four levels, each higher than the next'.[51] Great care was taken in assigning each student to the right class; ascending to the next class carried considerable prestige. As one student put it: 'I then went up into the domain of R. Shimon, and this was a great joy for me.'[52] He also explained that sometimes he would attend a more advanced *shiur* without permission: 'I sometimes used to attend the *shiur* given by R. Lezer [Gordon] or by R. Shimon, and I was not the only one. We did not sit together with the students from those *shiurim*, but they allowed us to sit there for a while and listen.' R. Me'ir Berlin points out another advantage of this system:

The *shiurim* at Telz, with their levels and classes, served not only to raise talented students, but were sometimes used to punish unworthy students . . . one of the students from the third *shiur* sinned and they imposed the worst possible punishment upon him: they demoted him to the second *shiur*. This had such an effect upon the young man that he wanted to kill himself. His friends, the elite of the *shiur*, went to R. Yosef Leib to ask for mercy, so that he would change the decree . . . but nothing helped. The compromise reached was that the young man would officially remain in the 'third *shiur*', but would leave the yeshiva. He later travelled to America and became a wealthy and important merchant in New York, far away from the *shiur* of Telz . . . he died young, but the memory that he had left Telz from the third and not the second *shiur* must have been a comfort to him.[53]

Berlin mentions another detail, unrecorded elsewhere and perhaps of limited duration. In other yeshivas, each student decided for himself which tractate of the Talmud to study, and at what pace he would learn. At Telz an attempt seems to have been made to change this practice: 'an unusual thing in my eyes was this, that all the students, apart from those in the rabbi's *shiur*, were studying the same tractate, unlike the custom at Volozhin'.[54] He also notes that 'they used to hold examinations each month, in order to establish the knowledge of each student and what he had learnt during that time'.[55]

---

[51] On *Kol kore* see §3 above.　　　　　　　　　　[52] B. Zuckerman, *Memoirs* (Yid.), 72.

[53] M. Berlin [Bar-Ilan], *From Volozhin to Jerusalem* (Heb.), i. 222–3.

[54] He seems to be talking about independent study. At Volozhin there was one *shiur* for all the students and everyone who attended it studied the same tractate. However, each student chose which tractate they would study independently.

[55] M. Berlin [Bar-Ilan], *From Volozhin to Jerusalem* (Heb.), i. 221.

R. Gordon was particularly proud of these examinations, devoting two paragraphs of his manifesto to this subject. He observed, however, that these examinations were also designed to improve study: 'And at the "test" they are asked questions about cases, for which they must bring proof from the Talmud that they have learned how to decide in each case, so that they become accustomed in this way, so that when they are older and have to judge and teach, they may bring proof from the Talmud in order to make a halakhic decision . . . so that they should not make decisions based upon the books of the *aharonim*.' His words echo R. Gordon's own words in paragraph six of his booklet and this might be a quote or paraphrase. The purpose of the examination is immaterial: its very existence represented a change in the structure of study. These and other deviations from the practices customary at other yeshivas show that the Telz system drew heavily on practices in modern secular schools, at the expense of the tradition of independent study.

5. The Admission Procedure

Telz also had an unusual admission procedure, totally different from that of the old *beit midrash*. Concern for order was prominent, whether for its own sake or for greater efficiency. The historian Ben-Zion Dinur, who started to study in Telz in 1897, describes it as follows:

Immediately upon our arrival we went to the yeshiva . . . it became clear that our admission to the yeshiva was not a simple matter. It was customary at the Telz yeshiva that a student who wished to be admitted to the yeshiva had to inform the administration in advance and send recommendations, and only after he had received notification that he had been accepted was he expected to turn up. Each student also had to ensure a certain minimum income for himself. It was forbidden for the yeshiva student to 'eat days' (or even 'weeks'), except on sabbaths, on which he was allowed to be a local householder's guest. The yeshiva administration was very strict about the conditions of entry and absolutely refused to accept students who had not sent a prior request and had not brought confirmation of their acceptance. In addition, we were very young, especially in my case; I would only become barmitzvah at Hanukah, and there were no students of this age at all in the yeshiva then. But since we came from a distant region and had brought numerous recommendations, and the Poltava district brought in a good income for the yeshiva, and we had brought recommendations from the emissaries of the Telz yeshiva who had passed through our district's towns at the end of the summer, it was not easy for the yeshiva's director to refuse to accept us.[56]

New students were required to take entrance examinations.[57] As R. Gordon wrote in the second point of his manifesto, 'No young man is

---

[56] Dinur, *In a World that Went Under* (Heb.), 64. This pattern of fundraising resembles that used at Volozhin. On the changes in this sphere at Telz, see below.

[57] B. Zuckerman, *Memoirs* (Yid.), 68.

accepted at the yeshiva until he is examined to ensure that he is talented and will rise in the levels of Torah in the best way, and there is a special committee for this purpose, to examine every young man before they accept him.' The emphasis on this principle, underlined by its position near the start of the document, demonstrates several things: (1) there was great demand for places at the yeshiva, so that it was possible to choose only the best students; (2) the yeshiva was concerned to maintain a high level; (3) there was a special framework for this—'there is a special committee for this purpose'; (4) the yeshiva was careful not to let the number of students exceed the institution's capacity. In paragraph 9, he adds: 'We cannot diminish these expenditures, for young men come to join the yeshiva at a greater rate than we can take them in, and although we warn the extra students that they will suffer from hunger, and many of them return to their homes, nevertheless many of them persist and enter the yeshiva.'

Students were not admitted in mid-term: 'You are travelling to Telz in the middle of *zeman*, and it must be supposed that you will have to manage without a home in Telz until Rosh Hashanah, and nobody will take care of you.'[58]

Another factor in accepting students was where they came from. Each region had its 'quota', as is apparent from the biography of R. Yosef Kahaneman:

The yeshiva gates were too narrow to admit all those who knocked for admission, and therefore the yeshiva administration were forced to adopt restrictions and strategies to halt the endless streams of students. For example, they decreed that only one student from each town would be accepted: up to two or three from a large city. Another decree stated that two students from the same family would not be accepted at the same time. The sons of rabbis and *rashei yeshivah* were excluded from this ruling and were accepted outside the quota . . . the son of Yehudah Kahaneman did not possess all the qualities required for admission to Telz. First of all, the eldest son, Ya'akov, was already studying at Telz. It thus emerged that Yosef Shelomoh was 'disqualified' on two counts: (1) his family already had a 'representative' at the yeshiva; (2) the quota from Kul [his parents' place of residence] was already full; and since he was not from a rabbinic family, all hope was lost.[59]

Geographical origins were also important in the allocation of financial support. As Zuckerman records: 'I was lucky. Zalman Ber of Kurenets left Telz . . . so I was now the only student from Kurenets. Therefore the sum I received from the fund was not inconsiderable, in terms of those days. I was

---

[58] B. Zuckerman, *Memoirs* (Yid.), 68.

[59] Kul, *Alone in his Generation* (Heb.), 34. There is a similar story in the memoirs of R. Alter Wasser, in Gindes et al. (eds.), *Festschrift for Rabbi Shimon Yehudah Shkop* (Heb.), 54–5. To gain admission he presented himself as coming from his grandfather's town, since there were no students from there at the yeshiva, while there were already three from his own town.

not accustomed to great luxuries, so my situation was not at all bad.'[60] It is not clear whether the policy of linking the income received from each town to the number of students at the yeshiva from these towns was intended to encourage the townspeople to increase their contributions to the yeshiva or was purely arbitrary. It was a decidedly non-egalitarian approach and was not even defensible in educational terms, but the students seem to have accepted it.

One of the factors behind the rigid admissions criteria, such as the demand that each student had to receive advance confirmation of admission, was undoubtedly the desire to make the administration and economic planning more efficient.[61] The yeshiva could not take everyone who wanted to study there, and imposing proper criteria prevented unpleasant situations, saved the candidates unnecessary expense, and reduced the administrative burden. The insistence that students should not have to rely on the hospitality of local families for meals (as was the practice when the yeshiva first opened) made things more difficult for the yeshiva, but it helped to increase the respect for the students and for the yeshiva in the local community. However, it seems that there was also a great concern for order and procedures, irrespective of the practical advantages.

6. Living Arrangements

The Telz students were organized to a level unknown at other yeshivas. One former student describes the process of entry to the yeshiva thus:

When I arrived, I first of all had to find a lodging. I went to the yeshiva building to learn how I might find a room, and there I was told that there was a special committee, organized by the students, called the 'lodgings committee' [*va'ad hame'onot*], and every student looking for a room had to go to this committee, where he would receive a list of rooms available for hire. Next to each room was its price, which was fixed by the committee, and it was forbidden to raise the fixed price . . . this committee was established in order to protect the students from exploitation by landlords. The committee . . . also kept a close watch to ensure that the landlords, or more correctly, the landladies, would treat the students with respect, keep [their rooms] clean, and be quiet, in order to avoid disturbing their studies and repose. The students took their meals at their lodgings and the committee also supervised the cost of the meals. If a student had complaints about his landlord and the committee found that they were justified, they would send a warning letter to the landlord. And if the appropriate response was not forthcoming, the committee would remove the student from the lodgings and stop sending other lodgers there.[62]

[60] B. Zuckerman, *Memoirs* (Yid.), 68.
[61] R. Gordon agreed to make the arrangements in Kelme more efficient and to hold examinations; see A. A. Friedman, *Memoirs* (Heb.), 100–3.
[62] S. Asaf, 'My Study Years at the Telz Yeshiva' (Heb.), 34–5.

Other committees dealt with other aspects of student life.[63] The highlight of
student organization seems to have been the election of student representatives at the yeshiva. Their status will be discussed later, but what Asaf has to
say is interesting in this context:

As a result of the bitter differences in opinion that broke out in later years between
the yeshiva and the students, the rabbi decided that it would be good for the students to have their own representatives, with whom the administration could negotiate when necessary. This was a great innovation. It must be remembered, however,
that those were the days of the first Russian Revolution, when the Russian people
was given its own parliament. A committee of eleven was elected by the students,
with representatives from all five *shiurim*, and I had the privilege of being elected as
one of them. This committee sometimes came up with rather extreme demands.[64]

Several factors contributed to the atmosphere of independence. There is no
doubt that the students were influenced by the general atmosphere of revolution and political activity, as they openly acknowledged. But there seem to
have been other factors too, if perhaps less important: first, R. Gordon's
emphasis on independent thought, which will be discussed further below; and
second, the students' complete economic independence of the yeshiva. This
was far less true of students at other yeshivas. Dinur, quoted earlier, says that
a student was only accepted if he could 'ensure a certain minimum income for
himself'.[65] The original practice of eating with local families soon disappeared,[66] and in fact became strictly forbidden. Asaf, who studied in Telz for
about ten years, records:

Most of the students were supported by their parents, with a supplement that they
received from the yeshiva fund. There were some poor students who were entirely
supported by the yeshiva fund and by giving private lessons to younger students,
the *ḥutsniks* . . . very few came from wealthy and prominent families and were studying Torah in luxury . . . [the custom of] 'eating days' was not practised. However, on

---

[63] Kul mentions committees for the following spheres: organizing festivities, lodgings,
organizing *shiurim*, health, spiritual assistance, and assigning Torah readings; there was also a
student *gemaḥ* (loan society). 'At the head of all these aforementioned committees stood the
central committee, which consisted of the senior and veteran students. This committee was
elected by the whole student body and appointed the other committees' (*Alone in his Generation*
(Heb.), 47–8). See further Z. A. Rabiner, *The Gaon Rabbi Eliezer Gordon* (Heb.), 90. Students
also played an important role in supervision; see Kul, *Alone in his Generation* (Heb.), 52; M. Berlin
[Bar-Ilan], *From Volozhin to Jerusalem* (Heb.), i. 221.

[64] S. Asaf, 'My Study Years at the Telz Yeshiva' (Heb.), 42.

[65] Dinur, *In a World that Went Under* (Heb.), 64.

[66] Druck wrote: 'Though there were students at Telz who were exceptionally rich spiritually,
they were equally destitute materially . . . following the custom that was universal, Telz students
too used to eat on a daily basis at other people's tables, with the God-fearing citizens of the town,
who wanted to share the students' reward in the next world by this meritorious practice, and
[they also ate] with the *rashei yeshivah*' (*Rabbi Levi Ginsberg* (Heb.), 33–4).

the sabbath some of the students were invited to the tables of the local townsfolk. There was also a fund, known as 'Oneg Shabat' [joy of the sabbath], which supported poor students so that they did not have to reduce their sabbath to the level of an ordinary day.[67]

It seems reasonable to suppose that the strict prohibition on taking hospitality from local families came from a desire to maintain the students' dignity. However, the yeshiva did not have the economic resources to support every needy student. This led to a preference for admitting students from prosperous families or wealthy towns and to encouraging ways of supporting students other than through the yeshiva—circumstances that ultimately lessened the yeshiva's influence on students. As we shall see, the extent of their independence was such that when a prolonged student strike at the yeshiva effectively closed the institution down, the students were able to continue studying without any financial support from the yeshiva. Another significant factor was that payments to landlords were made directly by the students, which made it impossible for the yeshiva to threaten students with eviction; whereas in Volozhin, any appeal to the landlords carried great weight because it was the yeshiva that paid for students' rent and board.

Asaf's observations suggest that most of the students were neither from poor families nor from wealthy families but were middle class. It seems that poor students found it more difficult to attend the yeshiva, both because of the necessity of support from home and because they would have been less likely to study at a good *ḥeder* and to reach the level required for more advanced studies. While the custom of relying on local hosts for food prevailed, financial support from home was less important; but under the new regime only the most exceptional poor student could cope, whether by receiving support from the yeshiva or doing some private teaching. It should be noted that the admission quotas that restricted the number of students from each town did not apply to the sons of rabbis and *rashei yeshivah*.[68] This seems to have stemmed from the perception that rabbis enjoyed special rights that should be passed on to their children.

7. Sources of Conflict

Telz was unusual not only in its administrative set-up but also the intensity of the conflicts that raged within the yeshiva. Most concerned two matters: the place of *musar* study and student opposition to staff appointments. Analysis of these disputes throws light on the power relationships in the yeshiva, the goals of the *rashei yeshivah* and of the students, and the mechanisms for resolving this type of disagreement in the Jewish society of the time.

[67] S. Asaf, 'My Study Years at the Telz Yeshiva' (Heb.), 42.

[68] Kul, *Alone in his Generation* (Heb.), 34; and see above.

The first dispute over the place of *musar* seems to have occurred in about 1885:

At that time a dispute broke out at the yeshiva over *musar* study, which they wanted to introduce into the yeshiva curriculum. R. Lezer [Gordon] himself was not too keen on the idea of establishing *musar* study at the yeshiva, but, in contrast, his son-in-law R. Yosef Leib Bloch stood fast like a mighty rock in favour of the idea. The yeshiva students themselves were utterly opposed to it, since they regarded it as a waste of Torah study time [*bitul torah*]. A compromise was eventually reached. It was ordained that *musar* study would not take place for all the classes at once, and would not be compulsory. But even so the yeshiva seethed like a cauldron.[69]

When Me'ir Berlin studied at the yeshiva in 1894, *musar* was already an integral—though minor—part of the curriculum:

Musar study too was a novelty for someone from Volozhin. At Volozhin they used to say: 'A page of Talmud is better than books of *musar*.' Even at Telz *musar* study was not carried on in those days in the way that developed later, but every evening we were compelled to study *musar* for half an hour. Each student was allowed to choose his favourite book . . . and just as each student's talents could be glimpsed during Talmud study, so too one could divine each student's character during *musar* study. But there was a difference in this too, in the way in which they studied *musar*. Those who saw *musar* as the principal subject used to express this with passion in the form of various exclamations, and sometimes even in gesticulations, expressing not only their thoughts but also their deep emotions as they meditated upon repentance [*teshuvah*], though it was clear that their repentance exceeded their sins.[70]

R. Gordon also alluded to *musar* in the manifesto he published in 1894, cited in entirety above, when M. Berlin was a student at Telz. He does not mention *musar* study and in fact seems to have deliberately refrained from emphasizing it: 'We will sum up: the students at the yeshiva are educated in an excellent way, both in Torah study and in behaviour, and we can justly say of the students of this institution that they combine Torah and fear [of Heaven] and good behaviour and all the qualities required of a man who intends to be a rabbi.'[71] However, the *musar* enthusiasts were not content with this and demanded the appointment of a *mashgiaḥ* (spiritual director) and greater emphasis on *musar* study. R. Gordon continued: 'An excellent *mashgiaḥ* will watch over all the yeshiva students. He watches and observes every student with attention; he is distinguished for his fear [of Heaven] and his spiritual nobility, is wise, and has the other qualities needed by one entrusted with inspiring the students to Torah study and fear [of Heaven] and good behaviour and good manners, so that they may find favour among God and men.'[72] It seems probable that there

[69] Druck, *Rabbi Levi Ginsberg* (Heb.), 35.

[70] M. Berlin [Bar-Ilan], *From Volozhin to Jerusalem* (Heb.), i. 221–2 (ellipsis in the original).

[71] *Kol kore*, para. 8; see n. 38 above.   [72] Ibid., para. 7.

had been *mashgihim* in Telz before this, but not *mashgihim* who belonged to the *musar* movement; the appointment of such a *mashgiah* in 1897 caused a crisis. R. Yeruham Wahrhaftig described the beginning of the conflict when R. Yosef Yehudah Leib Bloch persuaded his father-in-law, R. Gordon, and R. Shimon Shkop, then teaching at the yeshiva, to appoint a *mashgiah*:

They immediately set their sights on the rabbi, the righteous *gaon*, R. Aryeh Leib Chasman renowned as a master of *musar*, and appointed him as *mashgiah* and spiritual director of the yeshiva. However, R. Chasman had a forthright personality and carried out his duties in a high-handed manner; immediately upon his arrival he rebuked the yeshiva students for talking about Torah *hidushim* during prayers, and told them angrily that Torah study time and prayer time were quite separate. He began to make regulations and decrees, for instance, that anyone who did not come to *musar* study at the appointed time would be punished as though he had not attended the *shiur*; he would not compromise on anything . . . for he considered the value of *musar* to be as weighty as that of Torah study. Moreover, he was also very severe with the young students of the first and second classes, who were not obliged to study *musar* at all, and he decreed that these youngsters were not free to desist from it, and that they too would have fines deducted from their monthly stipends if they did not attend *musar* study. The *musar* adherents became very influential thanks to the spiritual direction of this *mashgiah* . . . therefore the students with the best reputations became fierce in the cause of Torah study and complained about the *mashgiah*, [saying] that his method and deeds had weakened Torah study at the yeshiva in comparison with *musar* study, which was becoming stronger and stronger . . . meanwhile a deep rift was developing between the hearts of the students and the *mashgiah*.[73]

A similar account appears in the memoirs of Ben-Zion Dinur, though he linked R. Chasman's arrival to the spread of the Haskalah and Zionism at the yeshiva.[74] The students' response to R. Chasman was to strike. According to Zuckerman, the strike broke out in response to a campaign targeted against students who possessed 'Haskalah pamphlets'. R. Bloch was also opposed to this, but R. Chasman was much more extreme in his fight against Zionism and the Haskalah.[75] A letter from R. Gordon to Eliezer Eliyahu Friedman reveals that the students had come to him with their complaints about the *mashgiah* and his doings: why was a *mashgiah* necessary? He had created a

---

[73] Wahrhaftig, *Offerings of Yeruham* (Heb.), intro. and p. i.

[74] Dinur, *In a World that Went Under* (Heb.), 71: 'The yeshiva made great efforts to introduce *musar* study, both because it was important in itself and as a barrier to the Haskalah and Zionism that had begun to spread among the students. R. Leib Hasman of Kelme, one of the most outstanding *musar* figures, was invited to be the yeshiva's *mashgiah*, and he made the students study half an hour every day, I think, between Minhah and Ma'ariv, R. Yisra'el Salanter's *Igeret hamusar* ['Musar Epistle'], R. Mendel Lefin's *Heshbon hanefesh* ['Spiritual Reckoning', which is really an adaptation of a book by Benjamin Franklin], and other *musar* books.'

[75] B. Zuckerman, *Memoirs* (Yid.), 70.

band of *musarniks* at the yeshiva and was forcing even the youngest students to study *musar*. Friedman summarizes R. Gordon's response:

(1) He had taken on the new *mashgiaḥ* because 'he saw in him the abilities required to supervise such an honourable yeshiva'; (2) as to the fact that the *mashgiaḥ* had begun to invite students to his house every sabbath eve, to teach them the principles of *musar*, and this, in the students' eyes, had become the foundation of a *musar* sect within the yeshiva, against which they had protested—all this had been done without his knowledge, and he had put a stop to it; (3) he had made a regulation in the yeshiva that only the older students from the fourth and fifth levels should study *musar*.[76]

We have two descriptions of the students' response, one by R. Wahrhaftig and one by Ben-Zion Dinur. R. Wahrhaftig records that the students demanded that the yeshiva should cancel R. Chasman's regulations, that R. Gordon and R. Shkop were inclined to do so, but that because of the intransigence of R. Bloch and R. Chasman the demand was refused:

When the *mashgiaḥ*'s opponents saw that their demands were refused, they began to hold secret meetings and to disseminate propaganda among the students, to spread a spirit of rebellion among them, until they had attracted so many students to them that they constituted the majority, and then they decided to rebel openly; on a winter night in the month of Shevat of 1897, with the very passion with which they usually studied, they stopped studying and began to argue as to whether the promotion of *musar* study weakened Torah study . . . conflict broke out among the students, and shouts and hellish noises rose to the heavens; the *mashgiaḥ* upbraided them for their waste of study time but his words went unheeded, and they stated clearly that they would stop studying until their demands were met.[77]

When R. Gordon learnt what had happened he was so overcome with grief that he could not respond. Only on the next day, 'shaking all over and as white as chalk', did he begin to reprove the students:

Seditious elements have led you astray; their intention was not pure, and the administration has decided to expel them from the yeshiva, for their own welfare and the welfare of all the yeshiva students; and these are the twelve students who rebelled, by name . . . it is with great sorrow that I must announce that we have also decided to remove from his post at the yeshiva the righteous *gaon*, the *mashgiaḥ ruḥani* [spiritual director] R. Aryeh Leib Chasman, since a great disaster has taken place because of him, and he will have to leave and live in another town . . . he made a mistake in his authoritarian ways, and did not raise the spirit of *musar* gradually but all at once, and thus tempers rose and the recent events took place; and in addition I announce that from now on the students of classes 1 and 2 are exempt from *musar* study, and thus I conclude my words.

[76] A. A. Friedman, *Memoirs* (Heb.), 109.
[77] Wahrhaftig, *Offerings of Yeruḥam* (Heb.), intro.

A student representative asked for mercy for his expelled comrades, and indeed 'the decree was cut in half; in other words, only six were subject to it, and considerable money was expended so that they would leave and go on their way in peace with nothing lacking. They took the righteous *gaon* R. Leib Chasman off to Kelme in secret.'

Dinur's account adds some details but is basically consistent with that of R. Wahrhaftig.[78] The yeshiva did not abandon its aim of introducing *musar* study,[79] and emotions continued to run high. According to Zuckerman, who studied at Telz four years later: 'The deep impression made by the strike did not seem to have weakened in the four years that had passed. Almost all the students who had been studying at the yeshiva then continued to speak of it.'[80] Elsewhere Zuckerman notes that some of the students who had left organized an 'underground movement'.[81]

The differences of opinion among the yeshiva staff seem to have continued for some time; Zuckerman records that 'domestic peace between father-in-law and son-in-law was not perfect'. He adds: 'I found out from the veteran students that R. Leib's strange behaviour stemmed from the fact that he had already received the post of rabbi of Varniai, a town near Telz.'[82] In 1902 R. Bloch resigned, and only then did peace return—though not for long. The *rashei yeshivah* did all they could to restore calm, and divided up R. Bloch's students between them.[83] Katz[84] and Kul[85] give similar descriptions. Shortly after R. Bloch's departure R. Chasman left too, and R. Shkop left in 1903. The reasons for his departure are unclear, though Dvorets seems correct when he says that: 'these *geonim* would never have taken these steps if it had not been for the dispute at the yeshiva'.[86] Thus three of the leading figures at Telz left it within a short period.

[78] Dinur writes that the leader of the disturbances was given a slap, and was expelled from the yeshiva together with his comrades. However, they received generous travel expenses (*In a World that Went Under* (Heb.), 71).
[79] See the continuation of Dinur's account (ibid. 71–2), where he describes the *mashgiah*'s unsuccessful attempt to attract students to *musar* study.
[80] B. Zuckerman, *Memoirs* (Yid.), 72.   [81] Ibid. 57, 59.   [82] Ibid. 69.
[83] Ibid. 72. R. Bloch was no longer R. Gordon's son-in-law since his wife had died, and this probably contributed to the weakening of the ties between them.
[84] D. Katz, *The Musar Movement* (Heb.), v. 27. He describes R. Gordon as a forgiving man and a great scholar, so that the yoke of discipline fell principally on R. Bloch; the latter, since he disagreed with other teachers on this issue, decided to leave the yeshiva. This description of R. Gordon's character is supported by Wahrhaftig (*Offerings of Yeruham* (Heb.), intro. and p. iv), who records that he discussed matters of Torah with the students who had been expelled 'until the moment that they left the yeshiva'.   [85] Kul, *Alone in his Generation* (Heb.), 64.
[86] Dvorets [Palin], *The Gaon Rabbi Moshe Mordekhai Epstein* (Heb.), 29. Kul writes that R. Shkop 'approved of the method [*musar*] . . . but did not have an aggressive personality' (*Alone in his Generation* (Heb.), 55). However, I have found no other evidence of his sympathy for the *musar* movement or of his intervention at the yeshiva to promote *musar* study. On the attempts to find a teacher to replace him at Telz, see below, and also Kamenetsky, *The Making of a Godol*, i. 423–6.

It was a difficult period for the yeshiva. Zuckerman writes of unrest following R. Bloch's departure;[87] others record that his departure caused consternation among the students.[88] It seems that R. Chasman could not maintain his position without the support of R. Bloch, which was why R. Bloch's departure forced R. Chasman to leave. R. Gordon made great efforts to find a replacement. One of the candidates seems to have been R. Yitshak Rabinowitz, known as R. Itzeleh Ponevezher. R. Kahaneman, later head of the Ponevezh yeshiva in Israel, records: 'When I left Telz I was very attached to R. Shimon [Shkop] and wanted to join him, in spite of the fact that they were preparing to welcome a new teacher, R. Itzeleh of Ponevezh who had been appointed to replace him. I could not imagine how I could leave the great rabbi, although R. Shimon ordered me to stay at Telz and told me in his great humility: "Truly, if it were up to me, I would myself stay at Telz and hear R. Itzeleh teach."'[89] Although R. Rabinowitz accepted the offer, he never went to Telz. According to Rabiner, 'the Ponevezh community increased R. Itzeleh's salary and undertook to give his daughters dowries, and R. Itzeleh changed his mind and stayed in Ponevezh.'[90] Rabiner adds that R. Gordon then asked R. Barukh Ber Leibowitz, but this did not work out either.[91] Apparently R. Leibowitz announced that he would have to receive the agreement of his teacher, R. Hayim Soloveitchik, and R. Gordon cancelled the appointment.[92] Eventually R. Hayim Rabinowitz was appointed as *rosh yeshivah*. He had been teaching at the Keneset Beit Yitshak yeshiva in Slobodka—the yeshiva that had not sided with the *musar* movement—and his post there was now filled by R. Barukh Ber Leibowitz.

R. Gordon's choice of candidates is interesting. Both Rabinowitzes had taught for some time in Slobodka, at R. Finkel's yeshiva, and had left because of their opposition to *musar*. R. Leibowitz had been a leading student of R. Hayim Soloveitchik, who also opposed the *musar* movement. The fact that R. Gordon chose these candidates suggests his disappointment with the *musar* movement, or at least a change in his attitude to it, though there is no explicit evidence of this.

The arrival of R. Hayim Rabinowitz solved the problem of a second teacher but then a new problem emerged: R. Rabinowitz was not related to R. Gordon, and up to this point all the senior posts at the yeshiva were held by family members. R. Gordon did have a son-in-law, R. Itsik Eizik Hirshowitz, and when R. Bloch had left, R. Gordon tried to appoint him but met with opposition from the students. After R. Rabinowitz's arrival, R. Gordon tried again—probably in response to family pressure, though there is no evidence

[87] B. Zuckerman, *Memoirs* (Yid.), 69.   [88] e.g. Kul, *Alone in his Generation* (Heb.), 64.
[89] Sorski, *Rabbi Shimon Shkop* (Heb.), 99–100.
[90] Z. A. Rabiner, *The Gaon Rabbi Eliezer Gordon* (Heb.), 66.   [91] Ibid.
[92] Edelstein, *Rabbi Barukh Dov Liebowitz* (Heb.), 24–5.

of this—but the students' response was not long in coming. Asaf describes it thus:

Shortly before Hanukah [1905], an open rebellion broke out among the students, which they called a *hopkeh*. The *hopkeh* used to begin with a *Sha!* The hundreds of students would be studying aloud, much louder than usual, and suddenly silence would fall. A whisper ran through the throng: *Sha!* And silence reigned, so absolute that one could hear the buzzing of a fly. After a few seconds the students would start to study again very loudly, and then came another *Sha!*, and a third and a fourth. This *Sha!* boded no good. It was a sign of the coming storm. At the end of the time set for study, the students would throw down the benches and *shtenders* [book stands] and leave the yeshiva hall in complete disarray.

A *hopkeh* occurred for the third year running, near the start of the study term, when the rabbi tried to appoint his second son-in-law, R. Itsik Eizik Hirshowitz, as the second teacher at the yeshiva . . . [he] had studied for several years at the Telz yeshiva, and after marrying R. Eliezer's daughter, he had been supported by him for eleven or twelve years, studying Torah. He was very diligent and had great knowledge of the Talmud and its commentaries, but he was not distinguished in sharp and original debate and had not acquired the affection of the students. He was a fierce opponent of Zionism, and this too brought him many opponents, since many of the students were Zionists.[93]

At first the students acceded to the appointment of R. Hirshowitz and he started teaching at the yeshiva. However, problems soon arose. The students harassed him during lessons, many failed to attend his classes,[94] and just before Hanukah a revolt against his appointment broke out. The rebellion was quite violent:

[There was] complete uproar, the lights were shattered, the benches were overturned, many windows were broken, and the students ran off home. Regular studies resumed after a couple of days, but R. Gordon, grieved and disappointed, especially by his own students from the fifth class, ceased to teach them. The students felt they had been rebuked and stopped visiting the rabbi's home. The affectionate ties between the rabbi and his students were broken. R. Gordon could not endure this situation for long, however; he had no life except in the yeshiva with his students, and after two months he began to teach again.[95]

A detailed letter by R. Gordon confirms most of Asaf's description, though he blames a small group for inciting the majority, and claims that most of the students had initially supported R. Hirshowitz's appointment.[96] However, his words seem to reflect wishful thinking rather than reality. If R. Hirshowitz

[93] S. Asaf, 'My Study Years at the Telz Yeshiva' (Heb.), 38–9.
[94] See the evidence from Asaf's account, quoted above on p. 305.
[95] S. Asaf, 'My Study Years at the Telz Yeshiva' (Heb.), 39.
[96] A. A. Friedman, *Memoirs* (Heb.), 109–11.

had been so popular, it is hard to understand how a minority of the students could have aroused such fierce opposition to him.

R. Hirshowitz did not resume teaching, and peace returned to the yeshiva, though not for long. At this time there were generally two *mashgihim*, whose function was to check attendance and to supervise everything that went on. *Musar* study remained obligatory. The scheduled time was between half past nine and ten o'clock in the evening, but there was no supervision of this. Many students disliked the *mashgihim*: we know of a booby trap that emptied a jug over one of them on a sabbath eve.[97] In 1905, after the conflict over R. Hirshowitz, it was decided that students who were liable to oppose further change in the yeshiva, particularly those who had been involved in recent events, should be kept at a distance:

Of the twelve students who attended the rabbi's *shiur*, eight were sent away . . . and several of the younger students were sent away too. Many of those who travelled home for the festival, thinking that they would return immediately afterwards, became *loyavoniks* [i.e. they were not permitted to return]. According to yeshiva regulations, every student who went home had to receive written permission to return to the yeshiva. Those with whom the yeshiva administration was not pleased received a negative answer: *Lo yavo!* [Let him not come!]

To replace the students who had been sent away and the *loyavoniks*, about thirty or forty students were brought in from the Slobodka yeshiva by agreement with the administration there, which was interested in bringing the renowned Telz yeshiva into the fold of the *musar* movement. Among the arrivals were all the 'lions of the company', some of whom eventually served as *mashgihim* and teachers at various yeshivas. These were the 'elders of the generation', students aged thirty and older, and we Telz students never became accustomed to the type.[98]

The veteran students were ferocious in their opposition to the *musar* students, and there were incidents in which yeshiva property was destroyed. The

[97] S. Asaf, 'My Study Years at the Telz Yeshiva' (Heb.), 36–8, 63. Shimon Kushnir, in his biography of Avraham Herzfeld, draws an interesting picture of the activities of the *mashgihim* and the students' responses: 'The yeshiva's *mashgihim* were very strict with every student who was late for prayers, even if by a few minutes. During the repetition of the Amidah one of the *mashgihim* used to walk between the benches, with a little notebook in his hand that contained a list of the students in order, and he would draw a little circle by the name of each student who was not in his place. This was also the custom with those who arrived late for their studies. This notebook used to strike fear into the yeshiva students . . . gradually the students came to despise the *mashgiah*'s notebook and little circles. As a result, one of the *mashgihim* had an idea—3 copecks would be deducted from a student's monthly stipend for each little circle he had earned. This aroused the students' ire . . . the yeshiva students rebelled and demanded the decree be abolished and the *mashgiah* be removed. The rebellion did not die down until their demands had been met' (Kushnir (ed.), *Fields and Heart* (Heb.), 32–3).

[98] S. Asaf, 'My Study Years at the Telz Yeshiva' (Heb.), 40; see also Dvorets [Palin], *The Gaon Rabbi Moshe Mordekhai Epstein* (Heb.), 40.

attempt to change the character of the yeshiva by importing new students
aroused extreme reactions: demands for the expulsion of the new students,
the firing of the *mashgiaḥ*, and the reduction or abolition of compulsory *musar*
study. When these demands were not met, the students called a general strike
that led to the closure of the yeshiva in 1905.[99] The students did not waste
their time during the strike: they collected funds, held *shiurim* by themselves
and maintained this situation for an extended period of time. This was possible as a result of their high level of organization, economic independence,
and habits of independent study. The reasons behind their success and
R. Gordon's ambiguous attitude towards it will be examined below.

The students managed to keep this arrangement going for several months.
After about six months the new *mashgiaḥ*, R. Eliezer Luft, left the yeshiva,
accompanied by the students from Slobodka, and normal studies were
resumed. Several students who had been active in the rebellion left at the same
time.[100] R. Gordon's son describes the relations between his father and the
students who were striking:

And his outstanding student, R. Yosef Kahaneman, told me of one incident. A
dispute once broke out at the yeshiva between the students and my father. As a
result, the yeshiva was closed and financial support for the students was halted. The
rebellious students were led by R. Kahaneman and Avraham Herzfeld, who was then
studying at Telz and was known as 'Avraham Stavisker'. They both went to my
father, as representatives of the students, in order to negotiate, and R. Kahaneman
happened to say, 'Your students are hungry and are studying Torah.' When my
father heard the dreadful words 'Your students are hungry' actually uttered by his
student, who was a *kohen*, he turned pale, and, trembling all over, went to the cup-
board and took out fifty-two roubles; without saying a word he handed the money
to the deputation, and thus lost his principal weapon—but gained the victory. No
considerations, no tactics could stand in the way of his love and compassion for his
students.[101]

The fact that the students turned up to study Torah even when hungry was
more important to R. Gordon than their unwillingness to accept his authority
on the *musar* issue, and this was why he was prepared to support them. This
would never have happened in Slobodka. The dispute seems to have ended
in a compromise, though the way in which it was reached is unclear; there is
no doubt, however, that the *musar* movement had suffered a setback.

Most sources see the *musar* issue as the cause of the student rebellion of
1905. However, the revolutionary mood in Russia at that time seems also to
have been a factor, since most of the anti-*musar* students who left the yeshiva

[99] S. Asaf, 'My Study Years at the Telz Yeshiva' (Heb.), 40–1; Kushnir (ed.), *Fields and Heart*
(Heb.), 34–6; Sheli, 'Droplets of Telz' (Heb.), 429–31.

[100] D. Katz, *The Musar Movement* (Heb.), v. 291.

[101] S. Gordon, 'The *Gaon* Rabbi Eliezer Gordon' (Heb.).

did not go on to other yeshivas or *batei midrash* but turned to other occupations. Shulman's memoir supports this and also reveals something about the interests of some of these students:

I arrived at the yeshiva at the beginning of 1906. 1905 had been a stormy year for the yeshiva. Several dozen of the best students had ridden high on the waves of the revolution. After bitter disputes between them and the administration they left the yeshiva for good; some of them worked in political organizations and others studied for the gymnasium examinations, while maintaining their links with the yeshiva students. They often used to come to the yeshiva and try to persuade the students to leave.[102]

The storms continued. Asaf mentions 'fierce disputes that broke out in the last years from time to time';[103] once again, *musar* was the source of the contention. After the strike ended in the summer of 1906, R. Gordon again changed course and turned once more to a *musar* rabbi, R. Shmuel Pundiler, to serve as *mashgiaḥ*. Like his predecessor, he brought several students with him. This caused another student revolt, as in the winter of 1905, but this time the rebels did not succeed: it is not clear whether this was due to R. Pundiler's personality and methods or to the departure of many of the students who were opposed to *musar*. Whatever the truth of the matter, R. Pundiler stayed at the yeshiva and the influence of the *musar* movement grew, though the conflict was not yet over.[104]

Peace finally prevailed only in 1910, following far-reaching changes. In 1908 there was a major fire in Telz, and the yeshiva building was burnt down. Rebuilding it involved the yeshiva in considerable debts. R. Gordon found it difficult to muster the necessary financial support, which induced a sense of personal humiliation,[105] and in 1910, when in London to lead a fundraising campaign, he died. After his death, his son-in-law R. Yosef Yehudah Leib Bloch returned to Telz; it is not clear whether this was a consequence of R. Gordon's death or had been planned earlier.[106] He quickly took control of the institution, starting a new page in the yeshiva's history. D. Katz describes it as follows:

[102] B. Shulman, 'The Spirit of Revolution in the Yeshivas' (Heb.), 135.

[103] S. Asaf, 'My Study Years at the Telz Yeshiva' (Heb.), 42.

[104] D. Katz, *The Musar Movement* (Heb.), v. 328; cf. iii. 63. See also B. Shulman, 'The Spirit of Revolution in the Yeshivas' (Heb.), 137–41. He identifies the new *mashgiaḥ* as R. Shmuel of Radun (p. 137), but his memory seems to have misled him, since R. Pundiler did not come from Radun. The other details he supplies do fit R. Pundiler.

[105] Mazeh, *Memoirs* (Heb.), iv. 120–6.

[106] See a letter written in Adar (i.e. before R. Gordon's death) that mentions that R. Bloch is about to leave Sadov; it is quoted in Gelbart, *The Great Yeshiva Torat Hesed* (Yid.), 18. His destination is not explicitly mentioned, but no other sources mentions any attempt by him to be appointed rabbi anywhere else, nor any problems in Sadov, so it seems likely that he was planning to return to Telz.

From the time that R. Yosef Leib was appointed as rabbi and *rosh yeshivah* of Telz, a new period began in his life and in that of the yeshiva. The moment he arrived at the yeshiva there was an uprising, but R. Shmuel [Pundiler] tried to direct matters so that the previous line was maintained . . . though this was not what R. Yosef Leib intended. He had another way and his own method. After a short while, he told R. Shmuel that he would take over the management of the yeshiva, and that there would thus be no room for two kings to share the same crown. Many asked him, was it not R. Shmuel who made great efforts to bring him to Telz and to raise him to this exalted position, and where was his sense of gratitude? And R. Yosef Leib answered, that we have never heard that people take back a favour because of [an issue of] gratitude; in other words, if he left R. Shmuel as administrator of the yeshiva, it would be his attitude that determined everything, while he, R. Yosef Leib, would have no influence at the yeshiva and it would be as though he had never received the favour.[107]

R. Pundiler did indeed leave, and the yeshiva continued to develop under the direction of R. Bloch up to and after the First World War. Several strictly Orthodox educational institutions grew up around the Telz yeshiva, which became one of the most important yeshivas in independent Lithuania.[108] The means by which R. Bloch engineered such a radical change will be discussed below in section 10.

In the last year of his life R. Gordon took an innovative step: he tried to set up an organization of Lithuanian yeshivas. His sudden death cut this process short, although it came to fruition after the First World War. As he wrote to R. Moshe Avigdor Haikin:

I am honoured to appeal to [you] . . . in the name of my dear friends, the rabbis and *geonim*, etc. etc., the members of the committee for the five holy yeshivas of our land, that is, our teacher the *gaon* R. Hayim Halevi Soloveitchik of Brisk in Lithuania, our teacher the *gaon* R. Tsevi Hirsh Rabinowitz of Kovno, our teacher the *gaon* R. Hayim Ozer Grodzinski of Vilna, and our teacher the *gaon* R. Eliezer Rabinowitz of Minsk . . . in the hope . . . that you might be willing . . . to be counted among them.

His honour the *gaon* surely knows of the great destruction wrought among our people since . . . last year, may God have mercy upon us, and that since in these days all the branches of trade are linked like a chain, therefore even those towns that were not actually affected by those disturbances have suffered and are suffering terrible damage, and general loss together with this, and terror is all around, may God have mercy.

It is thus easy to understand that the principal yeshivas among our people in our land, such as Volozhin, Telz, Lubavitch, Mir, Lomza, the two yeshivas of Slobodka,

---

[107] D. Katz, *The Musar Movement* (Heb.), v. 34–5.
[108] See Shoshanah, 'Chapters on History and Evaluation' (Heb.); Gifter, 'The Telz Yeshiva' (Heb.), 169–88.

the Kolel Perushim of Kovno, and some other great yeshivas such as Slutsk and Krinik...[109]

R. Gordon went on to explain how the economic and political situation had led to a substantial reduction in support for the yeshivas, and how money collected abroad for the needy of Russia had reached its destination only in part or not at all. He continued:

We therefore established this committee last winter and appealed to the committees that had been collecting contributions abroad for the destitute, and we described the situation of the yeshivas to them, and the committees in Berlin, Vienna, and Hungary, as well as the Jewish Colonization Association in Paris all recognized the truth of our description and extended aid to us ... the aid was insufficient ... we suggested that they send the support by means of Baron Guenzburg ... for since the money that arrives ... simply for the support of the destitute has to be accounted for to the government, may it be exalted, he cannot allocate a particular sum for the yeshivas ...

For many years now the modernist writers have been denigrating the reputation of the yeshivas . . . and especially since they spread malicious reports that the yeshivas only produce hordes of idlers and paupers among our people, whereas the situation is really the exact opposite. For apart from their holy spiritual purpose, the holy yeshivas give us rabbis, ritual slaughterers, elementary and secondary teachers, preachers, and the like, most of whom are gainfully employed.

The main outlines of his plan were adopted in setting up the Va'ad Hayeshivot (Council of Yeshivas) that was active in Poland from about 1924 until the Second World War. The claim that the yeshivas are actually institutions for the vocational training of rabbis and other religious personnel is interesting. Even if this was for the sake of public relations, it shows that there was already recognition among the public that the yeshiva was not intended purely for study. In another letter to R. Haikin, written in the winter of 1907, R. Gordon estimates the numbers of yeshiva students as 'more than ten thousand students, distinguished for their Torah and fear [of Heaven]'.[110]

R. Moshe Mordekhai Epstein, the head of the Keneset Yisra'el yeshiva in Kovno, which belonged to the *musar* movement, wrote to R. Michael Friedlander in London asking him to support his own yeshiva, as well as the Keneset Beit Yitshak yeshiva (which opposed the *musar* movement), and other Lithuanian yeshivas. He explained that since the yeshivas did not enjoy official recognition, they could not receive funds from charitable organizations in Russia. He therefore requested that donors from abroad send their contributions to R. Grodzinski in Vilna, who would assist the rabbis in Kovno, Brisk,

---

[109] This information is taken from a letter by R. Gordon published in Heiman, 'From the Archive of Rabbi Moshe Avigdor Haikin' (Heb.).

[110] Ibid. 173. A lower estimate was suggested above, p. 258 n. 10.

Telz, and Minsk, who would in turn distribute the money to the yeshivas. The letter was written on 'the eve of the holy sabbath of Beshalaḥ [that is, spring] 1906'—in other words, before R. Gordon wrote to R. Haikin.[111] This seems to reflect the same state of organization described by R. Gordon in his letter.[112]

8. Factors Leading to the Disturbances at the Yeshiva

Interruption to study plays a prominent role in the history of all the yeshivas described in previous chapters. There were serious disturbances at Volozhin as a result of R. Berlin's attempt to appoint his son as *rosh yeshivah*, as there were in Telz in response to R. Gordon's attempt to appoint R. Hirshowitz. There were fierce conflicts at Slobodka, too, which eventually led to the split into two yeshivas, Keneset Yisra'el and Keneset Beit Yitshak. At Slobodka the dispute was over attitudes to *musar*, as were most of the disturbances at Telz. However, the disruptions of regular study at Telz were on a far greater scale. Only in Telz did study stop completely, and only in Telz did the *rosh yeshivah* find himself totally isolated. Some of the leaders of the rebellion at Telz, such as Yosef Kahaneman and Avraham Herzfeld, were actually among those closest to R. Gordon, and the dispute did not lessen their affection for him. Moreover, unlike in Slobodka, the rebels in Telz received no support at all from any of the rabbis teaching at the yeshiva or from the press.

To understand the factors underlying the repeated disturbances at Telz, one needs to understand the motivations of both sides. The students' actions can be attributed, at least in part, to the revolutionary spirit of the times. There is no doubt that awareness of political activity in the wider society influenced behaviour at the yeshiva, though there are some fundamental differences. Students were free to leave the yeshiva, and so anyone studying there was doing so of his own free will. At that time, there were good economic and professional reasons for abandoning yeshiva study; and there were people interested in helping those who wanted to leave the yeshiva, so a student who remained was almost by definition committed. A significant distinction between the revolutionary spirit of the time and the struggles of the yeshiva students should be noted. The political activists in the wider society were attempting to change reality, whereas in Telz the rebels were the conservative elements who were opposing the innovations that the *rashei yeshivah* were trying to introduce.

Memoirs about Telz emphasize the devotion to study and the enthusiasm of many of the students who took part in the rebellion, rather than the abandonment of traditional values. Thus, even if the students adopted behaviour

---

[111] Unless there is an error in the year. See ibid. 169–70.

[112] This letter appears in A. Y. Katz, *Personalities and Deeds in the Mirror of the Past* (Heb.), 348–9.

they saw in the society around them, the cause of the dispute lay within the yeshiva rather than outside it. The yeshiva was not really affected by events in the outside world: students may have taken an interest in what was going on around them and may even have left the yeshiva to pursue a secular education, but the general framework continued as before. The relationship between staff and students was inconsistent, with the *rosh yeshivah* being less strict than the *mashgiḥim*. However, there is no evidence that greater strictness led to a change in students' values or behaviour:

All this [political and maskilic activity] was not hidden from the eyes of the authorities at the yeshiva, and the pressure upon R. Lezer [Gordon] for a change in discipline and an increase in restrictions [on students] became more intense; in particular the influence of the *mashgiḥim*, who always viewed the winds blowing in the yeshiva with suspicion, was directed more strongly towards him, and they tried to turn the rabbi's heart away from the group of student leaders, who were dear to him. This pressure was intensified by rabbis from *musar* circles in Kovno, who were working to spread *musar* to all the yeshivas; the special status of the Telz yeshiva, protected by the mighty wings of R. Lezer, was an obstacle to them.[113]

The age of the students was also a contributory factor in the unrest. Most of the students were in their mid-teens, an age characterized by intellectual curiosity and readiness to change attitudes. It is also an age when discipline is hard to accept. The ages of the students at Telz may not have been very different from those at Volozhin a century earlier, but circumstances had changed in the meantime, and what had been a routine situation in the past now caused instability. There were other yeshivas in this period where the students' ages were less of a problem. At Slobodka, where many of the students were in their twenties,[114] the atmosphere was somewhat calmer, though not entirely so.

The students' relationship with the *rosh yeshivah* was good,[115] and dislike of the *rosh yeshivah* did not exist nor could it have been the cause of the strikes and dispute. However, R. Gordon's own behaviour contributed to the unrest. He encouraged independence and commitment. Zuckerman says of him: 'He treated his students in a manner lacking in respect, with denigrating language. If one of them answered a question incorrectly [he] would lay into the wretch ... R. Shimon was the exact opposite in his treatment of the students and was warm, almost loving.'[116] Most of the students, however, saw such behaviour in a more positive light as teaching students not to accept authority.[117] This

---

[113] Sheli, 'Droplets of Telz' (Heb.), 427–8; B. Shulman, 'The Spirit of Revolution in the Yeshivas' (Heb.), 136.   [114] S. Asaf, 'My Study Years at the Telz Yeshiva' (Heb.), 40.

[115] See R. Gordon's speech when the rebellion broke out during Hanukah 1897, in which he emphasized his personal tie to the students; Wahrhaftig, *Offerings of Yeruham* (Heb.), intro. and p. 2.   [116] B. Zuckerman, *Memoirs* (Yid.), 2.

[117] S. Asaf, 'My Study Years at the Telz Yeshiva' (Heb.), 44–5: 'Anyone who has not seen R. Eliezer when he was giving a *shiur* to the students has never seen the joy of Torah ... he would

by-product of R. Gordon's *shiurim* was one of the characteristic features of Telz:

But the most amazing thing was the *shiurim* and the time at which the *shiur* was given . . . at Telz the *shiur* was a sort of *ḥavruta*.[118] From the moment the *rosh yeshivah* opened his mouth, one student would ask something, another would answer, a third would bring a proof, a fourth would counter with a refutation, and the *rosh yeshivah*, full of pleasure that his students were outdoing him, took an active part in these arguments. There would be quiet for a moment, and then they would be at it again. The *rosh yeshivah* delighted in complicated Torah argumentation, and the students were happy as they felt themselves 'ascending the levels of Torah'. The time of the *shiurim* at Telz was not fixed. In summer, when the days were long, the *shiur* would be at four o'clock in the afternoon, even on the sabbath. In winter R. Eliezer would give his *shiur* four hours before dawn.[119]

The atmosphere of freedom and equality existed not only in R. Gordon's *shiurim* but also with R. Shimon Shkop. In the Festschrift for R. Shkop, R. Amiel writes:

I was lucky enough to hear the *shiurim* given by the subject of this book about forty years ago, from 1895 to 1897. When I arrived I was only thirteen, and, as if it were only yesterday, still fixed in my memory, if not the *shiurim* themselves, is the manner in which the *shiurim* were given. The *shiur* usually lasted about two hours, but it was interrupted countless times. At each interruption of the *shiur* a confused babble issued forth from the best students, overwhelming the words of the rabbi, who in my eyes resembled an angel of the Lord of Hosts; nor did they act with *derekh erets* [courtesy] and take care to avoid interrupting each other, but whole gangs of students would attack the teacher at once, and it seemed as though it was a matter of life and death, and that they wanted to fight him in a struggle that knew no bounds or limits. At the same time the great teacher would sit there in perfect tranquillity and

begin seemingly at the lowest level . . . scarcely had five minutes passed when the atmosphere became electric, and the dialogue began—or more accurately, the duel—between him and the best students . . . a student would come up with a problem, and R. Eliezer would immediately charge him with theft: "You have stolen this problem from Maharit [Joseph of Trani, 13th-cent. commentator on Talmud] or from the *Ketsot* [*Ketsot haḥoshen*, commentary by R. Aryeh Leib Heller (1745–1813) on parts of the *Shulḥan arukh*] or from some Tosafot [composite commentary on the Talmud, 12th–13th centuries] on a tractate that not many people study" . . . sometimes he would hurl harsh words at the student who raised a problem, such as "You are a Torah fool!", "You don't know what you're talking about!", "A day-old baby has more intelligence than you!", and so forth; but no student was ever insulted by this. Everyone knew that he was talking to them as a father talks to his children.' It was recorded in the name of R. Kahaneman: 'Once the yeshiva students took an oath not to interrupt their rabbi's *shiur* . . . R. Eliezer arrived to give his *shiur*, and spoke for ten minutes without anyone saying anything or raising any problem . . . he stopped the *shiur* and said "I am not accustomed to giving a *shiur* in the cemetery" and left the room.' See Shurin, *Keshet giborim*, 51.

[118] The traditional form of study in pairs, characterized by lively argument and discussion.
[119] M. Berlin (Bar-Ilan), *From Volozhin to Jerusalem* (Heb.), i. 222.

calm, as though he were saying 'Rejoice my offspring!' Indeed, he was not pleased with the quiet students who sat there in admiring silence. Some of the students had wonderful memories and could repeat the *shiur* word for word without adding or omitting the least thing, but they did not please R. Shimon.[120]

The heady combination that characterized the student body at Telz—their youth, the encouragement of independent thinking, their arrogance,[121] their economic independence, and their organization—as well as R. Gordon's ambiguous attitude towards Zionism and the Haskalah, as will be discussed below, made the imposition of discipline very difficult, and this increased the atmosphere of conflict.

Another major source of strife was the attitude to *musar* in general and the place of *musar* study in Telz in particular. What impelled R. Gordon to introduce *musar* study to the yeshiva? Had he no idea of what the consequences might be? He seems to have thought it would be of benefit to the yeshiva, though he did not identify with the goals of the *musar* movement himself and his attitude to it was ambiguous in spite of—or perhaps because of—his close personal ties with R. Salanter. A hint of R. Gordon's ambiguity appears in a long letter sent to him by R. Simhah Zissel Ziv. The letter, which is undated, is in a sense a congratulatory note on the integration of Talmud study and the teaching of the fear of Heaven in the yeshiva.[122] For a true adherent of the *musar* movement, such a combination would have been obvious and would not have merited words of praise. However, it could not be taken for granted

---

[120] Gindes et al. (eds.), *Festschrift for Rabbi Shimon Yehudah Shkop* (Heb.), 42. Shulman emphasized this difference in his description of the first *shiur* he heard at Sadov, from R. Bloch, after he had left Telz: 'At first light we entered to debate with him, and discovered his expertise in Talmud and his understanding of the *rishonim*. Students who were his long-time admirers were surprised by our boldness and were even afraid that we would suffer for it, but the rabbi seemed to be pleased with it. He was happy that a new current had arrived, fiery and essential to his sleepy yeshiva' ('The Spirit of Revolution in the Yeshivas' (Heb.), 143).

[121] On the students' arrogance, see Sheli, 'Droplets of Telz' (Heb.), 426–7: 'This scale of values implanted in the students of Telz a certain intellectual arrogance and sense of elevation above all the other yeshivas, including Volozhin. As evidence, I remember a play . . . the subject of the play was the closure of the Volozhin yeshiva by the authorities . . . of all its verses I remember the one that ended "they will build you a new sanctuary in Telz". Obviously this was a special addition made by the Telz students . . . this fashion of giving preference to talent over creation, to intention over deed, nurtured in the hearts of many of the students a negative tendency to discount anything that lay outside the realm of their experience and also moulded their behaviour in matters of religion. One moment of deep inner intention was worth all verbal prayer, and true devotion to a religious principle was greater than all the practical commandments associated with it, which were a matter for individuals who could not distinguish between the essential and the marginal.' The play was published in Rivkind, 'From the Volozhin Collections' (Heb.), 365–75. Sheli continues with a description of R. Gordon's influence on his students' characters.

[122] The letter was published in *Moriyah*, 12/7–9 (Oct. 1983), 111–14. I thank Beni Brown for this reference.

because every attempt to introduce *musar* into the yeshiva brought disturbances and violent protests in its wake, yet the attempts were repeated again
and again. Asaf describes R. Gordon's reluctance to introduce *musar* study as
follows:

For a long time the chief *mashgiḥim* had planned to introduce a new spirit to the
yeshiva and to introduce the system of the elders of the *musar* movement. Only *musar*
could persuade students to keep away from the Zionist and more left-wing movements and from reading Haskalah books . . . but R. Eliezer, to whom Torah study
was the main thing and everything else was secondary, did not listen to them; he
feared that *musar* study had something about it that would deflect the students' attention from Torah study, which needs all the spiritual strength of young students.[123]

Friedman writes of R. Gordon in the same vein, both about the Kelme
yeshiva[124] and his attitude to it and about Telz,[125] and R. Me'ir Berlin similarly
comments on the ambiguity of R. Gordon's attitude to *musar*:

His attitude to the question of *musar*, which was then a 'burning issue' at Telz, was
not clear. In one of the talks that he used to give students from time to time, especially at the beginning of term, he spoke of the sons of Joseph, and said that Ephraim
was on a higher level than Manasseh because Ephraim studied Torah, but Manasseh
was only an adherent of the *musar* movement. But when the import of his words,
contradicting the spirit of the yeshiva, was pointed out to him, he immediately went
back and corrected himself, [and said that] in truth Ephraim too was closely associated with *musar* . . . however all this did not diminish his importance since everything flowed not from his spiritual qualities, which were completely perfect, but
from his superb intellectual talents.[126]

Asaf writes:

I remember that we once went to see the rabbi, because we wanted him not to
expel students, and not to write *lo yavo'u* ['shall not attend'] against students under
suspicion without first consulting the committee, and in order to set his mind at

---

[123] S. Asaf, 'My Study Years at the Telz Yeshiva' (Heb.), 40.

[124] A. A. Friedman, *Memoirs* (Heb.), 101: 'However, R. Simhah Zissel and his gang exerted
great pressure on the rabbi . . . once the rabbi called me to his special room and tried to persuade
me to agree to accept three young men from R. Simhah Zissel's *talmud torah*. "Surely you know",
said the rabbi, ". . . that I am forced to do this. For if I do not comply in this matter the flame of
a great controversy will be lit in the town by his devotees . . . therefore please agree to my request
and persuade your companions to agree to it, and I will be very grateful to them."'

[125] Ibid. 106: 'The rabbi himself, who, when he dwelt in Kelme, was a great opponent of R.
Simhah Zissel's group and of all the *musar* sects, allowed one of the *musarniks* of Kelme to come
to Telz as . . . a *mashgiaḥ* . . . this was in 1897 . . . when I found out about this I asked my rabbi
why he was allowing one of the *musarniks* to set foot in the yeshiva, since he had always opposed
them. He answered that his attitude to the *musarniks* had not changed in the least, but that he
had accepted this *mashgiaḥ* because he was a great expert in this subject and diligent in his work.'

[126] M. Berlin (Bar-Ilan), *From Volozhin to Jerusalem* (Heb.), i. 220.

rest we said to him: 'Rabbi, at Slobodka too some of the best students have some influence on the course of events at the yeshiva.' And he answered us: 'What, are you comparing Telz to Slobodka? Are there students at Slobodka? They are lumps of wood! If R. Neta Hirsh told them, "Jump into the water!", they would jump into the water, while every Telz student knows his own mind.' The rabbi's love for his students and his pride in them stood out in this conversation, in spite of the bitterness they caused him by their actions from time to time.[127]

Given all the above, the question of why R. Gordon wanted to introduce *musar* at Telz is mystifying. Was the state of study at the yeshiva so dire that he was compelled to accept his colleagues' opinions? Was he influenced by pressure from the rabbis of Kovno who supported the *musar* movement? Or perhaps the pressure came from nearer home, from his son-in-law R. Bloch? Perhaps it derived from his sense that traditional society was collapsing. In any case, it was not difficult for students to sense that they were getting conflicting messages from R. Gordon. Whatever the reason, it seems to have been associated with R. Gordon's general sense of crisis in Jewish society; however, before examining this we should first consider his attitude to the Haskalah and to Zionism.

9. R. Gordon's Attitude to the Haskalah and to Zionism

One of the goals of introducing *musar* study to the yeshiva was to counter the students' leanings towards openly modernizing movements, such as Zionism and the Haskalah. However, R. Gordon's own attitude to both of these was just as ambiguous as his attitude to *musar*.

There were almost no supporters of Zionism among the leaders of the *musar* movement.[128] R. Bloch was certainly no Zionist. However, the situation with regard to R. Gordon was more complex, as it was with R. Berlin. He commented on this in 1889 as follows:

For some seven years I supported the idea of the commandment of settling the Land of Israel with all my heart, as demonstrated by the two letters I wrote to two of the greatest rabbis of our generation, but afterwards, to the grief of our hearts and the hearts of the wise who fear God, by the fault of the freethinking members of the new generation, this idea was stripped of its holy character and took on another form, which God-fearing people who understand cannot approve, so I withdrew my support from this idea . . . and since this idea of the commandments of settling the Land of Israel is holy in my eyes, I suggest that it not be abandoned but that it should be carried out in holy purity as will be explained later . . . and in every town where there is a branch [of the Zionist movement whose members] are observant

---

[127] S. Asaf, 'My Study Years at the Telz Yeshiva' (Heb.), 42.

[128] This was not true of all rabbis in the movement, and there were indeed some, like R. Moshe Mordekhai Epstein, who were associated with Hibat Zion groups for a while.

Jews who love the commandment of settling the Land of Israel in all its practical and spiritual aspects, in order to observe the commandments that are related to the land or [if such a society] be founded from now onwards, let it be one of their basic principles that the money that is collected should not be sent to anyone at all except the committee in Jerusalem . . . for the committee will supervise the colonies so that they act in accordance with the law of Moses and Israel in all its most minute details, as is fitting for the inhabitants of the pure Holy Land, and in particular that they should observe the commandments related to the land.[129]

There is abundant evidence of R. Gordon's activity in Hibat Zion or the early Zionist movement before the militantly secular Leon Pinsker (1821–91) was elected as its chairman at the Katowice conference in 1884.[130] From the 1890s until his death in 1910 Gordon was close to several people who were fiercely opposed to Zionism, people such as R. Hayim Ozer Grodzinski, Ya'akov Lifschitz, R. Hayim Soloveitchik, and others. However, even though he became known as an opponent of the Zionist movement, his attitude was not like that of the others. R. Ya'akov Mazeh (1859–1924), the enlightened Zionist rabbi of Moscow, described him as 'one of the most excellent of the extremist rabbis';[131] the dialogue between them reveals that their opposition was tempered by tolerance. R. Mazeh claimed that 'every rabbi who opposes Zionism obstructs the people in this holy work; he has no right to ask for support for his institutions'. R. Gordon replied:

First of all, I do not obstruct the work of the Zionist emissaries, and there are also many Zionists in my town, and many of the town's inhabitants bring substantial donations to the Land of Israel fund, and I have never protested against this, Heaven forbid; secondly, according to all opinions Torah study is equivalent to everything, and if there is no Torah, what does Zion matter? Thirdly, the rabbi [meaning himself] cannot participate in Zionist matters, since the individual who leads the movement is not observant.[132]

His ambivalence is clear, however, from the fact that—as R. Mazeh noted— one of the most important emissaries of the Telz yeshiva was an enthusiastic Zionist.[133] R. Gordon was also tolerant of yeshiva students who engaged in the Haskalah and Zionist activity, as long as they were good students. Asaf recalls:

A Zionist circle was founded, composed of townsfolk and yeshiva students, in order to investigate and understand various current problems . . . and it was decided to arrange a course of public lectures on Jewish history; I was appointed to open the

---

[129] Epel, *At the Beginning of the Revival* (Heb.), 547–9. See also Z. A. Rabiner, *The Gaon Rabbi Eliezer Gordon* (Heb.), 125–35.

[130] Z. A. Rabiner, *The Gaon Rabbi Eliezer Gordon* (Heb.), 125–35.

[131] Mazeh, *Memoirs* (Heb.), iv. 120.   [132] Ibid. 124.

[133] Ibid. ii. 102; see also A. A. Friedman, *Memoirs* (Heb.), 58.

series of lectures . . . many people came to my lecture, including many yeshiva students . . . the *mashgiḥim* realized that many students were missing and found out the reason for this. Of course they were furious with me. Such a thing had never happened at the yeshiva, that a student should give a public lecture and attract many other students to it. On Sunday I was summoned to the rabbi again, and he said to me, 'They told me about your lecture and its contents. I did not find any heresy in it, God forbid, but you have caused many people to waste Torah study time, and why did you not ask me first? You were here on Friday!' I said to him, 'Rabbi, if I had asked your honour, would you have agreed?' He smiled and said, '*Nu, nu,* in future it would be better if you asked me. The *mashgiḥim* are very angry with you. But I have told them to leave you alone, since you are a diligent student in Torah.'[134]

It is thus not surprising that in 1905—in other words, two years after R. Gordon wrote the letter quoted above—R. Yitshak Ya'akov Reines suggested that he should join him in Mizrahi, the religious Zionist movement that he headed.[135] It is difficult to imagine that R. Reines would have made such an appeal if he expected a negative response.

R. Gordon's attitude to the Haskalah was similarly complex. Asaf writes:

I have to thank the rabbi for the fact that I was not sent away like many other students whose sins were fewer than mine. He stood up for me against all those who accused me. The yeshiva authorities knew perfectly well . . . that I had become a follower of the Haskalah, and I had been caught red-handed twice . . . one day I was summoned to the rabbi and he said to me, 'I think that you should learn Russian. I see that you are involved with your fellow men and interested in the questions of life, and it would be good for you to know the language of the state.' I was very surprised, and felt sure that he had never made such a suggestion to any other student. I immediately thought that he sought to distract me from reading heretical books by this device. I said to him, 'Rabbi, I too have been thinking of doing this.' I began studying Russian, and my teacher was the rabbi's son, who had taken an external gymnasium course. I used to do my homework in the attic of the rabbi's house.[136]

Ya'akov Marek, a contemporary of R. Gordon who knew the rabbinic world well, comments:

R. Eliezer was the first of the new type of rabbi in the last generation in Russia. Those rabbis who were also experienced in worldly affairs betook themselves to the service of the public and took public affairs out of the hands of the ignorant leaders . . . his house was always full of people coming to ask his advice, especially in matters related to the laws of the Russian government, and thanks to this one could see on

---

[134] S. Asaf, 'My Study Years at the Telz Yeshiva' (Heb.), 42–3.

[135] Y. Y. Reines, *Shenei hame'orot*, vol. ii, pt. 1, ch. 4, p. 38, on R. Gordon's appeal to R. Reines. R. Reines' message to R. Gordon is mentioned in Z. A. Rabiner, *The Gaon Rabbi Eliezer Gordon* (Heb.), 142.   [136] S. Asaf, 'My Study Years at the Telz Yeshiva' (Heb.), 43.

his desk, among other books, the Russian law code, in which he was more expert than a lawyer.[137]

The attitude in Telz to Haskalah literature varied over time. Asaf notes that in his time, reading secular books was seen as a sufficient reason for expulsion from the yeshiva,[138] but a few years later Shulman wrote:

> There was a tradition of freedom at the yeshiva from its very foundation; the students read newspapers, journals, and books in Yiddish and Hebrew without any opposition. There were people who obtained 'underground' literature for us from outside and some of the students were interested in it. Indeed, the *mashgiah*—a skinny man with a pointed little beard—knew all about this but did not take any punitive measures against those who indulged in this type of literature. He was with us at the yeshiva all day long, studying by himself or talking about talmudic issues with various students. There was no spying on how students occupied themselves at home. If a student stopped coming to the yeshiva and started going around with those who 'had left their studies and abandoned tradition', the yeshiva authorities would send a *lo yavo* letter [meaning that the student should not return to the yeshiva] at the end of term—before Pesah or Sukkot—when the students travelled home.[139]

As at Volozhin, punishments were meted out for wasting time, not for occupation in secular studies per se. Interest in the Haskalah existed within R. Gordon's own family. Asaf's evidence that the rabbi's son possessed considerable secular knowledge and had studied Russian has already been quoted. His son-in-law, R. Hirshowitz, was 'from Courland, and had a certain amount of secular education; he also knew German and had read German literature'.[140] R. Gordon's second son-in-law, R. Zalman Sorotskin, was reported to have 'completed secular studies' in a short time 'and passed the external matriculation examinations in Courland together with N. Y. Steinberg'.[141] R. Gordon himself was interested in the Haskalah and read maskilic literature.[142] It is

---

[137] Marek, *In the Company of the Great Men of the Generation* (Heb.), 24.

[138] See also B. Zuckerman, *Memoirs* (Yid.), 70, on the opposition of the *mashgihim* to Haskalah literature.   [139] B. Shulman, 'The Spirit of Revolution in the Yeshivas' (Heb.), 136.

[140] S. Asaf, 'My Study Years at the Telz Yeshiva' (Heb.), 38.

[141] Sorotskin, 'The Life of Rabbi Zalman Sorotskin' (Yid.), 233.

[142] Dinur, *In a World that Went Under* (Heb.), 73: 'The first person at Telz who aroused in me the will and desire to search in Haskalah books and who showed me how to find them was R. Eliezer Gordon, in his talks, during which he used to fulminate against the maskilim. The rabbi used to mention Graetz and Weiss in particular, and often used to quote from [Naftali Herz] Wessely and praise his *Sefer hamidot* [Book of Virtues]. He loved to mention the names of other early maskilim in his talks . . . once the rabbi took issue with Weiss over [the halakhic concept of] *halakhah lemoshe misinai* and the Oral Law, and he also mentioned Zekhariah Frankel's book *Darkhei hamishnah*. I deduced from this that there were many Haskalah books in the rabbi's house. I made friends with the rabbi's son, Shmuel . . . and he used to get me books regularly.' Dinur went on to describe a large group of students who clubbed together for a subscription to

clear that a man who himself displayed a certain openness to Zionism and the Haskalah would have found it difficult to take a strong stand against those who were interested in these spheres.

10. R. Gordon's Confrontation with the Social Crisis

Like those who supported the *musar* movement, R. Gordon acted out of a sense that east European Jewry was in crisis. This is clear from a letter he wrote near the end of his life, in 1907, responding to an invitation to become the rabbi of Jerusalem:

It would be desirable to accept the rabbinate of Jerusalem, since because of our many sins an unimaginable amount of heresy has broken out in our land among all the youth, boys and girls, and every day we see that the boys and girls who yesterday were at peace with God and his Torah have today become rebellious, Heaven have mercy; and even though my sons and daughters, thanks be to God, are walking in the way of Torah and fear [of Heaven], who can tell what will happen, God forbid, with them in a few years. And because of this, it is most necessary to escape from our country to Jerusalem, our holy city, where heresy is not so prevalent, as in all the cities of our holy land.[143]

On the other hand, he went on to point out that while there were greater Torah scholars than he in Jerusalem, the level of Torah study was lower in Palestine than in the yeshivas of Lithuania, and that he had greater experience in giving *shiurim* than the rabbis in Jerusalem. In other words, he saw his mastery of new methods of Talmud study as a skill he could contribute to the Jerusalem Jewish community.[144] Indeed, R. Gordon also adopted modern

the newspaper *Hamelits*. Dinur's description is very interesting, since it is usual to regard the yeshivas as fortresses against the Haskalah. Obviously the yeshiva leaders encouraged this view, since it helped them to raise money and strengthen their institutions' position in the rabbinic world. However, the reality was much more complex, and these institutions sometimes served as a channel for the Haskalah. This is why some parents were opposed to their sons studying at Telz. See A. Wasser's report in Gindes et al. (eds.), *Festschrift for Rabbi Shimon Yehudah Shkop* (Heb.), 55, describing a young man who wanted to go to yeshiva; his father opposed this precisely because he feared that his son would turn his back on religion, as had happened with a young man of his acquaintance who had gone to yeshiva and been corrupted.

[143] The letter is published in Ostrovsky (ed.), *Man of Jerusalem* (Heb.), 67–9.

[144] This was no exaggeration on the part of R. Gordon, since the new method developed by him and R. Shkop had indeed conquered all hearts. The importance of new study methods has been discussed above in my analysis of R. Hayim Soloveitchik (Ch. 4, §2). Here I will restrict myself to observing that the students who used the analytical method escaped from any feeling of inferiority towards Haskalah methods of study and found tremendous satisfaction in the possibilities of original thought available to them. An interesting reaction to this study method appears in R. Amiel's comment on R. Shkop: 'In truth, "there is nothing new under the sun", and this innovation that was invented in the *beit midrash* of the Telz yeshiva is no more than a restoration of former glories . . . the "analytical method", as R. Shimon himself called his

working methods in spheres other than education. We shall consider two cases of this that shed light, indirectly, on his tendency to innovate in education.

The first example is his failed attempt to found a strictly Orthodox daily newspaper that could compete with non-traditional journalism. His grandson describes it thus:

> Our rabbi saw the reasons for this [the weakness of traditional society] in the free press, which had begun to appear every day and penetrated every Jewish home, sowing poison and mockery of all holy Jewish things, and in the new outlooks which were flooding the Jewish street: the secular nationalism and socialism that had settled there. Our rabbi initiated and summoned meetings of rabbis to discuss how to strengthen and promote religion, and called for the faithful in Russia to organize in a single league in order to maintain religion and stand in the breach against the various freethinkers. Our rabbi saw the foundation of a daily religious newspaper of the highest literary quality as the most immediate goal; it would banish the free-thinking journalists from observant homes and would fight the war of religion against the secular streams of thought.[145]

The second example is R. Gordon's attempt to organize the traditional community into a political body, an idea which later was achieved in the form of Agudat Yisra'el. About this attempt, the same grandson wrote:

> Together with the great scholars the *gaon* R. Hayim Soloveitchik of Brisk and the *gaon* R. Hayim Ozer Grodzinski . . . he worked to set up a strictly Orthodox organization that would include all the rabbis and observant Jews of Russia, and several lively meetings were held for this purpose. Eventually the basis was laid for the Keneset Yisra'el organization, which was actually the foundation stone of the world-wide strictly Orthodox organization Agudat Yisra'el. He also took part in the Hamburg meeting, where the leaders and scholars of east European Jewry met for the first time.[146]

method, is a method used by the *rishonim*, though the original method was partly forgotten during the generations of the *aharonim* . . . R. Shimon came and made the analysis and the hidden depths public knowledge. When I arrived at Telz as a young lad, I had already heard "disputes" [*hilukim*, lit. 'divisions'] from various rabbis and scholars, and that was the right word for them in those days—they were an assemblage of different issues with no logical connection between them . . . but in Telz I heard disputation of a completely different type: this was R. Shimon's disputation, which was a genuine "division" between matters that from their external form could be classed together, but after deeper analysis is applied to their inner nature, are revealed as completely separate' (in Gindes et al. (eds.), *Festschrift for Rabbi Shimon Yehudah Shkop* (Heb.), 42–3). R. Amiel links the importance of the human intellect, the decline of study in recent generations, and the deep impression made by the Telz method of study on yeshiva students who had been educated in totally different way. In fact, the experience of the novelty of this method resembled the experience of the first encounter with *musar* study. Of course the author emphasized that ultimately this was not an innovation but a return to the ways of the *rishonim*.   [145] Sorotskin, 'These Are the Generations' (Heb.), 116.

[146] Ibid. 117. See also the material in Z. A. Rabiner, *The Gaon Rabbi Eliezer Gordon* (Heb.), 142–5, with other examples of R. Gordon's public activity.

Like the Jewish organizations with which it was competing, such as the Zionist movement and the Bund, Keneset Yisra'el and later Agudat Yisra'el adopted modern methods, though in this case the aim of doing so was to defend tradition rather than to bring about change. It should be noted that the leaders of the *musar* movement were conspicuous by their absence from the group that founded Keneset Yisra'el.

R. Gordon's strategy was similar but not identical to that of other rabbis of his time, and the comparisons are illuminating. For example, R. Gordon's attitude to Hibat Zion was very similar to that of R. Berlin: they both saw it in a positive light since its aims were very traditional. R. Gordon and R. Berlin similarly shared a belief in the centrality of Torah study and an admiration for—or more accurately, a lack of opposition to—engagement in intellectual spheres or membership of movements that did not oppose tradition. We have already seen R. Gordon's tolerant attitude towards the study of Russian, and to some extent, towards reading Haskalah literature. R. Berlin's position was similar.[147] He valued Hebrew literary style, which shows that he had a positive attitude towards aspects of culture that were not part of Torah study in the narrow sense.

R. Berlin's and R. Gordon's yeshivas both introduced changes to the traditional model, the one in content and the other in structure.[148] Certain biographical details that they shared may explain their willingness to accept change. Both grew up in an environment free of major conflicts and absorbed the idea of Torah study as the supreme Jewish value. Their exposure to other ideas came only after they were already mature, and it seems that the experience did not shake their basic confidence in the value system they had acquired in their youth. In contrast, most of the people who supported the *musar* movement had grown up in a more complex environment, as had R. Hayim Soloveitchik, and they tended to more extreme methods than those adopted by R. Berlin and R. Gordon, and even ventured to propose content-based changes that altered traditional patterns. Both R. Berlin and R. Gordon considered such steps unnecessarily extreme.[149]

Nevertheless, R. Gordon was aware of the collapse of traditional society and felt the need to act. He drew on the methods of the *musar* movement not only because of pressure from those close to him, but also because he saw the

---

[147] M. Berlin (Bar-Ilan), *From Volozhin to Jerusalem* (Heb.), i. 129–30.

[148] By making this distinction between change in content and in structure, it would at first seem that R. Gordon's innovations in methods of Talmud study are being ignored, since at first sight these would appear to be purely a matter of content. However, the terms 'content' and 'structure' are being used here in relation to organization and values and thus do not apply to innovations in study methods. It should be noted that, in fact, innovation in study methods is the most traditional feature of Lithuanian Talmud study. In contrast, the traditional scholarly world saw fewer attempts to make far-reaching changes in the sphere of values. It is clear that R. Gordon's activity at Telz was regarded as an innovation.

[149] I arrived at this analysis after reading Lipset, *Political Man*, ch. 8.

signs of crisis in the yeshiva, even if in the all-important area of Torah study it was functioning properly. Driven by this sense of crisis, he adopted *musar* methods even though they accorded with neither his personal educational views nor students' expectations. His attempt failed partly because he regarded *musar* methods purely as a means to an end, while the very nature of the *musar* system required that it be seen as central. Many of his students stayed faithful to him at the personal level, thanks to his greatness as a scholar and teacher and his other personal qualities, but they internalized only some of his values and thus strongly opposed the technique he wanted to introduce. In fact, his students often adopted his own ambiguous position to perfection. Their persistence in studying during their strike demonstrated the devotion to Torah study with which he had inspired them, proving to him just how much he had influenced them: their nominal allegiance to political and Zionist organizations and their interest in Haskalah literature were insufficient to counter the personal example he had set them.

R. Gordon's complex attitudes made it impossible for him to calm the unrest at the yeshiva. Some students wanted to study *musar* as well as Talmud, some opposed *musar*. There were Haskalah enthusiasts alongside conservatives, and political activists alongside those who desired nothing more than traditional Torah study. It was only when R. Bloch became *rosh yeshivah* and set out the educational approach in clear and uncompromising terms that calm returned. Any student who could not come to terms with his policy simply left. This is the only way to explain the peace that prevailed at Telz after 1910, in contrast to the troubles of previous years.

The change was due entirely to the personality and method of the new *rosh yeshivah*. One of the students describes R. Bloch as a strict, outstanding personality who stayed aloof from the students.[150] He records how everyone missed R. Gordon, who was 'simple, passionate, and natural'. Others wrote in a similar vein. Another student wrote in his memoirs: '[R. Bloch's] heart was as hard as his mind was penetrating and deep, especially in his youth, and thus he inspired hatred among some of the yeshiva students.'[151]

After marrying R. Gordon's daughter, R. Bloch had lived for several years in Kelme, where he saw the *musar* movement at close hand. He accepted its conceptual path but was not drawn to its leaders. He was a strict disciplinarian; affection for a student or recognition of special talents never led him to bend the rules. It was this and his attitude to *musar* that led to his departure from Kelme. When he returned to Telz, he placed great emphasis on the study of Jewish thought—of which *musar* could be regarded as a key element— together with Talmud study. An adherent of the *musar* movement describes his policy thus:

[150] B. Shulman, 'The Spirit of Revolution in the Yeshivas' (Heb.), 142.
[151] Sorski, *Torah and Musar Teachers* (Heb.), ii. 30.

The *gaon* R. Yosef Leib gave the fifth *shiur* instead of R. Eliezer, and *musar* talks began to be given at the yeshiva, with all the students compelled to attend; though our teacher R. Yosef Leib did not give '*musar* talks' to his students but 'lessons in the knowledge of God' [*shiurei da'at hashem*]. It should be noted that the *gaon* R. Yosef Leib was brilliant both in halakhah and in Jewish philosophy. His knowledge of the whole Talmud and all its commentators was deep and thorough. His *shiurim* on halakhah were renowned throughout Lithuania and thousands learnt how to study from them. In addition to all this he was a genius in Jewish philosophy—in faith, fear [of Heaven], and the knowledge of God; a divine philosopher to whom the paths of true wisdom lay open. In this field of study too, as in his Talmud knowledge, he blazed his own trails. From the time he was appointed *rosh yeshivah* there was no more need for a special spiritual director to encourage the students to acquire the fear of Heaven and refine their characters. Our teacher R. Yosef Leib taught that only one who is great in halakhah can also teach matters pertaining to the fear of Heaven. Halakhah and philosophical matters were not divided in his thought into two separate subjects, for he had the same attitude to each of them, built on the foundations of knowledge and understanding. In the *gaon* R. Yosef Leib's opinion, *musar* should be based on halakhic foundations; for without this, mistakes could be made in *musar*. But *musar* could also influence the halakhah; only by using both of them could an all-encompassing world view be created. R. Yosef Leib aspired to shape the entire spiritual stature of each student: he developed [a student's] talents in halakhah and instilled in him a Torah world view that illumined his duty in the world and his aim in life.[152]

Whether these words should be taken at face value or not, R. Bloch's policy of combining the teaching of *musar* and of Talmud is clear. In his opinion, they both came from the same authoritative source, and he believed passionately in their importance and in the importance of combining them. The yeshiva's policy was unambiguous, and those who did not agree with it left. The stormy years of the Telz yeshiva were over. R. Bloch succeeded in directing the yeshiva, consistently and methodically, without any further disturbances, until his death in 1930.

[152] Shoshanah, 'Chapters on History and Evaluation' (Heb.), 276.

ELEVEN

The Kolel Perushim of Kovno and the Institution of the Kolel

1. The Founding and Early History of the Kolel Perushim

IN 1880 A NEW TYPE of institution was founded in Kovno—the Kolel Perushim—and like the yeshiva it became an important element in the provision of a traditional Jewish education.

A *kolel* was, and is, an institution that regularly distributes money to a defined group of married men, usually young, who devote all their time to Torah study. *Perushim* are men who leave their families to study Torah in temporary celibacy, almost always in a place other than where their families live. The Kolel Perushim, then, was a framework for financial support for a group of married students. The *kolel* of eastern Europe was not a totally new innovation. The Torah scholars who emigrated to Palestine in previous generations organized themselves into *kolelim* according to their country of origin—though it should be noted that the members of the *kolelim* in Palestine were not *perushim*. These *kolelim* raised funds, usually in their country of origin and then distributed the money raised among the members of the *kolel*. The members of these *kolelim* did not necessarily study in a common, shared study hall nor did they have an obligatory programme of study. The *kolel* did not organize study but dealt with financial needs. Until 1880, there were no *kolelim* in eastern Europe. Hence the novelty of the one for married students established in Kovno in 1880. It was similar to those of Palestine, but membership was open not to all scholars from a given place or region but rather to a selected group of young married students; it provided its students with money but did not restrict them to study in a particular communal study framework or to follow a common curriculum.[1]

Support for young married scholars among European (and non-European) Jewry was not an innovation of the late nineteenth century. In previous generations, this had been done in a number of ways. One classic structure was the *kloyz*, a framework for supporting full-time students who would study in

---

[1] See D. Katz, *The Musar Movement* (Heb.), vol. iii, ch. 1, and ch. 16, §3, and the bibliography.

a private study hall (*kloyz*) that was usually named after a key donor. Funds usually came from local Jews and often solely from a single wealthy family.[2] Rich fathers-in-law supported their sons-in-law, economically active women supported their husbands, and young scholars found themselves employment as rabbis. In some communities this support was very organized. For instance, in 1864 an organization called Tomkhei Torah ('Supporters of the Torah') was set up in Minsk.[3] Funds were originally raised locally, but later came from the surrounding area too. However, the community's ability to support such an institution was limited. Minsk was an important community, but even with devoted volunteers making huge efforts it could not support more than about thirty scholars.

At the end of the nineteenth century, however, the situation changed completely. Wealthy men no longer wanted to marry their daughters to young Torah scholars, so the latter had to make do with less affluent wives or with rabbis' daughters. At the same time, urbanization meant that population growth was not matched by growth in the number of Jewish communities— or of rabbinical posts. This meant more competition for rabbinical posts. For those young men who anticipated becoming rabbis, the pressure for posts could easily lead to a delay in finding a position. Until they found such a post, they needed support. There was thus a need for a new way to fund young married men to continue devoting themselves to studying Torah, which meant that a new sort of institution was required.

The distinctive feature of the new type of *kolel*, like the new type of yeshiva, was that it was funded as a supra-community institution. Financial support came from people who shared a common attitude to Torah study rather than a common place of origin. The originator of the concept was R. Ya'akov Reines, who came up with the plan for such an institution in 1875:

What is most necessary in these times is to establish a special place, with a licence from the government, from whence Torah may emerge; there men of intellect, whom God has graced with great abilities, will gather to engage in God's Torah until they are worthy and trained to be adorned with the crown of the rabbinate, which will match the glory of their community, to guide the holy flock in the ways of Torah and the fear of Heaven. There are some who are worthy to ascend the steps to be a light to their people, but who have been torn away from the breasts of Torah because of the poverty and lack that oppress them and their families. How many have taken the rabbinate upon themselves before they were ready, and the teeth of their communities have been blunted because of them; how many have struggled to become rabbis using despicable and low means, and [as a consequence] all those who have thirsted for the assistance of a rabbi have found no help, for until we learn to tear out this disease by its roots, all our efforts will be in vain. And the surest

---

[2] See Reiner, 'Capital, Social Status, and Torah Study' (Heb.).

[3] Rosenstein, *Writings* (Heb.), 90–3.

medicine for this disease is that these students should have somewhere to sit and study Torah that will maintain them and their families with dignity. For all these have done what they did only because of the struggle with the terrible and pressing hand [of poverty].[4]

R. Reines intended his *kolel* to be associated with the Volozhin yeshiva,[5] although the nature of his relationship with R. Berlin is not entirely clear.[6] R. Berlin agreed in principle, however, and further agreed that R. Hayim Hillel Fried, his former rival for the post of *rosh yeshivah*, would be its director. However, the plan was shelved for lack of funds.

In 1878 it was proposed to persuade the Brodsky family to fund the *kolel*.[7] The Brodsky's were extremely wealthy, having made a fortune in sugar production, and they were involved in Jewish educational initiatives. Among those active in trying to establish it was Rebbetzin Reina, R. Fried's mother, who was concerned to find a suitable post for her son. It was suggested that donations be collected from all the men of the Brodsky family, but, for reasons unknown, this never happened, and the Volozhin yeshiva seems to have been unable to raise the necessary sum. R. Reines's son says that 'people opposed him', though he gives no further details.[8] There was an unexpected consequence of the initiative, however. During his search for people who might be interested in the idea of the *kolel*, R. Reines travelled to see R. Alexander Moshe Lapidot, the rabbi of Raseiniai. He was not there but in Janishok, so R. Reines followed him there.

No precise details are known of their meeting and its results, but the trip led to the growth of links between R. Reines and a Jew from Janishok, Eliezer Moshe Habas. According to Moshe Reines (son of R. Reines and a scholar in his own right),[9] Habas was 'an average Jew but a true God-fearer'.[10] He was excited by the idea of the *kolel* and decided to travel to Berlin to see his wealthy brother, Yosef Hayim Habas, in the hope that the latter would help raise funds through his circle of associates. In 1877 Habas left on his mission, bearing a letter of recommendation from R. Lapidot. He travelled first to Kovno to seek the support of R. Yitshak Elhanan Spektor, but R. Spektor's secretary, Ya'akov

---

[4] Y. Y. Reines, *Hotam tokhnit*, i. 17 n. 4; see also p. 18.

[5] On the plan to annex the *kolel* to the Volozhin yeshiva, see 'The Letters of R. Berlin', in M. Reines, 'Dwelling-Places of Torah' (Heb.), 23–5.

[6] The new edition of the responsa collection *Meshiv davar*, vol. v, para. 44, includes a letter from R. Berlin to R. Reines, written in 1887, which criticizes R. Reines's book *Orim gedolim*.

[7] See the letter to Rivkah Miriam, written in 1878; the original is in the Rabinowitz Collection, housed in the Manuscript Collection of the National and University Library in Jerusalem.   [8] M. Reines, 'Dwelling-Places of Torah' (Heb.), 25.   [9] Ibid. 27.

[10] Habas was a relative of Eliyahu Me'ir Feivelson and later became the father-in-law of R. Naftali Trop. When he married his daughter off, he wrote to his son-in-law, 'Thanks be to God that I have merited finding a bridegroom for my daughter who is capable of nothing except of being a great Jewish scholar.' See Kul, *Alone in his Generation* (Heb.), 90.

Lifschitz, thought the project unfeasible and turned him away.[11] Undeterred, Habas continued to Berlin and succeeded in persuading his brother Yosef to support the plan.[12] Yosef promised to donate 100 roubles a year, but more importantly he persuaded his wealthy friend Ovadiah Lachman to support the *kolel* too. In fact, Lachman was to become the *kolel*'s principal benefactor: he set up an endowment fund of about a 1,000 roubles per annum, 'which in those days was an extremely generous contribution', and the interest was set aside to support the institution.[13] It seems likely that the money was not donated for the express purpose of establishing a *kolel*, and that Habas was allowed to spend it as he saw fit.

Habas went to ask R. Yisra'el Salanter about how to use the money, and R. Salanter seconded the idea of establishing a *kolel*. Habas asked R. Lapidot to head the institution, but the latter refused and suggested R. Spektor in Kovno instead.[14] Both these rabbis had close ties with R. Salanter. All the sources record that R. Spektor hesitated, but eventually agreed to take responsibility for the *kolel*, which was given the name Kolel Perushim of Kovno.[15] In fact he did not intend to direct the *kolel* personally, and appointed his son R. Tsevi Hirsh Rabinowitz as *rosh kolel* (head of the *kolel*) in his stead. As will be seen however, the son similarly did not take on responsibility for the day-to-day administration.

This was a complicated process because, as mentioned above, the original initiative had come from R. Reines. However, by the time the *kolel* was established, he had ceased to play any role in it. According to Reines's son, when his father had originally come up with the idea, R. Lapidot had agreed that the *kolel* would be set up in Volozhin and that R. Berlin would act as its head, with R. Hayim Hillel Fried responsible for administration.[16] However, despite the fact the money was found, this is not what happened.[17] R. Reines's son explains that there was yet another intermediary, R. Yitshak Blaser, who was a well known figure in the *musar* movement:

[11] Lifschitz, *Zikhron ya'akov*, iii. 222.	[12] Ibid.

[13] Ibid. 223; see also Y. Y. Reines, *Ḥotam tokhnit*, i. 18. This is the same Lachman who later supported the yeshivas of Telz and Slobodka, as recorded above.

[14] D. Katz, *The Musar Movement* (Heb.), i. 192.	[15] Lifschitz, *Zikhron ya'akov*, iii. 223.

[16] M. Reines, 'Dwelling-Places of Torah' (Heb.), 27–8.

[17] R. Reines does not explain why R. Lapidot did not co-operate, but a possible explanation may be suggested. In 1882 R. Reines tried to found an institution at which both sacred and secular subjects would be studied, in order to train a new generation of rabbis (see below, and also Salmon, 'The Beginning of the Reform of East European Yeshivas' (Heb.)). It is possible that his opinions and plans were already common knowledge by 1879, and that R. Lapidot, who was a disciple of R. Salanter, withdrew from association with him and turned instead to R. Spektor. Appealing to R. Spektor, who was the most prominent rabbi of the generation, was a wise move in practical terms, since his very name was sufficient to ensure public support. However, there is a difficulty with this suggestion, since R. Reines did support the *musar* movement subsequently.

Then the matter of the *perushim* came to the *gaon* R. Yitshak Blaser . . . and the donation of the illustrious L. N. [= Lachman] was placed under his control. Who chose him? And why did they choose him and none else? I have found no answer to these questions. It seems that L. N. had his eye on R. Blaser because he was a disciple of the exalted *gaon* R. Yisra'el of Salant . . . who was valued and beloved in the eyes of the illustrious man.[18]

The establishment of the *kolel* in Kovno rather than in Volozhin seems to have been a consequence of opposition in some quarters to Volozhin. Moshe Tzinovitz writes:

The foundation of the Kovno *kolel* was something of an obstacle for the Volozhin yeshiva. The establishment of this important talmudic institution strengthened the 'other side' in the Torah world of Lithuania, which had always remained distant from this famous yeshiva, for several reasons. The chief opponent was R. Reuven, the *av beit din* of Dvinsk. The heads and administrators of the Volozhin yeshiva were grieved by this and made efforts to remove the enmity from his heart.[19]

He also claims that R. Hayim Soloveitchik travelled to meet R. Reuven in an attempt to win him over. The reference is apparently to R. Reuven Halevi Levine who was a rabbi in Dvinsk but it is not clear why he was opposed to the idea. Tzinovitz knew a great deal about the yeshiva world; if he did not want to offer details, he had his reasons. The existence of a party that was opposed to the Volozhin yeshiva is not attested elsewhere.

It seems very likely that one of those involved in locating the *kolel* in Kovno was R. Natan Tsevi Finkel, the founder of the Slobodka yeshiva.[20] R. Finkel was related to Habas; when the latter asked for his help he seems to have assembled a dozen men in Slobodka, some of them supporters of the *musar* movement, to form a *kolel*, without waiting for the official opening of the institution in Kovno.[21] A. A. Friedman suggests that all the men were associated with the *musar* movement, but his assessment may have been influenced by his own loathing of the movement:

When I went to Slobodka in order to study, I decided to study in this institution. It was late in the afternoon when I arrived at the *beit midrash*. I found the students

[18] M. Reines, 'Dwelling-Places of Torah' (Heb.), 428. In this context, a comment about R. Blaser in *Haḥavatselet*, written after his death, is interesting: 'and he hastened to the land of Ashkenaz to establish the *kolel* on a correct and enduring foundation' (*Haḥavatselet*, 37/41 (2 Aug. 1907), 326).   [19] Tzinovitz, *Personalities and Communities* (Heb.), 395a.

[20] The hypothesis about R. Finkel is based on the fact that he took an active part in establishing the *kolel* (see below), but there is no evidence for this in the writings of R. Reines and his son. However, during the *musar* controversy of the 1890s, R. Reines supported R. Salanter's students. He was one of the twelve signatories of the pamphlet 'Lema'an ha'emet' ('For Truth's Sake') issued in their support. See *Hatsefirah*, 24/175 (15 Aug. 1897); D. Katz, *The Musar Controversy* (Heb.), 144–7.

[21] D. Katz, *The Musar Movement* (Heb.), i. 196, which lists the members.

wrapped in *talit* and *tefilin*, rocking and wandering around the spacious *beit midrash*. One was silently humming a tune, pacing round the room and waving a finger in the air. Another was plunged in the depths of *Reshit ḥokhmah*,[22] humming quietly. Still another gave vent to a prolonged sigh that filled the entire *beit midrash*. When one spoke to another, it was in hints, a few broken, fragmentary Hebrew words. Some of them did not speak at all but communicated their needs by means of winks and hand motions—real *perushim* [lit.: 'renegades'], cut off from humankind, from the experience of the world, and also from the world of the Talmud. The study of Talmud and the halakhic literature—this was secondary, a withered limb . . . I saw all this and said to myself: This is not a house of God nor the gateway to heaven, the gates of Torah, for a man who truly aspires to perfect himself in the knowledge of the Torah, and I turned and went off to the centre of the town. There in Kovno I chose the *beit midrash* of Yosef Rabinowitz, which I made my place of study.[23]

Friedman adds that as a result of this experience and of the hardships suffered by the *perushim* studying in Kovno, R. Finkel appealed to the rabbi (perhaps this was R. Shraga Feivel Frank or R. Avraham Shenker of Aleksat—a suburb of Kovno) to join him in going to R. Spektor to ask him to assist in setting up a *kolel* for the *perushim* in Kovno; in other words, it was R. Finkel who came up with the idea of a *kolel* in Kovno. According to Friedman, R. Spektor approved the idea, and the Kolel Perushim in Kovno was founded at a meeting attended by R. Salanter, R. Lapidot, and others. Friedman himself wrote a flyer appealing for public support which was circulated in the names of R. Spektor and R. Salanter. Friedman's account explains neither what financial resources R. Finkel had at his disposal—though funds were of course essential—nor how he went from loathing to supporting—and no other source confirms Friedman's account of R. Finkel's central role. Even Ya'akov Lifschitz, who was opposed to the *musar* movement, but a personal friend of R. Salanter, does not mention Friedman at all in connection with the founding of the *kolel*, and therefore it is not clear how much Friedman can be relied on. Nevertheless, Friedman's description of the opening of a *kolel* in Slobodka before the institution officially opened in Kovno with R. Spektor's permission is consistent with the accounts given by Katz and Paltin.[24]

Funds for traditional Jewish education were in short supply in eastern Europe at that time, and it is quite understandable that the question as to who would control the funds of the *kolel* was complicated. The complex relationship between R. Spektor and the *musar* movement are also evident in a small book, *Ets peri*, that was published in 1881 and served in many respects as a manifesto for the new institution. It contained articles by the Hafets Hayim

---

[22] A 16th-cent. moralistic work by Eliyahu ben Moshe de Vidas.

[23] A. A. Friedman, *Memoirs* (Heb.), 131. On Friedman, see below.

[24] D. Katz, *The Musar Movement* (Heb.), iii. 12; see also Dvorets [Paltin], *The Biography of Our Master and Teacher* (Heb.), 2–3.

(R. Yisra'el Me'ir Hakohen of Radun, 1838–1933), R. Lapidot, R. Salanter (two articles), R. Spektor, and a closing article by R. Lapidot. The book has two parts. The first has a Russian title page that names the author as 'Yisra'el Salankah' (*sic*); the title page of the second part gives the author as R. Spektor. R. Spektor's article appears after this page, and the page numbering starts afresh. This seems to be something more than an attempt to show respect to two people. The first part was passed by the censor on 9 December 1880, while the second part was passed on 3 January 1881, implying that they were not presented to the censor together. It seems likely that the anonymous editor obtained articles from his acquaintances easily, but received the material from R. Spektor only later. This reinforces Friedman's account of the date of the opening of the *kolel*, if only in rather general terms. It is equally possible that other circumstances led to the double title pages and page numeration.[25]

R. Spektor was formally the head of the *kolel*, but it was actually run in part by his son, R. Tsevi Hirsh Rabinowitz and in part with the assistance of others, including R. Avraham Shenker. The function of the *kolel* was principally administrative rather than educational: it did not offer teaching, but rather allocated funds. In 1878 R. Spektor published a manifesto appealing for public support.[26] The funds donated by Lachman were only sufficient to support a limited number of students—five, according to one of those involved in the institution[27]—and much larger sums were required to meet the needs of the many suitable candidates. The exact sum Lachman contributed is not clear, and nor do we have details of the size of the allocations granted. An emissary was appointed for the purpose of raising funds;[28] an attempt to co-ordinate his activities with those of the Volozhin emissaries was unsuccessful.[29] The publication of *Ets peri* in 1881 was also part of the fundraising effort.

The approach adopted in raising funds in western Europe for the Kovno *kolel* is revealed by a letter written in support of the institution by R. Samson Raphael Hirsch at the request of R. Avraham Shenker.

---

[25] The identity of the publisher is not certain. Some suggest it was R. Finkel (see Dvorets [Paltin], *The Biography of Our Master and Teacher* (Heb.), 4), though Yashar, *The Hafets Hayim* (Heb.), i. 197, claims that it was Habas; in contrast, Lifschitz, *Zikhron ya'akov*, iii. 223, asserts that it was R. Tsevi Hirsh Rabinowitz, R. Spektor's son.

[26] It has been republished in Lifschitz, *Toledot yitshak*, 77–8. For partial quotations, see §2 below. It is dated 5 Kislev (1 Dec.) 1878.

[27] See the article, 'From Where Will Wisdom Come?' (Heb.) written by someone who signed himself 'One of the Keepers of the Sacred Watch in Russia'.

[28] On this emissary, see Lifschitz, *Zikhron ya'akov*, i. 225. The emissary he mentions, R. Barukh Ze'ev Mot, is mentioned on p. 4 of *Ets peri*, in a publisher's note.

[29] See a letter written by R. Berlin, in M. Reines, 'Dwelling-Places of Torah' (Heb.), 26. On the dispute between the Volozhin emissaries and the Slobodka yeshiva and on the court case between R. Hayim Soloveitchik and R. Finkel, see D. Katz, *The Musar Movement* (Heb.), ii. 306.

This institution trains young men destined to be outstanding scholars, while simultaneously providing them with education in the national language and other branches of knowledge important for their general enlightenment. This institution may be truly regarded as the salvation of the religion . . . this is the first, and so far the only, instance in which outstanding teachers, distinguished for their Torah and fear of Heaven, have decreed that study of the national language and general scientific enlightenment are permitted and indeed desirable. This confirms the principle upon which our community is founded . . . and behold, I declare it an illustrious exemplar beyond all doubt, and it is worthy of imitation. [30]

In publishing the letter, Mordechai Breuer added:

It is not our responsibility to check how it happened that the Kovno *kolel*, which followed the classic Lithuanian yeshiva style of study, was described to R. Samson Hirsch and his disciples as an institution that also provided secular education. It is possible that there was some misunderstanding here, and that perhaps R. Hirsch was misled by his enthusiasm to add extra details to ambiguous hints given by R. Avraham Shenker.

Obviously there are other ways of explaining this.

Most of R. Rabinowitz's income came from a commercial enterprise he owned, and when this collapsed in 1880 he was forced to take a post as the rabbi of Mitau.[31] As a result, changes were made in the administration of the *kolel*, as Lifschitz describes:

In 1880 the business of the *gaon*, our rabbi [Tsevi Hirsh Rabinowitz], son of our rabbi [Spektor], collapsed, and from then on he was forced to seek and accept a post in the rabbinate, and he was appointed as rabbi and *av beit din* of the town Mitau. Obviously, without his assistance it was difficult for our rabbi his father . . . to deal with all the management of the *kolel* by himself. Our master therefore called a meeting of the illustrious local rabbis who had participated in the establishment of the institution, such as his honour the *gaon* R. Alexander Moshe Lapidot of Raseiniai, the *gaon* R. Eliyahu Lezer Grodzinski of Vilna . . . to make arrangements to establish the *kolel* on an enduring basis. The *gaon* R. Yitshak Blaser . . . who had left the rabbinate in Petersburg and had moved to Kovno, took part in the meeting, and they discussed all the affairs of the institution very seriously. Treasurers were appointed to supervise and watch over everything—two prominent laymen of the town of Kovno, both God-fearing: Mr Eliyahu Merkel and Mr Barukh Broide, of blessed memory; and as the agent for the funds. To replace the *gaon* R. Tsevi Hirsh, son of our R. Yitshak Elhanan [Spektor], the *gaon* R. Yitshak Blaser [was chosen]. They chose me as scribe and chief secretary from this time onwards, with a salary of 6 roubles a month; the *gaon* R. Avraham Shenker did not take on any official post, but promised that he would help and assist those involved in all possible ways. The meeting achieved its object, that the above-mentioned appointees would assist our

[30] Breuer, 'Torah and Derekh erets' (Heb.), 26.
[31] Lifschitz, *Zikhron ya'akov*, iii. 224–5.

master R. Yitshak Elhanan . . . in the administration of the *kolel* and in improving its
position both physically and spiritually, and thus this institution was strengthened
in quality and size, in a most excellent fashion, until after several years the number
of students grew to almost 120, among them giants in Torah and the fear of Heaven.
This Kolel Perushim made a great and mighty impression everywhere and became
greater and greater![32]

This seems to have been a compromise between those who supported the
musar movement and those who opposed it. Each side could thus keep an eye
on the other. The supporters of the *musar* movement probably could not have
managed without the members of the local rabbinic establishment, while the
opponents of *musar* do not seem to have wanted complete control of the *kolel*,
for reasons that are not clear. They may have been worried about losing
Lachman's support, since he was a friend of R. Salanter, or there may have
been other reasons.

R. Yitshak Blaser became a major figure at the *kolel*.[33] He was born in 1837
in a suburb of Vilna, and after settling in Kovno he became a follower of R.
Salanter. In 1862, on R. Salanter's advice, he took a rabbinical post in St
Petersburg. He served there as a traditional rabbi for sixteen years, becoming
wealthy and embroiling himself in controversy with some of the local maskilim, including Yehudah Leib Gordon.[34] Around the time the *kolel* was
founded, R. Blaser returned to Kovno. He bought himself a large house and
his wife managed a tavern,[35] and he headed the *kolel* until 1891. He left after
a disagreement over how the institution was operated, how its finances were
administered, and the place of *musar* study there.[36]

[32] Ibid. 225–6.
[33] See D. Katz, *The Musar Movement* (Heb.), ii. 220–37. R. Blaser was not the only or even the
chief rabbi of St Petersburg (R. Mazeh was there part of the time), and seems to have been
associated with more conservative circles.
[34] Accusations of embezzlement of public funds were made against him but were never
proved; see Mazeh, *Memoirs* (Heb.), ii. 40. According to another source, he amassed 20,000
roubles in seven years—a very respectable sum for a rabbi; see Alexander Zederbaum in
Hamelits, 19/27 (16 Apr. 1883), 430. Both Zederbaum (who was the editor of *Hamelits*) and
Gordon objected to R. Blaser on personal grounds, so their evidence is not trustworthy.
However, R. Blaser was wealthy when he arrived in Kovno, according to all the sources. On R.
Blaser and Y. L. Gordon, see Stanislawski, *For Whom Do I Toil?*, 132.
[35] Malakhi, 'Rabbi Yitshak Blaser' (Heb.), 147.
[36] R. Blaser was a fascinating figure; Ya'akov Marek writes: 'I myself have never met such an
interesting personality, full of conflicting facets . . . his outlook was that of the early hasidim
who could not recognize a coin—but nevertheless he was a leader [*nagid*] all his life—and he
might have been the richest rabbi of his time' (Marek, *In the Company of the Great Men of the
Generation* (Heb.), 110–14). The *kolel*'s administrative practices damaged R. Blaser's reputation.
In 1887 Lachman bought a building in Kovno for 30,000 roubles and a courtyard for 48,000
roubles. He registered the courtyard under R. Blaser's name rather than his own. About a year
later Lachman asked R. Blaser for collateral for the property and demanded a sum equal to the

2. How the *Kolel* Operated

We shall now look at how the *kolel* operated and the special place occupied by *musar* study until the crisis of 1891.

The founders of the *kolel* had definite ideas about the need for the *kolel* and about its aims:

Everyone who knows and understands the ways of the Torah and its teaching will realize and understand that the existence and endurance of Torah in Israel cannot be continued without mighty heroes of war . . . indeed the time is not too late to act for the Lord and His Torah . . . and there are many young men among us who are mighty in intellect, who will surely become famous for their Torah, if only they are supported and assisted to avoid the buffets of the wind of life's worries, and are not scattered abroad because of want in their families, with none to help or aid them. Therefore have we arisen and taken courage, I and those who are aiding me, to support the elite of the students, who volunteer to devote their labour and time to the Lord's Torah, for from among them will arise rabbis, geniuses of the Torah, for the next generation, and—thanks be to God—there are already assembled in this city [Kovno] many of these young men, who are veterans in their Torah knowledge, and the needs of their families are being met, so that they should not be burdened by having to work for them and for their wives and children, and thus have to cease their Torah study.[37]

The *kolel* accepted only married students.[38] It was the practice in traditional Lithuanian Jewish society that only after marriage was it proper to study Torah for practical purposes such as determining halakhah, so the *kolel* could consciously present itself as a place for training rabbis. The practice of *perishut*, separation from one's family, allowed the young married men to concentrate on their studies and also helped to limit the number of their children.

A distinction should be made between the founders' concerns about the danger of diminishing numbers of great Torah scholars and the concerns of the young students. There was in fact no lack of men capable of serving as rabbis. If we look carefully at what the leaders of the *kolel* actually said, they were worried about a problem that had not yet arisen: that there might be a lack of scholars in the future. Thus, for instance, just before the *kolel* was

cost of the land. However, the real-estate market had declined in the meantime, and R. Blaser was only prepared to offer a guarantee at 1888 prices and not according to the value of the land when it was purchased. Lachman eventually transferred another house to R. Blaser's name, and the latter gave him a guarantee as requested. This is the description of their business dealings given in *Hamelits*, 28/186 (22 Aug. 1888), 1958–9. It is clear that matters were much more complicated, but the account presented here is sufficient to account for the gossip about R. Blaser.

[37] From R. Spektor's *Kol kore*, Nov. 1878. The pamphlet appears in Lifschitz, *Toledot yitshak*, 77. The style of this manifesto resembles that issued by R. Hayim of Volozhin upon the foundation of his yeshiva.   [38] Tchernowitz, *Pirkei hayim*, 122.

founded, a man from Telz wrote: 'I know full well that in my native city of Telz there are about ten men, aged from twenty-five to fifty, who are endowed with all the talents necessary for teaching, learned and expert in their knowledge, and there are others in all the towns of our district, and in all the towns of Russia there are *batei midrash* full of Torah scholars, whose Torah is their main activity.'[39] Many of the students were thus talented enough to serve as rabbis, but there were not enough rabbinic posts available. As we have already seen, this was a consequence of changes in the pattern of Jewish settlement: the migration from villages to towns meant that few new Jewish communities— and therefore few new rabbinical positions—were being established. The rise of new Jewish communities in the south, as in the area of Odessa, did not contribute a great deal to the job prospects of rabbis because the Jews were concentrated there, as elsewhere, in a few urban centres and not a multitude of small ones. In other words, the rise in the Jewish population of the large cities did not lead to a concomitant increase in the demand for rabbis. Torah students were forced to grapple with the problem of daily subsistence: where would they earn money for food? The young students and their wives were worried about their future, as the *kolel* leaders were aware. As *Ets peri* records:

And as for these few remnants, can we believe that they are already confident of achieving their aims and arriving at their desired goal without interruption? Are there not many obstacles in their way that could prevent them from succeeding; do not letters arrive daily from their wives, the delicate daughters of Israel, who remain lonely and sad in their towns, lacking everything and with no support or prop to aid them and their dear children, and who pour out their bitterness of spirit into the bosom of the husbands of their youth, saying, 'You may have acquired Torah—but what shall we eat?'; and with their words, questions pierce their husbands' hearts: 'What will become of us?'... And apart from this, a great host arises, poverty and want and crises and innumerable burdens, to fight fiercely against them, to deflect them from their purpose, to banish them from the houses of their delight, to steal the joy of their eyes from them with great cruelty, to push them into the markets and the streets and the haunts of the idle, [so that they must] pursue trade and commerce, and where will they beg for bread for their households? Ah! What a terrible and appalling threat is this painful and disheartening prospect![40]

There is a note of despair in the wife's question 'What will become of us?' In the new economic conditions of the 1880s, a yeshiva education was insufficient to prepare a man for a future life in commerce, and knowledge of the Talmud no longer guaranteed students the respect of society. The *kolel* did not offer its students a long-term solution for a livelihood, but merely freed them from this concern in the short term. In effect, the *kolel* was replacing the old *kest* system, in which the father-in-law supported the young couple. The

[39] *Halevanon*, 15/30 (28 Feb. 1879), 237–9, signed by the pseudonymous 'Ne'eman' ('Faithful'). [40] *Ets peri, Kol kore*, 3.

kolel was unable to solve the basic problem, but could only help the students study in the meantime and postpone the day that they would have to find themselves employment. In the words of the manifesto:

Nowadays it is not as it used to be, for even those who study *lishmah* [for the sake of study] and are so talented that they fit to be rabbis in Israel face the risk of falling into the category of those who quit in the middle of their study and find some way of supporting themselves, and must bear the yoke of sustaining a wife and children . . . if everyone would only urge his neighbour to strengthen and support the Torah, for then we would be able to restore the crown of the Torah to its former glory, and together we could support the Lord's students, that they might become rabbis in Israel in the days to come; if only our brethren, the children of Israel, might awaken to strengthen the tent of Torah among our people at this time; and if not now, when?[41]

Students were accepted to the *kolel* only after passing an examination. During the *kolel*'s first years, the examination was conducted by R. Spektor or his son,[42] and later by R. Blaser.[43] The level of support was set after the examination. At the beginning, it varied between 3 and 10 roubles a month.[44] A source dating from 1889 records that the allocation was then between half a rouble and 2 roubles a week.[45] Another source from the same period states that the sum received was inadequate as the students needed at least 5 roubles a week, though there seems to be some exaggeration here. The shortfall could have been met in several ways, one of which would have been for the student to receive supplementary funds from the *beit midrash* where he actually studied.[46] There seems to be no evidence that anyone managed to subsist solely on support received from the *beit midrash*.

The examination was not always the determining factor in deciding whether to accept a student; attention was paid to the student's background and the recommendations he had received. One student records:

Since I had no proper connections, I receive only the grant money, which amounts to 6 roubles a month. My lack of contacts is due to the fact that I did not obtain a recommendation from a prominent rabbi in our district who is known in Kovno. This is according to the custom of the *kolel*, that the students who come from Podolia and Kiev and Kherson, and so on, which are far distant from Kovno and few come to the *kolel* from there—they receive more financial support than those students who come from Lithuania and Zamut.[47]

[41] *Ets peri, Kol kore*, 10. [42] Yashar, *The Hafets Hayim* (Heb.), i. 156.
[43] Rosenfeld, *Rabbi Yisra'el Salanter* (Heb.), 36. [44] Ibid.
[45] M. Reines, 'Dwelling-Places of Torah' (Heb.), 32.
[46] Tchernowitz, *Pirkei hayim*, 126; see also Yashar, *The Hafets Hayim* (Heb.), ii. 156.
[47] From a letter by Shaul Gelman to R. Moshe Nahum Yerushalimski in 1898. The letter is in the Yerushalimski Collection in the Schocken Library, Jerusalem.

Once students were accepted, their only contact with the *kolel* was when they went to receive their stipends. They studied on their own, generally without supervision and without attending *shiurim*. These students generally concentrated on Jewish law and studied the classic codes rather than focusing on Talmud. As the *kolel* had no building of its own, they would spend their time in one of the *batei midrash* in the town. These *batei midrash* were 'shared' between the young full-time students and local men who used them a prayer houses and for occasional study. The choice of *beit midrash* was a matter of some importance, as emerges from an account of 1889:

The city's *batei midrash* were all different—according to the level of Torah study and piety of the men who frequented them, and their social and economic standing. Some were very devout, while others were inclined towards the Haskalah and free-thinking. The *perushim* too were distinguished by their level and their outlook. For example, those who were inclined to the *musar* movement used to study at the Nevaizer *beit midrash*, which was founded by R. Yisra'el Salanter, and where the regulars still secretly leaned towards the *musar* movement, even though R. Yitshak Elhanan [Spektor] disapproved of it. In the old *beit midrash*, where 'the Rabbi', R. Yitshak Elhanan, used to pray, were the outstanding students who studied constantly and were particularly devout and close to 'the Rabbi'. In contrast, those students who had maskilic tendencies studied at the new *beit midrash*, where the city's maskilim and intellectuals prayed.[48]

There was no formal or methodical framework for training for the rabbinate. A student studied whatever he wanted, but if he wanted to obtain ordination he would go to a well-known and veteran rabbi or rabbis to be examined on 'Yoreh de'ah', one of the four parts of Yosef Karo's great code, the *Shulḥan arukh*. Students received no preparation in practical rabbinics, or indeed in anything that would equip them to serve as rabbis—either as traditional rabbis or as government appointees. They generally did not work with established *posekim* to learn how to make halakhic decisions, nor was there any programme to hone their ability to preach sermons, or develop their knowledge of Russian, or help them acquire secular knowledge. There were cases where young scholars would serve an apprenticeship with community rabbis to learn how to decide everyday questions, but this was not required nor was there a structure that arranged such apprenticeships. The *kolel*'s goal was not actually to train rabbis, but rather, as the Hafets Hayim had said, to replace the *kest* system and solve the financial problem. The *kolel* was innovative in its system for financial support, not in the education it offered.

[48] Tchernowitz, *Pirkei ḥayim*, 125. It should be noted that the concentration of the first core of the *kolel* in a single *beit midrash*, as described by A. A. Friedman, was not characteristic of the rest of the *kolel*'s history (Friedman, *Memoirs* (Heb.), 131). The proliferation of *kolel* members would certainly have hampered any attempt to assemble them in one place. Likewise, there was no educational reason for doing this since there was no collective or guided study in the *kolel*.

The emphasis that was placed in fundraising literature and elsewhere on the *kolel* as an institution for training rabbis was largely a tactical strategy; the founders themselves may not have been aware of it. The great interest in the establishment of a rabbinical seminary in Russia has been described above.[49] The establishment of the *kolel* not only helped meet the young scholars' financial needs but also demonstrated that an effort was being made to train spiritual leaders in a traditional spirit. The emphasis on the goal of training rabbis was quite definitely important for fundraising, both in Russia and abroad: if the institution had been presented as just another yeshiva, donors would have questioned the need for it.

The *kolel*'s appeal to the general public who supported it raises the question of whether they too had ceased to regard Torah study as a value in itself and now only saw it as a means to ensure the training of rabbis. There is a hint of this in a description of the Volozhin yeshiva in *Hamelits* in 1891 as 'the only special university in our country for training rabbis'.[50] That description seems to have been inspired by practical considerations—the need to encourage support for the yeshiva. The author therefore presented the yeshiva in a way he knew would appeal to the public. The extent to which Jewish society absorbed ideas from the wider society is difficult to measure, but there seems to be proof of it here.

The number of *kolel* members rose from about sixty in the early 1880s to about 120 by the mid-1880s. There was a simultaneous rise in its income, which may have led to the rise in numbers. The relative speed with which the Kovno *kolel* became a success soon led to the development of a network of subsidiary branches in other cities, anticipating the foundation of branches of the Slobodka yeshiva by some years.[51] From an organizational perspective this was quite simple because all that was required was to make funds available at new locations. But in other respects it was a major step because it marked the beginning of an entirely new phenomenon in the Jewish community of eastern Europe: a network of linked educational institutions. Once established, a branch of an educational network enjoyed considerable independence from the local community, since a large percentage of its budget and its staff came from elsewhere. A branch was similarly generally free of the need to raise funds and search for students, since these functions were carried out by the central institution. In this way, members of the *kolel* in Minsk, for example, could make use of funds collected in the name of R. Spektor, just at the *kolel* in Kovno did. However, establishing a network of branches needs a

---

[49] See Lifschitz, *Zikhron ya'akov*, iii. 123. R. Salanter was not only active on behalf of the *kolel* but also played a role in the fight against the rabbinical seminary.

[50] Eli'ezer Braun in *Hamelits*, 31/45 (6 Mar. 1891).

[51] Lifschitz, *Zikhron ya'akov*, iii. 225; A. A. Friedman, *Memoirs* (Heb.), 133; D. Katz, *The Musar Movement* (Heb.), ii. 228.

more complex mechanism and a formal organization of authority and responsibility than a single institution does, and this sort of modern organization structure had not previously existed in Jewish eastern Europe.

The fact that the *kolel* concentrated exclusively on the distribution of funds rather than on imposing a curriculum affected relationships among the *kolel* students, between them and the *kolel*, and between the *kolel* and the general public. In this context, it is interesting to compare the *kolel* to the yeshiva. The central figure at the *kolel* was the man who distributed the funds, rather than the teacher who educated his students and served as a role model for them. At the yeshiva all the students studied in the same hall and there was a sense of being a group, while at the *kolel* the students studied separately, by themselves; their contacts were mainly with the person responsible for handing out the money or the students in the particular *beit midrash* they frequented.[52] The only overall framework the students had in common was provided by the *musar* movement:

And in every *beit midrash* where the *perushim* would sit over their Torah study—and they sat in every *beit midrash* in Kovno—there was always an older *perush* . . . distinguished for his fear of Heaven, and secretly keeping an eye on the doings of the *perushim* in matters of conduct. All these were supported by the *kolel* funds and were considered to be masters of *musar*. Those in charge of the *kolel* never required the *perushim* to go to the *beit musar* [a special *beit midrash* in Kovno that was used only for *musar* study] or to visit R. Yitshak Blaser's house on the sabbath to hear his *musar* talks, which he gave every sabbath. But the . . . [older] *perushim* of whom I have spoken, by talking to the students and spending time with them, knew them intimately and could tell which were inclined, or were capable of inclining, to *musar*, and which were incapable of this. Everything was recorded in a book and was relayed to R. Blaser.[53]

The students associated themselves with the *kolel* in order to receive financial support. There may have been an element of honour in being accepted to the *kolel* and this could also have attracted students. However, the *kolel* did not offer a better programme of study than elsewhere. Since the study was independent, it could be done anywhere. The association with the *kolel* was important because it gave them the money they needed to support their families; support for men studying at *batei midrash* was very limited. Their great dependence on the *kolel*, and particularly on the individual who distributed the funds, meant that they were very exposed to pressures and influence.

Even during the *kolel*'s earliest days, supporters of the *musar* movement tried to take a central place in the institution in order to use it to attract young

---

[52] It is not clear when this changed and the *kolel* members were required to study at a particular location, as is the practice today. It is clear, however, that this makes supervision easier.

[53] Rosenfeld, *Rabbi Yisra'el Salanter* (Heb.), 52.

men to *musar* study. Ya'akov Lifschitz writes of R. Avraham Shenker, the official assistant to R. Tsevi Hirsh Rabinowitz, as follows:

The rabbi and *gaon* R. Avraham Shenker . . . was one of the students of . . . R. Yisra'el Salanter . . . and was enthusiastic about the *musar* study method of the *gaon* R. Salanter . . . Most of the great rabbis of the generation did not approve of the *musar* method in the version that was then current . . . even though I had grown up and studied with many of the great rabbis who harboured these fears, and whose opinions had rubbed off on me, nevertheless I admired R. Avraham Shenker's dealings with this exalted institution, though I saw and realized that he was beginning to chase and hunt down those students who might incline towards this *musar* method, for I felt that he was very talented and was acting in good faith to strengthen the Torah and was also starting something new, and all beginnings are hard. And we should recognize and acknowledge his work with proper respect, and we are certain that since he was close to our rabbi and master R. Yitshak Elhanan [Spektor] and enjoyed the light of his Torah, and God forbid there should be any distress from his actions.[54]

After R. Rabinowitz left, R. Shenker had no formal position. When he in turn left, two men from Kovno—R. Eliyahu Merkel and R. Barukh Broide— were chosen to run the institution.[55] R. Broide was a follower of the *musar* movement and he appointed another follower, Yehoshua Tsadikov, as acting treasurer.[56] They used the power they had by virtue of their control over the distribution of funds in order to influence the *kolel* members. This was not always seen favourably:

A simple Jew, Yehoshua Tsadikov, who was also a *musar* adherent, was appointed as *mashgiah* over the *perushim*, to watch their behaviour; he used to go from one *beit midrash* to another and watch and spy and investigate: who was a conscientious student and who was not, who was studying with enthusiasm and who was studying as if forced to by a demon . . . and this R. Yehoshua was also a sort of treasurer, from whose hand the *perushim* used to receive their monthly stipend and also loans from the *gemilut hasadim* [charity] fund, for those who were worthy. Whenever a *perush* needed something and turned to the *kolel* for some 'favour', R. Yehoshua's opinion was decisive—whether the suppliant deserved to receive a favour from the *kolel* or not—for he knew the *perushim* very well and was familiar with each one's deeds. And the chief treasurer, the prominent R. Broide, was reckoned to be one of the oldest *musar* adherents. R. Blaser never told a *perush* that he was displeased with him because he had not adopted the *musar* way. But everyone knew that he was fonder of those *perushim* who were *musarniks* than of those who were not, and that the former received a more generous stipend than the latter, and there were also those who were supported with generous sums of money 'at appropriate times'.[57]

[54] Lifschitz, *Zikhron ya'akov*, iii. 224.
[55] Ibid. 225, and see above.   [56] Rosenfeld, *Rabbi Yisra'el Salanter*, 52.
[57] Ibid. Rosenfeld was a fanatical opponent of the *musar* movement but had information on

3. Opposition and Conflict

The favouritism shown to those students who were interested in *musar* aroused opposition both among the other students and in the wider community. However, the dispersion of the students between many different *batei midrash* and their complete dependence on the financial support of the *kolel* made it difficult for them to take united action. Within the wider community, opposition came from maskilim who regarded the *musar* movement as a threat to the spread of Enlightenment, but not only from them: they acquired some unexpected allies in the traditional rabbis who saw the *musar* movement as an unwelcome innovation that distracted youths from the study of Torah.

Opposition to the *kolel* was considerable, principally because of R. Blaser's pro-*musar* stance. There had been doubts about the need for such an institution from the beginning,[58] but from 1883 onwards critical articles began to appear in *Hamelits*, focusing on *musar* study and the indolence of the *perushim*.[59] The strange activities of a few *musar* adherents, such as R. Yosef Yosel Horowitz who shut himself up in a small house for many years and refused to come out, were given great prominence.

In 1890 R. Blaser faced a wave of criticism amidst claims that the *kolel* was collecting 60,000–80,000 roubles a year and that he was embezzling these funds.[60] R. Spektor responded by saying that the financial situation of the institution had been examined, that its income was about 20,000 roubles a year, the number of students being supported was 170, and administrative expenditure amounted to 450 roubles a year.[61] If we recall that the Volozhin yeshiva only managed to raise about 15,000 roubles a year in the mid-1880s,

what was happening within it. The writer Kadish Yehudah Silman wrote a short autobiography at the request of Moshe Yardeni, in which he noted: 'The writer Shmuel Rosenfeld received his first knowledge of this yeshiva [Slobodka] from me, which he then published in his letters "From Provincial Towns" in *Hamelits*. I meant what I said as praise but he meant it as criticism.' I would like to thank Silman's grandson, Ido Basuk, who gave me a photocopy of this autobiography, which was never published. There thus seems to be some truth in the story, even if not every detail is accurate. It seems likely that R. Blaser supported *musar* study, and this is consistent with other descriptions. If this were not true, it would be hard to understand why R. Spektor eventually dismissed him, even though he was not a fierce opponent of the *musar* movement (nor was he known for extreme views in any other sphere). Tsadikov's desire to check whether students who received stipends were in fact studying also seems probable.

[58] See *Halevanon* 15/30 (28 Feb. 1879), 237–9. The author claimed that there were plenty of young men willing to serve as rabbis.

[59] Some of this may even date from an earlier period. I am relying on material collected in D. Katz, *The Musar Controversy* (Heb.), ch. 2. Two more references should be added to this list: the article by Efrayim Shevah Dayan in *Hamelits*, 19/89 (7 Dec. 1883), 1404–5, and a letter from Pinsk entitled 'A Man of the House of Levi' (Heb.), *Hamelits*, 25/66 (14 Sept. 1885), 1063–5. It is possible that the criticism predated 1883 but this is not of decisive importance.

[60] D. Katz, *The Musar Controversy* (Heb.), 32–40.

[61] M. A. Eisenstadt, 'The Money of the Guilt-Offering' (Heb.).

it is clear that the sum specified by R. Spektor would have been very reasonable, and the higher sum seems exaggerated. According to R. Spektor's figures, the average stipend received would have been 2.26 roubles a week. Moshe Reines, who gives details of the *kolel's* financial situation in 1888, records that the stipends did not amount to more than 2 roubles a week, and the average stipend was 1.5 roubles. He adds that the members ate with local families since their stipends were insufficient,[62] and expressed his doubts about the fate of the large sums of money that were collected.[63] It is known that when R. Yitshak Rabinowitz was teaching at Slobodka, the *kolel* helped fund his salary even though he did not teach there.[64]

Criticism of the *kolel* continued, and seems to have had a certain basis, as R. Dov Katz writes:

The real reason that they never published a detailed financial report and made do with a declaration that the accounts were available to anyone who was interested was that the funds that the emissaries collected were also used to support the students of the Slobodka yeshiva, who numbered several hundreds, and in Russia it was forbidden by law at that period to run yeshivas that constituted colleges for the young. (For this reason, as is known, the Volozhin yeshiva was closed in 1892.[65]) The Slobodka yeshiva existed illegally at this time, and many of the students were eligible for conscription, so they could not engage in any publicity. Apart from this, fundraising campaigns for these purposes were forbidden in Russia, and everything had to be done in secret and underground.[66]

R. Blaser's response to the criticism and opposition was restrained, like that of R. Finkel.[67] According to Ya'akov Marek, who happened to meet him in Vilna when he was being attacked by the rabbis who opposed the introduction of *musar* study to yeshivas, 'although many people insulted him . . . he never harmed anybody. On the contrary, he defended them [on the grounds that] their intentions were for the sake of Heaven. This attitude of his made a great impression on me. There is no real proof of his misuse of the funds at his disposal, and he spent his old age living very modestly in Jerusalem.'[68]

Katz seems to be correct in claiming that the maskilim who criticized the *kolel* were not motivated by concern for the *perushim* but rather by their opposition to the institution, which they regarded as impeding the spread of

[62] *Hamelits*, 29/242 (19 Nov. 1889), 2–3. However, see the response in *Hamelits*, 30/7 (21 Jan. 1890), 1. According to R. Spektor, the signature was forged ('Insult to the Torah' (Heb.)).

[63] M. Reines, 'Dwelling-Places of Torah' (Heb.), 32, 35.

[64] Dvorets [Paltin], *The Biography of Our Master and Teacher* (Heb.), 2–33.

[65] On the reasons for the closure of the Volozhin yeshiva, see Ch. 8 above.

[66] D. Katz, *The Musar Controversy* (Heb.), 40.

[67] On R. Blaser, see Malakhi, 'Rabbi Yitshak Blaser' (Heb.). On the transfer of funds to Slobodka, see also Dvorets [Paltin], *The Biography of Our Master and Teacher* (Heb.), 2.

[68] Marek, *In the Company of the Great Men of the Generation* (Heb.), 111.

enlightenment among the Jewish community. They saw the *perushim* as a threat, since they could influence the wider Jewish public. An anonymous 'Jew' wrote in *Hamelits* in 1891:

Kovno has become a city of *perushim*. This event, even though in general good for the Jews, for in the opinion of many, were it not for them—the *perushim*—who have arisen in this stubborn and devious generation, who knows whether the entire world would not have returned to its original chaos . . . but their activities have a bad influence on the masses in our city, for there is not a single *beit midrash* in the city which does not have its *perush* giving his sermons and preaching his doctrine to a crowded audience, and they are far from any knowledge of [real] life and its necessities, and pour out their spirit on the masses, filling their hearts with a world full of nonsense and delusions, frightening them with the threat of death and his thousand-eyed angel, with demons of the deep and angels of terror, or stuffing them with *pilpul* and driving them away from knowledge and understanding.[69]

Most critics of the *kolel* claimed that R. Spektor was not aware of what was happening in the institution, even though it was nominally under his direction. This claim is typical of a situation in which the person at the head of the institution is admired by the critics, or is very popular with the general public, and the critics do not want to come into conflict with him.[70] However, the fact that R. Spektor was forced to appoint two men to examine the financial arrangements of the *kolel* reinforces the claim in this case. After this examination, R. Spektor answered the criticism levelled by Rosenfeld, 'Erez' (Zederbaum's pen-name—*erez* being the Hebrew for Zederbaum, meaning 'cedar tree'), and others in the Jewish press in a long article entitled 'An Insult to the Torah', in which he wrote: 'I hereby bear witness that all the leaders who engage with me in supporting the *perushim* are men of stature, upright and God-fearing, and far from loving money and honour, and they expose their dignity to blasphemers and accusers purely because of their love of the Torah.'[71] He wrote this even though he himself was opposed to the *musar* movement in its institutional forms.[72]

In spite of R. Spektor's support, R. Blaser resigned his position with the

---

[69] 'Letters from Kovno' (Heb.), *Hamelits*, 31/5 (19 Jan. 1891), 1–2.

[70] A good example of this appears in Friedman's comment on the foundation of the Kovno *kolel*; see A. A. Friedman, *Memoirs* (Heb.), 132–3. Opponents of the *kolel* even forged letters to the press; see 'A Word of Peace and Truth' (Heb.), an article signed by 'N. Natanson'. However, he does not seem to have written the article, as confirmed by R. Spektor himself, in his article 'Insult to the Torah' (Heb.).

[71] Spektor, 'Insult to the Torah' (Heb.). According to 'Erez' (i.e. Zederbaum), the author of the piece was Ya'akov Lifschitz. This is apparent from his article 'An Unfair Protest', in which he wrote that Lifschitz had written a critical response to another of his articles, 'A Fire Has Gone Out from Heshbon' (Heb.).

[72] He never defended the *musar* movement publicly. See Lifschitz, *Zikhron ya'akov*, iii. 224.

kolel shortly afterwards. The reasons for his departure are not clear. Y. Z. Paltin (who also published under the name Dvorets) writes:

It seems that these men were interested in ensuring that the *kolel* passed out of the hands of the *musar* supporters, and for this reason they made strenuous efforts to attack the *kolel* administration, until our master the *gaon*, the righteous pillar of the world, R. Yitshak Blaser, who had been appointed to run the *kolel* after he left his rabbinical post in Petersburg, realized that the odour of controversy clung to these attacks, and he resigned from the *kolel* administration. However, our master, the *gaon* R. Natan Tsevi Finkel did not cease directing the *kolel*'s affairs in secret, as was his practice, and he made an effort to correct what was possible in the *kolel*; but nevertheless, since the gates had been officially closed to *musar* supporters, he could not do much.[73]

There were probably other factors in R. Blaser's resignation. First, some individuals close to R. Spektor, such as his son, R. Tsevi Hirsh Rabinowitz,[74] and the rabbi of Slobodka, R. Moshe Danishevski,[75] opposed the *musar* movement; even though they did not share the goals of *Hamelits*, it seems likely that they exploited the attacks on R. Blaser to pressure him to resign. Second, the articles published about the *kolel* caused a sharp drop in its income:

The *perushim* are hardly receiving anything now, for since their income dropped after the controversy in this newspaper, their funders are telling them that there is no money for *kolelim*, and they are putting them off by promising them to pay them for several months at once, after the situation has improved. This is a sign that if there is no money to give the [*kolel*] *perushim*, there is plenty and more for the leaders, and this is the time for them to act, a time to meet and not a time to disperse, for who knows what will happen, and whether the *kolel* will fall into everlasting desolation. For there is no end to the tremendous harm that the controversy in the press has done them. Also the emissaries are now doing whatever they please and are sending as much money as they want to the administration, and if the administrators have a claim against them, the emissaries silence them by a single word whispered in their ears, for the emissaries know what is happening better than those who write in *Hamelits*, and they can do much harm.[76]

Given this situation, the opponents of *musar* could have claimed that R. Blaser had to leave, both for the financial good of the institution and for the sake of propriety. Indirect evidence of the importance of the economic factors appears in a condolence letter sent in 1893 by R. Spektor to the widow of Avraham Kupernik, a maskil who had also supported the *kolel*.[77] R. Spektor

---

[73] Paltin [Dvorets], 'In the Paths of Advanced Torah Study (Heb.), 53; see also D. Katz, *The Musar Controversy* (Heb.), 60.

[74] His signature appears on the pamphlet 'Lema'an da'at'; see Ch. 9 n. 63 above.

[75] He also signed the pamphlet.   [76] 'A Word of Peace and Truth' (Heb.).

[77] See Malakhi, 'Some Letters of Rabbi Yitshak Elhanan [Spektor]' (Heb.), 78.

expresses his hope that the *kolel* can rely on a contribution as in the previous year. The sum donated by her husband in the past had been 18 roubles; if R. Spektor took the trouble to write a personal letter of thanks for a sum this small, it is clear that he was very sensitive to anything that could destabilize the *kolel*'s financial basis.

The new director of the *kolel* was R. Spektor's son-in-law, Tsevi Soltsavski. The following is a description of him and of Yehoshua Tsadikov by Hayim Czernowitz, who studied at the *kolel* in 1890:

When war broke out against the *musarniks* and their leader R. Itsik [Blaser], who was forced to resign from the administration of the *perushim* yeshiva, the post was given to the son-in-law of R. Spektor, H. Soltsavski, who was already a widower . . . Soltsavski was a crude man, as hard as iron and not a great scholar. Before this he had been a merchant, and had had nothing to do with the rabbinate. In fact, his directorship was purely administrative; his main function was to accept students who came to study at the *perushim* yeshiva and to support them according to their level. Since he was not intelligent enough to assess the capabilities of the new student, he used to ask the advice of his cronies, who formed a sort of gang around him, advising and serving him. R. Moshe Danishevski of Slobodka was officially in charge of accepting students to the yeshiva, and would examine the students to see whether they were suitable. After Soltsavski received a note from this examiner that so-and-so was suitable to join the *perushim* yeshiva, he would decide the amount of support that the student would receive. Even so, Soltsavski was the sole judge and did not take much notice of R. Danishevski's opinion, for R. Spektor had entrusted him with the entire management of the yeshiva.

R. Itsik and those close to him, even though they had officially been removed from the administration, had left some *musarniks* who were connected in some way to the *perushim* yeshiva, and Soltsavski himself with all his aggressiveness could not get rid of them; they wove plots against him in secret among the students and the local people who supported the institution.

One of those responsible for administration was known as R. Yehosheleh. His main role was to find accommodation, somewhere to eat, and so on for newly accepted students. He used to do all this openly, but in secret he acted as a sort of detective for the *musarniks*. There was eternal hatred between Soltsavski and this R. Yehosheleh, whom he called 'Yehoshekeh', but it seems that he could not get rid of him. Soltsavski would openly speak ill of this R. Yehosheleh, and R. Yehosheleh would drop unpleasant hints about Soltsavski, for he was frightened of him.[78]

The source of Tsadikov's authority is not clear. He may have remained in his job as the result of a secret agreement between the *musar* supporters and their opponents, as a condition for the departure of R. Blaser. We know from other sources that money from the *kolel* funds was given to the Slobodka

[78] Tchernowitz, *Pirkei ḥayim*, 122–3.

yeshiva even after R. Blaser left,[79] so it is clear that his departure did not put an end to the *musar* movement's ties with the *kolel*. From this point until the First World War the *kolel* carried on its work with no major disruptions.[80]

4. The Brodsky Kolel

The idea of establishing a *kolel* had first been raised in 1875, and the possibility of enlisting support from the Brodsky family was suggested three years later. Nothing came of this idea for more than a decade. It was only after the project had been successfully realized in Kovno that the original plan was put into effect. However, by the time this was done, the *kolel* in Kovno had already made an impact, so the impression made by the establishment of a *kolel* in Volozhin was not great. None the less, the way in which it was carried out sheds light on a number of aspects of Jewish communal life.

The *kolel* in Volozhin was founded in 1886, thanks to the financial support of Yisra'el Brodsky, a sugar merchant from Kiev. The founding charter specified its aims:

The Lord has inspired the heart of the great and renowned man, our master Reb. Yisra'el Brodsky, may his light shine, to set up an endowment fund of sixty shares of the Kiev Land Bank, which yields 2,000 roubles annually; and this income will be for the maintenance of ten men expert in Torah study, either from among the yeshiva students or students who come to Volozhin from elsewhere to devote themselves to labour in the Torah and to study the traditions of the halakhah and to perfect themselves to become teachers of instruction in Israel.[81]

An announcement of the foundation of the *kolel* was published in *Hamelits*.[82]

The intermediary for the plan was R. Me'ir Levin, a businessman and scholar who in 1875 moved from Karlin to Kiev, where he and Brodsky became friends.[83] It is not clear what linked him to the yeshiva or how he managed to revive an idea that had been dropped over a decade previously.

The founding charter establishing the *kolel*'s programme included the following points. The *kolel* was to be funded by an endowment that would be administered by an agent of Yisra'el Brodsky. Fellows of the *kolel* were expected to stay for five years, though if they made good progress they could

[79] According to D. Katz, the Lachman fund remained under Blaser's control (*The Musar Controversy* (Heb.), 60); see also the unsigned article 'A Fire Has Gone Out from Heshbon' (Heb.), according to which R. Blaser refused to give Lachman the property bought for the *kolel* and registered in his name.   [80] On this period, see Tchernowitz, *Pirkei hayim*, 129–33.

[81] M. Rabinowitz published the regulations in 'Documents Relating to the History of the Volozhin Yeshiva' (Heb.), 230–3.   [82] *Hamelits*, 26/125 (11 Oct. 1886), 1573.

[83] See also Yanovsky, *Biography of Rabbi Me'ir Halevi Levine* (Heb.), 14–15. This source claims that the first *mashgiah* was Yitshak Tsevi Yanovsky; after his death in early 1890 his son Yisra'el took over his position.

leave after three years. The examination and acceptance of candidates would be solely in the hands of the administration of the Volozhin yeshiva.

Acceptance to the Brodsky Kolel in Volozhin bestowed not only great honour but also considerable economic benefits. Each of the members received 17 roubles a month—a very large sum. This *kolel* was very important to its members but had little influence on the yeshiva's history. It remained a small institution and made little impression on the general public, perhaps because it operated in the shadow of the yeshiva, did not run its own fundraising campaign, and made no effort to advertise itself.

In the long run, the *kolel* came to play an important role in the traditional education system of the Torah community. It provided an economic base for young couples at a critical stage of their lives. If in the past Torah study had been identified with the socio-economic elite, the *kolel* made it possible for boys from middle-class families to receive the benefits of Torah study too. The fundraising programme was able to draw on the resources of many people of very limited means who identified with the goals of the *kolel*. These people did not have the means to support a son-in-law studying Torah for several years. The programme could attract support from geographically isolated individuals who definitely identified with what they saw as traditional values but who were too few to form a cohesive social group and to establish traditionalist institutions themselves. The *kolel* as it was first founded had no educational programme. However, the structure and dependence of *kolel* students on the administration offered the potential for developing programmes of study under supervision. This potential was not realized immediately, but certainly developed in the twentieth century.

Conclusion

O N THE EVE OF the First World War, yeshivas were among the most important institutions of traditional east European Jewish society, and the *rashei yeshivah* were among its most prominent leaders. Whereas many rabbis born in the early or even the mid-nineteenth century never studied in a yeshiva at all, most rabbis born in the late nineteenth century most certainly had done (at least in mitnagdic circles). The yeshivas of eastern Europe at this time attracted young men from western Europe and even from America, and the trend intensified in the interwar period.[1] With some justification one may say that most of the world's Torah students at this time were to be found in the yeshivas of eastern Europe and particularly of Lithuania. The tremendous efforts made to raise funds for the yeshivas, and the success these efforts enjoyed despite the many competing philanthropic causes in the interwar period, also demonstrate their significance.[2]

As we have seen, however, the role of yeshivas had changed considerably since the Volozhin yeshiva was founded in the early nineteenth century. Whereas Volozhin reflected the values prevailing in Jewish society at that time and prepared its students to enter its elite, by the end of the century the yeshivas increasingly aimed to educate their students *away* from the values favoured by the Jewish elite, which was now increasingly defined in terms of wealth and integration into non-Jewish society rather than traditional talmudic scholarship. A related development was the rise of the *kolel*, an institution that provided financial support to young married men who were willing to devote themselves to Torah study. By allowing young men to continue their Torah learning for a few more years after marriage, it also protected them for longer from the dangers of the wider world. One by-product of this extension of study was that by the time a married man left the *kolel* he would already have a family, which would make it impractical for him to take up secular study even if he were interested.

Another change lay in the perception of the benefits of a yeshiva education. Whereas in the early nineteenth century a yeshiva was merely a place of study,

---

[1] On yeshiva students from the West, see for instance Vishnitzer, 'Material for the History of the Yeshiva in Eastern Europe' (Heb.), 606.

[2] On support for yeshivas in the interwar period, see ibid. 613–18.

by the end of the century the yeshiva came to be seen as a 'fortress of Torah', providing an experience that strengthened the student spiritually. The metaphor was well suited to a period in which the values of the yeshiva world were increasingly seen to be in opposition to those of the surrounding society, so that the yeshiva itself was seen as protecting its students from the dangers that lay beyond.[3]

This development was not anticipated. Volozhin, the first yeshiva to be founded in Lithuania and the model in many respects of the later yeshivas, was the first to be independent of the local community, but it developed in this way not because of an ideology of separation and exclusiveness but as a result of the particular personal circumstances of R. Hayim of Volozhin. However, the growth of the yeshiva, both in numbers and importance, and the adoption of the Volozhin model by other yeshivas was due, at least in part, to the fact that it proved to be effective in the new conditions of modernity. Analysis of the establishment of yeshivas elsewhere, for example in Hungary and Poland,[4] suggests that yeshivas would have developed in Lithuania even if Volozhin had not been founded; however, the process would probably have begun later and developed differently, and perhaps less successfully. The success and impact of the *musar* movement was a similar development. Most of R. Salanter's ideas were formed well before he came into contact with modernity. They could have been expressed in any period, and many of them had indeed been expressed earlier. The movement in fact became more influential after R. Salanter's time. This was not because he was ineffective; it was a question of circumstance. When there was a general sense of stability, the ideas of the *musar* movement had limited appeal. However, as the challenge of modernity grew in the latter part of the nineteenth century, ideas which had once interested only a small number of individuals were now seen as attractive by far more people.

By the end of the nineteenth century, the changes and conflicts that had struck the Jewish world had affected the yeshiva too. Contemporary discussion of the yeshiva was frequently in the context of the Haskalah and noted its

---

[3] This was obviously a broader process than just changes in yeshivas, but little has been written about it; see Bacon, '*Da'at torah*' (Heb.); M. Friedman, *Society and Religion* (Heb.); Samet, 'Strict Orthodoxy in Modern Times' (Heb.); Soloveitchik, 'Rupture and Reconstruction'; Y. Katz, 'Orthodoxy in Historical Perspective' (Heb.); Luz, *Parallels Meet*; Y. Shulman, *Religion and Zionism* (Heb.); and Silber, 'The Emergence of Ultra-Orthodoxy'.

[4] On Hungarian yeshivas, see A. Friedman, 'Major Aspects of Yeshiva Education in Hungary'; Fuchs, *Hungarian Yeshivas* (Heb.); Silber, 'The Limits of Rapprochement'; Stampfer, 'Hungarian Yeshivot, Lithuanian Yeshivot, and Joseph Ben David'; and Weingarten, *Hungarian Yeshivas* (Heb.). Less has been written about Polish yeshivas; see S. Mirsky (ed.), *The Rise and Destruction of the Torah Institutions of Europe* (Heb.). Much can be learnt from rabbinical biographies, but this is not the place to present a full bibliography. There is a considerable body of literature on the Hakhmei Lublin yeshiva; see Mandelbaum, *The Hakhmei Lublin Yeshiva* (Heb.); see also Sorski, *Hasidic Torah Teachers* (Heb.).

power to effect change.[5] Why the Haskalah had such influence and where the youngsters who abandoned tradition went are questions that have not yet been adequately investigated, and it is doubtful whether they can be. There is no clear answer as to what it was that persuaded young people to abandon traditional Jewish life, but the wholesale attribution of this to the Haskalah is not self-evident. It seems much more likely that the threat to traditional ways came from indifference to Jewish identity rather than from any desire to change that identity. Indifference is naturally hard to identify, and it was easier for conservatives to battle against a concrete enemy, equally eager to do battle, than to engage with an attitude that was so contemptuous of traditional approaches that it did not even bother to argue with them.[6]

There are good grounds for thinking that the changes that took place in the late nineteenth century threatened the very existence of traditional society. We have considered how the different yeshivas offered somewhat different explanations of the challenge of modernity, and somewhat different ways of meeting that challenge, but ultimately they all succeeded in doing so. It was this that in the late nineteenth and early twentieth centuries led both traditional circles and hasidic circles in Poland to adopt the Lithuanian model.[7] The social and educational advantages of assembling young men under one roof, with supervision and an organized and clear curriculum, were obvious to all.

Neither the process of concentrating Torah students in yeshivas nor the prominent place that the *rashei yeshivah* assumed in the Jewish leadership went unopposed. As is generally the case when new systems are introduced, the absence of clarity over authority and power caused conflict and jealousy. However, in this case it seems that opposition stemmed more from resistance to change than from personal factors. For example, the campaign by the rabbi

[5] On the conflict with the Haskalah, see articles in the anthology of Etkes (ed.), *Religion and Life* (Heb.), esp. Feiner, 'Annotated Bibliography' (Heb.), to which should be added Avital, *The Yeshiva and Traditional Education* (Heb.). See also Katzenelson, *The Literary War* (Heb.); Luz, *Parallels Meet*; Shifman, 'The Controversy between the Strictly Orthodox and the Zionists' (Heb.).

[6] The history of attitudes towards Jewish culture in eastern Europe has yet to be written. I mention this in my article 'What Did "Knowing Hebrew" Mean in Eastern Europe?' See also Zahavi, *The Jewish Assimilation Movement* (Heb.), though there is little there that is relevant to our purposes. Much can be learnt on this subject from the works of Y. Slutsky, *Russian Jewish Journalism in the Nineteenth Century* (Heb.) and *Russian Jewish Journalism in the Early Twentieth Century* (Heb.). Levinson, *The Hebrew Movement in the Diaspora* (Heb.), reveals the problems in maintaining knowledge of Hebrew in eastern Europe. The suppression of Hebrew and Yiddish by the Bolsheviks is well known, but even in Poland there was a transition to Polish. See also Mendelsohn, *Jews of East Central Europe*, 67; on the transition to secular studies in eastern Europe, see Kreiz, 'Russian-Language Jewish Schools' (Heb.).

[7] There has been no methodical research on the spread of the yeshiva in the hasidic world; see the sources cited in n. 4, above. On hasidic yeshivas see e.g. Mondschein (ed.), 'Chronicles of the Tomkhei Temimim' (Heb.), and Sorski, *Hasidic Torah Teachers* (Heb.). See also my article 'Hasidic Yeshivas in Poland' (Heb.).

of Mir to become head of the Mir yeshiva was fired by the traditional attitude that all local institutions had to be administered by the community,[8] and the hints of opposition to the foundation of the Volozhin yeshiva—if they are accurate—reflect reservations about whether the institution was needed at all rather than opposition to R. Hayim and his methods.[9] The subsequent opposition by R. Willowski to the new style of Torah study in Lithuania—the so-called 'analytical method'—stemmed from similar feelings: he opposed it because it was different from the traditional way, which he regarded as the correct way by definition.[10] R. Hayim Tsevi Hirsch Broda similarly expressed frustration at the fact that the younger generation, who had been brought up on the analytical method, rejected the traditional method on which his own work was based:

And behold, I am now standing in the gateway, ready to publish my book, *Otsar ḥayim*, and to disseminate it in Israel, and I know all too well my own lack of value and that of my book, a poor and inadequate treasure; for the study of Talmud today according to the ways of logic, which has been renewed by some of the great scholars of our generation, is beyond me; for they prolong a single investigation into the finest details.[11]

A sense of bitterness, though not of opposition or denigration, is palpable here.

The fiercest opposition to the leadership role that the yeshivas aspired to take on themselves was reserved for the yeshivas of the *musar* movement, both because of that movement's own criticism of traditional society and from fear within the traditional society that this new approach would do more harm than good.[12] The *musar* yeshivas may have seen themselves as bastions protecting the traditional Jewish world from dangerous external innovations, but this view was opposed by some elements even within that society.

The early nineteenth-century yeshivas were elitist. Despite the obvious differences between Torah study in yeshivas and the study of literature in other societies, it is instructive to compare Jewish society with other cultures in which knowledge of classical literature was central to the education of the elite. In such societies, a cultured man was one who could quote literary texts; a man who had mastered classical literature was assumed to have the mental ability to master any problem. Training in classical literature was considered superior to any vocational training. Nobody within these societies, whatever their social class, cast doubt upon the value of classical literature.[13]

---

[8] On this, see Lifschitz, *Toledot yitsḥak*, 66–7.

[9] See Ch. 1 above: the discussion of the yeshiva's foundation.

[10] See Ch. 4 above. [11] H. T. H. Broda, *Otsar ḥayim*, intro.

[12] On opposition to the *musar* movement, see Ch. 9 above; for more details, see D. Katz, *The Musar Controversy* (Heb.). [13] See Wilkinson, 'The Gentleman Ideal'.

This was the situation in classical China and in Victorian England, and the comparison with Torah study in Jewish society is interesting.[14] The sociologist Max Weber enumerated the three key features of Chinese culture in this regard as follows. First, the scholar was required to be meticulous in his behaviour, to be devoted to learning, and to follow the curriculum of study of classical literature. Second, this curriculum included a restricted selection of books. There was no lack of mathematicians, astronomers, scientists, and geographers in Chinese society, but these were all classified by scholars as members of the masses, or in today's parlance, non-academics. Thirdly, entry to the ruling elite was conditional on passing examinations in classical literature and the history of classical Chinese society. Anyone who was not educated was considered a boor. In Victorian England, too, education was based on the study of classical literature in Greek and Latin.[15] Education in classical literature was considered preferable to the study of practical subjects as the proper training for an English gentleman and future leader. On this view, anyone educated in the classics would subsequently be able to pick up any knowledge and skills he might need. The English gentleman was distinguished by his accent, but no less by his ability to quote the classics in the original, from memory—in other words, by his cultural rather than his practical knowledge. Thus in Weber's view, the content of this educational system resembled that of Chinese culture.

The parallels with the education of the Jewish elite in eastern Europe in the early nineteenth century are instructive. The principal subject of study was the Talmud, most of which was written in Aramaic—an ancient language no longer spoken. The commentaries that were studied alongside the Talmud were also not written in the Yiddish vernacular and dictionaries of the Talmud were still very rare. The language itself thus presented an obstacle to anyone wishing to study it. Other areas of Torah learning that might conceivably have been the focus of study—such as the Bible, philosophy, or aggadah—were excluded from the curriculum. Scholarly status was demonstrated not by honorific titles but by knowledge of talmudic literature.

Several characteristics of a culture based on textual literacy can be distinguished here. In traditional Jewish society, Talmud scholars were considered more refined in their behaviour than ordinary men; like English gentlemen, they could be identified by their speech and conduct.[16] Also, the emphasis was on textual study for its own sake: as with vocational subjects or science in the classical English education, practical halakhah was not usually part of the curriculum. Even though the *batei midrash* and yeshivas did produce rabbis, they were not intended to be places of vocational training, and those who studied

[14] This is based on Young, 'Curricula and Social Organization of Knowledge'.
[15] See Wilkinson, 'The Gentleman Ideal'.
[16] See e.g. comments on the Vilna Gaon in Y. H. Levin, *Aliyot eliyahu*, 46 n. 31.

with this aim in mind tended to conceal the fact. It was only towards the end of the nineteenth century that yeshivas began to present themselves as rabbinical seminaries, but this was largely due to external factors rather than because of any change in their own orientation. The Jewish public was asked to support the yeshivas simply as places of Torah study.

In many societies, education serves as a means of changing one's class affiliation because success in study appears to depend solely on ability rather than on wealth or family connections. The educational systems of China and Victorian England would at first glance seem to have made such social mobility possible. Their graduates should have been able to justify their membership of the elite by their personal achievements and intellectual ability, as expressed by their expertise in classical literature. In practice, however, placing classical literature at the centre of the curriculum prevented social mobility. Study of literature in a foreign language, such as Latin or Greek, or subjects that required mastery of a complicated script and constant study for several years, as in China, generally prevented members of the lower classes from having any chance to improve their social status. The preliminary training demanded considerable investment for the long term, thus necessitating confidence that the student would justify the investment and would continue to study. This obviously depended on the parents' ability to fund their child's studies, and to do without the income that he would have been able to bring to the family during these years. Moreover, in these societies, graduates of the educational system found good jobs, on the grounds that they were the most suitable candidates, even if they had no vocational training. Learning was thus a real asset, and these educational systems tended to perpetuate the class system.[17] This reality depended on the fact that society accepted the supremacy of the literature studied as self-evident.

Traditional Jewish society reflected a similar model: it accepted the centrality of rabbinic literature as self-evident, and regarded Torah study as a supreme value. Every boy was sent to study Torah, though few were lucky enough to have good teachers. In other words, even the very first level of education concealed an obstacle discouraging social mobility. The need for families to support yeshiva students financially, in addition to forgoing the contribution they might have made to the family income, tended to perpetuate the class distinctions within Jewish society. But just as sociological change led to crises in elitist education in England and in China, sociological change had repercussions in the traditional Jewish world too—although in Lithuania the yeshivas were part of the solution rather than the cause of the problem.

The yeshiva system developed in response to the collapse of the *batei*

[17] See Turner, 'Sponsored and Contest Mobility', 855. For a basis for the analysis of the hypothesis, see Bourdieu and Passeron, *Reproduction in Education, Society, and Culture*.

midrash and was seen as essential element in preserving the traditional values of a conservative society. In the early nineteenth century, the yeshiva was therefore presented as simply a place of Torah study; with no suggestion of practical advantage or reward. By the end of the century, the yeshiva still saw itself in this way but began to present itself to the Jewish public as an institution worthy of support because of its role in training rabbis and future leaders.[18] With the increased emphasis on training and formal education, students came to be seen as participants in a study programme rather than as responsible adults engaged in study for its own sake. This also reflected changes in concepts of maturity in this period.

If the yeshiva did not give students any practical training, how did yeshiva graduates make a living? Those with wealthy parents could go into the family business, just as the sons of rabbis hoped to succeed their fathers. A young man to whom neither option was open hoped to marry into a wealthy family so his father-in-law could support him financially or buy him a rabbinical position. Teaching young boys was of course also a possibility. None of this was directly linked to having studied at yeshiva because of the absence of a formal qualification. Indirectly, however, a yeshiva education did help students to find a good match or a rabbinical post because the concentration of talented students in one place was such that people naturally turned to yeshivas to find suitable candidates, whether as rabbis or as marriage partners. Even the emissaries who collected donations for the yeshivas were useful in this regard, since on their trips back to the yeshiva they could find out who were the best students and propose matches for them with girls who lived in more distant communities.

In the second half of the nineteenth century, a large proportion of the Jewish public ceased to regard Torah study for its own sake as being of value and placed greater emphasis on studying for a profession or acquiring vocational training, This view did not immediately filter through to the yeshivas and had no effect on the yeshiva curriculum, but in the long term the fact that students' aspirations and plans for the future were changing had its effect. To better understand some of the implications of these changes, let us look at the process of studying at yeshiva from a rather different aspect: the process of entry into a different world.

Leaving home to join a yeshiva in some ways resembled the puberty rites known from other cultures,[19] rites of passage that serve to mark the end of childhood and integrate the young person into life outside the family framework. In a similar fashion, leaving home and family to go to an all-male

---

[18] R. Yisra'el Salanter was prominent in this regard, as in other spheres. On his attitude to the rabbinate, see Etkes, *Rabbi Yisra'el Salanter* (Heb.), 235–7, 285–94.

[19] On a possible link between education and puberty rites, see the interesting article by Ong, 'Latin Language Study as a Renaissance Puberty Rite', 232–48. See also Ch. 5, §5, above.

yeshiva or *beit midrash* constituted a young man's break with his past and sig-nified his entry to adult Jewish society. Once at the yeshiva, many came to be known by nicknames, usually based on their town of origin, rather than by the surnames they would have used at home. This added to the sense of alien-ation from the past, another characteristic of puberty rites.

Descriptions of suffering and harsh conditions regularly appear in memoirs written by yeshiva students, and this too is characteristic of puberty rites. Yeshiva life is portrayed as a time of poverty, even by students who came from wealthy homes. Former yeshiva students proudly recall in their memoirs how they overcame all obstacles for the sake of Torah study. Study demanded endurance and tremendous persistence in the face of difficulties. It proved the triumph of the will over the body: the more time spent in study, the more praiseworthy the student. Those who studied for twenty hours a day rightly regarded this as an achievement, and recounted it with pride. This was the way in which a Jewish youth could demonstrate that he was worthy and eager to enter the adult world.

Another feature typical of puberty rites is supervision—adult control of those entering the new society. In the *beit midrash* this was the job of the veteran students, even though they had no official authority; in the yeshiva, the role was taken by the *rashei yeshivah*, who saw themselves *in loco parentis* in every respect. There are many accounts of *rashei yeshivah* who called their stu-dents 'sons' and of students who relied on their *rosh yeshivah* as on a father.[20] The fact that students remained at the yeshiva for festivals underscored the position of the *rosh yeshivah* in this role. On the other hand, the subconscious desire to rebel against a father figure seems to have been one of the factors behind the unrest in the yeshivas, even though ostensibly the conflict was always for other reasons.

Yet another element akin to a puberty rite was that students—notionally, the future elite of the society—temporarily acquired low social status. In the *beit midrash* system, students ate with different families on different days as a way of getting local people to support the institution while also giving them the opportunity to fulfil the religious obligation of giving charity to the poor—even though everyone knew that the students' poverty was temporary, and that after marriage they would return to take their rightful place in society. This was true of some yeshivas too in the early nineteenth century, but the yeshiva in Volozhin had more students than the town could support in this way so the yeshiva actually paid for students to eat with local families, which made the town dependent on the yeshiva rather than the other way round.

At the end of the nineteenth century, the changes in Jewish society were

[20] For an example of the fatherly attitude of R. Berlin at Volozhin, see M. Berlin [Bar-Ilan], *From Volozhin to Jerusalem* (Heb.), vol. 1, ch. 8, and see pp. 112–17 for a portrait of yeshiva life from within.

such that yeshiva students had many reasons to feel trepidation about their future. In order to maintain the attractiveness of Torah study, the yeshiva had to reinforce students' self-image. The move away from making students rely on the hospitality of individual families, as poor people had to do, was one expression of this. Another was the change in students' dress code. Many societies recognize a phenomenon by which people in powerful positions can allow themselves to dress simply, while those who are more concerned about their status take pains to dress elaborately, in a way that they think matches their aspirations. This was true of eastern Europe too. In the early part of the century students in the *batei midrash* and yeshivas were known for their unkempt appearance, whereas by the end of the century yeshiva students wore modern, even fashionable, clothes. Particular attention was paid to dress at Slobodka.[21]

Changes also took place in the composition of the student body, in terms of age and of geographical and social background, although it is difficult to document this. In the early nineteenth century there were many students at Volozhin who had not yet reached the age of thirteen. Arrival at the yeshiva at this age is not singled out for emphasis in the biographies, reinforcing the impression that it was not unusual. By contrast, at the end of the century most students were fourteen or fifteen, or sometimes much older,[22] and there was a similar increase in the age of marriage. In the mid-nineteenth century the traditional pattern of child marriage disappeared, and the average age of marriage rose to twenty or more.[23] Part of the reason seems to have been a change in the concept of maturity: the age of the onset of adolescence rose, and adolescence itself lengthened. This rise in the students' age had unforeseen consequences: institutions for 17- to 18-year-olds have different disciplinary problems from those of institutions for younger or older populations. Analysis of the rebellions at yeshivas in the late nineteenth century reveal the power of a group of young people with a high degree of solidarity.

It is even more difficult to trace the changes in the students' geographical background.[24] The nineteenth century saw a gradually accelerating process of urbanization. However, there were not many yeshiva students during this period who came from cities. The available sources give the impression that most students came from small towns or villages—places where the allure and possibility of acquiring a secular education did not yet exist. Some of the students from cities may have belonged to a special sub-group, such as the families of rabbis and other religious functionaries. The proportion of rabbis' sons

[21] D. Katz, *The Musar Movement* (Heb.), iii. 289.
[22] See Stampfer, 'Three Lithuanian Yeshivas in the Nineteenth Century', 223–30.
[23] I have written on this subject in 'The Social Significance of Very Early Marriage'.
[24] The only relevant source that I know from this period is the pamphlet 'Keneset yisra'el', analysed above, in the discussion of the Slobodka yeshiva (Ch. 9).

among yeshiva students should thus also be examined: many students' memoirs do indeed mention rabbis' sons, but unfortunately there are not enough sources to enable a methodical survey. It seems likely that the students who came from small towns or from rabbinical families were less influenced by new ideas in their youth, but this was not sufficient to protect them against the Haskalah and the changes in the surrounding society, both Jewish and non-Jewish. The background of many of these students did not shield them in the long run, but merely delayed the process undergone by their contemporaries in the cities. It seems that entry into yeshiva sometimes served as the first step in exposure to the new world.

How successful were the yeshivas? As I have said, nobody would question their importance in traditional Jewish society. The men who founded the yeshivas did not do so in order to make headlines: their goal was simply to strengthen Torah study in the Jewish community. From a qualitative point of view, success can be measured in the important developments in methods of study. From a quantitative point of view, success can be measured in the great increase in the number of yeshivas and in the number of students increasing through the century. However, the collapse of the *beit midrash* system on the one hand, coupled with the overall rise in the Jewish population of eastern Europe on the other, must also be taken into account in a comparison between the beginning and the end of the nineteenth century. The relative numbers of those studying Torah seems to have dropped considerably by the end of the century, but it would have been even lower without the yeshivas. It is also difficult to measure the success of the yeshivas in moulding students' characters, though the extent of student rebellions in the latter part of the century seems to suggest that success may have been limited. Nevertheless, it seems that, in the absence of the yeshivas, a larger proportion of the faithful and constant minority would have abandoned tradition.

The long-term influence of the Lithuanian yeshiva is unquestionable. R. Hayim of Volozhin's attempt to overcome the difficulties of running a large institution in a small town led to the development of a yeshiva characterized by its independence of the local community, the reinforcement of its internal links, and the organization of a supra-regional support system. As Jewish society ceased to see Torah study as a supreme value worthy of financial support, this pattern served as a model that could be adopted elsewhere. It is probable that the cultural disintegration at this time would have led to the emergence of a new institutional framework in any case—nature abhors a vacuum—but the existence of a ready-made model certainly helped to ensure that the tradition of Torah study survived, both within eastern Europe and beyond. The Lithuanian yeshiva model was also eventually adopted by hasidic circles, even though one of the original factors in the growth of hasidism had been rejection of the emphasis on a scholarly elite: eventually even hasidim reached the conclusion that the yeshiva was essential for the education of the younger generation. The seeds sown in early nineteenth-century Lithuania continue to flourish today.

Gazetteer of Place Names in Central and Eastern Europe

THIS gazetteer has been compiled using Gary Mokotoff and Sallyann Amdur Sack's comprehensive work *Where Once We Walked: A Guide to the Jewish Communities Destroyed in the Holocaust* (Teaneck, NJ, 1991). We are grateful to Avotaynu as the publishers of that work for their generosity in allowing us to do so. The style of the entries follows their conventions, except that diacritical marks have been added where necessary.

Names of countries have been abbreviated as follows: Bel. = Belarus; Cz. = Czech Republic; Est. = Estonia; Lat. = Latvia; Lith. = Lithuania; Pol. = Poland; Rus. = Russia; Slov. = Slovakia; Ukr. = Ukraine.

Aleksat *see* Aleksotas

Aleksotas Lith. (Aleksat); now a district of Kaunas

Amtchislav *see* Mstislavl

Antakalnis Lith. (Antokol); now a district of Vilnius

Antokol *see* Antakalnis

Bauska Lat. (Boisk); 69 km S of Riga

Belarus (Belorussia) part of the tsarist empire in the nineteenth century, later a republic of the Soviet Union (the western half was part of Poland before the end of the Second World War), now an independent state (Belarus) between Poland and Russia

Berdichev Ukr.; 82 km N of Vinnitsa

Berezen *see* Berezino

Berezino Bel. (Berezen); 95 km E of Minsk

Biała *see* Biała Podlaska

Biała Podlaska Pol.; 101 km NNE of Lublin

Bobruisk Bel.; 139 km WNW of Gomel

Boisk *see* Bauska

Bransk *see* Brańsk

Brańsk Pol. (Bransk); 50 km SSW of Białystok

Bratislava Slov. (Pressburg); the capital of Slovakia

Brest Bel. (Brest-Litovsk, Brisk); 163 km WSW of Pinsk

Brisk *see* Brest

Bukovina (Bucovina) a region now in north-eastern Romania and south-western Ukraine; part of the Austro-Hungarian Empire before the end of the First World War and then part of Romania until the end of the Second World War

Bychow *see* Bykhov

Bykhov Bel. (Bychow; formerly Stary Bykhov); 133 km NNW of Gomel

Chełm Pol.; 69 km E of Lublin

Cherven Bel. (Ihumen); 62 km ESE of Minsk

Ciechanowiec Pol.; 69 km SSW of Białystok

Courland a region in western Latvia

Danzig *see* Gdańsk

Daugavpils Lat. (Denenburg, Dvinsk); 189 km ESE of Riga

Denenburg *see* Daugavpils

Derechin Bel.; 150 km NNW of Pinsk

Dorpat *see* Tartu

Dvinsk *see* Daugavpils

Dyatlovo Bel. (Zhetel); 150 km WSW of Minsk

Eishyshok *see* Eišiškės

Eišiškės Lith. (Eishyshok); 62 km SSW of Vilnius

Galicia a region that since the Second World War has been part of southern Poland and Ukraine. Before 1772 it constituted the southern part of the Kingdom of Poland, then became part of the Austro-Hungarian Empire until the end of the First World War. It was then returned to Poland until the end of the Second World War

Gdańsk Pol. (Danzig); 240 km NNE of Poznań

Glusk Bel. (Helusk); 135 km SE of Minsk

Gorodeya Bel.; 94 km SW of Minsk

Gorodok Bel.; 50 km NW of Minsk

Grobin *see* Grobiņa

Grobiņa Lat. (Grobin); 182 km WSW of Riga

Grodno Bel.; 234 km NW of Pinsk

Helusk *see* Glusk

Haslowicz *see* Khislavichi

Ihumen *see* Cherven

Ilya Bel.; 62 km NNW of Minsk

Ivenets Bel. (Iwaniec); 56 km W of Minsk

Iwaniec *see* Ivenets

Jacobstadt *see* Jēkabpils

Jałówka Pol. (Yalovka); 56 km ESE of Białystok

Janishok *see* Joniškis

Jašiūnai Lith.; 26 km S of Vilnius

Jēkabpils Lat. (Jacobstadt); 82 km NW of Daugavpils

Jelgava Lat. (Mitau); 45 km SW of Riga

Joniškis Lith. (Janishok); 38 km NNE of Šiauliai

Kalisz Pol.; 94 km W of Łódź

Kalvarija Lith.; 70 km SW of Kaunas

Karlin Bel.; 6 km E of Pinsk

Katowice Pol.; 62 km S of Częstochowa

Kaunas Lith. (Kovno); 94 km W of Vilnius

Kėdainiai Lith. (Keidan); 50 km N of Kaunas

Keidan *see* Kėdainiai

Kelme *see* Kelmė

Kelmė Lith. (Kelme); 45 km SSW of Šiauliai

Kherson Ukr.; 146 km ENE of Odessa

Khislavichi Rus. (Haslowicz); 67 km S of Smolensk

Kiev Ukr.; the capital of Ukraine

Klaipėda Lith. (Memel); 137 km W of Šiauliai

Kolin *see* Kolín

Kolín Cz. (Kolin); 50 km E of Prague

Kopust *see* Kopys

Kopys Bel. (Kopust); 101 km S of Vitebsk

Kovno *see* Kaunas

Krakizov This place has not been identified

Kremenets Ukr. (Kremenitz); 69 km SSW of Rovno

Kremenitz *see* Kremenets

Krinik *see* Krynki

Krynki Pol. (Krinik); 45 km ENE of Białystok

Kul *see* Kuliai

Kuliai Lith. (Kul); 107 km WSW of Šiauliai

Kurenets Bel.; 88 km NW of Minsk

Libau *see* Liepāja

Lida Bel.; 146 km WSW of Minsk

Liepāja Lat. (Libau); 195 km WSW of Riga

Łódź Pol.; 114 km N of Częstochowa

Lomza *see* Łomża

Łomża Pol. (Lomza); 69 km W of Białystok

Lubavitch *see* Lyubavichi

Lyady Bel.; 38 km ESE of Minsk

Lyubavichi Rus. (Lubavitch); 60 km SE of Vitebsk

Maitchet *see* Molchad

Malech Bel. (Maltsh); 107 km WNW of Pinsk

Maltsh *see* Malech

Memel *see* Klaipėda

Międzyrzec Podlaski Pol.; 120 km E of Warsaw

Minsk Bel.; the capital of Belarus

Mir Bel.; 88 km SW of Minsk

Mitau *see* Jelgava

Mogilev Bel.; 150 km S of Vitebsk

Molchad Bel. (Maitchet); 139 km SW of Minsk

Mstislavl Bel. (Amtchislav); 163 km SE of Vitebsk

Nesvizh Bel.; 94 km SW of Minsk

Novoaleksandrovsk *see* Zarasai

Novogrudok Bel.; 120 km WSW of Minsk

Odessa Ukr.; 258 km SSE of Uman

Oshmyany Bel.; 120 km WNW of Minsk

Pale of Settlement a region in the western part of the tsarist empire in which Jews were allowed to reside

Panevėžys Lith. (Ponevezh); 69 km ESE of Šiauliai

Pilvishki *see* Pilviškiai

Pilviškiai Lith. (Pilvishki); 50 km SW of Kaunas

Pinsk Bel.; 221 km SSW of Minsk

Podolia a region in south-western Ukraine

Poltava Ukr.; 126 km SW of Kharkov

Ponevezh *see* Panevėžys

Posen *see* Poznań

Poznań Pol. (Posen); 157 km N of Wrocław

Pressburg *see* Bratislava

Radun Bel.; 170 km W of Minsk

Rakov Bel.; 35 km WNW of Minsk

Raseiniai Lith.; 69 km WNW of Kaunas

Rozhinoy *see* Ruzhany

Rozin *see* Ruzhany

Rubezhevichi Bel.; 50 km SW of Minsk

Ruzhany Bel. (Rozhinoy, Rozin); 120 km NW of Pinsk

Ruzhin Ukr.; 75 km NE of Vinnitsa

Sadov Ukr.; 94 km W of Rovno

Salakas Lith. (Saluk); 114 km NNE of Vilnius

Salant *see* Salantai

Salantai Lith. (Salant); 107 km W of Šiauliai

Saluk *see* Salakas

Samogitia *see* Žemaitija

Satanov Ukr.; 107 km N of Chernovtsy

Shklov Bel.; 114 km S of Vitebsk

Shkod *see* Skuodas

Shnipishak *see* Šnipiškės

Šiauliai Lith.; 120 km NNW of Kaunas

Skuodas Lith. (Shkod); 120 km WNW of Šiauliai

Slavuta Ukr.; 56 km ESE of Rovno

Slobodka *see* Vilijampolė

Slonim Bel.; 126 km NW of Pinsk

Slutsk Bel.; 101 km S of Minsk

Smorgon Bel.; 107 km WNW of Minsk

Šnipiškės Lith.; now a district of Vilnius

Stary Bykhov *see* Bykhov

Suvalk *see* Suwałki

Suwałki Pol.; 114 km NNW of Białystok

Švenčionys Lith. (Sventsyany); 75 km NE of Vilnius

Sventsyany *see* Švenčionys

Svir Bel.; 133 km NW of Minsk

Szczuczyn Pol.; 73 km NW of Białystok

Tartu Est. (Dorpat); 160 km SE of Tallinn

Telšiai Lith. (Telz); 69 km W of Šiauliai

Telz *see* Telšiai

Ukmergė Lith. (Vilkomir); 69 km NE of Kaunas

Varna *see* Varniai

Varniai Lith. (Varna); 62 km SW of Šiauliai

Veliuona Lith.; 45 km WNW of Kaunas

Vidaz *see* Vidzy

Vidzy Bel.; 176 km NNW of Minsk

Vilijampolė Lith. (Slobodka); now a district of Kaunas

Vilkomir *see* Ukmergė

Vilna *see* Vilnius

Vilnius Lith. (Vilna, Wilna); the capital of Lithuania

Vitebsk Bel.; 221 km NE of Minsk

Volhynia a region of north-western Ukraine

Volkovysk Bel.; 163 km WNW of Pinsk

Volozhin Bel. (Woloshin, Wolozin); 75 km WNW of Minsk

Warsaw Pol.; the capital of Poland

Wilna *see* Vilnius

Woloshin *see* Volozhin

Wolozin *see* Volozhin

Yalovka *see* Jałówka

Žagarė Lith.; 50 km N of Šiauliai

Zamut *see* Žemaitija

Zarasai Lith. (Novoaleksandrovsk);
133 km NNE of Vilnius

Zelva Bel.; 200 km WSW of Minsk

Žemaičių Naumiestis Lith.; 120 km

SW of Šiauliai

Žemaitija (Samogitia, Zamut) a region
in NW Lithuania

Zhetel *see* Dyatlovo

Zhitomir Ukr.; 120 km N of
Vinnitsa

Bibliography

ABEL, ABRAHAM ABA, 'Rabbi Shlomo Zalman Halevi Abell' (Heb.), *He'asif*, 4 (1888), 64–5.

ABEL, S., *Beit shelomoh* [A halakhic work dealing primarily with financial matters] (Vilna, 1893).

ABRAMOWICZ, HIRSZ, *Disappeared Images* [Farshvundene geshtaltn] (Buenos Aires, 1958).

ABRAMSON, GLENDA (ed.), *Jewish Education and Learning* (Chur, Switzerland, 1993).

ADAM HAKOHEN [ABRAHAM DOV LEBENSOHN], *Shir ḥavivim* [Song of the Beloved Ones] (Vilna, 1822).

AGRANOVSKY, GENRIKH, 'Materials on the History of the Volozhin Yeshiva' (Rus.), *Vestnik Evreiskogo universiteta v Moskve*, 11/29 (2006), 327–38.

——'Naftali Berlin and the Volozhin Yeshiva' (Rus.), *Vestnik Evreiskogo universiteta v Moskve*, 1/3 (1993), 130–4.

——and SID LEIMAN, 'Three Lists of Students Studying at the Volozhin Yeshiva in 1879', in Michael A. Shmidman (ed.), *Turim: Studies in Jewish History and Literature Presented to Dr Bernard Lander*, vol. ii (New York, 2008), 1–24.

ALBARELLI, G., *Teacha! Stories from a Yeshiva* (Thetford, Vt., 2000).

ALEXANDROVSKY, YITSHAK HAKOHEN, *Sha'arei yitsḥak* (Warsaw, 1898).

ALPEROWITZ, YITZHAK (ed.), *Telz* [Sefer telz] (Tel Aviv, 1984).

ALTMAN, Y., '"And his head reached heaven": The Teaching and Personality of R. Yosef Leib Bloch' [Verosho magia hashamaimah: harav yosef yehudah leib blokh—torato ve'ishiuto], MA thesis (Touro College, Jerusalem, 2002).

ARONSON, I. M., *Troubled Waters: The Origins of the 1881 Anti-Jewish Pogroms in Russia* (Pittsburgh, 1990).

ARYEH HALEVI OF VOLKOVYSK, *Penei aryeh* [Torah commentary] (Vilna, 1873).

ASAF, A., *Sources for the History of Jewish Education* [Mekorot letoledot haḥinukh beyisra'el], 4 vols. (Tel Aviv, 1925–48).

ASAF, S., 'A Pedigree' (Heb.), *Reshumot*, NS 4 (1947), 131–43.

——'My Study Years at the Telz Yeshiva' (Heb.), *He'avar*, 2 (1954), 34–45.

ASHKENAZI, ASHER HAKOHEN, *Birkat rosh* [Principal Blessing] (Piotrków, 1891).

ATTIA, ALI MOHAMED ABD EL-RAHMAN, *The Hebrew Periodical Ha-Shiloah (1896–1919)* (Jerusalem, 1991).

AUERBACH, M. (ed.), *Yitshak Eizik Halevi Memorial Volume* [Sefer zikaron lerabi yitsḥak eizik halevi] (Benei Berak, 1964).

AVITAL, M. N., *The Yeshiva and Traditional Education in the Literature of the Hebrew Enlightenment Period* [Hayeshivah vehaḥinukh hamasorti besifrut hahaskalah ha'ivrit] (Tel Aviv, 1996).

AVIVI, Y., *The Kabbalah of the Vilna Gaon* [Kabalat hagra] (Jerusalem, 1993).

AVRAHAM BEN HAGRA, *Sa'arat eliyahu* [Eulogy of the Vilna Gaon] (Jerusalem, 1970).

Avraham Dov Vaisfish Memorial Volume [Sefer zikaron likhevodam ulezikhram shel harav avraham dov vaisfish . . . verayato . . . shoshanah] (Jerusalem, 1992).

AVRAHAM SIMHAH OF AMTCHISLAV, *Binyan shel simhah* (Vilna, 1869).

——and SHALOM OF RUBEZHEVICHI, 'Correspondence between the *Gaon* R. Avraham Simhah of Amtchislav and the *Gaon* R. Shalom of Rubezhevichi' (Heb.), *Tevunah*, 1/12 (Sept. 1940), 145–50.

BACON, G., '*Da'at torah* and the Birthpangs of the Messiah' (Heb.), *Tarbits*, 52 (1983), 497–508.

——*The Politics of Tradition: Agudat Yisra'el in Poland 1916–1939* (Jerusalem, 1996).

BALOSHER, ABA, 'Bialik at Volozhin' (Heb.), *Moznayim*, 4 (1935), 120–36.

——*Hayim Nahman Bialik in Volozhin, Volozhin in Bialik* [Hayim nahman bialik bevolozhin, volozhin bebialik] (Kaunas, 1935).

BAR BEI RAV, *see* BERDYCZEWSKI, MICHA YOSEF

BAR-ILAN, ME'IR, *see* BERLIN, ME'IR

BARIT, YA'AKOV, 'Approbation for Levin's *Tsiyun yehoshua*' (Heb.), in Yehoshua Heshel Levin (ed.), *Moda'ah mevaseret tsiyon* (Vilna, 1880), 9.

BARIT, Z. L., 'Glory of Israel' (Heb.), in A. Y. Slutsky (ed.), *Return to Zion* [Shivat tsiyon], vol. ii (Warsaw, 1900), 55–9.

BARNET, Z., *Memoirs* [Zikhronot] (Jerusalem, 1929).

BAT-YEHUDAH, G., *Man of Light* [Ish hame'orot] (Jerusalem, 1985).

BEER-MARX, R., 'The Confrontation of the Rabbis who Wrote in *Halevanon* with the Challenges of Radical Haskalah (1868–74)' [Hitmodeduto shel hug rabanei 'Halevanon' im etgarei hahaskalah haradikalit], MA thesis (Hebrew University, Jerusalem, 1998).

BEN-EZRA, A., 'Kings of Purim' (Heb.), *Hado'ar*, 38/19 (20 Mar. 1959), 344–9.

BEN-SASSON, H. H., 'The *Musar* Movement in Lithuania in the Nineteenth Century' (Heb.), in B. Z. Dinaburg and N. H. Tur-Sinai (eds.), *[First] World Congress of Jewish Studies, 1947* (Heb.), (Jerusalem, 1952), 446–9.

BEN-SASSON, Y., 'The *Musar* Movement and the School of Volozhin: Continuation and Change—A Typological Comparison' (Heb.), *Mayim midalyo*, 1 (1990), 251–77.

BEN-TOVIM, YITSHAK EIZIK, 'In the Volozhin Yeshiva before its Closure' (Heb.), *Hahed*, 7/4 (Dec. 1931–Jan. 1932), 30.

BERDYCZEWSKI, MICHA YOSEF [BAR BEI RAV], 'A Bundle of Letters' (Heb.), *Hamelits*, 28/53 (4 Mar. 1888), 541–4; 28/56 (20 Mar. 1888), 573–4; 28/59 (23 Mar. 1888), 605–8.

——'History of the Ets Hayim Yeshiva' (Heb.), *He'asif*, 3 (1885), 231–42.

——'The World of Emanation' (Heb.), *Hakerem*, 1 (1880), 63–77.

BERGER, P., and T. LUCKMANN, *The Social Construction of Reality* (New York, 1966).

BERLIN, H., 'Forgotten Sheaf and Corner of the Field' (Heb.), *Beit hamidrash*, 1 (1888), 72–3.

—— *Ha'amek davar* [Biblical commentary] (Vilna, 1879).

—— *Meshiv davar* [Responsa], 2 vols. (Warsaw 1904; Jerusalem, 1993).

—— *Nishmat ḥayim* [Articles and letters], ed. Jacob Kosovski-Shahor (Jerusalem, 2003).

—— 'To Those Who Research the Past' (Heb.), *Hapeles*, 2/15 (1902), 140–3.

—— (ed.), *Ḥut hameshulash* [The Threefold Cord] (Vilna, 1882).

BERLIN, ME'IR [ME'IR BAR-ILAN], *Rabbi of Israel* [Raban shel yisra'el] (New York, 1943).

—— *From Volozhin to Jerusalem* [Mivolozhin liyerushalayim], 2 vols. (Tel Aviv, 1971).

BERLIN, NAFTALI TSEVI YEHUDAH, *Letters of the Netsiv* [Igerot hanetsiv], ed. Jacob Kosovski-Shakhor (Benei Berak, 2003).

—— *Sermons of the Netsiv* [Derashot hanetsiv], ed. Aryeh Shapira (Jerusalem, 1993).

BERNSTEIN, YISRAEL, 'Hastening Redemption' (Heb.), *Hashaḥar*, 10 (1880), 231–2.

BIALIK, HAYIM NAHMAN, *Devarim shebe'al peh* (Tel Aviv, 1935).

—— *Hamatmid* [The Eternal Student], ed. and introd. Dan Miron (Tel Aviv, 1975).

—— *The Letters of Hayim Nahman Bialik* [Igerot ḥayim naḥman bialik] (Tel Aviv, 1938).

BIALOBLOCKI, S., 'Rabbi Itzeleh of Ponevezh' (Heb.), in N. Goren et al. (eds.), *Lithuania* [Sefer lita] (Tel Aviv, 1960), 394–7.

BINYAMINI, Z. N., *Yesteryear* [Temol shilshom], ed. H. I. Yevin (Ramat Hasharon, 1960).

BLAU, YOSEF (ed.), *Lomdus: The Conceptual Approach to Jewish Learning* (Jersey City, 2006).

BLOCH, ELIJAH MEIR, 'The Telz Yeshiva' (Yid.), in Mendel Sudarsky et al. (eds.), *Lithuania* [Sefer lite], vol. i (New York, 1951), 623–30.

Book of Instructions and Guidelines of Our Rabbi Hayim of Volozhin [Sefer horaot vehanhagot mirabenu ḥayim mivolozhin] (Benei Berak, 1987).

BOURDIEU, P., and J.-C. PASSERON, *Reproduction in Education, Society, and Culture* (London, 1977).

BRAVERMAN, H., 'The Jewish Community in Kovno' (Heb.), *Keneset yisra'el*, 2 (1887), 163–76.

BREUER, M., 'The Ashkenazi Yeshiva in the Late Middle Ages' [Hayeshivah ha'ashkenazit beshalhei yemei habeinayim], Ph.D. thesis (Hebrew University, Jerusalem, 1967).

—— *Tents of Torah: The Structure and History of the Yeshiva* [Ohalei torah: hayeshivah tavnitah vetoledoteiha] (Jerusalem, 2004).

—— 'Torah and Derekh erets in the Thought of Rabbi Samson Raphael Hirsch' (Heb.), *Hama'ayan*, 9/1 (Dec. 1968–Jan. 1969), 1–16.

BRINKER, D. N., *The Shemuel [Salant] Charitable Foundation* [Otsar ḥesed keren shemuel] (Jerusalem, 1940).

BRODA, HAYIM TSEVI HIRSCH, *Otsar ḥayim* [Selected talmudic insights] (Vilna, 1899).

BRODA, Y., *Beit ya'akov* (Jerusalem, 1884).

BROIDES, Y., *Zionist Vilna and its Activists* [Vilna hatsiyonit ve'askaneiha] (Tel Aviv, 1940).

BROWN, BENJAMIN, *The Hazon Ish: Halakhist, Believer and Leader of the Haredi Revolution* [Haḥazon ish: haposek, hama'amin umanhig hamahpekhah haḥaredit] (Jerusalem, 2011).

BRUTSKUS, B. D. (ed.), *Statistics of the Jewish Population: The Territorial Distribution, and the Demographic and Cultural Features of the Jewish Population according to the Data of the 1897 Census* [Statistika evreiskogo naseleniya: Raspredelenie po territorii, demograficheskie i kul'turnye priznaki evreiskogo naseleniya po dannym perepisi 1897 g.] (St Petersburg, 1909): <http://www.census1897.com/source/books/ bruzkus.pdf>.

BUNIMOVITSH, DAVID, 'The Burden of Volozhin' (Heb.), *Hamelits*, 25/68 (21 Sept. 1885), 1097–8.

——*Mikhtav me'eliyahu* [Correspondence and ethical writings of Rabbi Eliyahu Dessler] (Vilna, 1901).

BURSTEIN, AVRAHAM AHARON, 'A Secret Society in Israel' (Heb.), *Hatsefirah*, 24/111 (27 May 1897), 568–9.

CHODZKO, I., *Lithuanian Figures* [Obrazy Litewskie] (Vilna, 1862).

CHWALBA, ANDRZEJ, *Empire of Corruption* [Imperium korupcji w Rosji i Królestwie Polskim w latach 1861–1917], 2nd edn. (Kraków, 2005).

COHEN, A. L., *The Life of R. Yisra'el Me'ir Hakohen* [Toledot vekorot ḥayav shel maran yisra'el me'ir hakohen] (New York, 1942).

COHEN, I., *Vilna* (Philadelphia, 1943).

COHEN, M., 'R. Yitshak Ya'akov Reines' (Heb.), in Y. L. Hakohen Fishman (ed.), *In Honour of Mizrahi* [Sefer hamizraḥi] (Jerusalem, 1946), 83–101 (second pagination).

COHEN, TOVA, 'The "Maskil" as "Lamdan": The Influence of Jewish Education on Haskalah Writing Techniques', in Glenda Abramson (ed.), *Jewish Education and Learning* (Chur, Switzerland, 1993), 61–73.

'Concerning the Volozhin Yeshiva' (Heb.), *Hamelits*, 32/46 (7 Mar. 1892), 1–2; *Hatsefirah*, 19/56 (18 Mar. 1892), 224; *Hatsefirah*, 19/57 (20 Mar. 1892), 228.

DAVID OF MINSK, *Beit david* (Warsaw, 1854).

DAVID OF NOVOGRUDOK, *Galya masekhet* [Responsa], 2 vols. in 1 (Vilna, 1845).

DEICHES, YISRA'EL HAYIM, *Sermons of Rabbi Yisra'el Hayim Deiches* [Derashot mahariḥ] (Leeds, 1920).

DESSLER, R., *Generations Gone By* [Shenot dor vador] (Jerusalem, 2000).

DINUR, BEN-ZION, *In a World that Went Under* [Be'olam sheshaka] (Jerusalem, 1958).

DOLBILOV, MIKHAIL, 'The "Cleansing" of Judaism: Confessional Engineering by the Department of Education' (Rus.), *Archive of Jewish History*, 3 (Moscow, 2006), 166–204.

——'Russifying Bureaucracy and the Politics of Jewish Education in the Russian Empire's Northwest Region (1860s–1870s)', *Acta Slavica Iaponica*, 24 (2007), 112–43.

DOLITSKI, M., *A Model for the Masses* [Mofet larabim] (Frankfurt am Main, 1894).

DON-YIHIA, YEHUDAH LEIB, 'Memoirs' (Heb.), *Netivah*, 11/29 (30 July 1936), 5; 11/34 (27 Aug. 1936), 2; 12/5 (4 Oct. 1936), 2; 12/11 (20 Nov. 1936), 3.

DRUCK, DAVID, *Rabbi Levi Ginsberg* (Heb.) (New York, 1924).

DRUYANOW, A., *Selected Writings* [Ketavim nivḥarim], 2 vols. (Tel Aviv, 1943–5).

——*Writings on the History of Hibat Zion* [Ketavim letoledot ḥibat tsiyon], 3 vols. (Tel Aviv, 1919–32).

DUBNOW, S. (ed.), *Lithuanian Recordbook* [Pinkas hamedinah lita] (Berlin, 1925; repr. Tel Aviv, 1969).

DVORETS, Y. Z. [*see also* PALTIN, Y.Z.], *Assembly of Israel* [Keneset yisra'el] (Kovno, 1912).

—— *The Biography of our Master and Teacher, of Blessed and Holy Memory* [Ḥoveret meyukhada [*sic*] mukdeshet lezikaron admor amud hatorah vehamusar maran harav natan tsevi finkel], *Tevunah* (20 Feb. 1928), special supplement.

—— *The Gaon Rabbi Moshe Mordekhai Epstein* (Heb.) (Jerusalem, 1944).

EDELBAUM, MEIR, 'Rabbi Dov Nahman Shapira' (Heb.), in Yitshak Ronkin and Bonim Heller (eds.), *The Book of Mezrich in Memory of the Martyrs of our Town* [Sefer mezritsh lezekher kedoshei ireinu] (Tel Aviv, 1978).

EDELMAN, S. R., *Hatirosh* (Warsaw, 1881).

EDELSTEIN, Y., *Rabbi Barukh Dov Liebowitz* (Heb.) (Tel Aviv, 1957).

EFRON, AHARON ELIEZER, *Ḥamishah alafin* (Vilna, 1914).

EISENSTADT, B. Z., *The Generation of Our Rabbi and its Scholars* [Dor rabenu vesoferav], 6 vols. (Warsaw, Vilna, and New York, 1895–1905).

—— *Rabbis and Scholars of Minsk* [Rabanei minsk vaḥakhameiha] (Vilna, 1899).

EISENSTADT, M. A., 'The Money of the Guilt-Offering' (Heb.), *Hamelits*, 29/233 (8 Nov. 1889), 1–2.

—— 'The Purim Rabbi' (Heb.), *Hatsefirah*, 42/66 (19 Mar. 1916), 2.

—— 'Revolution in the Yeshiva' (Heb.), *Hatsefirah*, 42/124 (2 June 1916), 1–2.

—— 'The Volozhin Yeshiva' (Heb.), *He'avar*, 14 (1967), 159–72.

ELIACH, D., *Father of the Yeshivas* [Avi hayeshivot], 2 vols. (Jerusalem, 1991).

—— (ed.), *Kol hakatuv leḥayim* [From the Wisdom of Rabbi Hayim of Volozhin] (Jerusalem, 1988).

ELIACH, YAFFA, *There Once Was a World: A 900-Year Chronicle of the Shtetl of Eishyshok* (New York, 1998).

ELIASBERG, M., *The Golden Path* [Shevil hazahav] (Warsaw, 1897).

ELIASHIV, ISRAEL, 'For the Sake of Knowledge' (Heb.), *He'avar*, 1 (Winter 1913), 107–16.

—— 'Grabin' (Heb.), *He'avar*, 2 (Spring 1918), 89–107.

ELIYAHU BEN SHELOMOH ZALMAN [VILNA GAON], *Likutei hagra* [ed. Nehemyah Fefer] (New York, 1999).

—— *Tsurat ha'arets* [The Form of the Earth] (Shklov, 1902).

Encyclopaedia of Education [Entsiklopediyah ḥinukhit], vol. iv: *History of Education* [Toledot haḥinukh], ed. Martin Buber and Chaim Ormian (Jerusalem, 1964).

Encyclopaedia Hebraica [Entsiklopediyah ivrit], 37 vols. (Tel Aviv and Jerusalem, 1984–95).

Encyclopaedia Judaica, 16 vols. (Jerusalem, 1971).

EPEL, Y., *At the Beginning of the Revival* [Betokh reshit hateḥiyah] (Tel Aviv, 1936).

EPSTEIN, BARUKH HALEVI, *Mekor barukh* [Autobiographical notes on life in Volozhin], 3 vols. (Vilna, 1928).

EPSTEIN, ZALMAN, 'A Forgotten Jubilee' (Heb.), *Hatsefirah*, 30/184 (21 Aug. 1903), 3; 30/185 (23 Aug 1903), 3; 30/186 (24 Aug. 1903), 4.

EPSTEIN, ZALMAN, *Minḥat yehudah* (Warsaw, 1877).

——*Writings* [Ketavim] (St Petersburg, 1903).

ETKES, IMMANUEL, 'The "Official Haskalah" and the Change in the Status of the Haskalah Movement in Russia' (Heb.), *Zion*, 43 (1978), 264–313.

——'R. Hayim of Volozhin's Method and Work as a Reaction of Mitnagdic Society to Hasidism' (Heb.), *PAAJR* 38–9 (1972), 1–45.

——*Rabbi Yisra'el Salanter* (Heb.) (Jerusalem, 1982).

——'Review of N. Lamm, *Torah lishmah*' (Heb.), *Kiryat sefer*, 50 (1975), 638–48.

——(ed.), *Religion and Life* [Dat veḥayim] (Jerusalem, 1993).

——(ed.), *Yeshivas and Batei Midrash* [Yeshivot uvatei midrashot] (Jerusalem, 2007).

——and SHLOMO TIKOCHINSKI, *Memoirs of the Lithuanian Yeshivas* [Yeshivot lita: pirkei zikhronot] (Jerusalem, 2004).

Ets peri (Vilna, 1881).

Evreiskaya entsiklopediya [Jewish Encyclopaedia], 16 vols. (St Petersburg, 1908–13).

EVRON, D., *The Register of the Qualified of the Community of Posen* [Pinkas hakasherim shel kehilat pozna] (Jerusalem, 1967).

FEINER, SHMUEL, 'Annotated Bibliography' (Heb.), in Immanuel Etkes (ed.), *Religion and Life* [Dat veḥayim] (Jerusalem, 1993), 456–75.

FEIVEL B. ZEEV WOLF, EZEKIEL, *Toledot adam* [History of a Man] (Dyhernfurth, 1801–9).

FEIVELSON, A., 'Memories from the Beginning of the Foundation of Torah Institutions in Lithuania' (Heb.), *Tevunah*, 2/3–4 (Dec. 1922–Feb. 1923), 3–7.

FELSENBERG, YIRMIYAHU, *Divrei yirmiyahu* (Vilna, 1927).

FESTINGER, L., et al. (eds.), *When Prophecy Fails* (Minneapolis, 1956).

'A Fire Has Gone Out from Heshbon' (Heb.), *Hamelits*, 30/22 (7 Feb. 1890), 1–4.

FISHMAN, D., *Russia's First Modern Jews: The Jews of Shklov* (New York, 1995).

'For Researchers of Antiquity' (Heb.) [text of a letter by R. Haim of Volozhin], *Hapeles*, 2/15 (1902), 140–3.

FRANK, TANHUM, *The History of God's House in Volozhin* [Toledot beit hashem bevolozhin] (Jerusalem, 2001).

FRIEDBERG, H., *The Hebrew Press in Poland* [Hadefus ha'ivri bepolaniyah] (Tel Aviv, 1950).

FRIEDENSTEIN, SHIMON, *City of Heroes* [Ir giborim] (Vilna, 1880).

FRIEDLAND, P. [HAD BEN HEVRAYA], 'Hibat Zion at Volozhin' (Heb.), *Hatur*, 4/40 (2 July 1924), 9–13.

FRIEDMAN, A., 'Major Aspects of Yeshiva Education in Hungary', Ph.D. thesis (Yeshiva University, New York, 1971).

FRIEDMAN, A. A., *Memoirs* [Zikhronot] (Tel Aviv, 1926).

——'On the History of the *Musarniks*' (Heb.), *Hator*, 6/10 (29 Jan. 1926), 8–10.

FRIEDMAN, DAVID, *Emek haberakhah* [Valley of Blessing] (Jerusalem, 1881).

FRIEDMAN, M., *Society and Religion: Non-Zionist Orthodoxy in the Land of Israel 1917–36* [Ḥevrah vedat: ha'ortodoksiyah halotsiyonit be'erets yisra'el 1917–36] (Jerusalem, 1978).

FRUMER, M., 'Memories of R. Zalman Sender' (Yid.), *Yidishe velt*, 3698 (20 Aug. 1923), 4–5.

FRUMKIN, A. L., *History of the Scholars of Jerusalem* [Toledot ḥakhmei yerushalayim], 4 vols. (Jerusalem, 1928–30).

—— *Toledot eliyahu* [Biography of his uncle, Eliyahu Rogoler] (Vilna, 1900).

FUCHS, A., *Hungarian Yeshivas in their Heyday, and their Destruction* [Yeshivot hungariyah bigedulatan uveḥurbanan], 2 vols. (Jerusalem, 1979, 1987).

FUENN, SHMUEL YOSEF, *Safah lane'emanim* [Language for the Faithful] (Vilna, 1881).

GELBART, S., *The Great Yeshiva Torat Hesed in Łódź* (Yid.) (Łódź, 1929).

GESSEN, YU., 'The Fate of the Volozhin Yeshiva' (Rus.), *Perezhitoe*, 1 (1908), 19–22.

GIFTER, MORDEKHAI, 'The Telz Yeshiva' (Heb.), in S. K. Mirsky (ed.), *The Rise and Destruction of the Torah Institutions of Europe*, 16–88.

GINDES, S., et al. (eds.), *Festschrift for Rabbi Shimon Yehudah Shkop* [Sefer hayovel lerav shimon yehudah shkop] (Vilna, 1936).

GINSBERG, ELI, *Keeper of the Law* (Philadelphia, Pa., 1966).

GOLDBERG, BINYAMIN, *Memories of the Past* [Zikhron la'aharonim] (Greyeve, 1924).

GOLDBERG, HILLEL, *Israel Salanter: Text, Structure, Idea* (New York, 1982).

GOLDBERG, MOSHE YEHUDAH, 'The Life of the *Gaon* of Maitchet' (Heb.), in Alexander Manor et al. (eds.), *Lida* [Sefer lida] (Tel Aviv, 1970), 122–4.

—— *Rabbi Hayim Yehudah (Tiktinski)* (Warsaw, 1902).

—— et al. (eds.), *Ideinu* [Memorial volume for Rabbi Solomon Polachek] (New York, 1929).

GOLDBLUM, ISRAEL, *Book Reviews* [Ma'amar bikoret sefarim] (Paris, 1886).

GOLDSTEIN, D., 'Bialik's Beginnings' (Heb.), *Davar*, 2897, supp. (23 Nov. 1934), 2–3.

GORDON, H. L., 'On the Banks of the Viliya and Neman' (Heb.), *Hado'ar*, 44/4 (27 Nov. 1964), 56–8.

—— 'The Son Will Honour the Father' (Heb.), *Hado'ar*, 44/33 (6 Aug. 1965), 614.

GORDON, SHMUEL, 'The *Gaon* Rabbi Eliezer Gordon' (Heb.), *Hane'eman*, 23 (May–June 1950), 12–13.

GORDON, YEHUDAH LEIB, *Letters of Y. L. Gordon* [Igerot yalag], ed. Y. Y. Weisberg (Warsaw, 1894).

GOREN, NATAN, et al. (eds.), *Lithuanian Jewry* [Yahadut lita], vol. i (Tel Aviv, 1959).

GOTTLIEB, JULIUS, 'Joshua Steinberg', *Encyclopaedia Judaica* (Jerusalem, 1971), xi. 542.

GOTTLIEB, S. N., *Ohel no'aḥ* (Pinsk, 1912).

GREENWALD, NAHUM, 'Soul and Hasidic Spirit: Hasidic Influences on *Nefesh haḥayim* and *Ruaḥ haḥayim*' (Heb.), *Heikhal habesht*, 5 (Dec. 2003), 25–47.

GRIES, ZE'EV, *Book, Scribe, and Story in Early Hasidism: From the Besht to Menaḥem Mendel of Kotsk* [Sefer sofer vesipur bereshit haḥasidut: min habesht ve'ad menaḥem mendel mikotsk] (Tel Aviv, 1992).

—— *The Literature of Correct Conduct: Its History and Role in the Life of the Hasidim of the Besht* [Sifrut hahanhagot: toledoteiha umekomah beḥayei ḥasidei habesht] (Jerusalem, 1990).

GRINBLAT, N., 'In the Secret Library' (Heb.), *Ha'olam*, 29/8 (28 Nov. 1940), 126–7.

GROSS, B., 'On the Weltanschauung of R. Hayim of Volozhin' (Heb.), *Bar-Ilan*, 22–3 (1988), 121–60.

HAD BEN HEVRAYA, *see* FRIEDLAND, P.

HALEVI, S., 'Rabbi Yisra'el of Shklov' (Heb.), *Sinai*, 5 (1939), 30–7.

HALEVI, Y. A., and Y. LIFSCHITZ, *Words of Peace and Truth* [Divrei shalom ve'emet] (Warsaw, 1884).

HALPERIN, Y. Z., *Mosedei yeshayah* [Talmudic commentaries and discourses] (Vilna, 1895).

'HAMASHKIF' [JOSEPH KLAUSNER], '"Steinberg, Yehoshua": Hebrew Outlook, pt. 23' (Heb.), *Hashilo'ah*, 18/4 (Apr. 1908), 380–4.

HANNOVER, NATHAN NETA, *Abyss of Despair*, trans. Abraham J. Mesch (New York, 1950); Hebrew edn.: *Yeven metsulah*, ed. Israel Halperin (Tel Aviv, 1966).

HARKAVI, MOSHE SHEMUEL, *Generation of the Upright* [Dor yesharim] (New York, 1903).

HASIN, Y., *Divrei yeshayah* [The Words of Isaiah], vol. iii (Jerusalem, 1955).

HASMAN, RAFAEL, et al. (eds.), *Lithuanian Jewry* [Yahadut lita], vols. ii and iii (Tel Aviv, 1960, 1967).

HAYIM OF VOLOZHIN, *Nefesh hahayim* [On the fundamentals of Jewish belief] (Vilna, 1824).

——*Ruah hayim* [Commentary on Mishnah, *Pirkei avot*] (Vilna, 1858).

——*Teachings and Practices* [Sefer horaot vehanhagot mirabenu hayim mivolozhin] (Benei Berak, 1987).

'He Who Sees But Is Not Seen' (Yid.), *Yidisher folksblat*, 4/45 (26 Nov. 1884), 706.

HEILPERN, M., *The Great Sage of Minsk* [Hagadol miminsk] (Jerusalem, 1991).

HEIMAN, D., 'From the Archive of Rabbi Moshe Avigdor Haikin' (Heb.), *Sinai*, 91 (1982), 168–77.

Hevrat Matsdikei Harabim, *Milhamah beshalom* [War on Peace] (Vilna, 1870).

HILDESHEIMER, M., 'R. Hayim of Volozhin's Opinion of Hasidism' (Heb.), *Hama'ayan*, 12/4 (June 1972), 42–57.

HILLMAN, D. T., *Letters of the Master of the Tanya and his Generation* [Igerot ba'al hatanya uvenei doro] (Jerusalem, 1953).

HIRSCH, YA'AKOV BEN TSEVI, *Shema ya'akov* (Lyck, 1860).

HIRSCHMAN, S., *Beit avot* (Berlin, 1889).

HOROWITZ, A. Z., *Memoirs of Two Generations* [Zikhronos fun tsvay doros] (New York, 1935).

HOROWITZ, M. M., *Derekh ets hayim* [The Way of the Tree of Life] (Kraków, 1895).

HUNDERT, GERSHON, and G. BACON, *The Jews in Russia and Poland*, pt. 2 (Bloomington, Ind., 1984).

JAWITZ, ZE'EV, *Jewish History* [Toledot yisra'el], 14 vols. (1895–1940; repr. Tel Aviv, 1963).

JONES, E., and R. NISBETT, 'The Actor and the Observer', in E. Jones et al. (eds.), *Attribution* (New York, 1972), 79–94.

JOSEPHUS, FLAVIUS, *The Jewish Wars* [Milḥamot hayehudim im haroma'im], trans. Kalman Schulman (Vilna, 1862).

KAHAN, ARCADIUS, *Essays in Jewish Social and Economic History*, ed. Roger Weiss, introd. Jonathan Frankel (Chicago, 1986).

KAHANA, Y., *Tosafot ma'aseh rav* [Additions to the Deeds of the Rabbi] (Jerusalem, 1896).

KAMENETSKY, NATAN, *The Making of a Godol*, 2 vols. (Jerusalem, 2002).

—— *Rebi Ya'akov* (Heb.) (Jerusalem, 1996).

KAPLAN, KIMMY, 'Rabbi Jacob Joseph' (Heb.), *HUCA*, 67 (1996), 1–43.

KAPLAN, Z., *From the World of Torah* [Me'olamah shel torah] (Jerusalem, 1974).

KAPLINSKI, B. (ed.), *Zhetel* [Pinkas zhetel] (Tel Aviv, 1958).

KARLINSKI, H., *The Founder of the Brisk Dynasty* [Harishon leshoshelet brisk] (Jerusalem, 1984).

—— 'The Shtetl Kelme' (Yid.), in Mendel Sudarsky et al. (eds.), *Lithuania* [Sefer lite], vol. i (New York, 1951), 1437–52.

KATZ, A., 'The Background to the Rabbis' Conference in Petersburg and its Consequences' (Heb.), in Y. Shapira (ed.), *Directions of Thought and Culture: Tartakover Jubilee Volume* [Binetivei hagut vetarbut: sefer tartakover)] (Tel Aviv, 1970), 61–74.

KATZ, A. M., 'On the Path Leading Up To Beit El' (Heb.), *Naḥalat tsevi*, 14–15 (1997), 136–43.

KATZ, A. Y., 'The Great Yeshivas of Volozhin and Mir' (Heb.), *Hado'ar*, 60/7 (19 Dec. 1980), 105–7.

—— *Personalities and Deeds in the Mirror of the Past* [Ishim uma'asim bire'i he'avar] (Jerusalem, 1972).

KATZ, DOV, *The Musar Controversy* [Pulmus hamusar] (Jerusalem, 1972).

—— *The Musar Movement* [Tenuat hamusar], 5 vols. (Tel Aviv, 1955–63).

KATZ, J., 'Jewish Civilization as Reflected in the Yeshivot', *Journal of World History*, 10 (1966–7), 674–704.

KATZ, Y., 'The "Ahuzot" Campaign in Palestine 1908–1917' (Heb.), *Cathedra*, 22 (Dec. 1981–Jan. 1982), 119–44.

—— 'Orthodoxy in Historical Perspective' (Heb.), *Kivunim*, 33 (1986), 89–100.

KATZENELLENBOGEN, ELIEZER BEN YA'AKOV, *Zekher tsadik* [The Memory of a Righteous Man] (Vilna, 1879).

KATZENELLENBOGEN, EZEKIEL B. ABRAHAM, *Tsava'at keneset yeḥezkel* (Vilna, 1871).

—— *Tsavat adonenu yeḥezkel* (Vilna, 1871).

KATZENELSON, G., *The Literary War between the Strictly Orthodox and the Maskilim* [Hamilḥamah hasifrutit bein haḥaredim vehamaskilim] (Tel Aviv, 1954).

KATZMAN, ELIEZER HAKOHEN, 'The Family of R. Hayim of Volozhin and the Hasidic Movement' (Heb.), *Yeshurun*, 20 (2008), 826–33.

—— 'On the *Gaon* R. Yehoshua Heshel Levin' (Heb.), *Yeshurun*, 5 (1999), 742–82; 6 (1999), 700–27.

KATZMAN, ELIEZER HAKOHEN, 'The Wonder of his Generation' (Heb.), *Yeshurun*, 4 (1999), 648–81.

KATZNELSON, H. Y., 'Yehoshua Steinberg' (Heb.), *Hado'ar*, 11 (29 Jan. 1932), 173–4.

KATZNELSON, Y., 'Why Was the Volozhin Yeshiva Closed Down?' (Rus.), *Voskhod*, 13/6 (June 1893) (separately numbered, at the end of the issue).

KETS [KEHAT], H., *The Doctrine of Rabbi Naftali Berlin* [Mishnat hanetsiv] (Jerusalem, 1990).

KINDER, YA'AKOV, *Terrible Stories* [Sipurim nora'im], ed. Gedalyah Nigal (Jerusalem, 1992).

KINSTLICHER, MOSHE ALEXANDER ZUSHA, 'A Chapter in the History of the Mir Yeshiva' (Heb.), *Tsefunot*, 14/2 (1992), 89–94.

—— 'Letters Concerning the Mir Yeshiva' (Heb.), *Moriyah*, 20/3–4 (1995), 73–5.

KLAUSNER, JOSEPH, *see* 'HAMASHKIF'

KLAUSNER, YISRAEL, *From Katowice to Basle* [Mikatovits ad basel], 2 vols. (Jerusalem, 1961).

—— *History of the Nes Ziona Association in Volozhin* [Toledot ha'agudah nes tsiyonah bevolozhin] (Jerusalem, 1954).

—— *Vilna, the Jerusalem of Lithuania: The First Generations, 1495–1881* [Vilna, yerushalayim delita: dorot rishonim] (Tel Aviv, 1988).

KLAUSNER, YOSEF GEDALIYAH, *History of Modern Hebrew Literature* [Historiyah shel hasifrut ha'ivrit hahadashah], 6 vols., 2nd edn. (Jerusalem, 1952–9).

KLIBANSKY, BEN-TSIYON, 'The Lithuanian Yeshivas in Eastern Europe between the Two World Wars' [Hayeshivot halita'iyot bemizrah eiropah bein shetei milhamot ha'olam], Ph.D. thesis (Tel Aviv University, 2009).

KLIER, JOHN, *Imperial Russia's Jewish Question* (Cambridge, 1995).

KOGAN, D., *In the Storm of History* [In shturm fun geshikhte] (Berlin, 1923).

KOOK, A. I., *Itur soferim* [Short-lived rabbinic journal] (Vilna, 1888).

—— *Letters* [Igerot hare'iyah], ed. B. Z. Shapira, 2nd edn. (Jerusalem, 1990).

KOPERNIK, A., 'And the Third Text Will Come and Decide the Issue' (Heb.), *Hamelits*, 17/6 (22 Feb. 1881), 119–20.

KOVNER, YITSHAK, *Sefer hamatsref* [An unknown maskilic critic of Jewish Society in Russia in the nineteenth century], ed. Shmuel Feiner (Jerusalem, 1998).

KREIZ, S., 'Russian-Language Jewish Schools in Tsarist Russia' [Batei sefer yehudiyim besafah harusit berusiyah hatsarit], Ph.D. thesis (Hebrew University, Jerusalem, 1994).

KRUMBEIN, ELIAKIM, 'From R. Hayim of Brisk...' (Heb.), *Netivim*, 9 (2002), 51–94.

KUL, S., *Alone in his Generation* [Ehad bedoro] (Tel Aviv, 1970).

KUSHNIR, SHIMON (ed.), *Fields and Heart: The Life and Work of Avraham Herzfeld* [Sadot velev: perakim bederekh hayav ufo'alo shel avraham hertsfeld] (Tel Aviv, 1962).

LACHOVER, P., *Bialik* (Heb.), 2 vols. (Tel Aviv, 1944).

LAMM, NORMAN, *Torah lishmah: Torah for Torah's Sake in the Works of Rabbi Hayyim of Volozhin and his Contemporaries* (Hoboken, NJ, 1989; original Hebrew edn. Jerusalem, 1972).

LANDA, H. Y., *Ḥayei ya'akov* (Vilna, 1913).

LANDAU, B., *The Pious Gaon of Vilna* [Hagaon heḥasid mivilna] (Jerusalem, 1968).

LEDERHENDLER, ELI, *The Road to Modern Jewish Politics* (New York, 1989).

LEHMAN, MENASHEH, 'Scattered Fruits from my Library' (Heb.), *Sinai*, 98 (1986), 68–79.

LEHREN, Z. H., *Igerot pakuam* (MS, Yad Ben Zvi Archive, Jerusalem).

LEIBOWITZ, YERUHAM, *The Torah Viewpoint* [Da'at torah] (Jerusalem, 1991).

LEONE, ELIEZER, 'History of the Volozhin [Jewish] Community' (Heb.), in id. (ed.), *Volozhin*, 19–65.

—— (ed.), *Volozhin* [Sefer volozhin] (Tel Aviv, 1970).

LESHCHINSKI, Y., *The Jewish Diaspora* [Hatefutsah hayehudit] (Jerusalem, 1960).

LEVIN, DOV (ed.), *Encyclopaedia of Jewish Communities: Latvia and Estonia* [Pinkas hakehilot: latviyah—estoniyah] (Jerusalem, 1988).

LEVIN, M., *Social and Economic Values in the Ideology of the Haskalah Period* [Erkhei ḥevrah vekalkalah be'ideologiyah shel tekufat hahaskalah] (Jerusalem, 1975).

LEVIN, SHALOM DUBER, 'The Tsemaḥ Tsedek and his Generation' (Heb.), *Pardes ḥabad*, 2 (June–July 1997), 79–104.

LEVIN, VLADIMIR, 'Jewish Politics in the Russian Empire during the Period of Reaction 1907–1914' [Hapolitikah hayehudit be'imperiyah harusit be'idan hare'aktsiyah 1907–1914], Ph.D. thesis (Hebrew University of Jerusalem, 2007).

LEVIN, YEHOSHUA HESHEL, *Aliyot eliyahu* [First book on the Vilna Gaon, originally published in 1855] (Jerusalem, 1970).

—— *Moda'ah mevaseret tsiyon* (Vilna, 1880).

—— *Peleitat soferim* (Vilna, 1863).

LEVIN-EPSTEIN, A. Z., *Memoirs* [Zikhronot] (Tel Aviv, 1932).

LEVINSKI, Y. T., 'A Home of Torah' (Heb.), in id. (ed.), *Łomża* [Sefer lomzah] (Tel Aviv, 1953), 103–22.

LEVINSON, A., *The Hebrew Movement in the Diaspora* [Hatenuah ha'ivrit bagolah] (Warsaw, 1935).

LICHTENSTEIN, AHARON, 'This Was the Rav's Method' (Heb.), *Alon shevut*, 2 (Mar.–Apr. 1994), 105–18.

LICHTENSTEIN, MOSHE, 'What Hath Brisk Wrought: The Brisker Derekh Revisited', *Torah U-Madda Journal*, 9 (2000), 1–18.

LIEBERMAN, H., 'Legends and Truth about Hasidic Printing Shops' (Yid.), *YIVO-bleter*, 34 (1950), 182–208; Heb. trans. in id., *Ohel raḥel*, vol. iii (New York, 1984), 103–14.

LIEBERMAN, Y., 'Musarniks in Lithuania' (Yid.), in Y. Lipschitz, *Biography of the World-Renowned Scholar R. Isaac Elhanan* [Lebensgeshikhte fun velt gaon rabi yitsḥok elḥonon] (Kovno, 1933), 60–4.

LIFSCHITZ, YA'AKOV, 'A Generation and its Authors' (Heb.), *Hakerem*, 1 (1888), 161–95.

—— *Toledot yitsḥak* [Biography of R. Yitshak Elhanan Spektor] (Warsaw, 1897).

—— *Zikhron ya'akov* [Ya'akov's memoirs], 3 vols. (Frankfurt and Kovno, 1924–30).

LILIENTHAL, MAX, 'My Travels in Russia', *American Israelite*, 2/52(33) (4 July 1856), 417–18; 3/1(34) (11 July 1856), 2; 3/2(35) (18 July 1856).

LIPMAN, D., *On the History of the Jews of Kovno and Slobodka* [Letoledot hayehudim bekovno uveslobodka] (Kaidan, 1935).

LIPSCHITZ, YISRAEL, *Tiferet yisra'el* [Commentary on the Mishnah], 1st edn. (Hanover, 1839; often reprinted).

LIPSET, S. M., *Political Man* (New York, 1960).

LITVIN, A., *Jewish Souls* [Yidishe neshomes] (New York, 1917).

LITVIN, Y., 'Rabbi Hayim, Founder of the Yeshiva' (Heb.), *Sha'arei tsiyon*, 13/4 (July 1959), 1–7.

LONDON, Y., 'The Hafets Hayim and the Struggle over the Form of Jewish Education in Eastern Europe 1833–69' [Hahafets hayim vehama'avak al demuto shel hahinukh hayehudi bemizrah eiropah 1869–1933], MA thesis (Hebrew University, Jerusalem, 2003).

LOZINSKY, SAMUIL, and SAUL GINZBURG, *Jewish Government Schools* [Kazennye evreiskie uchilishcha: Opisanie del byvshego arkhiva Ministerstva narodnogo prosveshcheniya] (St Petersburg, 1920).

LUNSKI, H., 'The *Gaon* Rabbi Hayim Hillel Fried' (Yid.), *Dos yidishe vort*, 657 (11 June 1937), 2.

—— 'The Rabbi's House: R. Yehoshua Heshel Levin' (Yid.), *Dos yidishe vort*, 663 (23 July 1937), 2.

LURIE, ILIA, *A Community and the State: The Habad Movement in Tsarist Russia 1828–1882* [Edah umedinah: hasidut habad be'imperiyah harusit 5588–5643] (Jerusalem, 2006).

LUTSKE, H., *History in their Hands* (Northvale, NJ, 1996).

LUVTSER, SHMUEL, *Olat shemuel* (Vilna, 1901).

LUZ, EHUD, *Parallels Meet: Religion and Nationalism in the Early Zionist Movement, 1882–1904*, trans. L. J. Schramm (Philadelphia, Pa., 1988).

LVOV, ALEKSANDER, 'Rabbi Isroel Salanter, the "Haskalah" and the "Theory of Secularization": An Analysis from a Folkloristic Point of View', *Central and East European Jews at the Crossroads of Tradition and Modernity* (Vilnius, 2006), 106–28.

MAGID, S., 'Deconstruction of the Mystical: The Anti-Mystical Kabbalism in Rabbi Hayyim of Volozhin's Nefesh Ha-Hayyim', *Journal of Jewish Thought and Philosophy*, 9 (2000), 21–67.

'Major Decrees' (Heb.), *Hapeles*, 1 (1901), 36–8, 122–6, 563–6.

MALAKHI, A. R., 'A Letter from Rabbi Yitshak of Volozhin' (Heb.), *Or hamizrah*, 11/1 (Dec. 1962–Jan. 1963), 19–20.

—— 'Rabbi Yitshak Blaser' (Heb.), *Talpiyot*, 5/1–2 (Dec. 1950–Jan. 1951), 140–56.

—— 'Some Letters of Rabbi Yitshak Elhanan [Spektor]' (Heb.), *Talpiyot*, 3/1–2 (Mar.–Apr. 1947), 72–80.

MANDELBAUM, D., *The Hakhmei Lublin Yeshiva* [Yeshivat hakhmei lublin], 2 vols. (Jerusalem, 1994).

MANE, M. M., *Collected Writings* [Kol kitvei m. m. mane] (Warsaw, 1897).

MAREK, YA'AKOV, *Great Men of Our Time* [Gedolim fun unzer tseit] (New York, 1927).

———*In the Company of the Great Men of the Generation* [Bimeḥitsatam shel gedolei hador] (Jerusalem, 1958).

MARKON, YITSHAK DOV, 'From Generation to Generation' (Heb.), *Metsudah*, 3–4 (1945/6), 341–50.

MARMER, K. Y., 'Ya'akov Tsevi Sobol' (Yid.), in Y. H. Pomerantz and A. Provotiner (eds.), *L. M. Stein Jubilee Volume* [L. m. stein yuvelbukh] (Chicago, 1938), 98–114.

MASHVITSKI, A., 'In the Dwelling-Places of Torah' (Heb.), *Baderekh*, 3/13(80) (30 Mar. 1934); 3/21(88) (25 May 1934), 4 [on the Mir yeshiva]; 3/23(90) (8 June 1934), 4 [on the Volozhin yeshiva]; 3/38(105) (12 Sept. 1934), 4 [on the Volozhin yeshiva].

MATHISSON, TSEVI, 'The Tragedy of a Great Man' (Heb.), *Hado'ar*, 45/18 (4 Mar. 1966), 284–5.

MAZEH, YA'AKOV, *Memoirs* [Zikhronot], 4 vols. (Tel Aviv, 1936).

MELTZER, TSEVI YEHUDAH, 'Ets Hayim Yeshiva' (Heb.), in S. Nahmani and N. Hinits (eds.), *Memorial Volume for Slutsk and Surrounding Towns* [Sefer slutsk uvenoteiha] (New York, 1962), 87.

MELTZER, YEDAEL, *Derekh ets ḥayim* [Way of the Tree of Life], 2 vols. (Jerusalem, 1986).

MENDELSOHN, EZRA, *Class Struggle in the Pale* (Cambridge, 1970).

———*Jews of East Central Europe between the World Wars* (Bloomington, Ind., 1983).

MILIKOVSKI-SAMSONOV, ELIYAHU AHARON, *Ohalei aharon* (Tel Aviv, 1937).

MILLER, Y. D., *Toledot menaḥem* [Biography of Menahem] (Piotrków Trybunalski, 1913).

MIRSKY, S., 'The Volozhin Yeshiva' (Heb.), in id. (ed.), *The Rise and Destruction of the Torah Institutions of Europe*, 1–86.

———(ed.), *The Rise and Destruction of the Torah Institutions of Europe* [Mosedot torah be'eiropah bevinyanam uveḥurbanam] (New York, 1956).

MIRSKY, YEHUDA, 'Intellectual and Spiritual Biography of Rabbi Avraham Yitzhaq Ha-Cohen Kook from 1865 to 1904', Ph.D. thesis (Harvard University, Cambridge, Mass., 2007).

MONDSCHEIN, YEHOSHUA, 'The Book *Matsref ha'avodah* and the Book *Vikuaḥ raba*' (Heb.), *Alei sefer*, 5 (1978), 165–75.

———'The Pious *Gaon* R. Yehonatan of Volhynia' (Heb.), *Morashah*, 21/5–6 (Mar. 1997), 28–39.

———'Suppressed Approbations from Volozhin and Vilna: "Accept the Truth from Whoever Speaks It"' (Heb.), *Kovets or yisra'el*, 16 (1999), 151–9.

———(ed.), 'Chronicles of the Tomkhei Temimim' (Heb.), *Kerem ḥabad*, 3 (Aug.–Sept. 1987), special supplement.

MORGENSTERN, ARYEH [ARIE], 'The 1840 Controversy in the Minsk Community over the Coming of the Messiah' (Heb.), *Zion*, 53 (1988), 199–210.

———*Hastening Redemption: Messianism and the Resettlement of the Land of Israel* (New York, 2006).

———*Natural Redemption* [Ge'ulah baderekh hateva], 2nd edn. (Jerusalem, 1997).

———'Two Traditions about the Beginning of the Emigration to Palestine of the Vilna Gaon's Disciples' (Heb.), *Shalem*, 6 (1992), 195–222.

NADAV, MORDECHAI, *The Jews of Pinsk, 1506 to 1880*, trans. Moshe Rosman (Stanford, 2008).

NATHANS, BENJAMIN, *Beyond the Pale: The Jewish Encounter with Late Imperial Russia* (Berkeley, 2002).

NEISHTATER, Y., *Words of Peace and Truth* [Divrei shalom ve'emet] (Vilna, 1873).

NERIYAH, M. Z., *On Rav Kook* [Tal hara'ayah] (Kefar Haro'eh, 1985).

—— *Rabbi Naftali Tsevi Yehudah Berlin* (Heb.) (Tel Aviv, 1943).

—— *Volozhin Studies* [Pirkei volozhin] (Jerusalem, 1964).

NISSENBAUM, YITSHAK, *Pages of My Life* [Alei ḥeldi] (Jerusalem, 1969).

'One of the Keepers of the Sacred Watch in Russia', 'From Where Will Wisdom Come?' (Heb.), *Halevanon*, 15/27 (7 Feb. 1879), 209–10.

ONG, W. J., 'Latin Language Study as a Renaissance Puberty Rite', in P. W. Musgrave (ed.), *Sociology, History and Education* (London, 1970), 232–48.

OSTROVSKY, M. (ed.), *Man of Jerusalem: In Honour of Gedaliah Broder* [Ish yerushalayim] (Jerusalem, 1937).

OVSAY, JOSHUA, 'The Yeshivas during the Revival Period' (Heb.), *Hado'ar*, 24/4 (24 Nov. 1944), 58–9; 24/5 (1 Dec. 1944), 73–5; 24/6 (8 Dec. 1944), 89–91; 24/7 (15 Dec. 1944), 110–11; 24/8 (22 Dec. 1948), 127–8; 24/9 (29 Dec. 1944), 149–50; 24/10 (5 Jan. 1945), 167–8.

PACHTER, M., 'Between Acosmism and Theism: R. Hayim of Volozhin's View of God' (Heb.), *Meḥkarim behagut yehudit*, 1 (1999), 139–57.

PAIMER, YOSEF, *Responsa of Our Master Rabbi Yosef of Slutsk* [She'elot uteshuvot rabenu yosef mislutsk] (Heb.) (Jerusalem, 1981).

PALTIN, Y. Z. [*see also* DVORETS, Y. Z.], 'In the Paths of Advanced Torah Study' (Heb.), *Tevunah* 11/117 (Oct.–Nov. 1954), 49–53.

—— 'On the History of the Keneset Yisra'el Yeshiva in Slobodka' (Heb.), *Tevunah*, 12/123 (June–July 1957), 4–8; 12/124 (Aug.–Sept. 1957), 2–6; 13/125 (Sept.–Nov. 1957), 8–11; 13/126 (Dec. 1957–Mar. 1958), 25–6; 13/127 (Mar.–May 1958), 46–9; 13/128 (May–July 1958), 64–7; 13/129 (July–Sept. 1958), 81–4.

PAPISH-BERLIN, A., *Unforgettable Sounds* [Tselilim shelo nishkeḥu] (Tel Aviv, 1988).

PERL, GIL SOLOMON, "Emek ha-Neẓiv: Window into the Intellectual Universe of Rabbi Naftali Ẓvi Yehudah Berlin', Ph.D. thesis (Harvard University, Cambridge, Mass., 2006).

PISIUK, MEIR, *Pages of Memories* [Bleter zikhronos] (Vilna, 1881).

POSNER, A. Z., 'Kalman Schulman' (Heb.), *Hatsefirah*, 26/23 (8 Feb. 1899), 1; 26/24 (9 Feb. 1899), 1; 26/25 (10 Feb. 1899), 1; 26/26 (12 Feb. 1899), 1.

PYATIGORSKY, REUVEN, 'The Point of a *Yod* from Volozhin' (Rus.), *Vesti* (23 Oct. 2003).

RABBINOVICZ, R. N. N., *An Account of the Printing of the Talmud* [Ma'amar al hadpasat hatalmud] (Jerusalem, 1952).

RABINER, S. A., 'At the Dawn of his Days' (Heb.), *Netivah*, 11/35 (3 Sept. 1936), 3.

RABINER, ZEEV ARYEH, *The Gaon Rabbi Eliezer Gordon* [Hagaon rabi eli'ezer gordon zts"l] (Tel Aviv, 1968).

—— *Or mufla* [Wonderful Light] (Tel Aviv, 1972).

—— 'Rabbi Itzeleh Ponevezher' (Heb.), *Bamishor*, 3/107–8 (17 Apr. 1942), 7–8; 3/110 (1 May 1942), 6–7.

RABINOWITZ, DAN, 'Rayna Batya and Other Learned Women: A Re-evaluation of Rabbi Baruch Halevi's Sources', *Tradition*, 35/1 (2001), 55–69.

RABINOWITZ, MIKHAL, 'Documents Relating to the History of the Volozhin Yeshiva' (Heb.), *Kovets al yad*, 15/5 (1951), 221–33.

RABINOWITZ, Z., 'Six Generations of the Great Persons of Pinsk and Karlin' (Heb.), in id. (ed.), *Pinsk*, ii. 409–66.

—— (ed.), *Pinsk* [Sefer pinsk], 2 vols. (Tel Aviv and Haifa, 1973, 1977).

RABINOWITZ-THEOMIM, ELIYAHU DAVID, *Seder eliyahu* [Autobiography] (Jerusalem, 1984).

RADUS, YEHOSHUA L., *Memoirs* [Zikhronot] (Johannesburg, 1936).

RAFAEL, Y., '*Peleitat soferim* and *Safah lane'emanim*' (Heb.), *Areshet*, 1 (1959), 327–95.

RAKOV, L. (ed.), *Vaya'al eliyahu* [Memorial volume for Eliyahu Gee] (London, 1991).

Record This for a Later Generation [Tikhtov zot ledor aḥaron] (Jerusalem, 1845).

REINER, ELHANAN, 'Capital, Social Status, and Torah Study: The *Kloyz* in Jewish Society in Eastern Europe in the Seventeenth and Eighteenth Centuries' (Heb.), *Zion*, 58 (1993), 287–328.

—— 'Transformations in the Polish and Ashkenazi Yeshivas during the Sixteenth and Seventeenth Centuries and the Dispute over *Pilpul*' (Heb.), in Israel Bartal, Ezra Mendelsohn, and Chava Turniansky (eds.), '*According to the Custom of Ashkenaz and Poland*': *Studies in Jewish Culture in Honour of Chone Shmeruk* ['Keminhag ashkenaz vepolin': sefer yovel leḥone shemeruk] (Jerusalem, 1989), 9–80.

REINES, MOSHE, 'Dwelling-Places of Torah' (Heb.), *Otsar hasifrut*, 3 (1885), 5–35.

REINES, YITSHAK YA'AKOV, *Hotam tokhnit* [A plan for a new method for studying the Talmud], 2 vols. (Pressburg and Mainz 1880, 1881).

—— *Shenei hame'orot* [Two Luminaries], 2 vols. (Piotrków, 1913).

RIVKIN, M., 'The Last Years of the Volozhin Yeshiva' (Rus.), *Voskhod*, 2 (May 1895), 1–17.

RIVKIND, Y., 'An Anonymous *Rosh Yeshivah* at Volozhin' (Heb.), in Y. Zilberschlag and Y. Twersky (eds.), *Turov* [Sefer turov] (Boston, Mass., 1938), 232–9.

—— 'From the Volozhin Collections' (Heb.), *Reshumot*, 5 (1927), 362–82.

—— 'History of the Volozhin Emissaries in the United States' (Heb.), *Hado'ar*, 45/11 (14 Jan. 1966), 169–70; 45/12 (21 Jan. 1966), 187–8.

—— 'Rabbi Rafa'el Shapira' (Heb.), in Eliezer Leone (ed.), *Volozhin* [Sefer volozhin] (Tel Aviv, 1970), 224–9.

RIVLIN, A., *The Tsadik Rabbi Yosef Zundel of Salant and his Teachers* [Hatsadik rav yosef zundel misalant verabotav] (Jerusalem, 1927).

ROSENFELD, SHMUEL, 'Letters from Provincial Towns' (Heb.), *Hamelits*, 37/52 (15 Mar. 1897), 1–2.

—— *Rabbi Yisra'el Salanter* (Heb.) (Warsaw, 1911).

ROSENSTEIN, H. D., *Writings* [Ketavim] (Jerusalem, 1973).

ROSENTHAL, HAYIM SHELOMOH, *They Shall Seek Torah from his Mouth* [Torah yevakshu mipihu] (Jerusalem, 2000).

ROSS, T., 'Conceptual Thought in the Writings of the Successors of R. Yisra'el Salanter in the *Musar* Movement' [Hamaḥshavav ha'iyunit bekhitvei mamshikhav shel r. yisra'el salanter bitenuat hamusar], Ph.D. thesis (Hebrew University, Jerusalem, 1986).

ROTSTEIN, YOSEF, 'Memoirs' (Heb.), in Y. Klausner (ed.), *History of the Nes Ziona Association in Volozhin* [Toledot ha'agudah nes tsiyonah bevolozhin] (Jerusalem, 1954), 115–24.

ROZANSKY, TSEVI, *Tsevi veḥamid* (Vilna, 1911).

SAGI, AVI, *Judaism: Between Religion and Ethics* [Yahadut: bein dat lemusar] (Tel Aviv, 1998).

SAIMAN, CHAYIM, 'Legal Theology: The Turn to Conceptualism in Nineteenth-Century Jewish Law', *Journal of Law and Religion*, 21 (2005–6), 39–100.

SALANTER, Y., *Or yisra'el* [Collected letters], ed. Yitshak Blaser (Vilna, 1900).

SALMON, Y., 'The Beginning of the Reform of East European Yeshivas' (Heb.), *Molad*, 4/19–20 (1971), 161–72.

—— 'The Yeshiva of Lida', *YIVO Annual*, 15 (1974), 283–308.

SAMET, M., 'Strict Orthodoxy in Modern Times' (Heb.), *Mehalakhim*, 3 (Mar. 1970), 15–27.

SCHACTER, J. J., 'Haskalah, Secular Studies and the Close of the Yeshiva in Volozhin in 1892', *Torah U-Madda Journal*, 2 (1990), 76–133.

SCHARFSTEIN, Z., *The History of Jewish Education in Modern Times* [Toledot haḥinukh beyisra'el bedorot ha'aḥaronim], 2 vols., 2nd edn. (Jerusalem, 1960).

SCHNEERSOHN, MENACHEM MENDEL, *Sacred Letters* [Igerot kodesh], vol. i (Brooklyn, NY, 1987).

—— *She'elot uteshuvot al tsemaḥ tsedek* [Responsa on *Even ha'ezer*] (Brooklyn, NY, 1995).

SCHNEERSOHN, SHALOM DOV BER, *Sacred Letters* [Igerot kodesh], ed. S. D. Levin (Brooklyn, NY, 1982).

SCHULWASS, M. A., 'The Torah and its Study in Poland and Lithuania' (Heb.), in Y. Halperin (ed.), *The Jews of Poland* [Beit yisra'el bepolin], vol. ii (Jerusalem, 1953), 13–35.

Seder hagadah shel pesaḥ ... im perush imrei shefer [Pesach Haggadah with commentaries] (Warsaw, 1894).

SEEMAN, DON, 'The Silence of Rayna Batya', *Torah U-Madda Journal*, 6 (1995–6), 91–128.

SEGALOVITZ, H., *Mekor ḥayim* (Vilna, 1898).

SHABAD, A., *Toledot hayamim* [What Transpired] (Vilna, 1904).

SHAIN, ISAAC, 'Tila Berlin', in M. Feigenbaum (ed.), *The Biała Podlaska Memorial Book* [Sefer biala podlaska] (Tel Aviv, 1961), 369–70.

SHAPIRA, M. S., *see* SHMUKLER, M. S.

SHAPIRO, MARC B., *Between the Yeshiva World and Modern Orthodoxy: The Life and Works of Rabbi Jehiel Jacob Weinberg, 1884–1966* (Oxford, 2004).

—— 'The Brisker Method Reconsidered', *Tradition*, 31/3 (1997), 78–102.

SHATZKY, YA'AKOV, *Cultural History of the Haskalah in Lithuania* [Kultur geshikhte fun der haskalah in lite] (Buenos Aires, 1950).

—— *History of the Jews of Warsaw* [Geshikhte fun yiden in varsha], 3 vols. (New York, 1947–53).

SHELI, M., 'Droplets of Telz' (Heb.), in S. Kushnir (ed.), *Fields and Heart: The Life and Work of Avraham Herzfeld* [Sadot valev: perakim bederekh ḥayav ufo'alo shel avraham hertsfeld] (Tel Aviv, 1962), 422–32.

SHIFMAN, Y., 'The Controversy between the Strictly Orthodox and the Zionists from the First Zionist Congress to the Appearance of *Hapeles*' [Hapulmus bein haharedim uvein hatsiyonim mehakongres hatsiyoni ad hofa'at 'Hapeles'], MA thesis (Hebrew University, Jerusalem, 1980).

SHIMOFF, E., *Rabbi Isaac Elchanan Spektor* (New York, 1959).

SHIMSHON OF VOLOZHIN, *Memoirs* [Zikhron shimshon] (Vilna, 1879).

SHIROTKIN, A., 'The Dew to which All Turn' (Heb.), *Hashaḥar*, 8/3 (1877), 112–19; 8/4 (1877), 161–9.

SHISHA, A., 'A Person's Feet . . .' (Heb.), *Hadarom*, 32 (1971), 194–6.

SHMUKLER [SHAPIRA], M. S., *Rabbi Hayim of Volozhin* [Rabenu ḥayim mivolozhin] (Vilna, 1909; 2nd edn., Jerusalem, 1968).

—— *Rabbi Moshe Shemuel and his Generation* [Rav moshe shemuel vedoro] (New York, 1964).

—— 'Rabbi Tsevi Hirsh Rabinowitz' (Heb.), *Talpiyot*, 3 (Apr. 1947), 81–6.

SHOCHAT, R., 'Messianic and Mystical Principles in Torah Study in the Vilna Gaon's *Beit Midrash*: A New Aspect of the Nineteenth-Century Crisis in Torah Study and the Concept of *Devekut*' (Heb.), in R. Shochat (ed.), *The Vilna Gaon and his Study Hall* [Hagra uveit midrasho] (Ramat Gan, 2003), 155–72.

SHOHET, AZRIEL, *The Official Rabbinate in Russia* [Mosad harabanut mita'am berusiyah] (Haifa, 1976).

—— 'The "Rekrutshchina" during the Reign of Tsar Nicholas I and the Proliferation of "Yeshivas" among Russian Jewry' (Heb.), *Historiyah yehudit*, 1/1 (Spring 1986), 33–8.

—— 'Study Groups in the Seventeenth and Eighteenth Centuries in the Land of Israel, Poland–Lithuania, and Germany' (Heb.), *Ḥinukh*, 20/4–5 (Nov. 1955), 404–18.

SHOMER [NAHUM MEYER SHAIKEVICH], *Poems and Memoirs* [Shirei shomer vezikhronotav] (Jerusalem, 1952).

SHOSHANAH, A., 'Chapters on History and Evaluation' (Heb.), in *Centenary Book of the Telz Yeshiva* [Sefer yovel hame'ah shel yeshivat telz] (Cleveland, Ohio, 1975), 263–325.

SHUK, M. M., 'The Grandfather of Slobodka' (Heb.), *Hado'ar*, 35/16 (17 Feb. 1956), 311.

SHULMAN, B., 'The Spirit of Revolution in the Yeshivas' (Heb.), *He'avar*, 12 (May 1965), 143–7.

SHULMAN, Y., *Religion and Zionism* [Dat vetsiyonut] (Jerusalem, 1990).

SHURIN, A., *Keshet giborim* [Biography of Rabbi Moshe Soloveitchik] (Jerusalem, 1964).

SILBER, M., 'The Emergence of Ultra-Orthodoxy: The Invention of a Tradition', in J. Wertheimer (ed.), *The Uses of Tradition* (New York, 1992), 23–84.

——'The Limits of Rapprochement: The Anatomy of an Anti-Hasidic Controversy in Hungary', *Studia Judaica*, 3 (1994), 124–47.

SLUTSKY, A. Y. (ed.), *Return to Zion* [Shivat tsiyon], 2 vols. in 1 (Warsaw, 1900).

SLUTSKY, Y., 'The Rabbinical Seminary of Vilna' (Heb.), *He'avar*, 7 (1960), 29–49.

——*Russian Jewish Journalism in the Early Twentieth Century* [Ha'itonut hayehudit-rusit bereshit hame'ah ha'esrim] (Tel Aviv, 1978).

——*Russian Jewish Journalism in the Nineteenth Century* [Ha'itonut hayehudit-rusit bame'ah hatesha-esreh] (Jerusalem, 1970).

Society for the Promotion of Culture among Jews, *Report for 1885* (22) [Otchet Obshch-estva dlya rasprostraneniya prosveshcheniya mezhdu evreyami v Rossii za 1885 (god 22)] (St Petersburg, 1886).

SOLOMON, NORMAN, *The Analytic Movement: Hayyim Soloveitchik and his Circle* (Atlanta, Ga., 1993).

SOLOVEITCHIK, H., 'Rupture and Reconstruction: The Transformation of Contemporary Orthodoxy', *Tradition*, 28/4 (1994), 64–130.

SOROTSKIN, ELHANAN, 'From the Paths of the *Tsadik*' (Heb.), *Tevunah*, 108 (Mar. 1950), 58.

——'The Life of Rabbi Zalman Sorotskin' (Yid.), in B. Kaplinski (ed.), *Zhetel* [Pinkas zhetel] (Tel Aviv, 1958), 233–5.

——'These Are the Generations' (Heb.) [Memoir of R. Gordon], in id., *Hade'ah vehadibur*, vol. iii (Jerusalem, 1968), 110–18.

SORSKI, A., *Hasidic Torah Teachers* [Marbitsei torah me'olam hehasidut], 8 vols. (Benei Berak, 1986–9).

——*Rabbi Shimon Shkop* (Heb.) (Benei Berak, 1971).

——*Torah and Musar Teachers* [Marbitsei torah umusar], 4 vols. (Tel Aviv, 1976).

SPEKTOR, YITSHAK ELHANAN, 'An Insult to the Torah' (Heb.), *Hamelits*, 30/20 (5 Feb. 1890), 1–2.

SPIEGEL, JACOB, *Studies in the History of the Hebrew Book* [Amudim betoledot hasefer ha'ivri] (Ramat Gan, 1996).

STAMPFER, SHAUL, 'Dormitory and Yeshiva in Eastern Europe', in id., *Families, Rabbis and Education*, 211–28.

——*Families, Rabbis, and Education: Traditional Jewish Society in Nineteenth-Century Eastern Europe* (Oxford, 2010).

——'Hasidic Yeshivas in Poland between the World Wars' (Heb.), in Immanuel Etkes et al. (eds.), *In Hasidic Circles* [Bema'agelei hasidim] (Jerusalem, 2000), 351–76.

——'Heder Study, Knowledge of Torah, and the Maintenance of Social Stratification', *Studies in Jewish Education*, 3 (1988), 271–89; updated in id., *Families, Rabbis, and Education*, 145–66.

——'Hungarian Yeshivot, Lithuanian Yeshivot, and Joseph Ben David', *Jewish History*, 11/1 (Spring 1997), 131–41.

——'On the History of the Dispute over Polished Knives between Hasidim and their Opponents' (Heb.), in Immanuel Etkes et al. (eds.), *Studies in Hasidism* [Meḥkarei ḥasidut] (Jerusalem, 1999), 197–210; updated in id., 'The Controversy over *Shiḥitah* and the Struggle between Hasidim and Mitnagedim', in id., *Families, Rabbis, and Education*, 342–55.

——'The *Pushke* and its Development', in id., *Families, Rabbis, and Education*, 102–20.

——'R. Hayim of Volozhin and his Approbations' (Heb.), *Alei sefer*, 4 (1977), 163–70.

——'The Social Significance of Very Early Marriage', in id., *Families, Rabbis, and Education*, 7–25.

——'Three Lithuanian Yeshivas in the Nineteenth Century' [Shalosh yeshivot lita'iyot bame'ah hatesha esreh], Ph.D. thesis (Hebrew University, Jerusalem, 1981).

——'What Did "Knowing Hebrew" Mean in Eastern Europe?', in L. Glinert (ed.), *Hebrew in Ashkenaz* (New York, 1993), 129–40.

STANISLAWSKI, M., *For Whom Do I Toil? Judah Leib Gordon and the Crisis of Russian Jewry* (New York, 1988).

——*Tsar Nicholas I and the Jews* (Philadelphia, Pa., 1983).

STEINSCHNEIDER, H. N., and MORDECHAI ZALKIN (eds.), *The City of Vilna* [Ir vilna], 2 vols. (Vilna and Jerusalem, 1900, 2003).

STERN, Y., *Ḥeder and Beit Midrash* [Kheder un beis medrash] (New York, 1950).

STERN, YEHIEL MIKHEL, *The Great Ones of the Generations* [Gedolei hadorot] (Jerusalem, 1996).

SUDARSKY, MENDEL, et al. (eds.), *Lithuania* [Sefer lite], vol. i (New York, 1951).

Supplement to the Book of Shiurim of Our Rabbi Hayim Levi [Mosaf lesefer shiurei rabenu ḥayim halevi] (New York, 1998).

Takanot sha'ah [Regulations for the Present Time] (Vilna, 1844).

TCHERNOWITZ, H., *Pirkei ḥayim* [Autobiography] (New York, 1954).

TEITELBAUM, MORDECHAI, *The Rabbi of Lyady and the Habad Party* [Harav miliadi umifleget ḥabad], 2 vols. (Warsaw, 1914).

TIKOCHINSKI, SHLOMO, 'The Methods of Learning in the Yeshivas of Lithuania in the Nineteenth Century' [Darkhei halimud beyeshivot lita bame'ah hatesha esreh], MA thesis (Hebrew University, Jerusalem 2004).

——'The *Musar* Yeshivas from Lithuania to Israel: Slobodka Yeshiva, its Emigration and Establishment in Mandate Palestine' [Yeshivot hamusar melita le'erets yisra'el: yeshivat slobodkah veshitatah haḥinukhit, aliyatah vehitbasesutah be'erets yisra'el hamandatorit], Ph.D. thesis (Hebrew University, Jerusalem, 2010).

TIKUCZYNSKI, NISAN AHARON, *The Teachings of R. Shemuel Salant* [Torat rabenu shemuel salant], 3 vols. (Jerusalem, 1998).

TISHBY, I., 'The Dissemination of Luzzatto's Kabbalistic Writings in Poland and Lithuania' (Heb.), *Kiryat sefer*, 45 (1970), 127–54.

——'God, the Torah and Israel Are One: The Source of the Quotation in Moshe Hayim Luzzatto's Commentary on the *Idra raba*' (Heb.), *Kiryat sefer*, 50 (1976), 480–92.

——'R. Yisra'el of Shklov's Criticism of the Hasidim' (Heb.), *Kiryat sefer*, 51 (1977), 300–3.

TRIVAKS, MOSHE HAYIM, *Nod demaot* (Warsaw, 1888).

TSCHERIKOWER, A., 'The Archives of Simon Dubnow', *Historishe shriftn*, 2 (1937), 565–604.

TSOREF, A., *Life of Rabbi Kook* [Ḥayei harav kuk] (Jerusalem, 1958).

TURBERG, PINHAS, *The Works of Pinhas Turberg* [Kitvei pinhas turberg], ed. A. R. Malakhi (New York, 1953).

TURNER, R., 'Sponsored and Contest Mobility and the School System', *American Sociological Review*, 25/6 (1960), 855–62.

TZINOVITZ, MOSHE, *The History of the Mir Yeshiva* [Toledot yeshivat mir] (Tel Aviv, 1981).

——*Personalities and Communities* [Ishim ukehilot] (Tel Aviv, 1990).

——*Tree of Life* [Ets hayim] (Tel Aviv, 1972).

VILNA GAON, *see* ELIYAHU BEN SHELOMOH ZALMAN

VINOGRAD, YESHYAHU, *A Treasury of the Hebrew Book* [Otsar hasefer ha'ivri], 2 vols. (Jerusalem, 1994).

——*A Treasury of the Works of the Vilna Gaon* [Otsar sifrei hagra] (Jerusalem, 2003).

VISHNITZER, M., 'Material for the History of the Yeshiva in Eastern Europe' (Heb.), *Talpiyot*, 5/3–4 (Jan. 1952), 603–18.

VITAL, HAYIM BEN JOSEPH, *Arba me'ot shekel kesef* [Kabbalistic text] (Korets, 1804).

WACHTFOGEL, MOSHE, *The Brisker Derech* (Jerusalem, 1993).

WAHRHAFTIG, YERUHAM, *Offerings of Yerucham* [Shalmei yeruḥam] (Jerusalem, 1900).

WEINBERG, YEHIEL, *Insights into the Talmud by the Author of Seridei esh* [Ḥidushei ba'al seridei esh . . . al hashas] (Jerusalem, 1998).

WEINBERGER, DAVID NETANEL (ed.), *The Grandfather of Slobodka* [Saba mislobodka] (Brooklyn, NY, 1986).

WEINGARTEN, S. HAKOHEN, *Hungarian Yeshivas: Their History and Problems* [Hayeshivot behungariyah: divrei yemeihen uv'ayoteihen] (Jerusalem, 1977).

WIENER, MOSHE, *A Beard Is the Glory of the Face* [Hadrat panim zakan], 2nd edn. (New York, 1978).

WILENSKY, MORDECAI, *Hasidim and Mitnagedim* [Ḥasidim umitnagedim], 2 vols. (Jerusalem, 1970).

WILKINSON, R., 'The Gentleman Ideal and the Maintenance of a Political Elite', in P. W. Musgrave (ed.), *Sociology, History, and Education* (London, 1970), 126–42.

WILLOWSKI, YA'AKOV DAVID BEN ZE'EV, *Beit ridbaz* [Responsa] (Jerusalem, 1908).

'A Word of Peace and Truth' (Heb.), *Hamelits*, 30/7 (21 Jan. 1890), 1–4.

WOZNER, SHAI, 'Legal Thinking in the Lithuanian Yeshivas as Reflected by the Works of Shimon Shkop' [Ḥashivah mishpatit biyeshivot lita bire'i mishnato shel harav shimon shkop], Ph.D. thesis (Hebrew University, Jerusalem, 2005).

YAMPOLSKI, P., 'Memories of my Youth' (Heb.), *Keneset yisra'el*, 1 (1887), 855–77.

YANOVSKY, YITSHAK TSEVI, *Biography of Rabbi Meir Halevi Levine* [Toledot haremah] (Berdichev, 1891).

YASHAR, M. M., *The Hafets Hayim* [Heḥafets ḥayim], 3 vols. (Tel Aviv, 1961).

YEHIEL MIKHAL BEN TSEVI HIRSH, *Lezekher leyisra'el* (Vilna, 1834).

YEHUDAH BEN ELIEZER, *Kol yehudah* (Józefów, 1827).

YITSHAK OF VOLOZHIN, *Milei de'avot* [Words of the Fathers] (Vilna, 1888).

—— *Peḥ kadosh* [Torah commentary] (Warsaw, 1890; repr. Jerusalem, 1994, ed. Elhanan Shapira).

YOUNG, M., 'Curricula and Social Organization of Knowledge', in R. Brown (ed.), *Knowledge, Education, and Cultural Change* (London, 1973), 348–99.

YUDLOV, Y., 'The Book of Ḥelkat re'uven' (Heb.), *Alei sefer*, 14 (1987), 139–41.

ZAHAVI, T., *The Jewish Assimilation Movement* [Tenuat hahitbolelut beyisra'el] (Jerusalem, 1941).

ZAKHEIM, E., *Nitei eitan* (Jerusalem, 1905).

ZALKIN, MORDECHAI, *At Dawn* [Ba'alot shaḥar] (Jerusalem, 2000).

—— 'City of Torah: Torah and its Study in the Lithuanian Urban Environment in the Nineteenth Century' (Heb.), in Immanuel Etkes (ed.), *Yeshivas and Batei Midrash* [Yeshivot uvatei midrashot] (Jerusalem, 2007), 131–61.

ZALMANOVICH, M. M., *Maḥazeh avraham* [Vision of Abraham] (Vilna, 1914).

—— *Zikhron hilel* [Memorial volume for Hillel] (Vilna, 1902).

ZALTZMAN, S., *From the Past* [Min he'avar] (Tel Aviv, 1943).

ZEDERBAUM, ALEXANDER, *Collected Articles* [Leket ma'amarim] (St Petersburg, 1889).

—— 'The Heavenly Yeshiva' (Heb.), *Hamelits*, 17/36 (21 Dec. 1880), 743–48.

—— 'An Unfair Protest' (Heb.), *Hamelits*, 30/37 (25 Feb. 1890), 1–2.

ZE'EV BEN YEHEZKEL FEIVEL, *Avodah tamah* (Vilna, 1836).

ZEIRA, M., *Our Sages in the Diaspora* [Raboteinu shebagolah], 2 vols. (Jerusalem, 1996, 1997).

ZEVIN, S. Y., *Personalities and Methods* [Ishim veshitot] (Tel Aviv, 1957).

ZHITLOWSKI, H., *Memories of My Life* [Zikhronos fun mein leben], 3 vols. (New York, 1935–40).

ZILBERZWEIG, Z., *Lexicon of Yiddish Theatre* [Leksikon fun yidishe teater], vol. iii (New York, 1959).

ZITRON, S. L., 'Dynastic Wars in the Volozhin Yeshiva' (Heb.), *Reshumot*, 1 (1925), 123–35.

—— *Intercessors* [Shtadlonim] (Warsaw, 1926).

—— *Three Literary Generations* [Dray literarishe doros] (Warsaw, 1920).

ZLATKIN, M., 'The Netsah Yisra'el Secret Society and H. N. Bialik' (Heb.), *Molad*, 5/27 (May–June 1950), 181–5.

—— 'The Volozhin Yeshiva in Bialik's Time' (Heb.), *Shevivim*, 1 (1955), 56–64.

ZUCKERMAN, A., 'Chaos' (Heb.), *Hashaḥar*, 7 (1876), 81–94, 285–90.

ZUCKERMAN, B., *Memoirs* [Zikhronos], 3 vols. (New York, 1962–7).

Index

Printed and bound by CPI Group (UK) Ltd, Croydon, CR0 4YY

09/06/2025

14685796-0004